THE NEW AMERICAN NATION 1775–1820

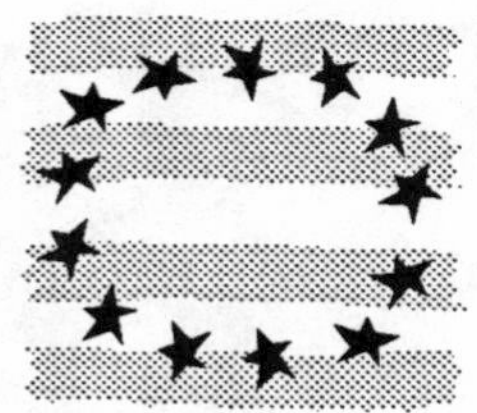

A Twelve-Volume Collection of Articles on the Development of the Early American Republic

Edited by

PETER S. ONUF
UNIVERSITY OF VIRGINIA

A GARLAND SERIES

THE NEW AMERICAN NATION 1775–1820

Volume

8

★

FEDERALISTS AND REPUBLICANS

Edited with an
Introduction by

PETER S. ONUF

GARLAND PUBLISHING, INC.
NEW YORK & LONDON
1991

Library of Congress Cataloging-in-Publication Data

Federalists and republicans / edited with an introduction by Peter S. Onuf.
p. cm. — (New American nation, 1776–1815 ; v. 8)
ISBN 0-8153-0443-9 (alk. paper)
1. United States—Politics and government—1797–1801. 2. United States—Politics and government—1801–1809. I. Onuf, Peter S. II. Series.
E164.N45 1991 vol. 8
[E321]
973 s—dc20
[973.4] 91-15475
CIP

Printed on acid-free, 250-year-life paper.
Manufactured in the United States of America

THE NEW AMERICAN NATION, 1775–1820

EDITOR'S INTRODUCTION

This series includes a representative selection of the most interesting and influential journal articles on revolutionary and early national America. My goal is to introduce readers to the wide range of topics that now engage scholarly attention. The essays in these volumes show that the revolutionary era was an extraordinarily complex "moment" when the broad outlines of national history first emerged. Yet if the "common cause" brought Americans together, it also drove them apart: the Revolution, historians agree, was as much a civil war as a war of national liberation. And, given the distinctive colonial histories of the original members of the American Union, it is not surprising that the war had profoundly different effects in different parts of the country. This series has been designed to reveal the multiplicity of these experiences in a period of radical political and social change.

Most of the essays collected here were first published within the last twenty years. This series therefore does *not* recapitulate the development of the historiography of the Revolution. Many of the questions asked by earlier generations of scholars now seem misconceived and simplistic. Constitutional historians wanted to know if the Patriots had legitimate grounds to revolt: was the Revolution "legal"? Economic historians sought to assess the costs of the navigation system for American farmers and merchants and to identify the interest groups that promoted resistance. Comparative historians wondered how "revolutionary" the Revolution really was. By and large, the best recent work has ignored these classic questions. Contemporary scholarship instead draws its inspiration from other sources, most notable of which is the far-ranging reconception and reconstruction of prerevolutionary America by a brilliant generation of colonial historians.

Bernard Bailyn's *Ideological Origins of the American Revolution* (1967) was a landmark in the new historical writing on colonial politics. As his title suggests, Bailyn was less interested in constitutional and legal arguments as such than in the "ideology" or political language that shaped colonists' perception of and responses to British imperial policy. Bailyn's great contribution was to focus attention on colonial political culture; disciples and critics alike followed his lead as they explored the impact—and limits—of "republicanism" in specific colonial settings. Meanwhile, the social historians who had played a leading role in the transformation of colonial historiography were extending their work into the late colonial period and were increasingly interested in the questions of value, meaning, and behavior that were raised by the new political history. The resulting convergence points to some of the unifying themes in recent work on the revolutionary period presented in this series.

A thorough grounding in the new scholarship on colonial British America is the best introduction to the history and historiography of the Revolution. These volumes therefore can be seen as a complement and extension of Peter Charles Hoffer's eighteen-volume set, *Early American History*, published by Garland in 1987. Hoffer's collection includes numerous important essays essential for understanding developments in independent America. Indeed, only a generation ago—when the Revolution generally was defined in terms of its colonial origins—it would have been hard to justify a separate series on the "new American nation." But exciting recent work—for instance, on wartime mobilization and social change, or on the Americanization of republican ideology during the great era of state making and constitution writing—has opened up new vistas. Historians now generally agree that the revolutionary period saw far-reaching and profound changes, that is, a "great transformation," toward a more recognizably modern America. If the connections between this transformation and the actual unfolding of events often remain elusive, the historiographical quest for the larger meaning of the war and its aftermath has yielded impressive results.

To an important extent, the revitalization of scholarship on revolutionary and early national America is a tribute to the efforts and expertise of scholars working in other professional disciplines. Students of early American literature have made key contributions to the history of rhetoric, ideology, and culture; political scientists and legal scholars have brought new clarity and sophistication to the study of political and constitutional thought and practice in the founding period. Kermit L. Hall's superb Garland series, *United States Constitutional and Legal History* (20 volumes, 1985), is another fine resource for students and scholars interested in the founding. The sampling of recent work in various disciplines offered in these volumes gives a sense of the interpretative possibilities of a crucial period in American history that is now getting the kind of attention it has long deserved.

Peter S. Onuf

INTRODUCTION

In his famous Farewell Address of September 1796, retiring President George Washington warned against the dangers of party divisions within the republic and of "entangling alliances" with foreign powers. Washington's "political testament" was a commentary on his own second administration when fundamental differences on foreign policy accelerated the process of party formation and jeopardized his own reputation as the "father of his country."

At first most Americans welcomed the French Revolution of 1789, but the efforts of successive British-led coalitions to destroy the Revolution created an increasingly dangerous foreign policy dilemma for the new nation's leaders. If they all agreed that the United States should avoid being drawn into the European war, it was another, much more controversial, matter to pursue a neutral course that was compatible both with American obligations under the French treaty of 1778 and with American interests as a weak power whose prosperity depended on cordial trade relations with the motherland. Cabinet disagreement over the language of Washington's Neutrality Proclamation of April 1793, which the Jeffersonians thought was tilted in favor of Britain, anticipated party polarization in Congress during the bitter debate over John Jay's English treaty, narrowly ratified in the summer of 1795. By submitting to this humiliating alliance, Republicans charged, the United States became Britain's satellite in its counterrevolutionary campaign against French republicanism. Federalists replied that the French revolutionary impulse had been hopelessly perverted, and that the survival of world civilization depended on beating back the forces of anarchy and infidelity.

Isolationism was no option for early national policymakers. Beneath the heated rhetoric and party polemics was a general agreement that the new nation's future prosperity and power depended on a vigorous trans-Atlantic trade. Disagreement centered on the Jeffersonians' conviction that Americans could open up new trade links and, by threatening retaliatory discrimination, force the British to offer more favorable terms of trade. Treasury Secretary Hamilton and his supporters followed a more circumspect policy, fearful that the disruption of Anglo-American trade would jeopardize the national government's revenues from import duties and retard economic growth. These opposing perspectives suggested broader conceptions of the new nation's future development that is articulated in partisan efforts to mobilize constituency support.

The development of the first party system has long been a favored topic of political historians. Among many others, important works by Joseph Charles, Noble Cunningham, Leonard White, and Richard Hofstadter have given us a good understanding of the imperatives of party organization and the process of government in a period still uncomfortable with institutionalized political conflict. More recently, students of political ideology influenced by the "republican" school of American Revolutionary historiography have explored the implications of partisan rhetoric for the continuing transformation of American political society. Building on seminal essays by Marshall Smelser and John R. Howe, Richard Buel and Lance Banning have demonstrated the continuing salience of Revolutionary themes in the political discourse of the early national period. In many ways, as the essays in this and the following volume make clear, the Revolution was not yet completed. American independence and the preservation of the union remained fundamentally problematic until the conclusion of the Napoleonic Wars in 1815.

Most of the essays in this volume are devoted to the histories of the administrations of John Adams and his successor Thomas Jefferson. Foreign policy concerns dominate the Adams historiography, with a focus on the second President's shifting course during the "Quasi-War" with France (1796–1800). Ultimately, Adams negotiated a peaceful resolution of the conflict and termination of the troublesome Franco-American alliance of 1778, but not before energizing the Republican opposition by sponsoring the ill-conceived and counterproductive Alien and Sedition Acts (1798) and dividing the administration party by alienating bellicose Hamiltonians. Adams's devotion to the national interest as he saw it is unquestionable, but his ineptitude as a party manager was unmatched.

By contrast, Jefferson's political talents have been the subject of much admiring commentary. Certainly, as James Sterling Young shows in *The Washington Community* (1966), the Virginian thrived in the rough and tumble, and necessarily informal, circumstances of the new national capital on the Potomac. Jefferson's moderate and pragmatic policies guaranteed a peaceful transition from Federalist to Republican rule. The successes of his first term, most notably the Louisiana Purchase of 1803, confirmed his enormous popularity and helped consign the Federalists to an increasingly marginal role in national politics.

Perhaps most crucial to the Jefferson administration's popular success, however, was a brief interval in the European wars after the Peace of Amiens (1802) and the great opportunities for neutral shippers in the years immediately following the resumption of war in 1803. Not for the first or last time in American history, a buoyant economy guaranteed the popularity of the party in power. Remarkably, however, the Republicans retained their hold on power despite the foreign policy failures of Jefferson's second term that disrupted the American economy and prepared the way for "Mr. Madison's War" in 1812.

Peter S. Onuf

Additional Reading

Lance Banning. *The Jeffersonian Persuasion: Evolution of a Party Ideology.* Ithaca, NY: Cornell University Press, 1978.

Richard Buel, Jr. *Securing the Revolution: Ideology in American Politics, 1789–1815.* Ithaca, NY: Cornell University Press, 1972.

Jerald A. Combs. *The Jay Treaty: Political Battleground of the Founding Fathers.* Berkeley: University of California Press, 1970.

Noble E. Cunningham, Jr. *The Process of Government under Jefferson.* Princeton, NJ: Princeton University Press, 1978.

David Hackett Fischer. *The Revolution of American Conservatism: The Federalist Party in the Era of Jeffersonian Democracy.* New York: Harper & Row, 1965.

Felix Gilbert. *To the Farewell Address: Ideas of Early American Foreign Policy.* Princeton, NJ: Princeton University Press, 1961.

Richard Hofstadter. *The Idea of a Party System: The Rise of Legitimate Opposition in the United States, 1780–1840.* Berkeley: University of California Press, 1969.

John R. Howe. *The Changing Political Thought of John Adams.* Princeton, NJ: Princeton University Press, 1966.

Ralph Ketcham. *James Madison: A Biography.* New York: Macmillan, 1971.

Stephen Kurtz. *The Presidency of John Adams: The Collapse of Federalism, 1795–1800.* Philadelphia: University of Pennsylvania Press, 1957.

Merrill D. Peterson. *Thomas Jefferson and the New Nation: A Biography.* New York: Oxford University Press, 1970

James Morton Smith. *Freedom's Fetters: The Alien and Sedition Laws and American Civil Liberties.* Ithaca, NY: Cornell University Press, 1956.

Leonard White. *The Jeffersonians: A Study in Administrative History, 1801–1829.* New York: Macmillan, 1951.

James Sterling Young. *The Washington Community, 1800–1828.* New York: Columbia University Press, 1966.

CONTENTS

Volume 8—Federalists and Republicans

Joseph H. Harrison, Jr., "*Sic Et Non*: Thomas Jefferson and Internal Improvement," *Journal of the Early Republic*, 1987, 7:335–349.

John Lauritz Larson, "'Bind the Republic Together': The National Union and the Struggle for a System of Internal Improvements," *Journal of American History*, 1987, 74(2):363–387.

Theodore Joseph Crackel, "The Founding of West Point: Jefferson and the Politics of Security," *Armed Forces and Society*, 1981, 7(4):529–543.

Robert R. Davis, Jr., "Pell-Mell: Jeffersonian Etiquette and Protocol," *Historian*, 1981, 43(4):509–529.

Constance B. Schulz, "'Of Bigotry in Politics and Religion': Jefferson's Religion, the Federalist Press, and the Syllabus," *Virginia Magazine of History and Biography*, 1983, 91(1): 73–91.

Duncan MacLeod, "The Political Economy of John Taylor of Caroline," *Journal of American Studies*, 1980, 14(3):387–405.

ACKNOWLEDGMENTS

Volume 8—Federalists and Republicans

Marshall Smelser, "The Federalist Period as an Age of Passion," *American Quarterly*, 1958, 10(4):391–419. Reprinted with the permission of the author, and the American Studies Association as publisher. Courtesy of Yale University Sterling Memorial Library.

John R. Howe, Jr., "Republican Thought and the Political Violence of the 1790s," *American Quarterly*, 1967, 19(2, Part I):147–165. Reprinted with the permission of the author, and the American Studies Association as publisher. Courtesy of Yale University Sterling Memorial Library.

Michael Lienesch, "The Role of Political Millennialism in Early American Nationalism," *Western Political Quarterly*, 1983, 36(3):445–465. Reprinted with the permission of the University of Utah, copyright holder. Courtesy of Yale University Sterling Memorial Library.

Wallace Evan Davies, "The Society of the Cincinnati in New England 1783–1800," *William and Mary Quarterly*, 1948, 5(1):3–25. Originally appeared in the *William and Mary Quarterly*. Courtesy of Yale University Sterling Memorial Library.

Gary B. Nash, "The American Clergy and the French Revolution," *William and Mary Quarterly*, 1965, 22(3):392–412. Originally appeared in the *William and Mary Quarterly*. Courtesy of Yale University Sterling Memorial Library.

Charles Ellis Dickson, "Jeremiads in the New American Republic: The Case of National Fasts in the John Adams Administration," *New England Quarterly*, 1987, 60(2):187–207. Reprinted with the permission of the *New England Quarterly*. Courtesy of Yale University Sterling Memorial Library.

William Stinchcombe, "The Diplomacy of the WXYZ Affair," *William and Mary Quarterly*, 1977, 34(4):590–617. Originally appeared in the *William and Mary Quarterly*. Courtesy of Yale University Sterling Memorial Library.

Jean S. Holder, "The Sources of Presidential Power: John Adams and the Challenge of Executive Primacy," *Political Science Quarterly*, 1986–87, 101(4):601–616. Reprinted with the permission of the Academy of Political Science. Courtesy of Yale University Sterling Memorial Library.

Michael Durey, "Thomas Paine's Apostles: Radical Emigres and the Triumph of Jeffersonian Republicanism," *William and Mary Quarterly*, 1987, 44(4):661–688. Originally appeared in the *William and Mary Quarterly*. Courtesy of Yale University Sterling Memorial Library.

Joyce Appleby, "Commercial Farming and the 'Agrarian Myth' in the Early Republic," *Journal of American History*, 1982, 68(4):833–849. Reprinted with the permission of the *Journal of American History.* Courtesy of Yale University Sterling Memorial Library.

Joyce Appleby, "What Is Still American in the Political Philosophy of Thomas Jefferson?" *William and Mary Quarterly*, 1982, 39(2) (Third Series):287–309. Originally appeared in the *William and Mary Quarterly.* Courtesy of Yale University Sterling Memorial Library.

John Ashworth, "The Jeffersonians: Classical Republicans or Liberal Capitalists" *Journal of American Studies*, 1984, 18(3):425–435. Reprinted with the permission of Cambridge University Press. Courtesy of Yale University Sterling Memorial Library.

Joseph H. Harrison, Jr., "*Sic Et Non*: Thomas Jefferson and Internal Improvement," *Journal of the Early Republic*, 1987, 7:335–349. Reprinted with the permission of Indiana University, Department of History. Courtesy of Yale University Sterling Memorial Library.

John Lauritz Larson, "'Bind the Republic Together': The National Union and the Struggle for a System of Internal Improvements," *Journal of American History*, 1987, 74(2):363–387. Reprinted with the permission of the *Journal of American History.* Courtesy of Yale University Sterling Memorial Library.

Theodore Joseph Crackel, "The Founding of West Point: JEFFERSON AND THE POLITICS OF SECURITY," *Armed Forces and Society*, 1981, 7(4):529–543. Reprinted with the permission of Transaction Publishers. Courtesy of Yale University Sterling Memorial Library.

Robert R. Davis, Jr., "Pell-Mell: Jeffersonian Etiquette and Protocol," *Historian*, 1981, 43(4):509–529. Reprinted with the permission of the International Honor Society in History. Courtesy of Yale University Sterling Memorial Library.

Constance B. Schulz, "'OF BIGOTRY IN POLITICS AND RELIGION': Jefferson's Religion, the Federalist Press, and the Syllabus," *Virginia Magazine of History and Biography*, 1983, 91(1):73–91. Reprinted with the permission of the Virginia Historical Society. Courtesy of Yale University Sterling Memorial Library.

Duncan MacLeod, "The Political Economy of John Taylor of Caroline," *Journal of American Studies*, 1980, 14(3):387–405. Reprinted with the permission of Cambridge University Press. Courtesy of Yale University Sterling Memorial Library.

by MARSHALL SMELSER
University of Notre Dame

The Federalist Period as an Age of Passion

THE YEARS of the administrations of Presidents Washington and Adams are usually regarded by the educated layman—although not by the few specialists in the era—as years in which public life was marked by statesmanlike decorum and a reliance on logic. This view has been encouraged by the overcompression of short popular accounts and the remarks of enthusiastic amateurs. While not wholly inaccurate, such a conception neglects to notice that the political activity of the Federalist period was strongly influenced by the passions of hate, anger and fear. It is possible to tell the story of this politically-conscious age so as to make it the narrative of a series of great statutes and treaties, enacted and ratified by heroes who set precedents which still serve us as guides. That is the way the tale is usually told. Yet the story can be organized quite differently by writing it as "emotional history," with the effect of emphasizing some almost forgotten motivations of the principal builders of the federal republic.

The ruling faction in the national politics of the United States, the group which controlled the three branches of government for the first twelve years of the federal republic (some months of congressional history excepted) were known as the Federalists—later, the Federalist Party. This group did not accept equalitarian principles. Their rejection was based on a theory of human nature which emphasized differences of individual abilities and the inherent depravity of passionate, self-interested human nature. When translated into the political jargon of the day this psychological analysis was much coarsened. For example, Edmund Burke's unfortunate epithet applied to the French people at large, "a swinish multitude," was widely used by the opposition party in America, the Republicans, to illustrate the contempt in which aristocracy held the people everywhere. And the Republicans were not misusing the phrase.[1]

To select illustrations of this attitude toward the populace is almost to call the roll of the best minds of Federalism. Alexander Hamilton, Fisher Ames, George Cabot, Timothy Dwight, John Quincy Adams, James Iredell —all have left ample literary evidence of their real fear of equalitarianism. Some of them explained themselves psychologically, some theologically and in others—evidence is clear—snobbery was sufficient ground.[2] About the only notable exception to the demophobia of Federalism was the political theory of the most able of Federalist constitutional historians, John Adams. Adams did not fear democracy more than other forms of government. It was absolute power that he feared, whether despotic, oligarchic or democratic.[3] But few of his collaborators were so dispassionate.

Whether a republic could be made to work, even with promising human material, was a question which was complicated by American geography. The vast area of the United States discouraged many, both Republicans and Federalists. It seemed very likely that the interstate and intersectional jealousies which had vexed the old Confederation would prove too strong for the union. The difficulties seemed so great that at every particular crisis there were fears of disunion and threats of secession. At the time of the congressional debates over Hamilton's proposal that the federal government assume the state debts—the "Assumption" controversy—there was a hint that New England and South Carolina might secede if Assumption

[1]Merle Curti, *The Growth of American Thought* (New York: Harper & Bros., 1943), p. 189; Edmund Burke, *Reflections on the Revolution in France* (New York: P. F. Collier & Son, 1909), XXIV, 227; Thomas A. Bailey, *A Diplomatic History of the American People* (2d ed.; New York: F. S. Crofts & Co., 1942), p. 58.

[2]Samuel Eliot Morison, *Sources and Documents Illustrating the American Revolution, 1764-1788* (2d ed.; Oxford: Clarendon Press, 1929), p. 259; Fisher Ames, "The Dangers of American Liberty," in Edwin H. Cady (ed.), *Literature of the Early Republic* (New York: Rinehart Co., 1950), pp. 108-16; Ames to Minot, July 9, 1789, Fisher Ames, *Works,* ed. Seth Ames (Boston, 1854), I, 62; Ames to Oliver Wolcott, Jr., April 22, 1798, George Gibbs, *Memoirs of the Administrations of Washington and John Adams, Edited from the Papers of Oliver Wolcott* (New York, 1846), II, 46 (Hereafter cited: Gibbs, *Memoirs*); Goodrich to Oliver Wolcott, Jr., March 23, 1790, *ibid.,* I, 42 illustrates a Federalist Congressman's contempt for the intellectual powers of his own constituents—see also Goodrich to Oliver Wolcott, Jr., Feb. 17, 1793, *ibid.,* I, 88; Edward Channing, *A History of the United States* (New York: Macmillan Co., 1932-36), IV, 65n. (Hereafter cited: Channing, *United States*); Cabot to King, August 14, 1795), April 10, 1797, Rufus King, *The Life and Correspondence of Rufus King,* ed. C. R. King (New York, 1894-1900), II, 25, 170; Leon Howard, *The Connecticut Wits* (Chicago: University of Chicago Press, 1942), pp. 345-46 (Hereafter cited: Howard, *Wits*); *ibid.,* pp. 368, 370; John Quincy Adams, *Memoirs of John Quincy Adams,* ed. C. F. Adams (Philadelphia, 1874-77), I, 83, where, among several mottoes at the head of his diary, is the sentence from the ancient writer Bias, "The many are evil."

[3]John Adams to Taylor, April 15, 1814, John Adams, *Works,* ed. C. F. Adams (Boston, 1850-56), VI, 477; Zoltán Haraszti, *John Adams and the Prophets of Progress* (Cambridge, Mass.: Harvard University Press, 1952), pp. 24, 198.

did not carry.[4] In 1792 George Washington was urged to accept a second term as President by Attorney General Edmund Randolph and by Secretary of the Treasury Alexander Hamilton because his presence would help to preserve the union, and this was no new idea to the President.[5] Northern Senators were again speaking privately of secession in the Third Congress.[6] During the hullaballoo over the Jay Treaty Virginians threatened secession if the treaty were ratified, and northerners threatened the same if southerners did not behave more responsibly.[7] In the presidential campaign of 1796 some Yankees hoped that New England would secede if Thomas Jefferson were elected to the presidency.[8] During the uproar over the X.Y.Z. Affair Jefferson thought that the Federalist outcry was aimed in part at justifying a secession which might soon occur, but he himself opposed secession when John Taylor of Caroline seriously suggested that Virginia and North Carolina leave the union.[9]

The leaders of the nation were dealing with hard facts when they contemplated the interstate and intersectional rivalries and jealousies. These were differences rooted in the psychology, the culture and the economy of the Americans. The weakness of the government under the Articles of Confederation had been its inability to harmonize local interests and to enforce a common will against stubborn sectionalism. With the ratification of the new constitution, national solutions of national problems might for the first time be possible. One national solution just *might* be the abolition of the states. Hamilton is well remembered as an extreme "consolidationist" who would have been pleased to see the states abolished. What is less well remembered is that he was not alone. Men of such views were disappointed when sectionalism did not quickly die. They did not think of sectionalism as the effect of deep and permanent causes but as the

[4]William Maclay, *Journal*, ed. E. S. Maclay (New York, 1890), [March 8, 1790] p. 209; Thomas Jefferson, "The Anas," *Writings*, Memorial edition, ed. A. A. Lipscomb (Washington: Thomas Jefferson Memorial Association of the United States, 1903-4), I, 274.

[5]Randolph to Washington, August 5, 1792, George Washington, *Writings*, ed. J. C. Fitzpatrick (Washington: U. S. Government Printing Office, 1931-44), XXXII, 135n.-136n.; Hamilton to Washington, July 30, August 18, 1792, Alexander Hamilton, *Works*, ed. Henry Cabot Lodge (New York: G. P. Putnan's Sons, 1904), X, 8, II, 465; Jefferson, "The Anas," ed. Lipscomb, I, 308.

[6]Henry H. Simms, *The Life of John Taylor* (Richmond: William Byrd Press, 1932), pp. 61-62.

[7]William Jay, *The Life of John Jay with Selections from his Correspondence and Miscellaneous Papers* (New York, 1833), I, 361n.; Oliver Wolcott, Jr. to Oliver Wolcott, Sr., August 10, 1795, Oliver Wolcott, Sr. to Oliver Wolcott, Jr., Nov. 23, 1795, Oliver Wolcott, Jr. to Hamilton, April 29, 1796, Gibbs, *Memoirs*, I, 224, 269, 334; Jefferson, "The Anas," ed. Lipscomb, I, 422.

[8]Oliver Wolcott, Sr. to Oliver Wolcott, Jr., Nov. 21, 28, Dec. 12, 1796, Gibbs, *Memoirs*, I, 397, 403, 409.

[9]Jefferson to Madison, March 21, 1798, ed. Lipscomb, X, 11; Jefferson to Taylor, June 4, 1798, *Jefferson Papers, Massachusetts Historical Society Collections*, Seventh Series, I (1900), 61-64.

product of selfishness or envy. Sectional opposition soon became malicious opposition or, at best, a quarrel of the "outs" and the "ins."[10]

Most of the sectional ill-feeling was the result of north-south clashes but there was also a discernible east-west jealousy. On the Federalist side its most articulate analyst was President Timothy Dwight of Yale who said that frontiersmen as a group were men who had been too shiftless for orderly society, men who were impatient of all restraints. Discouraged, fearing poverty, jail and public contempt, at length they went to the wilderness (where some of them were saved by acquiring property, since, to some extent, one must love property to have good morals).[11] Another Federalist disapproved of westward migration because a scattered population became "ignorant, savage, and ungovernable."[12] Whether they went because they were bad, or became bad because they went, westerners were generally odious.

Residence in Philadelphia was alone enough to excite provincialism in some of the northern executive officers and members of the Congress. For the first time some of them came into a genuine liberal atmosphere, Philadelphia being the first influential home of freedom in America.[13] Philadelphia had been a democratic center during the War for Independence. In the 1790's English republicans and revolutionary Irishmen were always to be found in Philadelphia.[14] Some Federalists were frank in expressing their mean opinions of the Pennsylvanians and their ill-informed and stormy politics.[15]

With their pessimistic view of human nature, their fear of localism and their almost universally held doubts of the permanence of the union, it is little wonder that the Federalists took an intolerant position regarding the opposition party, which seemed to be a race of marplots characterized by excessive ambition, unwholesome partisanship and a dangerous reliance upon the judgment of the voters. At best the Republicans often seemed

[10]Oliver Wolcott, Sr. to Oliver Wolcott, Jr., Dec. 23, 1789, Jan. 28, 1790, Oliver Wolcott, Jr. to Oliver Wolcott, Sr., Feb. 12, 1791, Oliver Wolcott, Jr. to Webster, May 20, 1793, Hopkins to Oliver Wolcott, Jr., August 21, 1793, Trumbull to Oliver Wolcott, Jr., Feb. 16, 1795, Gibbs, *Memoirs,* I, 33, 36, 63, 99, 105, 180; James Schouler, *History of the United States under the Constitution* (rev. ed; New York: Dodd, Mead & Co., 1894-1913), I, 219.

[11]Quoted in Howard, *Wits,* pp. 374-77.

[12]Oliver Wolcott, Sr. to Oliver Wolcott, Jr., March 21, 1796, Gibbs, *Memoirs,* I, 323.

[13]Samuel Eliot Morison, "John Adams and Thomas Jefferson," *By Land and by Sea, Essays and Addresses* (New York: Alfred A. Knopf, 1954), p. 225.

[14]William Cobbett, *Letters . . . to Edward Thornton Written in the Years 1797 to 1800,* ed. G. D. H. Cole (New York: Oxford University Press, 1937), p. xxviii.

[15]Oliver Wolcott, Jr. to Oliver Wolcott, Sr., Feb. 12, 1791, Oliver Wolcott, Sr. to Oliver Wolcott, Jr., June 17, 1793, Oliver Wolcott, Jr. to Oliver Wolcott, Sr., Nov. 27, 1796, Gibbs, *Memoirs,* I, 62-63, 102, 401, Hamilton to King, Oct. 30, 1794, King, *Life and Correspondence,* I, 575.

governed by obstinacy, envy, malice or ambition. At worst they were seditious and treasonable. Federalist private correspondence was peppered with references to Republican disloyalty, insincerity, intrigue and demagoguery, and similar allegations were made in the pamphleteering war.[16] To Federalists it was obvious that Republican opposition was malicious mischief. The conclusion almost forced upon the reader of these and hundreds more of Federalist condemnations is that the two-party system is immoral. Since both parties could not be correct, one must be the foe of order.[17] Protestations of the loyalty of an opposition party were insincere. It became almost normal to consider opposition as seditious and, in extraordinary cases, as treasonable.[18]

The appearance of the Democratic-Republican societies in 1793 seemed sufficient proof of an organized conspiracy against the liberty of the nation. These political clubs were formed by city workers and western farmers and, as we now see, were the nuclei of the Republican Party. Called "demoniacal" as a pun on the word "democratical" their seditious character was assumed and their legality denied.[19] They needed only to take up arms to be a revolutionary army.

Another evidence of the bad intentions of the Republicans was that they went to some trouble to gain popularity, and disgraced themselves by seeking votes.[20] To run for office was plainly beneath the dignity of the wellborn. Man must not seek office; office must seek the man. It was bad enough to canvass the opinions of the vulgar on the qualifications of men. It was worse to ask the mob to pass on questions of public policy. Young John Quincy Adams thought a victorious majority in a Boston Town Meeting "looked as if they had been collected from all the jails of the con-

[16]Gore to King, Dec. 3, 1789, *ibid.*, I, 369; Oliver Wolcott, Jr. to Oliver Wolcott, Sr., July 11, 1793, Goodrich to Oliver Wolcott, Jr., March 10, 1794, Gibbs, *Memoirs,* I, 103, 131; Hamilton to Washington, Aug. 18, 1792, Hamilton, *Works,* II, 458-59: "Civis to Mercator," Sept. 5, 1792, *ibid.*, III, 29-30; "Camillus," No. 1, July 22, 1795, *ibid.*, V, 190-91; John Quincy Adams to Abigail Adams, May 16, 1795, John Quincy Adams, *Writings,* ed. W. C. Ford (New York: Macmillan Co., 1913-17), I, 340n.

[17]Suggested by Eugene Perry Link, *Democratic-Republican Societies, 1790-1800* (New York: Columbia University Press, 1942), pp. 122-23.

[18]Quoted in John A. Krout and Dixon Ryan Fox, *The Completion of Independence, 1790-1830* (New York: Macmillan Co., 1944), pp. 156-57; Washington to Stone, Dec. 6, 1795, to Lafayette, Dec. 25, 1798, Washington, *Writings,* XXXIV, 385, XXXVII, 66-67; Carroll to McHenry, Dec. 5, 1796, Bernard C. Steiner, *The Life and Correspondence of James McHenry* (Cleveland: Burrows Brothers Co., 1907), p. 205.

[19]Washington to Ball, Sept. 25, 1794, Washington, *Writings,* XXXIII, 505-7; Murray to McHenry, Dec. 16, 1794, Steiner, *McHenry,* pp. 155-56.

[20]Gore to King, Oct. 23, 1790, King, *Life and Correspondence,* I, 393; Oliver Wolcott, Jr. to Oliver Wolcott, Sr., Feb. 14, 1792, Goodrich to Oliver Wolcott, Sr., May 6, 1796, Gibbs, *Memoirs,* I, 73, 337; Ames to Foster, Jan. 4, 1796, Ames, *Works,* I, 181-82.

tinent"[21] and a Federalist Secretary of State once stated it as a principle that the larger the attendance at a public meeting the less weight should be given to its resolutions.[22] It is hard now to imagine that an administration which was at once fearful and contemptuous of the people could expect to stay long in power. But the Federalists saw no weakness in their political theory. Weakness, they admitted, but it was a weakness of disposition and organization in their own followers whereby rich men evaded responsibility and thereby helped their natural enemies. Such renegades feared to make government strong enough to be workable and opposed a spirit of determination in government because they were too timid to risk the loss of public favor. One would gather that the American republic was dying of senility while still in its cradle.[23]

Once the newspapers had found their normal level of stridency, which had been pretty well established by the last year of Washington's first term, many Federalists felt that they lived permanently on the edge of doom. The harshness of partisanship made it seem unlikely that government could be administered or the union preserved.[24] Nevertheless, although they might claim to despise popularity-seeking and electioneering, Federalists worked hard to influence public opinion by means of the press. Hardly a Federalist leader can be named who did not at some time or other, over his own name or a pseudonym, engage in newspaper controversy. A reading of the polemics shows that a good deal of the writing was much less concerned with informing the intellect than it was with whipping up those same passions which the Republicans were accused of trying to arouse. The result was the publication of some of the ripest vituperation in American literary history.[25]

Before 1798 and the enactment of the Sedition Act, the Federalists had few remedies for the acute infection of the body politic. About the only constructive suggestions were those for the conduct of local political cam-

[21]John Quincy Adams to Thomas Boylston Adams, Feb. 1, 1792, John Quincy Adams, *Writings,* I, 110-14.

[22]Pickering to Williams, July [no day] 1795, Pickering to Washington, July 27, 1795, Charles W. Upham and Octavius Pickering, *The Life of Timothy Pickering* (Boston, 1867-73), III, 181-83.

[23]Ames to Oliver Wolcott, Jr., July 9, 1795, April 22, 1798, Gibbs, *Memoirs,* I, 210, II, 47; John Quincy Adams to John Adams, May 26, 1794, John Quincy Adams, *Writings,* I, 191; Ames to Gore, Dec. 17, 1794, Ames, *Works,* I, 156-57.

[24]Washington to Hamilton, Aug. 26, 1792, to Randolph, Oct. 16, 1794, to Henry, Oct. 9, 1795, Washington, *Writings,* XXXII, 132-34, XXXIV, 3, 335; Ames to Dwight, August 8, Sept. 3, 1794, Ames, *Works,* I, 146-48; John Quincy Adams to John Adams, Jan. 5, 1794, John Quincy Adams, *Writings,* I, 178; Ames to Oliver Wolcott, Jr., July 9, 1795, Oliver Wolcott, Jr. to Morse, Sept. 26, 1795, Oliver Wolcott, Jr. to Frederick Wolcott, Sept. 29, 1795, Goodrich to Oliver Wolcott, Sr., Feb. 21, 1796, Gibbs, *Memoirs,* I, 210, 247-48, 304.

[25]For examples of the poetry of vituperation see Frank Monaghan, *John Jay, Defender of Liberty* (New York: Bobbs-Merrill Co., 1935), p. 396 and Curti, *Thought,* pp. 192-93.

paigns.[26] But it seemed probable that the malevolence of the Republicans could be explained and counter-attacked by moral theology. In their discussions of the infidelity and immorality of their opponents, the Federalists owed much in their thinking to foreign writers, particularly to Edmund Burke who, in his *Reflections on the Revolution in France,* had described a systematic plan of literary men to destroy Christianity. The same trend was noticed by some commentators in America and in the course of identifying infidelity in religion with democracy in politics, Jefferson's private life was slanderously attacked in prose and verse[27]—an attack which established a false tradition that is still alive.

It was strongly suspected that the turbulent demagogues and their depraved followers were untrustworthy on the subject of the rights of property.[28] There seemed to be many evidences for this, but the unreliability of the Republicans was sufficiently shown by their consistent opposition to the Hamiltonian design for safeguarding property and establishing the national credit.

If the opposition to administration measures had been limited to words and votes the Federalists, in time, might have come to accept partisanship as the normal state of American politics, but in 1794 and 1795 opposition erupted into violence which appeared to justify the worst fears of the ruling group. Violence was used to prevent the enforcement of the federal excise law in western Pennsylvania, and large crowds, perhaps mobs, demonstrated in many places to show their disapproval of the Jay Treaty.

The news of the Whiskey Rebellion sent a shock wave of alarm through the country. The appearance of rebellion and anarchy was what Federalists had been predicting and fearing.[29] After the rioters dispersed before

[26]The best tactical proposals appear to have been those of Fisher Ames, Ames to Dwight, Sept. 11, Dec. 12, 1794, Ames, *Works,* I, 150, 155.

[27]John Trumbull, *Autobiography,* ed. Theodore Sizer (New Haven: Yale University Press, 1953), pp. 173-75; See the allegedly anti-Christian clause, Article XI, of a treaty with the Dey of Algiers, negotiated by the Republican Joel Barlow in 1796-97, United States, Navy Department, *Naval Documents Related to the United States Wars with the Barbary Powers* (Washington, 1939), I, 178—for an outraged comment thereon, Steiner, *McHenry,* p. 470; D. M. Ludlum, *Social Ferment in Vermont,* 1791-1850 (New York: Columbia University Press, 1939), p. 30; Curti, *Thought,* pp. 195-96.

[28]Link, *Democratic-Republican Societies,* pp. 175-86; Jay to Duane, Sept. 16, 1795, Jay, *Jay,* I, 375-76; Hamilton, "Vindication of the Funding System," 1791[?], Hamilton, *Works,* III, 11-12; See also a perceptive essay in the form of a review of the new publication of Griffith J. McRee, *Life and Correspondence* of James Iredell (New York: Peter Smith, 1949) by Elisha P. Douglass, in *William and Mary Quarterly,* Third Series, VII (July, 1950), 459-66.

[29]The best account is Leland D. Baldwin, *Whiskey Rebels: The Story of a Frontier Uprising* (Pittsburgh: University of Pittsburgh Press, 1939); See also J. S. Bassett, *The Federalist System, 1789-1801* (New York: Harper & Bros., 1906), Vol. XI, of *The American Nation, A History,* ed. A. B. Hart, 107-10; Fisher Ames thought it premature, hence perhaps a Good Thing in the long run: Ames to Dwight, Sept. 3, 1794, Ames, *Works,* I, 148.

the approach of troops sent by the President, a great deal of talk and writing, both public and private, of Federalist leaders in the next few months was devoted to the motives, causes and dangers of the whiskey disturbance. Washington's opinions on the subject are valuable, because he had the responsibility for suppressing the insurrection and he also had the most widespread network of correspondents. He was convinced that the troubles were the work of a conspiracy organized by the Democratic-Republican clubs, but set in motion prematurely. He was gratified by the popular support of the government. His views were formally summarized in his annual message to the Congress in November, 1794.[30] (The true view of responsible Republicans was glumly expressed by James Madison who thought the leaders of the rebellion did a service to despotism. Insurrections "increase the momentum of power" as had been shown by Shays's Rebellion in the 1780's.)[31]

The Whiskey Rebellion had been quieted only briefly when sporadic violence broke out in many towns as part of the opposition to the Jay Treaty. Jay's character was symbolically and systematically defamed. A Philadelphia crowd demonstrated before the house of the British Minister and smashed windows elsewhere. Hamilton was stoned by a hostile mob in New York. Several disturbances in Boston led to a charge that Governor Samuel Adams evaded responsibility for keeping public order. Anti-Jay rioting extended as far north as Portsmouth, New Hampshire.[32] It was very hard for Federalists to believe that these outbursts, these lawless proceedings so uncomfortably reminiscent of the French Revolution, were spontaneous. There simply had to be a plot.[33]

The partisan press appeared to be a principal tool of organized malevolence. And as early as the end of Washington's first term it was a settled conviction of the Federalists that the *National Gazette,* edited by the poet Philip Freneau, was the trumpet of treason. Hamilton detected subversion in it as early as the summer of 1792, and he often appeared in print (over pseudonyms) in John Fenno's *Gazette of the United States* in controversy with Freneau's paper, questioning Freneau's integrity, and blaming Jeffer-

[30]Washington to Fleming, Cook and McLenahan, Jan. 30, 1793, to Thruston, August 10, 1794, to Henry Lee, August 26, 1794, to Daniel Morgan, Oct. 8, 1794, to Jay, November 1[-5], 1794, Washington, *Writings,* XXXII, 321, XXXIII, 464-65, 475-76, 524, XXXIV, 17; Washington, "Sixth Annual Address to Congress," Nov. 19, 1794, *ibid.,* XXXIV, 29, 34-35.

[31]On the part played by the Democratic-Republican clubs see Link, *Democratic-Republican Societies;* Madison commented in Madison to Monroe, Dec. 4, 1794, James Madison, *Writings,* ed. Gaillard Hunt (New York, 1900-10), VI, 220-21.

[32]Bailey, *Diplomatic History,* p. 66; Monaghan, *Jay,* pp. 392-94; Hamilton to Oliver Wolcott, Jr., July 28, 1795, Gibbs, *Memoirs, I,* 218-19; Cabot to King, July 27, 1795, Gore to King, Sept. 13, 1795, King, *Life and Correspondence,* II, 20, 31-32; Lawrence Shaw Mayo, *John Langdon of New Hampshire* (Concord, N.H.: Rumford Press, 1937), pp. 268-69.

[33]Oliver Wolcott, Jr. to Washington, Sept. 26, 1795, Gibbs, *Memoirs,* I, 246.

son for the foundation of a paper which existed only to calumniate and blacken the reputations of responsible administrators. Others—Fisher Ames, Timothy Dwight, even Washington—questioned the honesty of the editor's purposes.[34] In Philadelphia the *National Gazette* and its successor, the *Aurora,* set the tone for anti-administration newspapers elsewhere. According to Hamilton the Republican press had mastered the technique of repetition. No reputation, however good, could survive constantly repeated lies. In time the public tires of holding out against the detractions and decides that anyone so often accused "cannot be entirely innocent."[35]

What was poison in a Republican paper was more tolerable in a Federalist sheet. The Federalist editors included some uncommonly skilled vituperators, most violent of whom was the Englishman, William Cobbett, who used the pen name Peter Porcupine. Freneau once called him "Porcupine Peter/The democrat eater," but he was praised by Washington. In asperity, strength and coarseness no Republican editor successfully competed with this master of malediction.[36]

The Federalists were quite willing to get down to individual cases. Not only did they damn the Republican Party en bloc as subversive but, in private letters, they named the traitors personally. Aaron Burr, George Clinton, Albert Gallatin, Thomas Mifflin, John Langdon, James Madison and many lesser men were tagged as intriguing, vile, mischievous, disloyal, overly ambitious or intellectually dishonest.[37] Thomas Jefferson, of course, was the arch-anarch. A socially conscious intellectual, both his learning and his morals were mocked.[38] Possessed of such an unpromising character, the author of the Declaration of Independence could hardly help being

[34]Hamilton to John Adams, June 25, 1792, John Adams, *Works,* VIII, 514; T. L. [Hamilton] to Fenno, July 25, 1792, "Catallus [Hamilton] to Aristides," Sept. 15, 29, 1792, Hamilton, *Works,* VII, 229 252, 270-71; Ames to Minot, Feb. 20, 1793, Ames, *Works,* I, 128; Timothy Dwight to Oliver Wolcott, Jr., 1793, Gibbs, *Memoirs,* I, 107; Washington to Henry Lee, July 21, 1793, to Pendleton, Sept. 23, 1793, Washington, *Writings,* XXXIII, 23-24, 95.

[35]John C. Miller, *Crisis in Freedom, The Alien and Sedition Acts* (Boston: Little, Brown & Co., 1951), p. 58.

[36]Philip Freneau, *Poems,* ed. F. L. Pattee (Princeton: Princeton University Press, 1907), III, 186; Washington to Stuart, Jan. 8, 1797, Washington, *Writings,* XXXV, 360; Cobbett's famous apostrophe to Democracy is quoted in Curti, *Thought,* p. 192.

[37]Hamilton, Sept. 21, 1792, Hamilton to Washington, Dec. 24, 1795, Hamilton, *Works,* X, 19-20, 138; Oliver Wolcott, Sr. to Oliver Wolcott, Jr., Dec. 5, 1792, Oliver Wolcott, Jr. to Oliver Wolcott, Sr., Sept. 23, 1794, Gibbs, *Memoirs,* I, 84, 159; John Adams to Cunningham, Feb. 11, 1809, *Correspondence Between the Hon. John Adams . . . and the Late Wm. Cunningham, Esq.* (Boston, 1823), p. 81, referring casually to the Whiskey Rebellion as "Gallatin's disturbance"; Bradbury to Parsons, April 13, 1796, Theophilus Parsons, Jr., *Memoir of Theophilus Parsons* (Boston, 1859), p. 474; Jeremiah Smith, quoted in Mayo, *Langdon,* pp. 248-49; Hamilton's explanation of the end of his collaboration with Madison is quoted in Alpheus Thomas Mason, "The Federalist—A Split Personality," *American Historical Review,* LVII (April, 1952), 626, 642.

[38]Oliver Wolcott, Jr. to Oliver Wolcott, Sr., Oct. 3, 1796, Gibbs, *Memoirs,* I, 385-86; Dumas Malone, *Jefferson and the Rights of Man* (Boston: Little, Brown & Co., 1951), pp. 473-74.

a conspirator against his country, in short, a traitor. This point was persistently developed over the years, both in letters and in print, by Hamilton,[39] but Hamilton was not alone in the matter.[40]

The extravagance and ferocity of Federalist assaults on the motives, character and reputations of Republicans, collectively and singly, can be partly explained as the tactics of resentful self-defense. They were responding to pain, suffered directly or vicariously in sympathy with men they admired. Washington was reasonably sure that Republican malignity would destroy the union.[41] Oliver Wolcott, Senior, could hardly praise Hamilton enough for the immense national benefits of his economic program and regretted that he was subject to attacks because of that "basest and vilest of human affections envy."[42] He was also convinced of a plot to drive the President to resign "by giving him constant disturbance." Hamilton had the expanded theory that "an unprincipled and daring combination" was trying to destroy Washington's popularity as the first step to the destruction of national independence.[43] As for Hamilton himself, his letters to Washington and to some others show a constant feeling of being persecuted.[44] But a plea of self-defense would go down better if the private records of the Federalists did not so plainly reveal their arrogant prior assumption of a monopoly of patriotism.

Just as the Republicans accused the Federalists of being the tools of a foreign power so the Federalists charged the Republicans with being instruments of France. But there were differences. For one thing, the Federalists circulated their slurs much more frequently than did their opponents. Surviving records show three or four denunciations of alleged disloyalty by the Federalists for every one by the Republicans. Secondly, unlike the followers of Jefferson, the Federalists were in a position to act on their convictions, to use the engine of the state to defend the people against the subversive conspiracy they claimed to recognize.

The French Revolution provided the occasion for the imputation. At its beginning probably most Americans were sympathetic[45] but some were

[39] "Catallus [Hamilton] to Aristides," Sept. 29, 1792, Hamilton, *Works,* VII, 264-66; the complete indictment is in Hamilton to Carrington, May 26, 1792, *ibid.,* IX, 513-35; see also Leonard D. White, *The Federalists: A Study in Administrative History* (New York: Macmillan Co., 1948), p. 231.

[40] See particularly Oliver Wolcott, Jr., in Gibbs, *Memoirs,* I, 121-22.

[41] Washington to Randolph, Aug. 26, 1792, Washington, *Writings,* XXXII, 136-37.

[42] Oliver Wolcott, Sr. to Oliver Wolcott, Jr., June 17, 1793, Gibbs, *Memoirs,* I, 101-2.

[43] Oliver Wolcott, Sr. to Oliver Wolcott, Jr., Nov. 9, 1795, *ibid.,* I, 264; Hamilton, "Explanation," Nov. 11, 1795, Hamilton, *Works,* VIII, 123-24.

[44] For example, Hamilton to Washington, April 9, 1794, *ibid.,* III, 192.

[45] Channing, *United States,* IV, 164-65; Irving Brant, *James Madison, Father of the Constitution, 1787-1800* (Indianapolis: Bobbs-Merrill Co., 1950), p. 371.

skeptical and regarded the enthusiasm for France as unbecoming (and dangerous to) the citizens of a sovereign republic.[46] A pre-revolutionary suspicion of French political philosophy had invaded the minds of many thoughtful men long before the stirring events in Paris.[47] A politically-minded people soon introduced the issue into politics. Charges of dangerous attachment to France and to Britain were exchanged in the campaign of 1792, and the Republicans were permanently tagged as "Jacobins" in that year at the same time as Thomas Jefferson was singled out as the head Gallican of the country.[48]

The internal conflict over the French Revolution and its influence in the United States is not only an episode of our political history; it is also a chapter in the history of the American intellect, in the course of which, to the satisfaction of most conservatives, the Jeffersonians were temporarily but completely identified as revolutionary corruptors of morality.[49] Each side fired salvos of books. The first pair of combatants were imports: Thomas Paine's *Rights of Man* and the book to which it was a reply, Edmund Burke's *Reflections on the Revolution in France.* In America Paine's work was also considered an answer to John Adams' *Discourses on Davila,* a constitutional treatise which had been read by Republicans as a royalist tract. Twenty-four-year-old John Quincy Adams contradicted Paine with his eleven *Publicola Letters,* which were attributed to his father and with that attribution reprinted in London; and pseudonymously in Glasgow and Dublin. All of this by the end of 1791. Thereafter the French Revolution and its controlling ideas remained the chief topic of journalistic and literary controversy, with special reference to the loyalty of American admirers.[50]

More oil was poured on the flames by the arrival of Paine's contemptuous attack on revelation, the *Age of Reason.*[51] Another frightening book was *Ruins; or, A Survey of the Revolutions of Empires,* by the history professor

[46]Samuel Eliot Morison (ed.), *Sources and Documents Illustrating the American Revolution,* p. 259, where Hamilton is reported in Yates's notes of the Federal convention, 1787, as speaking of the danger of foreign influence. He never changed his mind.

[47]Brant, *Madison,* p. 249 on Madison's "Frenchified" politics early in 1789, and Robert Beverley's view of French influence, p. 371.

[48]William B. Hatcher, *Edward Livingston, Jeffersonian Republican and Jacksonian Democrat* (University, La.: Louisiana State University Press, 1940), pp. 17-18; Cabot to Parsons, Oct. 3, 1792, Parsons, *Parsons,* p. 469; Jefferson to Thomas Pinckney, Dec. 3, 1792, ed. Lipscomb, VIII, 443-44; Oliver Wolcott, Jr. to Frederick Wolcott, Dec. 15, 1792, Gibbs, *Memoirs,* I, 84-85; John Quincy Adams to John Adams, Feb. 10, 1793, John Quincy Adams, *Writings,* I, 135.

[49]Curti, *Thought,* p. 199; Vernon Louis Parrington, *Main Currents in American Thought* (New York: Harcourt, Brace & Co., 1930), I, 292-356, is the best-known treatment.

[50]John Quincy Adams, *Memoirs,* I, 25-26; Gilbert Chinard, *Honest John Adams* (Boston: Little, Brown & Co., 1933), pp. 238-39.

[51]Curti, *Thought,* p. 159.

Constantin Volney, a work strongly anti-clerical which concluded that there could be no certain determination of the true religion—with easily imagined effects on the conservative clergy in America. Even more shocking was the translation of Paul Dieterich, Baron Holbach's *Christianity Unveiled,* avowedly hedonistic and anti-Christian.[52]

Worse than words were deeds, such as the founding of Deistical Societies in the United States, and of the synthetic (and short-lived) religion called Theophilanthropy which—it was rumored—was to be exported to the United States from France.[53]

The defenders sallied vigorously from the citadel of New England orthodoxy, led by clergymen and the legal profession.[54] The world view most influential in shaping arguments against France and French ideas was that of Edmund Burke. Apart from theoretical generalizations there is a remarkable coincidence of Burke and the Federalists in most points of applied political science.[55] Burke's ideas were adopted and expanded for domestic consumption by able controversialists, among them Fisher Ames and Noah Webster.[56]

Burke had recommended looking into the workings of a group which has been blamed or credited with full responsibility for starting the French Revolution, the Society of Illuminati, of Bavaria.[57] This society, it was said, aimed to control the world by corrupting its morals. The notion captured the imaginations of Federalists everywhere when they read John Robison's *Proof of a Conspiracy* and Abbé Barruel's *Memoirs, Illustrating the History of Jacobinism,* both on the same subject, which were reprinted in the United States. Abigail Adams circulated Barruel, Phi Beta Kappa was suspected of illuminism, the President of Yale, Timothy Dwight, denounced Jacobinism in America.[58] Gallophobia had become an obsession

[52]Curti, *Thought,* pp. 163, 165.

[53]Charles Downer Hazen, *Contemporary American Opinion of the French Revolution* (Baltimore, 1897), p. 268 (Hereafter cited: Hazen, *Opinion*); Curti, *Thought,* pp. 159-60; Lewis Leary, *That Rascal Freneau* (New Brunswick, N.J.: Rutgers University Press, 1941), pp. 281-82; John Quincy Adams to John Adams, Feb. 17, 1798, John Quincy Adams, *Writings,* II, 255-56; Abigail Adams, *New Letters . . . 1788-1801,* ed. Stewart Mitchell (Boston: Houghton, Mifflin Co., 1947), pp. 179-80, 180n.

[54]For example, Jedediah Morse in James K. Morse, *Jedediah Morse, A Champion of New England Orthodoxy* (New York: Columbia University Press, 1939), pp. 51-58.

[55]For a parallel of Burke and Hamilton see Edmund Burke, *Reflections on the Revolution in France,* p. 303; there are many other instances, *passim.*

[56]Hazen, *Opinion,* p. 143n.; Fisher Ames, "The Dangers of American Liberty," in Cady, ed., *op. cit.,* pp. 108-16; Harry Warfel, *Noah Webster, Schoolmaster to America* (New York: Macmillan Co., 1936), p. 264.

[57]Burke, *Reflections on the Revolution in France,* p. 303n.

[58]Abigail Adams to Mercy Warren, Oct. 5, 1799, *Warren-Adams Letters,* 2 volumes, *Massachusetts Historical Society Collections* (1917-25), Vols. LXXII-LXXIII, II, 341 (Hereafter cited: *Warren-Adams Letters,* the roman numerals referring to these two volumes, not to the over-all series numbers); Abigail Adams, *New Letters,*

which confined the minds and colored the rhetoric of Federalists, blinding the leaders to American political realities and distracting them from the kind of practical politics necessary to keep them in power. The provincializing effect of the mania was shown by the rejection of the metric system in 1795 because it was too French.[59]

The war between France and Britain brought to a peak the excitement previously stimulated by the overthrow of the monarchy and the proclamation of the French Republic. Successive military victories won by the French so heated the blood of their American well-wishers that in at least eighteen American cities and towns such French events were the occasions of civic celebrations. To the Federalists war against Britain was war against the chief bastion of civilization and the excesses of Republican enthusiasm for France seemed hardly credible unless—unless, it was all a great plot to involve the United States in the war on the side of France.[60] A nationwide plot requires a highly placed plotter, so leadership was accorded to Citizen Charles Edmond Genêt, the newly arrived Minister of France, aided, no doubt, or even directed by that same Thomas Jefferson who had probably helped to start the French Revolution when he represented the United States in Paris during the first days of the uprising.[61] Whether the Republicans had been bought or flattered by the French, leading Federalists were sure they saw evidence on all sides that they were pliant agents of France.[62]

Western expansionist projects were taken up and promoted by Genêt (who was condemned for originating more of them than he actually did). Where they involved the use of armies against British or Spanish colonies in the new world it was feared that the armies were really to be used against the United States.[63] The decline and dismissal of Genêt eased Federalist nervous tension somewhat but it appeared that he had left a

p. xxxi; Howard, *Wits,* p. 349; Timothy Dwight, "The Duty of Americans at the Present Crisis," July 4, 1798, W. Thorp, M. Curti and C. Baker, *American Issues* (Philadelphia: J. B. Lippincott Co., 1944), I, 358-63; For a contrary view of Dwight's part in arousing the excitement see Charles E. Cunningham, *Timothy Dwight, 1752-1817, A Biography* (New York: Macmillan Co., 1942), pp. 396-97.

[59]Hazen, *Opinion,* pp. 281-82.

[60]*Ibid.,* pp. 164-73, 214; Ames to Dwight, May 6, 1794, Ames, *Works,* I, 143; John Adams, *Correspondence between the Hon. John Adams . . . and the Late Wm. Cunningham,* pp. 35-37; Charles Adams to John Quincy Adams, July 29, 1793, John Quincy Adams, *Writings,* I, 147.

[61]Oliver Wolcott, Jr. [undated memorandum] Gibbs, *Memoirs,* I, 121-22; Hamilton, May, 1793, *Works,* X, 44; Bailey, *Diplomatic History,* pp. 76-77, gives John Adams' opinion of the nearness of another American Revolution in 1793.

[62]Hopkins to Oliver Wolcott, Jr., Aug. 21, 1793, Gibbs, *Memoirs,* I, 104; Hamilton, "Pacificus," No. 6, July 17, 1793, Hamilton, *Works,* IV, 481-82; King to Hamilton, Aug. 3, 1793, King, *Life and Correspondence,* I, 492-93; John Quincy Adams, "Columbus," No. 2, Dec. 4, 1793, John Quincy Adams, *Writings,* I, 155-56, 160; Link, *Democratic-Republican Societies,* pp. 191-92.

[63]Link, *Democratic-Republican Societies,* pp. 133-38; Cabot to Parsons, Jan. 8, 1794, Parsons, *Parsons,* p. 470.

legacy—the network of Democratic-Republican societies which coincided with the term of his mission. "Gallic Jackals" were carrying on the bad work in these seditious societies. The analogy with the Jacobin Clubs of France and her satellites was only too apparent (actually the Jacobin Clubs owed more to American examples than vice versa).[64] A first fruit of the founding of the Democratic-Republican societies appeared to be the Whiskey Rebellion. The alarm of the administration was shown by the size of the force sent into the west. As Bernard De Voto put it, thirteen thousand men were more than were needed "to collect an excise."[65]

It was charged that an important element of Jacobin tactics was to attempt to destroy the Hamiltonian system of public finance, thus protecting southern planter-debtors, and making it difficult for a then impoverished administration to govern at home or to war abroad.[66] Another Jacobin operation was a smear campaign against President Washington, to destroy his popular reputation which was the chief obstacle against French domination.[67] When a clumsy French spy visited the western country, one of his purposes was to campaign for Jefferson for the office of president; Gallatin, it was said, drafted the instructions and itinerary.[68] The heat of the Republican attack on the Jay Treaty convinced some of the Federalists that the Republican rancor was inspired by France, an inspiration which extended into the House of Representatives.[69] Outside the Congress,

[64]Ames to Dwight, August, 1793, August 8, Sept. 3, Sept. 11, 1794, Ames, *Works,* I, 129, 146-48, 150; Bailey, *Diplomatic History,* p. 58; John Quincy Adams to John Adams, March 2, 1794, to Randolph, June 24, 1795, John Quincy Adams, *Writings,* I, 180, 363; Warfel, *Webster,* p. 228; Johnston to Iredell, Dec. 10, 1794, McRee, *Iredell,* II, 430-31; Link, *Democratic-Republican Societies,* pp. 19-20, 24; John Adams to Abigail Adams, May 5, 1794, John Adams, *Works,* I, 473; Washington to Ball, Sept. 25, 1794, Washington, *Writings,* XXXIII, 505-7; Hamilton, "France," 1796, Hamilton, *Works,* VI, 212-13.

[65]Washington to Henry Lee, August 26, 1794, Washington, *Writings,* XXXIII, 475-76; John Quincy Adams to Pitcairn, March 3, 1797, John Quincy Adams, *Writings,* II, 133; Hamilton alone hinted that the Whiskey Rebels were pro-British: Hamilton, "Tully," No. 2, Aug. 26, 1794, Hamilton, *Works,* VI, 418; Parrington, *Main Currents,* I, 392, quotes a sympathetic contemporary, Hugh Henry Brackenridge, on the fright it gave even him; Bernard De Voto, *The Course of Empire* (Boston: Houghton, Mifflin Co., 1952), p. 342; Ellsworth to Oliver Wolcott, Sr., April 5, 1794, Gibbs, *Memoirs,* I, 134.

[66]*Ibid.;* Oliver Wolcott, Jr. to Oliver Wolcott, Sr., April 18, 1796, Goodrich to Oliver Wolcott, Sr., May 22, 1796, Tracy to Oliver Wolcott, Sr., Jan. 24, 1797, *ibid.,* I, 327, 341, 439; Ames to Gore, Dec. 17, 1794, Ames, *Works,* 157.

[67]John Adams to Abigail Adams, Jan. 9, 1794, John Adams, *Works,* I, 462; Hamilton, "Explanation," Nov. 11, 1795, Hamilton, *Works,* VIII, 123-24.

[68]George Victor Collot, "Plan for a Reconnaissance of the Ohio and Mississippi Valleys, 1796," trans. with an introduction by Durand Echeverria, *William and Mary Quarterly,* Third Series, IX (Oct. 1952), 512-20; Memoranda, May 19, 21, June 15, 1796, Gibbs, *Memoirs,* I, 350-54.

[69]Hamilton, "Horatius," May, 1795, Hamilton, *Works,* V, 182; Washington to Carroll, to Carrington, May 1, 1796, Washington, *Writings,* XXXV, 30, 32-33; John Quincy Adams to John Adams, June 6, 1796, John Quincy Adams, *Writings,* I, 491-92; Higginson to Pickering, Aug. 13, 1795, Williams to Pickering, July 17, 1795, Upham, *Pickering,* III, 195, 177-78.

French influence over the enemies of the Treaty was equally visible, whether in the press or, more alarming, in the riotous demonstrations against the administration.[70]

The office of Secretary of State very early showed its quality of making incumbents uncomfortable. The first Secretary retired out of frustration. The second resigned under a cloud, suspected of improper financial dealings with the French government. The third was dismissed for politicking against his President. It is with the second Secretary, Edmund Randolph, that we are here concerned. Of all high-ranking officers of government he was most severely damaged by the passions of the age. In the cabinet Randolph spoke in opposition to the Jay Treaty and seems to have persuaded the President to withhold assent until the British showed better faith by better treatment of American shipping. The British then intercepted a dispatch of the French Minister which appeared to show financial dealings with the American Secretary of State. The document was shown to Treasury Secretary Oliver Wolcott, Jr. To the fevered state of the Federalist mind "two" plus "x" immediately equalled "four." At a special cabinet meeting, without warning, the President confronted Randolph with the almost unintelligible dispatch in a way which amounted to a charge of bribery. Randolph resigned on the spot and prepared a poorly reasoned defense which had little effect. He argued irrelevancies, skipped over important points and weakened his case with misleading translations of French idioms. His guilt was easily accepted. Historians, up to the present decade, generally followed the contemporary Federalist opinion, or left the question open. (The truth was that he had asked the Minister to pay in advance for French purchases of western wheat so that certain western grain dealers could pay their debts to British creditors and be free to spy about for alleged British influence in fomenting the Whiskey Rebellion.)[71]

James Monroe, United States Minister to France, had almost as hard a time as Randolph had (but was consoled by prompt election to the office of Governor of Virginia and, later, by two terms in the White House).

[70]Monaghan, *Jay,* pp. 391-95; Hamilton, "Camillus," No. 2, 1795, Hamilton, *Works,* V, 202; Ames to Dwight, Sept. 13, 1795, Ames, *Works,* I, 174; Ames to Oliver Wolcott, Jr., Sept. 2, 1795, Oliver Wolcott, Sr. to Oliver Wolcott, Jr., March 21, April 25, 1796, Gibbs, *Memoirs,* I, 230, 323, 332.

[71]Channing, *United States,* IV, 144, 144n.-145n.; Oliver Wolcott, Jr. to Hamilton, July 28, 1795, Gibbs, *Memoirs,* I, 219; Ames to Dwight, Sept. 22, 1795, Ames, *Works,* I, 176; Murray to McHenry, summer, 1795, Steiner, *McHenry,* pp. 159-60; Dana to Parsons, Jan. 20, 1796, Parsons, *Parsons,* p. 472; Hamilton to Washington, Dec. 24, 1795, Hamilton, "France," 1796, Hamilton, *Works,* X, 137, VI, 213; John Quincy Adams to John Adams, Jan. 14, 1797, to Abigail Adams, Feb. 22, 1798, John Quincy Adams, *Writings,* II, 85-86, 261-62.

But see what appears to be the final word, a century and a half later, in Irving Brant, "Edmund Randolph, Not Guilty!" *William and Mary Quarterly,* Third Series, VII (April, 1950), 180-98.

Monroe's trouble was that while serving in Paris he could not bring himself to be enthusiastic about administration policies. The cabinet in Philadelphia came to believe that his reporting was inaccurate, that he misrepresented the United States to France, and France to the United States, in order to promote the interests of the Republican Party. From the first his behavior in France vexed the administration. His final undoing was his tepid and perfunctory defense of the Jay Treaty, an agreement which he cordially detested. He was recalled when the Cabinet memorialized President Washington to the effect that the public interest was not safe in his hands. Their opinion was based in part on a private letter written by Monroe to a friend, which showed an anti-federalist spirit. Back came Monroe to write an attack on Federalist foreign policy. As usual in such controversies he convinced his friends but not his enemies.[72]

Before the heat generated by the Jay Treaty contest had cooled, the election of 1796 occurred. Put in an elementary and almost oversimple way, the Anglo-French war was the central issue. On the one hand the nation was threatened with Jefferson and a French alliance to bring war on Britain, and, on the other, it was Adams and a continuation of the Jay Treaty spirit of appeasement to involve us in a war with France. It is reasonably certain that the French government actively interested itself in the result of the presidential election, through interference in the United States by its Minister, Adet. John Adams, heir presumptive to Washington, had predicted French opposition, and his fellow Federalists said the same.[73] For once they were right about French activity. As a reprisal against the Jay Treaty, in a note of very menacing tone, Adet announced that the French would treat American shipping in the same manner in which the United States allowed Britain to treat American shipping. The note was simultaneously given to the Republican press. Infuriated Federalists cried

[72] Monroe's first offense was the tone of his "Address to the National Convention," August 14, 1794, James Monroe, *Writings,* ed. Stanislaus M. Hamilton (New York, 1898-1903), II, 13-14. For the gathering of the storm see the following: Pickering to Washington, July 21, 1796, Monroe to Logan, June 24, 1796, to Jefferson, Jan. 8, 1798, *ibid.,* II, 482n., III, 6-7, 96-97; Washington, *Writings,* XXXV, 123n.-124n., and marginal notes on Monroe's vindicatory book, probably in March, 1798, a series of texts which gives one of the best insights into Washington's rarely revealed private thoughts, *ibid.,* XXXVI, 194-237; Oliver Wolcott, Jr. to Hamilton [no date] Brant, *Madison,* 442, *cf.* 443; Freneau, "The Republican Festival," *Poems,* III, 151, 151n.; John Quincy Adams to John Adams, April 3, 1797, to Abigail Adams, Feb. 22, June 27, 1798, to Murray, Dec. 8, 1798, John Quincy Adams, *Writings,* II, 157, 261-63, 323-25, 379-80.

[73] Chinard, *Adams,* p. 256; Samuel Eliot Morison, *The Life and Letters of Harrison Gray Otis, Federalist, 1765-1848* (Boston: Houghton Mifflin Co., 1913), I, 70-71; John Adams to Abigail Adams, Jan. 20, 1796, John Adams, *Works,* I, 485; John Quincy Adams to John Adams, April 4, Aug. 13, 1796, John Quincy Adams, *Writings,* I, 486, II, 17-18; Cabot to King, Sept. 24, 1796, King, *Life and Correspondence,* II, 91; Oliver Wolcott, Jr. to Oliver Wolcott, Sr., Oct. 17, 1796, Gibbs, *Memoirs,* I, 386; Upham, *Pickering,* III, 209.

that this was an electioneering trick arranged by the Republicans. Except that it was not arranged by the Republicans, the conjecture was reasonable, even obvious, since the note was published on the Monday before the Friday when Pennsylvanians were to choose their presidential electors.[74] Federalist anger was almost boundless.[75]

Meanwhile, back in the American legation in Paris, more trouble. Charles Cotesworth Pinckney had been sent to succeed Monroe but his presence was ignored by the Directory. Eventually he withdrew to the Netherlands. The rejection of Pinckney could only be part of the American Jacobin plot and Monroe was suspected of having arranged the humiliation.[76]

A good deal of the responsibility for the Federalist obsession with the American Jacobin plot must be attributed to the Adams family. Practically every time one of their letters touched on Franco-American relations it revealed an explicit or implicit conviction of the existence of a pro-French American faction which was a grave threat to the nation. John Quincy Adams, abroad in the foreign service, was their main source of information. For several years the younger Adams stated flatly in almost every one of his letters to the United States from his successive legations that a conspiracy existed between the French government and certain Americans. This correspondence flowed in a steady stream to two Secretaries of State, to Vice President and President Adams, to his mother, Abigail Adams and to neighboring Americans in the foreign service. The high regard in which he was held made his reports the more credible, and gained him the unofficial position of being the Department of State's chief expert on the French Revolution. The tone of his letters can be illustrated by his conclusion that a third of the members of the House of Representatives loved France and French doctrines more than their own country; no greater calumniation of the Congress has been put in writing by an American official since that time.[77]

[74]Brant, *Madison*, p. 445; Pickering to King, Nov. 14, 1796, King, *Life and Correspondence,* II, 108-9; Goodrich to Oliver Wolcott, Sr., Nov. 15, 1796, Gibbs, *Memoirs,* I, 394.

[75]Oliver Wolcott, Sr. to Oliver Wolcott, Jr., Nov. 21, 28, Dec. 12, 1796, Oliver Wolcott, Jr. to Oliver Wolcott, Sr., Nov. 27, 1796, Tracy to Oliver Wolcott, Sr., Jan. 7, 1797, *ibid.,* I, 397, 403, 409, 401, 415-16; Carroll to McHenry, Nov. 28, 1796, Steiner, *McHenry,* p. 203; Bingham to King, Nov. 29, 1796, Hamilton to King, Dec. 16, 1796, King to Pinckney, Jan. 14, 1797, Cabot to King, March 19, 1797, King, *Life and Correspondence,* II, 113, 126, 129, 161; Hamilton, "The Answer," Dec. 6, 1796, Hamilton, *Works,* VI, 215; Washington to Stuart, Jan. 8, 1797, Washington, *Writings,* XXXV, 357-59.

[76]Pinckney to Pickering, [no date] Timothy Pickering, *Review of the Correspondence between the Hon. John Adams . . . and the late Wm. Cunningham, Esq.* (Salem, 1824), p. 113; John Quincy Adams to John Adams, Feb. 23, April 30, 1797, John Quincy Adams, *Writings,* II, 126-27, 160-61.

[77]This paragraph is based on eighteen letters of John Quincy Adams, Feb. 15, 1795 to Jan. 8, 1798, *Writings,* I, II. For the estimate of the House of Representatives see John Quincy Adams to Murray, Jan. 27, 1798, *ibid.,* II, 244-45.

The Federalists kept up their high clamor, both publicly and privately. In his newspaper Noah Webster printed eleven of his own pieces on the French revival of the Roman institution of vassal states, and graphically described the coming partition of the United States. Hamilton wrote a series of newspaper articles entitled "The Warning," in which he cautioned against Americans who were heated enough to try to provoke war with Great Britain although they could excuse anything French. In private letters he supported the idea of sending another mission to France to succeed Pinckney, because the French might soon have an idle army which could be employed in America, assisted by an "INTERNAL INVASION. . ."[capitals his]. President Adams in his Inaugural Address expressed his fear for the freedom of American elections. To the first session of the Fifth Congress he said the French Directory revealed a hope of separating the American people from their government. Minister John Quincy Adams, in letters to his father, continued to sniff treason in the breezes and told how French policy was the joint product of the French government and the American Jacobins. But signals were sometimes confused. When President Adams decided to send a three-man mission to France, Hamilton suggested that Madison be appointed but Oliver Wolcott, Jr. wrote to Hamilton to tell him that Madison's name had been put in nomination by the French. Washington wrote of France "encouraged . . . by a party among ourselves." Secretary of War McHenry told Washington that France planned to dismember the American union, and himself received the identical news some months later from William Vans Murray, United States Minister at the Hague. Murray also blamed Vice President Jefferson's personal charm for much of the moral deterioration of the Senate. Writing to the younger Adams he confided—"His influence . . . does I am convinced immense mischief in the Senate." He invited Senators to "philosophising dinners," and blended "theories of universal benevolence and philanthropy . . . easily with the politics of the day." William Henry Harrison, Captain, First Infantry Regiment, the same who was to be called "Tippecanoe," advised the Secretary of War that it was the duty of all to expose traitors. But Fisher Ames had good news for his friends: Jacobinism was declining in Dedham.[78]

[78]Warfel, *Webster,* pp. 229, 231; Hamilton, "The Warning," No. 1, Jan. 27, 1797, No. 2, Feb. 7, 1797, No. 4, Feb. 27, 1797, No. 6, March 27, 1797, Hamilton, *Works,* VI, 232-33, 238-39, 245-46, 259; Hamilton to Pickering, March 22, 1797, J. C. Hamilton, *History of the Republic of the United States as Traced in the Writings of Alexander Hamilton* (New York, 1864), VII, 17, to McHenry, March 1797, *ibid.,* VII, 18; John Adams, "Inaugural Address," "Special Session Message," May 16, 1797, James D. Richardson (ed.), *Messages and Papers of the Presidents, 1789-1897* (Washington: Bureau of National Literature and Art, 1909), I, 230, 235-39 (Hereafter cited: Richardson, *Messages and Papers*); John Quincy Adams to John Adams, March 4, 1797, Murray to John Quincy Adams, Aug. 23, 1797, John Quincy Adams, *Writings,* II, 136, 193n.-194n.; Oliver Wolcott, Jr. to

While the President, the ex-President, cabinet officers and diplomatists were aggravating each other's quasi-paranoia, the judiciary did not remain silent. Supreme Court Justice James Iredell warned the Philadelphia Grand Jury against those Americans who had foreign attachments, and his colleague of the same bench, Samuel Chase, fretted about "a licentious press."[79]

Thus was an unstable compound balanced for detonation. The concussion which set it off has become memorable as the "X.Y.Z. Affair." Its touches of comic relief went unnoticed in the 1790's as, in the tension of the time, it produced an explosion which almost blew away the First Amendment. Put briefly the story was this. In 1797 the President sent a three-man mission to France, which was not received by the French Foreign Minister, Talleyrand. Instead the Americans were approached by several unofficial characters who told them that unless a private bribe and a public loan were offered there could be no negotiation. The Americans refused to be parties to this kind of diplomacy (which was standing procedure with the French Directory) and two of them, Charles Cotesworth Pinckney and John Marshall, withdrew. The third, Elbridge Gerry, stayed in Paris, apparently because he feared that a total severance would inevitably bring on war. In the United States the dispatches from the commissioners were published with the names of the French extortionists deleted and the letters "X," "Y" and "Z" substituted. The public reaction was, one might say, *bouleversé*. Forceful addresses from civic groups poured in upon the President and were answered with equal ardor. That remarkable woman his wife, Abigail, in letters to her sister and to the historian Mercy Warren showed great excitement; she saw conspirators everywhere.[80]

Federalist reaction in the Congress was equally intense. A pamphlet by Harrison Gray Otis, successor to the seat of Fisher Ames, warned of a French plan to establish Trans-Appalachian and Cis-Appalachian Republics. The Speaker of the House announced to the Representatives that an

Hamilton, March 31, 1797, Gibbs, *Memoirs*, I, 487; Washington to Pinckney, May 28, 1797, to Pickering, Aug. 29, 1797, to Pinckney, Dec. 4, 1797, Washington, *Writings*, XXXV, 452-53, XXXVI, 19, 90; McHenry to Washington, July 9, 1797, Murray to McHenry, Aug. 7, Sept. 22, 1797, Harrison to McHenry, Aug. 13, 1797, Steiner, *McHenry*, pp. 246, 257, 276-77, 264; Ames to Dwight, Oct. 25, 1796, to Pickering, Oct. 4, 1797, Ames, *Works*, I, 204, 217.

[79]McRee, *Iredell*, II, 501-2; Chase to McHenry, Dec. 4, 1796, Steiner, *McHenry*, p. 203.

[80]Morison, *Otis*, I, 110-11; some of the President's replies to public addresses are quoted in Manning J. Dauer, *The Adams Federalists* (Baltimore: Johns Hopkins Press, 1953), pp. 159-61; James Morton Smith, *Freedom's Fetters* (Ithaca: Cornell University Press, 1956), pp. 16-20, correctly attributes much of the popular excitement to the tone of Adams' replies; Abigail Adams, *New Letters*, March 20, 27, April 4, 7, 13, 1798, pp. 147-48, 151, 154, 156; Abigail Adams to Mercy Warren, April 25, June 17, 1798, *Warren-Adams Letters*, II, 337-39.

army had been assembling on the coast of France, not to invade Britain as previously believed, but for the invasion of the United States ("confirmed" in the *Gazette of the United States* a month later). Representative Robert G. Harper gave out tantalizing hints of treasonable correspondence between Americans and Frenchmen. Harper it was who also apologized to the House for attacking an opponent only verbally; the opposition Congressman was too old to be physically beaten.[81]

John Quincy Adams, now stationed in Berlin, expressed himself in his usual vein in several letters on the subject. William Vans Murray, Minister at the Hague, suggested a security measure to the President—organized counter-espionage. Rufus King, Minister at London, wrote to an English correspondent that much of the trouble in America was owing to the ease with which lower-class Irish immigrants could be organized for mischievous purposes. Governor John Jay of New York was convinced that American "Jacobins" were "numerous," "desperate," "active."[82]

These public officials were heartily supported by leading private citizens, the most influential and articulate being Hamilton, Ames and ex-President Washington. Hamilton returned to the press with sulphuric phrases—"Gallic faction," "subaltern mercenaries"—and an oblique reference to Vice President Jefferson as "so prostitute a character." Fisher Ames thought the Federalist leadership should take care to rouse the public. The government needed more force, more revenue, a more warlike use of ships, repudiation of the French treaties of 1778, presidential authority to embargo trade with the French West Indies, a sedition law, "more decision and dispatch." Half measures were weak. The country must wage full but undeclared war. Ex-President Washington, in letters to eminent friends, showed himself in general agreement with the Federalist world view.[83]

To blame all dangers on the Republican Party apparently did not give full emotional satisfaction. There had to be a personal culprit, scapegoat or sacrificial victim. He was easily identified as Elbridge Gerry, the uneasy gentleman-Democrat of Massachusetts, who lingered in Paris after Pinckney and Marshall left, motivated by the hope of making the mission a success

[81] Harrison Gray Otis, "Letter to General William Heath," March 30, 1798, Morison, *Otis,* I, 68-69; Dauer, *The Adams Federalists,* p. 150; Jefferson to Madison, June 21, 1798, ed. Washington, IV, 250.

[82] John Quincy Adams to Murray, June 7, 19, to Pickering, June 25, to Abigail Adams, June 27, to Murray, July 3, Aug. 14, 1798, Murray to John Quincy Adams, July 10, 1798, John Quincy Adams, *Writings,* II, 300, 309-10, 321-22, 323-28, 330-31, 339n.-40n., 350n.; King to Jackson, Aug. 28, 1799, King, *Life and Correspondence,* II, 645-46; Monaghan, *Jay,* p. 417.

[83] Hamilton, "The Stand," "Detector," "A French Faction," *Works,* VI; Ames to Oliver Wolcott, Jr., April 22, 1798, Gibbs, *Memoirs,* II, 47; Ames to Pickering, June 4, 1798, Ames, *Works,* I, 226-28; Washington to McHenry, March 27, to Pickering, April 16, to Hamilton, May 27, to Lafayette, Dec. 25, 1798, Washington, *Writings,* XXXVI, 191-92, 248-49, 272, XXXVII, 66-67.

alone, and by fear of war if he failed. A random sampling of the opinions of ten leading contemporaries who privately expressed decided views on Gerry's conduct shows that six regarded him as a dishonorable, deceitful *intriguant,* three—all southerners—thought he showed very bad judgment and only one acquitted him. (Fortunately for Gerry this solitary vote for acquittal was cast by the President of the United States who had employed him.) When Gerry came home he found himself boycotted by the Massachusetts Federalists. His family had been hooted at, obscenities shouted under Mrs. Gerry's window and effigies hung from the elms around his house. His mail was tampered with and his movements watched.[84]

Other men also felt the sanction of social ostracism. Chief Justice McKean, of the Pennsylvania judiciary, was removed from the Vice Presidency of the Order of the Cincinnati in Pennsylvania. Vice President Jefferson found life in Philadelphia almost unendurable.[85]

To a large number of the Federalists the one thing lacking was a declaration of war—a decision which has never been reached in this country except on the request of the executive. There were obvious advantages to be gained: a monopoly, with Britain, of world trade, weakening of the Republican Party, suppression of the domestic opposition, distraction from an otherwise probable civil war (to be started by Virginia). But the President did not ask it and the House of Representatives refused to consider it.[86]

One question remains to be examined. Just how spontaneous was the combustion of 1798? Almost everything that happens in practical politics is arranged to happen. Both John C. Miller and Gilbert Chinard have suspected that the hysteria was induced.[87] Events and opinions of 1797 can be marshaled to support a conclusion that the sentiment was whipped up by men who were themselves cool and calculating. The Bank of England was in distress and some were alarmed by the thought that Britain might therefore make peace with France. The hypothesis can be advanced

[84]Arthur B. Darling, *Our Rising Empire, 1763-1803* (New Haven: Yale University Press, 1940), pp. 290-91; Lloyd to Washington, July 4, 1798, Vol. 289, Washington Papers, Library of Congress; McHenry to Washington, June 26, 1798, *ibid.;* Higginson to Oliver Wolcott, Jr., Sept. 11, 1798, Gibbs, *Memoirs,* II, 107; Pinckney to King, April 4, 1798, John Quincy Adams, *Writings,* II, 277n.; Pinckney to Pinckney, April 4, 1798; Hamilton, *Hamilton,* VII, 207n.; Pickering to King, June 12, 1798, Pinckney to King, July 18, 1798, King, *Life and Correspondence,* II, 347, 369; Pickering to Marshall, Sept. 4, 1798, Albert Beveridge, *Life of John Marshall* (Boston: Houghton, Mifflin Co., 1916-19), II, 366; Leonard D. White, *The Federalists, A Study in Administrative History,* pp. 250-51; Morison, "Elbridge Gerry, Gentleman-Democrat," *By Land and By Sea,* pp. 192-196.

[85]Lloyd to Washington, July 4, 1798, Vol. 289, Washington Papers, Library of Congress; Jefferson to Lewis, May 9, 1798, ed. Washington, IV, 241; Jefferson to Martha Jefferson Randolph, May 17, 1798, Feb. 11, 1800, Sarah N. Randolph, *The Domestic Life of Thomas Jefferson* (New York, 1871), pp. 249, 262-63.

[86]Dauer, *The Adams Federalists,* pp. 168-70, 191, 195, 198-99, 208, 223-24.

[87]John C. Miller, *Crisis in Freedom, The Alien and Sedition Acts,* pp. 21-22 (Hereafter cited: Miller, *Crisis*); Chinard, *Adams,* p. 274.

that the British financial strains encouraged the American Federalists to use violence against France and terror against the Democratic-Republicans as a support of Britain, for economic reasons and for moral reasons that were equally if not more weighty in their minds. Letters of George Cabot, Alexander Hamilton, Chauncey Goodrich and Oliver Wolcott, Jr. in the first quarter of 1797, rumble and mutter with hopes and fears of the attitude of the Fourth Congress toward military matters. Certainly the enactments of that Congress were unsatisfactorily parsimonious to this group. Military and naval appropriations were cut, not raised. There had been hopes for enlargement of the army and the navy, for a policy of arming and convoying merchant shipping, for the fortification of ports and for a firm line with the French, but they were not fulfilled before the X.Y.Z. Affair. Certainly the emotional turbulence of 1798 could have been seen as a very opportune circumstance for the promotion of the military measures of 1797—that is, military measures and "some others" as Hamilton cryptically put it.[88]

But whether the passions were spontaneous or caused deliberately, they existed. The United States in the year 1798 was a scene of fear and hate, warmed by seven or eight years of heating. Then, subject to these temperatures and surrounded by political commotion, the Congress of the United States sat to enact laws for the internal security of the nation.

The year 1798 was a year of crisis in the history of constitutional liberty. It was a year in which fear of a foreign ideology and of its effects on fellow citizens goaded a party in power to attempt by statute to destroy free speech and a free press. In the same year there was legislation severely restricting the privileges of aliens but the Alien Laws are not our chief concern. Although harsh and probably impolitic, the Alien Laws were undoubtedly constitutional. But the Sedition Law of 1798 attempted to achieve what the First Amendment was written to prohibit. It is not necessary here to analyze the passage, provisions and enforcement of the Sedition Act. The story of that law, and of the three acts applicable to aliens, has been definitively written by James Morton Smith in his *Freedom's Fetters.*[89] It is sufficient to observe of the prosecutions under the Sedition Act that every defendant was a Republican, every judge and practically all jurors were Federalists.[90] The results of the prosecutions support the historical

[88]King to Low, June 6, 1797, Cabot to King, March 19, 1797, King, *Life and Correspondence,* II, 185, 160 (and *passim.*); Goodrich to Oliver Wolcott, Sr., Jan. 27, Feb. 10, 1797, Oliver Wolcott, Jr. to Oliver Wolcott, Sr., March 29, 1797, to Hamilton, March 31, 1797, Hamilton to Oliver Wolcott, Jr., April 5, 1797, Cabot to Smith, April 17, 1797, Gibbs, *Memoirs,* I, 441, 441-42, 482, 486, 490 (the "some others" letter), 495.

[89]James Morton Smith, *Freedom's Fetters, The Alien and Sedition Laws and American Civil Liberties.*

[90]Bassett, *Federalist System,* pp. 263-64.

generalization that in state trials, courts and juries have generally thought it a mark of patriotism to find the defendants guilty.

Although a few Federalists favored conciliation and moderation, the public mood was too excitable for them to prevail. Outside the courtrooms there was widespread social paranoia. A motion to censure Representative John Randolph of Roanoke for denouncing the manners of the military lost in the House by only two votes.[91] Minister Rufus King warned the Secretary of State that several suspicious French characters were leaving Hamburg for Charleston, with dispatches from the Directory concealed in tubs with false bottoms, which report was widely printed as a "diabolical plot" to incite a slave insurrection. The passengers went on from Charleston to Guadeloupe as they had intended, but no Federalist newspaper printed a correction of the story of the great Tub Plot.[92] In an outburst of personal passions, Federalist Representative Rufus Griswold and Republican Representative Matthew Lyon exchanged insults and twice fought on the floor of the House.[93] There was armed resistance—the Hot Water Riots, or Fries Rebellion—to direct federal taxation in Pennsylvania, led by one John Fries who was convicted of treason but pardoned by President Adams.[94]

Alexander Hamilton was zealous to change the nature of the federal republic in the interest of national security.[95] Perhaps because of his money troubles, [96] more likely out of a genuine fear of impending anarchy and civil war,[97] he proposed a vast extension of federal power.[98] He also seems to have been in the center of a scheme to conquer South America.[99] It is not impossible that the failure of Hamilton's political career prevented the prussianizing of the American state.[100]

At this point in their grand ascent John Adams tripped the Federalists and cast them down from the pinnacle by nominating William Vans Mur-

[91]Gerald W. Johnson, *Randolph of Roanoke, A Political Fantastic* (New York: Minton, Balch & Co., 1929), pp. 106-11.

[92]King to Pickering, Nov. 5, 1798, King, *Life and Correspondence,* II, 457; Charles Warren, *Odd Byways in American History* (Cambridge, Mass., 1942), pp. 117-26; Washington to Spottswood, March 25, 1799, Washington, *Writings,* XXXVII, 156; Miller, *Crisis,* pp. 146-50.

[93]Bassett, *Federalist System,* pp. 254-55.

[94]*Ibid.,* p. 280; McRee, *Iredell,* II, 575; Tracy to McHenry, May 6, 1799, Hamilton to McHenry, March 18, 26, 1799, Steiner, *McHenry,* pp. 433, 436, Hamilton, "John Adams," 1800, Hamilton, *Works,* VII, 353-55.

[95]Dauer, *The Adams Federalists,* p. 211; Sedgwick to King, November 15, 1799, King, *Life and Correspondence,* III, 147—on lack of results see Sedgwick to King, May 11, 1800, *ibid.,* III, 236.

[96]Cabot to King, April 26, 1799, Troup to King, June 5, 1799, *ibid.,* III, 8, 34.

[97]Dauer, *The Adams Federalists,* pp. 208, 208n.-209n.; Miller, *Crisis,* p. 175.

[98]Hamilton, *Hamilton,* VII, 280-85; Morison, *Otis,* I, 162.

[99]Marshall Smelser, "George Washington Declines the Part of El Libertador," *William and Mary Quarterly,* Third Series, XI (Jan., 1954), 42-51.

[100]Dauer, *The Adams Federalists,* p. 196.

ray to negotiate with France. This was shocking news to the Hamiltonian wing of his party. If peace with France were formally made, the Federalist position on domestic sedition and foreign foes was untenable. But from public officers and from private citizens the President had good reasons to think the French were ready to be conciliatory.[101] The best that outraged extremists of his own party could accomplish was to get the nomination of a commission of three instead of Murray alone.[102] In the Hamiltonian group all was execration. Their bitterness almost passes belief. Frantic, almost hysterical, they used the strongest polemic language yet heard or read in that decade. After the nomination, Secretary of State Timothy Pickering wrote letters to Hamilton and Washington dissociating himself from the decision. Hamilton expressed regret to Washington. Robert Troup, one of Hamilton's closest confidants, wrote to Rufus King in London that Adams' decision would lead to an attempt to prevent his re-election to the presidency—a pregnant remark. Treasury Secretary Wolcott revealed a lack of competitive spirit—he was beaten thirteen months before the presidential electors were to vote—as he predicted Federalist paralysis and Republican victory.[103] Senator Uriah Tracy threatened to quit the Party.[104] Ex-Senator George Cabot privately blamed the peace move on defects of Adams' character but defended him in the press.[105] Theodore Sedgwick, Speaker of the House, alluded to Adams' vanity and then burst into a colorful display of vituperative fireworks.[106] Fisher Ames and Jedediah Morse, the geographer, were dismayed and angry.[107]

[101]Darling, *Our Rising Empire,* pp. 333-40; Gibbs, *Memoirs,* II, 192; Channing, *United States,* IV, 201-3; Frederick B. Tolles, "Unofficial Ambassador: George Logan's Mission to France, 1798," *William and Mary Quarterly,* Third Series, VII (January, 1950), 20-25; Dauer, *The Adams Federalists,* pp. 190, 228; Ames to Gore, July 28, 1798, Jan. 11, 1799, Ames, *Works,* I, 237, 250; Barlow to Watson, July 26, 1798, Gibbs, *Memoirs,* II, 111-12, see also a quotation from John Adams, *ibid.,* II, 198; Washington to John Adams, Feb. 1, 1799, Washington, "Memorandum of an Interview," Nov. 13, 1798, Washington, *Writings,* XXXVII, 119-20, 18-20; King to Troup, Sept. 16, 1798, to Hamilton, July 14, 1798, to Pickering, Jan. 14, April 12, 1799, King, *Life and Correspondence,* II, 365, 415, 511, 594; John Quincy Adams to Bourne, Aug. 31, 1798, to Abigail Adams, Sept. 14, 1798, to Pickering, April 14, 1799, John Quincy Adams, *Writings,* II, 355, 360-63, 407; Lloyd to Washington, June 18, 1798, Vol. 288, Washington Papers, Library of Congress; Richardson, *Messages and Papers,* I, 282-83, 283n.

[102]Channing, *United States,* IV, 203-4; Pickering to King, March 6, 1799, to Hamilton, Feb. 25, 1799, King, *Life and Correspondence,* II, 548-49, 552n.

[103]*Ibid.;* Dauer, *The Adams Federalists,* p. 232; Pickering to Washington, Oct. 24, 1799, Oliver Wolcott, Jr. to Cabot, Nov. 7, 1799, Gibbs, *Memoirs,* II, 280, 286-87, and see also, *ibid.,* II, 279; Hamilton to Washington, Oct. 21, 1799, Hamilton, *Hamilton,* VII, 335; Troup to King, Nov. 6, 1799, King, *Life and Correspondence,* III, 141-42.

[104]Tracy to McHenry, June 24, Sept. 2, 1799, Steiner, *McHenry,* pp. 393, 416-17.

[105]Cabot to King, March 10, April 26, June 2, Sept. 7, Oct. 6, 16, 1799, also a selection from the Boston *Gazette,* King, *Life and Correspondence,* II, 551, III, 8, 27-28, 101, 113-14, 134-35, 39n.

[106]Sedgwick to King, Nov. 15, 1799, *ibid.,* III, 145-48; Darling, *Our Rising Empire,* p. 342.

[107]Ames to Pickering, March 12, Oct. 19, Nov. 5, 1799, Ames, *Works,* I, 253, 257, 260; Morse to Oliver Wolcott, Jr., Nov. 8, 1799, Gibbs, *Memoirs,* II, 287.

Despite delays deliberately arranged by several in the Cabinet, delays equivalent to contumacy,[108] the mission went to France. The political reaction, and the phrase is used literally, opened the eyes of the Adams family to the warlike and frenzied spirit of that part of the Federalist group which looked to Hamilton for inspiration.[109] Peace was made with France in the "Convention of 1800" but Federalist Senatorial die-hards unsuccessfully fought it to the last ditch.[110] It began to appear that Federalism was irreparably split. Adams regarded the French peace as his greatest achievement[111] which, perhaps, it was.

We can better understand the bitterness of the Hamiltonian Federalists when we realize how high they sat after the X.Y.Z. Affair. It seemed that everyone was anti-Gallican. The composition of the new Sixth Congress, elected in 1798, caused exultation in Federalist hearts and the elections in the spring of 1799 brought further cheer.[112] But all this was merely the last flare of the ember before it turned black. As Adams proved adamant on the question of his mission to France the Federalist correspondence lost its buoyancy and sank, until by the end of 1799 it began to show querulousness and irritation.[113] The drama played to its almost inevitable climax, an open break between Adams and the Hamiltonians, which began with a purge of two of his Cabinet who were more loyal to Hamilton than to him. His patience exhausted, in May, 1800, Adams rid himself of his Secretaries of State and War, Pickering and McHenry.[114] Thus in the year of a national election the angry President shook the pillars of the

[108]Cabot to King, Sept. 23, Oct. 16, 1799, Pickering to King, Nov. 7, 1799, King, *Life and Correspondence,* III, 110, 134, 143; John Adams, *Works,* IX, 255, John Adams to Boston *Patriot,* No. 10, 1809, to Abigail Adams [early 1799], *ibid.,* IX, 270-71, I, 547; John Adams to Abigail Adams, Feb. 22, 1799, J. Q. Adams and Charles Francis Adams, *The Life of John Adams* (Philadelphia, 1874), II, 276.

[109]John Quincy Adams to Murray, May 14, 1799, John Quincy Adams, *Writings,* II, 420; John Adams to Boston *Patriot,* No. 4, No. 9, 1809, Stoddert to John Adams, Sept. 13, 1799, John Adams, *Works,* IX, 248, 267-68, 28; Henry Adams, *The Life of Albert Gallatin* (New York: Peter Smith, 1943), p. 221.

[110]Channing, *United States,* IV, 207, 207n.; Cabot to King, Dec. 28, 1800, Pickering to King, Feb. 17, 1801, King, *Life and Correspondence,* III, 354, 392; Gallatin to Hannah Gallatin, Feb. 5, 1801, Adams, *Gallatin,* p. 259.

[111]*Adams-Cunningham Correspondence,* Feb. 22, 1809, p. 93.

[112]Johnston to Iredell, Nov. 21, 1798, Davie to Iredell, June 17, 1799, McRee, *Iredell,* II, 540, 577-78; Hindman to King, Dec. 13, 1798, Sedgwick to King, Jan. 20, 1799, Pickering to King, May 4, 1799, Troup to King, June 5, 1799, King, *Life and Correspondence,* II, 492, 516, III, 13, 35; Washington to Bushrod Washington, May 5, 1799, Washington, *Writings,* XXXVII, 200-1; Tables showing at least nominal party affiliations of members of the Congress are in U. S. Bureau of the Census, *Historical Statistics of the United States, 1789-1945* (Washington, 1949), p. 293.

[113]For example, Sedgwick to King, Dec. 12, 29, 1799, King, *Life and Correspondence,* III, 154-55, 162-63.

[114]Bassett, *Federalist System,* pp. 207-8; Channing, *United States,* IV, 217, 217n., 239-41; Wilfred Binkley, *President and Congress* (New York: Alfred A. Knopf, 1947), pp. 46-47; Dauer, *The Adams Federalists,* pp. 229, 239-42, 250-51; Goodhue to Pickering, June 2, 1800, King, *Life and Correspondence,* III, 263-64; John Adams to Boston *Patriot,* No. 17, No. 18, 1809, John Adams, *Works,* IX, 301, 303-4.

Federalist house. His political career was to perish in the wreckage of his party.

Thus far we have seen how the faction which administered the government attempted to discredit and suppress the other faction, and simultaneously suffered a serious internal cleavage. The national political events leading to the election of 1800—the publication of the Kentucky and Virginia Resolutions, the case of "Jonathan Robbins," the continued existence of endemic Anglophobia, the dislike of the tax load, the relevant local elections—all these things have been well studied and need no repetition. Only an emphasis on certain occurrences as part of the national emotional storm is here necessary to complete the picture of an age of passion.

There was, for example, John Marshall's "defection" from Federalism. Oddly enough the first effective blow at the repressive statute concerning sedition was his, in a letter to the press written while he was a Federalist candidate for the Congress. He thought the Sedition Act useless and disunifying. Northern Federalists showed by their fury that they felt betrayed,[115] by one who had so lately been a hero of the X.Y.Z.

When the Virginia and Kentucky Resolutions were passed, copies were sent to all the legislatures of the union. The result could only have been disappointing to Jefferson and Madison, the authors. Every state north of Virginia, and even North Carolina, condemned the Resolutions. So warm was the reaction that the Virginia sponsors feared for their personal liberty and took the precaution of passing a law which required state judges to issue the writ of habeas corpus whenever a legislator was arrested. They also strengthened the militia. Judge Iredell promptly predicted civil war and other Federalists responded in similar fashion.[116] To the extreme Federalists the Virginians and Kentuckians were merely pushing the same old plot. Massachusetts Federalists, in particular, took the matter very hard.[117]

Republican industry and confidence in this period made a sharp con-

[115] Beveridge, *Marshall,* II, 386, 387n., 574-77; Sedgwick to Pickering, Oct. 23, 1798, but see also, Pickering to Sedgwick, Nov. 6, 1798, *ibid.,* II, 391, 394; George Cabot [?], "A Yankee Freeholder," *Columbian Centinel,* Oct. 24, 1798, *ibid.,* II, 391-93; Ames to Gore, Dec. 18, 1798, Ames, *Works,* I, 246; John Quincy Adams to Murray, March 26, 1799, John Quincy Adams, *Writings,* II, 397.

[116] Channing, *United States,* IV, 227-28; Brant, *Madison,* p. 464; James Iredell to Hannah Iredell, Jan. 24, 1799, McRee, *Iredell,* II, 543; Washington to Henry, Jan. 15, 1799, Washington, *Writings,* XXXVII, 87-90; Hamilton, *Hamilton,* VII, 278-79.

[117] Pickering to King, Dec. 14, 1798, Sedgwick to King, Nov. 15, 1799, Hamilton to King, Jan. 5, 1800, King, *Life and Correspondence,* II, 493, III, 147-48, 173-74; Washington to Fairfax, Jan. 20, 1799, Washington, *Writings,* XXXVII, 92-94; John Quincy Adams to Murray, March 30, 1799, John Quincy Adams, *Writings,* II, 398; Channing, *United States,* IV, 228-29; Ames, "Laocoön," Boston *Gazette,* April, 1799, Ames, *Works,* II, 109-28.

trast with Federalist defeatism. An economic downturn caused a certain loss of confidence among the followers, and the Adams mission to France had certainly shaken the Federalist leaders.[118] One can only repeat the conclusion that their obsession with the French danger had blinded these men to their own excesses and to Republican tactics. While the Federalists stamped out a nonexistent treasonable conspiracy their opponents built a good political machine. Face-to-face with that machine the Federalists were quitters. There is plenty of evidence of defeatism, while all felt a consciousness of impending climax—the presidential election of 1800. Psychologically the Federalists were at a disadvantage in any election; for that kind of work they were too fastidious.

But before that event Alexander Hamilton indulged in the most eccentric bit of self-gratification in American political history. In the midst of the presidential campaign in which he and his friends were gravely interested, he published an attack on the competence of the incumbent who was his party's candidate for re-election. Hamilton took offense at Adams for having implied that Hamilton was pro-British. Against the advice of his wisest allies he wrote a fifty-three-page pamphlet for private circulation among party leaders, in which he enlarged on Adams' errors of judgment, bad temper, jealousy and "unfounded accusations," all of which, he concluded, were undoing the work of the great Washington.

The efficient Manhattan Republican organization, headed by Aaron Burr, put a copy of the pamphlet in Burr's hands before it reached the mails. Burr had it reprinted for wide distribution, to the glee of Republican partisans everywhere.

Hamilton's closest friends regretted his maneuver. The arrogant tone of the work and the self-praise of the author did nothing to restore their confidence in the judgment of the man they looked to as their natural leader. To the twentieth-century student it seems that a psychiatrist might build an interesting hypothesis on this episode considered in the light of illegitimate birth, insecure childhood, chronic gastric complaints, easy entrapment in Mrs. Reynolds' "badger game," contempt for the common people, yearning for military glory and some recent political shocks.[119] As

[118]Channing, *United States,* IV, 111; Taxation is mentioned as a grievance in Ames to Gore, Dec. 18, 1798, Ames, *Works,* I, 246-47; Ames to Oliver Wolcott, Jr., [tax grievance] Jan. 12, 1800, [the shattering effect of Adams' behavior is apparent in:] June 12, 1800, Oliver Wolcott, Jr. to Bingham [Federalist defeatism]: July 28, 1800, Ames to Oliver Wolcott, Jr. [the same]: Aug. 3, 1800; Bingham to Oliver Wolcott, Jr. [this and the next reveal defeatism]: Aug. 6, 1800, McHenry to Oliver Wolcott, Jr., Nov. 9, 1800, Gibbs, *Memoirs,* II, 320, 368, 393, 396, 398, 445.

[119]Bassett, *Federalist System,* pp. 288-90; Cabot to Hamilton, Aug. 21, 1800, Gibbs, *Memoirs,* II, 407-8; Hamilton, "John Adams," *Works,* VII, [his summary] 361-62; Troup to King, Nov. 9, Dec. 31, 1800, King, *Life and Correspondence,* III, 331, 359; A gastric note is in Lawrance to King, Oct. 15, 1796, *ibid.,* II, 98-99.

for the effect of the pamphlet on the national election it is imponderable, but certainly the Federalists might have exploited the "Jacobin Phrenzy" more profitably if the issue had not been partially eclipsed by the more interesting acrimony among the self-chosen wise, good and rich.

The Federalist press worked hard to influence the legislators who chose presidential electors, the presidential electors and the small body of voters at large. The *Columbian Centinel* of Boston had a department devoted solely to attacking Jefferson's morals, opinions and public record. Several newspapers carried a serial feature called "The Jeffersoniad" and intended to destroy his reputation. The *Connecticut Courant* and the *Gazette of the United States* were especially ferocious. The Philadelphia *Monthly Magazine* in November reviewed four pamphlets on Jefferson's atheism.[120]

But it was hate's labor lost. The final electoral count was Jefferson seventy-three, Burr seventy-three, Adams sixty-five, Pinckney sixty-four and Jay one. Burr's superb management in New York had been decisive. Outside of New York Adams ran as well or better, than he did in 1796 when he carried this state. Losing New York in 1800 he lost the presidency.[121] Of course the electoral vote did not settle the presidential contest, for Jefferson and Burr were tied (in a manner later made impossible by the Twelfth Amendment). The decision now had to be made in the House of Representatives—a "lame duck" House be it noted—where each state had one vote only.

The Federalists were going out of power, and nothing in their term of office so ill became them as the manner of their leaving it, for many congressional Federalists now decided to support Burr, who had been intended by the Republicans to be Vice President. Neither party in New York approved of this course, but even Hamilton's expostulations (legend to the contrary notwithstanding) had little weight.[122] As for Burr, he held his tongue and pen and waited it out. The votes of nine states were needed to elect. On the first ballot and on the next thirty-four ballots, Jefferson received eight and Burr six. At length Representative Bayard, sole member from Delaware, managed to learn indirectly that Jefferson had no thought of undoing every Federalist legislative work, and arrangements were made

[120]For a typical calumny see a quotation from the *New England Palladium* in Frank L. Mott, *Jefferson and the Press* (Baton Rouge: Louisiana State University Press, 1943), pp. 38-39.

[121]Channing, *United States,* IV, 235-37; Dauer, *The Adams Federalists,* p. 257; U. S. Bureau of the Census, *Historical Statistics of the United States,* p. 290.

[122]Hamilton to Oliver Wolcott, Jr., December 16, 1800, Gibbs, *Memoirs,* II, 458-60; Troup to King, Feb. 12, 1801, King, *Life and Correspondence*, III, 391; For the notion that Burr's reputation for dishonesty made him more eligible for the presidency than the quasi-doctrinaire Jefferson see Hale to King, Jan. 21, 1801, *ibid.,* III, 372.

by Bayard and friends to elect Jefferson on the thirty-sixth ballot.[123] And so was completed the "Revolution of 1800."

The Federalist period of American history can thus be presented as a span of twelve years in which every great public decision, every national political act, was somehow governed by fierce passions, by hatred, fear and anger. Although this view must not be stretched beyond proportion, certain it is that the founding fathers had less confidence in each other and in the Constitution than our generation has in both. From suspicion of each other it was a short step to fear and hate.

The Democratic-Republicans feared a centralization which would lead to monarchy. Their fear caused them to make angry and fantastic charges against men now venerated. They thought of their opponents as tools of the British crown, turned against republicanism and the rights of man. Their accusations wounded contemporaries but did no particular damage to posterity because they were not in control of the state; they could only write, speak and, occasionally, riot.

The Federalists feared democracy as mobocracy. They hated the French Revolution and its sympathizers. They could do much harm because they were in charge of the government and could make their enemies feel its force. They jailed and fined in a manner which the First Amendment was intended to prohibit, and they fired off accusations of treason or sedition like birdshot. The most extreme among them justified suspicions of a plot to new-model the government as a unitary, militarized state. They honestly believed that political opposition was founded on sloth, envy, senseless rage or treason. Fear of the "mob," and fear of subversives, made it impossible for them to build a real political engine capable of keeping them "in" and the Republicans "out." Their tragedy was that they were the prisoners of their own propaganda.

These verbal blows were not just "campaign oratory," but were delivered, on both sides, in dead earnest. The evidence is in their private letters to friends, close collaborators and relatives, and in memoranda noted privately for their own guidance. These private documents used the same passionate rhetoric as did the public literature. Some believed so intensely that —blinded by emotion—they willingly destroyed their party rather than admit to errors or excesses.

[123] John Bach McMaster, *A History of the People of the United States from the Revolution to the Civil War* (New York, 1883-1926), II, 524n.; Nathan Schachner, *Aaron Burr, A Biography* (New York: Frederick A. Stokes Co., 1937), pp. 204-9; William Sullivan, *Familiar Letters on Public Characters and Public Events, 1783-1815* (Boston, 1834), pp. 420-21; Baer to Bayard, April 19, 1830, *ibid.*, p. 424.

JOHN R. HOWE JR.
University of Minnesota

Republican Thought and the Political Violence of the 1790s

ONE OF THE CHARACTERISTICS OF THE 1790s that strikes the attention even upon first glance and demands explanation, is the peculiarly violent character of American political life during these years.[1] Throughout our history, politics has not been a notably calm or gentlemanly affair. One need only recall some of the contests of the Jacksonian period, the Populist tactics of the late nineteenth century, the demagogy of Huey Long, or the rough and tumble of Joe McCarthy to realize this. But evidence abounds that the last decade of the eighteenth century constituted a time of peculiar emotion and intensity.

Indication of this is on every hand; for example, in the physical violence, both actual and threatened, which appeared with disturbing regularity. Note the forceful resistance within the several states to the authority of the central government. In Pennsylvania, the flash-point of civil disturbance seemed particularly low, as the Whiskey Rebellion and John Fries' brief rising attest.[2] Or recall the high emotions generated first by such domestic measures as Hamilton's financial program and reinforced by the complex of issues, both foreign and domestic, revolving around the French Revolution and the near-war with France: the Alien and Sedition Acts and the Provisional Army, designed in substantial measure to rid the Federalists of effective political opposition at home; the bands of Jeffersonian militia, formed in the various states and cities from Baltimore to Boston, armed and openly drilling, preparing to stand against the Federalist army.[3] During the critical days of 1798 and 1799,

[1] This paper was first presented to the American Studies Group of Minnesota and the Dakotas, meeting at Minneapolis in the spring of 1966.

[2] Leland Baldwin, *Whiskey Rebels: The Story of a Frontier Uprising* (Pittsburgh, 1939); Harry M. Tinkcom, *Republicans and Federalists in Pennsylvania, 1790-1801* (Harrisburg, Pa., 1950); W. W. H. Davis, *The Fries Rebellion* (Doylestown, Pa., 1899).

[3] Descriptive accounts can be found, among other places, in Joseph Charles, *The Origins of the American Party System* (Williamsburg, Va., 1956); Stephen Kurtz, *The Presidency of John Adams: The Collapse of Federalism, 1795-1800* (Philadelphia, 1957); Dumas Malone, *Thomas Jefferson and the Ordeal of Liberty, 1791-1801* (Boston, 1962).

mobs roamed the streets of Philadelphia inspiring the President of the United States (as John Adams later recalled) to smuggle arms into his home secretly through the back streets.[4]

Events of this sort, however, constituted neither the only nor indeed the most impressive form of violence displayed during the decade. Even more pervasive and ominous was the intensity of spirit and attitude displayed on every hand—and in no place more emphatically than in the political rhetoric of the time. Throughout American political life—in the public press, in speeches, sermons, the private correspondence of individuals —there ran a spirit of intolerance and fearfulness that seems quite amazing. Foreign travelers commented frequently upon it. "The violence of opinion," noted one Frenchman, the "disgraceful and hateful appellations . . . mutually given by the individuals of the parties to each other" were indeed remarkable. Party spirit, he concluded, "infects the most respectable, as well as the meanest of men."[5]

Men in the midst of the political controversy noted the same thing. "You and I have formerly seen warm debates and high political passions," observed Jefferson to Edward Rutledge in 1797. "But gentlemen of different politics would then speak to each other, and separate the business of the Senate from that of society. It is not so now. Men who have been intimate all their lives, cross the streets to avoid meeting, and turn their heads another way, lest they should be obliged to touch their hats. This may do for young men for whom passion is an enjoyment," Jefferson concluded. "But it is afflicting to peaceable minds."[6] Virtually every political figure at some time or another expressed disgust at the abuse to which he was subjected. "I have no very ardent desire to be the butt of party malevolence," complained John Adams to his wife. "Having tasted of that cup, I find it bitter, nauseous, and unwholesome."[7]

Further evidence of the ferocity and passion of political attitudes

[4] John Adams to Thomas Jefferson, June 30, 1813, *The Adams-Jefferson Letters,* ed. Lester Cappon (2 vols.; Chapel Hill, N.C., 1959), II, 346-48. Witness, as well, the burning of John Jay in effigy, the stoning of Alexander Hamilton in the streets of New York and the physical scuffling within the halls of Congress, of which the exchange between Matthew Lyon and Roger Griswold, spittle for fire-tongs, was only the most sensational example. George Gibbs, *The Administrations of Washington and John Adams* (2 vols.; New York, 1846) I, 218-19. Charles Fraser, *Reminiscences of Charleston* (Charleston, S.C., 1854), p. 45. J. F. McLaughlin, *Matthew Lyon, The Hampden of Congress* (New York, 1900), pp. 226-30.

[5] Francis La Rouchefoucauld-Liancourt, *Travels through the United States of North America* (2 vols.; London, 1799), I, 470, 545; II, 514-18.

[6] Thomas Jefferson to Edward Rutledge, June 24, 1797, *The Writings of Thomas Jefferson,* ed. H. A. Washington (9 vols.; Philadelphia, 1871), IV, 191.

[7] John Adams to Abigail Adams, Jan. 20, 1796, *The Life and Works of John Adams,* ed. C. F. Adams (10 vols.; Boston, 1856). I, 485. See also Timothy Pickering to John Clarke, July 22, 1796, Pickering Papers, VI, 207. Massachusetts Historical Society.

abounds: in the editorializing of William Cobbett, Benjamin Bache and Philip Freneau; in the acidulous writings of Thomas Paine; in John Quincy Adams' *Publicola* articles. Perhaps most remarkable were the verbal attacks on the venerable Washington which mid-decade brought. In Virginia, men drank the toast: "A speedy Death to General Washington"; and one anti-Federalist propagandist (probably Pennsylvania's John Beckley) composed a series of articles with the express purpose of proving Washington a common thief.[8] Few men (perhaps with the exception of William Cobbett) could surpass Thomas Paine for sheer ferocity of language. Attend to his public comment on Washington's retirement in 1796: "As to you, sir, treacherous in private friendship, and a hypocrite in public life; the world would be puzzled to decide, whether you are an apostate or an imposter; whether you have abandoned good principles, or whether you ever had any."[9]

As one reads the political literature of the time, much of it seems odd and amusing, contrived and exaggerated, heavily larded with satire.[10] But the satire contained venom; it appears amusing to us largely because our own rhetoric of abuse is simply different.

All in all, then, this seems a quite remarkable phenomenon, this brutality both of expression and behavior that marked American political life with such force during these years. Involved were more than disagreements over matters of public policy—though these were real enough. For the political battles of the 1790s were grounded upon a complete distrust of the motives and integrity, the honesty and intentions of one's political opponents. Men were quick to attribute to their enemies the darkest of purposes. Jefferson acknowledged in 1792 his grim distrust of Hamilton. "That I have utterly, in my private conversations, disapproved of the system of the Secretary of the Treasury," he told Washington, "I acknowledge and avow; and this was not merely a speculative difference. His system flowed from principles adverse to liberty, and was calculated to undermine and demolish the republic, by creating an influence of his department over the members of the legislature."[11] James Madison was even more suspicious of Federalist intentions than was Jefferson.[12] And

8 Philip Marsh, "John Beckley: Mystery Man of the Early Jeffersonians," *Pennsylvania Magazine of History and Biography,* LXXII (1948), 59-60.

9 Thomas Paine to George Washington, July 30, 1796, *The Writings of Thomas Paine,* ed. Moncure D. Conway (4 vols.; New York, 1906-8), III, 213-52.

10 G. L. Roth, "Verse Satire on Faction, 1790-1794," *William and Mary Quarterly,* XVII (1960), 473-85.

11 Thomas Jefferson to George Washington, Sept. 9, 1792, *The Writings of Thomas Jefferson,* ed. P. L. Ford (10 vols.; New York, 1892-99), VI, 101-2. See also Jefferson to Philip Mazzei, Apr. 24, 1796; *Writings of Thomas Jefferson,* ed., H. A. Washington, IV, 139-40.

12 *Letters and Other Writings of James Madison* (4 vols.; Philadelphia, 1865), I, 535-36, 558.

Federalists were quick to find patterns of French Jacobinism in the Republican opposition at home. "I often think that the Jacobin faction will get the administration of our government into their hands ere long," worried Stephen Higginson; "foreign intriguers will unite with the disaffected and disappointed, with Seekers after places, with ambitious popular Demagogues, and the vicious and corrupt of every class; and the combined influence of all these . . . will prove too much for the feeble efforts of the other Citizens."[13] Similarly, John Quincy Adams warned in 1798 that "the antifederalism and servile devotion to a foreign power still prevalent in the style of some of our newspapers is a fact that true Americans deplore. The proposal for establishing a Directory in America, like that of France, is no new thing."[14]

By the middle of the decade, American political life had reached the point where no genuine debate, no real dialogue was possible for there no longer existed the toleration of differences which debate requires. Instead there had developed an emotional and psychological climate in which stereotypes stood in the place of reality. In the eyes of Jeffersonians, Federalists became monarchists or aristocrats bent upon destroying America's republican experiment. And Jeffersonians became in Federalist minds social levelers and anarchists, proponents of mob rule. As Joseph Charles has observed, men believed that the primary danger during these years arose not from foreign invaders but from within, from "former comrades-in-arms or fellow legislators."[15] Over the entire decade there hung an ominous sense of crisis, of continuing emergency, of life lived at a turning point when fateful decisions were being made and enemies were poised to do the ultimate evil. "I think the present moment a very critical One with our Country," warned Stephen Higginson, "more so than any one that has passed. . . ."[16]

In sum, American political life during much of the 1790s was gross and distorted, characterized by heated exaggeration and haunted by conspiratorial fantasy. Events were viewed in apocalyptic terms with the very survival of republican liberty riding in the balance. Perhaps most remark-

[13] Stephen Higginson to Timothy Pickering, Aug. 29, 1795, "Letters of Stephen Higginson," American Historical Association, *Annual Report, 1896* (Washington, 1897), I, 794.

[14] John Quincy Adams to Abigail Adams, May 16, 1795, *The Writings of John Quincy Adams*, ed. W. C. Ford (7 vols.; New York, 1913-17), I, 340 n. See also Oliver Wolcott Jr. to Oliver Wolcott, July 11, 1793, George Gibbs, *The Administrations of Washington and John Adams* (2 vols.; New York, 1846), I, 103.

[15] Charles, *Origins of the American Party System*, p. 6.

[16] Stephen Higginson to Timothy Pickering, Aug. 16, 1795, American Historical Association, *Annual Report, 1896* (1897), I. 792-93. See also Timothy Dwight, *The Duty of Americans in the Present Crisis* (New Haven, 1798); Jedediah Morse, *Sermon* (Boston, 1798).

ably of all, individuals who had not so long before cooperated closely in the struggle against England and even in the creation of a firmer continental government now found themselves mortal enemies, the bases of their earlier trust somehow worn away.

Now the violent temper of American political life during the 1790s has often been noted by political scientists and historians; indeed, one can scarcely write about these years without remarking upon it. But almost without exception, students of the period have assumed the phenomenon as given and not gone much beyond its description. Professor Marshall Smelser has made the most sustained effort at explanation. The key to an understanding of the decade he finds in differences of political and social principle, and in state and sectional rivalries.[17] Similar explanations are implicit in most other treatments of the period.[18]

This argument is certainly to the point, for very real differences of principle and belief did distinguish Federalists from Jeffersonians. As I shall argue more fully in a moment, matters of social and political ideology were of paramount importance to Americans of the late eighteenth century; and this generation divided sharply in its basic definition of social and political life—particularly over the degree of equality and the proper balance between liberty and authority believed desirable. Certainly any explanation of political behavior during the 1790s must take these differences closely into account; nothing in this paper is intended to deny their importance.

I should like, however, to suggest a different approach to the problem; one which emphasizes not the points of opposition between Federalists and Jeffersonians but the peculiar pattern of attitudes and beliefs which

17 Marshall Smelser, "The Jacobin Phrenzy: Federalism and the Menace of Liberty, Equality, and Fraternity," *Review of Politics,* XIII (1951), 457-82; "The Federalist Period as an Age of Passion," *American Quarterly,* X (1958), 391-419; "Jacobin Phrenzy: The Menace of Monarchy, Plutocracy, and Anglophobia, 1789-1798," *Review of Politics,* XXI (1959), 239-58.

18 For example, see Charles, *Origins of the American Party System;* Alexander DeConde, *Entangling Alliance; Politics and Diplomacy during the Administrations of George Washington* (Durham, N. C., 1958); John Miller, *The Federalist Era* (New York, 1960). Variations, however, do appear. Charles Beard detects the basis of Federalist-Jeffersonian antagonism in an economic split between commercially oriented capitalists and agrarians (*The Economic Origins of Jeffersonian Democracy* [New York, 1915]). Louis Hartz, on the other hand, explains the tendency of Jeffersonians and Federalists to exaggerate the "monarchical" or "democratic" intentions of their opponents by their common confusion of American and European social systems (*The Liberal Tradition in America* [New York, 1955]). Richard Hofstadter, finally, has identified a "paranoid style" running throughout American political history, but pays only passing attention to the late eighteenth century ("The Paranoid Style of American Politics," *Harper's,* CCXXIX [Nov. 1964]), 47, passim and *Anti-Intellectualism in American Life* (New York, 1963).

most Americans, both Federalists and Jeffersonians, shared—that is, the dominant republican ideology of the time.

Historians have recently claimed that the American people throughout their history have been profoundly nonideological; that they are now and were equally so during the revolutionary era. Daniel Boorstin is at present perhaps the most articulate spokesman of this point of view. The American Revolution, he argues, was a "revolution without dogma." The revolutionary years "did not produce in America a single important treatise on political theory." In fact, during the latter part of the eighteenth century, "a political theory failed to be born." Indeed, Professor Boorstin insists, the revolutionary generation had no "need" for system-building, for their protests were simply "an affirmation of the tradition of British institutions." Missing was any "nationalist philosophy"; the American revolutionaries "were singularly free from most of the philosophical baggage of modern nationalism." In sum, "the American Revolution was in a very special way conceived as both a vindication of the British past and an affirmation of an American future. The British past was contained in ancient and living institutions rather than in doctrines; and the American future was never to be contained in a theory. The Revolution was thus a prudential decision taken by men of principle rather than the affirmation of a theory. What British institutions meant did not need to be articulated; what America might mean was still to be discovered."[19]

Now this understanding of the revolutionary experience raises numerous difficulties. For one thing, the Revolution involved quite rash, even presumptuous, decisions. More importantly, the revolutionary generation was profoundly dogmatic, was deeply fascinated with political ideology —the ideology of republicanism. This was a generation of Americans which, perhaps more than any other, viewed the world about them very much through the lens of political ideology, and which found meaning in their own experience largely as republican theory explained it to them. This point emerges clearly enough from examination of early revolutionary tracts written during the 1760s and 1770s, the debates over the new constitutions constructed within the several states, argumentation over the proposed federal constitution, and the political wrangling of the 1790s. Recent studies of the Revolution's political ideology argue much the same point.[20]

19 Daniel Boorstin, *The Genius of American Politics* (Chicago, 1953), pp. 66, 71, 73, 94-95.

20 Bernard Bailyn, *Pamphlets of the American Revolution* (Cambridge, 1965) and "Political Experience and Enlightenment Ideas in Eighteenth Century America," *American Historical Review*, LXVII (1962), 339-51; Robert Taylor, *Western Massachusetts in the Revolution* (Providence, 1954); Cecelia Kenyon, "Men of Little Faith: The

The revolutionary break with England and the task of constructing new governments made the American people consciously, indeed self-consciously, republican in loyalty and belief. However lightly royal authority may have rested on the colonies prior to the Revolution, they had then been fully loyal to the idea of monarchy. The English constitutional system they had regarded as the wisest and most benevolent ever devised by man.

With independence, however, they turned their backs willfully not only upon the Crown but upon the whole conception of monarchical government and became aggressively, even compulsively, republican in orientation. Bernard Bailyn is quite right in suggesting that the break with England forced the American people to sit down and systematically explore political principles for the first time in at least half a century, to come to grips intellectually with the political systems which they had already developed, and to decide where their newly embraced republicanism would carry them in the future.[21] Indeed, the whole revolutionary era may be most profitably viewed as a continuing effort by the American people to decide what for them republicanism was to mean.

Republicanism, one quickly finds, is no easy concept to define. Certainly as used within the United States during the late eighteenth century the term remained supple and elusive. Most Americans agreed that republicanism implied an absence of monarchy and English-like aristocracy, and the establishment of governments directly upon the authority and will of the people. But beyond this, concerning the details of republican political forms, agreement vanished. The concept of republicanism was obviously subject to a variety of readings when individuals as diverse as Alexander Hamilton and Thomas Jefferson, John Adams and John Taylor could each claim allegiance to it.

If the men of this generation differed, however, over the specifics of republican theory, most of them shared a common body of assumptions about republican political society—the problems involved in its establishment and the prerequisites for its maintenance and survival—assumptions which together constituted what I would identify as a distinctive world-view, a republican set-of-mind encompassing certain patterns of thought common to both Federalists and Jeffersonians.[22]

Anti-Federalists on the Nature of Representative Government," *William and Mary Quarterly*, XII (1955), 1-43 and "Republicanism and Radicalism in the American Revolution: An Old-Fashioned Interpretation," *Wm. & Mary Quarterly*, XIX (1962), 153-82; Gordon Wood, "Rhetoric and Reality in the American Revolution," *Wm. & Mary Quarterly*, XXIII (1966), 3-32.

21 Bailyn, *American Historical Review*, LXVII, 339-51.

22 Let me emphasize once again that I in no way mean to minimize the points of difference between Federalists and Jeffersonians (or to obscure the disagreements within these two political groupings). I agree fully with Joseph Charles that "the fundamental

One of the fundamental elements of this republican world-view, indeed the most important element for the purposes of this paper, was a widespread belief in the essential frailty and impermanence of republican governments. This notion was founded jointly on the historical assumption that republics had never lasted for long at any time in the past and on the psychological premise that the moral prerequisites of a republican order were difficult if not impossible to maintain.[23]

The men of the revolutionary generation were quite aware that history offered little promise of the success of their republican experiments. From their study of examples both ancient and modern, they knew that the life-span of most republics had been limited. Unlike the English republican theorists of the seventeenth century, they were impressed not with the possibilities of establishing permanent republican orders but with the difficulties of maintaining them at all.[24] Nowhere outside of the United States, with the exception of certain Swiss cantons and scattered European principalities, did republican government prevail by the time of the American Revolution. Of this single, brute historical fact the revolutionary generation was profoundly aware.

For one thing, republics had proved vulnerable historically to hostile threats from the outside, both direct military attack and more subtle forms of influence and subversion. The reasons for this were understood to be several. Republican government, at least by American definition, was described as limited government, carefully restricted in its powers and duties. Republican political society was characterized by a broad permissiveness, by the free play of individual liberty, by the absence of any powerful, dominating central authority; in short, by the minimizing of power (that is, the capacity of some individuals to coerce and con-

issue of the 1790's [indeed, I would add of the whole revolutionary era] was no other than what form of government and what type of society were to be produced in this country" (*Origins of the American Party System*, p. 7). What I wish to emphasize, however, are certain values and understandings held in common by most Americans during the revolutionary era which contributed importantly to the display of political violence that I am seeking to explain.

23 The republican persuasion of the American revolutionary generation, compounded of their reading of classical and English republican theory and the writings of the Enlightenment, and of their own unique historical experience has not been adequately elaborated by students of the revolutionary era. Professor Bailyn has recently opened the problem anew; and Gordon Wood's forthcoming study of the political thought of the 1770s and 1780s will carry our understanding of the matter considerably further. For permission to read his manuscript ("The Creation of an American Polity in the Revolutionary Era") in dissertation form, I am most grateful. When completed, it promises to be the most provocative and illuminating study of late-eighteenth-century political thought yet produced.

24 For the fullest discussion of seventeenth-century English republican thought (which eighteenth-century Americans read with great avidity), see Zera Fink, *The Classical Republicans* (Evanston, Ill., 1945).

trol others).[25] Thus, republican governments proved particularly susceptible to outright attack (for by definition there should be no standing army, no military machine ready to discourage external foes) and to manipulation by outside powers (the people, after all, could be easily reached and their sensibilities played upon).

To be sure, certain circumstances rendered the United States less vulnerable in this regard than other republics had been: their isolated geographical location, the people's sense of identity with and loyalty to their governments and their willingness to stand in their governments' defense. (The recent struggle against England had demonstrated this.) But still the problem remained, as John Jay took pains to point out in the first numbers of *The Federalist.* In numbers two through five, he warned vigorously against the dangers the American states faced from inadequate coordination of their relations with the outside world. The difficulties experienced under the Articles of Confederation, of course, he offered as evidence. Safety against foreign domination, he explained, depended on the states, "placing and continuing themselves in such a situation as not to *invite* hostility or insult. . . ." Nations, he reminded, make war "whenever they have a prospect of getting any thing from it." And such prospects were increased when a people seemed either incapable or unwilling to stand firmly in their own defense. Sensing the continuing suspicion of centralized government, Jay urged upon his readers the importance of learning from past experience and providing their central government with powers adequate to its own preservation. "Let us not forget," he concluded, "how much more easy it is to receive foreign fleets into our ports, and foreign armies into our country, than it is to persuade or compel them to depart."[26] In the late eighteenth century, the American republic stood virtually alone in an overwhelmingly nonrepublican world; in a world, in fact, dominated by monarchies and aristocracies to which the very concept of republicanism was anathema. And the burden of this loneliness was keenly felt.

More importantly, republican governments were deemed frail because of their tendency toward internal decay. If there was one thing upon which virtually the entire revolutionary generation could agree, it was the belief that republican governments were closely dependent upon a broad distribution of virtue among the people. Virtue was one of those marvelously vague yet crucially important concepts that dotted late-eighteenth-century moral and political thought. As used within the United States, it signified the personal virtues of industry, honesty, frugality and

[25] Bailyn, "The Transforming Radicalism of the Revolution," *Pamphlets of the American Revolution.*

[26] *The Federalist,* ed. E. M. Earle, Modern Library edition (New York, nd), pp. 18, 26.

so forth. But more importantly, it meant as well a certain disinterestedness, a sense of public responsibility, a willingness to sacrifice personal interest if need be to the public good. Montesquieu had identified virtue as the animating spirit of republican societies; and the American people fully agreed. "The foundation of every government," explained John Adams, "is some principle or passion in the minds of the people."[27] The informing principle of republican government was virtue. "The only foundation of a free constitution," Adams repeated, "is pure virtue. . . ."[28] To Mercy Warren, he made the same point: "public Virtue is the only Foundation of Republics." There had to be among the people a positive passion for the public good, superior to all private passions. In short, "the only reputable Principle and Doctrine must be that all things must give Way to the public."[29]

Countless Americans echoed Adams' refrain. The problem was that virtue constituted a frail reed upon which to lean. For while men were capable of virtuous behavior, they were also and more often creatures of passion, capable of the most selfish and malicious actions.[30] Americans liked to believe themselves more virtuous than other people, and American behavior during the active years of the revolutionary struggle had convinced many of them of this. The revolution had made extraordinary demands upon their public spiritedness, and they had proved themselves more than adequate to the test. The revolutionary trials had constituted a "furnace of affliction," John Adams believed, testing and refining the American character. The success of the struggle against England had demonstrated virtue's strength among the American people.[31]

By the 1790s, however, the revolutionary crisis was over and it was widely believed that after a period of exhausting moral discipline, men were reverting to their more normal selfish, ambitious and extravagant ways. Evidence was on every hand. The greatest dissolvants of virtue, both private and public, were commonly recognized to be wealth and luxury, for these excited the selfish passions, set men into jealous competition with each other and dimmed their sense of obligation to the

27 "Thoughts on Government," *Life and Works of John Adams*, ed. C. F. Adams, IV, 194.

28 John Adams to Zabdiel Adams, June 21, 1776, *ibid.*, IX, 401.

29 John Adams to Mercy Warren, Apr. 16, 1776, "Warren-Adams Letters," Massachusetts Historical Society, *Collections*, LXXII and LXXIII (Boston, 1917 and 1925), LXXII, 222-23.

30 Concerning the views of human nature held generally by the revolutionary generation, see Clinton Rossiter, *The Political Thought of the Revolution* (New York, 1963), chap. 7 and Stow Persons, *American Minds* (New York, 1958), chap. 7.

31 John Adams, Diary, July 16, 1786, *The Diary and Autobiography of John Adams*, ed. L. H. Butterfield (4 vols.; Cambridge, 1961), III, 194. See also John Adams to William Gordon, June 23, 1776, Adams Papers Microfilm, Reel 89.

larger society. As Thomas Paine remarked in *Common Sense,* "commerce diminishes the spirit both of patriotism and military defence. And history informs us, that the bravest achievements were always accomplished in the non-age of a nation. . . ."[32] "Youth is the seed-time of good habits," he repeated, "as well in nations as in individuals."[33] After an extended period of economic dislocation, brought on by the break with the empire and the war with England, the late 1780s and 1790s witnessed an impressive economic recovery.[34] And this returned prosperity raised powerful questions about American virtue.

Throughout the revolutionary era, gloomy observers had wondered if American virtue would prove lasting. "The most virtuous states have become vicious," warned Theophilous Parsons. "The morals of all people, in all ages, have been shockingly corrupted. . . . Shall we alone boast an exemption from the general fate of mankind? Are our private and political virtues to be transmitted untainted from generation to generation, through a course of ages?"[35] Parsons and others had thought it doubtful. The dilemma was compounded by the belief that once begun, the erosion of virtue spiraled downward out of control. When the people grow lax, John Adams had explained, "their deceivers, betrayers, and destroyers press upon them so fast, that there is no resisting afterwards." Designing men forced their attack relentlessly. "The people grow less steady, spirited, and virtuous, the seekers more numerous and more corrupt, and every day increases the circles of their dependents and expectants, until virtue, integrity, public spirit, simplicity, and frugality, become the objects of ridicule and scorn, and vanity, luxury, foppery, selfishness, meanness, and downright venality swallow up the whole society."[36] Though written during an earlier year, this reflected the moral and political logic of an entire generation and was the logic of moral and political crisis.

America's economic recovery raised a further problem. Another postulate of republican theory, deriving most clearly from Harrington, declared that republican governments were suitable only for societies which

[32] Thomas Paine, *Common Sense, The Political Writings of Thomas Paine* (2 vols.; New York, 1830), I, 53.

[33] *The Complete Writings of Thomas Paine*, ed. Philip Foner (2 vols.; New York, 1945), I, 45.

[34] Stuart Bruchey, *The Roots of American Economic Growth* (New York, 1965), chap. 5; Douglass North, *Growth and Welfare in the American Past* (Englewood Cliffs, N. J., 1965), chaps. 4, 5. Other evidence, such as the wholesale price index, registration of patents and charters of incorporation supports this argument. *Historical Statistics of the United States* (Washington, D. C., 1965), pp. 232-33, 313.

[35] Rossiter, *Political Thought of the Revolution*, p. 211.

[36] *Ibid.*, pp. 209-10. For further elaboration on this point, see John Howe, *The Changing Political Thought of John Adams* (Princeton, 1966), chap. 5.

enjoyed a broad distribution of property. "Power follows property," ran the maxim; and republican government presumed the broad distribution of political power among the people. The problem arose from the fact that as wealth increased, its tendency was to consolidate in the hands of a few, thus threatening both the economic and political bases of republicanism. John Taylor in his *Enquiry into the Principles and Tendency of Certain Public Measures* (1794) made precisely these points. "It is evident that exorbitant wealth constitutes the substance and danger of aristocracy," he wrote. "Money in a state of civilization is power. . . . A democratic republic is endangered by an immense disproportion in wealth."[37] J. F. Mercer of Maryland warned the federal Congress of the same thing. "A love and veneration of equality is the vital principle of free Governments," he declared. "It dies when the general wealth is thrown into a few hands."[38] Both Taylor and Mercer found this insidious tendency at work during the 1790s. Indeed Taylor's whole book was aimed directly at Hamilton's financial program and what Taylor conceived to be its effect in promoting the growth of a monied aristocracy. Mercer's comments were uttered in the context of a sustained attack upon Hamiltonian "stock-jobbers." Not only Jeffersonians were disturbed about the matter, however; for by the 1790s, John Adams was warning vigorously against the social and political dangers posed by a growing aristocracy of wealth.[39]

One further element in the dominant republican ideology of these years contributed to the sense of vulnerability with which it seemed to be enveloped. This involved the problem of faction. Few notions were more widely held by the revolutionary generation than the belief that "faction," the internal splintering of society into selfish and competing political groups, was the chief enemy of republican political society. Republican government, as we have seen, depended essentially upon virtue's broad distribution among the people. Faction was virtue's opposite; instead of an overriding concern for the general good, faction presumed the "sacrifice of every national Interest and honour, to private and party Objects."[40] The disruptive effects of faction increased as a society developed, as wealth increased, as the people became more numerous and their interests more disparate. Gradually, differences of interest hardened into political divisions, with parties contesting against each other for power. Voters were organized and elections manipulated, thus destroying both

37 John Taylor, *Enquiry into the Principles and Tendency of Certain Public Measures* (Philadelphia, 1794).

38 *Annals of Congress, 1791-1793* (Washington, D.C., 1849), pp. 506 ff.

39 Howe, *Changing Political Thought of John Adams*, pp. 140-41.

40 John Adams to Thomas Jefferson, Nov. 15, 1813, *Adams-Jefferson Letters*, ed. Cappon, II, 401.

their political independence and integrity. Permanent party organizations took root, organizations which cared more for their own survival than for the society as a whole. In their resulting struggle, passions were further aroused, internal divisions deepened and ultimately civil conflict was brought on. Such was the deadly spiral into which republican governments too often fell.

Because of republicanism's vulnerability to faction, republican governments were widely believed suitable only for small geographic areas with essentially homogeneous populations. Even during the 1770s and 1780s, when the various states had set about constructing their own republican systems, fears had been voiced that some of them (New York and Virginia were frequently mentioned) were too large and diverse. The problem was infinitely compounded when talk began of a continental republic encompassing thousands of square miles, sharply opposed economic interests and radically different ways of life. To attempt a republican government of such dimensions was to fly in the face both of accepted republican theory and the clearest lessons of historical experience. This, of course, is what the anti-federalists repeatedly argued. "The idea of an uncompounded republik," remarked one incredulous observer, "on an average of one thousand miles in length, and eight hundred in breadth, and containing six millions of white inhabitants all reduced to the same standard of morals, of habits, and of laws, is in itself an absurdity, and contrary to the whole experience of mankind."[41] The argument had a powerful effect upon the whole course of constitutional debate, as is evidenced by the efforts of Madison and Hamilton in *The Federalist* to answer it.

As the decade of the 1790s progressed, the dangers of faction grew ever more compelling. Acknowledging the political divisions which had sharpened during his second administration, Washington spoke directly to the problem in his Farewell Address, issuing a warning which echoed the fears of the whole society.[42] The latter half of the 1790s witnessed further intensification of the struggle between Federalists and Jeffersonians, bringing ever closer what seemed to many the ultimate danger: a division of the nation into two powerful political parties locked in deadly struggle with each other. In such a setting, it was easy to believe

[41] The Agrippa Letters, *Essays on the Constitution of the United States*, ed. P. L. Ford (Brooklyn, 1892), p. 65. Cecelia Kenyon points out how basic this was to the whole anti-federalist position (*Wm. & Mary Quarterly*, XII, 12-13).

[42] The uneasiness with which both Federalists and Jeffersonians defended their party activities during the 1790s illustrates the force of this pervasive fear. See Noble Cunningham, *The Jeffersonian Republicans; The Formation of Party Organization, 1789-1801* (Chapel Hill, N. C., 1954) and David Fischer, *The Revolution of American Conservatism; The Federalist Party in the Era of Jeffersonian Democracy* (New York, 1965).

that the familiar pattern of republican collapse was threatening once more.

Again, republican governments were believed frail because liberty, which was peculiarly their product, was under constant attack from power. In this notion lay one of the basic political conceptualizations of the republican generation.[43] History was seen as comprising a continuing struggle between liberty and tyranny, between liberty and power. In this contest, power was the aggressive element, threatening relentlessly through the medium of ambitious and misguided men to encroach upon and narrow liberty's domain. The antagonism between the two was believed inevitable and endless, for by definition they stood unalterably opposed: liberty signifying law or right, the freedom of individuals to determine their own destiny, and power specifying dominion, force, the compulsion of some men by others. The whole course of recorded history displayed the ceaseless antagonism between the two, and America was not to escape the dilemma. "A fondness for power," Alexander Hamilton had declared knowingly, "is implanted in most men, and it is natural to abuse it when acquired."[44] With this belief, most Americans concurred. As Cecelia Kenyon has shown, the anti-federalists of 1787-88 were especially fearful of power's effects upon human nature.[45] But the federalists shared their fears.[46] The reality of this self-interested drive for power, as Professor Kenyon has shown, was "an attitude deeply imbedded and widely dispersed in the political consciousness of the age."[47]

The dilemma posed by power's continuing encroachment upon liberty's domain provided what Edmund Morgan has identified as "the great intellectual challenge" of the revolutionary era: that is, how to devise ways of checking the inevitable operation of depravity in men who sought and wielded power.[48] The devices most widely, indeed almost universally invoked to achieve this goal were the separation and balance of powers within government.[49] The hope was that in these ways power

[43] Bernard Bailyn has developed this point more fully in the introductory essay to his *Pamphlets of the American Revolution*. The following paragraph draws heavily upon his findings.

[44] *The Works of Alexander Hamilton*, ed. H. C. Lodge (9 vols.; New York, 1885-86), I, 114.

[45] Kenyon, *Wm. & Mary Quarterly*, XII, 13.

[46] See Madison's comments in *Federalist* no. 51.

[47] Kenyon, *Wm. & Mary Quarterly*, XII, 14.

[48] Edmund S. Morgan, "The American Revolution Considered as an Intellectual Movement," *Paths of American Thought*, eds. Arthur Schlesinger Jr. and Morton White (Boston, 1963), p. 26.

[49] John Adams was the most persistent spokesman for the idea of a balanced government, as his three-volume *Defense of the Constitutions of Government of the United States of America*, written during 1786 and 1787, attests.

could be kept under proper restraint by the prevention of its fatal accumulation in the hands of any single individual or group of men.

And yet problems immediately arose, for the American people were by no means in agreement concerning who or what was to be separated from or balanced against each other. Was the proper thing to separate executive, legislative and judicial powers? Or was the more important aim to balance the "constituted bodies" of society against each other: the rich versus the poor, the "aristocracy" versus the "democracy"? Throughout the revolutionary era, there remained substantial disagreement over what the notions of separation and balance really involved.[50]

Moreover, given power's restless and unrelenting character, it was hard to believe that any system of separation or balance could prove permanent. The only hope for liberty's preservation lay in posing power against itself, in setting at balance men's self-interests. And yet given the dynamic character of power's advance, it seemed unlikely that any system of counterpoise could be permanently maintained. This, indeed, was one of the most powerful arguments that critics of the balanced government, such as John Taylor, developed.

A still further consideration contributing to the prevailing belief in the frailty of republican government, one which underlay and informed the notions of virtue and power which we have already examined, involved the revolutionary generation's understanding of the cyclical character of history. In this view, history consisted of the gradual rise and fall of successive empires, each for a period dominating the world and then giving way to another.[51] Over the centuries, there had taken place a constant ebb and flow of ascendant nations, each rising to preeminence and then, after a period of supremacy, entering an era of decline and ultimately giving way to another. This process was often described in terms of a biological analogy; that is, political societies were believed to pursue a natural cycle of infancy, youth, maturity, old age and death. Every nation had unavoidably to pass through the full revolution. Governor James Bowdoin of Massachusetts described with particular clarity the law of cyclical development to which most Americans adhered. "It is very pleasing and instructive," Bowdoin declared,

> to recur back to the early ages of mankind, and trace the progressive state of nations and empires, from infancy to maturity, to old age and

[50] Francis Wilson, "The Mixed Constitution and the Separation of Powers," *Southwestern Social Science Quarterly,* XV (1934-35), 14-28; Benjamin Wright, "The Origins of the Separation of Powers in America," *Economica,* XIII (1933), 169-85; William Carpenter, "The Separation of Powers in the Eighteenth Century," *American Political Science Review,* XXII (1928), 32-44.

[51] This conception has been described in Persons, *American Minds,* chap. 7.

> dissolution: — to observe their origin, their growth and improvement . . . to observe the progress of the arts among them . . . to observe the rise and gradual advancement of civilization, of science, of wealth, elegance, and politeness, until they had obtained the summit of their greatness: — to observe at this period the principle of mortality, produced by affluence and luxury, beginning to operate in them . . . and finally terminating in their dissolution. . . . In fine — to observe, after this catastrophe, a new face of things; new kingdoms and empires rising upon the ruins of the old; all of them to undergo like changes, and to suffer a similar dissolution.[52]

Not only did empires wax and wane, but every phase in their life cycle of growth, maturity and decline could be traced out in the character and behavior of their people. David Tappan, Hollis Professor of Divinity at Harvard, explained how this was true. In the early stages of development, he observed, nations were inhabited by men "industrious and frugal, simple in their manners, just and kind in their intercourse, active and hardy, united and brave." Gradually, the practice of such virtues brought the people to a state of manly vigor. They matured and became flourishing in wealth and population, arts and arms. Once they reached a certain point, however, their manners began to change. Prosperity infected their morals, leading them into "pride and avarice, luxury and dissipation, idleness and sensuality, and too often into . . . impiety." These and kindred vices hastened their ruin.[53] A direct correlation existed, then, between national character and the stages of empire.

This cyclical theory of empire provided a perspective within which the events of the 1790s could be viewed, a way of reading their hidden—and ominous—meaning. For if it implied that in contrast to Europe, America was still young—an "Infant Country" it was frequently called—and on the ascent, it implied as well that eventually American must mature and enter its period of decline. And if this cyclical conception of moral and political change allowed success in the revolutionary contest to be interpreted as evidence of youthful virtue, it demanded that the moral decay, personal extravagance and internal bickering of the 1790s be accepted as indication that the American empire had reached its summit and begun its decline far more quickly than anticipated.

Few people, to be sure, jumped immediately to such a gloomy conclusion. The exhilaration of the Revolution continued to work its hopeful effects upon this generation of men. Even the most pessimistic individuals projected America's demise vaguely into the future; some refused to accept the theory's implications at all. Yet the logic of the argument

52 *Ibid.*, p. 123.
53 *Ibid.*, p. 125.

could not be entirely escaped. At the least, it encouraged people to examine with minute care evidences of public and private morality and to search out patterns of significance in them. The doctrine, moreover, had a certain manic quality about it. During moments of hopefulness and success, it acted as a multiplier to expand the future's promise. And yet when the society became troubled, when virtue seemed to fade, when internal divisions deepened and the sense of common purpose receded, the cyclical doctrine could work just as powerfully in the opposite direction to enhance the sense of crisis. For the logic of the doctrine was clear: a nation's position in its cycle could be clearly perceived in the behavior of its people. And the downward slide, once begun, could not be reversed.

Finally, this sense of the instability of republican government was heightened still further by the American people's understanding of the critical importance of the historical moment through which they were passing. Few generations of Americans have so self-consciously lived an historical epic as did these men of the late eighteenth century. Virtually every important action they took over a span of more than three decades seemed a turning point of great significance: their defense of basic liberties against England, the declaration of national independence, the establishment of republican governments in the several states, the creation of a new national constitution. This sense of historic grandeur carried into the 1790s. As the first administrative agents of the national government, they found themselves setting precedent with every decision made, every act taken: laying the bases of both foreign and domestic policy, determining by their decisions how the new government would function in practice, how popular or elitist it would be, what powers it would possess and what would be retained by the states. "Many things which appear of little importance in themselves and at the beginning," explained Washington, "may have great and durable consequences from their having been established at the commencement of a new general government. It will be much easier," he continued, "to commence the administration, upon a well adjusted system, built on tenable grounds, than to correct errors or alter inconveniences after they shall have been confirmed by habits."[54] Only with this in mind does the intensity of emotion generated by the debate over the use of titles or over President Washington's levees become understandable.

In effect, the American people were carrying further during the 1790s a process upon which they had been embarked for several decades: that is, of defining what republicanism within the United States should in fact mean. Every decision they made loomed as fundamentally important.

[54] *The Writings of George Washington*, ed. John C. Fitzpatrick (39 vols.; Washington, D.C., 1931-44), XXX, 321.

Their opportunity, they firmly believed, would come but once, and if mishandled could not be recovered. Given the cycle of empire, never again would the American be so competent for the task of understanding or defending liberty. The insidious pressures of power, the perpetual tendency of virtue to decay, the relentless historical cycle of nations promised that.

Their moment, then, was historically unique. "How few of the human race," noted John Adams in wonder, "have ever enjoyed the opportunity of making an election of government, more than of air, soil, or climate for themselves or their children." Throughout history, other peoples had suffered under governments imposed by accident or the wiles of ambitious men. Americans, however, now faced the prospect of modeling their governments anew, "of deliberating upon, and choosing the forms of government under which they should live."[55] To blunder in the face of such opportunity would be to compound their disaster.

Moreover, they firmly believed that upon the success of their venture hung the fate of republicanism not only for America but the entire world. "Let us remember that we form a government for millions not yet in existence," reminded one anxious soul. "I have not the act of divination. In the course of four or five hundred years, I do not know how it will work."[56] "I consider the successful administration of the general Government as an object of almost infinite consequence to the present and future happiness of the citizens of the United States," acknowledged Washington.[57]

And yet the success of this momentous undertaking was by no means assured. As late as the 1790s, the American people were painfully aware that theirs was still a political society in process of change; that their political institutions were new, lacking the habit of regularity which only long establishment could provide; that their republican faith was still undergoing definition. The whole venture, as witnesses repeatedly pointed out, remained very much an "experiment." They were embarked directly upon the task of "determining the national character"; of "fixing our national character," as one Jeffersonian remarked, and "determining whether republicanism or aristocracy [the Federalists would say democracy]" would prevail.[58] The society remained malleable, its understanding of "true" republican principles not yet firmly developed, the design of its social and political institutions still unclear.

[55] "Thoughts on Government," *The Life and Works of John Adams,* ed. C. F. Adams, IV, 200.

[56] *Debates in the Several State Conventions on the Adoption of the Federal Constitution,* ed. Jonathan Elliot (2nd ed.; 5 vols.; Philadelphia, 1861), IV, 215.

[57] *The Writings of George Washington,* ed. Fitzpatrick, XXX, 510.

[58] Charles, *Origins of the American Party System,* p. 7, 7n.

In sum, the Americans of this generation found themselves living on a balance, at a moment in history given to few men, when decisions they made would determine the whole future of mankind. Surely their reading of their own historic importance was overdrawn; but it seemed not in the least so to them. And altogether it posed at once an exhilarating and yet terrifying responsibility.

These, then, are some of the attitudes, some of the peculiar understandings which informed this republican generation. It was, I submit, a peculiarly volatile and crisis-ridden ideology, one with little resilience, little margin for error, little tradition of success behind it, and one that was vulnerable both psychologically and historically. Within this context, politics was a deadly business, with little room for optimism or leniency, little reason to expect the best rather than suspect the worst of one's political enemies. And in the end, this republican set of mind goes far to make understandable the disturbing violence of American political life during the 1790s.

THE ROLE OF POLITICAL MILLENNIALISM IN EARLY AMERICAN NATIONALISM

MICHAEL LIENESCH

University of North Carolina at Chapel Hill

AMERICAN NATIONALISM is often contradictory and sometimes extreme. It is seldom consistent or moderate. At times its character can be apocalyptic. Students of nationalism (Curti 1946; Friedman 1975; Gabriel 1940; Kohn 1957; Lipset 1963; Nagel 1971; Weinberg 1935) have described several contradictory characteristics. One element is interventionism, the assumption that America has a mission to make the world safe for democracy. A second feature is isolationism, the tendency to withdraw from the rest of the world in order to protect the nation at home. The third common characteristic is xenophobia, the sometimes irrational fear of foreign enemies. These contradictory and extreme characteristics have been common features of American nationalism. Yet little is known of their origins. This essay suggests that they are in part the product of religion.

The study of the role of religion in politics has a long intellectual heritage. At least since 1937, when H. Richard Niebuhr published *The Kingdom of God in America*, religious historians have sought to describe the influence of religious faith on secular culture. Inspired by Niebuhr, a full generation of scholars led by Sidney Mead (1975), Ernest Tuveson (1968), and Martin Marty (1970) has traced the role of evangelical themes in the creation of national character (see also Handy 1971; Sandeen 1970; Smith 1957). The religious scholars expressed their estimation of the importance of religion in their descriptions of America: "The nation with the soul of a church" (Mead 1975), the "redeemer nation" (Tuveson 1968), the "righteous empire" (Marty 1970). Intellectual historians have been slower to take up the study, but led by Perry Miller (1939, 1953, 1956), they have begun to discuss the role of religious ideas in political thought (see Bailyn 1970; Hatch 1977; May 1976). The religious scholars and the intellectual historians have often concentrated on their respective concerns of theology and ideology, and hence have worked in isolation from one another. But some recent writers, including Sacvan Bercovitch (1978), Alan Heimert (1966), and Cushing Strout (1974b), have described the common themes that unite the sacred and secular realms. In particular, the work of Robert Bellah (1967, 1975) on civil religion has attracted wide interest in the study of religion and politics.

Students of American nationalism, however, have said little of the role of religion. Among political historians, nationalism is most often described as the product of secular forces. The leading histories of the early

NOTE: I wish to thank the National Endowment for the Humanities for its support of this study, and, for their comments and suggestions, Donald Mathews and the members of the Comparative Politics Study Group at the University of North Carolina at Chapel Hill.

nation have examined the influence of economic interests (Beard 1915), state and sectional rivalries (Dauer 1953; Goodman 1964; Young 1967), social distinctions (Fischer 1965), and ideological disputes (Buel 1972; Kerber 1970). They have treated at some length the formative role of party organization (Chambers 1972; Cunningham 1957, 1963; Hofstadter 1969; Young 1966). At least one has considered the contribution of popular political thought (Howe 1967). Yet the political historians have said almost nothing about religion. Similarly among political scientists, the standard sources (Deutsch 1953; Kohn 1957; Lipset 1963) have been firmly fixed on secular interpretations. Political theorists as well have been slow to evaluate the religious content of popular political ideas. In a recent article, Eldon J. Eisenach (1979) discussed the impact of religion on revolutionary thought. On the whole, however, students of American politics continue to overlook its effect on nationalism. This study considers one example of its influence.

Introduction

American nationalism did not begin with the framing of the Constitution. Long before the constitutional founding, a sense of national identity had been developing. But with the creation of a national government, local and state ties increasingly gave way to national loyalties. In the process, myths, symbols, and rituals emerged to constitute the basis of the new national identity (see Merritt 1966). Many of these symbols originated in Christianity (Bellah 1975). Early nationalists were predisposed to view their politics through the filter of their Protestant faith (McLoughlin 1973). Some of them interpreted events according to the most radical brand of religion known, for many early nationalists were millennialists (Hatch 1974). At the end of the eighteenth century there was enormous popular interest in the apocalyptic books of the Bible. In fact, as the religious historian J. F. Maclear has observed, millennial ideas were "so common as to be canonical" (1971: 184). These frightening, fascinating prophecies promised that the end of the world would be preceded by a thousand-year kingdom of peace known as the millennium (for background, see Brown 1952; Davidson 1977: 12-36; Maclear 1975; Middlekauff 1971: 320-49; Tuveson 1968: 1-25). The millennial theme was pervasive in religion, where ministers promised millennial states that ranged from the literal heavenly kingdoms of the Calvinist conservatives to the metaphorical earthly states of the dissenters and deists. Yet it played a role in politics as well, because many nationalists relied on these prophecies concerning the end of the world to make predictions about the fate of the new nation. These political prophets assumed that the founding would usher in a new era of republican peace and happiness. They called this political heaven-on-earth the "political millennium."

These nationalistic millennialists were neither political philosophers nor party leaders. Most were small-town ministers (see Baldwin 1928), though some were lawyers, teachers, or public servants. All were respected in their communities — their selection as preachers and orators attests to their high local status — but many were probably not well known far beyond their own towns. The majority were New Englanders, though a few represented other regions. Almost all tended to be Federalists, or sympathetic to Federalism, but their party affiliation is not at issue here. For the millennial preachers did not pursue any unified national strategy. While some may have read the writings of others, they were part of no identifiable political movement. Instead, they were united by a strong sense of national loyalty and a millennial vision of the new nation. Together, though individually, they articulated a millennial brand of nationalism. They are called here "political millennialists."

In the 1790s, these political millennialists played a part in defining a popular form of nationalism. A review of their works reveals that almost every oration combined millennial and political themes. Nathan O. Hatch (1977: 176-82) has shown that most of the sermons were printed at the request of the listeners, and the same was true for the orations. Thus these sources can be seen to reflect the concerns of not only the speakers, but also their audiences, which included high public officials, local leaders, and citizens. In effect, the speeches helped to create a popular public discourse in which millennialism and republicanism were almost indistinguishable. In his study of revolutionary New England, Hatch (1977: 23) labeled this combination of apocalyptic and republican rhetoric as "civil millennialism." His term implies that by the late eighteenth century, millennial theory had become an essential feature of popular republican thought. Nevertheless, in the 1790s, the melding of millennialism and nationalism took place in an atmosphere of highly partisan political debate. For this reason, I have chosen to call this mixture of prophecy and politics "political millennialism."

Political Millennialism

Millennialism is in essence a theory of apocalypse (for an introduction, see Schwartz 1976; Tuveson 1949: 1-21). All millennialists believe that the end of the world is coming, and that a series of prescribed signs and preordained events will announce the beginning of the end. In some of the more radical biblical texts, such as the books of Joel, Isaiah, and Daniel, the signs are cataclysmic, including wars, earthquakes, and political revolutions. In other more moderate Scriptures, like the book of Micah, the events seem more subdued, as in the prediction that before the end there will be advances in piety, learning, and peace. All millennial Scripture seems to be consistent with the explanation found in the book of Revelation that a cosmological conflict will be joined on the plains of Armageddon, in which the forces of heaven led by the risen Jesus Christ will meet the powers of hell led by the Antichrist, Satan, or the devil. That battle is to end with the promised triumph of the armies of righteousness. With the victory at Armageddon the devil is to be bound in chains and held captive for the thousand-year reign of peace. At the close of that millennial age, however, Satan will break loose again, and aided by the allied armies of darkness, confront the heavenly host once more on the field of battle. In this final conflict Christ and his angels will triumph at last, the forces of evil will be banished forever, and the saints of all the ages will celebrate in chorus the glorious finale of Judgment Day.

Such millennial prophecy has often been applied to politics. The application, however, has been complex. One version of millennialism has emphasized the Second Coming of a warrior Christ who would usher in with the sword the millennial period of peace (Harris 1949; Hill 1971; Lamont 1979). This "pre-millennialism," with its assumption of imminent conflict and war, has been a deeply pessimistic brand of prophecy (Tuveson 1949: 22-70). At least in America, "pre-millennialists" have been found to be conservative and even reactionary in their politics (Smith 1965: 539). A second version, on the other hand, has looked more often toward the thousand years of peace (Toon 1970: 23-41). This "post-millennialism," which assumed that heaven-on-earth would be announced quietly, attained gradually, and marked by steady progress in religion, science, and the arts, has been supremely optimistic in its predictions (Miller 1956: 221-34; Maclear 1971: 188-200; Tuveson 1949: 113-203). Among Americans, "post-millennialists" have been described as pursuing progressive and reformist policies (Smith 1965: 539).

Unfortunately, scholars have seldom ventured beyond the standard ideal types of "pre-" and "post-" millennialism. Yet as James W. Davidson (1972, 1977: 129-41) has shown, millennialism in its truer and more common form has been a mixture of these strains. Prophecy, that is, has seldom been pure: the millennialists of most times have practiced neither pre-millennialism nor post-millennialism, but a complicated combination of each. Thus Davidson found that many millennialists have managed to be simultaneously pessimistic and optimistic. In essence, he suggested that because these prophets pursued what he called an "afflictive model of progress," they could be conservatives and progressives at the same time (Davidson 1977: 131-32). Other recent students have tended to agree. Robert Middlekauff (1971: 279-350) has shown that in early America many Puritan theologians combined pre-millennial mysticism with an interest in post-millennial enlightenment philosophy. In *The American Jeremiad*, Bercovitch (1978: 3-30) demonstrated how eighteenth-century ministers blended Protestantism with capitalism to create the concept of the jeremiad, a combination of pessimistic theology and optimistic economics. Most recently, James Moorhead (1978: 6-22) suggested that even activist nineteenth-century millennialist reformers saw periodic disaster as the price of ultimate progress.

Furthermore, standard historical scholarship has not only divided millennialism into separate pre- and post-millennial parts, but it has assigned each to its own political party, to Federalists and Republicans respectively. For example, in his celebrated and controversial *Religion and the American Mind,* Heimert (1966: 532-45) compared the pessimistic conservatism of the pre-millennial Federalist preachers to the optimistic progressivism of the post-millennial Republican politicians. As Davidson (1972: 251-61) has shown, however, the situation was otherwise; for regardless of party, political millennialists combined pre- and post-millennial themes, mixing their predictions of failure and success. This dualistic form of millennialism was particularly well suited to the 1790s. The early national period was a time of enormous uncertainty, in which the future seemed to hold equal potential for disaster and triumph. Thus the rhetoric of early nationalists could be deeply pessimistic, haunted by fears of international conflict and domestic disorder, and at the same time supremely optimistic, proud of the successful revolution, boastful about the recent founding, and captivated by the seemingly limitless potential of the new nation. Certain Federalists may have leaned more towards pessimism, and certain Republicans more towards optimism. Generally, however, supporters of both parties combined elements of each. In the contradictory 1790s, this contradictory millennialism was the perfect prophecy.

Millennial theory played an important part in defining early ideas of nationalism. Davidson (1972: 254-61) has contended that its prophetic contradictions were used to explain and interpret the political contradictions of this unsettling era. Thus he argued that the theory provided comfort to anxious citizens. But millennialism was in addition a political tool, used not only to explain and interpret events, but also to inspire actions. The 1790s was a period of conflict, with Federalists and Republicans contending over philosophical points and practical issues. But the conflicts of the time became even more heated because they took place in an environment of millennial expectation. In the course of the decade, political millennialism became increasingly intense. In the process, political debate grew increasingly irrational. The result was a volatile form of early nationalism, a contradictory and extreme combination of interventionism, isolationism, and xenophobia.

Interventionism

In 1789 American republicans could be found making the case for republican intervention (Strout 1974a: 42-43). The constitutional founding had announced the possibility of republican self-government. As the first new republican nation, the United States had the responsibility to export its perfect politics to all other countries, to "regenerate the old world" (Mercer 1792: 17). Federalists and Republicans alike, conservatives as well as liberals cheered the extension of revolution, not only to France, but to all oppressed people. "The sceptre of domination," intoned the Federalist Theodore Dwight (1792: 15), "trembles in the hands of every monarch in Europe." Among early nationalists, the more secular relied on enlightened rationalism to inspire their internationalist visions, but the more spiritual looked to millennial prophecy to foretell the future role of America in the world. Prophecy held that the chosen nation had the mission to spread its true religion over the earth, ushering in a new age of faith and announcing the end of time. The political millennialists, mixing prophecy with politics, expanded this millennial vision to include the export of republican liberty, leading eventually to the creation of a universal republic. The Congregationalist conservative Joseph Lathrop

(1794: 22-23) expressed their vision in common millennial terms: "The day is coming, when liberty and peace shall bless the human race. . . . The rod of the oppressor will be broken, and the yoke will be removed from the shoulders of the oppressed. . . . The whole earth will rest and be quiet: they will break forth into singing. . . . Joy and gladness shall be found therein; thanksgiving and the voice of melody."

Political millennialists relied on this prophetic theory to explain the spread of revolutionary republicanism. According to prophecy, world revolution was not only desirable, it was inevitable. The French Revolution seemed an auspicious indication that the predicted universal republic was near at hand. Protestant ministers began to announce the imminent arrival of the New Jerusalem, the "new heavens and a new earth" (McKnight 1794: 24), "the millennium state, or empire of holiness" (Eckley 1792: 20), "the general jubilee" (Robbins 1793: 17). But their prophecy crossed over frequently into politics with predictions that the millennial state would provide not only personal but also "political salvation" (Robbins 1793: 17). For twenty centuries anxious prophets had been searching the skies for the coming kingdom of heaven. With the French Revolution, millennialists could believe that heaven was being realized on earth. The events of the day, advised the theologian Samuel Deane (1794: 31), already presaged "no faint picture of the predicted millennial state." Some began to prepare for its arrival. "We doubt not," declared William Jones (1794: 19), a wealthy trader, "that we are upon the eve of that long predicted period. . . ." A few could see its outline already. "Methinks," concluded the influential Reverend Chandler Robbins (1793: 7), "I already see the dawn of that most auspicious day. . . ."

Millennial theory helped rationalize the excesses of revolution. By the early 1790s, many Americans were watching in horror as the French republic, the happy offspring of their revolutionary seed, became a raging brute that seemed dedicated to devouring all authority, convention, and religion. Paradoxically, however, among political millennialists such violence did not inspire despair. On the contrary, as the revolution seemed to turn toward chaos, they began to see cause for celebration. Apocalyptic theory explains their reaction. Prophecy promised that before the consummation there would be one final battle in which the devil would be bound by the forces of the Lord. Providential catastrophes could appear in many manifestations, and revolutionary France, whether avenging angel or devil in disguise, might be exactly the providential force to announce the end of time. Thus political millennialists were resigned to the conflict, whatever its duration or extent. "The world subsists by *revolutions*," explained one: ". . . if the voice from heaven cry, 'REVOLUTION!' in vain would all the powers upon earth attempt to arrest the motions of these wheels" (*Prophetic Conjectures* 1794: 59). While others cowered, most of the millennialists cheered their revolutionary brothers. "The present aspect of the world is wonderful, and above description affecting!" confided the Presbyterian clergyman Samuel Miller (1795: 31-32). "We behold nation rising up against nation, and kingdom against kingdom. . . . What designs the Governor of the Universe is carrying on, we know not. The Christian patriot, however, cannot help indulging in the confident hope, that all these things are designed to banish tyranny from the earth. . . ."

Millennial prophecy explained the violence of the revolution; enlightened rationalism did not. As events in France took their bloody course, rationalist writers found themselves unable to justify the extent of the carnage. "Perhaps a revolution from the extremes of *Arbitrary Power*, to the fair midway region of temperate LIBERTY," suggested a troubled Elisha Lee (1793: 12), "without a vibration towards *Anarchy* and *Licentiousness* is impossible." Millennialists, however, saw good reason for the bloodshed. David Austin (1794: 392-93), the eccentric but immensely popular preacher, was typical when he described the French revolution as the sword of righteousness leveled against the forces of evil. Americans could be proud that they had introduced the cleansing power of revolutionary war into the world. "Behold, then, this hero of America wielding the standard of civil and religious liberty over these United States!" Austin wrote. "— Follow him, in his strides, across the Atlantic! —See him, with his spear already in the heart of the beast! —See tyranny, civil and ecclesiastical, bleeding at every pore!" Millennial theory stated that as violence became more extreme, peace became more imminent. Thus some began to wish for even more death and destruction, applauding the exportation of the revolution to other nations in Europe. To the political millennialists, the ultimate end of universal freedom justified all the suffering. "It is indeed shocking to think of the present slaughter amongst conflicting powers and parties," admitted one anonymous millennialist (*Prophetic Conjectures* 1794: 58); "but prophecy holds out consolation," he continued, "that when the judgment written shall be accomplished, and the present convulsions subside, — *the remnant shall give glory to the God of heaven* — . . . ."

In fact, political millennialism made world revolution seem positively providential. With the extension of the French revolution, Protestant ministers began to argue in perplexing detail and with remarkable certainty that the prescribed 1260 years of Antichristian rule were finally coming to an end. In 1793 Samuel Hopkins (1793: 150), the dean of American millennialists, could foresee the end in no more than two hundred years, though neither, he calculated, "this or the next generation are like to see it." In 1794, as the revolution turned outward, it seemed much closer to scholars like William Linn (1794: 26-27, 166-71), who saw the end approaching so rapidly that the children alive at that time would experience its glorious arrival. By 1795, with international war raging, millennialists were predicting that the "*men of this generation*" (Watkins 1795: 35), would themselves witness the final scenes. Many predicted the coming end: "The present age is big with events" (Jones 1794: 19); the "GRAND AERA" was "approaching with a speed rapid as the flight of time" (Austin 1794: 425); the "seventh viol" — the final symbolic sign —would "e're long be emptied" (Blake 1795: 28). Yet again prophecy seemed often indistinguishable from politics. Predictions were meant to be read in a "figurative manner," the Reverend Joseph Eckley (1792: 8) told a Boston audience. The coming consummation did not necessarily imply the literal end of the world. Instead it symbolized the destruction of the corrupt monarchies that had long dominated the nations of the earth, "the final catastrophe of the tyrannical system." The political millennialists, exporters of republicanism, welcomed world revolution. "The grand consummation is at hand," announced an excited Samuel Worcester (1795: 9) to an audience of Dartmouth students, "— the conflagration of the political world. . . ."

Isolationism

In the early republic, however, intervention was never far removed from isolation. That is, while early republicans were eager to export the principles of revolution, their ideological forays were almost always exhortative and rhetorical. As soon as this moral intervention began to suggest military involvement, most retreated. The war between England and France was decisive in turning republicans from international revolutionaries into provincial seclusionists (DeConde 1958: 173). Members of both parties, frightened by the threat of European war — Republicans fearing the English, Federalists the French — began to pursue a policy of neutrality. "At a distance we hear the thunders roar, and see the lightnings play," declared one troubled observer (Johnson 1794: 19); "who can tell how soon they may slash across our sky, and enkindle all the fire of war?" As President Washington announced his proclamation of neutrality, many of the political millennialists, until this time ardent interventionists, added their assent, becoming suddenly and somewhat surprisingly isolationist. Millennial theory explains their dramatic reversal. The end of the world promised both chaos and salvation. With the frightening possibility of war, millennialists needed only to turn their attention from the threat of immediate conflict to the promise of ultimate peace. Americans had no need to worry, Worcester (1795: 11-12) told his Dartmouth students; "aloof from the din of battle, and the ravage of war," they could "anticipate the day when war and tyranny, with all their horrors, shall cease from the earth, and when uninterrupted peace, benevolence, and happiness shall prevail. . . ."

Political millennialism helped ease the transition from intervention to isolation. Beyond describing events, millennial theory could interpret circumstances and inspire responses. At times of despair, for example, it offered hope. The chaos of the Old World might well foreshadow the demise of despotism; the peace and plenty of the New World seemed, by contrast, to portend the triumph of republicanism. Americans could watch from afar ". . . the sublime, the awful, and tremendous prospect of the conflict of armies and of battles, and of the wreck and fall of empires," observed the New York physician Dr. Phineas Hedges (1795: 14), adopting the well-worn verse from the book of Micah; "while the political atmosphere of Europe is dissolving with fervent heat, consuming and sweeping away the vile fabrics of despotism, we are sitting under our vines and fig-trees enjoying the sweet fruits of our former exertions." Indeed, the distant conflict seemed to redound to their advantage. "The fruit, which the tempest is shaking from the vineyards of the nations," as one observer (Kellog 1795: 19) put it, was "falling into the lap of Columbia." While rationalists argued that a policy of isolation would profit them at home, their millennialist counterparts went one step further, arguing that isolation would be of benefit to the rest of the world as well. America was the model for other nations, a "miniature," as Worcester (1795: 8) suggested, "of what the world shall shortly be." Instead of plunging rashly into war, Americans could best serve mankind by maintaining their perfect peace. Their chosen nation had been set aside to be the site of the coming millennial kingdom; it was, contended one enthusiastic millennialist (Ellery 1796: 24), "the *fifth Empire*: . . . in us, *all the nations of the earth will be finally blessed*. . . ."

Many of the political millennialists turned to isolationism. The chosen nation had the responsibility not only to extend its influence in the world, but also to maintain itself at home. The United States had been blessed with riches. Others could go on contending for scarce resources; America would remain — "whatever may be the fate of other nations" (Thacher 1796: 24) — the land of abundance. As President Washington declared a Day of National Thanksgiving, the millennialists began to emphasize this theme of peace and prosperity. The ancient vision of Isaiah was commonly heard, as writers turned west to describe the unprecedented potential of their resource-rich continent: " 'The wilderness becomes a fruitful field, and the desert blossoms as the rose'." (Barnard 1795: 22). Some went so far as to extend the theme to the realm of marketplace economics, creating prospects of American lakes covered with sailing ships, canals and rivers teeming with vessels, harbors bulging with the produce of the world, and America, as one prophetic capitalist (Jones 1794: 16) put it, "the emporium of the earth." Blessed with providential resources, the continent itself was the certain sign that the millennium would arrive in the New World. "This continent which we inhabit," rejoiced one July Fourth orator (Lee 1797: 13), "presents to the contemplation of the astonished beholder, a theater for the noblest scenes of Time; and on which the last and finishing act of the World's grand drama will be displayed."

Nevertheless their isolationism was fearful and deeply defensive. Prophecy required, after all, that the coming kingdom could be brought about only through conflict. Thus even at times of hope — indeed, expecially at times of hope — this complex millennialism predisposed the prophets to look for the calamities that would usher in final success. A troubled Reverend Thomas Baldwin (1795: 19) expressed their anxiety: "We know not how soon the present scene may be reversed, and the dark clouds of adversity overshadow our brightest prospects." The prophets assumed that there would be threats to their domestic millennium. In particular they foresaw the danger of constitutional dissolution arising from internal subversion. Federalist ideologues fed their fears by calling attention to the revolutionary sympathies of their Republican enemies, and claiming their complicity in initiating the Whiskey Rebellion. Some even went so far as to intimate the existence of a Franco-Republican plot to overthrow the Constitution (Smelser 1958: 410). Republicans chimed in with allegations that Federalists had conspired in monarchical cabals with their English allies (Howe 1967: 149-50). With the controversy over Jay's Treaty, the United States seemed to become another front for the conflict that raged three thousand miles away. More secular writers, unable to explain the swing from harmony to conflict, became disillusioned and fell into despair. It was surely only a matter of time, a gloomy John Adams wrote to his wife (16 April 1796, in Adams 1841: II, 221), before "our country must be deformed with divisions, contests, dissensions, and civil wars. . . ." But millennialists were neither surprised nor disheartened. Their theory required that perfection be purchased with struggle. Thus Americans would be well advised, the Reverend Joseph Lathrop (1795: 19) told his flock, "to mingle prayers with our praises, and fears with our rejoicing."

The millennialism of the 1790s explained both failure and success. It insisted on destruction, complete with "confusion, dismay, and carnage" (Warner 1797: 19). At the same time, it promised deliverance, "a more improved and happy state . . . before the final consummation of all things" (Lee 1797: 15). Some rationalists assumed a similar dualism. It was a law of nature, stated Oliver Fiske (1797: 15), that "excess should be followed by its opposite extreme." Unlike their rationalist counterparts, however, the millennialists were certain of ultimate vindication, for God had promised to bring "good out of evil" (Mellen 1797: 29). Thus they seemed reconciled to the extremes of desperation and hope that characterized this time of uncertainty. "Those events which appear, at first, altogether threatening and sad," observed the Reverend Thomas Barnard (1795: 17), "are followed with agreeable consequences." Americans had little to fear. The victories of their enemies were transitory. Their own defeats could only, as the Presbyterian preacher John Mason (1797: 27) assured a New York audience, "confirm our faith," for the forces of darkness were "really, though ignorantly" working their own destruction. Thus Americans needed only to trust in their millennial Savior: "What, though Disorder spread from pole to pole, and mingle the nations in universal uproar?" asked a fearless Mason (1797: 28): ". . . *he* will bring order out of confusion, and light out of darkness."

It followed that the political millennialists became armed isolationists. Many writers of the time found themselves mourning the fate of the nation, warning that America would soon "break into parties," become "the dupes of foreign influence," or even "enter into destructive wars" (Taylor 1796: 20). Millennialists did not disagree. Comforted by their two-edged theory, however, they found these threats reassuring. In effect, they were never so content as in times of trouble. "Impending calamity," explained the Reverend Mason (1797: 36), "should stimulate, and not dishearten, the disciples of Jesus. The walls of Jerusalem are commonly built in troublous times. . . ." The millennial prophets stressed preparation for possible conflict; their sermons were filled with exhortations to vigilance. "Let us gird our loins and stand clad in the armour of our defence," exclaimed an excited Reverend Simeon Williams (1796: 21) in a sermon to the local militia, "and our banner will be terrifying to every invading foe." None seemed to suggest that preparation might lead to conflict. On the contrary, as Williams explained (1796: 23), their efforts were not aggressive but defensive: ". . . preparation for danger will never hasten it upon us. . . ." In short, these isolationists sought to create a fortress nation. Millennial theory held that attack was inevitable. When it came, they could look forward fearlessly to defending their land. After all, as Mason (1797: 38) informed his listeners, "With the Lord of Hosts on our side, whom or what shall we fear?" Besides, war was only the preparation for peace, announcing the time when, as the Reverend Williams (1796: 22) recited the familiar refrain from Isaiah, "swords shall be beaten into ploughshares, spears into pruning hooks, nation shall not lift up the sword against nation, nor learn war any more."

Xenophobia

In early nationalism, isolation seemed to lead logically to xenophobia, for the ideology of self-protection required enemies (see DeConde 1966: 3-108). With the turbulent events of the 1790s — the XYZ Affair, the rebellions in the West, the party warfare and partisan plots — American republicans seemed to find enemies everywhere, "foes from without," as one (Rockwell 1798: 5) put it, "and traitors within." Supporters of the new nation began to exhibit an irrational blend of paranoid fear and boastful belligerence. Federalists again led the way with the charge that secret societies, led by the international "Order of the Illuminati," were conspiring to overthrow the government from within (Dwight 1798; Morse 1799). Frantic Federalist ministers went to their pulpits to speak with extraordinary passion of the imagined threat. Republicans responded in kind with their own charges of conspiracy and cabal. Many of those who participated were partisan ideologues rather than millennial prophets. But the partisans were often faint-hearted, begging their fellow party loyalists to pull back from the brink, warning solemnly of "the most direful of calamities, a *Civil War*" (Parkhurst 1798: 12). The political millennialists, on the other hand, certain that the end was drawing near, seemed prepared for their fate. Millennial theory could comfort and reconcile, but it could also exhort and incite. Its logic was compelling. Salvation came only through crisis; it required violent conflict, demanded the constant threat of enemies, insisted on readiness. The political millennialists found themselves, many almost unwillingly, reiterating the importance of this element of conflict. The scriptures promised that the clash of kingdoms would precede the end of time. Hence millennialists could only conclude that their enemies were preparing to begin the final battle. All the signs, the redoubtable Timothy Dwight (1798: 30) assured his many readers, had been "marked out in prophecy, exhibited as parts of one closely united system, and [were] to be expected at the present time; they shew that this affecting declaration is even now fulfilling in a surprising manner, and that the advent of Christ is at least at our doors."

The millennialists became captives of their metaphor. Beyond explanation, beyond interpretation, their millennial faith seemed to exhort them to action. Thus they found themselves demanding — even inciting — the disorder that would bring on ultimate victory. As prophecies became more irrational, policies became more extreme. Federalists lobbied for passage of the Alien and Sedition Acts, called for the creation of a Provisional Army to put down their Republican opponents, and insisted on full pursuit of the "Quasi-War" with France. Republicans replied with calls for resistance and secession. Debate took place in an atmosphere of near hysteria (Smelser 1958: 411-19). Ideology can account for the content of the conflict (Howe 1967; Banner 1970, 44-45), but prophecy provided much of its frenzy. Republican millennialists like Austin (1799a: 3) announced that the last days were closer than ever, that the sixth trumpet had already sounded, and that the moment for the final battle was "at hand." Federalists like David Osgood concurred that the end was near: "Not in France only," Osgood (1799: 13) announced, "but in various other countries, is the devil let loose." The Antichrist seemed to be preparing his attack: ". . . the last vials of divine wrath," Osgood (1799: 14) declared, "are pouring forth upon a guilty world." The millennialist prophets exhorted their fellow citizens to prepare themselves for the fight. The Federalist Elijah Parish (1799: 18) was only one of many who called for total war against the powers of evil, meaning, in his case, France and the Republicans. "Go then, be the soldiers of God," Parish told his congregation. "Like David assaulting the giant of Gath, go in the name of the God of battles. Go and conquer; then shall there be a new song in heaven — 'BABYLON is fallen, is fallen'."

Preparing their audiences for this cosmological conflict, the millennialists seemed unafraid of the actual consequences of war or insurrection. While President Adams declared a Day of National Fast, and more moderate ministers led their flocks in earnest prayer, the millennial prophets, relying on the twin themes of doom and redemption, were pointing to the future with what one called the "most unreserved confidence" (Wells 1798: 21). The coming conflicts, they argued, would be nothing less than "the fulfillment of ancient predictions" (Mellen 1797: 28). War and revolution might well wreak devastation, but out of the rubble would arise, "like a phoenix" (Fessenden 1798: 16), a new, more righteous world. In effect, the approaching struggles would be wars to end all wars. In the final reckoning the armies of righteousness would triumph, while the legions of evil, which had "so disturbed and distressed the world," would "vanish like chaff before the wind" (Belknap 1798: 26). The political millennialists assured their listeners that heaven had intended from the start for America to witness the millennium. This certain promise, a confident Dwight (1798: 29) suggested, "shed the dawn of hope and comfort over this melancholy period." With the growing threat of conflict, the thousand years of peace seemed almost upon them. "The sorrows of present scenes — the expectation of many, and the testimony of Holy Writ all unite in teaching that the Great Day is at hand," announced Austin (1799b: 24). "The long predicted jubilee trump is about to sound."

Millennial theory demanded the inevitability of destruction. France had no intention of attacking the United States. Yet millennialists pictured the French as an army of evil, poised and ready to attack. Millennial ministers encouraged their congregations to pray to God, confess their sins, and humiliate themselves, lest God "suffer even this wicked nation [France] to scourge, if not wholly to destroy us" (Stone 1799: 29). Orators identified Bonaparte as the embodiment of the Antichrist, denounced French actions as examples of the "wiles of the Devil" (Doggett 1799: 20), and described how the revolutionary armies had "waged war with heaven as well as with earth" (Fiske 1799: 23). The United States was not in danger of invasion or insurrection. But frenzied millennialists, certain of their cosmological enemies, drew fantastic pictures of imminent conflict. Noah Worcester (1800: 26) spoke of the threat of "assassination and massacre." Thomas Grant (1799) described burning villages, desolated farms, violated wives, and murdered children. William Brown (1799: 20) pictured Haitian-style slave uprisings, with "white-men, butchered by their infuriate slaves, the shrieks of mothers, and of virgins, a prey to more than demonic lust and barbarity, and the cries of infants. . . ." By the close of the century, millennialists had come face to face with the ultimate implication of their theory: they found themselves demanding their own Armageddon. Even at that moment, stated a fearful Reverend Daniel Humphreys (1800: 35), God was pouring out his wrath. The political world would soon be destroyed. "Even so," prayed the resigned Humphreys, "come Lord Jesus."

The Decline of Millennial Nationalism

At the close of the 1790s, American nationalists found themselves surrounded by threats of invasion and insurrection. Few if any seemed to know how they had come to such a pass. But some began to search for the causes of the crisis, and to lay blame for the contradictory and extreme policies of the time. Some of their criticism was aimed at the partisan ideologues who had led them down what one called "the dark abyss of visionary speculation" (Woodward 1798: 15). But much was leveled against the political millennialists as well. The skeptics pointed out that their end-of-the-world predictions had not transformed the new nation into the New Jerusalem. Such prophecies had consisted of "one fine and glittering notion after another" (Mitchell 1800: 9). The prophets had foreseen "new *Edens,*" pictured "modern *Paradises,*" predicted the "golden age" (Mitchell 1800: 9; Bangs 1800: 5). Their promises, however, as the tough-minded David Daggett (1799: 18) put it, had proven "theoretic, speculative, and delusive." By the close of the century, many of these critics had come to contend that, in their search for an appropriate form of nationalism, Americans had looked too often to what one (Gould 1798: 12) called "the precarious credit of political prophecies."

Millennial prophecy began to be challenged by the idea of pragmatic reform. A new breed of nationalist — doctors, lawyers, merchants, even a few ministers — began to suggest that politics be based on more than the promise of heavenly perfection. The American people might well assume that God had led them to their present state. But providence alone would not suffice to lead them in the future. Americans, one of these new nationalists (Lewis 1799: 25) advised, must " 'work out our own salvation'." Though the United States had been set aside to be the chosen nation, it would retain its chosen status only by "proper management" (Andros 1799: 13). The new non-millennial nationalists demanded human action, informing their audiences that the future depended on the power of steady perseverence. In turn, the application of human action held out the possibility of incremental progress. These nationalists did not assume that progress would be inevitable: prosperity was only "considerably certain," according to the Reverend Samuel Austin (1798: 11), or "at least probable." Nevertheles, prophetic predictions were not necessary for success. Instead they relied on "prosperous enterprise, successful industry, and a long course of fortunate events" (Sullivan 1800: 11). In the future, Americans might best look to human will to take the place of heavenly predestination. "Our own happiness," concluded the realistic David Ogden (1798: 9), "is in our own hands."

The idea of progress seemed inimical to millennial theory. Yet the conflict was more apparent than real. For the new nationalists held visions of the future every bit as grand as any millennial prophecies. In the New World even a "short life" was "of more worth than Methuselah's term of years" (Whiting 1798: 18). In the space of only a decade a sleepy provincial colony had been converted into a rising world power. The future promised even more extraordinary advancement. Progress, ventured one excited nationalist (Andros 1799: 10), might "almost exceed the bonds of calculation." In fact, progressive reform provided its own version of prophecy. "We have no reason to pronounce visionary," observed the Massachusetts lawyer Edward Bangs (1800: 15), "the hope and faith of pious men who pray for a millennial state." Americans did not need to abandon the millennium. Instead they could set to work creating it themselves. The New Jerusalem, offered Woodward (1798: 26), would be "ushered in by human means."

The new nationalists replaced faith in prophecy with an even more ardent faith in progress. Millennial ideas seemed finally to fade. The spirit of the apocalypse was banished to the realm of radical religion, where hot-blooded preachers like David Austin (1800: 18) could persist in declaring that the end of the world had arrived at last, and that the "New Jerusalem-day," as he announced again and again, was "at the door." Similarly the vision of paradise was consigned to the domain of liberal theology, where cool-headed theologians like Jeremy Belknap (1798: 27; 29) could urge their flocks to work towards perfection "by slow degrees," cultivating "in our own minds and conduct," the moral virtues that would prepare the way "for the universal reign of the Prince of peace." But much of the old millennialism was absorbed into this new form of nationalism.

Throughout the final decade, millennialists had spoken of the end of the century as the time that would announce the end of the world. With the new century, they were forced to admit that the end had not yet come, and that the millennium, as the chastened Robert Fowle (1800: 14) conceded, "may be more distant than our wishes may lead us to expect." Yet as the certainty of a heavenly millennium retreated, the possibility of an earthly one seemed closer than ever. For to these new nationalists, the perfect future state would be the new American nation, "an empire," as one prophet of reform (Davis 1800: 21) phrased it, "shining with celestial splendour."

Conclusion

For years, American nationalism has been the topic of scholarly study. Many factors have been shown to contribute to its character. One influence that has long been overlooked, however, is the role of religion. In particular, scholars have underestimated the importance of millennialism in the shaping of early nationalism.

In the formative 1790s, millennialist preachers and orators were instrumental in creating and disseminating a complicated form of millennial theory. This theory, though the product of religion, became pervasive in politics, where it provided a cosmological framework within which republicans of all parties could interpret contemporary events. Millennial theory provided ready explanations for the contradictions and conflicts of this troubling time. But it also exacerbated party rivalries and heightened international tensions. In the process, it helped to forge an extreme form of nationalism, a volatile combination of interventionism, isolationism, and xenophobia.

Though later nationalists, led by the pragmatic reformers of the late eighteenth century, would reject this millennialism, its influence has endured. In his *Redeemer Nation* (1968), Ernest Tuveson found millennial themes to be prominent in westward expansion, the Civil War, and the entry into the First and Second World Wars. In our own time, they have almost certainly been present in the best and worst of policies: the Marshall Plan and the Vietnam War, the Nonproliferation Treaty and the Bricker Amendment, human rights campaigns and anticommunist crusades. We have seen these features often: the idealistic interventionism, the anxious isolationism, the fearful and blustering xenophobia. We will see them often in the future. For the millennial impulse, for better or worse, remains an indelible element of our nationalism.

REFERENCES

Adams, John. 1841. Letter to Abigail Adams, 16 April 1796. In Charles Francis Adams, ed., *Letters of John Adams, Addressed to His Wife*. Boston: Charles C. Little and James Brown.

Andros, Thomas. 1799. *An Oration, Delivered at Dighton, (Massachusetts), July 4, 1794.* . . . Newbedford: John Spooner.

Austin, David. 1794. "The Downfall of Mystical Babylon; or, a Key to the Providence of God, in the Political Operations of 1793-94." In David Austin, ed., *The Millennium, or the Thousand Years of Prosperity . . . Shortly to Commence. . . .* Elizabethtown: Shepard Kollock.

[______]. 1799a. *The First Vibration of the Jubilee Trump*! [Elizabethtown]: n.p.

[______]. 1799b. *The Millennial Door Thrown Open; or the Trump of the Latter Day Glory. . . .* East Windsor: Luther Pratt.

[______]. 1800. *The Dawn of Day, Introductory to the Rising Sun. . . .* [New Haven]: Reed and Morse.

Austin, Samuel, A.M. 1798. *An Oration, Pronounced at Worcester, on the Fourth of July, 1798. . . .* Worcester: Leonard Worcester.

Bailyn, Bernard. 1970. "Religion and Revolution: Three Biographical Studies." *Perspectives in American History* 4:85-169.

Baldwin, Alice M. 1928. *The New England Clergy and the American Revolution.* Durham: Duke University Press.

Baldwin, Thomas, A.M. 1795. *A Sermon Delivered February 19, 1795: Being the Day of National Thanksgiving. . . .* Boston: Manning & Loring.

Bangs, Edward. 1800. *An Oration on the Anniversary of American Independence, Pronounced at Worcester.* Worcester: Isaiah Thomas.

Banner, James M., Jr. 1970. *To the Hartford Convention: The Federalists and the Origins of Party Politics in Massachusetts, 1789-1815.* New York: Knopf.

Barnard, Thomas, D.D. 1795. *A Sermon, Delivered on the Day of National Thanksgiving, February 19, 1795.* Salem: Thomas C. Cushing.

Beard, Charles A. 1915. *Economic Origins of Jeffersonian Democracy.* New York: Macmillan.

Belknap, Jeremy, D.D. 1798. *A Sermon, Delivered on the 9th of May, 1798, The Day of the National Fast. . . .* Boston: Samuel Hall.

Bellah, Robert N. 1967. "Civil Religion in America." *Daedalus* 96: 1-21.

______. 1975. *The Broken Covenant: American Civil Religion in Time of Trial.* New York: The Seabury Press.

Bercovitch, Sacvan. 1978. *The American Jeremiad.* Madison: University of Wisconsin Press.

Blake, George. 1795. *An Oration, Pronounced July 4th, 1795 . . . at . . . Boston. . . .* Boston: Benjamin Edes.

Brown, Ira V. 1952. "Watchers for the Second Coming: The Millenarian Tradition in America." *The Mississippi Valley Historical Review* 39: 441-58.

Brown, William. 1799. *An Oration, Spoken at Hartford . . . July 4th, A.D. 1799.* Hartford: Hudson and Goodwin.

Buel, Richard, Jr. 1972. *Securing the Revolution: Ideology in American Politics, 1789-1815.* Ithaca: Cornell University Press.

Chambers, William N. 1972. *The First Party System: Federalists and Republicans.* New York: Wiley.

Cohn, Norman. 1970. *The Pursuit of the Millennium: Revolutionary Millenarians and Mystical Anarchists of the Middle Ages.* Revised and expanded version. New York: Oxford University Press.

Cunningham, Noble E. 1957. *The Jeffersonian Republicans: The Formation of Party Organization, 1789-1801.* Chapel Hill: University of North Carolina Press.

———. 1963. *The Jeffersonian Republicans in Power: Party Operations, 1801-1809*. Chapel Hill: University of North Carolina Press.

Curti, Merle. 1946. *The Roots of American Loyalty*. New York: Columbia University Press.

Daggett, David. 1799. *Sun-Beams May be Extracted from Cucumbers, But the Process is Tedious. An Oration*. . . . New Haven: Thomas Green and Son.

Dauer, Manning J. 1953. *The Adams Federalists*. Baltimore: Johns Hopkins Press.

Davidson, James W. 1972. "Searching for the Millennium: Problems for the 1790's and 1970's." *The New England Quarterly* 45: 241-61.

———. 1977. *The Logic of Millennial Thought: Eighteenth Century New England*. New Haven: Yale University Press.

Davis, M. L. 1800. *An Oration, Delivered in St. Paul's Church, on the Fourth of July, 1800*. . . . New York: W. A. Davis.

Deane, Samuel, D.D. 1794. *A Sermon, Preached Before His Honor Samuel Adams, Esq*. . . . *May 27th, 1794*. . . . Boston: Adams and Larkin.

DeConde, Alexander. 1958. *Entangling Alliance: Politics and Diplomacy under George Washington*. Durham: Duke University Press.

———. 1966. *The Quasi-War: The Politics and Diplomacy of the Undeclared War with France, 1797-1801*. New York: Charles Scribner's Sons.

Deutsch, Karl W. 1953. *Nationalism and Social Communication: An Inquiry Into the Foundations of Nationality*. Cambridge: The Technology Press.

Doggett, Simeon, Jun. 1799. *An Oration, Delivered at Taunton, on the Fourth of July, 1799*. New Bedford: John Spooner.

Dwight, Theodore. 1792. *An Oration, Spoken Before the Society of the Cincinnati, of the State of Connecticut*. . . *on the 4th of July, 1792*. Hartford: Hudson and Goodwin.

Dwight, Timothy, D. D. 1798. *The Duty of Americans, at the Present Crisis, Illustrated in a Discourse, Preached on the Fourth of July, 1798*. . . . New Haven: Thomas and Samuel Green.

Eckley, Joseph, A.M. 1792. *A Sermon, Preached at the Request of the Ancient and Honourable Artillery Company, June 4, 1792*. . . . Boston: Samuel Hall.

Eisenach, Eldon J. 1979. "The American Revolution Made and Remembered." *American Studies* 20: 71-91.

Ellery, Abraham. 1796. *An Oration, Delivered July 4th, A.D. 1796, in the Baptist Meeting-House, in Newport*. . . . Warren: Nathaniel Phillips.

Fessenden, Caleb Page. 1798. *An Oration, Delivered at Conway* . . . *on the Fourth day of July, 1798*. . . . Fryeburg: [Ezekiel Russell].

Fischer, David Hackett. 1965. *The Revolution of American Conservatism: The Federalist Party in the Era of Jeffersonian Democracy*. New York: Harper & Row.

Fiske, Abel, A.M. 1799. *A Discourse, Delivered at Wilton, November 15, 1798*. . . . Amherst: Samuel Preston.

Fiske, Oliver. 1797. *An Oration, Pronounced at Worcester* . . . *July 4, 1797*. Worcester: Isaiah Thomas, jun.

Fowle, Robert. 1800. *An Oration, Delivered at Plymouth, in New-Hampshire*. . . . Concord: Geo. Hough.

Friedman, Lawrence J. 1975. *Inventors of the Promised Land*. New York: Knopf.

Gabriel, Ralph Henry. 1940. *The Course of American Democratic Thought*. New York: Ronald Press.

Goodman, Paul. 1964. *The Democratic-Republicans of Massachusetts: Politics in a Young Republic.* Cambridge: Harvard University Press.

Gould, James. 1798. *An Oration, Pronounced at Litchfield*. . . . Litchfield: T. Collier.

Grant, Thomas, A.M. 1799. *A Sermon, Delivered at Felmington, on the 4th of July, 1799.* Trenton: G. Craft.

Handy, Robert T. 1971. *A Christian America: Protestant Hopes and Historical Realities.* New York: Oxford University Press.

Harris, Victor. 1949. *All Coherence Gone.* Chicago: University of Chicago Press.

Hatch, Nathan O. 1974. "The Origins of Civil Millennialism in America." *The William and Mary Quarterly* 31: 407-30.

———. 1977. *The Sacred Cause of Liberty: Republican Thought and the Millennium in Revolutionary New England.* New Haven: Yale University Press.

Hedges, Phineas, M.D. 1795. *An Oration, Delivered Before the Republican Society, of Ulster County, and Other Citizens*. . . . Goshen: David M. Wescott.

Heimert, Alan. 1966. *Religion and the American Mind.* Cambridge: Harvard University Press.

Hill, Christopher. 1971. *Antichrist in Seventeenth Century England.* London: Oxford University Press.

Hofstadter, Richard. 1969. *The Idea of a Party System: The Rise of Legitimate Opposition in the United States, 1780-1841.* Berkeley: University of California Press.

Hopkins, Samuel, D.D. 1793. *A Treatise on the Millennium*. . . . Boston: Isaiah Thomas and Ebenezer T. Andrews.

Howe, John R., Jr. 1967. "Republican Thought and the Political Violence of the 1790s." *American Quarterly* 19: 147-65.

Humphreys, Daniel. 1800. *A Plain Attempt to Hold up to View the Ancient Gospel*. . . . Portsmouth: Republican Press.

Johnson, John B. 1794. *An Oration on Union, Delivered in the New Dutch Church . . . May, 1794*. . . . New York: John Buel.

Jones, William, A.B. 1794. *An Oration, Pronounced at Concord, the Fourth of July, 1794*. . . . Concord: Nathaniel Coverly.

Kellog, Elijah, A.M. 1795. *An Oration, Pronounced at Portland, July 4, 1795*. . . . Newburyport: Blunt and March.

Kerber, Linda K. 1970. *Federalists in Dissent: Imagery and Ideology in Jeffersonian America.* Ithaca: Cornell University Press.

Kohn, Hans. 1957. *American Nationalism: An Interpretative Essay.* New York: Macmillan.

Lamont, William M. 1979. *Richard Baxter and the Millennium: Protestant Imperialism and the English Revolution.* London: Croom Helm.

Lathrop, Joseph D.D. 1794. *The Happiness of a Free Government, and the Means of Preserving it: Illustrated in a Sermon*. . . . Springfield: James R. Hutchins.

———. 1795. *National Happiness, Illustrated in a Sermon, Delivered at West Springfield, on the Nineteenth of February, 1795, Being a Day of General Thanksgiving.* Springfield: J. W. Hooker and F. Stebbins.

Lee, Chauncey, A.M. 1797. *An Oration, Delivered at Lansingburgh, on the Fourth of July, A.D. 1797*. . . . Lansingburg: E. Moffit & Co.

Lee, Elisha. 1793. *An Oration Delivered at Lenox, on the 4th of July, 1793*. . . . Stockbridge: Loring Andrews.

Lewis, Zechariah. 1799. *An Oration, On the Apparent, and the Real Political Situation of the United States. . . .* New Haven: Thomas Green and Son.

Linn, William, D.D. 1794. *Discourses on the Signs of the Times.* New York: Thomas Greenleaf.

Lipset, Seymour Martin. 1963. *The First New Nation: The United States in Historical and Comparative Perspective.* New York: Basic Books.

McKnight, John, D.D. 1794. *God the Author of Promotion, A Sermon Preached in the New Presbyterian Church, New-York, on the 4th of July, 1794. . . .* New York: William Durrell.

Maclear, J. F. 1971. "The Republic and the Millennium." In Elwyn A. Smith, ed., *The Religion of the Republic.* Philadelphia: Fortress Press.

______. 1975. "New England and the Fifth Monarchy: The Quest for the Millennium in Early American Protestantism." *The William and Mary Quarterly* 32: 223-60.

McLoughlin, William G. 1973. "The Role of Religion in the Revolution: Liberty of Conscience and Cultural Cohesion in the New Nation." In Stephen G. Kurtz and James H. Hutson, eds., *Essays on the American Revolution.* Chapel Hill: University of North Carolina Press.

Marty, Martin E. 1970. *Righteous Empire: The Protestant Experience in America.* New York: Dial Press.

Mason, John M., A.M. 1797. *Hope for the Heathen: A Sermon, Preached in the Old Presbyterian Church . . . November 7, 1797.* New York: T. & J. Swords.

May, Henry. 1976. *The Enlightenment in America.* New York: Oxford University Press.

Mead, Sidney E. 1975. *The Nation With the Soul of a Church.* New York: Harper & Row.

Mellen, John, Jun. 1797. *A Sermon, Delivered Before His Excellency the Governor . . . of the Commonwealth of Massachusetts . . . May 31, 1797.* Boston: Young & Minns.

Mercer, John. 1792. *An Oration Delivered on the Fourth of July 1792. . . .* Richmond: T. Nicolson.

Merritt, Richard L. 1966. *Symbols of American Community, 1735-1775.* New Haven: Yale University Press.

Middlekauff, Robert. 1971. *The Mathers: Three Generations of Puritan Intellectuals, 1596-1728.* New York: Oxford University Press.

Miller, Perry. 1939. *The New England Mind: The Seventeenth Century.* Boston: Beacon Press.

______. 1953. *The New England Mind: From Colony to Province.* Boston: Beacon Press.

______. 1956. "The End of the World." In Perry Miller, ed., *Errand Into the Wilderness.* Cambridge: Harvard University Press.

Miller, Samuel, A.M. 1795. *A Sermon, Delivered in the New Presbyterian Church, New-York, July Fourth, 1795. . . .* New York: Thomas Greenleaf.

Mitchell, Samuel. 1800. *An Address to the Citizens of New-York. . . .* New York: George F. Hopkins.

Moorhead, James H. 1978. *American Apocalypse: Yankee Protestantism and the Civil War, 1860-1869.* New Haven: Yale University Press.

Morse, Jedidiah, D.D. 1799. *A Sermon, Exhibiting the Present Dangers, and Consequent Duties of the Citizens of America. Delivered at Charlestown, April 25, 1799*. . . . Charlestown: Samuel Etheridge.

Nagel, Paul C. 1971. *This Sacred Trust: American Nationality, 1798-1898*. New York: Oxford University Press.

Niebuhr, H. Richard. 1937. *The Kingdom of God in America*. Chicago: Willett, Clark & Company.

Ogden, David B. 1798. *An Oration, Delivered on the Fourth of July, 1798*. . . Newark: Jacob Halsey & Co.

Osgood, David. 1799. *The Devil Let Loose*. . . *Illustrated in a Discourse Delivered on the Day of the National Fast, April 25, 1799*. Boston: Samuel Hall.

Parish, Elijah, A.M. 1799. *An Oration; Delivered at Byfield, July 4, 1799*. Newburyport: Angier March.

Parkhurst, Jabez. 1798. *An Oration, Delivered on the Fourth of July, 1798 in the Presbyterian Church, at Newark*. Newark: Bennington and Dodge.

[anon.]. *Prophetic Conjectures on the French Revolution, And Other Recent and Shortly Expected Events*. . . . 1794. Baltimore: John Hayes.

Robbins, Chandler, D.D. 1793. *An Address, Delivered at Plymouth, on the 24th Day of January, 1793*. . . . Boston: Belknap and Hall.

Rockwell, Samuel. 1798. *An Oration, Delivered at the Celebration of American Independence, at Salisbury, Fourth July, Ninety-Seven*. Litchfield: T. Collier.

Sandeen, Ernest. 1970. *The Roots of Fundamentalism: British and American Millenarianism, 1800-1930*. Chicago: University of Chicago Press.

Schwartz, Hillel. 1976. "The End of the Beginning: Millenarian Studies, 1969-1975." *Religious Studies Review* 2: 1-15.

Smelser, Marshall. 1958. "The Federalist Period as an Age of Passion." *American Quarterly* 10: 391-419.

Smith, David E. 1965. "Millenarian Scholarship in America." *American Quarterly* 17: 535-49.

Smith, Timothy L. 1957. *Revivalism and Social Reform: American Protestantism on the Eve of the Civil War*. Nashville, Abingdon Press.

Stone, Eliab, A.M. 1799. *A Discourse, Delivered at Reading, on the Day of the National Fast, April 25, 1799*. Boston: Manning & Loring.

Strout, Cushing. 1974a. *The American Image of the Old World*. New York: Harper & Row.

______. 1974b. *The New Heavens and New Earth: Political Religion in America*. New York: Harper & Row.

Sullivan, George. 1800. *An Oration, Pronounced at Exeter on the Fourth Day of July, 1800*. . . . Exeter: H. Ranlet.

Taylor, John, A.M. 1796. *An Oration, Delivered on the Anniversary of Independence, at Deerfield*. . . . Greenfield: Thomas Dickman.

Thacher, Samuel. 1796. *An Oration, Pronounced July 4, 1796, at* . . . *Concord*. . . . Boston: Samuel Hall.

Toon, Peter. 1970. "The Latter-Day Glory." In Peter Toon, ed., *Puritans, the Millennium, and the Future of Israel*. Cambridge: James Clarke & Co.

Tuveson, Ernest Lee. 1949. *Millennium and Utopia: A Study in the Background of the Idea of Progress*. Berkeley: University of California Press.

———. 1968. *Redeemer Nation: The Idea of America's Millennial Role.* Chicago: University of Chicago Press.

Warner, G. J. 1797. *Means for the Preservation of Public Liberty. An Oration. . . .* New York: Thomas Greenleaf and Naphtali Judah.

Watkins, John. 1795. *An Essay on the End of the World.* Worcester: Isiah Thomas, jun.

Weinberg, Albert K. 1935. *Manifest Destiny: A Study of Nationalist Expansionism in American History.* Baltimore: Johns Hopkins Press.

Wells, John. 1798. *An Oration, Delivered on the Fourth of July, 1798, at St. Paul's Church, Before the Young Men of the City of New-York. . . .* New York: McLean and Lang.

Whiting, Thurston. 1798. *An Oration, Delivered in the Baptist Meeting House, in Thomaston, July 4th, 1798. . . .* Hallowell: Howard S. Robinson.

Williams, Simeon Finley, A.M. 1796. *An Oration, Delivered on the Fourth of July 1796 . . . at Meredith Bridge.* Dover: Samuel Bragg, jun.

Woodward, Israel, A.M. 1798. *American Liberty and Independence: A Discourse, Delivered at Watertown, on the Fourth of July, 1798.* Litchfield: T. Collier.

Worcester, Noah, A.M. 1800. *An Election Sermon, Delivered at Concord, June 4, 1800. . . .* Concord: Elijah Russell.

Worcester, Samuel. 1795. *An Oration: Delivered, at the College Chapel, Hanover. . . .* Hanover: Durham and True.

Young, Alfred F. 1967. *The Democratic Republicans of New York: The Origins, 1763-1797.* Chapel Hill: University of North Carolina Press.

Young, James Sterling. 1966. *The Washington Community, 1800-1825.* New York: Columbia University Press.

The Society of the Cincinnati in New England 1783-1800

Wallace Evan Davies*

THE first American patriotic order, the Society of the Cincinnati, so startled the citizens of 1783 that they promptly denounced it as un-American and unpatriotic. As the precursor of all subsequent veterans' and hereditary associations, the vicissitudes it encountered through all the states and in New England in particular are of continuing interest. At the very outset of the nation's life the organization drew sharply into focus the problems posed by groups within the community claiming special privileges because of military service and special distinctions because of ancestry.[1]

On May 13, 1783, shortly before the Continental Army disbanded, a gathering of officers along the banks of the Hudson formed a society which, in accordance with the young republic's tendency to compare itself with the states of classical antiquity, they named the Cincinnati after the Roman soldier-citizen whose example they professed to follow. Its constitution, rather formally entitled the "Institution," provided that membership was to pass to the eldest male descendants of the founders, but also allowed the admission of honorary members "whose views may be directed to the same laudable objects with those of the Cincinnati." Each officer was to contribute one month's pay into a permanent charitable fund. Since general meetings of the entire order were to be held only every three years, it was suggested that each state society send occasional circular letters to all the other constituent societies "noting whatever they think worthy of observation respecting the good of the Society or the general union of the States. . . ." Finally, the Institution described in considerable detail the organization's badge, an elaborate medal in the form of a gold eagle to be hung by a blue and white ribbon.[2]

*Mr. Davies is a member of the Department of History at Yale University.

[1] The nearest to a comprehensive survey of the public's reaction is Edgar Erskine Hume's "Early Opposition to the Cincinnati," *Americana,* XXX (1936), 597-638, which is perhaps unduly anxious to absolve the order of any sinister intent and too prone to ascribe criticisms to personal pique. See also John Bach McMaster, *A History of the People of the United States* (New York, 1883-1913), I, 167-176.

[2] The Institution is reproduced in William S. Thomas, *The Society of the Cincinnati 1783-1935* (New York, 1935), 24-32.

The order soon developed branches in all the thirteen original states and even in France among the foreign volunteers recently returned from their romantic interlude. Excluding the large French contingent, New England had both the largest and smallest branches, Massachusetts claiming more than three hundred adherents, while New Hampshire could muster only thirty. In Connecticut there were about two hundred and fifty members, and Rhode Island garnered eighty more.[3]

Though opposition to the Cincinnati was widespread from its inception, New England proved to be the center of the hottest debate over its merits and influence. By February, 1784, the man who came nearest to being the founder of the society, General Henry Knox of Massachusetts,[4] a Yankee himself, had to admit to the president-general, George Washington, that sentiment was universally hostile throughout the section.[5] The intensity of animus was largely due to the excitement caused by Congress' first granting the officers of the Continental Army half pay for life and then early in 1783 commuting that settlement to five years' full pay in government securities bearing six per cent interest.[6] The uneasiness occasioned by this arrangement was just beginning to subside when news of the Cincinnati's formation aroused suspicion that the officers' chief motive was to perfect an organization that could bring pressure on the government to insure payment of this obligation and probably to advance their fortunes in other ways. Though Washington later declared that to ascribe the order's founding to such concern for their financial interests was "ridiculous," [7] unquestionably this problem was very much in the minds of the officers at the time they formed the Cincinnati.[8]

[3] *Ibid.*, 149.

[4] The original draft of the Institution, dated April 15, 1783, is in his handwriting. Henry Knox Papers, XII, Massachusetts Historical Society. Years later the irascible Timothy Pickering observed that "it bore marks of his pomposity." Notes on Judge Johnson's *Life of General Greene*, Feb. 11, 1823, Timothy Pickering Papers, Massachusetts Historical Society.

[5] Knox to Washington, Feb. 21, 1784, Knox Papers, XVII.

[6] William H. Glasson, *Federal Military Pensions in the United States* (New York, 1918), 24-37; Louis Clinton Hatch, *The Administration of the American Revolutionary Army* (*Harvard Historical Studies*, X, New York, 1904), 142-178.

[7] George Washington to Thomas Jefferson, May 30, 1787, Worthington Chauncey Ford, ed., *The Writings of George Washington* (New York and London, 1889-1893), XI, 157.

[8] Knox to Benjamin Lincoln, April 8, 1783, Knox Papers, XII; Constant Freeman, Jr., *Letter to Lieut. John Winslow, May 30, 1783* (Niagara Falls, N. Y., 1897); James Thacher, *A Military Journal During the American Revolutionary War* (Boston, 1823), 394-396.

The most virulent opposition to the commutation scheme came from Connecticut. There the charges and rebuttals of "A Farmer," "An Officer," "An Impartial Farmer," "A Continentalist," "Cives" and "Honorius" (he was actually Noah Webster of dictionary fame, a defender of the commutation) jostled each other in the press. Town meetings condemned the settlement. A statewide convention met at Middletown to consider the problem and, finally, the lower house of the legislature added its protest. The principal arguments against the arrangement were that it placed an undue financial burden upon the citizenry, that it began a pension system which implied mercenary motives for the officers' services, that it set up a "badge of distinction" within the community and that in taking such action Congress had encroached upon the sovereignty of the states.[9]

The formation of the Cincinnati only heightened this distrust of the officers as a class. A town meeting at Killingworth pointed out that Cincinnatus had never received half pay, that the ability of the members to contribute to a benevolent fund seemed to refute their claims of poverty and that the intended use of this capital "remains as yet a secret" but doubtless would be reprehensible. The securing of the passage by Congress of first the half pay and then the commutation, it predicted, would prove only the first examples of the officers' "skill in the arts of intreague."[10]

Presently a pamphlet by another determined classicist, "Cassius" (actually Aedanus Burke of Charleston, South Carolina), arrived to nurture the ill-feeling. This little volume, entitled *Considerations on the Order or Society of Cincinnati,* sounded the tocsin against the association wherever it appeared. Hartford gave the indictment two reprintings, the New Haven press advertised it extensively and the Middletown convention commended it "to the notice and perusal of the people at large. . . ."[11] For those desiring to learn what could be said in behalf of the society, an

[9] *The Connecticut Courant and Weekly Intelligencer,* Hartford, May 13-Nov. 4, 1783; *The Connecticut Journal,* New Haven, Feb. 11, March 31 and April 7, 1784; James Truslow Adams, *New England in the Republic 1776-1850* (Boston, 1926), 70-71; Glasson, *Federal Military Pensions,* 44-45; Hatch, *Administration of the American Revolutionary Army,* 194.

[10] *Conn. Courant,* Sept. 2, 1783.

[11] Aedanus Burke (Cassius, *pseud.*), *Considerations on the Order or Society of Cincinnati* (Hartford, [1783?] and 1784); *Conn. Journal,* Feb. 4, 1784; *The Pennsylvania Packet,* Philadelphia, Jan. 6, 1784.

attempted refutation by "An Obscure Individual," which had appeared earlier in Philadelphia, was also soon available.[12]

This ammunition led to a series of accusations and defenses that rang across the Connecticut hills throughout the spring of 1784.[13] Typical evidence of the current suspicion was an open letter to the state society urging its members, if it were really innocent, to "quit the matter and be content with the station and the honours you are entitled to in society" and to allow their descendants to "stand their chance with their coevals." Should they instead persist, "it will be decided beyond a question that your design is nothing short of the subversion of our constitution, which in short is treason against our rights." The vigilant citizens of Connecticut would never permit this. "You must be stupid beyond description to imagine such absurdities can be palmed upon the people without detection," rang the warning, "and to think that the fortitude and perseverance that has baffled the power and intrigues of Britain, will now be cajoled by such a farce of philanthropy and tamely stand to have your manacles riveted." The final plea was to abandon these schemes and not to "plunge a dagger into the bosom of the country that gave you existence. . . ."[14]

Meanwhile, the Middletown convention was keeping a watchful eye on this "new and strange order of men." In March it reminded the public that the Cincinnati had arisen "at the moment of the grant of five years pay; assuming to be the only saviours of the republic, to be distinguished from the rest of the citizens, wearing the badge of peerage, and to be paid from the purse of the people. . . ."[15]

Less frequently, champions of the society entered the journalistic arena. "It is ridiculous to suppose," declared one such advocate, "that every subaltern in the Society of the Cincinnati, by giving up part of his wages for the poor of the Society, is become in fact a peer of the realm; but it is easy to give names to persons and things, to hold them up in an odious light." Yet even if the members did aspire at nobility, "we have no right to believe Congress will aid them in their views, as *it is inconsistent*

[12] *Conn. Journal*, Feb. 4, 1784.

[13] *Ibid.*, March 24, March 31 and April 7, 1784; *The Independent Chronicle and the Universal Advertiser*, Boston, April 1, 1784; Thomas' *The Massachusetts Spy: or, Worcester Gazette*, May 13 and May 27, 1784.

[14] *Independent Chronicle*, April 1, 1784.

[15] *Conn. Journal*, April 7, 1784.

with the principles of the Confederation."[16] Another defender argued that if ever the society committed an unlawful act, punishment would inevitably follow; until such an unlikely event, the order should ignore its current odium.[17] But such jousters tilted against overwhelming hosts. Connecticut's representative at the Cincinnati's first national convention in 1784 reported that the organization labored under "a very general disapprobation of the People."[18]

Dislike of the commutation also caused tiny Rhode Island to swell the chorus of protest against the Cincinnati.[19] A few weeks after a Providence newspaper had printed the Institution,[20] a notice, cautiously signed "A Brother Officer," summoned the commissioned veterans to meet in that city on December 17 to form a state society "and to transact some other interesting Business, which will be laid before the meeting."[21] Even had this clandestine note not seemed ominous, the warnings of "Cassius" soon turned up in a Newport edition to make explicit any suspicions.[22] Noting that "Burke's address has sounded the alarm," the president of the Rhode Island branch, General Nathanael Greene, soon had to concede that, because of the hereditary feature and the honorary membership, "the current of public prejudice is directed against the Cincinnati." The order "is thought to contain dangerous designs, pregnant with mischief, and may be ruinous to the people." As a result, many persons "wish an alteration of the Order, but more a dissolution."[23]

But this miniscule commonwealth, whose democratic and even radical leanings were soon to be evidenced by the passage of the "Know-ye" laws and by its reluctance to ratify the Constitution, did not implement its objections as forcibly as has often been believed. Despite a rumor current

[16] Quoted from *Conn. Journal* in *The New-Jersey Gazette,* Trenton, May 3, 1784.

[17] An item from Hartford in *Mass. Spy,* May 13, 1784.

[18] Winthrop Sargent, "Journal of the General Meeting of the Cincinnati in 1784," *Memoirs of the Historical Society of Pennsylvania,* VI (Philadelphia, 1858), 79.

[19] Nathanael Greene to Washington, April 22, 1784, and May 6, 1784, Edgar Erskine Hume, ed., *George Washington's Correspondence Concerning the Cincinnati* (Baltimore, 1941), 142, 165.

[20] *The Providence Gazette and Country Journal,* Oct. 25, 1783.

[21] *Ibid.,* Nov. 29, Dec. 6 and 13, 1783.

[22] Burke, *Considerations* (Newport, [1783?]). A rebuttal, probably that of the "Obscure Individual," apparently soon followed. "We expect to print the answer to the Foregoing next week." *Ibid.,* 16.

[23] Greene to Joseph Reed, May 17, 1784, William B. Reed, *Life and Correspondence of Joseph Reed* (Philadelphia, 1847), II, 409.

in the newspapers of other states in April, 1784, that Rhode Island was about "to disfranchise any and every person who is a member [of the Cincinnati], and render them incapable of holding any post of honour and trust in that government," [24] there is no evidence that the legislature took any action.[25] The possibility, however, was soon being reported as fact. Count de Mirabeau's version of Burke's assault gave the legend wider currency, and even Jefferson accepted the story.[26] Though Washington eventually issued a formal denial that there had ever been any such measure, the tradition proved persistent and a century later was still being perpetuated by so reputable a historian as John Bach McMaster.[27]

Nevertheless, the drift of Rhode Island opinion was sufficiently clear and although Washington sent Greene "letter after letter" urging his attendance at the general meeting of the society, that gentleman decided that his health would not permit the trip. "The Doctor thinks my life would be endangered by attempting to cross the Water," he informed the president-general, "and pain in my stomach increased by riding by land." [28] He stayed home, and died within two years from the effects of a sunstroke.

Further to the north, New Hampshire displayed similar aversion to the new order. General Stark's disapproval delayed the organization of a state society in 1783, and its delegate to the general meeting at Philadelphia the following year announced that "the opinions of the State were very generally in opposition to the Institution on its present Establishment." [29]

In Massachusetts also vigorous objections to the commutation fore-

[24] *Independent Chronicle,* April 16, 1784; *The Freeman's Journal: or the North American Intelligencer,* Philadelphia, April 28, 1784; *Penna. Packet,* April 29, 1784.

[25] *Records of the State of Rhode Island and Providence Plantations in New England,* X (Providence, 1865), covers the period 1784-1792 and has no such law recorded.

[26] *Freeman's Journal,* June 2, 1784; *Independent Chronicle,* June 17, 1784; Count de Mirabeau, *Considerations on the Order of Cincinnatus* (Philadelphia, 1786), 50; Jefferson to Meusnier, June 22, 1786, Paul Leicester Ford, ed., *The Works of Thomas Jefferson* (New York, 1904-1905), V, 53.

[27] Washington to Jefferson, May 30, 1787, Washington, *Writings,* XI, 157; McMaster, *History,* I, 173.

[28] Greene to Washington, May 6, 1784, Hume, *Washington's Correspondence Concerning the Cincinnati,* 165.

[29] Albert Stillman Batchellor, ed., "The Institution and Records of the New Hampshire Society of the Cincinnati 1783 to 1823," *Early State Papers of New Hampshire,* XXII (Concord, 1893), 812; Sargent, "Journal," 80-81.

shadowed antipathy to the Cincinnati. The Bay State's representatives in Congress had voted against the half pay in 1780. Now, as in Connecticut, town meetings passed resolutions condemning the new arrangement, while the General Court protested to Congress that the new society tended to elevate some citizens in wealth and grandeur at the expense of others.[30] Throughout 1783, however, there was little alarm over the Cincinnati. The press concerned itself with the peace settlement, the evacuation of New York City and the proper treatment of Tories, and only a few more prescient individuals surmised that objections might develop. Timothy Pickering later claimed he had foreseen them but had joined the society to avoid the appearance of "Singularity."[31] William Heath privately voiced similar fears, but at last also signed the Institution.[32]

Hardly had the year 1784 begun when a copy of the Philadelphia edition of Burke's work came to the notice of the *Independent Chronicle* of Boston. Since it seemed *"to claim the serious attention of the free citizens of these States,"* the paper proposed to publish extracts of the pamphlet, along with a copy of the Institution, and the editor expressed his readiness *"to give place to the sentiments of any gentleman, on the subject, who shall favor us with them in season."*[33] Antagonism that had been merely smouldering now erupted spectacularly.

Widely read throughout the commonwealth, Burke's pamphlet was generally considered the greatest single influence in rousing the popular clamor.[34] Further fuel came with the news of an address Governor Guerard had made to the South Carolina legislature seconding the pamphleteer's indictment.[35] By March James Warren was informing John Adams,

[30] *Mass. Spy,* Aug. 7, 1783, March 25, April 1 and May 20, 1784; *Conn. Journal,* March 31 and April 7, 1784; Glasson, *Federal Military Pensions,* 34, 43; Hatch, *Administration of the American Revolutionary Army,* 194; Adams, *New England in the Republic,* 69-70.

[31] Pickering to John Marshall, Jan. 17, 1829, and notes on *Life of Greene,* Feb. 11, 1823, Pickering Papers.

[32] "I am told that at last general Heath saw his error, and that he became a member of the Society." Col. Gouvion to Knox, Sept. 18, 1783, Knox Papers, XIV. "Our friend Heath says 'I forewarned you of all that would happen.'" Knox to Baron Steuben, Feb. 21, 1784, *ibid.,* XVII.

[33] *Independent Chronicle,* Jan. 29, Feb. 5 and Feb. 12, 1784.

[34] Knox to Nathanael Greene, Feb. 14, 1784, Knox Papers, XVII; Knox to Washington, Feb. 21, 1784, *ibid.;* James Warren to John Adams, March 10, 1784, *Warren-Adams Letters* (Massachusetts Historical Society, *Collections,* LXIII, n.p., 1925), II, 237; Stephen Higginson to Elbridge Gerry, April 28, 1784, Higginson Papers, New-York Historical Society.

[35] *Independent Chronicle,* April 8 and May 6, 1784. For its effectiveness, see

then minister to Holland, "Nothing seems to be a more General Subject of Conversation than the Cincinnati Clubb," adding that he would have sent him the much talked about essay by "Cassius" if the postage had not been so great.[36] "The Cincinnati appears (however groundless) to be an object of jealousy," Knox admitted to Washington, ". . . The cool dispassionate men seem to approve the institution generally but dislike the hereditary descent." So strong was the public's hostility that when the state society met in February, "it was thought prudent not to make any honorary members at present."[37]

Fears concerning the new order now filled the newspapers.[38] It clearly intended, wrote one correspondent, "to establish a compleat and perpetual *Personal* distinction, between the numerous *military* dignatories of their corporation, and the whole remaining body of the people who will then be stiled Plebeans through the Community." It should be checked "if it tends to introduce even the mildest nobility, since nobility itself is reprobated by these confederated Republican States. . . ."[39] Another opponent predicted that the society would have dangerous political consequences, leading to the overthrow of the republic. He foresaw the officers being gradually drawn into measures "which they now would shudder at the thought of, and which I have no doubt will be the reality, unless this political monster is crushed in embryo." The forthcoming general meeting of the Cincinnati at Philadelphia would, he thought, propose drastic increases in the powers of Congress so as to secure payment of the commutation. The officers would next fill Congress with their adherents, who would then vote these enlarged federal powers.

Samuel Adams to Gerry, April 19, 1784, Henry Alonzo Cushing, ed., *The Writings of Samuel Adams* (New York and London, 1908), IV, 300; Higginson to Gerry, April 28, 1784, Higginson Papers.

[36] Warren to John Adams, March 10, 1784, *Warren-Adams Letters,* II, 237.

[37] Knox to Washington, Feb. 21, 1784, Knox Papers, XVII. Knox also described "the rising indignation against the institution of the Cincinnati" to William Hull, April 5, 1784, *ibid.* "Cincinnati is another subject of disgust," Nathaniel Sargent to Pickering, May 25, 1784, Pickering Papers.

[38] *Independent Chronicle,* March 18, April 1, 8, 15, 22, 29, May 6 and June 3, 1784; *Mass. Spy,* May 13 and 27, 1784. The Cincinnati even became the subject of topical banter: "A certain eminent Attorney General, whose disapprobation of the order of Cin-Cinnati is known, being asked his opinion concerning that intended institution, answered, 'I dislike it more particularly for having two *Cin's* in it.' " Attributed to Boston, *Conn. Journal,* March 24, 1784, and to Worcester, *Virginia Gazette* (Richmond), April 3, 1784.

[39] *Independent Chronicle,* March 18, 1784.

To insure ratification of these powers by the states they would also elect fellow-members to the state legislatures. Even if they formed but a small minority in the assemblies, "their address, ingenuity, perseverance and prowess, will undoubtedly, if we consider the manner of conducting business in such bodies, secure them success." Once the Cincinnati achieved these alterations, "then you may bid *adieu*, a lasting *adieu* to republican principles."[40]

The correspondence of persons prominent in Massachusetts public life at that time reveals that there was in the state a substantial group so strongly attached to abstract "republican principles" and so hostile to any suggestion of aristocratic or monarchical tendencies that they were compelled to view the Cincinnati with great alarm.[41] That many of these possessed considerable, if newly acquired, wealth and hence were far from being radically democratic in their outlook made no difference in their opinion of the Cincinnati. Elbridge Gerry, a successful merchant whose leanings were as pro-republican in theory as they were sometimes anti-democratic in practice, thought that the society established an *imperium in imperio,* distrusted the collection of indefinite sums of money and feared that the hereditary element would lead to a nobility.[42] His close friend, almost his mentor, Samuel Adams, thought the order "as rapid a Stride towards an hereditary Military Nobility as was ever made in so short a time."[43] Another mercantile member of this faction, Stephen Higginson, likewise opposed the distinctions created by the Cincinnati as being "most clearly anti republican, & while our People remain attached to the present Constitution, they can not but be averse to every thing of the kind."[44] From Holland, John Adams denied that he had spoken "very violently" against the society, arguing that he had "disapproved . . . with as much tranquillity and self-recollection, and phlegm, if you will, as if I had been a native, full-blooded Dutchman," he nevertheless considered the order "the first step taken to deface the beauty of our temple of liberty."[45]

[40] *Ibid.*, April 22, 1784.

[41] See Robert A. East, "The Massachusetts Conservatives in the Critical Period," in Richard B. Morris, ed., *The Era of the American Revolution* (New York, 1939), 351-352, 366-368.

[42] James T. Austin, *The Life of Elbridge Gerry with Contemporary Letters* (Boston, 1828-1829), I, 419-420.

[43] Adams to Gerry, April 23, 1784, Samuel Adams, *Writings,* IV, 301. See Adams to Gerry, April 19, 1784, *ibid.*, IV, 298-299.

[44] Higginson to Gerry, April 28, 1784, Higginson Papers.

[45] Lafayette to John Adams, March 8, 1784, Charles Francis Adams, ed., *The*

As it had only threatened to do in Rhode Island, the popular unrest successfully invaded the legislative chambers in Massachusetts. On February 10, 1784, the senate appointed a committee "to consider what measures are necessary to be taken in order to prevent the ill consequences of any combinations that are, or may hereafter be formed, to promote undue distinction among the citizens of this free State, & Tending to establish a hereditary nobility, contrary to the federation of the U. States, & the Spirit of the Constitution of this Com'th." The house quickly acted to make this a joint body. At the end of the month it recommended that, since the officers "pretend certain distinction from their fellow Citizens, and intend the same as honorary and hereditary," another committee should be appointed to investigate the Cincinnati specifically and to report what action was needed.[46]

On March 22 the legislature finally adopted resolutions condemning the Cincinnati. The society had assumed to itself the power of adopting measures "for the promoting certain important, publick and national purposes," although for these matters the American people had established their state legislatures and the Congress. It therefore "savors of a disposition aspiring to become independent of lawful and constitutional authority, tending, if unrestrained, to *Imperium in Imperio,* and consequently to confusion and the subversion of publick liberty." Its charitable funds, "although really intended for lawful and laudable purposes, may be converted to uses unlawful and dangerous." The provision for regular meetings and correspondence among the state societies may eventually be "destructive of the liberties of the State; and the existence of their free constitutions," a possibility that seemed all the more likely because the officers had been "accustomed to military laws, maxims, sentiments, habits and feelings, during a war of eight years. . . ." A particularly dangerous element in the membership were the foreigners, "who, however respectable their characters are, yet are the subjects of and strongly attached to a government essentially different in principles as well as form, from the republican constitutions of the United States."

Hereditary distinctions, continued the statement, were likely to lead

Works of John Adams (Boston, 1851-1856), VIII, 187; Adams to Charles Spencer, March 24, 1784, *ibid.,* IX, 524; Adams to Lafayette, March 28, 1784, *ibid.,* VIII, 192.

[46] Journal of the Senate of the Commonwealth of Massachusetts 1783-84, IV, 339, 366; Journal of the House of Representatives from May, 1783, to March, 1784, IV, 389, 420, Massachusetts State Library.

to a hereditary nobility, "which is contrary to the spirit of free government, and expressly inhibited by an article in the confederation of the United States." Yet posterity, grateful as it should be to the Revolutionary officers, might be tempted to reward their descendants who "hold what may have the appearance of hereditary honors, with the usual powers, as well as the ostentatious distinctions of nobility." The assembly therefore, "after mature deliberation, are of the opinion, that the said Society, called the Cincinnati, is unjustifiable, and if not properly discountenanced, may be dangerous to the peace, liberty and safety of the United States in general, and this Commonwealth in particular."[47]

Any specific measure of suppression, however, was left to the next General Court. Though Henry Knox predicted that its members would come prepared to demolish the society "with all their might and main—if so much should be required," and a town meeting at Cambridge instructed them to declare all efforts "to establish exclusive rights and hereditary honors" criminal offenses,[48] by the time the legislature met the association had drastically altered its constitution to meet just such criticism. In June, 1784, therefore, the legislature named a joint committee, of which Samuel Adams was a member, but took no further action, probably because the state society in July ratified the changes proposed earlier in the year by the national association.[49]

Meanwhile, with the press suggesting that town meetings direct their local officials "to disavow the institution, or in case of refusal, to inform them they cannot expect the suffrages of their countrymen for the civil offices of government for the future,"[50] it had become apparent that membership in the Cincinnati might be detrimental to an aspiring politician. For this reason the defection from the society of one prominent man, General William Heath, soon followed. About the time that the legislature first appointed its committee, Knox sardonically noted that "he left us in the lurch and did not attend the meeting having prudently caught cold."[51] Heath's candidacy for the state senate explained his caution. For campaign purposes he shrewdly circulated the rumor that he had

[47] *Independent Chronicle,* March 25, 1784.

[48] Knox to William Hull, April 5, 1784, Knox Papers, XVII; *Independent Chronicle,* June 3, 1784.

[49] Journal of Mass. Senate, V, 34; *Journal of the Honorable House of Representatives of the Commonwealth of Massachusetts,* V (Boston, 1784), 38.

[50] *Independent Chronicle,* April 29, 1784.

[51] Knox to Baron Steuben, Feb. 21, 1784, Knox Papers, XVII.

resigned from the order. Though this was "known by many to be wholly devoid of truth, so industriously was the *Lie* circulated that he had most of the Votes."[52]

Such staunch opponents of the society as Samuel Adams and Stephen Higginson were shocked at his success. Adams grieved that "the Citizens are not so vigilant as they used and still ought to be."[53] As Higginson viewed the maneuverings among political leaders that had secured Heath's election, he concluded "that some of our great men are in favour of the Institution. . . ." These individuals, who "have always been tickled with most trifling Baubles, a feather, a Cockade," perhaps found the prospect of honorary membership "so very flattering . . . that they cannot resist" and thus easily allowed thoughts of a medal to divert them from the public welfare.[54] Both Adams and Higginson agreed that Heath's stratagem of pretended resignation could not long be maintained; so ingrained was the legislature's republicanism that he would be forced to resign from either the senate or the society.

Meanwhile, New England's Congressional delegates had a chance to indicate their sentiments when Jefferson's committee on the organization of new states west of the mountains recommended that "their respective governments shall be republican, and shall admit no person to be a citizen who holds any hereditary title." Samuel Adams hastened to inform Gerry, "I hope Congress will not fail to make this an indispensable Condition."[55] Though the lawmakers finally struck out the clause, Massachusetts and Rhode Island's representatives voted solidly to retain it, while Connecticut's were evenly divided.[56]

So extensive was the ill-feeling and distrust aroused by the Society of the Cincinnati in its original form that most of its leaders soon concluded that they must make substantial modifications in the Institution when the association held its first general meeting in May, 1784. Though Nathanael Greene opposed a change, arguing the "public seems to want something in New England to quarrel with the officers about, remove one thing and they will soon find another,"[57] even the progenitor of the fraternity,

[52] Higginson to Gerry, April 28, 1784, Higginson Papers.

[53] Adams to Gerry, April 19, 1784, Samuel Adams, *Writings,* IV, 299.

[54] Higginson to Gerry, April 28, 1784, Higginson Papers.

[55] Adams to Gerry, April 23, 1784, Samuel Adams, *Writings,* IV, 303.

[56] Gaillard Hunt, ed., *Journals of the Continental Congress 1774-1789* (Washington, 1910-1936), XXVI, 250-251.

[57] Greene to Washington, April 22, 1784, Hume, *Washington's Correspondence*

Henry Knox, decided that it was necessary to introduce amendments abolishing the hereditary feature and the admission of honorary members.[58] "In constitutions like ours, public opinion already governs us," he later explained to one of the French members, "and it runs most furiously against our Society."[59] Indeed when the delegates assembled in Philadelphia, those from New Hampshire, Massachusetts and Connecticut testified that the order was in general disfavor in those states. It was the vehement insistence of the president-general, George Washington, however, that induced the members finally to consent to far more fundamental changes than they had at first intended. They abolished all inherited eligibility, honorary membership and correspondence among societies, and restricted the business of the local meetings to the election of officers and the disposal of charitable funds. State societies were to apply to their respective legislatures for charters and with their consent to lend the societies' capital to the various commonwealths, reserving only the interest for their own use.[60]

For these proposals to become operative, all the state societies had to approve them. Securing such unanimous consent proved no easier than inducing the thirteen states to endorse any change in the Articles of Confederation. Massachusetts and Rhode Island joined seven other states in ratifying the new constitution, though they later rescinded their votes. But Connecticut and New Hampshire were two of the four states whose intransigence blocked acceptance.[61]

The secretary of the Connecticut branch reported that "for my self, my Sentiments are fully in favor of the Alterations—but unhappily, I have to differ with most of my Brethren in this State Society, who cannot be persuaded that an Amendment is expedient, notwithstanding the very general opposition which is made to the original Institution by the Citizens

Concerning the Cincinnati, 142. See Greene to Washington, May 6, 1784, *ibid.*, 165.

[58] Higginson to Gerry, April 28, 1784, Higginson Papers.

[59] Knox to Gouvion, July 2, 1784, Francis S. Drake, *Memorials of the Society of the Cincinnati of Massachusetts* (Boston, 1873), 30.

[60] John C. Daves, ed., *Proceedings of the General Society of the Cincinnati* (Baltimore, 1925-1930), I, 9-13. "I confess I should have been better pleas'd with the institution in some respects, had not so material alterations have taken place, but we found our selves reduced to the single alternative of making such alterations as we have, or attempt to stand without the President Genl, he was very much alarm'd. . . ." Henry Dearborn to Gen. Sullivan, June 8, 1784. Batchellor, "Records of the N.H. Cincinnati," 809.

[61] Hume, *Early Opposition*, 24-27.

of the State."[62] A circular letter issued by the New Hampshire society in 1785 expressed the die-hards' attitude of injured innocence. "We viewed with grief and astonishment the uneasiness which the establishment of our Society gave to some of our Fellow-Citizens," it announced, "and were no less surprised to find the pen of Malice so successfully employed in construing actions that flowed from the purest motives into secret and dangerous attempts to subvert a Government which we had toiled and bled to rear up and defend." The members saw no need for action. "Nothing could afford us more pleasure, than to quiet the minds and remove the fears of our fellow-citizens," they protested, but they could not be expected "to yield to Arguments that have no force, to acknowledge dangers that cannot exist, to recede from a Plan founded on the most laudable Principles. . . ." Such a decision would stamp "the mark of suspicion on the most virtuous actions" and "imply a concession that by our serving as Soldiers we have forfeited our right as Citizens, and are not entitled to those Privileges which our fellow subjects enjoy without controul. . . ." The manifesto defended the right to establish funds and to wear badges as did other fraternities such as the Masons. Furthermore, why should officers be denied the right of correspondence when other societies and individuals were not? Why should the desire of any group of citizens to devote part of their property to philanthropic purposes be challenged? Finally, the idea of surrendering their funds to the state legislature and thus losing control of their disposal was strongly offensive.[63]

The newspapers meanwhile had widely publicized the revised Institution. The subsequent failure of ratification escaped editorial attention, however, and gradually the press turned the public's attention away from the threat of the new order to the infant nation's commercial difficulties, the government's inability to remedy them and the fresher sensation of the balloon craze.

But in spite of the good press the order's revised constitution received,

[62] Jonathan Trumbull, Jr., to Adam Boyd, May 1, 1786, *Papers of the Connecticut State Society of the Cincinnati* (Hartford, 1916).

[63] Batchellor, "Records of the N.H. Cincinnati," 783-785. In April, 1787, the society voted against submitting funds to the assemblies or leaving their existence dependent on charters that might never be obtained. The abolition of inherited membership was condemned as "repugnant to the Design of the Institution" and "Destructive to the principles on which it was originally founded. . . ." The right of correspondence, it insisted, was "the right of freemen of every denomination in America. . . ." MS in handwriting of Gen. John Sullivan, April 16, 1787, Sullivan Papers, New-York Historical Society.

it was some time before the appearance of even such substantial concessions alleviated all misgivings. In Massachusetts the society did not dare apply for a charter as proposed in the new constitution.[64] When its president, Benjamin Lincoln, sought the lieutenant-governorship, he found his leadership in the Cincinnati a liability. The attack against his receiving any political preferment was led by Samuel Adams.[65] Stationed now at the Court of St. James, John Adams inveighed more strongly than ever against the order. "It is the deepest piece of cunning yet attempted," he wrote to Elbridge Gerry. "It is sowing the seeds of all that European courts wish to grow up among us, viz. of vanity, ambition, corruption, discord, and sedition." He was not surprised that men like Steuben and Lafayette, "born and bred to such decorations and the taste for them," favored the association, but "I could not have believed, if I had not seen it, that our officers could have adopted such a scheme, or that the people, the legislatures, or congress have submitted to it one moment." He was little impressed by the alterations that had been proposed. Despite the abolition of hereditary membership, the officers' offspring would continue to wear their ancestors' badges, which eventually would be "considered as the only proofs of merit. Such marks should not be adopted in any country where there is virtue, love of country, love of labour."[66] And as late as the meeting of the Constitutional Convention in 1787 Gerry reiterated his distrust during the deliberations on how to select the president. As an argument against popular choice, he contended that the Cincinnati, acting in concert throughout the union, "will in fact elect the chief Magistrate in every instance, if the election be referred to the people."[67]

Nevertheless, the current of opinion had begun to run the other way. "As to the Cincinnati," Knox took satisfaction in reporting to Washington early in 1785, "the objections against it are apparently removed."[68]

[64] "In this State, it is pretty evident from communicating with the members of the legislature that we should not succeed." Knox to Washington, Jan. 31, 1785, Drake, *Memorials*, 558.

[65] John Quincy Adams to John Adams, June 30, 1787, Worthington Chauncey Ford, ed., *Writings of John Quincy Adams* (New York, 1913-1917), I, 32-33.

[66] Adams to Gerry, April 25, 1785, Austin, *Life of Gerry*, I, 427-430.

[67] Max Farrand, ed., *The Records of the Federal Convention of 1787* (New Haven, 1937), II, 114.

[68] Knox to Washington, Jan. 31, 1785, Drake, *Memorials*, 558. See Knox to Washington, July 26, 1784, Hume, *Washington's Correspondence Concerning the Cincinnati*, 201. Benjamin Lincoln declared that the new plan "appears to give great satisfaction to the citizens at large." Lincoln to Washington, July 15, 1784, *ibid*.

Boston newspapers began to publish defenses of the society and laudatory accounts of its meetings.[69] When the officers assembled on July 4, 1784, a committee from another meeting celebrating the day, "being ever ready to show a respect to such distinguished characters," visited the Cincinnati to announce that they were about to drink the following toast: "May the members of the honorable Society of Cincinnati ever retain that Honor in Present Establishment, which their bravery and Virtues had acquired in their Military."[70] A few years later the society's aversion to Shays' Rebellion won it further favor in previously hostile conservative circles.[71]

Critics found themselves increasingly in the minority, and staunch republicans viewed with dismay how the order flourished. "It is daily acquiring strength," young John Quincy Adams informed his father in 1787. After the death of General Greene his son had inherited his membership in the Rhode Island society. "I was perfectly astonished to see no notice taken of this measure by the public," Adams continued, "But as they are not immediately dangerous, and there are so many other difficulties that engage the attention of the public, nothing is said, or done upon the subject, and they are suffered to take their own course." He still felt that the order "will infallibly become a body dangerous, if not fatal to the Constitution."[72] And James Warren, who also suspected that "the Barefaced and Arrogant System of the Cincinnati Association is not fully matured, but it is rapidly progressing," could only lament that the people "have almost forgott this Insolent Attempt at distinction and are Introducing the members into the Legislature, and the first Civil and Military Offices."[73]

In the 1790's the repercussions of the French Revolution temporarily revived hostility toward the society among Francophiles who felt obliged to disown aristocratic pretensions wherever found. "While we are celebrating in high festivity the conduct and success of our French friends," declared William Heath, "let us, if not already practising, imitate such of their examples as appear to be evidently marked with propriety, and calculated to establish those principles which form the permanent basis of a genuine Republick." Tidings that in France General Dumourier had

[69] *Independent Chronicle,* July 1 and 15, and Oct. 7, 1784, July 7 and 14, 1785.

[70] *Freeman's Journal,* July 21, 1784.

[71] Knox to Washington, March 19, 1787, Drake, *Memorials,* 560; East, "The Massachusetts Conservatives," 389.

[72] J. Q. Adams to John Adams, June 30, 1787, J. Q. Adams, *Writings,* I, 32-33.

[73] James Warren to John Adams, May 18, 1787, *Warren-Adams Letters,* II, 291.

renounced the Cross of St. Louis caused Heath, ever sensitive to shifts in public opinion, again to evaluate the wisdom of his connection with the Cincinnati. "If the *Cross of St. Louis,* long worn in France as an emblem of the distinguished merit of the wearer, is judged by this great man as improper to be worn in a Republick," reflected this determined democrat, "how can I, a *citizen* of the *renowned American Republick,* allow my name to stand affixed to an *institution,* or to wear a *device* which is construed by many of our fellow citizens the indication of an *order* and *distinction* in society." The answer seemed unmistakable. "Animated by this recent example of the Gallic Citizen General," in January, 1793, he asked the secretary-general "to *erase* my name from the *institution* of the Society of the Cincinnati, as I do from this moment for *myself, renounce* the institution. . . ."[74] But this episode represented the afterglow of an ancient animus rather than the dawn of a renewed clamor.

Connecticut, where vigilant citizens had been so quick to scent nefarious designs, displayed an even more striking reversal of opinion. In the press, once so critical, a supporter, modestly known only as "A Farmer," hailed the organization as one "from which I expect infinite advantage will acrue to the Continent; they will watch over our liberties like faithful veterans, and be a firm band to support Congress, with the illustrious American Cyrus at their head. . . ."[75] Prominent citizens of the Nutmeg State willingly accepted honorary membership with expressions of high esteem for the order. According to the distinguished clergyman and patriot, James Dana, the association "must meet the full approbation of all who have any claim to patriotism, learning, liberality or benevolence."[76] President Ezra Stiles of Yale was so carried away as to prophesy that the "Fraternity will figure beyond any that was ever instituted in any part of the World, and will build its Perpetuity and Universality of Estimation upon an Achievement, which will be as immortal, or shall I rather say as durable as the World."[77] Finally, three of the Connecticut Wits, David Humphreys, Joel Barlow and John Trumbull, came to the defense of the

[74] Heath to Knox, Jan. 18, 1793, John Schuyler, *Institution of the Society of the Cincinnati . . . With Extracts . . . from the Transactions of the New York State Society* (New York, 1886), 72.

[75] *Independent Chronicle,* Oct. 7, 1784. See *Conn. Journal,* July 14, 1784.

[76] James Dana to Samuel Parsons, president of the Connecticut Society, Aug. 13, 1784, *Papers of the Conn. Cincinnati.*

[77] Ezra Stiles to Parsons, July 24, 1784, *ibid.* Another announced his acceptance in "honest Conviction that the Society was formed, and is now influenced by the most Honorable Principles. . . ." Nathan Strong to Parsons, July 24, 1784, *ibid.*

Cincinnati in their Federalist satire, "The Anarchiad," written in 1786-1787.[78]

Meanwhile, an examination as to what extent and in what ways the Cincinnati carried out its professed intentions of perpetuating wartime friendships, aiding the unfortunate and preserving "union and national honor" among the states might afford some insight as to the validity of the numerous accusations and rebuttals that were in such wide circulation. For most members the order was chiefly attractive for the convivial aspects of the annual reunions, usually held on the Fourth of July and marked by a symbolic thirteen toasts. Certainly the preparations for the Bay State's gathering in 1789 belie any stereotyped tradition of Puritan austerity and sobriety:

> Your committee beg leave further to report, that they have agreed with Mrs. Lobdell, at the Bunch of Grapes, to have the entertainment at her hotel, for fifty gentlemen; pay her four shillings lawful money, each; she to provide the best dinner the season and market will afford, agreeable to a memorandum furnished her; we finding our own wine, paying her one shilling lawful money a bottle for drawing the corks, and three lawful money a double bowl of punch.
>
> As we are of the opinion that the best liquors will be most acceptable to the Society, we have agreed for the best Madeira wine at fourteen shillings lawful money per gallon, and the best claret wine at two shillings per bottle.[79]

The greater orthodoxy of Connecticut gave its gatherings a more sedate and even pious tone. The official report of the assembly in New Haven on July 4, 1801, ran as follows:

> The meeting having formed at the Court house moved in procession to the brick meeting house, where the public exercises of the day were introduced by prayer; after which the declaration of independence was read by the Secretary;—an oration was delivered by Theodore Dwight Esq at the request of the president;—sundry select pieces of sacred music were performed by the ladies and gentlemen of the City, highly to the credit of the performers, and to the enter-

[78] Humphreys was later vice-president of the Connecticut society, while Trumbull was its secretary during these years. Barlow delivered the first annual oration before the society. Frank Landon Humphreys, *Life and Times of David Humphreys* (New York and London, 1917), I, 382-383.

[79] Report of the subcommittee for the July 4, 1789, meeting, Drake, *Memorials,* 53-54.

tainment of the society and audience; the exercises were closed by prayer. The Society moved in like order of procession to the assembly room, where they partook of a very elegant dinner, composed of all the varieties of the season.[80]

In either case, whether on the frivolous or pompous side, these sessions certainly lacked any sinister undertones.

In the years immediately following the Revolution the eleemosynary enterprises of the Cincinnati did not loom as large as in later years. The Massachusetts and Connecticut societies did not make their first grants to distressed members until 1789, but as the war's survivors became more infirm or left needy widows and orphans, the order found the demands upon its charitable funds increasing until the business of its meetings consisted chiefly of passing upon such applications.[81]

Politically and economically the order proved a strong conservative force. In Massachusetts its hostility to Shays' Rebellion was unmistakable. "In the only instance in which it has had the least political operation," Knox pointed out to Washington, "the effects have been truly noble." Although "the officers are still unpaid and extremely depressed in their private circumstances," nevertheless, "the moment the government was in danger they unanimously pledged themselves for its support, while the few wretched officers who were against the government were not of the Cincinnati."[82] He doubtless referred to the resolution adopted by the Massachusetts branch in October, 1786, when events were moving toward a crisis. The "Society are interested in the preservation of the Constitution," ran this statement, "and so long as life and its attendant blessings, so long as public faith and private credit are made the sacred objects of government agreeably to the original institution, this Society pledge themselves to support it by every means, and by every exertion in their power."[83] The leader of the forces that eventually suppressed Shays' uprising was the president of the state society, Benjamin Lincoln, while the

[80] *Records of the Connecticut State Society of the Cincinnati 1783-1804* (Hartford, 1916).

[81] *The Institution and Proceedings of the Society of the Cincinnati . . . with the Proceedings of the Massachusetts State Society from . . . 1783, to July 4, 1811* (Boston, 1812), *passim; Papers of the Conn. Cincinnati, passim; Records of the Conn. Cincinnati, passim;* Batchellor, "Records of the N.H. Cincinnati," *passim.*

[82] Knox to Washington, March 19, 1787, Drake, *Memorials,* 560.

[83] James M. Bugbee, ed., *Memorials of the Massachusetts Society of the Cincinnati* (Boston, 1890), 41.

vice-president, William Eustis, served as a surgeon on the expedition.[84] Actually, despite Knox's assurances to the contrary, two persons affiliated with the order, Luke and Elijah Day, did participate in the rebellion. In July, 1787, the society, declaring that such action made them "particularly odious and obnoxious," ordered their month's pay returned to them and a statement published in the press that "they are not and never have been considered as members of this Society."[85]

In New Hampshire, General John Sullivan, president of the local Cincinnati, was active in checking the paper money riots. Here the leader of the government's troops was the society's vice-president, Joseph Cilley.[86] The Rhode Island society furnished an even more drastic example of the order's financial conservatism. In 1789 it expelled Joseph Arnold of Warwick, who "by a late tender of the paper currency for a specie demand, notwithstanding the most pressing and repeated admonitions to the contrary, has forfeited all claims to those principles of honor and justice which are the basis of the institution, and thereby rendered himself no longer deserving the friendship of that class of his fellow-citizens, or the patronage of good men."[87]

Whether approvingly or disapprovingly, persons of all factions came more and more to view the society as a bulwark of conservatism. "The men who have been most against it," Knox reported, "say that the Society is the only ban to lawless ambition and dreadful anarchy to which the imbecility of government renders us so liable. . . ."[88] Anxious democratic partisans, however, still feared that this zeal for strong government might even lead the order to overthrow the republic. Mrs. Mercy Warren viewed dourly "the whole class of Cincinnati who are panting for nobility and with the eagle dangling at their breast assume distinctions that are yet new in this Country. . . ." Leagued with other monarchist groups, to her mind they formed "a formidable body, ready to bow to the sceptre of a King, provided they may be the lordlings who in splendid idleness may riot on the hard earnings of the peasant and the mechanic."[89]

[84] *Dictionary of American Biography* (New York, 1928-1944), XI, 261, and VI, 194.

[85] Drake, *Memorials*, 50.

[86] *Dictionary of American Biography*, XVIII, 193, and IV, 107-108.

[87] Rhode Island society to the Connecticut society, July 13, 1789, *Papers of Conn. Cincinnati.*

[88] Knox to Washington, March 19, 1787, Drake, *Memorials*, 560.

[89] Mercy Warren to Catharine Macaulay, Aug. 2, 1787, Charles Warren, *The Making of the Constitution* (Boston, 1929), 378. At least one member of the order

Not surprisingly, the Cincinnati reacted favorably to the drive for a new federal constitution in 1787. While it took no official stand, several of its leaders played an active part in the struggle for ratification. The head of the New Hampshire society, John Sullivan, presided over the state convention there, while the presidents of the branches in Massachusetts and Connecticut, Benjamin Lincoln and Jeremiah Wadsworth, labored for approval in their respective meetings.[90] A touchstone of the order's sympathies was the message that the New Hampshire society sent to Washington "congratulating him and the Gen Society on the Ratification of the federal Constitution in this State manifesting our hearty approbation thereof."[91]

Under the new government the Cincinnati quickly developed close affiliations with the Federalist regime. In the cabinet of the first president, who was simultaneously president-general of the order, two Yankee members, Henry Knox and Timothy Pickering, filled the post of secretary of war in sequence. The president of the Massachusetts branch, Lincoln, received an appointment as collector of the port of Boston, while his successor, John Brooks, who later also became vice-president-general of the national organization, served in the state senate and eventually became the last Federalist governor of the state. In Connecticut the officers' chief, Jeremiah Wadsworth, was a Federalist member of the legislature; Benjamin Tallmadge, successively their treasurer, vice-president and president, served several terms as a Federalist Congressman; and their secretary, Jonathan Trumbull, Jr., after three terms in Congress, became first, United States Senator and then, governor.[92]

To be sure, a few of the association's followers identified themselves with the opposition. Joseph Cilley, New Hampshire's president in the 1790's, was a Jeffersonian member of both houses of the legislature and later became a councillor. Its first vice-president and treasurer, Henry

did feel that monarchy was necessary and that the Cincinnati would have to take the lead. Benjamin Tupper to Knox, April, 1787, Anson Ely Morse, *The Federalist Party in Massachusetts in the Year 1800* (Princeton, 1909), 42 n. It is on this evidence that the leading student of monarchist tendencies in this period attributes such sentiments to the New England Cincinnati. See Louise Burnham Dunbar, "A Study of 'Monarchial' Tendencies in the United States from 1776 to 1801," *University of Illinois Studies in the Social Sciences*, X (March, 1922), 73-74.

[90] *Dictionary of American Biography*, XVIII, 193; XI, 261; XIX, 310.

[91] Batchellor, "Records of the N.H. Cincinnati," 788.

[92] *Dictionary of American Biography*, III, 80; XI, 261; XIX, 310; XVIII, 285; XIX, 18.

Dearborn, was a Republican member of Congress who later became Jefferson's secretary of war. The vice-president of the Massachusetts society, William Eustis, despite his part in the expedition against Shays, became an anti-Federalist member of the legislature.[93] But these apostates were few in number compared to the upholders of orthodoxy. Even so, these data prove nothing more than that there was a high correlation between Cincinnati membership and political conservatism, a not too startling finding in view of the social status of most officers. That the society itself acted as an independent political force, moulding the thoughts and actions of its members, seems dubious, though its meetings and inter-correspondence among branches certainly made it easier than it would otherwise have been for the commissioned veterans to exchange opinions and discover their mutual compatability.

In any case, after 1800 the combination of such factors as the westward migration of officers, the fear of popular hostility, the members' own apathy and the general difficulties in maintaining an organization before the development of modern transportation and communication made the order increasingly moribund in New England.[94] The Connecticut society, reacting with "infinite pain and mortification" to the legislature's refusal to grant the charter of incorporation which they thought essential to protect their charitable funds, disbanded in 1804.[95] After the early 1790's the New Hampshire society never had as many as ten members present at its sessions and, since by the early 1800's the number was usually only two or three, it ceased functioning in 1825.[96] After Rhode Island's association became dormant in 1832, the Massachusetts group, of the original branches in New England, alone remained active, quietly changing from a veterans' to a hereditary society as sons and nephews replaced the original members.[97]

[93] *Ibid.*, IV, 108; V, 175; VI, 194. For a list of state officers of the Cincinnati in these years, see the appendix in Thomas, *Society of the Cincinnati*, 125-149.

[94] For an account of the migration of a considerable number of the Massachusetts members to Ohio, for example, see *Proceedings of the Massachusetts State Society 1783-1811*, 83-85.

[95] *Records of the Conn. Cincinnati.*

[96] Batchellor, "Records of the N.H. Cincinnati."

[97] The last original member of the Massachusetts society, Dr. Joseph Prescott, died in 1852. Drake, *Memorials*, 82. With the wave of interest in hereditary patriotic societies that marked the late nineteenth century came the revival of defunct branches of the Cincinnati: Rhode Island in 1878, Connecticut in 1889 and New Hampshire in 1899. Thomas, *Society of the Cincinnati*, 181.

Hence the feeble remnants of the Cincinnati no longer occasioned suspicion or alarm. At the outset of an era far more truculently democratic than the 1780's had ever been, the son-in-law and biographer of one of the society's early opponents, himself on the road from Republican to Whig allegiance, finally dismissed the order in 1829 as a group "which at the present day is beheld with veneration and respect, whose weakness and not their power excites the public sympathy; whose devotion to the country's services in the gloomiest hours should have been their guaranty for future patriotism, and secured their gallant name from reproach. . . ."[98] The fears aroused by the Society of the Cincinnati never materialized, and in retrospect it seems a singularly innocuous order. Yet it does not follow that the apprehensions were entirely imaginary, for what might have developed had there not been so instant and so extensive an outcry, in New England as elsewhere, can remain only surmise.[99]

[98] Austin, *Life of Gerry*, I, 416-417.

[99] Admittedly the early critics of the order based much of their attacks on a greatly exaggerated idea of its size ("Cassius" attributed to it some 10,000 followers rather than the 2,300 it ever had at most) and in estimating its future influence did not foresee the society's steadfast refusal to increase its membership by allowing more than one descendant of a Revolutionary officer to belong at a time, or to permit new branches to be established outside of the thirteen original states. Much less could they imagine the inundation of the colonial stock by subsequent immigration.

The American Clergy and the French Revolution

Gary B. Nash*

ON May 9, 1798, responding to President Adams's call for a day of "solemn humiliation, fasting and prayer," Jedidiah Morse rose to the pulpit, once in the morning at New North Church in Boston, again in the afternoon before his own congregation in Charlestown. Using the same text for his sermon at each service, Morse electrified his parishoners. Agents of a secret European organization dedicated to the destruction of all civil and ecclesiastical authority, he revealed, had invaded the United States. This same organization, which he identified as an offshoot of Freemasonry called the Illuminati, had kindled the French Revolution and currently stood behind the successes of the French army in Europe. "Kings, princes, and rulers in all governments, . . . priests and ministers of religion of all denominations . . . are reviled and abused," he declared, and "fraud, violence, cruelty, debauchery, and the uncontrolled gratification of every corrupt and debasing lust and inclination of the human heart" exist in the place of religion throughout the western world. Such was the final fruit of the French Revolution.[1]

The response to Morse's sermon was immediate. Already inflamed by the XYZ affair, newspaper editors, clergymen, politicians, and private citizens echoed the charges, calling for the extermination of the alien influence and affirming the need for social unity, conservative government, and a revival of religion. France and the French Revolution were subjected to the most unrestrained criticisms as the source of American impiety and social disorder. Deism, and its inevitable partner atheism, were reviled as dangerous imports from France. The suppression of French

* Mr. Nash is a member of the Department of History, Princeton University.

[1] Jedidiah Morse, *A Sermon, Delivered at the New North Church . . . May 9th, 1798 . . .* (Boston, 1798), 18-23. Morse later revealed that his sermon was inspired by a reading of John Robison's *Proofs of a Conspiracy . . .*, which had just arrived in America. Morse, *A Sermon, Exhibiting The Present Dangers, and Consequent Duties of the Citizens of the United States of America* (Charlestown, 1799), 33.

ideas must be immediate and total, for the very fabric of American society was threatened.[2]

Morse had not always breathed such Francophobic fire. In fact neither the September Massacres in 1792, the execution of the King the following year, the period of so-called de-Christianization, nor the Reign of Terror had aroused his hostility. "Liberty is the birthright of all mankind" usually stolen away by despots and tyrants, Morse reminded his congregation at a Thanksgiving Day sermon in 1794. The French cause was "unquestionably good"; as for the massacres, the guillotine, and atheism, the "errors and irregularities" of the revolutionaries, he said, "proceeding almost necessarily from the magnitude and the difficulties of their undertaking, are not to be justified, nor yet too severely censured. All circumstances taken into view, they ought, perhaps, in a great measure, to be excused."[3] In February 1795, Morse was more direct. Although regretting its excesses, he compared the revolution in France to our own, predicting that once she had defeated her external enemies, France would achieve political and social stability. The full extent of Morse's commitment to the revolutionary cause is best measured by his justification of French atheism. "The rejection of the Christian Religion in France," he said, "is less to be wondered at, when we consider, in how unamicable and disgusting a point of view it has been there exhibited, under the hierarchy of Rome. When peace and a free government shall be established, and the people have liberty and leisure to examine for themselves, we anticipate, by means of the effusions of the Holy Spirit, a glorious revival and prevalence of pure, unadulterated Christianity."[4]

Among the "publishing clergy," those ecclesiastics whose pulpit oratory was committed to print, such views were held with virtual unanimity during the first five years of the Revolution. Primarily from New England and the middle states, and representing in most cases the Calvinist wing of the Protestant church, these men were highly influential in forming public opinion in the 1790's. Few voices in the community outweighed

[2] See Vernon Stauffer, *New England and the Bavarian Illuminati* (New York, 1918), 239-287.

[3] Jedidiah Morse, *The Present Situation of Other Nations of the World, Contrasted with our Own* (Boston, 1795), 15*n*, quoting from his unpublished Thanksgiving Day sermon of Nov. 20, 1794.

[4] *Ibid.*, 11-14. Morse also rejoiced at "the increasing harmony and union between this country and the French nation, in consequence of the recent happy change in the measures of their government," an allusion, no doubt, to the Thermidorean reaction. *Ibid.*, 30-31.

that of the clergyman; and, apart from newspapers, sermons were probably the principal reading matter of the literate public. The attitudes of southern clergymen are extremely difficult to measure as only a few of their sermons were published. It is likely that opinion of the French Revolution in the South was strongly influenced by the uprisings in St. Domingo and the fear of slave insurrections.[5]

That the American clergy should respond with enthusiasm to the early stages of the Revolution in France is hardly surprising. What is surprising, and little recognized, is that the clergy's Francophilia persisted through its most violent and most anticlerical phase. In the beginning, Americans of all classes and religious beliefs, seeing a consanguinity between their own Revolution and the upheaval in France, rejoiced at the prospect of liberty flourishing on a second continent.[6] Even if a clergyman had not shared this general enthusiasm, he would have been reluctant to attack a cause regarded by most of the members of his congregation as a part of their own Revolutionary heritage, particularly at a time when clergymen were attempting to rebuild their congregations in the face of widespread religious backsliding. Besides, few outdid the clergy in welcoming the overthrow of the Catholic church in France, an institution stigmatized by Protestants since the Revocation of the Edict of Nantes and before. Illustrative of this mood was the publication in 1793 of *The French Convert,* the pretty tale of the "happy conversion of a noble French lady from the errors and superstitions of popery to the reformed religion by means of a Protestant gardener, her servant." An immediate best-seller, *The French Convert* went through ten printings in four years.[7] Also popular was James Bicheno's *The Signs of the Times: or, the Overthrow of the Papal Tyranny in France, the Prelude of Destruction to Popery and Despotism But of Peace to Mankind,* an English concoction imported to America and reprinted in five cities.

[5] The extensive listing of printed sermons may be traced in Charles Evans, *American Bibliography* . . . (Chicago, 1903-59). The membership of the late 18th-century clergy may be followed in William B. Sprague, *Annals of the American Pulpit* . . . , 9 vols. (New York, 1857-69).

[6] For American response to the French Revolution see Charles D. Hazen, *Contemporary American Opinion of the French Revolution* (Baltimore, 1897), 140-152; and Howard M. Jones, *America and French Culture, 1750-1848* (Chapel Hill, 1927), 530-538.

[7] First printed in New York. Later editions bear the imprint of presses as far removed as Walpole and Amherst, New Hampshire.

Among the clerical Francophiles was Ezra Stiles, Congregationalist president of Yale. A fervent supporter of the Revolution—a "Yale Jacobin" as his recent biographer calls him[8]—he welcomed news of the King's arrest at Varennes, reflecting that his failure to escape would "convince all the Sovereigns of Europe the Vanity of withstanding the general and popular Resolutions of a Nation of enlightened Subjects."[9] In the execution of Louis XVI and the declaration of war against England and Holland he saw ultimately "the Tameing, the Moderation and Amelioration [of] all the European Governments." By August 1794 Stiles was commenting with satisfaction on the inability of "all Europe and its Kings" to break up the Republic of France. Even the execution of the Brissotins did not alter his warmth for the Revolution, for in that event he saw all further monarchical tendencies expurged. Stiles remained an enthusiast of the Revolution up to his death in May 1795, pronouncing no word of hostility toward the Revolution or dismay at the "de-Christianization" process sweeping France in these years.[10]

Stiles might be thought an atypical example, for, though without deistical or unitarian leanings, he was a theological liberal and an enthusiastic partisan of the Enlightenment—an American philosophe. But his views of the Revolution were shared by a large part of his confreres in the clergy. Samuel Stillman, for example, told his congregation at the First Baptist Church of Boston in 1794 that whereas the numerous executions and the rejection of religion in France could not be countenanced, these excesses could no doubt be attributed to the bottomless evils of the old regime which the revolutionary leaders had to overthrow. The Revolution remained, Stillman asserted, a mighty triumph over "papal corruptions and tyrannies," for never had a people been so martyred as the Protestants of France. That this "very important pillar of Popery . . . her kings, nobles and priests . . . impiously combined against the civil and religious liberties of the people," should fall, he stated, was the judgment of God. Even in the revolutionary calendar Stillman found reason for comfort. The calendar would obliterate from the peoples' minds, he felt, the remembrance of "saints days, feasts and fasts, etc. which make a great

[8] Edmund S. Morgan, *The Gentle Puritan: A Life of Ezra Stiles, 1727-1795* (New Haven, 1962), chap. 27.

[9] Aug. 25, 1791, in Franklin B. Dexter, ed., *The Literary Diary of Ezra Stiles* (New York, 1901), III, 428.

[10] Apr. 7, 1793, June 7, 1793, Aug. 21, 1794, and Mar. 11, 1795, *ibid.*, 488-490, 496, 530, 559. See also Morgan, *Life of Stiles*, 453-461.

part of the superstition of the Romish Church."[11] Joseph Lathrop in West Springfield held similar views. He saw the Revolution as "a continuation of the late AMERICAN war," and viewed irreligion as a natural but temporary side effect of the "civil convulsions" by which the corrupt clergy and the tyrannical monarchy would be overthrown.[12]

In July 1794, John M'Knight, Presbyterian clergyman of New York, openly endorsed the cause of liberty in France, a conflagration started by the "Sparks of that fire of liberty which has burned so bright in America." Samuel Kendal, at the Congregational Church in Weston, Massachusetts, in November 1794 celebrated the Revolution as the political regeneration of France, proceeding with "as much wisdom, firmness, and moderation, as was reasonable to expect." Though deploring the Jacobins as the usurpers of national authority and fearing that their factionalism would exhaust the cause of liberty, Kendal insisted that the "cause in which the nation is embarked . . . is just and must prevail."[13]

Even as late as 1795 clergymen warmly applauded the Revolution. Benjamin Wadsworth of the Congregational church in Danvers, Massachusetts, reminded his parishioners that it was America who taught the world how to be free. In France the cause of liberty must prevail. James Malcomson, pastor of the Presbyterian Church at Williamsburgh, South Carolina, applauded the demise of "priestcraft as well as king-craft." The Revolution in France was for him "the cause of humanity, the cause of religion, the cause of God." In Boston, Samuel West warmed to the "candid spirit [which] prevails at present in the French Republic" and expressed his confidence that France was proceeding to the establishment of a "wise, liberal and energetic government, under which, they and their posterity may be happy for ages to come." Samuel Miller, later the celebrated president of the Princeton Theological Seminary, exhorted his listeners in New York to "support the banner of freedom . . . in those TWO REPUBLICS which have lately cast off the yoke."[14]

[11] Samuel Stillman, *Thoughts on the French Revolution* (Boston, 1795), 12-14, 17-20.

[12] Joseph Lathrop, *Sermons on Various Subjects . . .* (Worcester, Mass., 1796), II, 195-198; *National Happiness, Illustrated in a Sermon* (Springfield, Mass., 1795), 16-17.

[13] John M'Knight, *God the Author of Promotion* (New York, 1794), 14-15; Samuel Kendal, *A Sermon, Delivered on the Day of National Thanksgiving* (Boston, 1795), 8-13.

[14] Benjamin Wadsworth, *America Invoked to Praise the Lord* (Salem, 1795), 25-26; James Malcomson, *A Sermon Preached on the 14th of July, 1794 . . .* (Charles-

Through at least the first five years of the Revolution, then, including the periods of most pronounced antireligious activity, the clergy steadfastly supported the French cause. They applauded its continuation of the American struggle for liberty, condoned violence and the worst excesses of the Committee of Public Safety, and blinked at the openly deistical and atheistical manifestations of this turbulent epoch. Searching the sermons of the time, one finds but a single American cleric, David Tappan, Professor of Divinity at Harvard College, who attacked the Revolution in France.[15] But Tappan's voice was a cry in the wilderness. This was so even though Federalist leaders had long been importuning their friends in the clergy to join them in the battle against France and things French. William Cobbett, the acid-tongued and bitterly Francophobic journalist, admitted as late as 1795 that much of the clergy was inclined toward the Revolution whether, as he said, by disposition or—significantly—by fear of offending their congregations.[16]

Not until late 1794, when the most violent and anticlerical phases of the Revolution were over, did the clergy begin to turn against the French cause. In September of that year from his pulpit in Medford, Massachusetts, David Osgood attacked the Revolution as an exercise in anarchy and irreligion. Two months later he repeated his indictment in a strongly worded Thanksgiving Day sermon, charging that some Americans were embracing irreligion along with their enthusiasiasm for the Revolution in France. For citizens to copy the iniquitous French at such a time was plainly leading to disorder and spiritual decay in their own country.[17]

Within four months of Osgood's pronouncements the tide of clerical opinion was turning swiftly; many of the clergy, especially in New England, made Fast and Thanksgiving Days in 1795 the occasion for rabidly anti-French sermons. February 19, 1795—by presidential proclamation a

ton, 1795), 29, 38-42; Samuel West, *A Sermon* (Boston, 1795), 19; Samuel Miller, *A Sermon* (New York, 1795), 31-32. Among the other outspoken friends of the Revolution were Joseph Dana of Ipswich and Thomas Barnard of Salem.

[15] David Tappan, *A Sermon, Delivered . . . On Occasion of the Annual Fast . . .* (Boston, 1793). As far as his sermons and published writings indicate, Tappan had never found occasion to criticize the Revolution before this.

[16] William Cobbett, *A History of the American Jacobins, Commonly Denominated Democrats,* in appendix to William Playfair, *The History of Jacobinism . . .* (Philadelphia, 1796), II, 40-41.

[17] David Osgood, *The Wonderful Works of God are to be Remembered* (Boston, 1794), 23-26; see also Bernard Fäy, *The Revolutionary Spirit in France and America* (New York, 1927), 366.

day of fast and thanksgiving—marked a turning point for the rallying opponents of the Revolution. On that day, Tappan, who had been first in the field, stepped up his attacks from Charleston, styling the French an "uninformed and furious populace, intoxicated with undigested notions of their own sovereignty." The "detestable principles of an atheistical philosophy" were ruining the country.[18] Tappan, like others, gave no hint that he had long been aware of the Thermidorean reaction in France. At Medford, David Osgood was at the same time lamenting the melancholy situation in France where "statesmen and legislators . . . should have been distinguished for opinions that would shock the reason of men, and would disgrace the understanding of an Hottentot," and spoke of the "ferocious and atheistical anarchy in France," which its authors were attempting to spread abroad.[19]

William White, Bishop of the Protestant-Episcopal Church of Pennsylvania, was another who spoke out on February 19. Discoursing on the "reciprocal influence of civil policy and religious duty," White decried the "'madness'* of popular tumult and insurrection" and called for a renaissance of religious feeling as a "counterpoise, to the basest passions of our nature."[20] Samuel Stanhope Smith, president of Princeton, offered additional testimony to the changing spirit among clergymen. A moderate and tolerant Presbyterian clergyman, Smith had studied the eighteenth-century rationalist philosophers in the 1760's under John Witherspoon at Princeton. Strongly influenced by his tutor, Smith sought to reconcile the Enlightenment philosophy with orthodox religion.[21] Before he became president of the college in 1795 he had evinced no hostility to the Revolution in France. But now he too saw the French in a new light. The revolutionists were "apostles of atheism more fanatical than the disciples of Omar . . . and more bloody than the votaries of Moloch."[22]

But the French Revolution still had friends among the clergy in 1795, principally among those who were staunch supporters of the Jeffersonian

[18] Tappan, *Christian Thankfulness Explained and Enforced* (Boston, 1795), 22-29.

[19] Morse, *Federalist Party in Mass.*, 99-100, citing Osgood's sermon of Feb. 19, 1795; Stauffer, *New England and the Bavarian Illuminati*, 93, citing the same.

[20] William White, *A Sermon, on the Reciprocal Influence of Civil Policy and Religious Duty* (Philadelphia, 1795), 22-32.

[21] See William H. Hudnut III, "Samuel Stanhope Smith: Enlightened Conservative," *Journal of the History of Ideas*, XVII (1956), 540-542.

[22] Samuel Smith, *The Divine Goodness to the United States of America . . .* (Philadelphia, 1795), 34-37.

party; but their numbers were dwindling rapidly. Throughout New England and the middle states clergymen were lining up against the movement.[23] Lathrop, Stillman, Dana, Ashbel Green in Philadelphia, and virtually all the former friends of the Revolution in the clergy felt compelled to alter the position they had held from 1789 to 1795. Jedidiah Morse accurately described this changing mood when he wrote in the autumn of 1796 that "very few of the clergy in the circle of my acquaintance seem disposed to pray for the success of the French . . . and I apprehend the complexion of the thanksgiving sermons throughout New England this year is very different from those of last in respect to this particular."[24]

Morse's spectacular charges against the Illuminati two years later represented only the climax of the clerical indictment of the French Revolution. The attacks of the clergy became progressively more bitter after 1795 when the clergy first began to turn against the Revolution. That so many clergymen gave credence to Morse's accusations reveals how far the pendulum of clerical opinion had swung. The French Revolution, so widely celebrated for five years and more, had become the object of scorn and hatred among the American clergy.

The timing of the clergy's change in its view of the French Revolution makes it clear that the change was the product not so much of the drift of events in France as of movements—ideological, political, and social—at home. Of chief importance were the rise of militant deism, the threat of social disorder, and the growing intensity of national political issues. It was perhaps the first of these, the threat to religious orthodoxy, that figured most prominently.

Deism in America, as in Europe, was an aspect of the eighteenth-century Enlightenment. Reflecting the optimistic, rational, scientific spirit of the age, deists rejected the theocentric piety of doctrinal Calvinism and adopted instead a "rational" approach to religion. Whereas Unitarians worked within the context of the Christian church in culling out the

[23] Of the clergymen who were previously pro-French, I can find only one, Ebenezer Bradford, who still supported the Revolution by 1796, and Bradford was increasingly uncomfortable with his pro-French inclinations. See his *Mr. Thomas Paine's Trial . . .* (Boston, 1795) and *The Nature of Humiliation, Fasting and Prayer Explained* (Boston, 1795).

[24] Quoted in William De Loss Love, Jr., *The Fast and Thanksgiving Days of New England* (Boston, 1895), 373.

nonrationalist elements of Calvinist theology, the deists labored to fashion a rationalist religion out of the materials of natural law.[25]

The secularization of the Revolutionary generation and the influx of French rationalist ideas at the time of our own Revolution added to the popular appeal of deism. Many of the most widely admired figures of the young nation subscribed to deistical thinking. Some, like Franklin, Jefferson, George Mason, Edmund Randolph, Philip Freneau, and Joel Barlow, openly espoused "natural" religion. Others, such as Washington, Noah Webster, James Madison, George Wythe, Robert T. Paine, and John Randolph, indulged the unorthodox faith though remaining nominally within the established churches.[26] Stephen Girard, the fabulously wealthy Philadelphia merchant who owned seventy-five printings of Voltaire's works, openly displayed his admiration for the French philosophers by giving the names *Voltaire, Rousseau,* and *Montesquieu* to three of his ships.[27] The foremost symbol of American intellectual achievement, the American Philosophical Society, leaned strongly toward the ideas of the Enlightenment, including rationalist religion.[28]

Clergymen, though they had long opposed rationalist religion, were reluctant to attack individual deists, especially as so many were highly respected figures in society. Deism was an intellectually fashionable religious philosophy, not an institution. Until the mid-1790's it had no leaders, publications, meeting places, or systematic theology. Indeed, the only published statement of the deists' creed before 1794 was Ethan Allen's *Reason, the Only Oracle of Man;* and few copies of this hastily-written tract survived a fire in the printer's garret in 1784, the year of its publication.[29] Nor did deists indicate any desire to institutionalize their beliefs.

[25] The origins of American deism are traced in Herbert M. Morais, *Deism in Eighteenth Century America* (New York, 1934), chaps. 1 and 2.

[26] Morais, *Deism in Eighteenth Century America,* 17; Russel B. Nye, *The Cultural Life of the New Nation, 1776-1830* (New York, 1960), 206-215; Harry R. Warfel, ed., *Letters of Noah Webster* (New York, 1953), 162, 229-230, 310-313. Webster is a revealing case of a nominal Congregationalist who privately imbibed deistical ideas. Although commonly denominated a rigid Congregationalist, Webster, as his letters indicate, rejected "regeneration, election, salvation by free grace, the atonement, and the divinity of Christ." In 1808 he underwent a conversion to orthodox Calvinism. See Webster to Thomas Dawes, Dec. 20, 1808, *ibid.,* 310-313.

[27] Nye, *Cultural Life of the New Nation,* 209n.

[28] Jones, *America and French Culture,* 403-405.

[29] John Pell, *Ethan Allen* (Boston, 1929), 253; Stauffer, *New England and the Bavarian Illuminati,* 71n. The clergy was quick to reply to Allen's book. Stiles, Dwight, Jeremy Belknap, Lemuel Haynes, and Nathan Perkins among others,

Their animus toward Biblical revelation, for example, was not based on any desire to undermine the clergy's source of authority but rather on a belief that revelation could not meet the all-important criterion of reason. Further, American deists, unlike those in France, were not actively anticlerical, for the clergy in the United States upheld no reactionary or tyrannical cause. All in all, deism and the early deists provided a most elusive target.

All of this began to change rapidly in the early 1790's. Ethan Allen's *Reason, the Only Oracle of Man,* though not widely circulated, had struck a responsive note when it attempted to identify deism with American democratic ideals and orthodox religion with feudal Europe. A reprinting in 1790 of Thomas Emlyn's *Humble Inquiry concerning the Deity of Jesus Christ,* a deistical argument first published in England in 1756, disturbed American clergymen and provoked replies from Aaron Burr and Caleb Alexander, both of which were published in Boston in 1791.[30] A rising flood of rationalist literature imported from Europe and reprinted in this country further aroused apprehensions among the clergy. Though an outspoken foe of deism and atheism and a pillar of the Philadelphia Unitarian church, Joseph Priestley upset the orthodox with the string of rationalist pamphlets he fed the presses of Philadelphia, New York, and Boston; and his *Appeal to the Serious and Candid 'Professors of Christianity'* (1784), reprinted in Philadelphia in 1792, evoked a feverish reply from the Reverend Samuel Wetherill of that city.[31]

In the meantime, a small number of deists began in the early 1790's to seek a wider audience for their views. Intent on popularizing and organizing their religion, these militant believers, only a handful in number, aroused disproportionate fears among the clergy who were already alarmed by the general religious apathy.[32] In 1790 John Fitch, inventor of the steamboat, founded a deistical club, the Universal Society, in Philadelphia. But it was not until 1794 when Elihu Palmer began trekking up

---

answered the deist's work, many of them magisterially interpreting the fire in the printer's garret as divine intervention. For a fresh consideration of Allen see Darline Shapiro, "Ethan Allen: Philosopher-Theologian to a Generation of American Revolutionaries," *William and Mary Quarterly,* 3d Ser., XXI (1964), 236-255.

[30] Aaron Burr, *The Supreme Deity of our Lord Jesus Christ Maintained;* Caleb Alexander, *An Essay on the Real Deity of Jesus Christ.*

[31] Samuel Wetherill, *The Divinity of Jesus Christ Proved . . .* (Philadelphia, 1792).

[32] The rise of militant deism is most extensively treated in G. Adolph Koch, *Republican Religion: The American Revolution and the Cult of Reason* (New York, 1933), chaps. 2 and 3; and Morais, *Deism in Eighteenth Century America,* chap. 5.

and down the coast to deliver lectures and organize deistical societies that clergymen became truly alarmed.[33]

It was in 1794, too, that the first part of Thomas Paine's *Age of Reason* reached this country from France. Of all the blows struck at revealed religion by Old World writers in the service of the Enlightenment, none had greater effect than this book. Paine was widely admired by all classes as the fiery polemicist of both the American and French Revolution. The presses could scarcely keep up with the demand for his *Rights of Man,* written in answer to Burke's hostile *Reflections on the Revolution in France.* Nineteen editions of Paine's treatise appeared in America between 1791 and 1793, while Burke's work was printed only twice. So popular was *The Age of Reason,* in turn, that eight American editions appeared in 1794, seven in 1795, and two in 1796, including printings in Boston, Hartford, New York, Philadelphia, and Worcester. Paine attacked traditional theological doctrine with all the skill of his trenchant pen, noting an association between despotic political systems and revealed religion. Selling for a pittance, the book was used as a catechism by democratic clubs and deistical societies, purchased by college students, who confronted their professors with the heretical arguments, and discussed in taverns and on street-corners everywhere.

By 1795 there was real reason for dismay among the ranks of orthodox clergymen. In that year, Baron Paul von Holbach's *Christianity Unveiled* appeared from a New York printer under the pseudonym of Boulanger.[34] So did Count Constantin de Volney's *Common Sense; or Natural Ideas Opposed to Supernatural,* in Philadelphia as well as in New York. In 1796 came Volney's *Law of Nature,* William Godwin's *Enquiry Concerning Political Justice,* the first edition in translation of Voltaire's heralded *Dictionnaire philosophique,* and, most notably of all, the second part of Paine's *Age of Reason.* As Timothy Dwight of Yale lamented, France, Germany, and England were all "vomiting" irreligious literature on America.[35] In Philadelphia Benjamin Bache alone sold fifteen thousand

[33] See Morais, *Deism in Eighteenth Century America,* 130-131.

[34] The authorship of *Christianity Unveiled* is disputed but attributed to Holbach by the Library of Congress and by Evans.

[35] Charles E. Cuningham, *Timothy Dwight, 1752-1817* (New York, 1942), 299. The wide variety of French literature, especially of a rationalist and liberal genre, available to the residents of Philadelphia and New York in both original and translation is discussed by Howard M. Jones, "Importation of French Books in Philadelphia, 1750-1800," *Modern Philology,* XXXII (1934-35), 157-177; and "The Im-

copies of *Age of Reason,* sent from France by Paine. New York and Philadelphia printings were required to supplement the Paris edition. Everywhere Paine was read. A young graduate of Yale and Williams noted in 1796 that the *"Age of Reason* is greedily received in Vermont," while in Connecticut a Presbyterian clergyman declared that everything from Paine's pen was "read with avidity by all parties."[36]

The clergy's deep concern is evident from the more than thirty-five printed replies to Paine's book, many as abusive as the work they attacked.[37] Shouted down from virtually every pulpit in the country, the *Age of Reason,* like other works proscribed by defenders of orthodoxy, aroused even wider curiosity and attracted even greater attention.

The state of the colleges gave the clergy additional cause for alarm. The post-Revolutionary decade had been a difficult one for these institutions, poised as they were on the brink of financial collapse. Now they were beset by the growing addiction of the students, presumably the leaders of the next generation, to the rationalist philosophers. Yale in 1795, Lyman Beecher later recalled, was in "a most ungodly state." "That was the day of infidelity of the Tom Paine School," remembered Beecher. "Boys that dressed flax in the barn as I used to read Tom Paine and believed Him." Classmates hailed each other as Voltaire, Rousseau, and D'Alembert. Another student of the time later recalled that "an aspiring ambitious youth, hardly dared avow his belief in the Christian doctrine."[38]

Harvard, as William E. Channing remembered it in 1794, "was never in a worse state, with the tendency of all classes to skepticism." The students at Cambridge, noted a fellow student of Channing, were deeply infected with the *"French mania";* an "infidel and irreligious spirit" prevailed. The college in 1796 felt compelled to distribute to every student a copy of Bishop Richard Watson's *Apology for the Bible,* widely regarded

portation of French Literature in New York City, 1750-1800," *Studies in Philology,* XXVIII (Oct. 1931), 235-251. Jones notes that books were frequently imported almost upon publication.

[36] Nye, *Cultural Life of the New Nation,* 214; Increase N. Tarbox, ed., *Diary of Thomas Robbins, D.D., 1796-1854* (Boston, 1886-87), I, 17; Sept. 10, 1803, in *The Diary of William Bentley, D.D. . . .* (Salem, Mass., 1905-14), III, 42. See Richard Purcell, *Connecticut in Transition, 1775-1818* (Washington, 1918), 20.

[37] For tracts published in response to *Age of Reason,* see Stauffer, *New England and the Bavarian Illuminati, 75n-76n;* and Morse, *Federalist Party in Mass.,* 217-219.

[38] Barbara Cross, ed., *The Autobiography of Lyman Beecher* (Cambridge, Mass., 1961), I, 27; Charles R. Keller, *The Second Great Awakening in Connecticut* (New Haven, 1942), 17.

as the most efficacious antidote to Paine's poison.[39] At Princeton, professed Christians were oddities among the student body. Moreau de Saint-Méry, a prominent traveler of the day, remarked after stopping at Princeton in 1794 that the college was greatly deteriorated and the "sport and licentious habits are said to absorb the pupils more than study."[40]

By 1795 the clergy was thoroughly frightened. Once the philosophical concern of only the upper-class elements, deism was now infiltrating the lesser ranks of society where it was accepted as the religious component of equality and liberty, the very bywords of the French Revolution. Conversely, revealed religion was being made by Paine and others to seem a part of a retrogressive scheme which sought to impose limitation of suffrage, a rigid class structure, and other antidemocratic measures. Deism was, apparently, the voice of modernity, a natural aspect of man's inevitable progress, the religious expression of an era which had liberated itself from outworn, nonrational concepts.

The course of political events during the early 1790's paralleling this increased deistic agitation gave clergymen further reasons to think themselves challenged by both internal and external forces. By 1792 an open split had appeared in American political life, and among the divisive forces the French Revolution loomed large. As Stephen Higginson later observed, it "drew a red-hot ploughshare through the history of America as well as through that of France."[41] In domestic terms the division was not just an argument over the relative merits of the French Revolution and its European opponents; it also involved the broader question of the nature and proper functions of national government. The Federalists, who sought a strong central government and rule by the "wealthy, wise, and well-born," saw a natural identification of British and American interests. On the other side stood the Republicans, viewing the abilities of the common man more optimistically and seeing the strongest principles of the American Revolution reaffirmed in the French struggle. In short, the European crisis required Americans to think out their political and social beliefs. All of the thinking of the Revolutionary and Confederation decades was crystallized by the polarity of France and Great Britain—the

[39] William H. Channing, *Memoir of William Ellery Channing* (Boston, 1848), I, 60-61.

[40] Varnum L. Collins, *President Witherspoon* (Princeton, 1925), II, 198-199; Moreau de St. Méry, *American Journey,* trans. and ed. by Kenneth and Anna M. Roberts (Garden City, N.Y., 1947), 105.

[41] Stephen Higginson, as quoted in Hazen, *Opinion of the French Revolution,* ix.

rhetorical symbols of the emerging Republican and Federalist parties.[42]

When England and France joined battle in 1793, Americans everywhere began choosing sides. Despite Washington's efforts to keep his country clear of the European maelstrom, this country could never really free itself from economic, emotional, and intellectual involvement. European books, newspapers, and ideas were as indispensable as European goods. Americans, while content to withdraw behind a political *cordon sanitaire,* had no wish to sever economic and intellectual ties with Europe. And virtually nobody could maintain a neutral position in regard to the amazing events in France.

As admirers of the British political and social order, which by definition made them less than enthusiastic about the changes being wrought in France, the Federalists in 1792-93 were placed in the difficult position of opposing a cause which was immensely popular at all levels of society. To discredit the French Revolution thus became a political necessity for the Federalists. This they sought to do by several devices. They charged that the Revolution, while pure in conception, had led to inexcusable and corrupting excesses; that the French were forcing their Revolution on other sovereign nations; and that by 1793 the Revolution was in the hands of atheists who, not content to extinguish Christianity in their own country, were spreading infidelity to other shores.

This last charge the Federalists exploited to the full in cultivating an alliance with the clergy. France was identified as the source of American infidelity, and the pro-French faction in the United States—the Jeffersonians—were charged with atheistic sympathies. Even though they blurred the distinctions between deism and atheism and ignored the spectrum of religious beliefs to be found among supporters of both parties, the Federalists succeeded in arousing clerical apprehensions at the rise of the Republicans.

Noah Webster provides an interesting example of the Federalists' early use of French irreligion as a political weapon. Urged by prominent Federalists to take up his pen for the conservative cause, Webster established a newspaper, the *Minerva,* in New York in 1793. Like other Federalist-

[42] The prelude to this debate had been carried on in 1790-91. It was initiated by Paine's *Rights of Man,* written in 1790 as a rebuttal of Burke's *Reflections on the Revolution in France.* When Paine's polemic appeared in this country, John Adams and his son, John Quincy Adams, felt compelled to answer. Writing under the pseudonyms of *Davila* and *Publicola,* they set forth the conservative position as to the division of the powers of government.

oriented papers, the *Minerva* opposed the French Revolution, its supporters in this country, and its scandalous minister, Edmond Charles Genêt.[43] In the following year Webster struck a telling blow against the Republicans. In a pamphlet printed anonymously, he assailed the French Jacobins and their "atheistic attacks on Christianity." More pointedly, Webster suggested the parallel between the Jacobin clubs and the Democratic-Republican societies in this country. Admiration for the American clubs, he warned, might reproduce the situation in France, a condition "dangerous to government, religion and morals." Deism and atheism—the two terms were used interchangeably—would lead to anarchy and complete immorality.[44]

Two events, following close upon each other in 1794 and 1795, served to raise the temperature of political debate while filling Federalist hearts with fears for the future: the Whiskey Rebellion and Jay's Treaty. The passions aroused by the Rebellion and the Treaty seemed almost to exceed those excited by the debate over independence two decades before. As Isaac Weld, a British traveler, observed, "it is scarcely possible for a dozen Americans to sit together without quarreling about politics" and Jay's Treaty. La Rochefoucauld-Liancourt noted the "violence of opinion," the intensity of national political issues, and the "disgraceful and hateful appellations . . . mutually given by the individuals of the parties to each other." "Party spirit," he observed, "infects the most respectable, as well as the meanest of men."[45]

Nothing less than a groundswell of apprehension, a general sense of crisis, swept over the conservative-minded in 1794-95. War with either France or Great Britain seemed imminent, if civil war itself did not spread from the insurrection in western Pennsylvania. So great was the state of public excitement that President Washington on January 1, 1795, set

[43] Emily E. F. Ford, *Notes on the Life of Noah Webster* (New York, 1912), I, 364-370. There is reason to believe that Webster was privately much pleased with the French Revolution although as a Federalist editor he found it necessary to condemn that cause. In a letter to Volney, July 10, 1796, Webster congratulated the French philosopher on the course of the Revolution, an event, as he said, "that will result in immense advantages to the French people, and which seems to be but a prelude to a general regeneration in Europe." Warfel, ed., *Letters of Webster*, 136-138.

[44] [Noah Webster], *The Revolution in France considered in Respect to its Progress and Effects* (New York, 1794), [3-4], 40-50.

[45] Isaac Weld, *Travels through the States of North America . . .*, 4th ed. (London, 1807), I, 102-103; Francois La Rochefoucauld-Liancourt, *Travels through the United States of North America . . .* (London, 1799), I, 470, 545; II, 514-518.

aside the following February 19 as a day of public thanksgiving and prayer. During such a time few of the clergy, as we have seen, could remain wholly unmoved by the warnings of the Federalist leaders, particularly as they themselves were stricken with the fear that theirs was a languishing cause.

Federalists had long brooded over the incipient lawlessness, present in any society, which threatened property, stable government, and civil order. In the Whiskey Rebellion and in the emotions aroused by Jay's Treaty men such as Hamilton, John Adams, and Fisher Ames, not in any case inclined to optimism about the virtues of mankind, saw their worst fears confirmed. Faction, the first problem of any government, was growing. Unless hemmed in by vigorous measures it would loosen irreparably the bonds of society. Federalists saw—or thought it useful to point out—the parallel to events in France where Jacobin clubs were turning the Revolution to their own ends. When the popular societies of western Pennsylvania closed ranks with the democratic militia to enforce popular demands —an alliance which figured importantly in the Whiskey Rebellion of 1794—conservatives predicted the ultimate destruction of orderly society.[46]

In these parlous times fears that the tide was running against them overtook the Federalist camp, making them all the more ready to employ French irreligion as a weapon in their domestic battles. Only "a revolutionary effort," said Fisher Ames late in 1794, "a rising, in mass, at the elections, to purify Congress from the sour leaven of antifederalism" would preserve the Federalist hegemony—and order. A few days later Ames remarked despondently that "the federal cause will go down, or I am no conjurer."[47] Stephen Higginson, leading merchant of Boston, reflected this mood in 1795 when he said: "I often think that the Jacobin faction will get the administration of our government into their hands ere long . . . foreign intrigurs will unite with the disaffected and disappointed, with Seekers after places, with ambitious popular Demagouges, and the vicious and corrupt of every class; and the combined influence of all these . . . will prove too much for the feeble efforts of the other

[46] See Richard Hofstadter, *The American Political Tradition and the Men Who Made It* (New York, 1948), 1-17; Eugene P. Link, *Democratic-Republican Societies, 1790-1800* (New York, 1942), 179-183; and John C. Miller, *The Federalist Era, 1789-1801* (New York, 1960), 108-121.

[47] Ames To Christopher Gore, Dec. 17, 1794, in Seth Ames, ed., *Works of Fisher Ames* (Boston, 1854), I, 156; Ames to Thomas Dwight, Dec. 27, 1794, *ibid.*, 158.

Citizens."[48] Said Christopher Gore, another Federalist luminary, "the friends of government are disheartened and discouraged."[49]

Increasingly obsessed by such apprehensions, the Federalists redoubled their efforts to wed the clergy to their cause. When Osgood's anti-French sermon appeared in November 1794, a group of Federalists, quick to sense that their efforts to change the drift of clerical opinion were taking effect, offered to underwrite the cost of printing the tract for wholesale distribution. The sermon was printed twice in Boston before the year was out, and in 1795 was reissued at Boston, Albany, Newburyport, Philadelphia, and Stockbridge.[50] "I love your plain speaking ministers—they do good and will become more useful if encouraged by our federalist rulers," wrote Peter van Schaak, New York Federalist and former loyalist, to Thomas Sedgwick. Fisher Ames also quickened to this assistance from the clerical quarter. "Mr. Osgood's sermon is extolled," he wrote a fellow Federalist. "The good sense and boldness of the sentiments will work their way. . . The sermon is reprinting here." The forthcoming Fast Day would "afford an opening for other clergymen to seek glory" in the Federalist cause.[51]

Pressing their advantage, the Federalists in late 1794 and in 1795 emphasized the issue of irreligion in France as a means of combatting Republicans at home. What followed was a barrage of vitriolic pamphlets and letters, answered in kind by the Republicans, which amounted to a civil war of belles lettres, as Vernon Parrington called it. Satire, slander, invective, and abuse in both prose and poetry aroused the passions of participants and onlookers alike. John Adams had advocated literary warfare of this sort as early as late 1792. "Nothing," he avowed, "[must] pass unanswered; reasoning must be answered by reasoning; wit by wit, humor by humor; satire by satire; burlesque by burlesque and even buffoonery by buffoonery."[52]

Federalist newspapers also took up the cry in 1794 and 1795. The Boston *Centinel* reminded its readers that religion was the first pillar

[48] Higginson to Timothy Pickering, Aug. 29, 1795, in "Letters of Stephen Higginson," in American Historical Association, *Report, 1896* (Washington, 1897), I, 794.

[49] Gore to Rufus King, Aug. 14, 1795, in Charles R. King, ed., *The Life and Correspondence of Rufus King* (New York, 1894-1900), II, 23.

[50] Link, *Democratic-Republican Societies*, 198.

[51] Van Schaak to Sedgwick, Dec. 20, 1794, as cited in Link, *Democratic-Republican Societies*, 198; Ames to Thomas Dwight, Jan. 7, 1795, in Ames, ed., *Works of Fisher Ames*, I, 160.

[52] Quoted in Page Smith, *John Adams* (Garden City, N. Y., 1962), II, 833.

of government and that the Republicans were the "advocates for the irreligious sentiments of France." Impiety in France, as in America, said the *Massachusetts Spy,* would pervert the best hope of mankind. The *Hampshire Gazette* and the *Western Star* expressed similar opinions as did the *New York Herald* and the *Gazette of the United States.*[53]

Prominent Federalist leaders pushed the offensive: the Revolution in France had discredited itself; between political liberals and atheists there was a marked affinity, a nexus which threatened the United States just as it despoiled France. William Smith and Oliver Wolcott, both important Federalist politicians, stated the equation without equivocation in 1796: "The late impious and blasphemous works of Thomas Paine, reviling the *christian religion,* have been much applauded in France, and have been very industriously circulated in the United States, by all *that class* of people, who are friendly to Mr. Jefferson's politics."[54]

A number of pamphleteers emphasized the interlocking nature of French anarchy and irreligion and sharpened the image of the Revolution as the source of American infidelity. The naturalized Englishman, James Rivington, for example, translated and published in 1795 Mallet du Pan's *The Dangers Which Threaten Europe.* Simultaneously, he issued Henry J. Pye's novel, *The Democrat; or Intrigues and Adventures of Jean le Noir.* Central to both works was the theme of the ravages inflicted by the Revolution and the resultant decay of order and stability.[55] Further fuel for the flames was added by John S. Gardiner's *Remarks on the Jacobiniad,* a scurrilous attack in verse on the "American Jacobins."

For sheer abusiveness William Cobbett's writings were without equal. This irrepressible Englishman, who appropriately signed his articles "Peter Porcupine," reversed his early enthusiasm for the French Revolution in 1795 with two biting anti-French diatribes.[56] In the following year he broadened his attack, offering a *History of the American Jacobins Commonly Denominated Democrats* as an appendix to his Philadelphia print-

[53] See Morse, *Federalist Party in Mass.,* 78-87; and Hazen, *Opinion of the French Revolution,* 268-269.

[54] [William Smith and Oliver Wolcott], *The Pretensions of Thomas Jefferson to the Presidency Examined . . .* (Philadelphia, 1796), 36.

[55] See Fäy, *Revolutionary Spirit in France and America,* 361-362.

[56] *A Bone to Gnaw, for the Democrats* (Philadelphia, 1795), and *A Little Plain English, Addressed to the People of the United States . . .* (Philadelphia, 1795). Cobbett's political inconstancy is discussed in William Reitzel, "William Cobbett and Philadelphia Journalism: 1794-1800," *Pennsylvania Magazine of History and Biography,* LIX (1935), 223-244.

ing of William Playfair's *The History of Jacobinism.*[57] Agents of the revolutionary government (presumably Genêt and his American sympathizers), Cobbett asserted, had joined the malcontents of society to subvert both civil and religious order in America—a process described metaphorically as "a sort of flesh flies, that naturally settle on the excremental and corrupted parts of the body politic." These carriers of disease, continued Cobbett, treated the irresponsible elements of American society to "a variety of . . . nonsensical, stupid, unmeaning, childish entertainments, as never were heard or thought of, till Frenchmen took it into their heads to gabble about liberty." Conspicuous among these imported heresies was atheism—or deism—the two terms being synonymous or nearly so.[58]

Cobbett's exposures of the "bacillus gallicus" touched off a round of journalistic charges and countercharges that only added fuel to the already highly combustible situation. In 1795 and 1796 he produced a succession of inflammatory pamphlets with such suggestive titles as *The Bloody Buoy, Thrown Out as a Warning to the Political Pilots of America: or, a Faithful Relation of a Multitude of Acts of Horrid Barbarity Such as the Eye Never Witnessed, the Tongue Never Expressed, or the Imagination Conceived, Until the Commencement of the French Revolution; A Letter to the Infamous Tom Paine; A Kick for a Bite;* and *A New Year's Gift to the Democrats.* Cobbett was answered in full measure by such tracts as John Swanwick's *A Rub from Snub . . . Addressed to Peter Porcupine,* Samuel Bradford's *The Imposter Detected,* and James Carey's *A Pill for Porcupine; Being a Specific for an Obstinate Itching Which That Hireling has Long Contracted for Lying and Calumny.*

Europe in flames, American society in flux, civil disorder, threats of war, widening schisms, faction rampant, irreligion rife, deist-tinged politicians on the upsurge—by 1795 conservative hearts quaked. No doubt many of the clergy, dedicated to a peaceful, ordered society, shared Federalist apprehensions. Far from continuing our own Revolutionary heritage, the leaders of the French upheaval appeared to sanction license instead of liberty, anarchy instead of order, blasphemy instead of religion. And Americans, led by Republican politicians and religious liberals, appeared all too susceptible to the misguided French ideas. As one orthodox New

[57] Playfair's book had originally been published in London in 1795.
[58] Cobbett, *History of the American Jacobins,* 8, 15, 23-32.

England clergyman was to remark, "the old foundations of social order, loyalty, tradition, habit, reverence for antiquity, were everywhere shaken, if not subverted. The authority of the past was gone. The old forms were outgrown, and new ones had not taken their place."[59] Everywhere in New England and in the middle states sermons took on a strong tone of hostility toward France, a development which Jedidiah Morse confided to his friend Oliver Wolcott did "a vast deal of good in a *political view.*"[60] As orthodox clergymen and Federalist leaders discovered a community of interest, sermons became the occasion for quasi-political and rabidly anti-French pronouncements. One listener described the election day pulpit oratory as "a little of governor, a little of council, a little of congress, much of puffing, much of politics and a very little religion—a strange compost, like a carrot pye, having so little of the ingredients of the vegetable, that the cook must christen it."[61] The *Age of Reason* coupled with deep-rooted anxieties over social and political instability was making its mark. "The Thanksgiving has helped tone the public mind," wrote Fisher Ames in 1795 of the February Fast Day. "Tom Paine has kindly cured our clergy of their prejudices."[62] In Salem, Massachusetts, the Reverend William Bentley at about the same time recorded in his diary: "The Clergy are now the Tools of the Federalists, and Thanksgiving Sermons are in the order of the Day." Nathaniel Ames, as Republican as his brother Fisher was Federalist, noted disgustedly, "Priests made politicians by Boston Torys."[63]

Clearly by 1795 so general a fear had overtaken the clergy that few, even if they still sympathized with the French cause, could resist using the issue of the French Revolution as a weapon in the war at home against religious stagnation. Nor could they resist the natural alliance with the Federalist party, which so assiduously bent itself to the Francophobe cause.

[59] Channing, *Memoir,* I, 60.

[60] Cited in Love, *Fast and Thanksgiving Days of New England,* 371-372. Other examples of the newly awakened Francophobia are given in Morse, *Federalist Party in Massachusetts,* 100-102.

[61] Quoted in William A. Robinson, *Jeffersonian Democracy in New England* (New Haven, 1916), 131-132. For an example of the tightening alliance between Federalists and clergymen see Morse, *Federalist Party in Mass.,* 116-139.

[62] Ames to Christopher Gore, Feb. 24, 1795, in Ames, ed., *Works of Fisher Ames,* I, 168. See also Ames to Thomas Dwight, Feb. 24, 1795, *ibid.,* 169.

[63] *The Diary of William Bentley, D.D.* (Salem, Mass., 1905-14), II, 129; Charles Warren, *Jacobin and Junto; or, Early American Politics as Viewed in the Diary of Dr. Nathaniel Ames, 1758-1822* (Cambridge, Mass., 1931), 66.

Given the facts of the domestic situation, it is not altogether surprising that the clergy should renounce its previous endorsement of the Revolution. Probably in most instances the reversal was not simple expediency but reflected a genuine change in feeling toward events in France. But it was events at home, not abroad, that had wrought the dramatic reversal of clerical attitudes toward France and led finally to Morse's spectacular charges of 1798.

Jeremiads in the New American Republic: The Case of National Fasts in the John Adams Administration

CHARLES ELLIS DICKSON

RONALD Reagan is not the first American president to be concerned with religious issues. Although partisans may quarrel about abortion, school prayer, and tax credits for parochial education, almost no one objects to the annual presidential Thanksgiving Day proclamation. For years it has been one of the most obvious ways in which the president of the United States officially recognizes the relationship between religion and the federal government. Acting under a supposedly secular Constitution and supported by long custom, he regularly acknowledges the need to express gratitude to a God who has provided many benefits to the American people. He does not, however, at any time formally acknowledge the need to express contrition to a God who might find the American people and their government lacking. In modern America, unlike colonial New England, government may encourage acts of thanksgiving but not acts of confession.

New England colonial governments had a more balanced view of their obligations toward God. Rather than just feasting on turkeys, they also called upon their peoples to fast. On these fast days and on other official occasions, clergymen preached jeremiads emphasizing New England's failings. Such views did not die with the Revolution but lingered in the minds of many Americans during the early years of the new federal government.

Massachusetts-born John Adams continued to worry about

the effect of sin on the new American republic. His administration provides a link between the old New England way and what has since become the politically sanctioned relationship between God and the American people. During Adams's four years as president, this man of strong principles openly expressed a Puritan-style awareness of individual and national sins rarely noted publicly by his successors. He did what his Virginia-born predecessor had not thought to do and issued two New England–style proclamations appointing days of "solemn humiliation, fasting, and prayer." On 23 March 1798 he recommended that on Wednesday, 9 May 1798, his countrymen "acknowledge before God the manifold sins and transgressions with which we are justly charged as individuals and as a nation"; and a year later (6 March 1799) he recommended that on Thursday, 25 April, Americans "call to mind our numerous offenses against the Most High God, confess them before Him with the sincerest penitence, implore His pardoning mercy, through the Great Mediator and Redeemer, for our past transgressions, and [pray] that through the grace of His Holy Spirit we may be disposed and enabled to yield a more suitable obedience to His righteous requisitions in time to come."[1]

After the Revolution, the American community's perception of a citizen's relationship both with civil and divine authority had altered fundamentally. In New England and elsewhere Adams's fellow countrymen were ignoring the admonitions of preachers and refusing to behave deferentially toward their elected leaders. Religious and political developments at the end of the eighteenth century encouraged them to see their corporate role as God's new chosen people in a different way. Whether the jeremiads delivered on the occasion of his two fast days were simply outworn colonial traditions or unacceptable national innovations, they fanned the flames of American

[1] James D. Richardson, ed., *A Compilation of the Messages and Papers of the Presidents, 1789–1908*, 11 vols. (n.p.: Bureau of National Literature and Art, 1908), 1:268–70, 1:284–86. On 12 April 1798 Adams issued a proclamation postponing his first fast until 16 May 1798 in Connecticut because a general election was being held in the state on the date he had originally set.

political discontent and helped make Adams a one-term president.

⁂

Adams's Puritan forebears usually opposed the observance of regular, fixed holy days other than the Sabbath, but they had long held an annual governmentally declared fast on a weekday in the spring. It was a plain affair of sabbatical character. Most communities had two services, and most people abstained from food until after the second service. The time of this spring fast was influenced by the "beginning of their Old Style year, the planting of their fields, the end of their long winters, the incoming of ships with foreign news, and the reflex influence of their annual thanksgiving."[2] The reenactment of this ritual over the generations reminded New Englanders of their fathers' errand into the wilderness and provided opportunities for political sermons, now usually called jeremiads, "to direct an imperiled people of God toward the fulfillment of their destiny, to guide them individually toward salvation and collectively toward the American city of God."[3]

During the American Revolution, New England's observance of the fast spread to the other colonies. On 12 June 1775 the First Continental Congress echoed the familiar New England penitential tone in a proclamation drafted by a committee including John Adams. This proto-national fast, held on 20 July 1775, set the precedent for confessional fast days which Congress continued to declare every spring throughout the Revolutionary War.[4] During the war the New England states no

[2] W. DeLoss Love, Jr., *The Fast and Thanksgiving Days of New England* (New York: Houghton, Mifflin and Company, 1895), p. 250; see also pp. 249, 416.

[3] Sacvan Bercovitch, *The American Jeremiad* (Madison: University of Wisconsin Press, 1978), p. 9.

[4] Bercovitch, *American Jeremiad*, pp. 334–39; *Journals of the Continental Congress, 1774–1789*, 34 vols. (Washington: Government Printing Office, 1904–37), 2:87–88, 3:507, 4:201, 4:208–9, 6:1014, 6:1022, 10:207, 10:229–30, 16:252–53, 19:257, 19:284–86, 22:137; *Diary and Autobiography of John Adams*, ed. L. H. Butterfield, 4 vols. (Cambridge: Belknap Press of Harvard University Press, 1961), 3:353, 3:371; and Perry Miller, "From the Covenant to the Revival," in *The*

longer called for their own separate fasts but looked to Congress for the day's appointment.

Possibly Southerners in Congress were merely seeking to humor their Yankee colleagues by supporting fast resolutions with a New England theological inspiration, but the congressional acceptance of the New England fast was a useful weapon in a propaganda war. It encouraged intercolonial unity by providing a stated day on which all Americans could consider their objectives. These observances therefore had, as one nineteenth-century historian maintained, "a great political as well as religious force."[5] In his *Origin & Progress of the American Rebellion* (1781), the Tory Peter Oliver blamed "Mr. [James] *Otis's* black Regiment, the dissenting clergy," for inflaming public opinion as they proceeded to "preach up" the Revolution, but, as Perry Miller points out, "The really effective work of the 'black regiment' was not an optimistic appeal to the rising glory of America, but their importing a sense of crisis by reviving Old Testament condemnations of a degenerate people." Miller contends that the Puritan concept of the covenant incorporated not only the social compact idea associated with John Locke but also "the philosophy of the jeremiad, which required abject confession of unworthiness from an afflicted people." By the time of the American Revolution, this "wonderful fusion of political doctrine with the traditional rite of self abasement . . . had become . . . a dynamo for generating action"; for "once we have purged ourselves and recovered our energies in the act of contrition . . . [we can then] act upon the principles of John Locke!"[6]

Shaping of American Religion, ed. James Ward Smith and A. Leland Jamison (Princeton: Princeton University Press, 1961), pp. 322–26. Congress issued several fast proclamations before its first thanksgiving proclamation. The first fast day connected with the Revolution did not occur in New England but in Virginia, where the House of Burgesses appointed a fast (without the usual New England formula calling upon the whole society to confess its sins and renew its covenant with God) for 1 June 1774, the day the Boston Port Bill went into effect. (As in Massachusetts, the governor had refused to proclaim such an observance, but the Virginians defied his wishes and held one anyway.)

[5] Love, *Fast Days*, p. 345.

[6] *Peter Oliver's Origin & Progress of the American Rebellion: A Tory View*, ed. Douglass Adair and John A. Schutz (San Marino, Calif.: Huntington Library, 1963),

After the war was won, Congress no longer declared fasts. Miller finds evidence that the providential victory over the British encouraged some patriotic preachers to argue "in effect, that the jeremiad had also triumphed, and that we, being a completely reformed nation, need no longer be summoned to humiliation!"[7] Rationalism, deism, and anticlericalism were also fashionable during this period. Enough traditional believers remained, however, to convince political leaders on the state level that, according to Cornelis de Witt, it was wise "to appeal to their religious feelings; and prayers and public fasts continued to be instruments resorted to whenever it was found desirable, whether by agitators or the State, to act powerfully on the minds of the people."[8]

Since the Confederation Congress issued no further religious proclamations in the post-Revolutionary period and since the new federal Constitution recognized no formal connection between government and God, it took a request by a joint committee of the First Congress to persuade George Washington on 3 October 1789 to appoint Thursday, 26 November 1789, a day of national thanksgiving and to urge his countrymen, without elaboration, to beseech Almighty God on that day to pardon the nation. Washington's next proclamation in this vein was not issued until almost six years later (1 January 1795). After his administration had successfully put down the Whiskey Rebellion, Washington set aside Thursday, 19 February 1795, as a day of public thanksgiving and prayer.[9] Neither of Washington's religious proclamations appointed a true New England–style fast, and the second one contained no

p. 63; Miller, "Covenant to Revival," pp. 336–40; cf. Winthrop S. Hudson, *Religion in America* (New York: Charles Scribner's Sons, 1965), pp. 96–97, and Alan Heimert, *Religion and the American Mind: From the Great Awakening to the Revolution* (Cambridge: Harvard University Press, 1966), p. 423.

[7] Miller, "Covenant to Revival," p. 348; see also Nathan O. Hatch, *The Sacred Cause of Liberty: Republican Thought and the Millennium in Revolutionary New England* (New Haven: Yale University Press, 1977), p. 147.

[8] Cornelis de Witt, *Jefferson and the American Democracy: An Historical Study*, trans. R. S. H. Church (London: Longman, Green, Longman, Roberts & Green, 1862), p. 17.

[9] Richardson, *Messages of Presidents*, 1:64, 1:179–80.

penitential language at all. Although the Virginian's two official proclamations did have a religious cast, many Christians still felt that their new nation should be called to repent. By 1795, for instance, the Methodist Church demanded a return to the custom of declaring fast days because it was appalled by "our manifold sins and iniquities."[10]

The John Adams administration was more in tune with the wishes of these tradition-minded Christians. When America's troubles with France arose in 1798, President Adams asked his cabinet to suggest solutions. Immediately after the cabinet meeting Secretary of War James McHenry wrote his mentor, the West Indies–born New Yorker Alexander Hamilton, to solicit advice concerning the president's formal request to his department heads, a copy of which was enclosed. The Federalist party leader, responding with a long list of recommendations, ended his letter to McHenry with these words:

> In addition to these measures Let the President recommend a day to be observed as a day of fasting humiliation & prayer. On religious grounds this is very proper—On political, it is very expedient. The Government will be very unwise, if it does not make the most of the religious prepossessions of our people—opposing the honest enthusiasm of Religious Opinion to the phrenzy of Political fanaticism. The last step appears to me of the most precious importance & I earnestly hope, it will by no means be neglected.[11]

As usual, McHenry promoted Hamilton's advice within the Adams administration and, without acknowledgment, incorporated Hamilton's letter almost verbatim into his own formal recommendations to the president.

Meanwhile, Hamilton bombarded other officials with similar letters. He told Timothy Pickering, the secretary of state

[10] Quoted by Miller, "Covenant to Revival," p. 351; see also Gary B. Nash, "The American Clergy and the French Revolution," *William and Mary Quarterly*, 3d ser. 22 (July 1965): 397–98.

[11] Hamilton to McHenry, 27 January–11 February 1798, *The Papers of Alexander Hamilton*, ed. Harold C. Syrett, 27 vols. (New York: Columbia University Press, 1961–81), 21:341–46; see also Adams to heads of departments, 24 January 1798, *The Works of John Adams*, ed. Charles Francis Adams, 10 vols. (Boston: Charles C. Little and James Brown, 1851), 8:561–62; McHenry to Hamilton, 26 January 1798, Hamilton, *Papers*, 21:339. McHenry replied to Adams on 15 February 1798.

and another close political associate, that he had "the last measure [the fast] at heart." He advised United States Senator Theodore Sedgwick (an Adams Federalist from Adams's home state and a frequent correspondent of Hamilton's) that the president should use the fast to "call to his aid the force of religious Ideas." He added, "This will be in my opinion no less proper in a political than in a Religious View. We must oppose to political fanaticism religious zeal."[12]

Years later Adams recalled seeing one of the many versions of Hamilton's letter but denied that Hamilton's campaign had influenced him: "I had determined on this measure long enough before Mr. Hamilton's letter was written." He believed that

> there is nothing upon this earth more sublime and affecting than the idea of a great nation all on their knees at once before their God, acknowledging their faults and imploring his blessing and protection, when the prospect before them threatens great danger and calamity. It can scarcely fail to have a favorable effect on their morals in general, or [he added significantly] to inspire them with warlike virtues in particular.

He "despised and detested" Hamilton's letter, which "recommended a national Fast, not only on account of the intrinsic propriety of it, but because we should be very unskillful if we neglected to avail ourselves of the religious feelings of the people in a crisis so difficult and dangerous."[13] Probably at Adams's direction, Secretary Pickering replied to Hamilton:

> Prior to the receipt of your letter, the President had determined to recommend the observance of a general fast; and had desired one or both the chaplains of Congress to prepare the draught of a proclamation. This has since been issued.[14]

Adams justified the first national fast requested by an American president by arguing that the American republic ought to

[12] Hamilton to Pickering, 17 March 1798, and Hamilton to Sedgwick, 1–15 March 1798, Hamilton, *Papers*, 21:364–67, 2:361–63.

[13] Correspondence from Boston *Patriot* (1809), *Works of Adams*, 9:289–91; see also Adams to Benjamin Rush, 28 August 1811, *Works of Adams*, 9:635–40.

[14] Pickering to Hamilton, 25 March 1798, Hamilton, *Papers*, 21:370–77.

acknowledge its dependence upon Almighty God, especially in dangerous times. He had heard this argument advanced during every spring fast called during his childhood. His first fast proclamation contended that America's deteriorating relations with France and the accompanying political discord at home made the spring of 1798 a dangerous time indeed. France's "unfriendly disposition, conduct, and demands . . . evinced by repeated refusals to receive our messengers of reconciliation and peace" had placed the United States "in a hazardous and afflictive situation" which required Americans to pray "that our country may be protected from all the dangers which threatened it" and that it may again be united in "bonds of amity and mutual confidence."[15] In other words, the friction with America's first ally—the XYZ Affair was about to become a political bombshell—should prompt all good Americans unequivocally to support the president and his political colleagues.

In the spring of the next year Adams again used the power of religion and the prestige of his office to drive home the Federalist claim that its political opposition was Jacobin. In a new fast proclamation he stated that "the most precious interests" of the American people were "still held in jeopardy by the hostile designs and insidious acts" of France "as well as by the dissemination among them of those principles, subversive of the foundations of all religious, moral and social obligations, that have produced incalculable mischief and misery in other countries." He urged his countrymen to ask God to "withhold us from unreasonable discontent, from disunion, faction, sedition, and insurrection" as well as to "preserve our country from the desolating sword." Clearly, he wanted his two fasts to be national acts which would "teach and inculcate" important truths, truths denied by the opposition party. In his second proclamation he went so far as to imply the Lord's particular displeasure with the political unrest stirred up by the Jeffersonian faction when he recommended that sinful Americans petition Almighty God to "save our cities and towns from a

[15] Richardson, *Messages of Presidents*, 1:268–70.

repetition of those awful pestilential visitations [yellow fever and cholera] under which they have lately suffered so severely."[16]

Adams's decision to reinstitute the fast may have been the instinctive act of a conservative leader using a time-honored means of calling a wayward people back to submission to those in authority, but, despite Adams's protestations to the contrary, it was also part of a Hamilton-inspired Federalist campaign to eradicate the Jeffersonian opposition. The Alien and Sedition Acts represented the iron fist of Federalist coercion and the fasts the open hand beckoning a politically divided nation back to unity.

Adams's designated fast days did not renew Americans' sense of corporate mission, as he had intended; instead, they intensified differences. Respected spiritual leaders found the fast days wonderful opportunities for employing partisan rhetoric to denigrate France and its Jeffersonian sympathizers; for the opposition, the fast days provided a fit occasion to rally against the Federalists.

Many Federalist clergymen applauded the president for proclaiming the fast. In Philadelphia Presbyterian minister Dr. James Muir chortled, "Let this day's devotion excite and strengthen the spirit of religious and civil freedom. It will tear the disguise from foes within; it will overawe those without, who meditate our ruin."[17] The Reverend Alden Bradford, minister of the Christian Congregational Society in Wiscasset, reported that "all the inhabitants of this great nation, except the atheistical and impious, and those who are influenced by an obstinate spirit of party," assembled for prayer on Adams's first fast day.[18] Bradford's final exception alludes to the many Americans who would have nothing to do with the activities

[16] Richardson, *Messages of Presidents*, 1:284–86.

[17] James Muir, *A Sermon Preached in the Presbyterian Church in Alexandria* . . . (Philadelphia: William Cobbett, 1798), p. 13.

[18] Alden Bradford, *Two Sermons, Delivered in Wiscasset (Pownalborough)* . . . (Wiscasset: Henry Haskins & John W. Scott, 1798), 1st sermon, pp. 3–4.

they considered, in Perry Miller's words, "Federalist plots to ensnare Republicans into praying for John Adams."[19] The Reverend John Thornton Kirkland, minister of New South Church in Boston, found it necessary to answer adverse Jeffersonian criticism that his fellow clergymen were "going out of our sphere, being tools of a party and contravening the spirit of our office."[20] Dr. Jedidiah Morse, a leading Federalist clergyman of a Congregational church near Boston, exclaimed in horror:

> But that we should have men among us, so lost to every principle of religion, morality, and even to common decency, as to reprobate the measure [the fast]; as to contemn the authority who recommended it [Adams], and to denounce it as hypocritical, and designed to effect sinister purposes, is indeed alarming.[21]

The sermons of Federalist clergymen like Morse aroused the very sentiments they sought so desperately to mollify. In Philadelphia on the evening of Adams's first national fast day, thousands of people took to the streets. The *Aurora* reported, "The passions of our citizens which have been artfully inflamed by war speeches and addresses, as well as threats against the Republicans burst out in such a manner as to endanger the peace of the city."[22] Pennsylvania Governor Thomas Mifflin had to order out a patrol of horse and foot soldiers to preserve that peace. The mood of the crowd around Adams's house was so ugly that some of his servants feared for his life. Writing to Thomas Jefferson years later, after the two former presidents had been reconciled, Adams revealed that he still had not completely forgiven Jefferson and his party for the events that night in Philadelphia, which had occurred when "I have no doubt you were fast asleep, in philosophical tranquility!"[23]

[19] Miller, "Covenant to Revival," p. 357.

[20] John Thornton Kirkland, *A Sermon, Delivered on the 9th of May, 1798* ... (Boston: John Russell, 1798), p. 19.

[21] Jedidiah Morse, *A Sermon Delivered at the New North Church in Boston* ... (Boston: Samuel Hall, 1798), p. 12; there are 2 editions.

[22] Philadelphia *Aurora*, 10 May 1798.

[23] Adams to Jefferson, 30 June 1813, in *Works of Adams*, 10:46–49.

Jefferson's supporters also expressed their displeasure in print. One partisan, protesting on economic grounds, estimated that in Philadelphia alone the fast day wasted $12,000 in lost labor.[24] Although they rarely objected on constitutional grounds, the Jeffersonians certainly offered many political objections. In the *Aurora General Advertiser* "a good Christian and an Enemy to hypocrisy" blamed the crisis with France on the administration, claimed that the people's only sin was having elected Adams, and contended that Adams was the one who ought to repent his errors. He and his cabinet ministers, in the spirit of the fast, ought to give up half their salaries to the state to support "those families who have been reduced to poverty and misery by their rash manoeuvres."[25]

Pacifistic Jeffersonians particularly resented Adams's appropriation of religion, as this extract from "Psalm of the Federalist Fast" makes abundantly clear:

Ye Clergy in this day
  On Politicks discourse
And when ye rise to pray
  Both France and Frenchmen curse
    For you've a right
    To pray and preach
    Exhort and teach
    Mankind to fight.

. . . .

Let all the States attend
  At this his [Adams's] solemn call
To curse their ancient *friend*
  And bless our rulers all:
    For this the day
    That heart and hand
    Thro' the whole land
    For WAR we pray.[26]

[24] Philadelphia *Carey's United States Recorder*, 19 May 1798, cited by Donald H. Stewart, *The Opposition Press of the Federalist Period* (Albany: State University of New York Press, 1969), p. 79.

[25] *Aurora General Advertiser*, 30 March 1798.

[26] Boston *Independent Chronicle*, 30 April 1798, cited by Stewart, *Opposition Press*, p. 295.

Since so many clergymen were Federalist sympathizers, the Jeffersonian press had for some time opposed political discussion from the pulpit. Hoping to silence a vocal and articulate group of leaders who disagreed with their position, the Jeffersonians warned that if thinking men began to doubt the clergy's views on politics, they would begin to question their views on religion. The Reverend Hugh Mitchell, in condemning the very idea of calling the nation to fasting and prayer, used religious rather than constitutional arguments. He pointed out that "in the new testament scriptures, there is neither warrant, example, nor precept for political prayer"; that, since both warring nations were wrong, "the political supplications of their nations . . . must be abominable to the God of justice and truth"; and that, if the United States were in the right, "God will maintain his own cause, whether the righteous nation pray for his interposition or not."[27]

While Jeffersonians strongly objected to the fasts Adams proclaimed, Federalist clergymen took full advantage of them. Their words had influence far beyond their own congregations, for printed sermons were still, apart from newspapers, the principal reading matter of literate Americans. At the request of their listeners in several congregations in Massachusetts—as well as congregations in South Carolina, North Carolina, Pennsylvania, and New York—about a score of well-known clergymen agreed to the publication of their fast-day sermons. In addition to those of the Congregational faith, the sermons of Jewish, Roman Catholic, Episcopal, Dutch Reformed, and Presbyterian preachers were printed by public subscription. Some sermons were so well received that they went through several editions and undoubtedly served as models for other preachers.

The colonial jeremiads had had a political function insofar as they commemorated the God-ordained social order established by the first generation in New England, but the printed

[27] Reprint in *Aurora*, 14 May 1798, of an extract "a subscriber" had submitted to the *Argus;* cf. Stewart, *Opposition Press*, p. 403.

fast sermons issued during the Adams administration were blatantly partisan documents. Many clergymen therefore felt the need to apologize for preaching on such controversial political matters. The Reverend Samuel Miller, a New York City United Presbyterian, said he was "not accustomed to carry political discussion into the pulpit" but claimed that "the occasion permitted, and even dictated some deviation from his ordinary habits in this respect."[28] Of course, he did not consider the Adams proclamation a partisan act. One prominent Boston preacher, Kirkland of New South Church, justified preaching on politics as a worthy habit emerging from the American Revolution.[29] Most preachers seemed to agree with Dr. William Linn, a Reformed Dutch minister in New York City, that "Religion, morality and obedience to government are inseparably connected" as well as with the Reverend Eliphalet Porter, who at Brookline in the morning and at his own Roxbury parish in the afternoon, said that "Silence with respect to the political concerns of our country, on an eventful occasion like the present, would be unnatural and therefore not free."[30]

Many fast-day preachers proclaimed nothing less than an orthodox manifesto of Federalist ideology. The words of Philadelphia's Dr. Muir are typical: "We have amongst us true patriots. Both the present and the late Presidents knew the true interests of their country and did, and still do steadily adhere to that interest."[31] Dr. Jedidiah Morse reminded members of the New North Church (Boston) in the morning and his own flock at the Charlestown Congregational Church in the afternoon that the government was "of our own forming, and administered by men of our own choice, and therefore

[28] Samuel Miller, *A Sermon, Delivered May 9, 1798*. . . (New York: T. & J. Swords, 1798), preface.

[29] Kirkland, *Sermon, Delivered on the 9th of May, 1798*, p. 18.

[30] William Linn, *A Discourse on National Sins* . . . (New York: T. & J. Swords, 1798), p. iv; Eliphalet Porter, *A Discourse, Delivered at Brookline, in the Morning, and at the First Parish in Roxbury, in the Afternoon* . . . (Boston: John Russell, 1798), p. 23.

[31] Muir, *Sermon Preached in the Presbyterian Church in Alexandria*, p. 14.

claims our confidence and support."[32] Clearly, the concept of a loyal opposition had not yet developed in America. The Reverend Nathanael Emmons argued, "That it is proper for a people, under a good government, to pray that God would defeat the designs of those who are aiming to subvert it." His Federalist doctrine was of the highest order when he added, "Just so far as any civil constitution allows the people to assist or control their Rulers, just so far it is weak, deficient, and contains the seeds of its own destruction."[33]

President Adams heard a relatively impartial discourse at the First Presbyterian Church in Philadelphia. There Dr. Samuel Blair demonstrated that he had some idea of how the two-party system might work. He admonished both sides, "As good Christians, it is our bounden duty to consider, and to treat, with charity and candor the political opinions of those, who may differ with us," but then showed which side he supported by adding, "and, as good Republicans, it is our bounden duty to accommodate ourselves to the decisions . . . of those who legislate for us."[34] The published fast sermons usually dwelt at some length on the evils of factionalism and lack of respect for government. Dr. David Osgood of the Congregational Church in Medford, Massachusetts, considered ministers of religion "a bulwark against the spirit of faction," even though his political attacks from the pulpit had been creating unrest in his congregation for some time.[35] Dr. John Prince of the Salem Congregational Church urged his listeners to "avoid all party spirit and contention."[36] Certainly Jeffersonians did not appreciate it when the Reverend John Thayer of the

[32] Morse, *Sermon Delivered at the New North Church*, p. 27.

[33] Nathanael Emmons, *A Discourse, Delivered May 9, 1798* . . . (Wrentham, Mass.: Nathaniel and Benjamin Heaton, 1798), pp. 5–6.

[34] Samuel Blair, *A Discourse Delivered in the First Presbyterian Church of Philadelphia* . . . (Philadelphia: James Watters & Co., 1798), pp. 29–30.

[35] David Osgood, *Some Facts evincive of . . . French Republicans* (Boston: Samuel Hall, 1798), p. 21; see also Nash, "American Clergy," p. 397, and Hatch, *Sacred Cause*, p. 122n.

[36] John Prince, *A Discourse, Delivered at Salem, on the Day of the National Fast* . . . (Salem: Thomas C. Cushing, 1798), p. 43; this popular sermon went through 3 editions.

Roman Catholic Church in Boston called political opposition "highly criminal" or when Dr. Osgood labeled certain Republican newspapers "traitorous" for supporting the French and denounced the "editors, patrons and abettors of those vehicles of slander upon our government" as "wet nurses of a French faction in the bowels of our country."[37]

While fast-day preachers were busy attacking the Jeffersonian faction, they were also quick to cite the French as the cause of America's unhappy divisions. According to Morse,

> Their too great influence among us has been exerted vigorously, and in conformity to a deep-laid plan, in cherishing party spirit, in vilifying the men we have, by our free suffrages, elected to administer our Constitution; and have thus endeavored to destroy the confidence of the people in the constitutional authorities, and divide them from the government.[38]

They accused Jefferson of being the French candidate for the presidency: "We have a great reason to be thankful that . . . God did not permit the intrigues of a foreign, insidious nation to succeed in raising the man of their choice to the presidential chair."[39] The title of Osgood's fast sermon demonstrates how blatantly the Federalist clergymen denounced France and, by implication, its Republican sympathizers in the United States: he spoke on "Some Facts evincive of the atheistical, anarchical, and, in other respects, immoral Principles of the *French Republicans.*"

The harsh criticism of the French and their revolution had two main sources. The first was the irreligious character of the French Revolution: "If France obtains the dominion and government of our country, the christian religion . . . will soon be utterly discarded," warned the Reverend Alden Bradford in the second of his two sermons to his congregation in

[37] John Thayer, *A Discourse, Delivered at the Roman Catholic Church in Boston* . . . (Boston: Samuel Hall, 1798), p. 8; there are 2 editions. Osgood, *Some Facts*, p. 22.

[38] Morse, *Sermon Delivered at the New North Church*, pp. 23–24; see also Nash, "American Clergy," pp. 392 and 399.

[39] Thayer, *Discourse, Delivered at the Roman Catholic Church*, p. 9.

Wiscasset.[40] Also of concern were France's unfriendly acts, which culminated in the XYZ Affair. (The dispatches from France had just been printed, much to the dismay of the Jeffersonians.) The Reverend John Wilder of the First Church in Attleborough noted this latest insult in his list of how "these scourges of mankind have done everything in their power to injure us."[41] The Reverend Gershom Seixas of the New York synagogue foresaw "all the horrors of war" resulting from France's threats; and Morse called such a war "a *just* and *necessary* one."[42] Thayer suggested that, while Americans had earlier been victims of inadequate and fallacious information concerning the French Revolution, the reports from American emissaries which Adams had just released now revealed the true nature of that revolution and should thus discourage any more sympathy from Americans. Thayer urged his listeners to counterbalance French indignities by signing addresses in support of Adams: "Let us all resolve to give him a generous and cordial support, and openly avow this resolution by setting our names to the manly and spirited addresses which are now proposed for the signature of all citizens."[43]

Jeffersonians did not agree with this analysis of France. The Boston *Independent Chronicle and the Universal Advertiser* argued that Federalist newspapers like the *Centinel* wanted to have France cursed from the pulpits but that only the corrupt would do what God Himself had not done. It concluded that France should be blessed because it was doing God's work: "How goodly are thy tents O Frenchmen, and thy Tabernacles ye true Republicans."[44]

But preachers in 1798 did not forget the customary purpose of the fast day. In addition to emphasizing political matters

[40] Bradford, *Two Sermons, Delivered in Wiscasset (Pownalborough)*, 2d sermon, p. 19; see also Nash, "American Clergy," p. 411.

[41] John Wilder, *A Discourse . . . on the Importance of Special Humiliation* (Wrentham, Mass.: Nathaniel and Benjamin Heaton, 1798), p. 15.

[42] Gershom Mendez Seixas, *A Discourse, Delivered in the Synagogue in New York . . .* (New York: William A. David, 1798), p. 6; Morse, *Sermon Delivered at the New North Church*, p. 17n.

[43] Thayer, *Discourse, Delivered at the Roman Catholic Church*, pp. 10–28.

[44] Boston *Independent Chronicle and Universal Advertiser*, 30 April–3 May 1798.

from a Federalist perspective, all their sermons were old-fashioned jeremiads warning their listeners not to break their special covenant with God. Ministers reminded their congregations that Almighty God had raised up the French to punish America just as He had raised up enemies against ancient Israel, and they promised that repentance would bring divine protection.

Even those not of the New England Puritan tradition spoke in this vein. The Reverend Simon Francis Gallagher (or O'Gallagher), a Roman Catholic priest in Charleston, South Carolina, demonstrated that "all human events are under the immediate direction and controul of divine providence and national depravity is ever punished with national calamity."[45] The Reverend James Abercrombie, an assistant in Philadelphia's Christ Church and St. Peter's, echoed this last remark when he stated, "That national calamities are induced by national corruption and guilt is a truth, clearly inculcated by the deductions of human reason, enforced by the history of mankind in all ages, and incontestably confirmed by the repeated declarations of Holy Writ."[46]

Like thousands of Puritan preachers of the covenant before him, Dr. Ashbel Green reminded his listeners at the Second Presbyterian Church in Philadelphia that "when a nation is *characteristically pious* it will be ultimately protected, and that when it becomes *characteristically impious* it will be fast hastening to destruction."[47] "Let us regard our existing and threatening calamities, as a loud call to repentance," warned Kirkland.[48] Bradford repeated his cry: "We certainly have need of repentance and reformation. . . . vice has greatly pre-

[45] S. F. O'Gallagher, *A Sermon Preached by the Rev. Mr. S. F. Gallagher* . . . (Charleston, S.C.: W. P. Harrison, 1798), p. 2.

[46] James Abercrombie, *A Sermon, Preached in Christ Church and St. Peter's, Philadelphia* . . . (Philadelphia: John Ormrod, 1798), p. 12.

[47] Ashbel Green, *Obedience to the Law of God* . . . (Philadelphia: John Ormrod, 1798), p. 17. Porter, *Discourse, Delivered at Brookline*, p. 15, added: "To rely on divine providence for protection, without employing the means of security which were in their power, would have been to tempt God."

[48] Kirkland, *Sermon, Delivered on the 9th of May, 1798*, p. 13.

vailed in this country within a few years past."[49] Sermons usually contained a long list of national sins including everything from neglecting the due observance of the Sabbath to, in Dr. William Linn's words, "the want of union."[50]

So grave were the apparent dangers to America from within and from without that clergymen of a variety of faiths spoke in eschatological terms. Thayer told Boston's Roman Catholics that the present events were "the predicted forerunners" of the anti-christ's "approaching reign."[51] Preaching in English at the New York synagogue, Seixas looked expectantly at the "situation and circumstances of the present wars, and the depravity and corrupt state of human nature, that prevails throughout the world" as a sign that God would soon "make manifest his intention of again collecting the scattered remnant of Israel."[52] Basing his assertion on events of the past ten years and a calculation that the millennium was less than two hundred years away, Miller told United Presbyterians in New York emphatically, "THE DAYS IN WHICH WE LIVE MAY BE CONSIDERED AS THE LAST DAYS."[53]

After the defeat of the Adams's administration, political leaders rarely called upon their fellow Americans to seek God's forgiveness for their corporate and individual transgressions. Having felt the public pressure of fast proclamations and fast sermons used against them, the victorious Jeffersonians realized that the American political system should not support the use of such religious practices for divisive political purposes.[54] Adams's immediate successors in office, emphasizing

[49] Bradford, *Two Sermons, Delivered in Wiscasset (Pownalborough)*, 1st sermon, p. 14.

[50] Linn also added to his list of sins "the retention of a multitude of our fellow creatures in slavery"; *Discourse on National Sins*, pp. 11, 33.

[51] Thayer, *Discourse, Delivered at the Roman Catholic Church*, p. 21n.

[52] Seixas, *Discourse, Delivered in the Synagogue in New York*, p. 10.

[53] Miller, *Sermon, Delivered May 9, 1798*, p. 11.

[54] The spring fast continued on the state level in parts of New England (it became "Patriots' Day" in Massachusetts by the end of the nineteenth century), but it was observed "more as an occasion for feasting and excess," as C. F. Adams remarked

the First Amendment and other constitutional considerations, argued that the president did not have the power to issue such edicts and that religion was not a proper area of concern for the national government. In his well-known response to the Danbury Baptist Association in 1802, Jefferson spoke of "a wall of separation between Church and State"; and in a private letter in 1808, he objected on constitutional grounds even to recommending a day of fasting and prayer.[55]

Despite the Jeffersonian political, religious, and constitutional objections to Adams's fast proclamations, at the beginning of the War of 1812, James Madison—the president who had helped father the Constitution and the Bill of Rights—reverted to the policy of his New England predecessor and proclaimed a national fast. He believed that he had a limited power to do so because, as he told Edward Livingston in 1822, he always made his religiously oriented proclamations "absolutely indiscriminate, and mere recommendatory; or, rather, mere *designations* of a day on which all who thought proper might unite in consecrating it to religious purposes."[56]

Since that is exactly what Adams had done, Madison was

in his diary for 4 April 1833 (see *Diary of Charles Francis Adams*, ed. Aïda Dipace Donald and David Donald [vols. 1–2] and Marc Friedlaender and L. H. Butterfield [vols. 3–6] [Cambridge: Belknap Press of Harvard University Press, 1964–74], 5:61).

[55] *The Writings of Thomas Jefferson*, ed. Andrew H. Lipscomb and Albert Ellery Bergh, 20 vols. in 10 (Washington: Thomas Jefferson Memorial Association, 1905), 16:281–82; and, Jefferson to the Rev. Mr. Millar [or Robert Miller], 23 January 1808, *The Writings of Thomas Jefferson: Being His Autobiography, Correspondence, Reports, Messages, Addresses, and Other Writings, Official and Private*, ed. H. A. Washington, 9 vols. (Washington: Taylor & Maury, 1853–54), 5:236–38; cf. Mark DeWolfe Howe, *The Garden and the Wilderness: Religion and Government in American Constitutional History* (Chicago: University of Chicago Press, 1965), pp. 7, 18.

[56] Quoted in Anson Phelps Stokes, *Church and State in the United States*, 3 vols. (New York: Harper & Brothers, 1950), 1:491. This first national fast was opposed by many New England Federalists who were against Mr. Madison's war. Like Madison, both Washington and Adams had phrased their proclamations as recommendations, as had Congress during the Revolutionary War. Adams (in the Boston *Patriot* in 1809 and *Works*, 9:291) appreciated but did not agree with the Jeffersonians' states rights argument: "When most, if not all of the religious sects in the nation, hold such fasts among themselves, I never could see the force of the objections against making them, on great and extraordinary occasions, national; unless it be the jealousy of the separate States, lest the general government should become too national."

having difficulty justifying yet another Republican use of a policy—like supporting a national bank—that Jeffersonians had previously condemned when instituted by Federalists. Like Madison, Adams did not think he was discriminating against other religions. Early in the Revolution he indicated his toleration, while at the same time revealing his New England religious bias, when he stated, "I am for the most liberal toleration of all denominations of religionists, but I hope that Congress will never meddle with religion further than to say their own prayers, and to fast and to give thanks once a year."[57] Unlike the first congressional fast proclamation, which had specifically called only upon "Christians of all denominations to assemble for public worship," Adams's presidential proclamations were phrased in more general terms, even though he still ended up giving governmental recognition to such specific Christian concepts as the—albeit unnamed—Mediator and Redeemer, the Holy Spirit, and the doctrine of grace.[58]

Despite Adams's attempt—or perhaps due to it—the American government moved away from the colonial idea of proclaiming fasts, as it found itself becoming an increasingly large and pluralistic society. The successful reception of the colonial jeremiad had depended upon the assent of a relatively homogeneous New England audience. By the end of the eighteenth century, even in New England, the fast-day speaker no longer issued the only clarion summons to reformation and renewal. A rising chorus of conflicting voices rang out from people who in the colonial period had rarely been able to express their contrary sentiments publicly.

Opponents of the Adams fasts undoubtedly included Christians of a new type, who condemned what was for them the empty religious content of conservative Federalist sermons. After a post-Revolutionary low water mark came a wave of revivals in the early nineteenth century. Many reawakened Americans repudiated the exclusionary, deferential

[57] Adams to Benjamin Kent, 22 June 1776, *Works of Adams*, 9:291.

[58] *Journals of the Continental Congress*, 2:87–88, 3:507.

world in which the jeremiad had been conceived.[59] To many Americans Christianity became a private affair, separate from their political life. The new system of personal religion had little place for the old-fashioned concept of the covenanted community.[60]

In this heterogeneous, if not heterodox, environment of an expanding America, religious leaders could no longer speak either *to* or *for* all believers. Neither could political leaders. Adams had wrongly assumed that the whole nation shared his fundamental spiritual beliefs and failed to understand that the rest of the country might not appreciate federal recognition of what was primarily a colonial New England religious practice. With religion becoming a private matter, Adams had also offended too many people by calling for a public fast. As a result of political, constitutional, intellectual, and sociological changes, a more innocuous civil religion developed in the United States. Political leaders could appeal to the least common denomination in their large and complicated society by publicly thanking Providence for singling out America for special favors, but they could no longer call the nation to repentance.[61]

[59] In 1765 John Adams himself had praised enthusiasm in his influential *Dissertation on the Canon and Feudal Law* (see David S. Lovejoy, *Religious Enthusiasm in the New World: Heresy to Revolution* [Cambridge: Harvard University Press, 1985], pp. 227–29).

[60] Sidney E. Mead discusses "the privatization of religion" in *The Old Religion in the Brave New World: Reflections on the Relation Between Christendom and the Republic* (Berkeley: University of California Press, 1977), pp. 46–57; see also, Heimert, *Religion and the American Mind*, pp. 126, 295–97, 423, 425, and Martin E. Marty, *The Public Church: Mainline-Evangelical-Catholic* (New York: Crossroad, 1981), pp. 4, 7.

[61] Heimert, *Religion and the American Mind*, p. 297, argues that evangelical Americans were ready to join in days of thanksgiving, as distinguished from days of humiliation, because such occasions "were a happy reminder of the Calvinist doctrine that the very nature of society prescribed collective praise, since God's earthly dispensations were, after all, communal."

Charles Ellis Dickson, *Assistant Professor of History at Wright State University, is currently studying the founding of a church on North Dakota's frontier.*

The Diplomacy of the WXYZ Affair

William Stinchcombe

HISTORIANS have long recognized the significance of the WXYZ affair of 1797-1798. They have emphasized its important effects on domestic politics in the United States—and rightly so, for such matters as the balance between the Republican and Federalist parties, the divisions among the Federalists, the politics of the provisional army, and the passage of the Alien and Sedition acts cannot be understood apart from the WXYZ affair. Less attention has been given, however, to the diplomatic ramifications of the episode. Interest has focused on the break between the United States and France, with its threat of armed hostilities. Yet the Quasi-War did not expand into a general conflict, neutrality was preserved, and a second mission to France was soon dispatched. To explain this outcome, the inner history of the WXYZ affair must be freshly explored.

President John Adams inherited a growing problem arising from French hostility to the ratification of the Jay Treaty with Great Britain in 1796. By the time he assumed office French privateers had captured hundreds of American vessels in the West Indies, and the French government had expelled Charles C. Pinckney, the United States minister to France. During Adams's term the abortive negotiations conducted by the commission consisting of Pinckney, John Marshall, and Elbridge Gerry, together with the publication of the WXYZ dispatches, led to a near-rupture between the two nations. Federalists portrayed the WXYZ affair as grounds for severing French-American relations, and Republicans feared that it was. Adams, however, detected limited but solid progress toward his foreign policy aims.

A close study of the WXYZ negotiations themselves will confirm Adams's judgment. The tentative, precarious diplomacy between the two republics was not fruitless. By July 1798 the French had dropped their bribery and loan demands, and an order had been issued calling for cessation of attacks on American vessels. Nor were the French diplomats as hostile to United States interests as many contemporary Americans and later historians concluded. The WXYZ agents and the less familiar second-line emissaries

Mr. Stinchcombe is a member of the Department of History at Syracuse University. He wishes to thank Charles Cullen, J. Roger Sharp, and W. Allan Wilbur for comments on the article during its preparation, and to acknowledge the financial support of the Penrose Fund of the American Philosophical Society and the Appleby Fund of the Maxwell School, Syracuse University.

whom Talleyrand manipulated knew the United States, and several had investments in America. Like Talleyrand himself, these men were more disposed toward peace than were the members of the Directory. Observers, then and later, rarely noted that the French first excluded the honor-bound Pinckney, whom they considered less amenable to peace than Marshall and Gerry. The later bitter division in the commission in April 1798, when Gerry remained in Paris after Marshall and Pinckney had left, marked the last stage in the negotiations. Even so, none of the envoys returned to the United States expecting the French to go to war. After the passage of defensive measures in the summer of 1798, the danger of war was already subsiding when Adams risked the unity of the Federalist party by resuming negotiations with France. To understand this conclusion we must return to the negotiations that set these events in train.

When Adams took office, his defeated opponent Thomas Jefferson wrote that Adams's predecessor had been "fortunate to get off just as the bubble is bursting."[1] Not only had French-American antagonism intensified with French retaliatory raids against American shipping in the West Indies, but Adams himself was widely believed to be unfriendly toward France. The president, however, privately disclaimed any such animus,[2] and to show a conciliatory spirit he proposed to appoint Jefferson as special minister to the French Republic. He hoped that his selection of the principal leader of the opposition party would demonstrate his desire both for peace and for domestic harmony. When Jefferson declined the offer, Adams explored the idea of appointing James Madison to the post, and even after Madison declined,[3] he continued to be Adams's preference. The president remained determined to name a Republican envoy—a point rarely acknowledged by historians.

By late March 1797, Adams had received official dispatches from Pinckney describing the French government's refusal to accept him and his abrupt ouster from France.[4] Adams then called a special session of Congress for mid-May to outline a policy toward France, and he continued to discuss the selection of an envoy or commission. During the six weeks that followed,

[1] Jefferson to James Madison, Jan. 8, 1797, Madison Papers, XX, Library of Congress.

[2] John Adams to Abigail Adams, Dec. 18, 1796, Adams Papers, Massachusetts Historical Society.

[3] Manning J. Dauer, *The Adams Federalists*, 2d ed. (Baltimore, 1968), 124-126; Franklin B. Sawvel, ed., *The Complete Anas of Thomas Jefferson* (New York, 1903), 184-185; Ralph Ketcham, *James Madison* (New York, 1971), 367-368.

[4] LeRoy, Bayard, and McEvers to P. and C. van Eeghen, Mar. 23, 1797, Holland Land Company Papers, 153, Gemeentearchief, Amsterdam; John Adams to Abigail Adams, Mar. 27, 1797, Adams Papers.

speculation centered on the choice of envoys; Federalists outside the cabinet most often mentioned the names of Jefferson and Madison.[5]

After opening the special session of Congress with renewed demands for military spending, Adams waited until the end of May before approaching his strongly Federalist cabinet on the selection of envoys. The cabinet decided to renominate Pinckney as head of a commission. Next Adams suggested Elbridge Gerry, but all members of the cabinet objected to Gerry's lukewarm Federalism. Acquiescing, Adams chose Francis Dana of Massachusetts, a friend who had had diplomatic experience in the Revolutionary War. The deliberations on the third appointment are uncertain. Adams made a list of six men from Virginia and Maryland to be considered as possible nominees. In consistency with his earlier feelings, he placed Madison at the head of the list, but John Marshall, second on the list, was named instead.[6] Adams had yielded to his cabinet on the selection of the envoys, thus foregoing a significant opportunity to reconcile Republicans to his leadership. In 1799 he would overrule his cabinet in selecting a second commission to France. In 1797, however, he unwisely allowed a partisan cabinet to dictate his choices and negate his desire for a conciliatory gesture to France.

When Dana refused to serve, Adams again moved the nomination of Gerry, and this time the cabinet accepted him, although with reservations. The Senate ratified the appointments, a few Republicans voting against Marshall and Pinckney, and a larger number of Federalists opposing Gerry.[7]

[5] Alexander Hamilton to William L. Smith, Apr. 15, 1797, William L. Smith Papers, I, Lib. Cong.; Hamilton to Timothy Pickering, May 11, 1797, Timothy Pickering Papers, XXI, Mass. Hist. Soc. After several conferences with the president, John Fenno suggested that a three-man commission be appointed, including Madison. Fenno to Joseph Ward, Apr. 17, 1797, Ward Papers, Chicago Historical Society. Abigail Adams hoped that Madison would be appointed. Page Smith, *John Adams*, II (New York, 1962), 916; LaRochefoucauld-Liancourt to Talleyrand, Mar. 1797, in Jean Marchand, ed., *Journal de Voyage en Amèrique en d'un sojour à Philadelphie* (Baltimore and Paris, 1940), 145-148; Elihu Smith to Uriah Tracy, Apr. 16, 1797, in James Cronin, ed., *The Diary of Elihu Hubbard Smith* (Philadelphia, 1973), 310.

[6] The one document that has the list of names and gives an idea of the order of selection is "Questions to be proposed" [May 27-28, 1797], Adams Papers, filed under the date of Oct. 1797. See also John Adams to Elbridge Gerry, June 20, 1797, *ibid.;* Timothy Pickering to Charles C. Pinckney, June 1, 1797, Pickering Papers, VI; James McHenry to Pickering, Feb. 23, 1811, in Henry Cabot Lodge, ed., *Life and Letters of George Cabot* (Boston, 1877), 204; George Gibbs, Jr., *The Administrations of Washington and Adams,* I (New York, 1846), 467, 469, 471; John Adams's letters to the *Boston Patriot,* in Charles Francis Adams, ed., *The Works of John Adams, Second President of the United States: With a Life of the Author . . .*, IX (Boston, 1854), 286-287; and Timothy Pickering, *A Review of the Correspondence between the Honorable John Adams and William Cunningham, Esq.*, 2d ed. (Salem, Mass., 1824), 79-80.

[7] Executive nominations and accompanying papers, Record Group 46, Records of the United States Senate, May 31, June 5, 20, 22, 1797, National Archives.

By mid-June, Adams had a commission with geographic, if not political, balance, and in mid-July Marshall and Gerry took ship to join the patient Pinckney, waiting at The Hague.

The political situation in Paris was precarious as the American envoys made their way to France. A weak Directory found itself increasingly dependent on military power and under attack by a small group in the upper chamber, the Council of Five Hundred. Critics led by Emmanuel Pastoret castigated the Directory for its policy toward the republican governments of Geneva, Venice, and the United States. These critics were not pro-American or even pro-republican; their purpose was to gain greater power for the legislative branch of government. To stave off any diminution of its power, the Directory responded by dismissing four ministers in June 1797, including the anti-American foreign minister Charles Delacroix. A compromise within the Directory allowed Paul Barras to advance his own candidate, Talleyrand, for foreign minister.[8]

Assuming his first ministerial position in a career that would span almost four decades, Talleyrand had yet to acquire the power he would enjoy under Napoleon and the Restoration. The Prussian minister to France, Sandoz Rollin, informed his government that Talleyrand had little or no influence on European policy, which remained under Director Jean Reubell's watchful eye.[9] Only in policy toward the United States could Talleyrand operate relatively free of interference.

Many Americans viewed the choice of Talleyrand as a good omen for French-American relations.[10] The new foreign minister had lived in the United States from 1794 to 1796, and his acquaintance with American customs and government exceeded that of most Frenchmen. Joseph Pitcairn, a New York merchant and Paris neighbor of Talleyrand, remarked that Talleyrand "has for us many advantages over his predecessor—he is superior in natural talents and in acquired—but above all he knows America and particularly her leading men very well."[11]

[8] R. R. Palmer, *The Age of the Democratic Revolution: A Political History of Europe and America, 1760-1800*, II (Princeton, N.J., 1964), 255-260; Georges Lefebvre, *The French Revolution from 1793 to 1799*, trans. John H. Stewart and James Friguglietti, II (New York, 1964), 171-182, 197-199; Isser Woloch, *Jacobin Legacy* (Princeton, N.J., 1970), 77, 364; Georgia Robison, *Revellière-Lépeaux, Citizen Director, 1753-1824* (New York, 1938), 48.

[9] Sandoz Rollin dispatches, Aug. 13, Oct. 29, 1797, in Paul Bailleu, ed., *Preusen und Frankreich von 1795 bis 1807: Diplomatische Correspondenzen*, I (Leipzig, 1881), 142-143, 155.

[10] Gouverneur Morris to James Mountflorence, Aug. 18, 1797, Gouverneur Morris Papers, XXIV, Lib. Cong.; Robert Morris to Talleyrand, Jan. 8, 1797, Robert Morris Papers, Letterbook II, *ibid.;* William L. Smith to Talleyrand, Nov. 8, 1797, Smith Papers, I; Rufus King to Talleyrand, Aug. 3, 1797, Rufus King Papers, LXIII, New-York Historical Society.

[11] Joseph Pitcairn to Rufus King, Aug. 3, 1797, King Papers, XXIX, N.-Y. Hist. Soc.

Talleyrand had indeed judged American leaders, and he had his preferences for the American envoys, specifically Aaron Burr or Madison.[12] Throughout the negotiations he was to insist on the need for envoys who professed friendship to France. His agents were even to taunt the envoys by saying that they had failed where pro-French appointees would have succeeded. Adams's original inclination on the selection of envoys had been well founded.

Talleyrand had indicated his thoughts about the United States in two public lectures given before he assumed office.[13] During his years in America he had become interested in the new relations developing between the United States and Great Britain. In his lectures he warned that bonds of culture, language, and commerce would inevitably tie the Americans more closely to Great Britain than to France, despite French aid in the American Revolution. He predicted that most European colonies in the Americas, including Santo Domingo, would become independent, and he recommended that reciprocal relations be developed between the United States and the French West Indies. Analyzing Talleyrand's speeches, John Quincy Adams concluded "that he was better disposed than many persons have represented him, and I have believed that pains were taken to misrepresent him to Mr. P[inckney] while he was in Paris."[14]

In September a triumvirate within the Directory moved to regain control of the government by ordering the arrest of Directors Lazare Carnot and François Barthélemy, cancelling the results of the 1796 elections, closing over thirty newspapers in Paris alone, and exiling many critics in the Council of Five Hundred. Marshall and Pinckney predicted that the slim chances of peace between France and the United States had been permanently damaged by this coup.[15] Even before the coup, however, a majority of the Directory opposed acknowledging the Jay Treaty and sought an apology from the United States for compromising with Great Britain. The victorious Directors Jean Reubell, Paul Barras, and Louis La Revellière-Lépeaux showed open hostility to the United States. Even the deposed Lazare Carnot argued for expansion into Louisiana and Florida; by way of warning to other neutrals he

[12] Pitcairn to John Q. Adams, Oct. 20, 1796, Adams Papers.

[13] *Memoir concerning the Commercial Relations of the United States with England,* Apr. 4, 1797, and *An Essay upon the Advantages to be derived from New Colonies,* July 3, 1797, trans. and publ. as one pamphlet (Boston, 1809).

[14] Adams to Joseph Pitcairn, Aug. 14, 1797, Joseph Pitcairn Papers, I, Cincinnati Historical Society.

[15] Pinckney to Timothy Pickering, Sept. [14], 1797, Diplomatic Dispatches, France, V, Record Group 59, Nat'l. Arch.; John Marshall to George Washington, Sept. 15, 1797, Washington Papers, Lib. Cong.; Marshall to Charles Lee, Sept. 22, 1797, Emmett Collection, New York Public Library, New York City.

suggested that the free city of Hamburg pay France to preserve its neutrality.[16] To the envoys of the Cisalpine Republic, La Revellière-Lépeaux stated in August 1797 that "the Directory will not treat with the Enemies of the Republic."[17] Reubell insisted that Adams had insulted France and betrayed it by supporting the Jay Treaty, further maintaining that peace with the United States would be impossible as long as Adams served as president. Neither the Directors nor Talleyrand saw a serious threat of war from the United States; they found no need for haste in the negotiations.[18]

Marshall reached Europe before his colleague Gerry. Arriving in Amsterdam after having been delayed by a British blockade of the Netherlands, he joined Pinckney at The Hague, where they waited for Gerry. After a delay of two weeks, during which time they heard only pessimistic appraisals of the anti-American effects of the recent coup, the two envoys decided to leave for Paris to begin negotiations without Gerry.[19] It is not clear what Marshall and Pinckney thought they could gain by hurrying to Paris, but en route they received news that Gerry would soon arrive. Two days after Gerry reached Paris, in the first week of October, the envoys requested a meeting with Talleyrand.[20]

Talleyrand received them two days later and, in contrast to the treatment given Pinckney earlier in the year, offered the cards of hospitality necessary to guarantee them against deportation by the police. During the fifteen-minute conversation Talleyrand remarked that he was writing a report on French-American relations.[21] He asked the envoys to postpone a request to begin negotiations until the Directory had approved his report.

[16] Marcel Reinhard, *Le Grand Carnot: L'Organisateur de la Victoire, 1792-1823*, II (Paris, 1952), 374, n. 10, 375, n. 15; Rollin dispatch, May 6, 1796, in Bailleu, ed., *Preusen und Frankreich*, I, 67.

[17] Georges Lefebvre, *The Thermidorians and the Directory: Two Phases of the French Revolution*, trans. Robert Baldick (New York, 1964), 334; Robison, *Revellière-Lépeaux*, 218.

[18] Bernard Narbonne, *Le Diplomatie du Directoire et Bonaparte d'après les Inédits de Reubell* (Paris, 1951), 85-86, 172-173; Gerlof Homan, "The Revolutionary Career of Jean François Reubell" (Ph.D. diss., University of Kansas, 1958), 347-348.

[19] Marshall to Pickering, Sept. 15, 1797, Diplomatic Dispatches, Fr., VI, RG 59.

[20] American Envoys to Talleyrand, Oct. 6, 1797, Correspondance Politique, Archives du Ministère des Affaires Étrangères, États-Unis, XLVIII, Paris, hereafter cited as Correspondence Politique.

[21] This report, which does not appear in the regular diplomatic series, is entitled "Memoir on Relations between France and the United States from 1792-1797" [Oct. 8-14], 1797, DeSages, Archives des Affaires Étrangères, États-Unis, XXXVI, hereafter cited as Talleyrand's Report. Other authors have cited the second Talleyrand memoir, Feb. [3-18], 1798, Correspondance Politique, XLIX, but the first report explains in detail the policy which Talleyrand pursued from October to February. See E. Wilson Lyon, "The Directory and the United States," *American Historical Review*, XLIII (1938), 522; Alexander DeConde, *The Quasi-War: The Politics and*

Less than a week later, Talleyrand opened negotiations on the basis of the report approved by the Directory. In his report he had reviewed French-American relations from 1792 to 1797. He advocated a slow pace for the negotiations, an approach in accordance with the Directory's previous policy. As a delaying tactic Talleyrand proposed to seek an explanation of Adams's speech to Congress in May. He declared that he did not expect an apology, but he did not clarify the distinction between an apology and an explanation. Talleyrand expected that this procedure would reveal whether the envoys had a friendly attitude toward France. Until the envoys had offered an adequate answer on the subject of Adams's "harmful" remarks, the Directory would postpone receiving them officially and thus put off the start of serious negotiations.[22]

Talleyrand's report noted that Adams seemed more conciliatory than George Washington had been during his last two years in office. Talleyrand went on to predict that the new president's slight electoral majority would deter him from adopting a strongly anti-French policy. Furthermore, Adams's prompt repudiation of William Blount's intrigues with the Spanish and British on the western frontier convinced Talleyrand that Adams was not the tool of what the foreign minister labeled the British party in the United States. In support of his view that the United States would not go to war, Talleyrand cited congressional resistance to Adams's defense proposals in the special session of Congress the previous spring. Even if the United States were to declare war, he believed that the American public would not support it. Nor should France declare war, because this would only harm the French West Indian colonies and drive the United States into the British orbit.[23] The tenor of Talleyrand's analysis made clear that the French had no reason to conclude the negotiations quickly.

But at the same time Talleyrand did not ignore the conflicts between the two countries. He considered the West Indies the most dangerous situation. He blandly noted that in the course of French-American differences "our agents in the Colonies accordingly took certain measures which pressed

---

Diplomacy of the Undeclared War with France, 1797-1801 (New York, 1966), 44, 56-57; Marvin R. Zahniser, *Charles Cotesworth Pinckney: Founding Father* (Chapel Hill, N.C., 1967), 179; and Albert Hall Bowman, *The Struggle for Neutrality: Franco-American Diplomacy during the Federalist Era* (Knoxville, Tenn., 1974), 312-316, 321. Bowman cites a document written on Oct. 2, 1797, as another report approved by Talleyrand, but Talleyrand did not accept any of this report's recommendations on indemnities, cessation of hostilities, and the revision of treaties during the next 9 months. For a discussion of the memoirs written for the American negotiations see William Stinchcombe, "Talleyrand and the American Negotiations, 1797-1798," *Journal of American History*, LXII (1975), 576-583.

[22] Talleyrand's Report, 22, 23, 29-30.

[23] *Ibid.*, 22, 32.

heavily on American trade with English Colonies." Later Talleyrand concluded that "the time has come to remove the despotic actions and violence which are carried out against Americans in our Antilles."[24] Unfortunately, he did not persuade the Directory to change its policy in this area until the much different circumstances of the summer of 1798.[25]

The first development in the negotiations came on October 14, when Antoine-Eustache, Baron d'Osmond, a private secretary to Talleyrand, told James Mountflorence, an assistant to American consul Fulwar Skipwith and a confidant of Pinckney, that the Directory was angered and expected an explanation of certain parts of Adams's May 16 speech before the envoys would be officially received.[26] One of the envoys' closest advisers and the unofficial leader of the American community in Paris, Joel Barlow, wrote that Talleyrand "gave our Ministers several indirect hints not to press any thing, but to have patience," but Barlow's judgment was ignored.[27] The envoys decided to make no response to d'Osmond, since his information was indirect. They also determined, in what was a critical decision, to make no explanation of the president's speech. This decision remained unaltered during the next six months, despite the repeated insistence of Frenchmen, including Talleyrand directly, that an explanation would be required.[28]

Three days later Nicholas Hubbard, identified as W in the envoys' published dispatches, called on Pinckney to request that he accept a visit from Jean Conrad Hottinguer, X of WXYZ.[29] Hubbard was an Englishman by

[24] *Ibid.*, 20, 37.

[25] Stinchcombe, "Talleyrand," *JAH*, LXII (1975), 576n-577n.

[26] American Envoys to Pickering, Oct. 22, 1797, Diplomatic Dispatches, Fr., VI, RG 59; John Marshall Journal, Oct. 14, 1797, Pickering Papers, LI, hereafter cited as Marshall Journal. For the identification of d'Osmond see Edmund Burke to Comtesse d'Osmond, Dec. 8, 29, 1794, in R. B. McDowell, ed., *The Correspondence of Edmund Burke*, VIII (Cambridge, 1969), 91-95, 102-103; G[eorges] Lacour-Gayet, *Talleyrand, 1754-1838* (Paris, 1930), II, 33, 237; and Frédéric Masson, *Le Department des Affaires Étrangères pendant la Révolution* (Paris, 1877), 472, 473, 479, 490. Masson says that Osmond was of humble birth, but in fact he was a priest from a noble family; he emigrated to Great Britain during the Terror and became a bishop after the Restoration. On d'Osmond see also Gabriel Debien, *Les Colons de Saint-Domingue et la Révolution* (Paris, 1953), 146, 383, 392. On Mountflorence and Skipwith, who was a close associate of Gerry, see Samuel M. Hopkins's letter in the *Pennsylvania Gazette* (Philadelphia), Feb. 11, 1799.

[27] Joel Barlow to James Cathalan, Oct. 29, 1797, Barlow Papers, IV, Harvard University. Fulwar Skipwith agreed with Barlow's assessment. Skipwith to James Monroe, Oct. 20, 1797, James Monroe Papers, Lib. Cong.

[28] Marshall Journal, Oct. 14, 1797; Caron de Beaumarchais to Gerry and Marshall, Jan. 17, 1798, Gerry Papers, Pierpont Morgan Library; American Envoys to Pickering, Mar. 9, 1798, Diplomatic Dispatches, Fr., VI, RG 59.

[29] W was Nicholas Hubbard; X was Jean Conrad Hottinguer; Y was Pierre

birth and a junior partner in the Amsterdam banking firm of Van Staphorst and Hubbard, which was the American government's European bank. He assured Pinckney that Hottinguer was a man of honor, an explanation which Pinckney accepted without seeking more detail. On the evening of October 18, Hottinguer informed Pinckney that the American government was expected to assume all of the claims of American citizens against the French government, pay an indemnity to American merchantmen for French confiscations, grant a loan to the French government of thirty-two million Dutch guilders, and provide an additional *pot de vin*, or bribe, of fifty thousand pounds to Talleyrand.[30]

When Pinckney informed his amazed colleagues, they jointly requested that Hottinguer present the proposal to all of the envoys. Without realizing it, the Americans had allowed the opening of informal negotiations with

---

Bellamy; and Z was Lucien Hauteval. There has been some confusion over the identification of Hubbard as W, but in the Marshall Journal, Oct. 30, 1797, and in American Envoys to Pickering, Oct. 22, 1797, Diplomatic Dispatches, Fr., VI, RG 59, Hubbard is named, and there is no doubt that he is W. In a note inserted in the Adams Papers, Oct. 22, 1797, the date of the envoys' dispatch, Adams wrote W over Hubbard's name. William V. Murray, in his Commonplace Book, July 13, 1798 (Murray Papers, II, Lib. Cong.), also identified Hubbard as W. But DeConde (*Quasi-War*, 72) identifies Caron de Beaumarchais as W, a mistake repeated by Bowman (*Struggle for Neutrality*, 317n). Albert J. Beveridge says W was a Paris businessman, which he was not (*The Life of John Marshall*, II [Boston, 1916], 259).

The French identification of the agents is more confusing and lacks documentation. [L. G. Michaud], *Biographie Universelle ancienne et moderne*, LXXXIII (1855), 201, 203, names Bellamy as X and adds that the approach to Pinckney was made by three associates of Talleyrand: Casimir de Montrond, André d'Arbelles, and Pierre Sainte-Foy. This mistake is continued by Raymond Guyot, *Le Directoire et la paix de l'Europe* (Paris, 1911), 561-562, and Lacour-Gayet, *Talleyrand*, I, 238. Bernard Fay, *L'Esprit révolutionnaire en France et aux États-Unis à la fin du XVIIIe siècle* (Paris, 1925), 405, uses American sources but mentions only Bellamy and Hauteval as agents. Henri Malo, however, in *Le Beau Montrond* (Paris, 1926), 41, combines the two traditions by incorrectly naming Hottinguer, Bellamy, and Hauteval as the official agents, while incorrectly identifying Montrond, Sainte-Foy, and d'Arbelles as the unofficial agents. Bowman, *Struggle for Neutrality*, 317n, variously names for W, X, Y, and Z, Beaumarchais, Hottinguer, Bellamy, Hauteval, Sainte-Foy, Montrond, and d'Arbelles.

For the latter career of Hubbard see P. J. Van Winter, *Het Aandeel van de Amsterdamschen handel ànn den pobouw van het Amerikaansche Gemeenebest* (The Hague, 1927-1933), I, 200, II, 283, 282, and Nicholas Hubbard to J. Van Beech Vollenhoven, Nov. 13, 1812, Brants Archives, 206, Gemeentearchief, Amsterdam. For the later career of Hottinguer see Romauld Szramkiewicz, *Les Régents et Censeurs de la Banque nommès sous le Consulat et l'Empire* (Geneva, 1974), 168-176, and Herbert Lüthy, *La Banque Protestante en France*, II (Paris, 1961), 544, 722-726.

[30] American Envoys to Pickering, Oct. 22, 1797, Diplomatic Dispatches, Fr., VI, RG 59; Marshall Journal, Oct. 18-[19], 1797.

unofficial French agents, and these discussions were to continue throughout the envoys' stay in Paris, despite their avowed determination not to conduct such unofficial negotiations. Hottinguer outlined the proposal to the three envoys, mentioning that he made his request in the name of a man close to Talleyrand. Faced with an abrupt American refusal, Hottinguer introduced this man—Pierre Bellamy, Y of WXYZ—at a meeting the next day, when they elaborated on the proposals.[31] In the first days of negotiations with Hottinguer and Bellamy the inexperienced envoys were aghast at their situation; they would agree only to send one of their number back to the United States for more instructions, provided the French government ceased attacks on American shipping during the interim. Having broken off peace talks with Great Britain during the week, the French refused the condition.[32]

Responding to the Americans' resolute stand, Talleyrand sent an emissary to call upon Gerry. This was Lucien Hauteval, Z of WXYZ, a wealthy West Indian sugar planter. Forced to flee Santo Domingo in 1792, Hauteval had moved to Boston, where he met Gerry. By 1796 he was in Paris, scheming to be named French minister to the United States. Hauteval assured Gerry that Talleyrand deeply desired peace and would welcome more private contacts with the envoys.[33] From this time forward Hauteval's role in the negotiations would be to proclaim Talleyrand's sincerity whenever the talks seemed to be breaking down. On this occasion he explained that a loan to France and a bribe to Talleyrand were necessary. But he also wanted it understood that he did not come as a representative bearing Talleyrand's proposals, as had Hottinguer and Bellamy. Talleyrand distinguished between those who approached the Americans to keep the negotiations open and those associates whom he trusted to negotiate in his name. Although Hauteval was devoted to French-American peace and sought to influence Talleyrand, he served only as a high-level errand boy without responsibility in the negotiations.[34]

[31] For background information on Bellamy see John Q. Adams to Rufus King, July 11, 1798, Adams Papers, and Jacques Galiffe, *Notices Généalogiques sur les Familles Geneovises,* III (Geneva, 1836), 43; for Bellamy's public explanation of his services to Talleyrand see his statement, June 25, 1798, Correspondance Politique, Supplement, II.

[32] John Marshall to Charles Lee, Oct. 12-[27], 1797, Diplomatic Dispatches, Fr., VI, RG 59; American Envoys to Pickering, Oct. 22, 1797, *ibid.*

[33] American Envoys to Pickering, Nov. 8, 1797, *ibid.* For the background on Hauteval and his American connections see John Q. Adams to William V. Murray, July 17, 1798, Adams Papers; William Lee Diary, Mar. 20, 1796, Lee-Palfrey Papers, II, Lib. Cong.; Gabriel Debien, *Études Antillaises* (Paris, 1956), 156, 156n; and Carl Seaburg and Stanley Paterson, *Merchant Prince of Boston: Colonel T. H. Perkins, 1765-1854* (Cambridge, Mass., 1971), 77-79.

[34] Talleyrand later characterized his messenger as officious. Talleyrand to the Directory, June 1, 1798, Correspondance Politique, LXIX; Marshall to Pickering, Sept. 28, 1798, Adams Papers; Lucien Hauteval to John Adams, Aug. 26, 1798, *ibid.*

A week passed after Hauteval's visit before Hottinguer and Bellamy reappeared. Probably this timing was related to the signing of the triumphant settlement with Austria at Campo Formio. French demands now became tougher and more threatening. The United States would suffer the same fate as Venice, which was given to Austria by the French. Under the genius of Napoleon, France would soon launch an attack on Great Britain, after which the United States would have to face French displeasure alone. Hottinguer and Bellamy suggested that if Madison or Burr had been sent, a settlement would have been reached; they threatened to provoke civil war in the United States by encouraging the partisans of France against the Federalists. Before this blustering the envoys held firm, rejecting all claims, although they did accept a copy of the parts of Adams's speech that had offended the Directory. At this time Pinckney made his well-known response to Hottinguer's insistence on a bribe: "No, No, not a sixpence."[35]

The first phase of the negotiations ended, and it was the record of these meetings that was published in April 1798, for the American public to read. Privately, in Paris, both sides showed frustration over the initial results. Gerry wrote, "The fact is, as I conceive it, that a small cargo of Mexican dollars would be more efficient in a negotiation at present than two Cargoes of Ambassadors." Pinckney took a sterner view, placing the emphasis on national honor, a standard he would maintain more earnestly than the other two envoys in the following months. "We experience a haughtiness which is unexampled in the history and practice of nations," he wrote to the United States minister to the Netherlands, William Vans Murray, "and feel ourselves under the necessity of submitting to circumstances which make an impression to be worn out, you may be assured, only with life. I would give a handsome fee for one half hour with you. I could a tale unfold."[36]

The impasse in the negotiations caused the resourceful Talleyrand to change his agents, if not his tactics. Historians have given undue emphasis to the infrequent meetings of the envoys with Hottinguer and Bellamy after November; they have failed to note the new intermediaries who kindled the envoys' hopes and kept them in Paris for five more months. This second group of intermediaries, including Louis d'Autremont, Caron de Beaumarchais, Joseph Pitcairn, and Pierre Du Pont de Nemours—to name several of the more important—now maintained contacts between Talleyrand and the envoys. In the last months of the mission these new agents

[35] American Envoys to Pickering, Nov. 8, 1797, Diplomatic Dispatches, Fr., VI, RG 59.

[36] Gerry to William V. Murray and Pinckney to Murray, Oct. 30, 1797, both enclosed in Murray to Pickering, Nov. 10, 1797, Diplomatic Dispatches, Netherlands, III, RG 59.

conducted the negotiations, under the close supervision of Bellamy and Talleyrand.

Despite the American rebuff, the French continued to apply pressure. Hauteval called on Gerry to ask if the envoys had informed other ministers of the bribe demands. Gerry informed him that the subject was considered confidential; he added, however, that he would not meet with Hauteval again, since Hauteval had no authority to negotiate. The French also approached James Mountflorence, through whom they had made their first overture to the envoys, but Pinckney shut off that avenue of access. Acting on Talleyrand's instructions, Pitcairn called on Marshall and Pinckney to determine if they were ready to reconsider the loan question. Pinckney ruefully mentioned that the idea had been discussed, but explained that because it was against their instructions the envoys would not consider it.[37]

Talleyrand did not cease his probing of the individual envoys. A day after Hauteval's visit to Gerry, Caron de Beaumarchais sent a note to Marshall asking if he were the lawyer whom Beaumarchais had hired to pursue his claims against Virginia for supplies furnished during the American Revolution. Beaumarchais had known of Marshall's presence weeks before, but he had not requested a meeting, even though he claimed to be desperate for funds.[38] Scholars have long suspected, and evidence now reveals, that Beaumarchais took direction from Bellamy and Talleyrand. Marshall received Beaumarchais, and the latter reported that he could detect no change in American attitudes.[39]

Talleyrand now entered the picture directly for the first time, taking the occasion of a dinner party to express his displeasure with the envoys. To John Trumbull he remarked that the envoys were three thousand miles from home and should take it upon themselves to reach the right decision to preserve peace without waiting for new instructions. The Americans, moreover, should realize that the "French were impatient" and that the problem required a quick solution, which meant acceding to the bribe and loan demands.[40]

Still resolute, the envoys attempted no appraisal of the situation in Paris.

[37] Hauteval to Gerry, Nov. 4, 1797, Gerry Papers, Pierpont Morgan Lib.; Pinckney to James Mountflorence, Nov. 7, 1797, Knight-Gerry Papers, Mass. Hist. Soc.; Marshall Journal, Nov. [22-28], 1797.

[38] Beaumarchais to Marshall, Nov. 6, 1797, Marshall to Beaumarchais, Nov. 7, 1797, Beaumarchais to Jean Chevallié, Oct. 1797, all in private archives, Paris.

[39] Beaumarchais to Talleyrand, Oct. 17, 1797, and Beaumarchais to Pierre Bellamy, Dec. 26, 1797 (with copy to Talleyrand); Bellamy to Beaumarchais, *ibid.*

[40] Notebook, Nov. 1797, King Papers, LXXIII, N.-Y. Hist. Soc.; Mary Pinckney to Margaret Manigault, Nov. 5, 1797, Manigault Family Papers, II, University of South Carolina. Trumbull arrived in London on Nov. 11, 1797. Rufus King to American Envoys, Nov. 15, 1797, Gerry Papers, Pierpont Morgan Lib.

They viewed French interests and conduct almost as if the French Revolution had not occurred. Their interpretation of Talleyrand's tactics focused only on the foreign minister's corruption. The envoys failed to analyze the group of agents and secretaries whom Talleyrand had chosen to confer with them. Rumors of bribes were rampant in Paris. During the seven months the envoys spent in Paris, Talleyrand accepted bribes channeled through intermediaries, particularly Bellamy, from Portugal and Great Britain. Sandoz Rollin heard that Spain had contributed a vast sum and suggested that Prussia do likewise for self-protection.[41] Nicholas Hubbard and Wilhelm Willink, another Dutch banker, told the envoys that bribery was indispensable in Paris.[42] Even though they would have no guarantee of success, to do business with the French government at this time the Americans would have to offer a bribe, or otherwise play the dangerous game of outwaiting Talleyrand. He and his associates had in fact turned the ministry of foreign affairs into a house of commerce. Talleyrand's partners, Hottinguer, Bellamy, and Hubbard, sought to use the foreign minister's position to enhance their private speculations.

We can better understand the insistence on the bribe and loan demands if we examine the economic interests linking Hottinguer, Bellamy, Hubbard, and Talleyrand. Neither Bellamy nor Hottinguer concealed his land investments in the United States from the envoys.[43] Hubbard, moreover, was not simply a partner in Van Staphorst and Hubbard, the firm that financed the American national debt. He was also a member of an openly acknowledged Dutch banking syndicate that speculated in land and currency in the United States.[44] Hottinguer had met Pinckney earlier in Amsterdam, if not in Charleston. John Marshall knew that his own brother James had negotiated

[41] Rollin dispatches, Jan. 21, Mar. 28, 1798, in Bailleu, ed., *Preusen und Frankreich*, I, 168, 182; Guyot, *Le Directoire*, 444, 446n, 469; Lüthy, *La Banque Protestante*, II, 662. For contemporary accounts of bribery under the French at this time, mostly involving Bellamy, see Rufus King to American Envoys, Nov. 24, 1797, King Papers, XXXII, N.-Y. Hist. Soc.; King to American Envoys, Dec. 24, 1797, King Papers, Lib. Cong.; John Trumbull to Elbridge Gerry [Jan. 1798], Trumbull Papers, Memo Book, 1792-1799, *ibid.;* Commonplace Book, July 6, 13, 1798, Murray Papers, II, *ibid.*

[42] Marshall Journal, Oct. 30, 1797.

[43] American Envoys to Pickering, Oct. 22, Nov. 8, 1797, Diplomatic Dispatches, Fr., VI, RG 59. In the printed edition of the dispatches all references to visits to the United States and land ownership were omitted.

[44] Van Staphorst and Hubbard was one of six houses that owned the Holland Land Company, in which Theophile Cazenove was the head American agent. In the summer of 1797 James Marshall contracted a loan from the firm to pay interest on shares of the North American Land Company. Statement of Bankruptcy Proceedings made by Robert Morris, Oct. 12, 1801, Holland Land Co. Papers, 144.

a loan through Hottinguer the previous summer in Amsterdam.[45] Of the four, Bellamy was perhaps the least known to Americans, although Pitcairn and Rufus King were acquainted with him.[46]

The activities of Talleyrand's three partners reveal the instability of French society in 1797. These were men temporarily set adrift by the French Revolution and seeking new outlets for investment safe from the vicissitudes of European wars. Jean Conrad Hottinguer was a former Zurich banker who came to Paris in the 1780s as a representative of Swiss banking interests. He established his own bank in Paris but was forced to leave in 1793, when he fled to London to avoid imprisonment and probable death. While in London, he married an American, Elizabeth Redwood of Newport, Rhode Island.[47] Hottinguer directed a group of German emigrants settling in Georgia in 1794 on behalf of a company, the Georgia Agricultural Company, of which he was part owner.[48] By mid-1795 he moved to Philadelphia, conducting business with Talleyrand and with Theophile Cazenove, the head of the Holland Land Company in America.[49]

Cazenove had worked with Talleyrand in Paris in the 1780s. He advised Talleyrand on American speculations and employed him to write reports on prospects for buying land in Maine and New York. Later, Cazenove lived with Talleyrand in Paris as a financial adviser.[50] Hottinguer joined a consortium with Cazenove and Talleyrand to purchase land in Pennsylvania, certainly from Robert Morris and probably from others.[51] In 1796 Hottin-

[45] John Marshall was also responsible for the loan. *Ibid.* Beveridge, *Life of Marshall,* II, 259, speculates that Hottinguer was connected with James Marshall. Van Winter, *Amsterdamsche Handel,* II, 280, was the first to suggest the connection between the loan and the WXYZ affair. For Pinckney's acquaintance with Hottinguer see American Envoys to Pickering, Oct. 22, 1797, Diplomatic Dispatches, Fr., VI, RG 59.

[46] Pitcairn to King, June 29, 1798, King Papers, XXIX, N.-Y. Hist. Soc.

[47] Szramkiewicz, *Les Régents,* 158-176.

[48] Van Winter, *Amsterdamsche Handel,* II, 341, 344; Theophile Cazenove to Nicholas Hubbard, Feb. 12, 1795, Holland Land Co. Papers, 300.

[49] James Cazenove to Theophile Cazenove, July 13, 1796, *ibid.,* 268.

[50] A. de Cazenove, ed., *Journal de Madame de Cazenove d'Arlens* (Paris, 1903), xxx-xxxi, 124-125.

[51] Edwin R. Baldrige, "Talleyrand in the United States, 1794-1796" (Ph.D. diss., Lehigh University, 1963), 100-114. Baldrige's argument that one land deal did fall through is confirmed by the Statement of Bankruptcy Proceedings by Robert Morris, Oct. 12, 1801, Holland Land Co. Papers, 144. Baldrige expands the argument: "Various authors have stated that Talleyrand participated in numerous land deals in America. Most of their remarks are nebulous, never citing exactly where the lands were situated, the size of the purchase, or the dates of the transactions. Furthermore, they never explain what he did with the lands he supposedly bought" ("Talleyrand's Visit to Pennsylvania, 1794-1796," *Pennsylvania History,* XXXVI [1969], 159). Given 18th-century business practices, however, and Talleyrand's custom of putting

guer returned to London and went on to Hamburg, where he formed a new land company to sell American property to emigrés. He named Bellamy as secretary of the company, and the banking firm of Bellamy and Ricci invested in the scheme.[52] After a visit to Amsterdam, Hottinguer returned to Paris to raise money for the company and opened his own bank there once again in 1798.[53] He and Talleyrand were to remain close associates for the following three decades.

Talleyrand himself had gone to the United States after being exiled from France and Great Britain. When he returned to Europe in the spring of 1796, he left his papers in the hands of Cazenove, some land in Cazenove's name, and investments in United States bank stock in the name of James Cazenove, a nephew of Theophile.[54] Talleyrand was met in Hamburg by Gabriel-Marie, comte de Ricci, a French emigré and Bellamy's partner.[55] He then traveled to Amsterdam, where he conducted business with his associate Hubbard on their American investments.[56] Probably not coincidentally, Talleyrand and Hottinguer returned from Amsterdam to Paris on the same day to continue their business ventures.[57]

---

his holdings in someone else's name, it is difficult to be precise. For land around Cazenovia, N.Y., held in Cazenove's name from 1795 to 1830, see Cazenove, ed., *Journal de Madame de Cazenove d'Arlens,* xxx-xxxi, 147n. Robert Morris wrote that Talleyrand did not want his American land deals known in Europe. Morris to Theophile Cazenove, Oct. 23, 1797, Robert Morris Papers, Letterbook II. For Talleyrand's land in Pennsylvania see I. H. LeCombe to Conderc, and LeCombe to Changuion, Apr. 28, 1797, Brants Archives, 648. On the land held in Virginia with Charles de la Forest, Geoggray de Grandmaison, *Correspondance du Comte de La Forest,* I (Paris, 1905), xii. For a loan to Du Pont de Nemours on Kentucky lands see Ambrose Saricks, *Pierre Samuel Du Pont de Nemours* (Lawrence, Kan., 1965), 305-306. For contemporary accounts that Talleyrand purchased American lands see Elbridge Gerry to John Adams, July 8, 1799, Adams Papers. John Stone reported that Talleyrand had visited his house and purchased land in the United States. Stone to Joseph Priestly, Feb. 12, 1798, *Lettres au Docteur Priestly en Amerique* (London, 1798), 21.

[52] Extrait de la lettre de M. H. à notre maison, Hamburg, Mar. 30 [1796], Brants Archives, 648; Lüthy, *La Banque Protestante,* II, 726n; Bellamy and Ricci to Campagnie de Ceres, May 21, Aug. 16, 1796, July 6, 25, Sept. 26, Nov. 17, 1797, Brants Archives, 648.

[53] Szramkiewicz, *Les Régents,* 173.

[54] Inventoire des Papiers, no. 25, Holland Land Co. Papers, 108; Cazenove, ed., *Journal de Madame de Cazenove d'Arlens,* xxx-xxxi, 147n.

[55] Lacour-Gayet, *Talleyrand,* I, 208, 229. The author identifies Ricci and Riccé as two different men, but see Fanny Burney Journal, Nov. 22, 1798, in Joyce Hemlow, ed., *The Journals and Letters of Fanny Burney: Madame d'Arblay,* IV (Oxford, 1973), 172-173.

[56] Theophile Cazenove to Nicholas Hubbard, June 26, 1796, Holland Land Co. Papers, 300.

[57] Lacour-Gayet, *Talleyrand,* I, 211; Szramkiewicz, *Les Régents,* 172.

Pierre Bellamy, a onetime clergyman, served on Geneva's Council of Two Hundred and conducted a banking business there until forced into exile by the Revolution in 1794.[58] In Hamburg he formed a new bank with Ricci, combining the traditional business of banking with that of an import merchant. After the French Revolution he returned to his native city, again to become a leading member of the business community.

Another figure who became prominent in the American negotiations could be included in this group—Caron de Beaumarchais. Exiled to Hamburg during the Revolution, he returned to Paris just after Talleyrand and Hottinguer. Talleyrand became Beaumarchais's financial adviser, recommending that he conduct business through Bellamy and Ricci, appoint Theophile Cazenove as his head agent in the United States, and hire Alexander Hamilton as his lawyer.[59] Beaumarchais boasted that Talleyrand had promised to use his position as foreign minister to secure payment of Beaumarchais's claims against the Americans.[60]

Thus the agents who approached the American envoys not only knew the United States but had heavy financial interests in American lands. All of them therefore had a vested interest in maintaining peace with the United States. As often happened in eighteenth-century diplomacy, the line between public and personal interests became blurred.[61] The WXY (Hubbard, Hottinguer, Bellamy) affair, as it might be called in view of Hauteval's minor role, resulted from the action of a group of recently returned exiles working with Talleyrand to preserve peace while rebuilding their fortunes. Because their interests had no connection with profits from privateering, these men were more willing than others to limit maritime abuses. For all the

[58] John Q. Adams to Rufus King, July 11, 1798, Adams Papers.

[59] Beaumarchais to Samuel Sterett, Oct. 29, 1796, Beaumarchais to Jean Chevallié, Oct. 29, 1796, June 26, and, Oct. 1797, Beaumarchais to Alexander Hamilton, Oct. 26, 1797, Beaumarchais to Talleyrand, Oct. 17, 1797, Hamilton to Beaumarchais, Feb. 13, 1798, private archives.

[60] Beaumarchais to Jean Chevallié, Oct. 1797, and Theophile Cazenove to Beaumarchais, Oct. 26, 1798, *ibid.;* Cazenove to Chevallié, Oct. 9, 1797, Holland Land Co. Papers, 302.

[61] John Marshall had the same situation on the American side with his loans from Van Staphorst and Hubbard arranged by Hottinguer, but Marshall firmly opposed giving in to France and was willing to risk war, even though he needed a loan to finance the Fairfax purchase. For the material on John, James, and Louis Marshall's financial dealings in Europe in 1797 see Robert Morris to Henry Lee, June 3, Sept. 18, 1797, Morris to Rawleigh Colston, July 10, Oct. 14, 1797, and Morris to James Marshall, May 29, 1797, Robert Morris Papers, Letterbook II; John Marshall to Mary Marshall, July 3, 1797, Marshall Papers, College of William and Mary; John Q. Adams Diary, June 2, 8, 11, 1797, Adams Papers; Charlotte Murray to Eliza Wolcott, June 14, 1797, Oliver Wolcott Papers, LIV, Connecticut Historical Society; and Mary Pinckney to Margaret Manigault, June 11, 1797, Manigault Family Papers, II.

public outcry in the United States when the dispatches were published, the agents whose actions seemed nefarious were more inclined to prevent war with the United States than were members of the Directory. In delaying the negotiations, Talleyrand and his associates did not intend to risk the peace but only to reward themselves.

The American delegation itself was divided on the importance of keeping the negotiations open. From the time of his appointment Gerry believed that the best strategy was to prolong the talks as long as possible. This attitude explains, in part, his receptivity to Talleyrand's delaying tactics. The mission's total failure, Gerry thought, would bring war and "disgrace republicanism, and make it the scoff of despots."[62] Pinckney quickly became disenchanted with Gerry, complaining that his colleague was "habitually suspicious, and hesitates so much, that it is very unpleasant to do business with him." Pinckney further noted French "attempts to divide the envoys" and observed that "some civilities are shewn to Mr. G[erry] and none to the two others."[63]

Marshall, too, became increasingly restive and sought to force the French to negotiate or suspend the mission, a reaction which Alexandre Hauterive, a confidant of Talleyrand, had predicted before the negotiations began.[64] Marshall did not expect war if the negotiations failed, and this was the basis of his disagreement with Gerry. And he differed with Gerry on the republican nature of France. "That she is not and never will be a republick is a truth which I scarcely dare whisper even to myself," Marshall wrote. "It is in America and America only that human liberty has found an asylum."[65]

The differences among the envoys became apparent to the French by mid-December, when Bellamy and Hottinguer intervened directly for the last time. Hottinguer called on Pinckney under the pretense of seeking advice on his Georgia landholdings. But his main interest was to determine if the envoys had changed their minds on financial aid during the previous six weeks. Meeting as a group for the first time in almost a month, the envoys reemphasized their position and added that they would treat only with officially accredited agents. A few days later, a woman told Pinckney at a dinner party, perhaps Talleyrand's, that the Americans must offer a loan or

[62] William V. Murray reported that "Mr. Gerry's idea is to delay and gain time." Murray to John Q. Adams, Oct. 1, 1797, Murray Papers, Pierpont Morgan Lib. See also Gerry to Murray, Dec. 28, 1797, Gratz Collection, Historical Society of Pennsylvania, Philadelphia; Gerry to John Adams, July 3, 1797, Adams Papers.

[63] Charles C. Pinckney to Thomas Pinckney, Dec. 22, 1797, Pickering Papers, VIII; Charles C. Pinckney to Rufus King, Dec. 14, 1797, King Papers, Lib. Cong.

[64] Alexandre Hauterive to Pierre Adet, July 16, 1797, Correspondance Politique, Supplement, II.

[65] Marshall to Charles Lee, Oct. 12-[27], 1797, Diplomatic Dispatches, Fr., VI, RG 59.

they would not be received.[66] The envoys then began to draw up a memorial listing United States' grievances. They originally intended to request their passports, but Gerry refused to take such a step, thus enabling the informal negotiations to continue.[67]

Bellamy now approached Marshall, undoubtedly in conjunction with Hottinguer's visit to Pinckney, to inquire if Marshall would consider the use of Beaumarchais's claim against Virginia as the personal bribe to Talleyrand, a step that would allow the negotiations to begin again. Bellamy explained that the Beaumarchais claim could be included in the final peace settlement, with the United States accepting responsibility for its payment. The new bribe proposal would allow Talleyrand and his associates immediate access to needed capital. Beaumarchais had urged Bellamy to present his claim in just such a context.[68]

Marshall replied equivocally that he would consider the proposal, but only if Americans' claims against the French government were also included in the final settlement. When he informed Pinckney of the new plan, however, he said that he would not commit himself on the question, since he was Beaumarchais's lawyer. Pinckney rejected the idea out of hand as another bribe request. After the dispatches were published, Bellamy complained to Beaumarchais that it had been a simple proposition bearing no implications of corruption. To Joseph Pitcairn, however, Bellamy gave another explanation, saying that he wanted to get the "£100,000 throu[gh] his hands." Bellamy had conceived the idea "from having heard that Marshalls brother had bought one similarly situated for 50 p[er] cent."[69]

[66] This woman has long been identified as Reine Philiberte de Varicourt, Madame de Villette. Theodore Lyman, *The Diplomacy of the United States* (Boston, 1826), 336, appears to have been the first to claim this. James T. Austin, *Life of Elbridge Gerry* . . . , II (Boston, 1829), 202n, refutes Lyman. Bowman, *Struggle for Neutrality*, 317, DeConde, *Quasi-War*, 51-52, and Zahniser, *Pinckney*, 175-176, all identify the woman as Madame de Villette and as an agent of Talleyrand. They do not, however, cite any document that demonstrates the connections, if any, between Madame de Villette and Talleyrand. Zahniser and DeConde cite the letter of Mary Pinckney to Margaret Manigault, Mar. 9, 1798, Manigault Family Papers, II, as their source. Mary Pinckney's letter does discuss Madame de Villette as a person unknown to Margaret Manigault, but she does not hint of any French connections. She speaks of Madame de la Forest, who had approached Charles C. Pinckney at a party about three months before. Madame de la Forest had known both Mary Pinckney and Margaret Manigault when her husband served as French consul in Charleston. He was a close associate of Talleyrand in the foreign office. Pinckney's account of the episode is in American Envoys to Pickering, Dec. 24, 1797, Diplomatic Dispatches, Fr., VI, RG 59.

[67] Charles C. Pinckney to Rufus King, Dec. 27, 1797, Pickering Papers, XXII.

[68] American Envoys to Pickering, Dec. 24, 1797, Diplomatic Dispatches, Fr., VI, RG 59; Beaumarchais to Pierre Bellamy, and Beaumarchais to Talleyrand, Dec. 21, 1797, Bellamy to Beaumarchais, Dec. 26, 1797, private archives.

[69] Joseph Pitcairn to Rufus King, July 6, 1798, King Papers, XXIX, N.-Y. Hist. Soc.

Bellamy's allusion was to John and James Marshall's purchase of the Fairfax claims in northern Virginia in 1797 during James's negotiations with Hottinguer in Amsterdam.[70]

Marshall's response, as contrasted with Pinckney's blunt refusals to Bellamy and Hottinguer, dictated Talleyrand's next move. Historians have long agreed that Talleyrand now selected Gerry as the most amenable of the envoys and chose to deal with him alone. In reality, Talleyrand's strategy was to exclude only Pinckney; he meant to continue negotiations with both Marshall and Gerry. Scholars have accepted Marshall's account in his journal, in which he depicted himself and Pinckney as equally adamant against the French. Actually, this was not the case. Nor can the division within the commission be attributed to Gerry alone, for Marshall accepted and participated in the gradual exclusion of Pinckney.

Talleyrand presented his new strategy at a party which Gerry gave for American guests and for Talleyrand, Bellamy, Hottinguer, and Hauteval; neither Marshall nor Pinckney was present. At the dinner Bellamy and Hottinguer renewed the demand for a bribe, which Gerry angrily rejected. More important, Gerry was informed that the French would no longer negotiate with Pinckney.[71]

In mid-January Beaumarchais assumed an important role in the negotiations. He asked Marshall and Gerry to discuss Adams's address to Congress and submitted a short memorial, approved by Bellamy, in which he analyzed portions that the French considered offensive and renewed the demand for an explanation. The negotiations had now reverted to the pattern of the original encounters in October, except that the bribe went unmentioned. Gerry and Marshall discussed the memorial with Beaumarchais, in Pinckney's absence. Again they refused to give an explanation.[72]

After January, Beaumarchais dealt with Marshall, while Louis d'Autremont, a former exile who had lived in Asylum, Pennsylvania, and returned to Paris with Talleyrand, met with Gerry.[73] Pinckney's contact was

[70] Van Winter, *Amsterdamsche Handel,* II, 280.

[71] Gerry to John Adams, July 8, 1799, Adams Papers. This was the last time the bribe request was made. According to the Marshall Journal, Dec. 31, 1797, the decision was reached not to give money, but, significantly, no mention was made of Pinckney's role: "We had another meeting in my room in which it was again determined that we should give no money and that Mr. Gerry should make this determination known to those who should apply to him."

[72] Notation of two drafts of Beaumarchais to Elbridge Gerry and John Marshall, Jan. 13, 15, 1798, Gerry to Beaumarchais, Jan. 15, 1978, private archives; Beaumarchais to Gerry and Marshall, Jan. 17, 1798, Gerry Papers, Pierpont Morgan Lib.

[73] D'Autremont's name is spelled as Dutrimont in the dispatches and in Marshall's Journal, Feb. 3, 1798. For an identification of d'Autremont see William Rawle

Pierre Du Pont de Nemours, who called on the third envoy two days after Gerry's party. Knowing that the foreign office had decided to exclude Pinckney from further discussions, Du Pont did not mention the negotiations but stated that he wanted advice on land purchases in the United States.[74]

A shift in lodging by Gerry and Marshall in November had facilitated Pinckney's later exclusion. The two envoys had moved to a house leased by Madame de Villette. A devoted follower of Voltaire, Madame de Villette supported the United States and had many American acquaintances, including Fulwar Skipwith and Joel Barlow. Barlow had probably recommended her apartments to the envoys, since Madame de Villette found herself in financial straits. Explaining to his wife why he had moved into the house of an attractive widow in her thirties, Gerry said that Paris crowds and burglars had made the Pinckney house so dangerous that he had to sleep with a "pair of pistols under my pillow." The Pinckney family never perceived this danger. In their new setting Madame de Villette offered her American tenants several social services: she accompanied Marshall to the theater, taught Gerry French, and organized parties and dinners for the two envoys.[75]

Madame de Villette's role in the negotiations has long intrigued scholars. Two recent accounts of the WXYZ affair declare that she was an agent of Talleyrand.[76] However titillating it would be to have a *femme fatale* influencing the course of the negotiations, we have no evidence that Madame de Villette was Talleyrand's agent. The Paris police did have an informer who watched her house for visitors. Posing as a wine merchant, this police

---

to Pickering, Oct. 31, 1798, Pickering Papers, XXIII. On the d'Autremont family in Asylum, Pennsylvania, see Theophile Cazenove's report on the Asylum Company in Holland Land Co. Papers, 268.

[74] Du Pont was establishing a land company in the United States with the expected financial backing from Talleyrand and Beaumarchais. Mack Thompson, "Causes and Circumstances of the Du Pont Family's Emigration," *French Historical Studies*, VI (1969), 66-68, 70. Du Pont complained of the hostile feeling toward Pinckey in the foreign ministry. He argued that officers there had confused Charles C. Pinckney with Thomas Pinckney, the former minister to Great Britain. It was not confusion, however, but deliberate French policy to exclude Pinckney. Pierre Du Pont de Nemours to Victor Du Pont, Jan. 2, 1798, Du Pont Family Papers, Winterthur MSS, 6-40, Eleutherian Mills Historical Library, Wilmington, Del.

[75] The quotation is from Elbridge Gerry to Ann Gerry, Nov. 25, 1797, Gerry Papers, Lib. Cong.; John Marshall to Charles C. Pinckney [Dec. 17, 1797], Pinckney Papers, Box B, South Carolina Historical Society. For other descriptions of Madame de Villette see John Marshall to Mary Marshall, Nov. 27, 1797, Marshall Papers; Mary Pinckney to Margaret Manigault, Mar. 9, 1798, Manigault Family Papers, II; Thomas H. Perkins Diary, Apr. 3, 1795, Thomas H. Perkins Papers, Journal in Paris, 1795, Mass. Hist. Soc.; Joel Barlow to Fulwar Skipwith, Aug. 9 [1798 or 1799], Beinecke Library, Yale University. For a biography of Madame de Villette see Jean Stern, *Belle et Bonne* (Paris, 1938).

[76] DeConde, *Quasi-War*, 51-53; Zahniser, *Pinckney*, 176.

agent, known as Kahion, regularly entered the house but was unable to steal any papers. The police did not inform Talleyrand of their surveillance until after Marshall and Pinckney had left Paris. Because most of the visitors to Madame de Villette's house were Talleyrand's agents, he demanded that the surveillance be dropped.[77]

The only public results of the final three months of the negotiations were memorials—manifestos might be a better word—and countermemorials. These served the interests of posterity rather than those of diplomacy. At the end of January the envoys sent Talleyrand a lengthy statement of the United States's position, written mainly by Marshall and called by his biographer Albert Beveridge, with exaggeration, "one of the ablest state papers produced by American diplomacy."[78] The paper reiterated American grievances based on the doctrine of neutrality as Jefferson had enunciated it to the British in 1793. Talleyrand made no response, commenting to Henry Rutledge, Pinckney's nephew and secretary, that the French were not accustomed to receiving such long epistles.[79] After waiting three weeks, Marshall pressed Gerry to request their passports. Gerry agreed, but matters of state were postponed while Marshall and Gerry escorted Madame de Villette and another Frenchwoman on a long weekend at Madame de Villette's country chateau.[80]

In February, Talleyrand devised new tactics, which the Directory approved without debate. He sought approval for a loan, which he had not done in his first memoir in October, and he again insisted that the Americans offer an explanation of Adams's speech. The strategy of delay was thus to continue. Now, however, Talleyrand proposed to negotiate only with the most receptive envoy and send the other two away.[81] Another month was to pass before he selected Gerry over Marshall.

As soon as the Directory approved the new memorial on American policy, members of the American community in Paris sent home letters warning of the possibility of war. As it had during Monroe's ministry in

[77] See Marquisse de Villette, La Famille de Beaumarchais, dossier 918, F7, 6152, Archives Nationales, Paris, for the items on surveillance.

[78] American Envoys to Talleyrand, Jan. [31], 1798, Correspondance Politique, XLIX; Beveridge, *Life of Marshall*, II, 297.

[79] American Envoys to Pickering, Feb. 7, 1798, Diplomatic Dispatches, Fr., VI, RG 59.

[80] Mary Pinckney to Margaret Manigault, Mar. 9, 1798, Manigault Family Papers, II; Charles C. Pinckney to Thomas Pinckney, Mar. 13, 1798, Free Library of Philadelphia; John Marshall to [Charles Lee], Mar. 4, 1798, *ibid;* American Envoys to Nathaniel Cutting, Feb. 27, 1798, Gerry Papers, Henry E. Huntington Library; Elbridge Gerry to John Adams, July 8, 1799, Gerry Papers, Lib. Cong.

[81] Talleyrand, Memoir, Feb. [3-18], 1798, Correspondance Politique, XLIX.

1796, the French government dropped strong hints that war was in the offing and appealed to France's friends to help prevent it. Without exception, those Americans who made the strongest statements were ideologically committed to republicanism and had backed Jefferson against Adams in 1796. Barlow, for example, described Pinckney and Marshall as captives of the British interest. "The first [Pinckney] was a man who had just been refused and could not be offered again without an insult, as it was so received. The second [Marshall] was a man whose effegy had been burnt in Virginia for his violent defense of the English treaty, at least it was so reported and believed in this place, the third [Gerry] was a little make-weight man appointed with the intention that he should have no influence. . . . if Gerry had been sent alone, and not been shackled with the other two, the Directorie would have negotiated with him without any difficulty."[82]

Skipwith advocated a policy which Pinckney and Marshall would have regarded as abject surrender. Although he called Gerry "one of the tryed patriots of '75 and one of the remaining republican chiefs of the American states," Skipwith doubted Gerry's ability to stand up to the other envoys and take decisive action. He believed that the United States should "confess some of our errors" and "lay their sins heavily upon the shoulders of a few persons who perpetrated them." The United States, he wrote to Jefferson, must determine to "modify or break the English treaty with Jay, and to lend France as much money, should she ask for it, as she lent us in the hour of distress."[83]

Gerry and Marshall returned from their visit to the country to find a different situation, at least in Gerry's eyes. After meeting with d'Autremont on the day of his return, Gerry reported that Talleyrand sought a loan to be granted at the end of the war with Great Britain, an arrangement thus preserving the facade of American neutrality. Gerry argued that this represented a change in the French position; Marshall and Pinckney disagreed, finding it only a tactic to keep the envoys in Paris. Compromising their differences on these points, the envoys asked for their first meeting with Talleyrand since October. It was understood that Pinckney would not reveal that their instructions positively forbade any loan to France.[84]

In the first week of March the envoys twice met with Talleyrand, for the first time discussing substantive issues. Rather than serving to open formal talks, these meetings convinced each side that an impasse had been reached. Talleyrand was disappointed to learn that the envoys had not asked for new

[82] Barlow to Abraham Baldwin, Mar. 4, 1798, Barlow Papers, IV.

[83] Skipwith to Jefferson, Mar. 17, 1798, Wolcott Papers, XII.

[84] Memorandum of American Envoys [Mar. 5, 1798], Pinckney Family Papers, Lib. Cong.; American Envoys to Pickering, Mar. 9, 1798, Diplomatic Dispatches, Fr., VI, RG 59.

instructions in December. At the second meeting Pinckney informed Talleyrand that their instructions prevented them from agreeing to a loan of any kind. Although the envoys thought they detected a look of surprise on Talleyrand's face at this information, he had received the same report from Pitcairn in November. More important for Adams's later decision to reopen the negotiations, Talleyrand now dropped his demand for the loan.

The maneuvers by each side to cast blame on the other for the collapse of negotiations obscured what had been accomplished. Talleyrand still declined to abandon French maritime attacks or discrimination against American vessels, and the envoys still refused to acknowledge any contradiction between the Jay Treaty and the French alliance. But the envoys now met with the foreign minister rather than his unofficial agents; the bribe and loan ultimata had not been renewed. Each side had assessed the position and determination of the other. The negotiations were deadlocked, but not hopelessly so.

As a result of his meetings with the envoys, Talleyrand released his February memorial and arranged to have it sent to the United States for translation and publication in American newspapers. He now demanded that one American who was "impartial" stay in Paris and negotiate.[85] The March meetings had convinced him that Marshall was as obstinate as Pinckney. Rather than accepting the invitation to depart, however, Marshall and Pinckney set to work on an answer to Talleyrand. They, too, took special care to see that copies of their memorial reached the United States quickly.[86] It was almost as if the negotiations were being conducted by newspapers three thousand miles from Paris.

Publication of charges and countercharges was the mode of French-American diplomacy in the first half of 1798. Within a day of the submission of the envoys' April memorial to Talleyrand, Congress ordered publication of their first dispatches, thus touching off the WXYZ affair in the United States. Gerry had reported Bellamy's statement

> that it was worthy of the attention of the Envoys to consider whether by so small a sacrifice [a loan] they would establish a peace with France, or whether they would risk the consequences; that if nothing could be done by the envoys, arrangements could be made forthwith to ravage the coasts of the United States by frigates from Santo Domingo; that small States which had offended France were suffering by it; that

[85] Talleyrand to American Envoys, Mar. 18, 1798, Gerry Papers, Pierpont Morgan Lib.; copy with marginal notation ordering translation in Correspondance Politique, XLIX.

[86] American Envoys to Talleyrand, Apr. 3, 1798, Correspondance Politique, XLIX; copy in American Envoys to Pickering, Apr. 3, 1798, Diplomatic Dispatches, Fr., VI, RG 59.

> Hamburg and other Cities in that quarter would within a month or two have their Government changed; that Switzerland would undergo the same operation, and Portugal would probably be in a worse predicament; that the expedition against England would be certainly pursued; and that the present period was the most favorable, if we wished to adopt any measures for pacification.[87]

Gerry also quoted Talleyrand to the effect "that the information Mr. Bellamy had given me was just and might always be relied on." No amount of argument by Talleyrand or by a few Americans in Paris could begin to counteract the revulsion caused by these revelations. Talleyrand's report, which was published over two months later, discussed consuls' rights, prize courts, and American violations of treaties, while his agents spoke of crushing the United States if that nation did not submit to France.[88]

In Paris, Gerry informed his colleagues that he would remain there if his presence would prevent war.[89] Marshall and Pinckney had little doubt that Gerry had long since made his decision. In early April they prepared to depart without demanding their passports or being officially asked to leave. The situation produced no expulsions or ultimata but, rather, a tacit acknowledgment that Gerry would remain. Gerry complained to John Adams that he now found himself virtually a hostage, sacrificing his reputation to the hope for peace with France.[90] The other two envoys left Paris with animus toward Gerry. Mary Pinckney charged that he "had been false to his colleagues and wanting to his country."[91]

But Talleyrand's hope that he would have an "impartial" Gerry with whom to deal was quickly dispelled. From the beginning of the mission, Gerry had seen the United States as right and France as wrong in the dispute, but he considered the prevention of war paramount. He informed Talleyrand that he could not negotiate officially and that France had no right to choose which American would represent the United States. He further explained that he would remain only long enough to receive instructions from Adams, which he hoped would assure the continuation of diplomatic relations.

[87] The quotation is from American Envoys to Pickering, Dec. 24, 1797, Diplomatic Dispatches, Fr., VI, RG 59; in *Message of the President of the United States submitted to both Houses of Congress, April 3, 1798* (Philadelphia, 1798), 67. Pickering substituted Y for Bellamy.

[88] *Aurora* (Philadelphia), June 16, 1798.

[89] Marshall Journal, Mar. [19]-20, 1798.

[90] John Marshall to Talleyrand, Apr. 13, 1798, Correspondance Politique, XLIX; Talleyrand to Pinckney and Marshall, Apr. 13, 1798, *ibid.;* Gerry to John Adams, Apr. 16, 1798, Adams Papers.

[91] Mary Pinckney to Margaret Manigault, Apr. 15, 1798, Manigault Family Papers, II.

Nonetheless, in July Talleyrand informed the Directory that the best way to prevent war was to keep Gerry in Paris as long as possible.[92]

By mid-May the published copies of the envoys' dispatches had reached Great Britain, where they were reprinted by the British government. The dispatches carried the initials W, X, Y, and Z, which Pickering had inserted for the names of Talleyrand's first group of agents. Sandoz Rollin called on Talleyrand the day the published dispatches reached Paris; from Talleyrand's comments he deduced that the bribery charges were true. Talleyrand asserted to Rollin that the American government was trying to force him out of office.[93] In reality, the publication of the dispatches only prevented Talleyrand from resigning his office in order to assume the ambassadorship to Constantinople, a step he had planned in conjunction with Napoleon's Egyptian campaign.[94]

Talleyrand did not need to fear for his position. While the war with England continued, the Directory saw little need for immediate peace with the United States. Unlike Talleyrand, a majority of the Directory remained adamant on the question of an apology for the Jay Treaty. The release of the dispatches could not force Talleyrand's resignation unless other policy considerations came into play. The foreign minister had secured Napoleon's support, and no attempt was made to replace him, despite growing attacks in the newspapers. Within a month of the publication of the dispatches, Talleyrand had regained control of American policy.[95]

In the United States, where he arrived in mid-June, Marshall was feted as a symbol of the staunch American resisting the corruptions of Europe. Not a little of the outpouring reflected Federalist efforts to secure the newly won political advantage gained through the WXYZ exposé. Marshall, however, was not the man the extreme Federalists in Adams's cabinet wanted at that moment. He argued, as he had for six months in Paris, that France did not want war and would not declare it. He believed that if Adams's defensive measures proposed in May 1797 had been adopted, they would have been "the best negotiator we could have employed." When Marshall returned to Philadelphia, Gerry's defense of his decision to stay in Paris was printed. The president announced that he would not send another representative to France

[92] Gerry to Talleyrand, Apr. 20, 1798, Pickering Papers; Talleyrand to Directory, July 10, 1798, in G. Pallain, ed., *Le Ministère de Talleyrand sous le Directoire* (Paris, 1891), 304-305, 309, 310.

[93] Rollin dispatch, May 31, 1798, in Bailleu, ed., *Preusen und Frankreich*, I, 210.

[94] Carl Lokke, "Pourquoi Talleyrand ne fut pas Envoyé à Constantinople," *Annales Historiques de la Révolution Française* (1933), 157-158.

[95] Rollin dispatch, June 28, 1798, in Bailleu, ed., *Preusen und Frankreich*, I 213. For one attack on Talleyrand see *Nouvelle Manière de négocier le paix, les Rapprochements, les Réconciliations ou l'art du Négociation Perfectionné & Simplifié* (Paris[?], 1798).

unless assured beforehand that he would be officially received by the Directory.[96] The anti-French atmosphere generated by many Federalists notwithstanding, prospects for peace had improved. Gerry still hoped for a settlement, Marshall did not expect a war to occur, and Adams publicly spoke of new representatives and future negotiations with the French government.

The Republicans had been almost paralyzed by the WXYZ affair. Unable to make any effective reply to the dispatches, they agreed to increased defense appropriations. Jefferson told John Rutledge, Jr., that the United States "was much too weak to resist france, and we ought to rub thro' our difficulties as well as we c[oul]d preserving peace *in all events*."[97] Edward Livingston, a Republican leader in the House, optimistically noted that France had dropped its bribe request and halved the amount sought for a loan, but he made no proposals. From Madison came the exclamation that he could not believe France's stupidity in its policy toward the United States. Monroe went so far as to refuse to answer any letters from France for almost two years for fear of being tarred again with the pro-French label.[98]

Reviewing the situation, Jefferson expressed optimism that the Republicans would regain their strength, but almost solely on domestic issues. Clearly, the Adams administration had not been bent on war, and, most important for Jefferson, Gerry remained in Paris.[99] The WXYZ affair had its most profound consequences in eliminating Republican opposition to Adams's foreign policy, as the president had failed to do in 1797. For the first time since the signing of the Jay Treaty, issues relating to policy toward France were debated among Federalists, particularly Adams and a majority of his cabinet, and not between Federalists and Republicans.

Historians have viewed events after the publication of the WXYZ dispatches as separate and distinct from the negotiations in Paris. In fact, the

[96] Quotation from Abigail Adams to Jeremy Belknap, June 21, 1798, Adams Papers; Thomas Jefferson to James Madison, June 21, 1798, Madison Papers, XXI; George Cabot to Rufus King, Oct. 6, 1798, Feb. 16, 1799, King Papers, XLI, N.-Y. Hist. Soc.; *[Annals of Congress] Debates and Proceedings in the Congress of the United States, 1789-1824*, IX (Washington, D.C., 1851), 5th Cong., 2d Sess., June 21, 1798, 3459-3460.

[97] John Rutledge, Jr., to Edward Rutledge, Mar. 6, 1798, Dreer Collection, Hist. Soc. Pa.

[98] Edward Livingston to Robert Livingston, Apr. 8, 1798, Robert R. Livingston Papers, XXX, N.-Y. Hist. Soc.; James Madison to Thomas Jefferson, Apr. 29, May 13, 1798, Madison Papers, XX; James Monroe to George Ervin, Apr. 4, 1800, in Stanislaus M. Hamilton, ed., *The Writings of James Monroe*, III (New York, 1899), 171-173.

[99] Thomas Jefferson to J. W. Eppes, May 6, 1798, and Jefferson to Martha Randolph, June 15, 1798, Jefferson Papers, Misc. MSS, Mass. Hist. Soc.; Jefferson to James Madison, June 21, 1798, Madison Papers, XXI.

summer and fall of 1798 saw continued progress, and that progress had its origins in the abortive peace mission. Talleyrand gained the Directory's approval to stop French piracy in the West Indies, a policy he had advocated almost a year before.[100] He now felt uncertain whether the United States intended to go to war, and this made it more urgent for him to start to settle the issues. He sent Louis Pichon to The Hague to open talks with the American minister William Vans Murray. In a direct response to Adams's invitation, in his June speech on Marshall's return, Talleyrand gave assurances that any new envoy would be officially received. Murray, who passed the news on privately to the president, would accept only an informal statement from Talleyrand, although the foreign minister took pains to inform Americans in Paris that he would offer an official one if so requested.[101]

In October 1798, Gerry returned to Boston and made additional reports on the last months of his mission. Much of this information he conveyed to Adams alone. Adams persuaded Gerry not to respond to Secretary of State Pickering's public attacks on his performance in Paris. In return, the president never repudiated Gerry's decision to remain in Paris and break up the commission. Marshall and Pinckney refused to enter into public controversy with Gerry, even though Pickering urged them to reveal Gerry's "treachery."[102] Although the silent Republicans did not recognize it, their prospects depended on the growing division between Adams and some members of his cabinet over French policy. At the new session of Congress, Adams made the surprise announcement that he had reopened negotiations with the French, acting on reports from Murray, Gerry, John Q. Adams, Barlow, and George Logan.[103]

Adams had always understood the critical difference between diplomacy and war. Independence based on neutrality had been his policy, inherited from Washington as set forth by Jefferson. The WXYZ affair was an eruption caused by French reaction to the Jay Treaty. Adams led the country,

[100] Stinchcombe, "Talleyrand," *JAH*, LXII (1975), 576, 576n.

[101] Peter P. Hill, *William Vans Murray, Federalist Diplomat: The Shaping of Peace with France, 1797-1801* (Syracuse, N.Y., 1971), 103-115, 123-131; marginal note by Fulwar Skipwith on Talleyrand to Louis Pichon, Sept. 28, 1798, Clausten-Pickett Papers, VII, Lib. Cong.; Skipwith to St. George Tucker, Apr. 18, 1799, Tucker-Coleman Papers, College of William and Mary.

[102] Gerry to John Adams, July 8, 1799, Adams Papers; Pickering to John Marshall, Oct. 15, Nov. 5, 1798, Pickering Papers, IX; Marshall to Gerry, Nov. 12, 1798, Marshall Papers.

[103] Adams's letters to the *Boston Patriot*, in Adams, ed., *Works of Adams*, IX, 241, 244-246; Stephen G. Kurtz, "The French Mission of 1799-1800: Concluding Chapter in the Statecraft of John Adams," *Political Science Quarterly*, LXXX (1965), 543-557.

slowly and unsteadily, to be sure, but consistently, toward the settlement with France which he achieved two years later. He knew that diplomacy was a continuing process affected by many considerations; progress and peace did not depend on clear choices. In a delicate situation Adams was willing to ignore the improprieties of Talleyrand's agents because of the possibility of gains through increased American strength and French compromises.

More than most of his contemporaries in 1798, Adams grasped the nature of relations between the United States and Europe. But he was not alone, and many leaders in his own party approved his second mission to France, including Washington, Hamilton, Pinckney, Marshall, and Gerry. Beneath the bombast following the WXYZ revelations, Americans knew that if France, as personified by Talleyrand, was corrupt, it was nevertheless powerful. "Our nation is, as it were," David Austin, Jr., wrote to an unbelieving Oliver Wolcott, "united in the figure of a triangle with Great Britain and France." Any attempt to improve upon one of these points, he explained, meant only that "you are followed by the other." Austin concluded, "Here we hang, and here we must consent to hang until propitious heaven lend its propitious aid."[104] In the WXYZ affair, John Adams realized that a settlement with France was essential if the United States was to begin to extricate itself from the crosscurrents of European war and diplomacy.

[104] Austin to Oliver Wolcott, Oct. 7, 1799, Wolcott Papers, X.

The Sources of Presidential Power: John Adams and the Challenge to Executive Primacy

JEAN S. HOLDER

Americans have characteristically held ambivalent views toward power—particularly presidential power. In the decade that began in 1970 the pendulum moved full swing as critics of various stripes first deplored the "imperial presidency" of Richard Nixon and then rejected the leadership of Jimmy Carter who tried to strip the presidency of its regal trappings. The present-day ambivalence is, in part, a legacy from the Founding Fathers who resolved their own inner and interpersonal conflicts in regard to power by creating an executive office of minimal definition in the Constitution. These men who had fought to free themselves from what they perceived to be the threat of enslavement to royal tyranny were caught between their fear of creating a quasi-regal leader and their belief that strength in the executive was essential to effective, balanced government. In providing a merely skeletal description of the presidential role, the framers of the Constitution skirted their own dilemma but set the stage for a power struggle that would essentially begin with the second American presidency. As the idol of the entire nation, George Washington conducted a magisterial administration; his personal prestige and stature made his word fiat among contemporaries. John Adams enjoyed no such advantage and would, therefore, be the first president to test the viability of the executive office on its constitutional basis. Because Adams experienced a unique combination of obstacles to the exercise of extra-constitutional authority, his presidency provides an ideal test case for evaluating recent arguments concerning the sources of presidential power.

In his influential study, *Presidential Power: The Politics of Leadership*, Richard

JEAN S. HOLDER is an assistant professor of history at Gettysburg College.

Political Science Quarterly Volume 101 Number 4 Centennial Year 1886–1986 601

Neustadt set the stage for an ongoing debate, contending that the power of the presidency lies in the power to persuade: formal powers are no guarantee of actual power, but translate into command only under unusual circumstances. The chief executive is a negotiator who enjoys specific advantages in terms of his constitutional power and status, but success in office depends largely upon the president's ability to convince others in authority that their own interests will be advanced by support of presidential policy. Neustadt draws analogies to the president's relations with leaders of foreign nations in which "power is persuasion and persuasion becomes bargaining." Although he uses the term "persuasion" in its broadest sense to include the tools for bargaining that are inherent in the executive office, Neustadt emphasizes that "the probabilities of power do not derive from the literary theory of the Constitution."[1]

In a more recent and detailed study, Richard M. Pious argues the opposite view, contending that constitutional power is indeed the foundation of the president's authority and ability to command. Pious emphasizes the developmental nature of the executive office: the ambiguous language of the Constitution predetermined the evolutionary character of the American presidency. The Constitution confers neither the title nor the plenary authority of "chief executive" but states that "the Executive Power shall be vested in a President of the United States," phrasing that allows for a wide variety of interpretations. The key to the developing presidency is the president's initiative in the exercise of constitutional power and implied prerogatives; the president's unilateral assertion of power provokes a response that shapes the office. A successful initiative that benefits the country and is approved by the public as well as Congress and the courts strengthens the office, creating what Pious terms a "frontlash" effect. A president can implement initiatives successfully and yet weaken the office if the policies provoke an extremely adverse reaction, a "backlash" effect. When a president is checked in his efforts to exert executive initiatives, then the authority of the office is diminished. By this process of recurrent effort presidents have expanded or contracted their executive influence and the power of the office as well.[2]

Pious acknowledges that political factors such as election mandates, mobilization of public opinion, and party lineups in Congress have a marginal effect but contends that they do not determine what a leader can accomplish in office: "The fundamental and irreducible core of presidential power rests not on influence, persuasion, public opinion, elections or party, but rather on the successful assertion of constitutional authority to resolve crises and domestic issues."[3]

Although recent studies tend to focus on the modern presidency, the ideal case study for an analysis of the sources of presidential power appears in the period of the early republic, the administration of John Adams from 1797 to 1801. The

[1] Richard Neustadt, *Presidential Power: The Politics of Leadership* (New York: John Wiley, 1961), 78–87, 32–37, 114.

[2] Richard M. Pious, *The American Presidency* (New York: Basic Books, 1979), 38–50, 213.

[3] Ibid., 10.

Adams presidency was distinctive in a number of respects, not the least of which was the second president's position as successor to George Washington. No other chief executive would succeed a leader of Washington's stature or have a former president serve as commanding general of the army. Adams was handicapped in having received no endorsement from his illustrious predecessor; Washington's favor and reflected glory fell upon Adams's intraparty adversary, Alexander Hamilton.[4] Adams was further handicapped politically in having been elected by a narrow margin, opposed in the election by a small but powerful faction of Federalists led by Hamilton, who saw Adams as a threat to his control of party policy. Hamilton's supporters dominated the Senate and played an influential role in the evenly divided House of Representatives. Vice-President Thomas Jefferson served as the able leader of the Republican opposition, putting Adams in a position of crossfire between opponents in government.

Public expectation that he would honor George Washington's political appointments served as a double handicap to Adams, depriving him of even the minimal degree of patronage that other early presidents enjoyed as well as burdening him with a holdover cabinet whose three principal members worked actively to defeat the presidential policies and to advance the interests of Hamilton, whom they regarded as the oracle of political wisdom as well as their personal mentor. Until mid-1798 Adams's working cabinet consisted of only three men. The attorney general was considered merely an adviser to the government and was expected to continue the private practice of law. This was particularly unfortunate for Adams because Attorney General Charles Lee was the only supporter of the President in the cabinet until Benjamin Stoddert became the first secretary of the navy in 1798.[5] Adams experienced a unique handicap in office in that he had a major resistance movement in his own cabinet.[6] Replacing Washington's appointees in order to distribute the political plums of patronage would have been unthinkable in the public view. When opportunities for making new appointments occurred, Adams was limited in his options by the need for approval from Hamilton's clique of supporters in the Senate.

Having neither cabinet members nor party leaders who would attempt to advance his interests in Congress, Adams was forced to rely upon the formal, constitutionally prescribed means of speeches, written recommendations, and messages. He accepted his isolated position and tolerated what would today be considered overbearing opposition from cabinet members because he shared to some extent the antipower outlook, the abhorrence of executive despotism that had become characteristic of the American political climate as a result of British

[4] For a discussion of Hamilton's role, see James MacGregor Burns, *Presidential Government, the Crucible of Leadership* (Boston: Houghton Mifflin, 1966), 17, 371n. See also James Thomas Flexner, *George Washington: Anguish and Farewell, 1793–1799* (Boston: Little, Brown, 1972), 337–39.

[5] George Gibbs, ed., *Memoirs of the Administration of Washington and John Adams, Edited from the Papers of Oliver Wolcott, Secretary of the Treasury*, 2 vols. (New York: n.p., 1856), 2:313–16.

[6] Pious, *American Presidency*, 211.

rule. A particular holdover fear from the colonial experience was apprehension of executive encroachment upon the legislature. Had Adams attempted to approach Congress in any direct, extra-constitutional way, he would have met with fierce resistance and hostility.[7]

Adams confronted a Congress that had polarized along lines of foreign orientation in the debates over the Jay Treaty, a document that brought into focus two irreconcilable views of the fundamental bases of American foreign policy. The Federalist followers of Alexander Hamilton believed that America's economic and commercial well-being depended upon trade with Britain and upon credit received from that country. Federalists tended to regard the British naval depredations on American commerce as an aberration, a necessity of their war of survival with France, and were willing to make substantial concessions to maintain peace with Britain. Republican followers of James Madison and Thomas Jefferson believed that America should counterbalance British power and dominance, increasing trade with France and other European countries and diminishing the British connection. The Republican leaders had tried repeatedly, without success, to secure legislation that would penalize Britain for its refusal to grant the United States a commercial treaty. The Jay Treaty, in relinquishing for twelve years the right of the United States to retaliate against British commercial policy and in appearing to accept British definition of neutral rights and freedom of the seas, committed the United States to Federalist foreign policy, placed France in a disadvantaged position in trade relationships, and outraged Republicans. Republican resentment was revived full force when France retaliated with naval war in 1797.[8]

Because Adams restored balance to foreign policy with conciliatory approaches to France and ultimately achieved a diplomatic settlement that minimized damage to Franco-American relations resulting from the British treaty, Jay's document appears more acceptable today than it did to Republican contemporaries. Indeed, few Federalists of the day defended the treaty except on the grounds that it prevented war with Britain or, at the least, forestalled a punitive commercial policy and further depredations, an argument that historians continue to advance.[9] The Jay Treaty set the framework for the intense party battle that would dominate the Adams years.

The Jay Treaty provided a pretext, if not a reason, for France to launch naval war on the United States as Adams began his administration. The French government's decree of 2 March 1797, an apparent response to the news of Adams's election, confirmed and extended a policy of naval aggression that had begun in the

[7] For a discussion of Jefferson's approach to Congress, see Robert M. Johnstone, *Jefferson and the Presidency: Leadership in the Young Republic* (Ithaca: Cornell University Press, 1978), 24–26. For a discussion of the anti-power attitude that prevailed, see James Sterling Young, *The Washington Community, 1800–1828* (New York: Columbia University Press, 1966), 59–64.

[8] Republicans believed that Federalists were deliberately provoking a quarrel with Britain's enemies. James Madison to Thomas Jefferson, 5 May 1798, James Madison, *Letters and Other Writings*, 4 vols. (Washington, D.C.: Congress, 1865), 2:134–40.

[9] The most complete recent discussion of the Jay Treaty is found in Jerald A. Combs, *The Jay Treaty: Political Battleground of the Founding Fathers* (Berkeley: University of California Press, 1970).

last months of Washington's administration.[10] The new policy would present Adams with a dual challenge, that of reconciling differences with France and resolving a conflict between political parties that would soon reach crisis proportions.

The combination of foreign and domestic crisis might have taxed Washington's successor to the utmost, but John Adams would face a third challenge in his relationship with the former president. Because the luster of George Washington has dimmed a bit over the years, it is difficult today to recapture the image of the "godlike" first president or to understand the influence that he wielded in his time. While other presidents have had cults and constituencies of admirers, George Washington's cult was the nation; and he carried his great prestige and influence into retirement with him. Republican leaders had rejoiced at his retirement, declaring that they were helpless in the face of his popularity.[11] When Washington returned to public life as commanding general of the army and demanded that President Adams's adversary, Alexander Hamilton, be awarded the second military position that would carry with it the actual command of the army, Adams was confronted with a major challenge to the exercise of his constitutional power.

When Adams took office in 1797, the citizenry of the new republic had looked to the transition with foreboding, questioning the ability of any successor to maintain public confidence and command of the office as Washington had done. Concern that the transition would be traumatic proved unfounded, but the stage was set, nevertheless, for a test of the viability of the office. Adams would face a turbulent four years with the starkest of political assets. What could a president accomplish without the support of party leaders or cabinet members, without patronage to dispense or an election mandate to provide a psychological advantage? Within this framework of imposing restrictions Adams began his administration.

Adams faced three immediate and interrelated challenges as president: finding a diplomatic solution to the French crisis; preparing the defenseless nation for war in the event that diplomacy failed; finding a middle ground in policy that would ease the polarization between Federalists and Republicans. He would eventually meet the three challenges, although not without frustration and defeat along the way.

Adams began his administration with action for which his constitutional authority was clear: he called a special session of Congress and addressed that body. The first message created a wave of enthusiasm for presidential policy among Federalists and elicited minimal grumbling from Republicans. Convinced that the country's most effective line of defense was the navy, Adams asked for immediate expansion of the nation's embryonic naval force. For the army he requested a minimal increase along with authority for further expansion if needed.[12] In his plans

[10] See William Stinchcombe et al, eds., *The Papers of John Marshall*, vol. 3 (Chapel Hill: University of North Carolina Press, 1979), 73–75, for a discussion of French naval policy in 1796–97.

[11] Thomas Jefferson to Aaron Burr, 17 June 1797, Thomas Jefferson Papers, Reel 21.

[12] Address to Congress, 16 May 1797, *Annals of Congress*, Fifth Congress, 2:54–59. Adams maintained throughout his life that the navy was "the most powerful, the safest, and the cheapest national defense for the country." To Thomas Jefferson, 13 October 1822, Adams Family Papers, Reel 119.

for defense Adams confronted a major challenge from Hamilton, who was already pressuring his supporters in Congress for a large increase in the army, a force that he expected to command and for which he had great ambitions. Hamilton made no secret of his desire to acquire the Floridas and Louisiana.[13]

Adams moved to check Hamilton's ambitions by appointing George Washington commanding general of the army, a move that backfired when Washington accepted the command on condition that he would not take the field until it should become "indispensable by the urgency of circumstances."[14] Adams would have had difficulty rejecting Washington's conditional acceptance in any event; but he accepted with alacrity, confident that he held the constitutional authority to name the commander in the field. Although Washington acknowledged after accepting command that Adams as president held the power to make field appointments, he soon succumbed to pressure from Adams's cabinet members to throw his great weight behind the appointment of Hamilton, threatening to resign should Adams refuse to comply.[15] Adams yielded of necessity, temporarily surrendering a power that was clearly his; but the defeat had not disarmed him. He was still commander-in-chief of the military and in charge of the nation's diplomacy.

Adams had begun his administration with a plan to conciliate Republicans and achieve rapprochement with France by sending a bipartisan mission to Paris to negotiate differences with the nation's former ally. He particularly wanted James Madison to serve; Madison was in good favor with the French government and also would provide reassurance to Republicans that their views were represented. Adams's cabinet members presented a wall of opposition to the appointment. Speaking for Secretary of State Timothy Pickering and Secretary of War James McHenry as well as himself, Treasury Secretary Oliver Wolcott, Jr. told Adams that the three would resign if Madison were appointed.[16] A brief flurry of confusion occurred as the secretaries channeled Adams's directives to Hamilton and received instructions from him in New York. The secretaries were astonished to learn that their mentor approved both the mission and the appointment of Madison. Hamilton warned that the measure should be adopted to allay public suspicions that the Hamiltonian clique wanted war: "I ought to apprize you . . . that a suspicion begins to dawn among the friends of the Government that the *actual* Ad-

[13] Hamilton outlined his plans for congressional action on defense to his spokesman, William L. Smith, 10 April 1798. Alexander Hamilton, *Papers of Alexander Hamilton*, Harold C. Syrett, ed., 26 vols. (New York: Columbia University Press, 1961–77), 21:29–41. Hamilton to Timothy Pickering, 17 March 1798, ibid., 364–67. Directions for a tax program to support the defense effort went to Oliver Wolcott, 6 June 1797, ibid., 543–47. Smith and Wolcott presented Hamilton's program to Congress as directed. Hamilton stated openly his opinion that the United States should acquire the Floridas and Louisiana. Hamilton to Harrison Gray Otis, 26 January 1799, Hamilton, *Papers*, 22:440–41.

[14] George Washington to John Adams, 4 July 1798, Adams Family Papers, Reel 390.

[15] Washington to Adams, 25 September 1798, George Washington, *The Writings of George Washington*, John C. Fitzpatrick, ed., 39 vols. (Washington, D.C.: U.S. Government Printing Office, 1931–44), 36:458–62.

[16] Adams to the Boston *Patriot*, 7 June 1809.

ministration is not much averse from war with France. How very important to obviate this."[17]

Unaware of Hamilton's views, Adams deferred to his secretaries' wishes on Madison's appointment, believing that party spirit made a bipartisan mission impossible and also fearing that Hamilton's supporters in the Senate would reject the nomination, further inflaming animosities between Republicans and Federalists. In succumbing to his cabinet members' proscription of the Madison appointment, a response that had the aura of political blackmail, Adams smoothed the way for the mission's progress; but in doing so, he may have committed the greatest mistake of his political career. For more than three years the secretaries connived to reduce Adams's presidential status to that of a figurehead and to make Hamilton's leadership the "actual administration."

Adams's willingness to defer to his department heads at the beginning of his administration was not evidence of weakness on his part but represented a reasonable effort to extend his resources for leadership. Had he been successful in securing the support of the Hamiltonian Federalists, he might have unified the party and established liaison with Congress, as Jefferson did after him. Midway in his administration when Adams realized that his cabinet members presented a threat to his command of the presidential office, he concluded that the heads of departments should function only as aides, to be consulted at the president's pleasure. From that time forward the Adams presidency assumed a new character.

Adams had determined from the beginning of his administration that the nation's interest lay with a negotiated settlement of differences with France and would have pursued such a course had he not seen a threat to his command of the presidential office. With Hamilton in charge of the army, the President had further reason to repair the relationship with France and to proceed with all possible speed. The first attempt at rapprochement, the famous "XYZ affair," presents one of the most colorful episodes in American diplomatic history and has received attention beyond its importance. Adams's first mission to France was predestined to failure because of timing. In September of 1797 a triumvirate within the French Directory had succeeded in crushing the moderates in government who might have been receptive to American overtures. Although France's celebrated foreign minister, Charles Maurice de Talleyrand-Perigord, had come to office in July 1797 and was directing American policy, he had not established the position of power he would later command. Talleyrand's attempt to elicit a bribe from the American diplomats represented a commonplace practice at the time and fit in well with his strategy of delaying a settlement of the quasi-war. The undeclared naval war was presenting optimum advantage to France at the moment and providing an additional advantage to the foreign minister in opportunities for extorting bribes. While French corsairs and privateers happily plundered America's neutral shipping, Talleyrand and his associates seized the opportunity afforded for personal

[17] Hamilton to Wolcott, 30 March 1797, Hamilton, *Papers*, 20:556–57.

gain. A delay in negotiations also served Talleyrand's purposes in minimizing conflict with the anti-American Directory.[18]

Publication of the American ministers' dispatches in April 1798, describing the details of the mission, brought a great wave of nationalism and anti-French sentiment that sent Republicans into temporary eclipse. Talleyrand had apparently not anticipated the sensational reaction and quickly began an about-face in diplomacy. Privately, he made known his desire for peace.[19]

Although Talleyrand continued to demonstrate the seriousness of his intent to negotiate by ordering a cessation of depredations on American shipping, the crisis was by no means over. News of the order was long in reaching the United States; its sincerity was questioned, and official control of the privateers was limited. Marauding of American shipping continued although on a much lower scale.[20] Meanwhile, a cycle of reaction and counterreaction set in, shattering domestic unity. Federalists remained skeptical of Talleyrand's overtures, while Republicans became increasingly convinced that Anglophile American policy was responsible for the French crisis.

With President Adams's cabinet standing ready and willing to do his bidding, Hamilton set out to direct both foreign and domestic responses to the French threat. The ease with which he began the effort is apparent in letters exchanged with Secretary of War James McHenry, who began his service to Adams by forwarding confidential executive documents directly to Hamilton for advice, asking that the arrangement continue in absolute secrecy.[21] The department heads plied Hamilton with privileged information concerning every aspect of executive function, sometimes relaying Hamilton's responses with his original language intact. George Washington became a silent partner to the arrangement; he neither criticized nor supported Adams but encouraged the flow of information which formed a triangle of communication with Hamilton at the apex funneling unabashed directives to the secretaries at the seat of government and more discreetly worded counsel to Mt. Vernon. Washington played a passive but important role in the intrigue against Adams, lending tacit consent to Hamilton's continual attempts to dominate executive policy.[22]

Unaware at first of his colleagues' disloyalty, Adams set out to unify the country and win bipartisan support for the administration by appoinfing influential Republicans to important military positions. George Washington and Alexander Hamilton, supported by their clique of admirers in the Senate, defeated Adams's

[18] For a recent discussion of the French mission see William Stinchcombe, *The XYZ Affair* (Westport, Conn.: Greenwood Press, 1960); George Athan Billias, *Elbridge Gerry: Founding Father and Republican Statesman* (New York: McGraw Hill, 1976). See also Marshall, *The Papers of John Marshall*, vol. 3.

[19] Billias, *Elbridge Gerry*, 282; Stinchcombe, *The XYZ Affair*, 125–26.

[20] Ibid., 113.

[21] 14 April 1797, Hamilton, *Papers*, 21:41. Ibid., May 1797, 85. Ibid., 26 January 1798, 22:339.

[22] For the Washington-Hamilton correspondence see Fitzpatrick, ed., *The Writings of George Washington*, vol. 33; Hamilton, *Papers*, vols. 19–23.

strategy, withholding approval of even the most moderate and well-qualified Republican leaders. Washington had fallen victim to paranoid suspicions of Republican adversaries, expressing his belief as early as January 1797 that Republican leaders were dangerous and a threat to security. Although Hamilton would have consented to a few Republican nominees, particularly for inferior grades, Washington was determined that commissioned officers would be men of the Federalist persuasion.[23]

Dismayed by his defeat on army appointments and convinced that the nation's security lay with the navy, Adams demonstrated the negative power of the executive office by delaying formation of the army until the need for force had passed, defeating Hamilton's ambitions to use military command as a means of personal and national aggrandizement. Although Congress provided the President with extensive and detailed legislation for organizing new units of military force in the period May-July 1798, and renewed expiring legislation in March 1799, no new army was raised. In the interval between the passage of the army bills and the reconvening of Congress in December 1798, Adams made no effort to recruit for the provisional army. When legislation for the provisional army expired, Congress renewed the bill. Adams submitted no nominations for officers in the period of the new law. Sensing quite correctly that Adams was purposely delaying formation of the army, Washington attempted to pressure the executive department into action.[24]

In February 1799 Hamilton informed Washington that "obstacles of a very peculiar kind stand in the way of an efficient and successful management of our military concerns." Hamilton indicated that it "would be unsafe at present" to explain the situation and suggested corresponding in code about matters relating to the administration. Washington sanctioned the arrangement, asking Hamilton to reply "with the utmost unreservedness.[25]

The attempt to undermine Adams's authority in this critical period posed a threat to the functional stability of the executive office, a fact of which Adams was very much aware. A decade after the French crisis, Adams wrote at length of his concern for the independence of the executive office. He feared that a president might have difficulty resisting the power of his commanding general in time of war. A commanding general is apt to be more popular than the president, he noted, and with thousands under his command could pose a threat to the independence of

[23] Washington to David Stuart, 8 January 1797, George Washington Papers, Reel 9; to Charles Cotesworth Pinckney, 4 December 1797, Fitzpatrick, ed., *Writings of George Washington*, 36:89–91; to Dr. James Anderson, 25 July 1798, ibid., 364–65; to William Heth, 5 August 1798, ibid., 388–89; to Brigadier General William Davie, 24 October 1798, ibid., 515–16.

[24] Hamilton, *Papers*, 22:383–88 contains a convenient synopsis of army legislation. George Washington attempted to pressure Adams through McHenry. Washington to McHenry, 13 December 1798, Fitzpatrick, ed., *Writings of George Washington*, 37:35.

[25] Hamilton, *Papers*, 22:483–84. Washington to Hamilton, 25 February 1799, ibid., 507–8. The coded correspondence does not appear in Washington's papers.

the chief executive. Adams wrote from bitter experience; his own struggle for independence had been a difficult one.[26]

Jefferson had declared in 1790 that if the presidency could be preserved for a few years until habits of authority were established, the nation had nothing to fear, a statement that suggests the attitude of insecurity that prevailed in the early period of the new national government.[27] Adams's success in maintaining command of the office was crucial at this juncture, demonstrating that a lesser chief executive than Washington could resist a formidable combination of adversaries supported by the first president himself. The struggle over the army was a unique situation that has not been repeated in American history. Adams demonstrated that the president as commander-in-chief, acting on the basis of his constitutional power, can indeed command.

Adams brought to the presidency the skills and perceptions gained from a decade of experience representing the new American republic in the courts of Europe. His talents for diplomacy and experience as a diplomat would serve him well as president for it was in the conduct of foreign relations that he found his last, bittersweet success as president. Isolated from party leaders, betrayed by his cabinet, undermined by the lack of support from George Washington, Adams was yet able to use his constitutional power as chief of foreign relations to reassert command and bring his administration to a successful conclusion.

In resisting the attempts at encroachment on his executive powers, Adams had shown resourcefulness and fortitude; but his strategy had been that of delay and holding. Real triumph would come with resolution of the French crisis. From a variety of sources Adams had been receiving indirect word that the French government wanted to resume a peaceful relationship with the United States.[28] The immediate impetus for initiating a new negotiation came in the form of a letter from George Washington, a message about which there has been much misunderstanding. Washington enclosed a letter that he had received from expatriate Joel Barlow, now residing in Paris, declaring that the French Directory was anxious to avoid formal war with the United States, was willing to retract its former demands and to assure the United States that all illegal restraints of American ships would cease. Washington assured Adams that he would reply to Barlow "with pleasure and

[26] Comments on the Hillhouse Amendment to the Constitution (1808), Adams Family Papers, Reel 406.

[27] Quoted in Morton Borden, *Parties and Politics in the Early Republic, 1789–1815* (New York: Thomas Crowell, 1967), 9.

[28] In the summer of 1798 John Quincy Adams had written from his post in Berlin that France gave every indication of wanting to settle differences with the United States. 29 July 1798, Adams Family Papers, Reel 391. William Vans Murray reported from The Hague that Talleyrand had been "deeply alarmed" at the American reaction to the XYZ mission and wished to reopen the door to negotiation. Talleyrand appointed as a representative to the French legation at The Hague a former acquaintance of Murray's, Louis Andre Pichon, who acknowleldged to the American minister that he had been sent to effect reconciliation; the French intermediary bore what appeared to be genuine peace offers. For a discussion of Murray's role, see Peter Hill, *William Vans Murray, Federalist Diplomat: The Shaping of Peace with France 1797–1801* (New York: Macmillan, 1972), chaps. 9 and 10.

alacrity" if Adams wished that he do so and thought that such an approach might restore peace, "which I am persuaded is the desire of all the friends of the rising empire."[29]

Adams declined Washington's offer to act as an intermediary on the grounds that Barlow was not a suitable person to act as an American agent. One can surmise that the more important reason for the refusal of Washington's offer was that Adams wished to retain control of the negotiation and to avoid enlarging the role of his commanding general, whose influence was of overwhelming proportions already. Under the umbrella of Washington's prestige, Adams could have begun a new negotiation with assurance of party support, but the price was too great. Adams would not court popularity at the expense of executive independence.

The Barlow letter and Washington's offer to act as an intermediary have led many historians to assume that Adams enjoyed the first president's support in the new diplomatic initiative that he announced on 18 February 1799, nominating William Vans Murray as minister plenipotentiary to France. Such was not the case. After the initial effort encouraging Adams to respond to French overtures, Washington remained aloof. Adams felt that it would be a violation of confidence to make the correspondence public, and Washington chose to conceal his role in the proceedings, criticizing the timing and procedure of Adams's move in language that suggested disapproval of the mission itself. "I was surprised at the measure, how much more at the manner of it," he informed Hamilton.[30] To Pickering he voiced stronger criticism, declaring that Adams should have waited for unequivocal proof. Washington encouraged opposition to Adams in cabinet and party, revealing to no one the information in the Barlow letter or the credence he had placed in it.[31]

Adams's opponents needed no encouragement to begin their efforts to thwart the President's plan for a new negotiation with France. A Senate committee of Hamiltonian supporters met with Adams privately, warning that they would reject the Murray appointment unless the President withdrew the nomination voluntarily.[32] Adams withdrew the nomination but named a commission of three, including Murray, in its place. Adams had sent the original nomination to the Senate without consulting cabinet members or party leaders, a move that astonished the nation. It was "the event of events" in Jefferson's view.[33] Adams moved quickly,

[29] George Washington to John Adams, 1 February 1799, Fitzpatrick, ed., Washington, *Writings*, 37:119–20. The Barlow letter of 2 October 1798, appears in the letter to the Boston *Patriot* of 15 April 1809, and also in the Adams Family Papers, Reel 393.

[30] 27 October 1799, Syrett, ed., Hamilton, *Papers*, 23:573–74.

[31] 3 March 1799, Fitzpatrick, ed., *Writings of George Washington*, 37:141–43.

[32] Theodore Sedgwick to Alexander Hamilton, 25 February 1799, Hamilton, *Papers*, 22:503. Sedgwick to Rutherford, 1 March 1799, Adams Family Papers, Reel 393. Adams's account of the meeting appears in a letter to the Boston *Patriot*. John Adams, *The Works of John Adams, Second President of the United States*, Charles Francis Adams, ed., 10 vols. (Boston: Charles C. Little and James Brown, 1850–56), 9:250–51.

[33] To James Madison, 19 February 1799, Thomas Jefferson, *The Works of Thomas Jefferson*, Paul L. Ford, ed., 12 vols. (New York: G. P. Putnam's Sons, 1904), 7:361–63. "We have all been shocked

he explained in later years, because his intraparty opponents were trying to dominate executive policy and defeat his aims. The committee from the Senate, in its effort to use that body's veto over executive appointments to check a major presidential initiative in foreign policy, was attempting to alter the constitutionally established balance of power, Adams believed. Adams's suspicions were not paranoid; a member of the committee acknowledged to Hamilton that the Senate committee was violating principle in approaching Adams privately on the nomination.[34] Adams moved precipitously because the stakes were high. The Hamiltonians were challenging the President's constitutional authority and personal leadership, forcing Adams to move boldly to maintain the power and primacy of the office.

Adams's decision to send a second mission to France outmaneuvered his intraparty opponents. As Talleyrand continued to furnish evidence of the new, conciliatory French policy, the Hamiltonian Federalists were checked and became increasingly isolated from the political mainstream. In reporting to Hamilton on the Murray nomination, Congressman Theodore Sedgwick had admitted that while he opposed the move, "that is not the inclination of the majority." Pressuring Adams to expand the mission and appoint a commission was "everything which, under the circumstances, could be done."[35] The most extreme High Federalists acknowledged that they could not effectively oppose the president's decision.[36]

The nomination of a new mission to France left the Hamiltonians without a weapon except the hope of a delay of the mission. Having secured Senate approval of the mission, Adams was content to wait for further assurances from France and to improve the American negotiating position by proceeding with defense measures. Construction of the new fleet was well underway with three naval squadrons nearing completion. With the new attempt at negotiations Adams was in command again, hoping for a peaceful resolution of the crisis but prepared for any outcome.[37]

Pickering dissassociated himself from Adams's diplomacy and renewed a campaign that he had begun earlier, writing a succession of letters to friends and acquaintances deriding Adams. The Secretary of State began to speak openly against the President, but his attacks proved to be counterproductive, alienating the moderate Hamiltonians who saw the potential for destruction in party schism. Harrison Gray Otis, formerly one of Hamilton's most enthusiastic supporters,

---

and grieved at the nomination," Pickering informed Hamilton, 25 February 1799. Hamilton, *Papers*, 22:500. George Cabot declared that "Surprise, indignation, grief and disgust followed each other in quick succession." To Rufus King, 10 March 1799, Rufus King, *The Life and Correspondence of Rufus King*, Charles R. King, ed., 6 vols. (New York: G. P. Putnam's Sons, 1894-1900), 2:551.

[34] Theodore Sedgwick to Alexander Hamilton, 25 February 1799, Hamilton, *Papers*, 22:399-400.

[35] Sedgwick to Hamilton, 25 February 1799, ibid., 22:503.

[36] Fisher Ames to Timothy Dwight, 27 February 1799, Fisher Ames, *Works of Fisher Ames*, Seth Ames, ed. (New York: Burt Franklin, 1971), 252; George Cabot to Timothy Pickering, 7 March 1797, Henry Cabot Lodge, ed., *The Life and Letters of George Cabot* (Boston: Little, Brown, 1877), 224.

[37] Peter B. Hill, *William Vans Murray*, 147; Lawrence Kaplan, *Colonies Into Nation: American Diplomacy 1763-1801* (New York: Macmillan, 1972), 289.

deserted the clique and supported Adams.[38] Rufus King and John Jay, members of Hamilton's most intimate circle, expressed reservations about the mission but supported the President.[39] John Marshall, the rising star of Federalism, threw his weight behind Adams and the moderates.[40] The extremist clique declined in numbers if not in virulence.

France's conciliatory gestures and the growing prospect of peace increased Adams's popularity and weakened the Hamiltonians further. Federalist Samuel Dexter warned extremists in the party that they could not oppose Adams because he was popular and "deemed the best qualified to perform the duties of President."[41] Dexter's warning did not deter the Hamiltonians who proceeded to consider two unlikely plans for displacing Adams: a third term for George Washington; an attempt to manipulate vice-presidential candidate Charles Cotesworth Pinckney into the first position. George Washington adamantly refused to run for a third term, declaring that party lines had hardened to the point that he could not get a single vote more than other Federalist candidates. Washington reproached the plotters for the division within the party, seemingly unaware that he had encouraged the schism by withholding support of President Adams's decision on the second mission.[42]

Frustrated that they could no longer control the party or influence executive policy, a small clique of Hamilton's supporters continued to play the spoiler role. They chose schism and the likelihood of defeat rather than accept a position within the party that involved compromise. Long delays in the completion of the French negotiation and communicating news of its success to the United States weakened Adams's position in the critical period in which electors were chosen. Hamilton seized the opportunity to make a last, desperate attempt to undermine Adams and establish the ascendancy of his own wing of the party, destroying himself and his rival in the process. In the end he acted alone—against the advice of the Federalists who remained most loyal to him. His decision appears to have been one of desperation.

The year that launched a new century began on a melancholy note as news spread of the sudden death of George Washington. Since his youth Hamilton had based his career on Washington's prestige and influence; he candidly acknowledged the

[38] Samuel Eliot Morison, *Harrison Gray Otis, The Urbane Federalist, 1765–1848* (Boston: Houghton Mifflin, 1969), 162.

[39] John Jay to Theophilus Parson, 1 July 1800, John Jay, *The Correspondence and Public Papers of John Jay, 1794–1826*, Henry P. Johnston, ed., 4 vols. (New York: G. P. Putnam's Sons, 1890–1893), 4:274–75.

[40] On 14 March 1799, Charles Lee wrote to Adams: "I presume it will afford you satisfaction to know that a measure which has excited so much agitation here has met the approbation of so good a judge as Mr. Marshall." Adams Family Papers, Reel 394.

[41] Theodore Sedgwick to Alexander Hamilton, 7 May 1800, Hamilton, *Papers*, 24:467–68.

[42] George Washington to Jonathan Trumbull, 21 July 1799, Fitzpatrick, ed., *Writings of George Washington*, 37:312–14.

loss of the "essential aegis" of his destiny.[43] His position with the army was vanishing with the army itself, nor could he have expected under any circumstances that Adams would promote him to the first position, now vacant. Hamilton was newly incensed that Adams had in May 1800 dismissed two of the disloyal secretaries, Pickering and McHenry. The influence of the Hamiltonians was clearly ending.[44]

Hamilton began a tour of New England in June, ostensibly to conduct a final review of the army; the tour was, in fact, the first effort in a campaign to defeat Adams and make Charles Cotesworth Pinckney the president in 1800. Hamilton was open in attacking Adams as he spoke to groups in New England. He told New Hampshire Federalists that Adams was "a very unfit and incapable character. . . ."[45] In the summer Hamilton began to prepare his famous publication attacking the President. Hamilton's biographers do not attempt to provide a rationale for his actions in this period, concluding that he was simply a victim of passionate rage. Recent biographer Jacob Cooke agrees with earlier writers that Hamilton "lost his grip, his sense of reality" because he could not bear the loss of his public role and stature.[46] Hamilton may have been encouraged by a series of misfortunes that weakened Adams's position.

The envoys to France experienced long delays on their journey; proceedings were postponed further by Joseph Bonaparte's month-long illness, and once begun, negotiations proceeded slowly with frequent interruptions occasioned by the absence of Talleyrand. In the critical months of September and October 1800 rumors began to spread that the mission had failed. In August 1800 a ship brought a newspaper report that the mission had been suspended, an account that appeared authentic. Those who wished most for the mission to succeed found the report credible. Except for false rumors that the mission had terminated unsuccessfully, no news of the outcome reached the United States until after electors were chosen.[47]

In October, after at least three months of preparation, Hamilton began circulating his *Letter from Alexander Hamilton Concerning the Public Conduct and Character of John Adams*, at first restricting the distribution to Federalist leaders.[48] The material predictably fell into opposition hands, and after the Republican press began publishing excerpts, Hamilton took out a copyright and published the document—a

[43] To Tobias Lear, 2 January 1800, Hamilton, *Papers*, 24:155.

[44] By mid-1798 Adams had become aware that at least one cabinet member was betraying his confidence. Adams discusses his relationship with the cabinet in a lengthy document (unpublished) entitled "Draft of a Reply to Hamilton's Pamphlet," 1800–1801, Adams Family Papers, Reel 399. See also Adams to James Lloyd, 11, 14, 21 February 1815, Adams, *Works*, 10:116–20, 129–31.

[45] John C. Miller, *Alexander Hamilton, Portrait in Paradox* (New York: Harper, 1959), 518–19.

[46] Jacob E. Cooke, *Alexander Hamilton* (New York: Scribner's, 1982), 219–20. Cooke is quoting biographer Broadus Mitchell.

[47] For a complete account of the negotiations see Alexander DeConde, *The Quasi-War: The Politics and Diplomacy of the Undeclared War with France, 1797–1801* (New York: Scribner's, 1954), chap. VII; see also Hamilton, *Papers*, 25:128–30n.

[48] See Hamilton, *Papers*, 25:169–234 for a complete account of the pamphlet episode with commentary. See also, Miller, *Alexander Hamilton*, 520.

compendium of trivia and hearsay, vaguely stated charges of incompetence, some material that was already well known, and some new allegations based on confidential information obviously furnished by one or more of Adams's cabinet members. The verbal missile proved to be a devastating boomerang, perhaps injuring Hamilton more than its intended victim. Hamilton's friends were "shocked and appalled."[49]

The damage to Adams appears to have been largely indirect, a result of party disarray and public loss of confidence in the Federalist party. While Hamilton attempted to reestablish his personal influence at the expense of party unity, the Republicans were moving smoothly and effectively to organize their forces and capitalize on Federalist disintegration. The Republicans were the ascendant party in 1800, pioneering a new and creative approach to political campaigning and party dynamics that would affect the functioning of the executive office itself when Republican leadership took over the government. Adams's near-victory in an election that brought a flood tide of Republican success demonstrated that he enjoyed impressive public support. Election year caught Adams and his moderate followers in a transitional stage of establishing their own leadership and displacing the Federalist old guard. The moderate new wing of Federalists had barely begun to organize their efforts when the election took place.

Because Adams failed to unite the Federalist party and win reelection, the significance of his contribution to the presidential office has been overlooked. The second president faced a unique challenge in the starkness of his political assets. Opposed by the leadership of his own party, elected by a narrow margin, bereft of patronage, and heir to a legacy of disloyal, obstructionist cabinet members, he nevertheless conducted a successful administration. After one term in office he left the nation at peace, the conflict with France resolved, a domestic crisis between political parties defused for the moment, the defense establishment strengthened by construction of a navy. Adams had dealt with the challenges of his war-crisis administration with few of the appurtenances of power that Neustadt describes as essential to command, making his presidency an ideal test case for the conflicting Pious-Neustadt theses. Although one cannot absolutely divide a president's constitutional powers from the political tools of bargaining and persuasion, Adams's achievements as president demonstrate that in the period of the early republic the executive office was viable on its constitutional basis in the hands of an able leader.

A president himself remains the crucial variable. Adams asserted his constitutional power and implied prerogatives aggressively but with perceptive restraint, pursuing a middle course that served to ameliorate the extreme polarization of political views. By taking a bold initiative in foreign policy on the basis of his constitutional power alone and achieving wide public acceptance of that policy, Adams

[49] Syrett concludes that the pamphlet ruined Hamilton's career, shattered the confidence of his closest supporters, and revealed that he had become an inept politician and a burden to the party. *Papers of Alexander Hamilton*, 25:170.

achieved the frontlash effect that Pious describes, strengthening his own position and the presidential office thereby. He continued the precedent of forceful action in foreign affairs begun by George Washington and did so without the undergirdings of personal prestige and power that had facilitated policy making for his predecessor. He inherited a position that has been correctly described as "woefully weak" and left the office strengthened by his accomplishments.[50]

Critics who fault Adams for his inability to please either Republican or Federalist extremists are focusing on his failure to win reelection rather than upon his goals as president. Adams's purpose in policy formation was to find a workable middle ground congruent with the nation's interest as he perceived that interest: peace; internal security and tranquility; neutrality; complete independence of foreign powers. Measured in terms of the nation's welfare or his own goals as president, Adams was a successful chief executive. Although he failed to win reelection, popularity had never been his primary goal. Adams had earlier set a standard for leadership and is best judged by his own measure: "Tis better to serve than to please the People; and they in time will be sensible of it."[51]

[50] Johnstone, *Jefferson and the Presidency*, 24–26.
[51] To Abigail Adams, 17 February 1794, Adams Family Papers, Reel 377.

Thomas Paine's Apostles: Radical Emigrés and the Triumph of Jeffersonian Republicanism

Michael Durey

THE key to understanding eighteenth-century American political discourse since the publication of Caroline Robbins's *The Eighteenth-Century Commonwealthman* in 1959 and Bernard Bailyn's *The Ideological Origins of the American Revolution* in 1967 has been the recognition that political ideas from England and Scotland underpinned republican ideology. In developing Robbins's and Bailyn's insights, both for the period of the American Revolution and for the Federalist years, historians have tended to gravitate toward one or the other of two general interpretations. "Classical" historians, represented most forcefully by J.G.A. Pocock and Lance Banning, seek the roots of American republicanism in the political writings of James Harrington, Algernon Sidney, John Trenchard, Thomas Gordon, Viscount Bolingbroke, and Joseph Addison.[1] In contrast, "liberal" historians such as Joyce Appleby and Isaac Kramnick include John Locke, Thomas Mun, Adam Smith, Richard Price, and Joseph Priestley.[2] The controversy over American republican ideol-

Mr. Durey is a member of the History Programme at Murdoch University, Western Australia. Acknowledgments: Ruth Bogin, Richard Buel, Jr., Eric Foner, Geoffrey Gallop, and Richard K. Matthews read versions of this essay and offered many valuable suggestions. Edward C. Carter II, Terry Parssinen, and Richard Twomey gave me useful advice when I first began research on the émigrés in 1981. Gwyn A. Williams was my inspiration. Steven Walker assisted me greatly in locating materials on the Scottish radicals and offered many sensible ideas. I am grateful to Murdoch University's Board of Research and Postgraduate Studies for significant financial assistance since 1982.

[1] Robbins, *Eighteenth-Century Commonwealthman* (Cambridge, Mass., 1959); Bailyn, *Ideological Origins of the American Revolution* (Cambridge, Mass., 1967); J.G.A. Pocock, *The Machiavellian Moment: Florentine Political Thought and the Atlantic Republican Tradition* (Princeton, N.J., 1975), and "Virtue and Commerce in the Eighteenth Century," *Journal of Interdisciplinary History*, III (1972), 119-134; Lance Banning, *The Jeffersonian Persuasion: Evolution of a Party Ideology* (Ithaca, N.Y., 1978); John Murrin, "The Great Inversion, or Court versus Country: A Comparison of the Revolution Settlements in England (1688-1721) and America (1776-1816)," in Pocock, ed., *Three British Revolutions: 1641, 1688, 1776* (Princeton, N.J., 1980), 368-453.

[2] Joyce Oldham Appleby, *Economic Thought and Ideology in Seventeenth-Century England* (Princeton, N.J., 1978); "Liberalism and the American Revolution," *New*

ogy concerns which of these two lines of thought was the more influential in late eighteenth-century American political discourse.

Whatever the relative merits of these two approaches for an understanding of American republicanism, one notable absentee from historians' deliberations on the 1790s is Thomas Paine. This omission is surprising, for recent historiography on the Revolutionary period has emphasized both Paine's role in securing popular acceptance of Independence and his wartime political propaganda.[3] But his long-term influence in the United States has been strangely neglected. Eric Foner's perceptive study of Paine in America, for instance, deals with his career after 1787 in an epilogue, as if his impact on the New World rapidly diminished after the crisis years of war became a memory.[4] Kramnick notes that Paine returned in 1802 to a very different America from the one in which *Common Sense* and the *Crisis* papers created mass support for the patriot cause: "*Common Sense* was a thing of the distant past. Paine was no longer the celebrated author of the pamphlet so influential in its day. He was now the notorious author of the godless *Age of Reason*"—and, it might be added, of the bitter *Letter to George Washington*.[5] Neither Banning nor Appleby, from their different vantage points, feels it necessary to dwell on Paine's contribution to American political thought after the acceptance of the Constitution.[6]

Paine's absence becomes even stranger when it is appreciated that much of the debate on republicanism in the 1790s revolved around political and economic issues such as egalitarianism, natural rights, and national economic development, on all of which Paine wrote copiously. The essence of Paine's radicalism—its singular politico-economic combination of democratic egalitarianism and support for national economic development in a market-oriented society—appears anomalous when one considers the classical-liberal debate. Paine, writes Pocock, "remains difficult to fit into any kind of category"; even *Common Sense*, the most unproblematic of his

---

England Quarterly, XLIX (1976), 3-26; "The Social Origins of American Revolutionary Ideology," *Journal of American History*, LXIV (1978), 935-958; and "What Is Still American in the Political Philosophy of Thomas Jefferson?" *William and Mary Quarterly*, 3d Ser., XXXIX (1982), 287-309; Isaac Kramnick, "Republican Revisionism Revisited," *American Historical Review*, LXXXVII (1982), 629-664, and "Religion and Radicalism: English Political Theory in the Age of Revolution," *Political Theory*, V (1977), 505-534; John Patrick Diggins, *The Lost Soul of American Politics: Virtue, Self-Interest, and the Foundations of Liberalism* (New York, 1985).

[3] David Freeman Hawke, *Paine* (New York, 1975); David Powell, *Tom Paine: The Greatest Exile* (London, 1985).

[4] Eric Foner, *Tom Paine and Revolutionary America* (New York, 1976), chap. 7.

[5] Thomas Paine, *Common Sense*, ed. Isaac Kramnick (London, 1976), 36.

[6] Joyce Appleby, *Capitalism and a New Social Order: The Republican Vision of the 1790s* (New York, 1984), and "Republicanism in Old and New Contexts," *WMQ*, 3d Ser., XLIII (1986), 20-34; Lance Banning, "Jeffersonian Ideology Revisited: Liberal and Classical Ideas in the New American Republic," *ibid*., 3-19.

works for American politics, fails "consistently [to] echo any established radical vocabulary."[7] In other words, Paine's radicalism does not fit neatly into the categories posited by historians, for when the patriots who guided the Constitution through Congress and the state ratifying conventions split in the 1790s, they did so in a way that sundered Paine's political from his economic ideology. They divided along lines leading to a federalism that rejected democratic politics but accepted economic progress or to a republicanism that accepted egalitarian politics yet held grave reservations concerning the nation's transformation into a commercial-manufacturing society. But the general debate over republicanism in the 1790s has as one major interest the question of how, and to what extent, Jeffersonian republicanism came to incorporate a more positive attitude toward commercial development.[8] Thus, although not recognizing Paine as a formative influence, this part of the debate is concerned with the process by which Jeffersonianism moved toward a political economy that, by combining egalitarianism with an acceptance of market economics, had many of the hallmarks of Paine's own ideology.

Moreover, some historians appear to suffer from telescopic longsightedness that enables them to see the impact of political ideas dating from as far back as Machiavelli but blinds them to much closer influences. One such influence on Jeffersonian republicanism was brought to bear by the political emigrants who arrived in numbers from Britain and Ireland in the 1790s. Although many studies focusing on individual émigrés have been published, only a few have essayed an assessment of their collective role in the formation and dissemination of republican ideology in this period.[9]

[7] J.G.A. Pocock, "The Variety of Whiggism from Exclusion to Reform: A History of Ideology and Discourse," in *Virtue, Commerce and History* (Cambridge, 1985), 276.

[8] Appleby, "What Is Still American?" *WMQ*, 3d Ser., XXXIX (1982), 287-309; Drew R. McCoy, *The Elusive Republic: Political Economy in Jeffersonian America* (Chapel Hill, N.C., 1980).

[9] Arthur Sheps, "Ideological Immigrants in Revolutionary America," in Paul Fritz and David Williams, eds., *City and Society in the Eighteenth Century* (Toronto, 1973), 231-246; Dumas Malone, *The Public Life of Thomas Cooper, 1783-1839* (New Haven, Conn., 1926); Caroline Robbins, "Honest Heretic: Joseph Priestley in America, 1794-1804," American Philosophical Society, *Proceedings*, CVI (1962), 60-76; Kim Tousley Phillips, "William Duane, Revolutionary Editor" (Ph.D. diss., University of California, Berkeley, 1968); Colin Bonwick, "Joseph Priestley: Emigrant and Jeffersonian," *Enlightenment and Dissent*, II (1983), 3-26; Edward C. Carter II, "The Political Activities of Mathew Carey, Nationalist, 1760-1814" (Ph.D. diss., Bryn Mawr College, 1962); G. S. Rowell, "Benjamin Vaughan—Patriot, Scholar, Diplomat," *Magazine of History*, XXII (1916), 43-57; Willis G. Briggs, "Joseph Gales, Editor of Raleigh's First Newspaper," *North Carolina Booklet*, VII (1907), 105-130; W. T. Latimer, "David Bailie Warden, Patriot 1798," *Ulster Journal of Archeology*, XXIII (1907), 29-38; D. H. Gilpatrick, "The English Background of John Miller," *Furman Bulletin*, XX (1938), 14-20; Sir James Fergusson, *Balloon Tytler* (London, 1972); Joseph I. Shulim, "John Daly

As a consequence, an important dimension of republicanism has been neglected.

The most impressive general analysis of the emigrants can be found in Richard Twomey's thesis of 1974, from which, unfortunately, only a small fragment has yet been published.[10] Ironically, it is Appleby who has most clearly tied the radical emigrants into American politics in the 1790s, but in such a way that their possible influence went unremarked. She has shown, by relying on James Cheetham, Thomas Paine, and especially Thomas Cooper to explicate Jeffersonian ideology, how important were their ideological and propagandist roles. Yet Appleby remained unaware that she was considering a new and significant element in the Republican equation. Recognizing that "no fewer than twenty [British radicals] played an active role in Republican politics," she nevertheless included with the "Jacobins" who arrived in the 1790s men of British extraction such as Eleazer Oswald, Blair McClenachan, William Findley, and even the West Indian–born Alexander Dallas, all of whom had left the British Isles many years previously.[11] Indiscriminately blending all those prominent in Republican politics who had connections with the British Isles, she has failed to distinguish those whose political sensibilities had been shaped less by Commonwealth ideology and the politics of the 1760s and 1770s than by the growth of popular Painite radicalism in the early 1790s and by the French Revolution.

John Ashworth has recently stated that "a definitive explication of Republican ideology will have to take full account of the factional composition of the party."[12] A major purpose of this article is to demonstrate that one important component of the Republican party in the 1790s consisted of political émigrés from Britain and Ireland, who brought with them to the "asylum for oppressed humanity"[13] a stock of political ideas acquired in the popular radical societies of the British Isles—ideas that were Painite in inspiration.

On their arrival in the United States many became deeply involved in national and local politics. Some, such as William Duane, James Thomson Callender, John Binns, and James Carey, through their writings played a

---

Burk: Irish Revolutionist and American Patriot," Am. Phil. Soc., *Transactions*, LIV (1964), pt. 6, 5-60.

[10] Richard Jerome Twomey, "Jacobins and Jeffersonians: Anglo-American Radicalism in the United States, 1790-1820" (Ph.D. diss., Northern Illinois University, 1974), and "Jacobins and Jeffersonians: Anglo-American Radical Ideology, 1790-1810," in Margaret Jacob and James Jacob, eds., *The Origins of Anglo-American Radicalism* (London, 1984), 284-299. The thrust of Twomey's work is to emphasize the *diversity* of the radicals in their political ideology and social composition. See *ibid.*, 285. Subsequent citations to Twomey, "Jacobins and Jeffersonians," are to the dissertation.

[11] Appleby, *Capitalism and a New Social Order*, 60-61.

[12] John Ashworth, "The Jeffersonians: Classical Republicans or Liberal Capitalists?" *Journal of American Studies*, XVIII (1984), 427.

[13] Callender in *Recorder* (Richmond), Aug. 18, 1802.

significant role in national Republican politics. Others participated more in local political affairs, either through membership in Republican clubs or by working to recruit immigrant votes for the Republican cause. A surprising number gained sufficient respect from their neighbors to be asked to give Fourth of March Jeffersonian or Fourth of July Independence Day orations.[14]

Although they did not supply original ideas to American political discourse, I will argue that the émigrés helped to rearrange the priority order of some of the more contentious elements of Republicanism in the 1790s, assisting both in the defeat of Federalism and in the development of a Jeffersonian image of America's future as an egalitarian society in which agriculture, commerce, and industry interacted in harmony. What exactly their political ideology was and how effectively they broadcast their Painite message are additional concerns of this study. By examining the role of the exiles I hope to demonstrate that British radical ideology, emerging from the popular societies, was influential in the United States in the 1790s.

I

> Down yonder rough beach, where the vessels attend,
> I see the sad emigrants slowly descend;
> Compell'd by the weight of oppression and woe,
> Their kindred, and native, and friends to forego.
> In these drooping crouds that depart every day,
> I see the true strength of the state glide away;
> While countries that hail the glad strangers to shore,
> Shall flourish, when Britain's proud pomp is no more.[15]

Historians have failed to appreciate the significant *number* of British and Irish radicals who fled to the United States in the 1790s. Many thousands of ordinary people emigrated in that decade; most of them, claimed

[14] Alexander Wilson, *Oration, on the Power and Value of National Liberty* (Philadelphia, 1801); John Binns, *An Oration Commemorative of the Birth-Day of American Independence, Delivered before the Democratic Societies of the City and County of Philadelphia* (Philadelphia, 1810); John D. Burk, *An Oration, Delivered on the 4th. of March, 1803, at the Courthouse, in Petersburg: To Celebrate the Election of Thomas Jefferson, and the Triumph of Republicanism* (Petersburg, Va., 1803); [Richard Dinmore], *A Long Talk, Delivered before the Tammany Society . . .* (Alexandria, Va., 1804).

[15] Alexander Wilson, "Tears of Britain," in [Thomas Crichton], *Biographical Sketches of the Late Alexander Wilson, Communicated in a Series of Letters to a Young Friend* (Paisley, Scot., 1819), 40.

Callender, went "not in search of a republic, but of *bread*."[16] But the emigrants also included politically conscious exiles whose vision of the new American polity was conditioned by strongly held republican perceptions forged from Paine's political works and from their experiences in opposition to William Pitt's government. At least seventy-four can be confirmed as having been active in the popular radical movements in Britain and Ireland in the 1790s. Of these, one-half were Irish; three-fifths of the remainder were English, and two-fifths Scottish.[17]

Until the end of the eighteenth century, politics in Britain was the province of the aristocracy and the landed classes. The radical societies that were springing up by the end of 1791 reflected a new phenomenon: for the first time political awareness was becoming widespread in the British Isles. These societies represented a groundswell of opinion in favor of significant parliamentary reform as the first and essential step toward reforming social and political institutions. Avowedly constitutionalist—at least in the early years—the radicals sought by petitioning Parliament to persuade the government to reform itself.

The extent of political reformation regarded as necessary was never universally agreed upon, but the majority of men who joined the Society for Constitutional Information, the London Corresponding Society, the Society of United Irishmen, and the English provincial corresponding societies favored eventual introduction of manhood suffrage and annual parliaments. In London, reformers who desired a slighter degree of change, and who could afford the high subscriptions, joined the Friends of the People, the society of the Foxite parliamentary Whigs; two of the emigrants, Robert Merry and Benjamin Vaughan, were associated with this group. The Scottish Friends of the People, founded in July 1792, began as an amalgam of conflicting groups, with the most moderate reformers—who wanted the franchise extended only to the middle classes—trying to persuade the moderate radicals to disown the small body of revolutionary extremists. The United Irishmen, whose membership included Roman Catholics, communicants of the Church of Ireland, and Protestant Dissenters, agitated for Catholic emancipation in addition to parliamentary reform. In the early years, national independence was not a major part of the radical program in either Scotland or Ireland, although it was to become so, especially in Ireland, by 1796.[18]

[16] [James Thomson Callender], *A Short History of the Nature and Consequences of the Excise Laws . . .* (Philadelphia, 1795), 45n.

[17] These are revised figures from Michael Durey, "Transatlantic Patriotism: Political Exiles and America in the Age of Revolutions," in James Walvin and Clive Emsley, eds., *Artisans, Peasants and Proletarians, 1760-1860: Essays Presented to Gwyn A. Williams* (London, 1985), 12-15. Twomey believes that there were more English radical émigrés than Irish ("Jacobins and Jeffersonians," 20-21).

[18] The literature on the popular societies in the 1790s is considerable. The last two paragraphs are based on E. P. Thompson, *The Making of the English Working Class* (London, 1969); Gwyn A. Williams, *Artisans and Sans-Culottes: Popular Movements in France and Britain during the French Revolution* (London, 1968);

The government responded to these new societies with policies of repression. In addition, in a semiofficial way, through local Church and King clubs and John Reeves's Association for the Preservation of Liberty and Property against Republicans and Levellers (founded in November 1792), the government harnessed popular loyalism in defense of the state. Thus the radicals, always a small minority, were harassed from all sides.[19]

The stage at which individual radicals decided to accept defeat and emigrate varied according to local circumstances and to the tactics used by government. Joseph Priestley and his Unitarian followers in Birmingham and London, for instance, experienced the force of Church and King mobs as early as July 1791, and Thomas Cooper's Unitarian group in Manchester was attacked by Edmund Burke in Parliament in 1792. In December 1792 a mob sacked the house and shop of Matthew Falkner and William Young Birch, publishers of the radical *Manchester Herald*. In March 1793 Falkner and Birch "discontinued the *Herald* and fled before the storm" to America. In July the government indicted a number of Cooper's friends on charges of sedition. They were acquitted in April 1794, but by that time most of them had decided to join Priestley and other Unitarians in the United States.[20]

One of those acquitted, James Cheetham, persevered in Manchester. His career thereafter exemplifies the way in which radicals who did not at first fold under loyalist pressure were gradually forced into secret societies aimed at overthrowing the state. By 1798 he was, with his two brothers, a member of the revolutionary United Englishmen. Loyalist rioters forced him to flee to America; he was carried on board ship at Liverpool in a chest marked "dry goods."[21]

In Scotland a similar combination of government repression and loyalist activism had similar results: the open radical movement collapsed and its most intransigent members laid insurrectionist plots, culminating in the Watt conspiracy of 1794. Robert Dundas, lord advocate of Scotland and a nephew of Henry Dundas, Pitt's close colleague, acted as soon as the Scottish Friends of the People held their first convention in Edinburgh in December 1792. Using the authority of a royal proclamation against seditious writings, Dundas prosecuted extremist writers such as Callender

---

Albert Goodwin, *The Friends of Liberty: The English Democratic Movement in the Age of the French Revolution* (Cambridge, Mass., 1979); Edward Royle and James Walvin, *English Radicals and Reformers, 1760-1848* (Lexington, Ky., 1982); Marianne Elliott, *Partners in Revolution: The United Irishmen and France* (New Haven, Conn., 1982); Roger Wells, *Insurrection: The British Experience, 1795-1803* (Gloucester, 1983); and John D. Brims, "The Scottish Democratic Movement in the Age of the French Revolution" (Ph.D. diss., University of Edinburgh, 1983).

[19] Clive Emsley, "Repression, 'Terror' and the Rule of Law in England during the Decade of the French Revolution," *English Historical Review*, C (1985), 801-825; Goodwin, *Friends of Liberty*, 264-265.

[20] R. B. Rose, "The Priestley Riots of 1791," *Past and Present*, No. 18 (1960), 68-88; Malone, *Thomas Cooper*, 65-70, quotation on p. 69.

[21] *Recorder* (Rich.), Dec. 1, 1801.

and James Tytler for seditious libel. Both failed to appear in court and were outlawed. Tytler fled to Belfast, whence he sailed to Boston in 1794. Callender escaped with his family only hours before the authorities searched his lodgings. After two months in Dublin, the Callender family set sail for Philadelphia.[22] Tytler and Callender were sensible; the Scottish courts gave extremely harsh sentences for crimes like theirs.

Radicals who persevered found themselves ostracized and their employment opportunities diminished. In her autobiography Mrs. Eliza Fletcher, wife of an Edinburgh lawyer, pointed out that "every man was considered a rebel in his heart who did not take a decided part in supporting Tory measures of government. . . . Such was the terror of Liberal principles in Scotland that no man at the Bar professing these would expect a fair share of practice." In the spring of 1795 the lawyer John Craig Millar, son of a professor at Glasgow University and a moderate reformer in the Friends of the People, was unable to find professional employment. "Disgusted with the state of public affairs," he took his family to America.[23]

Schoolmasters and university professors faced the same pressures. In Scotland their every word was carefully scrutinized for "Jacobin" connotations; even the famous were not exempt.[24] And, of course, men who received patronage of any kind could not afford to arouse even slight suspicions. In London, in January 1792, the poet and playwright Robert Merry made the mistake of presenting his play "The Magician No Conjuror" at Covent Garden. (Playhouses, like newspapers, were battlegrounds for partisan propaganda.) Though Merry's play had no Jacobin signification, it satirized William Pitt as "The Magician." In June the popular actress Miss Brunton, Merry's wife, was suddenly dismissed by the theater. With the government subsidizing the theaters and Merry associated with the Friends of the People, her career was finished. After a period in France the Merrys emigrated to the United States.[25]

Under such pressures, men of progressive views found their options shrinking in the 1790s. They could recant, and hope that their sins would soon be forgiven and forgotten. Many middle-class reformers did so, especially after the Jacobins had seized control of the French Revolution and Britain went to war with France. Most radical artisans, laborers, and small shopkeepers followed suit by 1796, except, of course, in Ireland.[26] Alternatively, radicals could continue efforts to gain parliamentary reform,

[22] Brims, "Scottish Democratic Movement," chap. 4; Fergusson, *Balloon Tytler*, 132-134; John Pringle to Henry Dundas, Jan. 7, 1793, H.O. 102/5, Public Record Office; *Recorder* (Rich.), Feb. 9, 1803.

[23] [Eliza Fletcher], *Autobiography of Mrs. Fletcher, with Letters and Other Family Memorials*, 3d ed. (Edinburgh, 1876), 65-71, quotations on pp. 66, 71; A. Hook, *Scotland and America: A Study in Cultural Relations, 1750-1835* (Glasgow, 1975), 241.

[24] Henry Cockburn, *Memorials of His Time* (Edinburgh, 1856), 85.

[25] Lucyle Werkmeister, *A Newspaper History of England, 1792-1793* (Lincoln, Neb., 1967), 92-93.

[26] Thompson, *English Working Class*, 162-164; Williams, *Artisans*, 101.

but this became increasingly difficult as the decade progressed: first the government stopped the spread of information by prosecuting newspaper editors and booksellers, then it banned public meetings, and, finally, it proscribed the popular societies by name. Only the most thick-skinned and intransigent could withstand this onslaught; they retaliated—in Scotland, Ireland, and England—by forming themselves into revolutionary cells.[27]

The only other viable option was emigration. The choice of country, for radicals, was confined to revolutionary France and to the republican United States. By and large, especially from 1793, only the most committed opponents of despotism, prepared to endorse the excesses of the Jacobins, fled across the Channel. United Irishmen, who realized the importance of intervention by foreign troops to the success of their intended revolution, made up the great majority of émigrés to France, where they squabbled amongst themselves in their efforts to obtain a French invasion force. Most prospective emigrants—disillusioned by the Terror, during which Paine was imprisoned and nearly executed—perceived the United States as a personally safer haven of liberty, even if its distance from Britain precluded their continued involvement in the politics of the popular societies.[28]

Most members of the popular societies in the British Isles in the 1790s were artisans, journeymen, and small shopkeepers, yet more than 70 percent of the radicals who emigrated to the United States had middle-class backgrounds or were attempting—before their political activities intervened—to rise into the solid middle ranks of society. In other words, emigration to the United States was less appealing to rank-and-file radicals, who possibly could not afford to go even if they wanted to, than to the educated and ambitious, who expected opportunities for advancement in republican America. At least seven were qualified in medicine; the United Irishman Edward Hudson was a dentist; the English Unitarian John Edmonds Stock was an Edinburgh medical student when he became embroiled in the Watt conspiracy.[29] John Craig Millar and the United Irishmen William Sampson, Harman Blennerhassett, and Thomas Addis Emmet were lawyers or barristers, while Callender, the son of a tobacconist, claimed to have been "bred to the law."[30] Thomas Ledlie Birch was

[27] Emsley, "Repression," *Eng. Hist. Rev.*, C (1985), 825; Wells, *Insurrection, passim.*

[28] Elliott, *Partners in Revolution, passim;* Foner, *Tom Paine*, 244; Hawke, *Paine*, 291-306.

[29] Those qualified in medicine included William James MacNeven, Stock, Reynolds, Edward Sweetman, Henry Toulmin, McLean, and Emmet. For Stock see *Edinburgh Evening Courant*, Sept. 6, 1794; *Scots Magazine*, LVI (1794), 652; and *Gentleman's Magazine*, N. S., IV (1835), 557. For Hudson, R. B. McDowell, *Ireland in the Age of Imperialism and Revolution, 1760-1801* (Oxford, 1979), 135, and *Dictionary of American Biography*, s.v. "Hudson, Edward."

[30] For Millar see Sir Francis J. Grant, *The Faculty of Advocates in Scotland, 1532-1943, with Genealogical Notes* (Edinburgh, 1944), 149, and *Autobiography of*

a Presbyterian minister; David Baillie Warden, James Hull, and John Miles were probationer Presbyterian ministers; Denis Driscol had been a clergyman before taking up the pen—in Ireland he edited the "wicked" *Cork Gazette* and in America the deist *Temple of Reason*—and Priestley was an eminent, if controversial, divine.[31]

Some of the émigrés had wealthy backgrounds. Thomas Cooper was a prosperous calico manufacturer until his business collapsed in 1793; the United Irishman Henry Jackson, who named his country seat "Fort Paine," was a well-to-do ironfounder.[32] When in 1798 the British army's attempt to forestall revolution by arresting most of the United Irish leadership failed, and the bloody and disastrous Irish rebellion erupted, John Devereaux, who owned an estate worth $10,000 per annum in Waterford, led 2,000 tenants against the British army. Banished, he became a merchant in Baltimore with business interests in South America, where he frequently visited. In 1815 he became a Bolivian general, returned to Ireland to enlist troops, and was eventually rewarded by Gen. Simón Bolívar with some of the profits of a goldmine. He died once again a rich man.[33]

At least four refugees secured professorships at American institutions of higher learning: Cooper at Central College (the University of Virginia) and at South Carolina College (the University of South Carolina); the chemist William James MacNeven at the New York College of Physicians and Surgeons; the Scotsman John Maclean at Princeton; and the United Irishman Daniel McCurtin at Washington College, Maryland. In addition, Warden was offered a professorship at Union College, Schenectady, but became for a while principal tutor at the Columbia Academy in New York, and John Wood, a Scotsman, tutored Aaron Burr's accomplished daughter. No fewer than eighteen exiles had attended university, although by no means all of these took a formal degree.[34]

Finally, nearly one-half of the émigrés were involved at one time or another in journalism and pamphleteering, and sixteen made the media their career. They ranged from hack writers Callender and James "Balloon" Tytler, who wrote much of the second edition of the *Encyclopaedia Britannica,* and struggling newspaper owners and editors such as James

---

Mrs. Fletcher, 64, 71. For Sampson, Twomey, "Jacobins and Jeffersonians," 36. For Blennerhassett, McDowell, *Ireland in the Age of Imperialism,* 134-135. For Emmet, Thomas P. Robinson, "The Life of Thomas Addis Emmet" (Ph.D. diss., New York University, 1955), 23-24. For Callender, *Recorder* (Rich.), Apr. 30, 1803.

[31] Latimer, "David Bailie Warden," *Ulster Jour. Arch.*, XXIII (1907), 29-38; A. Aspinall, *Politics and the Press, 1780-1850* (London, 1949), 62; Twomey, "Jacobins and Jeffersonians," 33-34.

[32] Malone, *Thomas Cooper,* 6; McDowell, *Ireland in the Age of Imperialism,* 480-481.

[33] [John Binns], *Recollections of the Life of John Binns* (Philadelphia, 1854), 317-318.

[34] Hook, *Scotland and America,* 241; Carter, "Political Activities of Mathew Carey," 244; *American Patriot* (Baltimore), Jan. 13, 1803.

Carey and John Mason Williams, to successful media barons such as William Duane, John Binns, and Joseph Gales.

This résumé of the respectable social origins of so many of the radical emigrants is a reminder that Paine's ideas influenced not only the lowest classes in the 1790s.[35] It also highlights the fact that his appeal centered partly in his belief in a meritocracy. In 1792 he wrote,

> Experience, in all ages, and in all countries, has demonstrated, that it is impossible to control Nature in her distribution of mental powers. She gives them as she pleases. . . . It appears to general observation, that revolutions create genius and talents; but these events do no more than bring them forward. There is in man, a mass of sense lying in a dormant state, and which, unless something excites it into action, will descend with him, in that condition, to the grave. As it is to the advantage of society that the whole of its faculties should be employed, the construction of government ought to be such as to bring forward, by a quiet and regular operation, all that extent of capacity which never fails to appear in revolutions.[36]

Much of Paine's popularity in Britain stemmed from his ability to mirror the sentiments of large numbers of people who resented their marginality in a society where a small privileged elite manipulated the levers of power. Professional men, and men aspiring to professional careers, in particular regarded their social position with ambivalence, for although they strove for independence and eminence, by tradition the lawyer, the cleric, the doctor, the teacher, and the man of letters were regarded as mere auxiliaries to the ruling elites. They were dependent satellites in a highly structured social world controlled by what Jonathan Clark has called "an *ancien régime* state."[37] At a time when the professions had neither the social status nor the popular esteem of today, and when professional power was confined to small oligarchies, many professionals found their social and economic aspirations stifled by a social structure that denied opportunities to advancement on merit. Thus to an important degree the émigrés represented the radicalism of ambitious but socially blocked classes in late eighteenth-century Britain. Their resentments multiplied when, as with most of the exiles, their dissenting religious opinions further reduced their status in the eyes of the powerful social elites.[38]

[35] Foner, *Tom Paine*, 99.

[36] Philip S. Foner, ed., *The Life and Major Writings of Thomas Paine* (Secaucus, N.J., 1974), I, 367-368.

[37] J.C.D. Clark, *English Society, 1688-1832: Ideology, Social Structure and Political Practice during the Ancien Regime* (Cambridge, 1985). This is a sustained and brilliant argument against the "bourgeois" nature of 18th-century British society that throws new light on late 18th-century radicalism.

[38] Goodwin, *Friends of Liberty*, 65-98; Thompson, *English Working Class*, 28-58; Michael R. Watts, *The Dissenters: From the Reformation to the French Revolution* (Oxford, 1978), 478-490.

The émigrés' writings echoed Paine's theme of wasted or underutilized talent. For the Reverend Thomas Dunn, in 1794, this was a perpetual condition: "from the murder of righteous Abel, down to Dr. Priestley, the first philosopher of the present age, superior integrity and superior talents have always been persecuted by narrow-minded, malignant, and wicked men." James Carey was more precise; in 1799 he claimed that John Adams's form of Federalism was no different from "the [Pittite] constitution," which aimed "above all to cramp the inventive genius and the enterprising spirit of Englishmen." For Cooper, "strength, and wisdom, and talents, and good dispositions, superior capacity of body or mind—superior industry or activity, do, and ought to create proportionate distinctions, and to bring with them their own reward."[39]

Under Pitt's government radicals had few illusions that their talents would be permitted effective expression. Recognizing this, Paine had written that republican government offered the best prospects of an open society. He defined republican government as one "established and conducted for the interests of the public, as well individually as collectively," and noted that "it most naturally associates with the representative form."[40] He had, since 1776, always carefully distinguished between society and government, the former a blessing, the latter "but a necessary evil."[41] The radicals accepted this distinction. Dunn, in a 1794 discourse at the New Dutch Church in Nassau Street, New York, went so far as to quote *Common Sense* almost verbatim: "At best, Government is but an imperfect remedy for the various evils of this imperfect state. 'Tis more a badge of lost innocence, than any positive advantage. SOCIETY is, indeed, a blessing; as it promotes our happinesss, unites our affections. . . . Government is only a negative advantage; a mere curb upon our vices: the necessity for government . . . arises from our wickedness."[42] So pervasive was Paine's view of government that Callender, near the end of his remarkable career in the United States, even when in the name of independence and political purity he was attacking the Jeffersonians and their newly imported propagandist, Thomas Paine, still adhered to it. "Government," he declared, "is chiefly known by the expence which it occasions. It is a sort of complex constable, a *something* hired to keep the peace, and nothing more. In 'Common Sense,' Mr. Paine has fully explained this doctrine. He observes that society arises from our *wants*, and government, from our *vices*. The definition is perfect. Government is

[39] Thomas Dunn, *A Discourse, Delivered in the New Dutch Church, Nassau Street* . . . (New York, 1794), 4; Timothy Telltruth [James Carey], *The Collected Wisdom of Ages, the Most Stupendous Fabric of Human Invention, the English Constitution* (Philadelphia, 1799), v; Thomas Cooper, *A Reply to Mr. Burke's Invective against Mr. Cooper, and Mr. Watt, in the House of Commons, on 30th of April, 1792* (Manchester, 1792), 22.

[40] Foner, ed., *Writings of Paine*, I, 369.

[41] Paine, *Common Sense*, ed. Kramnick, 65. This distinction can, of course, be traced back to Locke.

[42] Dunn, *Discourse Delivered in the New Dutch Church*, 13-14.

to society, what a bridle is to a horse, or a dose of salts to the human body. They produce no positive good; but they prevent the existence of evil."[43]

Paine's ideal form of republican government was that of the United States, in which "representation [is] ingrafted upon democracy." The American people had solved their political problems in 1787 "by the simple operation of constructing government on the principles of society and the rights of man.... There the poor are not oppressed, the rich are not privileged. Industry is not mortified by the splendid extravagance of a court rioting at its expense. Their taxes are few, because their government is just; and as there is nothing to render them wretched, there is nothing to engender riots and tumults."[44] As enthusiasm for reform in Britain gave way in 1792 first to the recognition that loyalism was immensely strong, and then to despair of success, Paine's vision of America as an asylum of liberty with an exemplary political system became more and more attractive. From Dublin in April 1792 John Chambers, whose bookshop was a meeting place for the United Irishmen, informed Mathew Carey in Philadelphia that the American Constitution was increasingly admired in Europe: "even that of France shrinks from a contrast."[45] Cooper, following a short sojourn in America at the end of 1793, wrote that "there is little fault to find with the government of America, either in principle or in practice;... we have few [disputes] respecting political men or political measures: the present irritation of men's minds in Great Britain, and the discordant state of society on political accounts, is not known there. The government is the government *of* the people, and *for* the people."[46] A Painite utopian vision filled the radicals' minds as they took flight across the Atlantic.

II

Utopian expectations are normally disappointed when confronted with reality, and the émigrés' dreams were no exception. Many radicals were unpleasantly surprised by their initial reception in America. Disembarking at New Castle in 1794, Alexander Wilson walked to Wilmington and then to Philadelphia. Virtually penniless, he and his nephew "made free to go into a good many farm-houses on the road, but saw none of that kindness and hospitality so often told of them."[47] In 1795 Wolfe Tone, the United Irishman, found the country to be "beautiful, but it is like a beautiful scene in a theatre; the effect at a proper distance is admirable, but it will not bear a minute inspection." Americans were unfriendly and selfish, and "they do

[43] *Recorder* (Rich.), Dec. 1, 1802.

[44] Foner, ed., *Writings of Paine*, I, 371, 360.

[45] John Chambers to Mathew Carey, Dublin, Apr. 12, 1792, Lea and Febiger Collection, Historical Society of Pennsylvania, Philadelphia.

[46] Thomas Cooper, *Some Information Respecting America*... (London, 1794), 52-53.

[47] Alexander Wilson to his parents, July 25, 1794, in Clark Hunter, ed., *The Life and Letters of Alexander Wilson* (Philadelphia, 1983), 150.

fleece us émigrés at a most unmerciful rate."[48] Their poverty or even notoriety does not explain the treatment the émigrés received. A respectable English lawyer, Charles William Janson, visiting a market in 1793 with other new arrivals, soon found "that we had paid at least a halfpenny per pound more than the market price," although he conceded that in other countries "the perversion of the scriptural expression 'I was a stranger and you took me in,' is perhaps still more strikingly exemplified."[49] Sooner or later, however, most émigrés came to terms with contemporary "republican mores" and settled down, usually with the assistance of radicals who had arrived earlier and who thus had already experienced the adapting process. Mathew Carey gave work to Callender, for instance, and Archibald Binny, the typefounder, assisted his fellow Scottish radical David Bruce.[50]

The émigrés' personal experiences, however, were less painful in the longer term than their dismay at Alexander Hamilton's perversion of the new Constitution. The pattern of radical reactions to Federalist policies was to some extent determined by the length of time émigrés had spent in America. The early emigrants' confidence in republican institutions *gradually* diminished as Hamilton's program systematically unfolded. Those arriving after 1795 already knew what to expect. All, however, condemned the growing convergence of Federalist policies and those of successive British governments in the eighteenth century. They had fled from the effects of such policies; many reacted in America by becoming actively involved in Jeffersonian Republican politics.

The émigrés strongly opposed Hamilton's apparent intention to recreate in America a stratified society based on finance capitalism, high taxation, a national debt, and a "placeman" system, with "the British and stock-jobbing faction" holding power only by "the countenance of England."[51] Richard Dinmore's succinct retrospective analysis of John Adams's presidency neatly underlined the émigrés' fears of Federalism. "Your national expences were encreased," he stated, and "placemen became numerous and governmental influence enormous."[52] According to Cheetham, Adams's administration "copied implicitly the acts of the English government, even in the worst and most vitiated period of its history. . . . The will of the executive became the animating principle of our federal legislature, and that will was palpably in favour of monar-

[48] Joseph James St. Mark, "The Red Shamrock: United Irishmen and Revolution, 1795-1803" (Ph.D. diss., Georgetown University, 1974), 154.

[49] Janson, *The Stranger in America, 1793-1806* (London, 1807), 20.

[50] Mathew Carey to James Thomson Callender, Oct. 5, 1793, Lea and Febiger Letter Book, IV, 1st Ser.; Rollo G. Silver, *Typefounding in America, 1787-1825* (Charlottesville, Va., 1925), 73; Twomey, "Jacobins and Jeffersonians," 66-75.

[51] [James Thomson Callender], *The Prospect before Us* (Richmond, Va., 1800), I, 101.

[52] [Dinmore], *Talk before the Tammany Society,* 13.

chy."[53] As usual, it was Callender who made the most virulent attacks on the Federalist system. Languishing in Richmond jail in 1800, he bemoaned the constitutional provision giving "an unqualified power of taxation" to Congress. "Out of every dollar which they could raise," he wrote, "at least three fourths have been misapplied. The public officers have rushed to public plunder, like as many dogs to a dead carcase. . . . [T]he federal government feels anxious . . . *to have a finger in every pye;* to swell the public debt as much as may be; and to raise its own power by the depression of the state governments, by the useless and endless multiplication of places, and of jobs."[54]

The émigré radicals, having discovered similar features in Federalist and Pittite policies, attacked the former with the weapons they had honed in their war against the latter. Faced in America with the menace of excessive governmental power, of a financial system supported by the state, and of a corrupt officialdom, the émigrés responded with political arguments that mingled the natural rights theories of Paine with residual elements of Commonwealth ideology. They laid much heavier emphasis on promoting the Painite vision of a socially harmonious, egalitarian, and commercialized society than on defending the older and by now—for both Britain and the United States—less relevant Commonwealth ideal of a closely integrated, relatively static, hierarchical agrarian polity. Much of the exiles' importance in America stems from the relative weighting of Commonwealth and Painite ideas in their political thought, for compared to contemporary American republican thought, theirs was more significantly informed by liberal than by classical ideology. Both American and British strains of republicanism were in transition,[55] but the latter had been developed further. Thanks to Paine's influence, British republicans were quicker to accept the benefits of a commercial society. In the battles of the Federalist decade, the émigrés' political arguments helped to nudge Jeffersonian Republicanism away from classical political thought.

Commonwealth ideology's limited appeal to the radical exiles is exemplified by their conception of virtue. Appleby has argued that in the United States "by the end of the century virtue more often referred to a private quality, a man's capacity to look out for himself and his dependents—almost the opposite of classical virtue."[56] The radicals easily accepted such a privatized version of virtue. The defrocked Irish priest and newspaper editor Denis Driscol, for instance, when extolling the middling class of free and independent citizens, equated virtue with the

[53] "A Citizen of New York" [James Cheetham], *A Narrative of the Suppression, by Colonel Burr, of the History of the Administration of John Adams* . . . (New York, 1802), 6-7.

[54] [Callender], *Prospect before Us*, II, 97, 116. Callender, of course, was incorrect to state that Congress's taxing power was unqualified.

[55] McCoy, *Elusive Republic*, 10.

[56] Appleby, *Capitalism and a New Social Order*, 15.

quintessentially personal values of honor and integrity.[57] Similarly, Cooper, while analyzing the inequities of a hierarchical society based on privilege and birth, also associated virtue with personal qualities. The privileged, although ignorant and vice-ridden, received all the honors and rewards, and thus undermined the morals of those with "abilities and virtue."[58] Callender gave short shrift to the nostalgic view of a virtuous golden age under an ancient constitution. "At what era this *freedom* and *virtue* existed, no body could ever tell. . . . British annals . . . [are] full of calamity and disgrace. . . . Some people talk of restoring the constitution to its *primitive* purity. They would do well to inform us what that purity was, and where its traces are to be found."[59]

Far more important than the language of virtue for the émigrés was the language of natural rights and the ethic of individualism. Their political discourse was founded less on the Commonwealth tradition of Harrington, Sidney, Bolingbroke, and Montesquieu than on the political and economic ideas of Locke, Smith, and Paine. In all their published writings there is only one reference to Harrington—by Cooper, who in a discussion of monarchy claimed that the subject was covered "more profoundly" by Paine, Joel Barlow, and the Abbé Siéyès than by Milton, Harrington, or Sidney.[60] Only Daniel Isaac Eaton, whose sojourn in America was brief, openly espoused the ideas of Montesquieu, reprinting the section "On Liberty" from *The Spirit of the Laws* in 1795. Eaton was also eccentric in believing that "talent was conferred on mankind, undoubtedly, for the promotion of public virtue."[61] Sidney was mentioned only rarely, and then usually in a general litany of heroic names that coupled him with Locke. Cheetham, in his dying speech to his children in 1810, after "raving mania" had set in, did mention Bolingbroke, but not for his political perspicacity. "With herculean strength he now raised himself from his pillow; with eyes of meteoric fierceness, he grasped his bed covering, and in a most vehement but rapid articulation, exclaimed to his sons, 'Boys! study Bolingbroke for style, and Locke for sentiment.' He spoke no more."[62]

On the other hand, the names and ideas of Locke, Smith, and "the immortal Paine" punctuate the writings of the radicals.[63] Dumas Malone

[57] *Am. Patriot,* Nov. 13, 1802; "A Quaker in Politics" [Joseph Priestley], "Maxims of Political Arithmetic, Applied to the Case of the United States of America," *Aurora, General Advertiser* (Philadelphia), Feb. 27, 1798.

[58] Cooper, *Reply to Mr. Burke's Invective,* 37.

[59] [James Thomson Callender], *The Political Progress of Britain; or, An Impartial History of Abuses in the Government of the British Empire* (Philadelphia, 1795), pt. 2, 55-56.

[60] Cooper, *Reply to Mr. Burke's Invective,* 17.

[61] Daniel Isaac Eaton, *The Philanthropist; or, Philosophical Essays on Politics, Government, Morals and Manners* (Philadelphia), Mar. 16, 1795, 1, Nov. 2, 1795, 1-3.

[62] Twomey, "Jacobins and Jeffersonians," 56-57.

[63] Cooper, *Reply to Mr. Burke's Invective,* 23.

showed how influential were Locke in the development of Cooper's early views and Smith for his political economy.[64] William Duane quoted with approval both Locke and Smith in an 1804 pamphlet on banking.[65] Callender was uncharacteristically effusive. "No man," he wrote, "has done more honour to England, than Mr. Locke." He added that Smith's *Wealth of Nations* "deserves to be studied by every member of the community, as one of the most accurate, profound, and persuasive books that ever was written."[66]

It was Paine's writings above all others that spoke to the radicals' needs. The publishing history of *Rights of Man* is astonishing. Part one, published in March 1791, was promoted by the Society for Constitutional Information in London and by the new provincial radical societies. The Manchester Constitutional Society asked Cooper to abridge it for popular use, and in January 1792 Joseph Gales of the Sheffield Constitutional Society obtained Paine's consent to print the first cheap edition.[67] The book became a bestseller, but it was eclipsed by the phenomenal success of part two, published in February 1792. As many as 200,000 copies of part two, in various forms and editions, may have been distributed in the British Isles by the end of the year.[68]

The effect of *Rights of Man* on many of the émigrés was electric. Cooper told James Watt, Jr., that "it has made me still more politically mad than I ever was. . . . It is choque full, crowded with good sense and demonstrative reasoning. . . . I regard it as the very jewel of a book."[69] Cheetham, one of three Manchester brothers known as "the three Jacobin infidels," rushed "from tavern to tavern and from brothel to brothel with *Rights of Man* in one hand and *Age of Reason* in the other."[70] Eaton gained notoriety for repeatedly publishing Paine's works, even after they had been banned as seditious libel.[71] Incarcerated in Kilmainham jail in 1793, Dr. James Reynolds took comfort from a print of Paine hanging on the wall of his cell.[72]

Paine was by no means an original thinker; it is possible to trace all his ideas to previous theorists, especially to those in the Lockean tradition. It

[64] Malone, *Thomas Cooper*, 13, 98, 216.

[65] [Duane], *Observations on the Principles and Operation of Banking* (Philadelphia, 1804), 3; [Richard Dinmore], *An Exposition of the Principles of the English Jacobins . . .*, 2d ed. (Norwich, 1797), 10.

[66] [J. T. Callender], *Deformities of Dr. Samuel Johnson. Selected from His Works*, 2d ed. (London, 1782), 69, 89.

[67] Goodwin, *Friends of Liberty*, 177.

[68] Royle and Walvin, *English Radicals*, 54.

[69] Frida Knight, *The Strange Case of Thomas Walker: Ten Years in the Life of a Manchester Radical* (London, 1957), 63-64.

[70] Twomey, "Jacobins and Jeffersonians," 29-30.

[71] Daniel Lawrence McCue, Jr., "Daniel Isaac Eaton and *Politics for the People*" (Ph.D. diss., Columbia University, 1974), 90.

[72] R. R. Madden, *The United Irishmen, Their Lives and Times*, rev. ed., 4 vols. (London, 1857-1860), I, 83.

was his tone that so stimulated the radicals, encouraging their sense of individual worth and desire for change. Paine, Edward Thompson has written, "destroyed with one book century-old taboos."[73] His contemptuous dismissal of the hereditary principle, his promotion of egalitarianism, individualism, and natural rights (Paine's two major points, wrote Callender, were an attack on hereditary right and a defense of equal representation),[74] and his faith in the future galvanized thousands into political action. Although some of the exiles were to have intellectual and emotional difficulties coming to terms with the deist principles in *Age of Reason,* in the 1790s they widely disseminated Painite radicalism so that it became a potent force in American Republican circles.

III

A recent examination of late eighteenth-century British radicalism shows that it consisted of two main ideological tendencies, one agrarian and the other commercial. According to Geoffrey Gallop, agrarian radicalism "exerted a powerful influence on a radical generation searching for solutions to . . . moral and political decay. The ideas of the self-sufficient village community and the independent freeholder . . . became intermixed with classical republican ideals of equality, simplicity and virtue to produce the agrarian radicalism of the late eighteenth century." In contrast, commercial radicalism "emphasised material progress and connected it with private property, self-interest and commercial society." Commercial radicals, including Paine and Priestley, "argued that the society and economy said by the agrarians to be the basis and fulfilment of the ethic of universal benevolence—the agrarian utopia—was antithetical to real human needs and aspirations. They . . . believed that commerce expanded and humanised the mind by way of increased contact and the encouragement of mutual interdependence."[75] This vision of a commercialized society appealed most to those radicals who looked to the establishment of a polity in which socially formed obstacles to growth and personal advancement were obliterated and opportunities for the exercise of talents were maximized. A commercial society obviously had more attractions for aspiring professionals than a hierarchical agrarian polity, for, as long as the political, social, and educational contexts were organized to promote equality of opportunity, their chances of advancement and independence were considerably enhanced.

The émigrés' emphasis on individual freedom and opportunity made their acceptance of commercial society inevitable. It was Paine who linked individualism and commerce most clearly. "Commerce," he wrote, "is no other than the traffic of two individuals, multiplied on a scale of numbers; and by the same rule that nature intended the intercourse of two, she

[73] Thompson, *English Working Class,* 92; Williams, *Artisans,* 17-18.

[74] *Recorder* (Rich.), Dec. 1, 1802.

[75] Geoffrey I. Gallop, "Politics, Property and Progress: British Radical Thought, 1760-1815" (D. Phil. diss., Oxford University, 1983), 22-24.

intended that of all."[76] Thus a commercial society had to be free and open to all. The émigré radicals strongly opposed what John Thelwall, the foremost theorist of the London Corresponding Society, called "speculation-commerce"—that is, commerce based on mercantilism, in which world trade was controlled "by a few engrossers and monopolists" who, by accumulating commodities "in the hope of exciting artificial wants" within a mercantilist system, manipulated trade to their own advantage.[77] Similarly, the views on commerce put forward by Cooper and Priestley in 1799, which some historians seem to have misinterpreted,[78] were aimed not at commerce per se but at commercial *speculation* and at government support for such artificial trade. Both men opposed the tendency of merchants to rush into the Atlantic carrying trade, opened up temporarily by the war between Britain and France, partly because the naval support necessary to defend a merchant marine increased the Federalist mania for government defense spending and the risk of war, and partly because it represented "forced" or "unnatural" trade. Merchants should be left alone to seek their own best interests, said Cooper: "prohibit nothing, but protect no speculation." If foreign commerce was threatened, it should, "like every other losing scheme . . . be left to its own fate."[79] In like manner, Callender's oft-reprinted *Political Progress of Britain,* much admired by Jefferson, was a virulent attack not on commerce itself but on British mercantilist policies that had led to numerous wars and millions of deaths in the eighteenth century.[80]

"Speculation-commerce" conflicted with the radicals' vision of an open society where every individual had the same opportunities to use his talents to the full. The ideal system of commerce was "commission-commerce," whereby countries exchanged abundant commodities for scarce but desired ones.[81] In this process the state should have no role to play. As Dinmore wrote, radicals "oppose all laws which cramp industry. . . . [E]very man has a right to get his bread wherever he pleases, and by whatever honest means."[82] In the American context, "commission-commerce" condoned the supremacy of agricultural products within the

[76] Foner, ed., *Writings of Paine,* I, 400.

[77] Gallop, "Politics, Property and Progress," 144.

[78] This is not the place to discuss in detail the misunderstandings, but compare Twomey, "Jacobins and Jeffersonians," 146, with McCoy, *Elusive Republic,* 176, and Appleby, *Capitalism and a New Social Order,* 88-89. Twomey's thesis is the most thorough examination of the émigrés' political economy.

[79] Twomey, "Jacobins and Jeffersonians," 146-147; [Priestley], "Maxims of Political Arithmetic," *Aurora,* Feb. 26, 1798.

[80] [James Thomson Callender], *The Political Progress of Britain; or, An Impartial Account of the Principal Abuses in the Government of This Country, from the Revolution in 1688* . . . (Edinburgh, 1792), pt. 1. It was reprinted in London in 1792 and in 1795 (by Daniel Isaac Eaton), and in America in 1794, 1795, and 1796.

[81] Gallop, "Politics, Property and Progress," 144.

[82] [Dinmore], *Principles of the English Jacobins,* 8; [Priestley], "Maxims of Political Arithmetic," *Aurora,* Feb. 26, 1798.

nation's economy; trade links with the rest of the world were naturally to be based on the exportation of agricultural products and the importation of manufactured goods.

Thus the British and Irish radicals' political economy incorporated without difficulty Smith's—and the French physiocrats'—belief that, in a "natural" and unfettered economic world, investment would logically flow into agriculture first, then into home manufactures, and finally into domestic and foreign commerce.[83] They did not oppose either commerce or manufacturing in the 1790s; they merely argued, as did Cooper in 1799, that individual and rational investment decisions in the United States would normally favor agriculture.[84]

But at the same time some were aware, at an earlier date than most Americans and probably as a result of their anglophobia, that to be truly independent Americans ought to be ready to promote home manufacturing when favorable conditions arose. Although in 1794 Cooper felt that large-scale domestic manufacturing would be unprofitable in America as long as land was a better investment and there remained "a prejudice in favour of British goods," he was not opposed to its eventual development. His unfortunate experiences as a failed manufacturer in England partly determined his opinions; "the common lot of inventors and first improvers [is that] they usually enrich the country and impoverish themselves," he wrote bitterly. In the same year Morgan John Rhees argued that Americans should "strain every nerve to patronize their manufactural as well as their agricultural interest." Callender, too, believed in the 1790s that home manufacturing would be unprofitable, at least while the circulation of excessive paper money left wages too high and excise taxes encouraged British imports, thus entombing American manufactures "in the grave of her independence." Nevertheless, by 1798, trying to wean Americans from Federalist support for Britain, he was arguing for the self-sufficiency of America ("America should, like the armidilla, withdraw within her shell") in both agriculture and home manufactures, the latter being more important than foreign commerce. No one was more useful to American society, he suggested, than the "industrious and intelligent manufacturer."[85]

The radical exiles envisaged a society in which agricultural, manufacturing, and commercial pursuits were carried out in harmony, without the danger of economic class conflict. In this they again echoed Paine, who had written that "the landholder, the farmer, the manufacturer, the merchant, the tradesman, and every occupation, prospers by the aid which each receives from the other, and from the whole. Common interest regulates their concerns."[86] As

[83] D. D. Raphael, *Adam Smith* (Oxford, 1985), 81-82.

[84] Thomas Cooper, *Political Essays, Originally Inserted in the Northumberland Gazette, with Additions* (Northumberland, Pa., 1799).

[85] Cooper, *Information Respecting America,* 59, 2; Twomey, "Jacobins and Jeffersonians," 155; James Thomson Callender, *Sketches of the History of America* (Philadelphia, 1798), 185-187, 207-209, and *Sedgwick & Co.; or, A Key to the Six Per Cent Cabinet* (Philadelphia, 1798), 87.

[86] Foner, ed., *Writings of Paine,* I, 357.

early as 1788 Mathew Carey looked to a United States where a manufacturing North and an agricultural South worked together to promote national unity. It would be "a patriotic undertaking," wrote Gales in 1802, for Americans to wear home manufactured cotton goods, for "it must be obvious . . . that every manufacture that consumes cotton, would be highly profitable to this country," most particularly to its agricultural interest. In 1806 Cheetham asserted that "if the commercial interest of this country is called upon to suffer, its *agricultural interest* cannot possibly escape. They are both too closely connected to stand alone; they must rise or fall together." And Binns in the *Democratic Press* continually emphasized the message that "manufacturing and commerce are the sisters, the friends, and the handmaidens of agriculture."[87]

In the 1790s, however, the mercantilist implications of this commercial and industrial political economy remained latent amongst the émigrés. While the Federalists held power, and state influence, in the opinion of Republicans, promoted the interests of a monied minority, anglophobia, and political necessity, the continued authority of Paine's teachings ensured radical adherence to a laissez-faire program. The alternative would merely have played into the hands of the Federalists. Under a Republican regime in the following decade, however, a mercantilist political economy became a patriotic desideratum, and as Paine's vision of a peaceful world predicated on commercial reciprocity stubbornly failed to materialize, one is not surprised to find at the forefront of demands for an independent and self-sufficient United States most of the surviving émigrés of the 1790s, including Cooper, Mathew Carey, Binns, Gales, and Sampson.[88] Government promotion of manufactures and of the infrastructure required for a modern commercial society was no longer regarded as creating a "forced" or "unnatural" economy; patriotic necessity ensured its "naturalness." With its emphasis on national economic development, such a political economy still conformed to Painite radical parameters.[89]

IV

Appleby has noted that in the 1790s the democrats in America found "a national voice where in the past their strength had been local."[90] Certain prerequisites were necessary for this to occur; one of the most important was a nationwide system for disseminating information by print. In media

[87] Carter, "Political Activities of Mathew Carey," 160; *Raleigh Register, and North-Carolina State Gazette*, June 2, 1801, Mar. 9, Aug. 3, 1802; "Politicus" [James Cheetham], *An Impartial Enquiry into Certain Parts of the Conduct of Governor Lewis, and a Portion of the Legislature* . . . (New York, 1806), 18, 51; [Binns], *Recollections*, 164-166.

[88] "Autobiography of Mathew Carey," *New England Magazine*, 1834, letters 22, 23; Mathew Carey, *The Olive Branch; or, Faults on Both Sides* (Philadelphia, 1814); [Binns], *Recollections*, 165-166; Twomey, "Jacobins and Jeffersonians," 147-170.

[89] The best study of Paine's nationalist political economy is Foner, *Tom Paine*, esp. chaps. 5, 6.

[90] Appleby, *Capitalism and a New Social Order*, 4.

communications in particular can be seen most clearly the influence of the émigré radicals on the development of Jeffersonianism. As one historian has written, "foreigners seemed to get one sniff of printers' ink and become loyal Jeffersonians."[91]

The extent of the radicals' involvement in newspaper production has never been fully appreciated. It has been estimated that 450 newspapers and 75 magazines were founded in the United States between 1783 and 1800.[92] The appendix indicates which ones were edited by émigrés from 1783, when the ex-Wilkite and later Democratic Society member John Miller founded the *South Carolina Gazette*.[93] All told, eighteen British and Irish radicals edited no fewer than 49 newspapers and magazines, mostly in the politically sensitive middle states but at one time or another covering all the eastern seaboard, from Georgia to Massachusetts.

It is obviously very difficult to determine their newspapers' general influence in spreading ideas, news, and propaganda. Circulation figures are almost impossible to calculate, although the common practice of copying from other newspapers ensured that major views were widely disseminated. Undoubtedly, most of these newspapers worked on a shoestring. The émigrés' efforts were predictably weak in Federalist New England, where the United Irishman John Daly Burk briefly edited the first daily newspaper in Boston, and elsewhere many of their prints were ephemeral. James Carey, for example, failed with newspapers in Richmond, Charleston (twice), Savannah, Wilmington, N.C., and Philadelphia (three times). Still, financially insecure though his newspapers were, their value was recognized in high places. As *Carey's United States' Recorder*, devoted to "the American constitution" and "true republican principles," and the *Aurora* tottered in 1798, Jefferson, who had subscribed to Carey's first newspaper in 1792, told Madison that "we should really exert ourselves to procure them, for if these papers fall, republicanism will be entirely brow-beaten."[94] He then organized a group of Philadelphia Republicans, including John Beckley, Israel Israel, and Mathew Carey, to subsidize Callender, who was then the assistant editor of the *Aurora*.[95] *Carey's United States' Recorder* collapsed, partly owing to the yellow fever epidemic, but the *Aurora*, edited by William Duane after Benjamin Franklin

[91] Walter Francis Brown, Jr., "John Adams and the American Press, 1797-1801: The First Full Scale Confrontation between the Executive and the Media" (Ph.D. diss., University of Notre Dame, 1974), 45.

[92] *Ibid.*, 72.

[93] Gilpatrick, "English Background of John Miller;" *Furman Bulletin*, XX (1938), 14-20; Eugene P. Link, *Democratic-Republican Societies, 1790-1800* (New York, 1942), 90; Donald H. Stewart, *The Opposition Press of the Federalist Period* (Albany, N.Y., 1969), 649.

[94] Jefferson to Madison, Apr. 26, 1798, in Worthington Chauncey Ford, ed., "Thomas Jefferson and James Thomson Callender," *New England Historical and Genealogical Register*, L (1896), 328n; *Carey's United States' Recorder* (Philadelphia), June 30, 1798; Carter, "Political Activities of Mathew Carey," 200.

[95] *Recorder* (Rich.), Aug. 25, 1802.

Bache's death in 1798, went from strength to strength. In his first year Duane nearly doubled the *Aurora*'s circulation, to a peak of 1,700 subscribers.[96] As the political crisis deepened in the last years of Adams's presidency, the Republican newspapers, with the émigrés to the fore, acted as a "conduit between [the party's] leaders and philosophers, and the masses."[97] Newsprint became the circulating medium that brought Republicans together under Jefferson's banner. As Callender wrote, "it is certain that the citizens of America derive their information almost exclusively from newspapers."[98]

The émigré newspaper editors represented perhaps 15 to 20 percent of all Republican printers in this period.[99] Their importance, however, was greater than their numbers suggest, for at crucial times, especially in the years leading to Jefferson's victory in 1800, they controlled some of the country's most widely circulating, strategically placed newspapers. Duane, for example, developed the *Aurora* almost into a national daily; not only did it circulate beyond the borders of Pennsylvania, but many other Republican newspapers reprinted its most important political articles. In North Carolina, the Federalist Abraham Hodge, with four presses and three newspapers, held almost a monopoly of printing until Sen. Nathaniel Macon persuaded Gales to move from Philadelphia in order to establish an opposition newspaper in Raleigh. The first number of Gales's *Register* was printed in October 1799, and within a few months Hodge was forced to shift one of his newspapers from Fayetteville to Raleigh to meet the competition. It was to no avail; Gales soon had a statewide readership. After 1800, for his services to Republicanism, Gales was rewarded with the state government's printing contract.[100]

Meriwether Jones's Richmond *Examiner* had the widest circulation of any Republican newspaper in Virginia. In the crucial months from mid-1799 to early 1801, as a "Scots Correspondent," Callender wrote for it almost one hundred columns of political news and opinion, and the newspaper's circulation rose by nearly 400, an increase of about 40 percent.[101] So much more dangerous did the tone of the newspaper become after Callender's arrival that a group of young Federalists tried, unsuccessfully, to drive him out of town.[102]

[96] *Carey's U.S. Recorder*, Aug. 30, 1798; Ray Boston, "The Impact of 'Foreign Liars' on the American Press (1790-1800)," *Journalism Quarterly*, L (1973), 722-730.

[97] Stewart, *Opposition Press of the Federalist Period*, 13.

[98] *Recorder* (Rich.), Dec. 1, 1802.

[99] This is an estimate. Fewer than one-half of the printers in America in the 1790s were Republicans. If together they edited just under half of the 550 serial publications, and individually two each, there would have been 18 émigré editors in a total of 110 Republicans.

[100] Briggs, "Joseph Gales, Editor of Raleigh's First Newspaper," *N.C. Booklet*, VII (1907), 117-118.

[101] *Recorder* (Rich.), May 12, 1802.

[102] *Ibid.*, Feb. 9, 1803.

Federalists perceived the émigré printers as major threats to their political supremacy. It was no accident that they regarded Duane, Cooper, and Callender as fit candidates for the rigors of the Alien and Sedition acts. If John Adams and Fisher Ames can be believed, Jefferson's election in 1800 was partly the consequence of the émigré newspapermen's concerted campaigns from 1799. In 1801 a distraught Adams lamented, "Is there no pride in American bosoms? Can their hearts endure that Callender, Duane, Cooper and Lyon should be the most influential men in the country, all foreigners and degraded characters?" Ames was equally devastated: "The newspapers are an overmatch for any Government. They will first overawe and then usurp it. This has been done; and the Jacobins owe their triumph to the unceasing use of this engine."[103]

Newspapers at that time, as today, were reading material one day, fire lighters the next, effective only if, as was the case from 1799 to 1801, the message was repeatedly hammered home and widely diffused by the copying system, which, according to Ames, was precisely why the Republican press was so effective. Somewhat less ephemeral were the numerous political pamphlets published in the 1790s. Again, émigré radicals were to the fore in disseminating political information, both original and borrowed. In addition to the printers listed in the appendix to this article, at least five other émigrés—Matthew Falkner, John Chambers, Daniel Isaac Eaton, Patrick Byrne, and Thomas Stephens—published and sold books and pamphlets in this period.[104] In 1796 Callender noted a preponderance of émigré booksellers: "take away all the Scots and Irish booksellers from Philadelphia, and [a reader] could hardly supply his library. With three or four exceptions the whole trade centres among foreigners. The case is much the same in New York and Baltimore."[105]

The émigrés had a two-fold publishing strategy: they printed original materials, and they reprinted political pamphlets from overseas. Mathew Carey, for example, who was probably the most prolific publisher and certainly the greatest risk-taker in the publishing world, reprinted Mary Wollstonecraft's *Vindication of the Rights of Women* (1794), Helen Maria Williams's *Letters Containing a Sketch of the Politics of France* (1796), and

[103] James Morton Smith, *Freedom's Fetters: The Alien and Sedition Laws and American Civil Liberties* (Ithaca, N.Y., 1956); Brown, "John Adams and the American Press," 272, 258. Brown argues that opposition to Adams from the High Federalist press was as important as Republican propaganda in Jefferson's election (*ibid.*, iv).

[104] The major source for the publishers and printers is Charles Evans, *American Bibliography*, vols. 9-13, (Worcester, Mass., 1925-1955). Another émigré, either Alexander Kennedy or his brother James, both of whom fled Scotland in 1794 during the Watt trial, was "a theological bookseller" in Washington in 1830. See Hook, *Scotland and America*, 240; *Edinburgh Evening Courant*, May 29, Aug. 28, Sept. 4, 6, 1794; *Scots Magazine*, Oct. 1794, 627. Another Scottish émigré, Archibald Binny, manufactured most of the type for the printers in Philadelphia, including Mathew Carey. See Silver, *Typefounding in America*, 22.

[105] *Recorder* (Rich.), Apr. 3, 1802.

Condorcet's *Outlines of an Historical View of the Progress of the Human Mind* (1796); "Citizen" Richard Lee reprinted Charles Pigott's *Political Curiosities* (1796); James Carey reprinted the *Trial of Margarot* (1794) and William Godwin's *Memoirs of Mary Wollstonecraft* (1799); and Thomas Stephens republished *The Proceedings of the Society of United Irishmen, of Dublin* (1795), and Volney's *The Law of Nature* (1796).[106] Although the émigrés had no monopoly on Paine's works, they reproduced his writings in a number of ways. Mathew Carey republished both parts of *Rights of Man* in 1796, and his brother James printed a two-volume edition of Paine's works in 1797, which could be bought with or without *The Age of Reason* and with or without Bishop Richard Watson's reply to Paine's deist pamphlets.[107]

Some also published their own or their fellow émigrés' original works. Callender wrote a second part to *The Political Progress of Britain* (1795) and *A Short History of the Excise* (1795)—both of which Mathew Carey reprinted in 1796—as well as an infamous but extraordinarily effective *History of 1796* (1797) and two volumes of *The Prospect before Us* (1800). The "O'Careys," as William Cobbett called them, published numerous squibs and satires in their private war against "Porcupine." Birch and Burk wrote histories of the United Irishmen. Cooper published his *Political Arithmetic* (1798) and *Political Essays* (1799).[108] In addition, the émigrés ensured the wide circulation of important speeches and political opinions. Mathew Carey published A. J. Dallas's *Features of Mr. Jay's Treaty* (1795), *An Address to the House of Representatives on Lord Grenville's Treaty* (1796), and Tench Coxe's *The Federalist* (1796), a defense of Jefferson. Gales printed Albert Gallatin's speech against naval expansion (1799), and Duane, at the height of the debates on the constitutionality of the Alien and Sedition acts, printed George Hay's *Essay on the Liberty of the Press* (1799).[109]

To recite this record is not to diminish the effectiveness or courage of native Republican editors and booksellers in the battle against Federalism. But throughout the 1790s Republican propaganda outlets were far fewer than those available to the Federalists, who where possible gave both state and federal patronage to politically reliable printers. The Republicans therefore needed all the help they could get, and although Callender may have exaggerated when he claimed that "it is [the newspapers'] weakness, or ability, which must decide the fate of every administration,"[110] there can be little doubt that in the propaganda battle against Federalism the radical émigré printers were of more value to the Republicans than their numbers suggest.

[106] Evans, *American Bibliography*, nos. 27592, 28122, 28590, 30257, 31010, 31516, 31634.

[107] *Ibid.*, nos. 31174, 32633.

[108] *Ibid.*, nos. 28381, 28384, 31173, 31174, 31906, 37083, 37084.

[109] *Ibid.*, nos. 28527, 30156, 30293, 30294, 35531, 34605.

[110] *Recorder* (Rich.), Dec. 1, 1802.

In the current debate on republicanism in the 1790s too little attention has been given to the role of the radical émigrés. Banning's failure to recognize their influx into the Republican party in the 1790s enables him to state that the party "was dependent to an important and unrecognized degree on an Americanization of eighteenth-century opposition thought."[111] Appleby, moreover, is only partly correct when she writes that "the particular ideas the Republicans and Federalists thought and fought with came from an English frame of reference, but it was only a frame of reference. They gave the ideas their operative meaning, working within their own situation in the polemics of the early national period."[112] This may have been true for English writers of earlier generations, but it ignores the influence of the emigrants of the 1790s. These radicals brought with them a peculiarly Painite political discourse that combined, without strain, egalitarianism, advocacy of commercial development, and a vision of unlimited progress. The Jeffersonian Republican party eventually stabilized around just such a political economy. This is certainly not to claim that the exiles determined by themselves the direction of Republican discourse; rather, it suggests that they were especially well equipped to promote Republican ideology as it developed in the Federalist decade. Their propagandizing was effective in vulgarizing Republican discourse, making it more suitable for a society that was becoming increasingly politicized and in which popular participation in politics was coming to be taken for granted. They therefore continued Paine's role of demystifying political principles and offering them to the masses.

In addition, their very foreignness helped to consolidate the Republican party, for, at least before 1800, they were not burdened with the factionalism that stemmed from earlier political battles. Their perception of America, unfettered by sectional or local interests and fueled by an intense anglophobia, was predicated on a demand for national unity and independence. They instilled this demand, together with other true Painite republican sentiments, into both native-born Americans and fellow immigrants, in the latter through relief-cum-political societies such as the Hibernian Society in Philadelphia and the Friendly Sons of St. Patrick in New York, or through patriotic militia companies such as the Republican Greens.[113]

Thus recent disputes over a Court-Country dichotomy and the emergence of a commercialized republicanism in the 1790s can perhaps be resolved more satisfactorily if it is recognized that there was offered to the American public a prepackaged Painite political economy, stamped "Made in Britain," that sought to destroy Britain's other exports, both manufactured and ideological. If we are fully to appreciate the meaning of

[111] Banning, *Jeffersonian Persuasion*, 129.

[112] Appleby, *Capitalism and a New Social Order*, 23.

[113] "Autobiography of Mathew Carey," *N. E. Mag.* (1834), letter 6; *Carey's U.S. Recorder*, May 19, 1798; St. Mark, "Red Shamrock," 147; Carter, "Political Activities of Mathew Carey," 120; Callender, *Prospect before Us*, I, 37.

Jefferson's success in 1800, and to understand what Republicanism meant in the early national period, we cannot afford to ignore the achievements of the radical émigrés as a major component of the Jeffersonian movement.

Appendix

Radical Emigre Serial Publications

Editor	*Title and Place*	*Dates*
J. Binns	*Republican Argus* (Northumberland, Pa.)	1802-1807
	Democratic Press (Philadelphia)	1807-1829
J. D. Burk	*Daily Advertiser* (Boston)	1796
	Polar Star (Boston)	1796-1797
	Time-Piece (New York)	1798
J. T. Callender	*Aurora* (Philadelphia)	1797-1798
	Examiner (Richmond)	1800-1802
	Recorder (Richmond)	1802-1803
J. Carey	*Virginia Gazette* (Richmond)	1792
	Star (Charleston)	1793
	Georgia Journal (Savannah)	1793-1794
	Wilmington Chronicle (N.C.)	1795
	Daily Evening Gazette (Charleston)	1795
	Telegraph (Charleston)	1795
	Daily Advertiser (Philadelphia)	1797-1798
	Carey's United States' Recorder (Philadelphia)	1798
	Constitutional Diary (Philadephia)	1799-1800
M. Carey	*Pennsylvania Evening Herald* (Philadelphia)	1785-1788
	Complete Counting House Companion (Philadelphia)	1785-1788
	American Museum (Philadelphia)	1787-1792
J. Cheetham	*Republican Watchtower* (New York)	1800-1801
	American Citizen (New York)	1801-1810
T. Cooper	*Sunbury & Northumberland Gazette* (Pa.)	1797
R. Davison	*Messenger* (Warrenton, N.C.)	1802-1809
R. Dinmore	*National Magazine*	1801-1802
	American Literary Advertiser (Washington, D.C.)	1802-1804
	Alexandria Expositor (Va.)	1802-1807
	Washington Expositor (D.C.)	1807-1809
D. Driscol	*Temple of Reason* (New York and Philadelphia)	1800-1801
	American Patriot (Baltimore)	1802-1803
	Augusta Chronicle (Ga.)	1804-1811

W. Duane	*Merchants' Daily Advertiser* (Philadelphia)	1797
	Philadelphia Gazette	1797-1798
	Aurora (Philadelphia)	1798-1829
	Apollo (Washington, D.C.)	1802
J. Gales	*Independent Gazetteer* (Philadelphia)	1796-1797
	Raleigh Register (N.C.)	1799-1833
R. Lee	*American Universal Magazine* (Philadelphia)	1796-1797
T. Lloyd	*Merchants' Daily Advertiser* (Philadephia)	1797-1798
J. Miller	*South-Carolina Gazette* (Charleston)	1783-1785
	Back Country Gazette (Pendleton, N.C.)	1795
	Miller's Weekly Messenger	1807
M. J. Rhees	*Western Sky* (Beula, Pa.)	1798
J. M. Williams	*Columbian Gazette* (New York)	1799
	Democrat (Boston)	1804
J. Wood	*Virginia Gazette* (Richmond)	1802-1804
	Western World of Kentucky (Frankfort)	1806
	Atlantic World (Washington, D.C.)	1807
	Petersburg Daily Courier (Va.)	1814

Commercial Farming and the "Agrarian Myth" in the Early Republic

Joyce Appleby

Nineteen forty-three marked the two-hundredth anniversary of the birth of Thomas Jefferson and the occasion for bestowing yet another honor on the Sage of Monticello. Amid salutes to Jefferson's politics and philosophy, historians and agronomists seized the opportunity to herald his contributions to scientific agriculture. Quoting from Vice-President Henry A. Wallace, M. L. Wilson claimed that farmers identified Jefferson with "the application of science to agriculture," and he then admiringly listed Jefferson's scientific achievements: the invention of a threshing machine, the improvement of the plow, the introduction of Merino sheep, and the advocacy of soil conservation.[1] August C. Miller, Jr., called Jefferson the father of American democracy and "a scientific farmer and agriculturist in the most comprehensive sense" of the term.[2] On this bicentennial anniversary, according to A. Whitney Griswold, people paid tribute to Jefferson as "preeminently and above all a farmer." Noting that Jefferson's enthusiasm for farming had always included commerce, Griswold agreed with William D. Grampp that Jefferson's concern about marketing farm commodities had made him an ardent proponent of international free trade.[3] Thus, like the Department of Agriculture experts who gathered in the auditorium that bore his name, Jefferson in 1943 was depicted as an early-day New Dealer, a modernizer dedicated to helping ordinary farmers become efficient producers.

In 1955—just twelve years later—Richard Hofstadter published *The Age of Reform*, and Jefferson was captured for an altogether different historiographical tradition. Looking for the roots of the nostalgia that flowered with the Populists, Hofstadter described how Jefferson and other eighteenth-century

Joyce Appleby is professor of history at the University of California, Los Angeles.

[1] M. L. Wilson, "Thomas Jefferson—Farmer," *Proceedings of the American Philosophical Society*, 87 (1944), 217–19.

[2] August C. Miller, Jr., "Jefferson as an Agriculturist," *Agricultural History*, XVI (April 1942), 65.

[3] A. Whitney Griswold, *Farming and Democracy* (New York, 1948), 18–19, 26–32; William D. Grampp, "A Re-examination of Jeffersonian Economics," *Southern Economic Journal*, XII (Jan. 1946), 263–82.

writers had been drawn irresistibly to the "noncommercial, nonpecuniary, self-sufficient aspects of American farm life." The Jeffersonians, Hofstadter said, had created an "agrarian myth" and fashioned for the new nation a folk hero, the yeoman farmer, who was admired "not for his capacity to exploit opportunities and make money," but rather for his ability to produce a simple abundance. Underlining the mythic aspect of this literary creation, Hofstadter noted the actual profit orientation of the farmers who, he said, accepted the views of their social superiors as harmless flattery.[4]

The instantaneous popularity of Hofstadter's "agrarian myth" owes a good deal more to trends in the writing of history than to the evidentiary base upon which it rested. That, in fact, was very shaky. Hofstadter directed his readers to two writers, neither of whom drew the distinction he had made between the romantic myth of rural self-sufficiency created by writers and the reality of farming for profit acted upon by ordinary men. Griswold, whom Hofstadter claimed had produced "a full statement of the agrarian myth as it was formulated by Jefferson," in fact explored Jefferson's views on agricultural improvements and commercial expansion in order to point out that what had made sense in Jefferson's day no longer held true in the twentieth century.[5] The second writer to whom Hofstadter referred, Chester E. Eisinger, addressed Hofstadter's theme of national symbols, but his freehold concept can be readily differentiated from Hofstadter's agrarian myth. Tracing the appearance of independent freehold farmers to the destruction of feudal tenures, Eisinger explained how in England the same commercial forces that destroyed the manorial system had also worked to eliminate the small, freeholding producer. In America the reality of vacant land gave substance to a vision of a society of independent farmers; so the freehold concept, like so many other ideas, got a new lease on life by crossing the Atlantic. Where Hofstadter stressed the appeal of yeoman self-sufficiency, however, Eisinger linked the freehold concept to the emerging capitalistic economy. In the era of commercial agriculture, Eisinger wrote, "not only could a man possess his own farm, but he was his own master, rising and falling by his own efforts, bargaining in a free market."[6] Thus where Hofstadter's introductory chapter juxtaposed the agrarian myth and commercial realities, Eisinger distinguished between the poetic yearning for a bygone age of peasants and the modern reality of market-oriented farmers. All of Hofstadter's sources had traced the eighteenth-century literary preoccupation with farming to the rising population and the consequent importance of food production, but Hofstadter snapped this connection between material reality and intellectual response by stressing the purely mythic power of what two of his students have recently characterized as the

[4] Richard Hofstadter, *The Age of Reform: From Bryan to F.D.R.* (New York, 1955), 23–24, 30.

[5] *Ibid.*, 25; Griswold, *Farming and Democracy*, 12–15.

[6] Chester E. Eisinger, "The Freehold Concept in Eighteenth-Century American Letters," *William and Mary Quarterly*, IV (Jan. 1947), 46–47. See also Chester E. Eisinger, "Land and Loyalty: Literary Expressions of Agrarian Nationalism in the Seventeenth and Eighteenth Centuries," *American Literature*, 21 (May 1949), 160–78; and Chester E. Eisinger, "The Farmer in the Eighteenth Century Almanac," *Agricultural History*, XXVIII (July 1954), 107–12.

ideal of "'the self-sufficient' yeoman dwelling in a rural arcadia of unspoiled virtue, honest toil and rude plenty."[7]

Without looking firsthand at the literature of the 1790s, Hofstadter wrote his thesis about the nostalgic politics of the Populist era back into the earlier period. His indifference to a time that provided only a backdrop to the central drama in the age of reform is understandable. Indeed, what sustained the attractiveness of the yeoman ideal was not Hofstadter's book but a much stronger tide coursing through scholarship on eighteenth-century America. As a quick survey of titles and expository prose produced in the last twenty years will reveal, *yeoman* has become a favorite designation for the ordinary farmer of postrevolutionary America. Losing its definition as a rank in a hierarchical society of tenants, yeomen, gentlemen, and lords, it has become instead a code word for a man of simple tastes, sturdy independence, and admirable disdain for all things newfangled. In this form the yeoman archetype has become particularly congruent with the recent work of social historians, who have sought to reconstruct the basic character and structure of colonial society.

Using continuous records on family formation and landholding patterns, these scholars have given special attention to the collective experience of whole communities. The models of the social scientists that they have employed, moreover, have encouraged them to look for the similarities between early American society and its counterpart in Europe. Where earlier historians had emphasized the idea of an America born free and modern, the new practitioners of social history have been more open to the possibility that America, too, had once been a traditional society. Indeed, they have found that, like traditional men and women of sociological theory, colonial Americans created the community solidarity and familial networks that encouraged resistance to change.[8] Instead of the contrast between old-fashioned and up-to-date that had been employed to describe the essentially external transformation from rural to industrial America, recent writings have concentrated on the connection between visible social action and invisible cultural influences. Traditional society as an abstract concept has been invested with the normative values of stability, cohesion, and neighborly concern, while the changes that came with economic development have been characterized as intrusive, exploitive, and class-biased. Where Hofstadter played off myth against reality, the new interpreters of early America are more likely to insist that a genuine conflict existed between farm communities and the modern world of money, markets, and merchants.

It is this more refined and subtle model of rural life that has turned the Jeffersonians into nostalgic men fighting a rearguard action against the forces of modernity. Thus J. G. A. Pocock has named Jefferson as the conduit through which a civic concept of virtue entered "the whole tradition of American

[7] Stanley Elkins and Eric McKitrick, "Richard Hofstadter: A Progress," in *The Hofstadter Aegis: A Memorial*, ed. Stanley Elkins and Eric McKitrick (New York, 1975), 316.

[8] For a review of this literature, see John J. Waters, "From Democracy to Demography: Recent Historiography on the New England Town," in *Perspectives on Early American History: Essays in Honor of Richard B. Morris*, ed. Alden T. Vaughan and George Athan Billias (New York, 1973), 222–49.

agrarian and populist messianism."[9] Less concerned with political issues, James A. Henretta has stressed the farmers' concern with protecting the lineal family from the centrifugal forces of individual enterprise and economic competition.[10] According to Lance Banning, the Republican party appealed to "the hesitations of agrarian conservatives as they experienced the stirrings of a more commercial age," while John M. Murrin has concluded that the Jeffersonians were like the English Country opposition on political and economic questions because "they idealized the past more than the future and feared significant change, especially major economic change, as corruption and degeneration."[11] For Drew R. McCoy the tension between tradition and innovation is more explicit. The Jeffersonians, he has said, were forced to reconcile classical ideals with social realities; their ambiguities and contradictions reflected "an attempt to cling to the traditional republican spirit of classical antiquity without disregarding the new imperatives of a more modern commercial society."[12] In *The Elusive Republic* McCoy has recovered the centrality of commercial policy in the Jeffersonians' program, but he has assumed that the values of civic humanism gave shape and direction to their recommendations.

In contrast to these characterizations of early national attitudes, I shall argue that the new European demand for American grains—the crops produced by most farm families from Virginia through Maryland, Pennsylvania, Delaware, New Jersey, New York, and up the Connecticut River Valley—created an unusually favorable opportunity for ordinary men to produce for the Atlantic trade world. Far from being viewed apprehensively, this prospect during the thirty years following the adoption of the Constitution undergirded Jefferson's optimism about America's future as a progressive, prosperous, democratic nation. Indeed, this anticipated participation in an expanding international commerce in foodstuffs created the material base for a new social vision owing little conceptually or practically to antiquity, the Renaissance, or the mercantilists of eighteenth-century England. From this perspective, the battle between the Jeffersonians and Federalists appears not as a conflict between the patrons of agrarian self-sufficiency and the proponents of modern commerce, but rather as a struggle between two different elaborations of capitalistic development in America. Jefferson becomes, not the heroic loser in a battle against modernity, but the conspicuous winner in a contest over how the government should serve its citizens in the first generation of the nation's territorial expansion.

[9] J. G. A. Pocock, "Virtue and Commerce in the Eighteenth Century," *Journal of Interdisciplinary History*, III (Summer 1972), 134. See also J. G. A. Pocock, *The Machiavellian Moment: Florentine Political Thought and the Atlantic Republican Tradition* (Princeton, 1975), ix, 529–33.

[10] James A. Henretta, "Families and Farms: *Mentalité* in Pre-Industrial America," *William and Mary Quarterly*, XXXV (Jan. 1978), 3–32.

[11] Lance Banning, *The Jeffersonian Persuasion: Evolution of a Party Ideology* (Ithaca, 1978), 269; John M. Murrin, "The Great Inversion, or Court versus Country: A Comparison of the Revolution Settlements in England (1688–1721) and America (1776–1815)," in *Three British Revolutions: 1641, 1688, 1776*, ed. J. G. A. Pocock (Princeton, 1980), 406.

[12] Drew R. McCoy, *The Elusive Republic: Political Economy in Jeffersonian America* (Chapel Hill, 1980), 10.

Anyone searching for the word *yeoman* in the writings of the 1790s will be disappointed. A canvass of titles in Charles Evans's *American Bibliography* failed to turn up the designation *yeoman* in the more than thirty thousand works published in the United States between 1760 and 1800. The word *yeomanry* appeared only three times, all in works by a single author, George Logan.[13] Noah Webster, America's first lexicographer, defined *yeoman* as "a common man, or one of the plebeians, of the first or most respectable class; a freeholder, a man free born," but went on to explain that "the word is little used in the United States, unless as a title in law proceedings . . . and this only in particular states." *Yeomanry*, on the other hand, was much used, according to Webster, and referred to the collective body of freeholders. "Thus the common people in America are called the yeomanry."[14] For Webster, an ardent Federalist, the word retained the social distinction of its British provenance but conveyed nothing as such about farming. I have never found the word *yeoman* in Jefferson's writings; it certainly does not appear in his one book, *Notes on the State of Virginia*, where undifferentiated people in political contexts are called "citizens," "tax-payers," or "electors"; in economic references, "husbandmen," "farmers," or "laborers"; and in social commentary, "the poor," "the most discreet and honest inhabitants," or "respectable merchants and farmers." When Jefferson spoke in theoretical terms, ordinary persons were often discussed as "individuals," as in a passage where he says the dissolution of power would leave people "as individuals to shift for themselves."[15] Like Jefferson, the writers who filled Evans's bibliography with titles chose such socially neutral nouns as *farmers, planters, husbandmen, growers, inhabitants, landowners*, or more frequently, simply *countrymen*, a term whose double meaning reflected accurately the rural location of the preponderance of American citizens.

The absence of the word *yeoman* is negative evidence only, although its occasional use by contemporary Englishmen and New Englanders suggests a lingering reference to a status designation.[16] The error in current scholarly usage, however, is not lexical, but conceptual; it points Jefferson and his party in the wrong direction. Despite Jefferson's repeated assertions that his party was animated by bold new expectations for the human condition, the agrarian myth makes him a traditional, republican visionary, socially radical perhaps,

[13] Charles Evans, C. K. Shipton, R. P. Bristol, comps., *American Bibliography* (14 vols., New York, 1959); George Logan, *Letters Addressed to the Yeomanry of the United States* (Philadelphia, 1791); George Logan, *Five Letters, Addressed to the Yeomanry of the United States Containing Some Observations on the Dangerous Scheme of Governor Duer and Mr. Secretary Hamilton* (Philadelphia, 1792); George Logan, *Letters Addressed to the Yeomanry of the United States Containing Some Observations on Funding and Bank Systems* (Philadelphia, 1793).

[14] Noah Webster, *An American Dictionary of the English Language* (2 vols., New York, 1828), s.v. "Yeoman" and "Yeomanry." See also Noah Webster, *A Compendious Dictionary of the English Language* (Hartford, 1806), where *yeoman* is defined as "a gentleman-farmer, freeholder, officer."

[15] Thomas Jefferson, *Notes on the State of Virginia*, ed. William Peden (Chapel Hill, 1955), 125, 127, 130, 164–65, 213.

[16] For the use of *yeoman* in this period, see *Boston Gazette*, April 15, 1790, March 3, 1794, May 25, 1796; *Independent Chronicle* (Boston), Dec. 15, 1786, April 9, 1789.

but economically conservative. The assumed contradiction between democratic aspirations and economic romanticism explains why his plans were doomed to failure in competition with the hard-headed realism of an Alexander Hamilton. To this form of the argument, interpretive schemes much older than Hofstadter's have contributed a great deal. Viewed retrospectively by historians living in an industrial age, Jefferson's enthusiasm for agriculture has long been misinterpreted as an attachment to the past. So dazzling were the technological triumphs of railroad building and steam power that the age of the marvelous machines came to appear as the great divide in human history. Henry Adams offers a splendid example of this distorting perspective. Describing America in 1800, Adams said that "down to the close of the eighteenth century no change had occurred in the world which warranted practical men in assuming that great changes were to come." The connection between industrial technology and a modern mentality for him was complete, for he then went on to say, "as time passed, and as science developed man's capacity to control Nature's forces, old-fashioned conservatism vanished from society."[17] In fact, an American who was forty years old in 1800 would have seen every fixed point in his or her world dramatically transformed through violent political agitation, protracted warfare, galloping inflation, and republican revolutions. Yet for Adams the speed of travel held the human imagination in a thrall that the toppling of kings could not affect.

Two interpretative tendencies have followed from this point of view. One has been to treat proponents of agricultural development as conservative and to construe as progressive those who favored manufacturing and banking. The contrast between Jefferson cast as an agrarian romantic and Hamilton as the far-seeing capitalist comes readily to mind. The other retrospective bias has been the characterization of industrialization as an end toward which prior economic changes were inexorably moving. Both classical economic and Marxist theory have contributed to this determinism which recasts historical events as parts of a process, as stages in a sequential morphology. Under this influence, the actual human encounter with time is reversed; instead of interpreting social change as the result of particular responses to a knowable past, the decisions men and women made are examined in relation to future developments unknown to them.[18] The situation in America at the end of the eighteenth century is exemplary.

Ignorant of the industrial future, Americans were nonetheless aware that their economy was being reshaped by the most important material change of the era: the rise of European population and the consequent inability of Euro-

[17] Henry Adams, *The United States in 1800* (Ithaca, 1955), 42. Contrast this with Duc Francois de La Rochefoucauld-Liancourt's firsthand observation that America was "a country in flux; that which is true today as regards its population, its establishments, its prices, its commerce will not be true six months from now." David J. Brandenburg, "A French Aristocrat Looks at American Farming: La Rochefoucauld-Liancourt's *Voyages dans les États-Unis*," *Agricultural History*, 32 (1958), 163.

[18] For a critique of this tendency in economic history, see Robert E. Mutch, "Yeoman and Merchant in Pre-Industrial America: Eighteenth-Century Massachusetts as a Case Study," *Societas*, VII (Autumn, 1977), 279–302.

pean agriculture to meet the new demand for foodstuffs. After 1755 the terms of trade between grain and all other commodities turned decisively in favor of the grains and stayed that way until the third decade of the nineteenth century.[19] In *Common Sense*, Thomas Paine dismissed colonial fears about leaving the security of the English navigation system by saying that American commerce would flourish so long as "eating is the custom of Europe."[20] Eating, of course, had long been the custom of Europeans. What made their eating habits newly relevant to Americans was their declining capacity to feed themselves. More fortunate than most of her neighbors, England benefited from a century and a half of previous agricultural improvements so that pressure from her growing population meant that harvest surpluses, which had once been exported, after mid-century were consumed at home. The withdrawal of English grains, however, created major food deficits on the Iberian peninsula. No longer able to rely upon Britain's bounteous harvests, the Spanish and Portuguese began looking anxiously across the Atlantic to North America. The impact of food shortages had a differential impact upon European nations, but for Americans the consequences, particularly after 1788, were salubrious. The long upward climb of prices enhanced the value of those crops that ordinary farmers could easily grow.[21] Combined with the strong markets in the West Indies for corn and meat products, the growth of European markets for American foodstuffs had the greatest impact on the ordinary farmer who pursued a mixed husbandry.

The first and most conspicuous response to these economic changes came in the prerevolutionary South where large planters and small farmers alike began planting wheat instead of tobacco. While soil exhaustion offered an incentive to make the switch, rising prices for grains financed the conversion. In the frontier areas of the Piedmont and Shenandoah Valley, selling grain and livestock surpluses offered a speedy avenue of integration into the Atlantic trade world.[22] As historians have recently made clear, this changeover to grains in the Upper South involved more than agricultural techniques, for the marketing of wheat and corn had a decisive influence upon the area's urban growth. The switch to grains and livestock along the Eastern Shore, the lower James, the upper Potomac, and in the Piedmont promoted in two decades the cities, towns, and hamlets that had eluded the Chesapeake region during the previous

[19] B. H. Slicher Van Bath, "Eighteenth-Century Agriculture on the Continent of Europe: Evolution or Revolution?" *Agricultural History*, XLIII (Jan. 1969), 173–75.

[20] [Thomas Paine], *Common Sense, Addressed to the Inhabitants of America*, in *The Writings of Thomas Paine*, ed. Moncure Daniel Conway (4 vols., New York, 1894–1896), I, 86.

[21] For some important interpretative points in regard to agricultural productivity and to exports as its measure, see Claudia D. Goldin and Frank D. Lewis, "The Role of Exports in American Economic Growth during the Napoleonic Wars, 1793 to 1807," *Explorations in Economic History*, 17 (Jan. 1980), 6–25; William N. Parker, "Sources of Agricultural Productivity in the Nineteenth Century," *Journal of Farm Economics*, 49 (Dec. 1967), 1455–68; and Andrew Hill Clark, "Suggestions for the Geographical Study of Agricultural Change in the United States, 1790–1840," in *Farming in the New Nation: Interpreting American Agriculture, 1790–1840*, ed. Darwin P. Kelsey (Washington, 1972), 155–72.

[22] Robert D. Mitchell, *Commercialism and Frontier: Perspectives on the Early Shenandoah Valley* (Charlottesville, 1977), 40, 173–78; Malcolm J. Rohrbough, *The Trans-Appalachian Frontier: People, Societies, and Institutions, 1775–1850* (New York, 1978), 99–106.

century of tobacco production. Equally important to the character of these new urban networks was capturing what Jacob M. Price has termed "the entrepreneurial headquarters" of the grain trade. Unlike tobacco, the capital and marketing profits for the commerce in food remained in American hands.[23] For planters and farmers the switch to wheat could mean liberation from British factors and merchants who controlled both the sales and purchases of Tidewater tobacco planters. Such a possibility can be read in more personal terms in the writings of the young planter George Washington, who pledged himself to economic freedom by raising wheat.[24] Fanning out from Baltimore, Norfolk, and later Richmond, an array of market towns sprang up to handle the inspection, storage, processing, and shipping of the grains and livestock being pulled into the Atlantic trade from the rural areas of North Carolina, Virginia, Maryland, and Pennsylvania. During these same years Philadelphia and New York, both drawing on a grain-raising hinterland, surpassed Boston in population, wealth, and shipping.[25]

The dislocations of the American Revolution were followed by a five-year depression, but in 1788 a new upward surge in grain and livestock prices ushered in a thirty-year period of prosperity. Even in England the shortfall between grain production and domestic demand led to net grain imports for twenty-seven out of these thirty years. Southern European demand remained strong. A printed solicitation for American business sent from a Barcelona firm in 1796 described American wheat and flour as much esteemed and constantly in demand "in this Place & Province, which," as the handbill explained, "in years of abundance never produces more than for four Months provisions."[26] In the longer run, sustained profits in grain-raising encouraged investments in agricultural improvements and prompted heroic efforts to increase output. By 1820, especially in England, Belgium, and the Netherlands, food production again had caught up with population growth, and prices returned to the levels of the mid-1790s.[27] Higher yields abroad, not the end of the Napoleonic wars, curbed demand for American farm products.

Coinciding as it did with the adoption of the United States Constitution, the new climb of food prices meant not only that the market could penetrate further into the countryside but also that the national government could extend its reach with improvements in communication and transportation sys-

[23] Carville Earle and Ronald Hoffman, "Staple Crops and Urban Development in the Eighteenth-Century South," *Perspectives in American History*, X (1976), 5-78; Jacob M. Price, "Economic Function and the Growth of American Port Towns in the Eighteenth Century," *Ibid.*, VIII (1974), 121-86.

[24] James Thomas Flexner, *George Washington: The Forge of Experience, 1732-1775* (Boston, 1965), 279-84.

[25] Price, "Economic Function and the Growth of American Port Towns," 151-60.

[26] Arabet, Gautier & Manning handbill, Barcelona, May 18, 1796, file 1215, Miscellaneous Material Regarding Philadelphia Business Concerns, 1784-1824 (Eleutherian Mills Historical Library, Wilmington, Del.). British imports of American grain can be followed in Great Britain, *Parliamentary Papers* (Commons), "An Account of the Grain of All Sorts, Meal, and Flour, Stated in Quarters, Imported into Great Britain in Each Year from January 5, 1800 to January 5, 1825" (no. 227), 1825, XX, 233-67. For the earlier period, see Great Britain, *Parliamentary Papers* (Commons), "Accounts Relating to Corn, Etc." (no. 50), 1826-1827, XVI, 487-501.

[27] Slicher Van Bath, "Eighteenth-Century Agriculture," 175.

tems. In the single decade of the 1790s, America's 75 post offices increased to 903 while the mileage of post routes went from 1,875 to 20,817. The number of newspapers more than doubled; circulation itself increased threefold. In the middle of the decade turnpike construction began.[28] With each decadal increase in grain prices the distance wheat and flour could be carted profitably to market increased dramatically. At 1772 price levels, farmers and grain merchants could afford to ship flour 121 miles and wheat 64 to reach the grain-exporting seaports of Norfolk, Baltimore, Richmond, Philadelphia, and New York. Between 1800 and 1819 the range had extended to 201 miles for flour and 143 for wheat. For the farmer who wished to earn his own teamster's wage, the distance could be extended further.[29] The population doubled during the first twenty-three years of the new national government, but even more important to the burgeoning trade in American foodstuffs, the preponderance of American farmers lived within marketing range of the inland waterways that flowed into the sea-lanes of the great Atlantic commerce. As the volume of grain exports grew, country stores replaced rural fairs, and millers, bakers, butchers, brewers, and tanners turned from the custom trade of their neighbors to the commercial processing of the farmer's surpluses.

For the gentlemen planters of the Upper South, the switch to wheat represented a calculated response to new market opportunities, but for the mass of ordinary farmers the growing demand for foodstuffs abroad offered an inducement to increase surpluses without giving up the basic structure of the family farm. The man with seventy-five to one hundred acres who relied principally upon his own and his family's labor to grow Indian corn and wheat and to tend his livestock and draft animals could participate in the market with increasing profits without taking the risks associated with cash crops.[30] European population growth had enhanced the value of the little man's harvests, not that of the rich man's staples. It also blurred the old textbook distinction between the commercial agriculture of the South and the subsistence farming of the North. The wheat farmer's replication of European crops was no longer a commercial liability, for it was exactly the foods and fibers indigenous to Europe that were in demand. Published prices current of American produce in Liverpool, Amsterdam, Le Havre, Bordeaux, Barcelona, Saint-Domingue, and

[28] Allan R. Pred, *Urban Growth and the Circulation of Information: The United States System of Cities, 1790–1840* (Cambridge, 1973), 58–59, 80, 153.

[29] *Ibid.*, 114. Max G. Schumacher has calculated the "approximate maximum commercial range from Baltimore and Philadelphia of wheat and flour dependent on land-carriage" for price levels in 1755 and 1772. I extended Schumacher's ratios to the price range from 1800 to 1819. Max G. Schumacher, *The Northern Farmer and His Markets during the Late Colonial Period* (New York, 1975), 63.

[30] As this relates to Maryland, see Paul G. E. Clemens, *The Atlantic Economy and Colonial Maryland's Eastern Shore: From Tobacco to Grain* (Ithaca, 1980). See also Mitchell, *Commercialism and Frontier*, 234; David Maldwyn Ellis, *Landlords and Farmers in the Hudson-Mohawk Region, 1790–1850* (New York, 1967), 76–82; Sarah Shaver Hughes, "Elizabeth City County, Virginia, 1782–1810: The Economic and Social Structure of a Tidewater County in the Early National Years," (Ph.D. diss., College of William and Mary, 1975), 406–07; and David C. Klingaman, *Colonial Virginia's Coastwise and Grain Trade* (New York, 1975). For some of the theoretical implications of the market involvement of self-sufficient family farms, see Mutch, "Yeoman and Merchant," 279–302.

Havana convey the situation: wheat, flour, Indian corn, clover seed, flax seed, hemp, deerskins, beeswax, staves, and timber all commanded good prices, while West Indian markets took beef, pork, fish, cider, apples, potatoes, peas, bread, lard, onions, cheese, and butter as well. The mixed husbandry through which the farmer supplied his family also fed into the stream of commerce that linked rural stores and backcountry millers to the Atlantic commerce. To be sure, as Diane Lindstrom has pointed out, the farmer's family remained his best customer, but this held true well into the nineteenth century.[31]

The diversity of demand for American farm commodities in the generation after 1788 encouraged the adoption of the up-and-down husbandry that had revolutionized English and Dutch agriculture a century earlier. Here diversification, not specialization, held the key to raising crop yields and maintaining soil fertility in an age without chemical fertilizers.[32] Livestock and wheat raising required dividing land among meadows, pastures, and fields. When these were rotated, yields could be increased and fertility maintained. Livestock fed with soil-enriching grasses could also produce manure for fields of wheat and corn. While foreign visitors judged American farmers improvident and wasteful, American writers insisted that European practices had been adapted to American needs. Fertility in the grain- and livestock-producing areas evidently held up.[33]

Economies of scale had practically no bearing on the enhancement of the harvests that produced the food surpluses of the eighteenth and early nineteenth centuries. Attention to detail was the key. As the agricultural writer

[31] Diane Lindstrom, "Southern Dependence upon Western Grain Supplies," (M.A. thesis, University of Delaware, 1969), 10. Printed prices current and merchant handbills can be sampled in manuscript files 1303, 667, 1097, 1144, 1215, and 1457 (Eleutherian Mills Historical Library). Comparisons were made between advertised export items and farm account books in the collections at the Delaware State Archives (Dover, Del.); the University of Delaware Library Special Collections (Newark, Del.); and the Historical Society of Delaware (Wilmington, Del.).

[32] Eric Kerridge, *The Agricultural Revolution* (London, 1967), 39–40, 107, 214–15, 299, 347–48.

[33] For a foreign view of American agriculture based on a tour in 1794–1795, see William Strickland, *Observations on the Agriculture of the United States of America* (London, 1801). A rebuttal is provided by William Tatham, *Communications Concerning the Agriculture and Commerce of America* (London, 1800). The controversy over William Strickland's report to the English Board of Agriculture is covered by G. Melvin Herndon, "Agriculture in America in the 1790s: An Englishman's View," *Agricultural History*, XLIX (July 1975), 505–16. Other contemporary writers who stressed both the differences and the profitability of American agriculture were Timothy Matlack, *An Oration Delivered March 16, 1780* (Philadelphia, 1780), 14=16; Francois Alexandre Frederick, duc de La Rochefoucauld-Liancourt, *Voyages dans les États Unis d'Amerique Fait en 1795, 1796, et 1797* (8 vols., Paris, [1799]), I, 101–17, II, 325, III, 50; John Spurrier, *The Practical Farmer* (Wilmington, Del., 1793); John A. Binns, *A Treatise on Practical Farming* (Frederick-town, Md., 1803); George Logan, *Fourteen Experiments on Agriculture* (Philadelphia, 1797); and J. B. Bordley, *Essays and Notes on Husbandry and Rural Affairs* (Philadelphia, 1801). Estimates on yields vary widely. William Guthrie estimated that yields in Delaware after fifty years of planting continued at levels of fifteen to twenty-five bushels per acre for wheat and barley and two hundred for Indian corn. William Guthrie, *A New System of Modern Geography* (2 vols., Philadelphia, 1795), II, 458. Sarah Shaver Hughes has confirmed Guthrie's conclusion that fertility held up. Hughes, "Elizabeth City County, Virginia," 90–91. An elaborate tabular computation of wages, prices, and yields done by La Rochefoucauld-Liancourt indicates yields ranging from eight to twenty-five bushels per acre for various areas in the Delaware, Maryland, and Pennsylvania wheat-raising belt. "Tabulation of Commerce in the United States, 1795–97," file 501, P. S. Du Pont Office Collection (Eleutherian Mills Historical Library).

John Dabney explained, the farmer who does not "cart out his summer dung, nor plough those lands in the fall, which he means to feed in the following spring" could not grow rich.[34] In no other husbandry was it more true that the best manure was the tread of the master's foot. Moreover, the capital investments that could improve output—folding animals, bringing uncultivated land under the plow, laying down new pastures—could be made by the ordinary farmer willing to exchange leisure for off-season labors.[35] Increasing surpluses required, above all, a better management of time and a close watch on the market. Here too the range of farm commodities in demand redounded to the benefit of the small farmer, for each nook and cranny had a potential use. Hemp, according to John Alexander Binns, could be raised on every conceivable hollow just as bee hives, whose wax commanded good prices in England, could be lodged near the ubiquitous stands of white clover.[36] The relative success of the farmers who harvested wheat in the Middle Atlantic states can be gauged by Stanley L. Engerman's findings that the wealth of the North surpassed that of the South for the first time in the period from 1774 to 1798.[37] Without any of the qualities that characterized commercial agriculture in the colonial period—slave labor, specialization, large holdings—northern farmers had been brought into the thriving trade in foodstuffs.

Although high food prices greatly increased the ambit of the market, soil and climate more rigidly delimited the domain of up-and-down husbandry. The optimal mix of livestock and grain raising depended on crops of timothy, alfalfa, and clover, which were not easily grown in the lower South where heavy rains leached the land, leaving severe lime deficiencies. Hot, humid summers exposed cattle to ticks and mosquitos which kept herds small. Agricultural improvements in these areas had to await later developments in fertilizers and soil amendments.[38] In New England the thin soils and rocky terrain also barred farmers from effectively competing with the rich farmlands of the South and West. Even before the Revolution, Massachusetts had become an importer of wheat.[39] The New England situation did not encourage the embrace of an expansive, market-oriented, food-raising economy. In time the reexport trade breathed new life into the mercantile sector, but manufacturing, with its very different cultural imperatives, held out the long-range prospect for develop-

[34] [John Dabney], *An Address to Farmers* (Newburyport, 1796), 5. John Dabney continued: "A complete Farmer is also a man of great carefulness and solicitude; without care, the severest labor on the best of Farms, will never produce riches nor plenty."

[35] For theoretical discussion of this point, see Stephen Hymer and Stephen Resnick, "A Model of an Agrarian Economy with Nonagricultural Activities," *American Economic Review*, LIX (Sept. 1969), 493–506.

[36] John A. Binns, *A Treatise of Practical Farming* (Richmond, 1804), 63. Dabney maintained that a farmer could clear £6 profit from an acre of flax. Dabney, *Address to Farmers*, 51. Substantial British imports of American beeswax are reported in Edmund C. Burnett, "Observations of London Merchants on American Trade, 1783," *American Historical Review*, XVIII (July 1913), 776.

[37] Stanley L. Engerman, "A Reconsideration of Southern Economic Growth, 1770–1860," *Agricultural History*, XLIX (April 1975), 348–49.

[38] Julius Rubin, "The Limits of Agricultural Progress in the Nineteenth-Century South," *Agricultural History*, XLIX (April 1975), 362–73.

[39] Klingaman, *Colonial Virginia's Coastwise and Grain Trade*, 38.

ment.[40] Thus, despite the easy entry into the mixed husbandry of grain and livestock raising, climate and topography drew the borders around the wheat belt that passed through Virginia, Maryland, Delaware, Pennsylvania, New Jersey, and New York. As long as food prices remained high, the conventional divisions of North and South, subsistence and commercial, yielded to a core of common interests among American farmers, food processors, and merchants in this favored region.[41]

The acknowledged novelty of the new American nation's political experiments has too often obscured the equally strong sense contemporaries had that they were entering a new economic era as well. Gouverneur Morris, for instance, called his fellow countrymen of 1782 "the first born children of extended Commerce in modern Times."[42] Americans were repeatedly characterized as eager market participants—certainly when it came to spending and borrowing—and commerce itself was associated with a remarkable augmentation of wealth-producing possibilities. "The spirit for Trade which pervades these States is not to be restrained," George Washington wrote to James Warren in 1784. Jefferson, eager to build canals linking the Chesapeake to the interior valleys of Virginia, wrote Washington that since all the world was becoming commercial, America too must get as much as possible of this modern source of wealth and power.[43] Timothy Matlack predicted for an audience in Philadelphia the rise of America to a "Height of Riches, Strength and Glory, which the fondest Imagination cannot readily conceive," going on to specify that "the Star-bespangled Genius of America . . . points to Agriculture as the stable Foundation of this rising mighty Empire."[44] Without any major technological breakthrough, the late-eighteenth-century economy nonetheless suggested to men that they stood on the threshold of major advances.

By isolating in time and space the golden era of grain growing in the early national period, one can see more clearly the material base upon which Jefferson built his vision of America, a vision that was both democratic and capitalistic, agrarian and commercial. It is especially the commercial component of Jefferson's program that sinks periodically from scholarly view, a submersion that can be traced to the failure to connect Jefferson's interpretation of economic developments to his political goals. Agriculture did not figure in his plans as a venerable form of production giving shelter to a traditional way of life; rather, he was responsive to every possible change in cultivation, processing, and marketing that would enhance its profitability. It was exactly the promise of progressive agricultural development that fueled his hopes that ordinary men

[40] Charles L. Sanford, "The Intellectual Origins and New-Worldliness of American Industry," *Journal of Economic History*, XVIII (March 1958), 1–16.

[41] For discussion of the problem of discriminating between a subsistence and a commercial agriculture, see Clark, "Suggestions," 166.

[42] Gouverneur Morris to Matthew Ridley, Aug. 6, 1782, quoted in Clarence Ver Steeg, *Robert Morris: Revolutionary Financier* (Philadelphia, 1954), 166–67.

[43] George Washington to James Warren, Oct. 7, 1785, *The Writings of George Washington, from the Original Manuscript Sources; 1745–1799*, ed. John C. Fitzpatrick (39 vols., Washington, 1931–1944), XXVIII, 290–91; Thomas Jefferson to Washington, March 15, 1784, *The Papers of Thomas Jefferson*, ed. Julian P. Boyd et al. (19 vols., Princeton, 1950–1974), VII, 26.

[44] Matlack, *Oration*, 25.

might escape the tyranny of their social superiors both as employers and magistrates. More than most democratic reformers, he recognized that hierarchy rested on economic relations and a deference to the past as well as formal privilege and social custom.

The Upper South's conversion from tobacco to wheat provided the central focus for Jefferson's discussion of commerce and manufacturing in his *Notes on the State of Virginia.* Throughout the Tidewater, planters were shifting from the old staple, tobacco, to the production of cereals. Made profitable by the sharp price increases occasioned by European and American population growth, foodstuffs were much less labor-intensive than tobacco and were therefore suitable for family farms. Large and small Virginia planters became integrated into the new grain-marketing network that connected American producers from the James to the Hudson with buyers throughout the Atlantic world. As Jefferson wrote, wheat raising "diffuses plenty and happiness among the whole," and it did so, he noted, with only moderate toil, an observation that evokes the unstated, invidious comparison with slave labor.[45] Whether talking about consumption or production, he took for granted the importance of the market in influencing developments. For instance, he predicted that wheat would continue to replace tobacco because growers in Georgia and the Mississippi Territory would be able to undersell their Chesapeake competitors. Similarly the weevil might threaten the profits of the Virginia wheat grower, for the expense of combating the infestation would "enable other countries to undersell him." Looking to the future Jefferson hailed the "immensity of land courting the industry of the husbandman," but he assumed that the husbandman would participate in international trade. Popular taste, that final arbiter for Jefferson, guaranteed that Americans would "return as soon as they can, to the raising [of] raw materials, and exchanging them for finer manufactures than they are able to execute themselves." The country's interest, therefore, would be to "throw open the doors of commerce, and to knock off all its shackles." At the same time it was entirely natural to Jefferson to mix shrewd assessment of market realities with homiletic commentary. Thus, he said, relying on European manufacturing would forestall the corruption of "the mass of cultivators," and he condemned tobacco raising as "a culture productive of infinite wretchedness."[46]

Working with a completely commercial mode of agriculture, Jefferson projected for America a dynamic food-producing and food-selling economy which promised the best of two worlds: economic independence for the bulk of the population and a rising standard of living. Even the word *farmer* captured some of the novelty of the new prospect. As William Tatham explained to his English readers, the cultivator "who follows the ancient track of his ancestors, is called a *planter*" while he "who sows wheat, and waters meadows, is a

[45] Jefferson, *Notes on the State of Virginia*, 168.

[46] *Ibid.*, 164–68, 174. For a description of the Founding Fathers as having "commerce-phobia," citing Jefferson's expressions of enthusiasm for free trade as the result of his years in France, see James H. Hutson, "Intellectual Foundations of Early American Diplomacy," *Diplomatic History*, 1 (Winter 1977), 6, 8.

farmer."[47] The concrete policy measures that emanated from this prescription for American growth were both political and economic: making new land in the national domain accessible to the individual farmer-owner, using diplomatic initiatives to open markets around the world, committing public funds to internal improvements, and, negatively, opposing fiscal measures that bore heavily upon the ordinary, rural taxpayers.[48] William N. Parker has described just what these policies meant to mid-nineteenth-century agriculture: "an ambitious farmer might buy more farms, but he gained no economies by consolidating them" because "enterprise was too vigorous and too widely diffused, competition for finance, land, and labor too intense to permit large concentrations of wealth in land." The larger farmer, moreover, "suffered the disadvantages of the liberal land policy and the prevailing sentiment in favor of the settler."[49]

Jefferson was not alone in joining political democracy to economic freedom; these themes coalesced in a number of local movements that in time found a national base in the opposition to Hamilton's program. Typical of this new view was Logan's declaration that the sacred rights of mankind included farmers deriving "all the advantages they can from every part of the produce of their farms," a goal that required "a perfectly free commerce" and "a free unrestricted sale for the produce of their own industry."[50] In a similar spirit John Spurrier dedicated *The Practical Farmer* to Jefferson because of his interest in agricultural science and his efforts "to promote the real strength and wealth of this commonwealth" on rational principles.[51] Writing at the same time Tench Coxe described the overwhelming importance of farming to America. Capital and labor investments in agriculture were eight times those in any other pursuit, Coxe estimated. More pertinently, he gave almost exclusive attention to the range of foodstuffs produced by family labor from Virginia to Connecticut.[52]

The nationalism implicit in these descriptions of America's economic future helps explain the breadth of the Republican movement, and the emphasis upon the commercial value of the grains, livestock, and beverages produced on family farms indicates how market changes affected early national politics. Jefferson's own nationalism was closely tied to the issues of international free trade and the disposition of the national domain. In this he was representative of the Virginia nationalists who dominated American politics after 1783 and led the campaign to establish "a more perfect union" four years later. With peace and

[47] Tatham, *Communications Concerning the Agriculture and Commerce of the United States*, 46.

[48] For excellent discussions of Thomas Jefferson's commercial policies, see Merrill Peterson, "Thomas Jefferson and Commercial Policy, 1783–1793," *William and Mary Quarterly*, XXII (Oct. 1965); Richard E. Ellis, "The Political Economy of Thomas Jefferson," in *Thomas Jefferson: The Man, His World, His Influence*, ed. Lally Waymouth (New York, 1973), 81–95.

[49] William N. Parker, "Productivity Growth in American Grain Farming: An Analysis of Its 19th Century Sources," in *Reinterpretation of American Economic History*, ed. Robert Fogel and Stanley L. Engerman (New York, 1971), 178.

[50] Logan, *Five Letters*, 25, 28.

[51] Spurrier, *Practical Farmer*, iii.

[52] Tench Coxe, *A View of the United States of America* (Philadelphia, 1794), 8–9, 87–99.

the failure of William Morris's impost scheme, attention in the Continental Congress passed to matters of vital concern to Virginians—the taking-up of western land and the marketing of America's bounteous harvests. Both goals encouraged a national perspective. To expel the British from the Northwest, to ease the Indians out of Ohio territory, to negotiate new commercial treaties abroad—these things required more than confederal cooperation. Just how long-range their view was can be gauged by the passions aroused by the idea of closing the port of New Orleans at a time when settlers had reached Kentucky. The implicit social values of this southern program, as H. James Henderson has pointed out, were secular rather than religious, anticipatory rather than regressive, individualistic rather than corporate. The leaders of the Old Dominion "looked forward to continental grandeur rather than back to ancestral virtue."[53] East of the Hudson there was little support for an expansive American republic. The stagnating Massachusetts economy made the past a more reliable guide to the future than dreams of a new age of prosperity and progress. In the middle and southern states, however, the depressed 1780s reflected less the limits of growth than the failure to unlock America's rich resources.

From Georgia to New York a hinterland ran westward that gave the new American nation what no other people had ever possessed: the material base for a citizenry of independent, industrious property holders. And Virginia, the largest and wealthiest state, produced the leaders who turned this prospect into a political program. Most national leaders recognized the economic potential in America; the question that emerged was how and in deference to which values would this potential be realized. The issues that clustered around the opening of the national domain reveal very well how choices would affect the character of American society. Manufacturing, proponents argued, would provide jobs for sons and daughters at home; uncontrolled movement into the west would scatter families.[54] Recognizing the class difference in migration rates, an article addressed to the working people of Maryland urged support for the Constitution on the gounds that the common people were more properly citizens of America than of any particular state, for many of them died far away from where they were born.[55] The congressional debates on the Land Act of 1796 swirled around the question whether these sons and daughters who moved west would become independent farmers or the tenants of land speculators. The geographic base of the Jeffersonian Republicans can be traced in the votes for 160-acre sales.[56] Because grains were raised throughout the United States and required ancillary industries for their processing and sale, the Republican program was neither regional nor, strictly speaking, agrarian. It

[53] H. James Henderson, "The Structure of Politics in the Continental Congress," in *Essays on the American Revolution*, ed. Stephen G. Kurtz and James H. Hutson (Chapel Hill, 1973), 188.

[54] "On American Manufactures," *American Museum or Repository of Ancient and Modern Pieces, Prose and Poetical*, I (Jan. 1787), 18.

[55] *Pennsylvania Gazette*, April 2, 1788, p. 3.

[56] Rudolph M. Bell, *Party and Faction in American Politics: The House of Representatives, 1789–1801* (Westport, Conn., 1973), 85–89; Murray R. Benedict, *Farm Policies of the United States, 1790–1950: A Study of Their Origins and Development* (New York, 1953), 12–15.

should be emphasized that it involved neither American isolation nor a slowed pace of growth. It was in fact a form of capitalism that Jefferson seized as the ax to fell Old World institutions because free trade offered the integrative network that social authority supplied elsewhere. Hamilton's response to the Louisiana Purchase makes this point negatively: the extension of America's agricultural frontier, he maintained, threatened to remove citizens from the coercive power of the state.[57]

The Revolution had made possible Jefferson's vision of a great, progressive republic, but developments during the first years of independence brought to light two different threats to its fulfillment. The one was old and predictable: the tendency of the rich and mighty to control the avenues to profit and preferment. The other came from the very strength of common voters in revolutionary America. The war effort itself had democratized politics, and without royal government, the broad prerevolutionary suffrage was translated into comprehensive popular power.[58] Emboldened by the natural rights rhetoric of the resistance movement, political newcomers began to challenge the old merchant oligarchies in the cities, while their counterparts in state legislatures pushed through radical measures affecting taxation, inheritance, insolvency, debt retirement, and land sales.[59] The ensuing conflicts, which Progressive historians made familiar as part of the struggle between rich and poor, aroused fears that cannot be categorized so easily. The new aggregate power of the people channeled through popularly elected legislatures alarmed men as philosophically different as Jefferson and Hamilton, as unalike temperamentally as Benjamin Rush and Robert Livingston. When ordinary Americans used their new voting power to push for legislation favorable to themselves, they made committed democrats as well as conservatives apprehensive. The anxieties expressed during the late 1780s cannot be ascribed solely to an elitist distrust of the poor, the ill-born, and the untalented many. Men destined to become the champions of political equality found the augmentation of power in the first state governments a genuine threat. A historiographical tradition that reads all fears of popular, unrestricted governmental power as evidence of upper class sympathies is in danger of missing the most compelling political goal to emerge in late eighteenth-century America—the limitation of formal authority in deference to individual freedom. Disaggregating society, the Jeffersonians redirected the sovereign people away from exercising power as a body and toward enjoying free choice as private persons. Leaders of both the Federalist and Republican parties had cooperated in 1787 because a national

[57] Gerald Stourzh, *Alexander Hamilton and the Idea of Republican Government* (Stanford, 1970), 192–93.

[58] Jackson Turner Main, "Government by the People: The American Revolution and the Democratization of the Legislatures," *William and Mary Quarterly*, XXIII (July 1966), 391–407; John Shy, "The American Revolution: The Military Conflict Considered as a Revolutionary War," in *Essays on the American Revolution*, ed. Kurtz and Hutson, 21–56; Edward Countryman, "Consolidating Power in Revolutionary America: The Case of New York, 1775–1783," *Journal of Interdisciplinary History*, VI (Spring 1976), 645–77.

[59] Jon C. Teaford, *The Municipal Revolution in America: Origins of Modern Urban Government, 1650–1825* (Chicago, 1975); Jackson Turner Main, *Political Parties before the Constitution* (Chapel Hill, 1973).

political framework and a unified economy were essential to their differing conceptions of America's future. The new government created by the Constitution, however, proved to be a double-edged sword for the democratic nationalists. Strong enough to provide the conditions for freedom and growth, it could also be used to concentrate power and thereby raise a new national elite.

In resisting Hamilton's policies the Republicans eschewed the very divisions that historians have dwelt upon in explaining party formation. Far from pitting merchants against farmers, rich against poor, or the commercially inclined against the self-sufficient, the Jeffersonians assumed that a freely developing economy would benefit all. The eradication of privilege and the limitation of formal power would stimulate the natural harmony of interests. Thomas Paine with his usual directness gave expression to this liberal view in the fight over Robert Morris's bank. In a republican form of government, he wrote, "public good is not a term opposed to the good of individuals; on the contrary, it is the good of every individual collected. . . . the farmer understands farming, and the merchant understands commerce; and as riches are equally the object of both, there is no occasion that either should fear that the other will seek to be poor."[60] Making a slightly different point, the Jeffersonian congressional leader, Albert Gallatin, opposed the Federalists' 1800 bankruptcy bill because its provisions could not be restricted to merchants. In America, he argued, "the different professions and trades are blended together in the same persons; the same man being frequently a farmer and a merchant, and perhaps a manufacturer."[61] What was distinctive about the Jeffersonian economic policy was not an anticommercial bias, but a commitment to growth through the unimpeded exertions of individuals whose access to economic opportunity was both protected and facilitated by government. Treated for so long as a set of self-evident truths, the flowering of liberal thought in America owed much to specific developments. The advantageous terms of trade for American farm commodities, the expulsion of Europeans and Native Americans from the trans-Appalachian west, the people's commercial tendencies that Jefferson described—all these made men and women receptive to a new conception of human nature that affirmed the reciprocal influences of freedom and prosperity. What had given a sacred underpinning to Locke's contract theory was his assumption that men living under God's law were enjoined to protect the life, liberty, and property of others as well as their own. Jefferson perceived that Locke's identity of interests among the propertied could be universalized in America and thereby acquire a moral base in natural design. It was indeed a *novus ordo seclorum*.

[60] [Thomas Paine], *Dissertations on Government: The Affairs of the Bank; and Paper Money*, in *The Complete Writings of Thomas Paine*, ed. Philip S. Foner (2 vols., New York, 1945), II, 372, 399–400.

[61] *Annals of the Congress*, 5 Cong., 3 sess., Jan. 14, 1799, 2650–51.

What Is Still American in the Political Philosophy of Thomas Jefferson?

Joyce Appleby

SHORTLY after leaving the presidency, Thomas Jefferson undertook the translation of a manuscript by the French philosopher Antoine Louis Claude Destutt de Tracy. At the same time he prevailed on his friend William Duane to publish it anonymously, and in due course Tracy's *Commentary and Review of Montesquieu's Spirit of Laws* appeared in Philadelphia.[1] For Tracy this American imprint offered his ideas safe conduct into the hostile territory of Napoleonic France. For Jefferson the *Review of Montesquieu* became a new weapon in his old war against pernicious ideas. He sent copies to friends and got the book adopted as a text at the College of William and Mary while venturing the hope that it might be placed in the hands of every American student as "the elementary and fundamental" work on the science of government. Such an outcome, Jefferson confided to Lafayette, would more than repay the five hours daily he had expended on Tracy's manuscript over the course of three months. To Pierre Samuel Du Pont de Nemours he revealed more clearly his motives: "The paradoxes of Montesquieu have been too long uncorrected."[2] Probably not many young men in America still read Montesquieu, but Jefferson's unabated desire to combat his influence offers us an Ariadne's thread through the ideological labyrinth of the early national period. In addition, Jefferson's endorsement of Tracy's economic theory gives us an idea of his mature thinking on commercial development and its moral implications. These well-documented reactions to the work of Montesquieu and Tracy raise serious doubts about the wisdom of the

Ms. Appleby is a member of the Department of History at the University of California, Los Angeles.

[1] Merrill D. Peterson, *Thomas Jefferson and the New Nation: A Biography* (New York, 1970), 947-948; Jefferson to Duane, Aug. 12, 1810, in Andrew A. Lipscomb and Albert Ellery Bergh, eds., *The Writings of Thomas Jefferson* (Washington, D.C., 1903-1905), XII, 407-408.

[2] Jefferson to Duane, Jan. 22, 1813, in Lipscomb and Bergh, eds., *Writings of Jefferson*, XIII, 213-214; Jefferson to Joseph Milligan, Oct. 25, 1818, *ibid.*, XIX 263; Jefferson to Thomas Cooper, Jan. 16, 1814, *ibid.*, XIV, 54-63; Jefferson to Lafayette, May 17, 1816, *ibid.*, XIX, 237-238; Jefferson to Du Pont de Nemours, Nov. 29, 1813, in Dumas Malone, ed., *Correspondence between Thomas Jefferson and Pierre Samuel du Pont de Nemours, 1798-1817* (Boston, 1930), 145. On Tracy's motives see Emmet Kennedy, *A Philosophe in the Age of Revolution: Destutt de Tracy and the Origins of 'Ideology'* (Philadelphia, 1978), 210.

recent scholarly effort to assimilate Jefferson into the Country party tradition of eighteenth-century England.[3]

During the years of constitution writing in America, Montesquieu's name acted as a code reference to the small-republic theory and the principle of the separation of powers. European readers, on the other hand, associated Montesquieu with an elaborate rationale for aristocratic power. All of these positions emerged from his schematic analysis of governmental types in *The Spirit of the Laws*. The maintenance of liberty and order in a society of any size, Montesquieu had said, required a "standing body" to mediate between the king and the people. Taking England as his model, he showed how the English constitution not only disentangled the executive, legislative, and judicial functions of government but also balanced the power of the people and the nobility. Here Montesquieu produced an eighteenth-century gloss on the ancient theory of politics that had been revived by Machiavelli and anglicized by James Harrington. The sovereign authority of the English king-in-parliament thus became the modern version of the constitutional balance of the one, the few, and the many recommended by Aristotle and Polybius.[4] Fractured and checked in this way, the august power of government could be moderated, which for Montesquieu was the great goal of politics. Republics, however, by their very nature had no such tripartite division, and the moderating influence had to come from another source. A virtuous citizenry could sustain a republic through the disorders endemic in human society, but this essential civic virtue could survive only among a people of frugal habits who lived in a limited area where a rough equality of property prevailed. From this chain of reasoning came Montesquieu's celebrated small-republic theory.[5]

Our knowledge of the significance of the Renaissance revival of classical political thought has been enormously enriched by J.G.A. Pocock, who has traced the tangled threads of civic humanism from sixteenth-century Florence through the political clash between the Court and Country parties in eighteenth-century England to what he considers the replay of

[3] J.G.A. Pocock, "Virtue and Commerce in the Eighteenth Century," *Journal of Interdisciplinary History*, III (1972), 133-134, and *The Machiavellian Moment: Florentine Political Thought and the Atlantic Republican Tradition* (Princeton, N.J., 1975), ix, 529-533; Lance Banning, *The Jeffersonian Persuasion: Evolution of a Party Ideology* (Ithaca, N.Y., 1978); Forrest McDonald, *The Presidency of Thomas Jefferson* (Lawrence, Kan., 1976); John M. Murrin, "The Great Inversion, or Court versus Country: A Comparison of the Revolution Settlements in England (1688-1721) and America (1776-1816)," in Pocock, ed., *Three British Revolutions: 1641, 1688, 1776* (Princeton, N.J., 1980); Rowland Berthoff, "Independence and Attachment, Virtue and Interest: From Republican Citizen to Free Enterpriser, 1787-1837," in Richard L. Bushman *et al.*, eds., *Uprooted Americans: Essays to Honor Oscar Handlin* (Boston, 1979).

[4] Pocock, *Machiavellian Moment*, 478-485.

[5] Charles Secondat, Baron de Montesquieu, *The Spirit of the Laws*, trans. Thomas Nugent (New York, 1962 [orig. publ. Paris, 1748]), 20-22, 40-48.

that conflict in America in the 1790s. Sensitive to the way ideas suggest and legitimate lines of action, Pocock connects the emergence of civic-humanist values to the political disorders of seventeenth-century England. Because the traditional monarchy left English subjects with no duties save obedience, the Civil War necessitated a search for ideas to inform a new consciousness.[6] After the failure of the Puritan commonwealth, Englishmen turned to classical political theory for explanations that could accommodate their reverence for the ancient constitution to the imperatives of a modern ruling class. There they found a chaste model of civil society where men exercised their virtue by putting the common good before their own and thus realized their fulfillment as Aristotle's political animal. Civic humanism offered a concept of public life that served the moral as well as the intellectual needs of the English gentry. However, the ancients did not give of their wisdom without a price. Their precepts were inseparable from the dreary record of tyrannies, rebellions, and usurpations from which they were gleaned. Human nature is flawed; civil order is always at risk; cycles of degeneration await all societies. History furnishes the important lesson that the rule of law alone preserves liberty and the balancing of the few and the many alone preserves the law. From this classical paradigm, Pocock believes, most Englishmen took their political soundings, discovering therein reasons for alarm as well as prescriptions for stability. This paradigm also generated the suspicion of novelty and the fear of self-interest. Politics had to be reduced to ethics if it were not itself to be reduced to corruption. This "sociology of civic ethics," according to Pocock, "had to be restated with paradigmatic force and comprehensiveness for the eighteenth-century West at large," and it fell to Montesquieu's *Spirit of the Laws* to do the job.[7]

Despite its character as a learned treatise, Montesquieu's book was immediately drawn into polemical warfare, in large part because his depiction of England's mixed monarchy was more ideological than empirical. His source of information had been the leader of the English Country opposition, Henry St. John, Viscount Bolingbroke, who had fashioned the theory of balanced government into an attack on the ruling Whig oligarchy. With the wisdom of the ancients at his back, Bolingbroke contended that his enemies at court were not merely wrong, but highly dangerous, that indeed their consolidation of executive power placed the entire British constitution in jeopardy.[8] Montesquieu's Bolingbrokean bias made the *Spirit of the Laws* highly useful to the Country party in England, while in France it offered new weapons for the fight against the absolutism of Louis XV. His theoretical justification for the autonomy and authority of political elites lent support to the campaign to strengthen the power of the French *parlements*, the provincial courts staffed by a

[6] Pocock, *Machiavellian Moment*, 333-347.

[7] *Ibid.*, 527, 484.

[8] Isaac Kramnick, *Bolingbroke and His Circle: The Politics of Nostalgia in the Age of Walpole* (Cambridge, Mass., 1968), 142-152.

hereditary magistracy.[9] These partisan responses, however, had little effect on Montesquieu's reception in America, where he exercised the influence of a mighty savant of the age of enlightenment and was, as Pocock puts it, "the greatest practitioner" of the "science of virtue."[10]

Jefferson began reading Montesquieu in 1774 when he was thirty-one and a member of the First Continental Congress. He devoted more space in his commonplace book to the *Spirit of the Laws* than to any other work.[11] Sixteen years later he began to write about its "falsehoods" and "heresies." To Tracy he admitted that his initial admiration was shaken only when he recognized so much of "false principle and misapplied fact" as to render equivocal the whole. Thereafter he took increasing note of the "inconsistencies," "apocryphal facts," and "false inferences" that, in his judgment, marred Montesquieu's great book.[12] In view of Jefferson's reputation as a guardian of virtue, an admirer of simplicity, and a patron, if not a person, of frugality, this mounting criticism of Montesquieu may seem puzzling. In fact, the two men began with diametrically opposed assumptions about human nature, which in turn impinged on their conception of the problem of order, and more important to Jefferson, the prospect for political equality.

Jefferson became aware of the elitist implications of Montesquieu's civic humanism during his years in Paris.[13] When he took up his duties as American minister in 1785, most educated Frenchmen believed that reform of their antiquated institutions was imminent. Debates in the famous Paris salons frequented by Jefferson swirled around the questions raised by this expectation. Must a newly constituted French monarchy include a role for the nobility, as Montesquieu had insisted? Did political realities dictate that the French legislature contain both a house for the people and a house for the privileged few, as in England? In the two years preceding the convocation of the Estates General, reform-minded Frenchmen divided into hostile camps. One comprised the *Anglomanes* who said yes to Montesquieu and his balanced-government theory; the other, the *Americanistes* said no, and rallied to the slogan "one king, one nation, one house." They also spurned the lessons encoded in the English example and maintained that Montesquieu's "standing bodies" had been the principal obstacles to improvements in France.[14] Jefferson's sympathies lay wholly

[9] *Ibid.*, 150-152.

[10] Pocock, *Machiavellian Moment*, 484.

[11] Gilbert Chinard, ed., *The Commonplace Book of Thomas Jefferson: A Repertory of His Ideas on Government* (Baltimore, 1926), 9, 31-37.

[12] Jefferson to Thomas Mann Randolph, May 30, 1790, in Lipscomb and Bergh, eds., *Writings of Jefferson*, VIII, 31; Jefferson to Duane, Aug. 12, 1810, *ibid.*, XII, 408; Jefferson to Nathaniel Niles, Mar. 22, 1801, *ibid.*, X, 232; Jefferson to Cooper, July 10, 1812, *ibid.*, XIII, 177-178; Jefferson to Tracy, Jan. 26, 1811, *ibid.*, 13. See also Peterson, *Jefferson*, 948.

[13] Chinard, ed., *Commonplace Book*, 31-37.

[14] Joyce Appleby, "America as a Model for the Radical French Reformers of 1789," *William and Mary Quarterly*, 3d Ser., XXVIII (1971), 267-286.

with the latter group, among whom he made warm friends. Though the question at hand concerned bicameralism, it unavoidably touched the entire classical paradigm: the esteem for ancient wisdom, the hostility to change, and the acceptance of ranks and orders as permanent features of human society. The civic-humanist tradition also fostered suspicions about commercial development and economic innovations, which both Jefferson and his *Americaniste* friends strongly favored.

The *Americanistes* were drawn from the ranks of the *Economistes*, who had long agitated for agricultural improvements and a free trade in grain. They disliked England's mercantilistic policies as much as its aristocratic constitution. America's unique economic situation, in their view, helped explain the bold political experiments of the new nation; both made the United States a powerful symbol of reform.[15] Shortly before he died, Anne Robert Jacques Turgot, the famous leader of the *Economistes*, had expressed to Richard Price his dismay at the slavish imitation of English forms to be found in the American state constitutions. Published after Turgot's death, this letter provoked John Adams, then minister at the Court of St. James, to write a three-volume rebuttal. Appearing in the midst of the French debates on political reform, Adams's *Defence of the Constitutions of Government of the United States of America* clearly ranged him on the side of the *Anglomanes*.[16] Fearing that the *Defence* would tarnish the fresh image of America, Jefferson's French friends, possibly with his connivance, rushed into print with an anonymous American pamphlet that explicitly dissociated Adams's veneration of Old World political theory from mainstream American thought. "Had Mr. Adams been a native of the old, instead of the new world," the author, John Stevens, wrote, "we should not have been so surprised at his system."[17] Having shed their provincial status by revolution, Americans like Stevens were ready to give ideological import to what were once considered egregious departures from European norms. Novelty no longer frightened them.

The political perceptions of Adams, like those of Jefferson, had been sharpened during his long sojourn in Europe. Writing the *Defence* on the eve of his return home, Adams was acutely aware that his ideas might not be well received in the United States. In a letter accompanying a presentation copy sent to Benjamin Franklin, he declared somewhat defensively, "if it is heresy, I shall, I suppose, be cast out of communion. But it is the only sense in which I am or ever was a Republican."[18]

[15] See Pierre Samuel Du Pont de Nemours's article in *Ephémérides du citoyen*, VI (1770), 210-211, and Durand Echeverria, *Mirage in the West: A History of the French Image of American Society to 1815* (Princeton, N.J., 1957), 24-26, 56.

[16] Joyce Appleby, "The Jefferson-Adams Rupture and the First French Translation of John Adams' *Defence*," *American Historical Review*, LXXIII (1968), 1084-1091.

[17] [John Stevens], *Observations on Government, Including Some Animadversions on Mr. Adams's Defence of the Constitutions of Government* . . . (New York, 1787), 25-26.

[18] John Bigelow, ed., *The Works of Benjamin Franklin*, XI (New York, 1904), 298-299.

Fortunately for Adams, his fellow New Englanders shared his preoccupation with the civic-humanist values of the classical republican tradition. In the years immediately following the end of the war, they had dwelt obsessively on the necessity of civic virtue and the threats posed by the riotous appetites oi a liberated people. As Nathan O. Hatch has recently detailed, clergymen of both evangelical and rationalist strains had revitalized John Winthrop's sense of mission by fusing the themes of an embattled Calvinism with the secular ideals of classical republicanism. Originally directed against the French Canadian menace, this civil millenarianism offered a rationale for opposing the British and for turning the resistance movement in Massachusetts into "the sacred cause of liberty." American Independence presented these Puritan descendants with yet another occasion for putting their countrymen to the question, "Are we a virtuous people?" Without endorsing formal political privilege, upper-class New Englanders insisted on the traditional deference of the many to the few. Both classical political theory and conventional Christian dogma heightened fears about individual self-interest. Like members of the English Country party, many New Englanders espied in the quickening pace of commercial life the triumph of license and luxury. Such concerns lay ready to trigger powerful emotions when the many actually spoke. Thus the court closings by western farmers led by Daniel Shays evoked the old refrains of "savage independence," "unthinking multitude," and "the sad corruption of republican virtue." The civil millenarianism that put Massachusetts in the Revolutionary vanguard, however, laid the groundwork for that unbending Federalism that would later set New England at odds with the rest of the nation.[19]

As Jefferson's and Adams's references to heresy suggest, contemporaries continued to think in terms of orthodoxy, while republicanism itself became a protean concept. With the first stirrings of American intellectual independence, republicanism flooded its classical channels, especially outside New England. In response to these new currents James Madison worked out an answer to Montesquieu's small-republic theory in his *Federalist* No. 10. Drawing on the experience of a socially diverse and economically expansive people, he argued that the mortal effects of majority faction could best be controlled in a large pluralistic society through the competition of interests. In Madison's eyes, Adams's endorsement of the ancient doctrine of balanced government represented a betrayal of American political forms. Four years after the publication of the *Defence* he charged that Adams, "under a mock defence of the Republican Constitutions of his Country," had attacked them with all his force.[20] Such hyperbole can be ascribed to partisan rhetoric, but the assertion of theoretical differences in the meaning of republicanism

[19] Hatch, *The Sacred Cause of Liberty: Republican Thought and the Millennium in Revolutionary New England* (New Haven, Conn., 1977), 36-55, 13-18, 121.

[20] Madison to Jefferson, May 12, 1791, in Gaillard Hunt, ed., *The Writings of James Madison*, VI (New York, 1904), 50.

deserves investigation, especially because historians of the early national period have recently claimed that the classical model that Adams endorsed dominated American politics well into the nineteenth century.

Jefferson's metaphorical response to Shays's Rebellion—"the tree of liberty must be refreshed from time to time with the blood of patriots and tyrants"—alerts us to a set of values easily distinguished from those flourishing in Adams's New England. In his conception of human nature, his expectation of progress, his enthusiasm for economic growth, and his irreverence toward the past, Jefferson explicitly distanced himself from the civic humanism that Adams had espoused. Far from fearing a decline of virtue in his fellow Americans, he laid it down as an axiom that they would remain healthy in spirit and body so long as they pursued farming. "Corruption of morals in the mass of cultivators," he wrote in a much-quoted passage in the *Notes on the State of Virginia*, "is a phenomenon of which no age nor nation has furnished an example." As Hatch has observed, most New Englanders would have gaped in disbelief at such faith in the beneficent influence of a social occupation.[21] Jefferson had freed himself from worries about the moral fiber of his countrymen by embracing a different construction of reality. Abandoning the eternal Adam of Christianity as well as the creature of passions portrayed in ancient texts, he had embraced a conception of human nature that emphasized its benign potential.

Where traditional thinkers traced the source of social evils back to wayward human propensities, Jefferson reversed the influence and ascribed the lowly state of man to repressive institutions. Nowhere better described than in Daniel Boorstin's *The Lost World of Thomas Jefferson*, this naturalistic view was at once mechanistic and moral.[22] The environment could create vice and virtue—typically, Jefferson described tobacco raising as "a culture productive of infinite wretchedness"—but the innate qualities of man held out great promise.[23] The purpose of government was therefore not to raise power to check power but rather to ensure the conditions for liberating man's self-actualizing capacities. If the authoritarian institutions of the past could be reformed, then a different and happier future could be imagined. Again he reversed the priorities implicit in the classical tradition. The private came first. Instead of regarding the public arena as the locus of human fulfillment where men rose above their self-interest to serve the common good, Jefferson wanted government to offer protection to the personal realm where men might freely exercise their faculties. It is to this complex set of values that one must look for the

[21] Jefferson to William Stephens Smith, Nov. 13, 1787, in Julian P. Boyd *et al.*, eds., *The Papers of Thomas Jefferson* (Princeton, N.J., 1950-), XII, 356; Jefferson, *Notes on the State of Virginia*, ed. William Peden (Chapel Hill, N.C., 1955), 164-165; Hatch, *Sacred Cause of Liberty*, 108.

[22] Boorstin, *The Lost World of Thomas Jefferson* (New York, 1948).

[23] Jefferson, *Notes*, ed. Peden, 166.

reasons behind Jefferson's prolonged campaign against the heresies of Montesquieu.

Montesquieu's veneration of ancient wisdom ran athwart Jefferson's oft-expressed optimism that the future would outshine the past; the American celebration of the balanced government theory in the *Spirit of the Laws* led Jefferson to fear that his countrymen would accept as inevitable the dominance of a new elite of wealth and privilege. Coining the term "Americanism," he put it to polemical use as an alternative to an Anglo-inspired "aristocracy."[24] As a Virginia politician during the Revolution, Jefferson had given highest priority to laws that would prevent concentrations of landed wealth. "Legislators cannot invent too many devices for subdividing property," he wrote to Madison from Paris, going on to suggest progressive taxes for large holders with total exemptions for small ones. Looking back in his autobiography on his own legislative record, he claimed to have created a system "by which every fibre would be eradicated of antient or future aristocracy." Tradition held no charms for him, nor did precedent. He was not at all surprised that "time and trial have discovered very capital defects" in the Virginia constitution when it had reached the ripe old age of eight years. Even more indicative of the iconoclastic cast of his mind was his idea of submitting the country's laws to a plebiscite every generation. By lifting the dead hand of the past Jefferson expected to give life to the latent human capacity for personal fulfillment. Science and education pulled his carriage of hopes, as he revealed when he ordered a composite portrait of the life-sized busts of Bacon, Locke, and Newton. They had, he told John Trumbull, laid the foundation for the physical and moral sciences and should not be confounded "with the herd of other great men," because they were "the three greatest men that have ever lived, without any exception."[25]

More than any other figure in his generation Jefferson integrated a program of economic development and a policy for nation building into a radical moral theory. What emerges from his own writings is a fairly coherent description of the kind of economic base that would support a democratic republic. Believing that industrious, self-reliant farmers made superior citizens, Jefferson advocated measures to increase the number of freeholders. He ingeniously suggested a fifty-acre qualification for voting in Virginia, coupled with a proposal to give fifty acres to every landless white adult male. His efforts to abolish primogeniture represented yet another way to diffuse property holding.[26] He successfully opposed the

[24] In a letter to C.F.C. de Volney, Feb. 8, 1805, Jefferson predicted that Delaware would be split until "Anglomany with her yields to Americanism" (Lipscomb and Bergh, eds., *Writings of Jefferson*, XI, 68). The *Oxford English Dictionary* credits Jefferson with coining the word Americanism but cites an 1808 passage as the first one.

[25] Jefferson to Madison, Oct. 28, 1785, in Boyd *et al.*, eds., *Jefferson Papers*, VIII, 682; *ibid.*, II, 308; Jefferson, *Notes*, ed. Peden, 118; Boyd *et al.*, eds., *Jefferson Papers*, XV, 384-398; Jefferson to Trumbull, Feb. 15, 1789, *ibid.*, XIV, 561.

[26] Boyd *et al.*, eds., *Jefferson Papers*, I, 362; II, 308.

speculative land companies in working out the details of Virginia's cession of western claims, and he guided the first land ordinance through the Continental Congress. There he wrote into American policy the goals of easy access to the national domain and speedy statehood for the territories. Where classical economic theory stressed that the poor could not act as citizens because they were dependent on the will of others, Jefferson unmasked the self-fulfilling prophecy in that formulation. Assessing the party divisions in the Constitutional Convention, he charged that many then had believed the experience of Europe "to be a safer guide than mere theory." Many, too, had come to accept the political domination of the poor by the rich and had further aimed at constraining "the brute force of the people" by hard labor, poverty, and ignorance.[27] As early as 1784 Jefferson had charted a different course: use constitutional and statutory measures to make the poor independent. Here his environmentalism merged imperceptibly into his convictions about the basic human endowment. What today would appear as social engineering presented itself to Jefferson as a liberation of those natural forces long held in check by the Old World artifices of monarchy, nobility, and established religion.

More basic to the issues here, Jefferson was an early advocate of the commerical exploitation of American agriculture. His vision of a nation of farmers involved him in long-range programs for expanding international free trade in basic farm commodities. The marketing of American surpluses engaged his attention from his days as Virginia's representative in the Continental Congress, through his years in Paris, as secretary of state, as president, and as advisor to his successors. In the *Notes* Jefferson adumbrated a prescription for American growth which he followed with some consistency through a long political career. Here he extolled the production of wheat because it "feeds the labourers plentifully, requires from them only a moderate toil . . . and diffuses plenty and happiness among the whole." Farmers, he assumed, would participate in the world market, not seek self-sufficiency. Their rising standard of living would lift them from the miserable life of their European counterparts. His countrymen, Jefferson predicted, would go back to buying European manufactured goods after the Revolution while moving rapidly westward to exploit the natural resources that could pay for them.[28] No partisan of Spartan endurance, he exonerated Americans from the charge of lukewarm patriotism by pointing to "the pennyless condition of a people, totally shut out from all commerce . . . and therefore without any means for converting their labor into money."[29] It was not the slave-worked staple crops that fueled Jefferson's hopes but the prospects opened to

[27] Jefferson to William Johnson, June 12, 1823, in Paul Leicester Ford, ed., *The Writings of Thomas Jefferson* (New York, 1892-1899), X, 226n-227n.

[28] Jefferson, *Notes*, ed. Peden, 168, 164.

[29] Jefferson to Johnson, Oct. 27, 1822, in Ford, ed., *Writings of Jefferson*, X, 222-223.

ordinary farmers. The burgeoning Atlantic trade in grains gave him the material base for a program that was both national and democratic.

The steady increase of world population that had raised the price of wheat prompted the pessimism of Thomas R. Malthus, but Jefferson stuck by his guns of optimism. Indeed, what is fascinating in both Jefferson's and Madison's responses to Malthus is their complete transformation of the problem. Expecting a diminishing return from agriculture, Malthus asserted that population would outstrip food; assuming an enhanced capacity to feed people, Madison and Jefferson instead feared that there would be more people than jobs.[30] Writing to Jean Baptiste Say in 1804, Jefferson explained why Americans would be exempted from Malthus's gloomy prophecies. The uncultivated expanses of the national domain promised harvests increasing "geometrically with our laborers." Americans would then be able to produce surpluses "to nourish the now perishing births of Europe, who in return would manufacture and send us in exchange our clothes and other comforts."[31] It was the same formula he had proposed a score of years earlier in the *Notes*. Meanwhile he had wrested much of the land in the Northwest from speculators, ensured the political parity of new states, and presided over the dismantling of the national financial establishment that had threatened to narrow the ambit of economic freedom for ordinary Americans.

In a recent article on Virginia's Revolutionary leadership Marc Egnal describes the coalescence of a party of expansionists among the Virginia gentry. Quick to identify themselves with "America's cornucopian future," burgesses from the Northern Neck and the piedmont took the lead in claiming the Ohio Valley. After the British made good that claim in the French and Indian War, these same expansionists fought the efforts of Parliament to control their hunger for land. Committed to expansion, they pursued what Egnal characterizes as "forthright measures against any power that hindered the colonies from becoming prosperous, self-assertive states."[32] In tracing the bold plans of the Lees and Washingtons

[30] Madison to Jefferson, June 19, 1786, in Boyd *et al.*, eds., *Jefferson Papers*, IX, 659-660. See also Drew R. McCoy, "Jefferson and Madison on Malthus: Population Growth in Jeffersonian Political Economy," *Virginia Magazine of History and Biography*, LXXXVIII (1980), 259-276. Although McCoy argues that there was a "significant interest in population growth in late eighteenth- and early nineteenth-century America" (p. 261), his review of Jefferson's four references to Malthus indicates that Jefferson held to his "basic vision of a predominantly agricultural America that would continue to export its bountiful surpluses of food abroad" (p. 268). See also Peterson, *Jefferson*, 771-773. No American publication on the subject of Malthus appeared until twenty years after the 1798 appearance of *An Essay on the Principle of Population*.

[31] Jefferson to Say, Feb. 1, 1804, in Lipscomb and Bergh, eds., *Writings of Jefferson*, XI, 2-3.

[32] Marc Egnal, "The Origins of the Revolution in Virginia: A Reinterpretation," *WMQ*, 3d Ser., XXXVII (1980), 404, 416, 424-428. See also H. James Henderson, "The Structure of Politics in the Continental Congress," in Stephen G. Kurtz and James H. Hutson, eds., *Essays on the American Revolution* (Chapel Hill, N.C., 1973), 187-191.

who led the expansionist party, Egnal provides roots for Jefferson's enthusiasm for economic progress. Indeed, it was in a letter to George Washington that Jefferson dismissed doubts about America's commercial future on the ground that the people had had too full a taste for manufactured comforts to be closed off from them. "We must," he wrote in 1784, "endeavor to share as large a portion as we can of this modern source of wealth and power."[33] Where Jefferson went beyond the expansionists was in imagining how the agricultural prospects of America could nurture the unfolding of a human potential long blocked by poverty and ignorance. Virginia's size, its population, its suitability for raising food, and its access to the West help explain why Virginians spearheaded the drive for a constitutional convention and won eight of the first nine presidential elections under the new federal government. The nationalism of Virginians drew sustenance from a favorable material situation, but it was the genius of Jefferson to give that vision of expansion a powerful moral character.

Jefferson's optimism and the hopes it promoted came out most clearly when he pushed against the limits of reform advocated by his radical French friends. As Gilbert Chinard long ago pointed out, Jefferson rejected Du Pont's premise that it was the *proprietaires* who formed the political nation. "You," he chided Du Pont, "set down as zeros all individuals not having lands," adding significantly that the landless "are the greater number in every society of long standing." Governments, Jefferson insisted, did not exist to protect property but rather to promote access to property or, more broadly speaking, opportunity. It was in deference to this distinction that he changed Locke's "life, liberty and property" to make the Declaration of Independence affirm the natural rights to "life, liberty, and the pursuit of happiness." A decade later, when Lafayette submitted to him a draft declaration of rights for France, he again excised the offending word, property. Investing faith in the profoundly revolutionary ideal of a natural capacity for personal autonomy, Jefferson resolutely put his influence to work to minimize social distinctions, eschewing as well the didacticism that came too readily to upper-class reformers. Writing to Du Pont at age seventy-three, he acknowledged that they shared a paternal love for their people, "but you love them as infants whom you are afraid to trust without nurses; and I as adults whom I freely leave to self-government."[34]

The linkage between Jefferson's basic assumptions about human nature and his ideas about commerce can be traced through the *Review of Montesquieu* upon which Jefferson lavished so much attention after he left the presidency. Describing Tracy's book as the "most profound and logical work" addressed to the present generation, he predicted that it would

[33] Jefferson to Washington, Mar. 15, 1784, in Boyd *et al.*, eds., *Jefferson Papers*, VII, 26.

[34] Gilbert Chinard, ed., *The Correspondence of Jefferson and Du Pont de Nemours* (Baltimore, 1931), lxiii; Jefferson to Du Pont, Apr. 24, 1816, in Malone, ed., *Correspondence*, 184.

finally reduce Montesquieu to his true value.[35] Tracy's own intellectual debts were owed to Thomas Hobbes, John Locke, and Adam Smith, whose cold analyses of social relations he warmed with infusions of a moralism reminiscent of Jean-Jacques Rousseau. From Hobbes he took his fundamental stance on human nature: men are creatures of will. Their liberty consists in the power of executing that will and accomplishing their desires, and their happiness in the gratification of the will. Hence happiness and liberty are the same. The pursuit of self-interest is both natural and irresistible, but Tracy escaped from the Hobbesian war of all against all by asserting that in a free government men would pursue possessions by exercising their own faculties rather than by invading the rights of others. This resolution reflected Jefferson's own environmentalism and his expectation that the reform of social institutions would activate hitherto suppressed human capacities. Like Frenchmen of an earlier generation, Tracy considered America's political forms as revolutionary breakthroughs: representative democracy was "a new invention, unknown in Montesquieu's time." With this new type of government came written constitutions, which Tracy described in Lockean rather than classical terms. They did not exist to establish a balance of power, as in the ancient constitution of England, but rather to define the power given to the people's representatives and to fix the limits beyond which they must not trespass. "This," he explained in Madisonian terms, "is democracy rendered practicable for a long time and over a great extent of territory."[36]

Tracy devoted a great deal of attention in both works to economics. Montesquieu, he said, had worked with too narrow an idea of trade. What he should have seen was that because all exchanges are acts of commerce, commerce is "not only the foundation and basis of society but . . . the fabric itself." Tracy declared that to understand economic relations was the principal end of the social sciences. He gave Smith and Say high marks but lamented that they had failed to see that only human beings create the utility that determines market value. Had they grasped this, a hundred thousand superfluous distinctions might have been avoided, including especially the physiocratic notion that agriculture possessed a special value. Emphasizing utility, Tracy gave to the capitalist an importance altogether lacking in Smith's mere accumulator. Whether an entrepreneur used his own labor or commanded the labor of others, he invested natural goods with utility when he organized productive resources and by doing so became a force for good. Tracy elaborated many of these points in his *Treatise of Political Economy,* which Jefferson also translated.[37]

[35] Jefferson to Du Pont, Nov. 29, 1813, in Lipscomb and Bergh, eds., *Writings of Jefferson,* XIX, 195; Jefferson to Cooper, July 10, 1812, *ibid.,* XIII, 177-178; Jefferson to Tracy, Jan. 26, 1811, *ibid.,* 13.

[36] [Antoine Louis Claude Destutt de Tracy], *A Commentary and Review of Montesquieu's Spirit of Laws . . .* (Philadelphia, 1811), 97-98, 232, 19-20, hereafter cited as Tracy, *Review of Montesquieu.*

[37] *Ibid.,* 204-211, 183-192; Tracy, *A Treatise on Political Economy . . .* (Georgetown, D.C., 1817).

Tracy's eudaemonism explains his rejection of the civic-humanist tradition. Montesquieu, he charged, made virtue consist in voluntary privations, a fundamental error because "no human being is so constituted by nature." We cannot say too often, he wrote, that liberty is happiness and that happiness flows from a civic order that enables men to multiply and perfect their enjoyments. When Montesquieu based republican government on self-denial, he made it depend on "a false and fluctuating virtue. . . . which, by exciting men to hardihood and devotedness, renders them at the same time malignant, austere, ferocious, sanguinary, and above all unhappy."[38]

Unlike Smith, whose invisible hand of the market required the competition of self-interested bargainers, Tracy generously gave human beings their own harmonizing qualities of good sense and moderation. He thus avoided both the problem of power and the problem of order. Montesquieu, he conceded, had recognized that taxes were generally bad but had failed to explain how they threatened human happiness: "We desire society to be well organized in order that our enjoyments may be more multiplied, more perfect, and more tranquil; and so long as this end is not well understood, we are liable to a number of errors, from which our celebrated author is not always exempt."[39] The emphasis in Tracy's strictures on taxation fell not on the transfer from private to public funds but rather on the diminution of the means of personal gratification, which he considered to be the source of happiness in human society. Reflecting more conventional ways of thinking, he also noted that public expenditures, unless for bridges and roads, were economically sterile and that swollen revenues encouraged corruption and oppression. Far from enhancing productivity, public indebtedness raised the price of money and thereby discouraged investment in agriculture, manufacturing, and commerce. Even more pernicious, paper money required the intrusion of government into the private economic system of voluntary bargains. Montesquieu was also faulted for his preoccupation with international trade and his error in thinking that profits could only be made off strangers. By contrast, Tracy asserted that internal commerce was in all cases much more important, especially for large countries. Moreover, commercial development in a representative democracy would level the rich and raise the poor, causing both "to approach that middle point, at which the love of order, of industry, of justice and reason, naturally establish themselves."[40] Men are thus not naturally corrupt, lazy, or avaricious; they become so only when special privilege exalts the few and depresses the many. If given scope for their innate inclinations, ordinary men would realize their true vocation as sober and industrious producers. This was a gratuitous endowment, as John Adams pointed out, but for

[38] Tracy, *Review of Montesquieu*, 20-24, 184, 35.
[39] *Ibid.*, 159-164, 184-185.
[40] *Ibid.*, 240-244, 214-218, 33.

believers it offered an escape from the predicament posed by the classical dichotomy between virtue and commerce.[41]

Jefferson had an exalted opinion of Tracy and his work. He thought his ideas should supplant those of Adam Smith and claimed that Tracy had produced "the best elementary book on the principles of government." It marked "an epoch in the science of government" and should be recognized as "the most precious gift the present age had received."[42] By joining this praise with criticism of Montesquieu's shortcomings, Jefferson made clear just what in the *Review* and *Treatise* prompted these accolades.[43] Considering the extended scholarly treatment of Jefferson's thought, this unbounded enthusiasm for Tracy expressed at the end of his life has special value as an indication of the ideas that he found enduringly attractive.[44] Tracy had dissolved society into its individual human components and given to them a fundamentally economic character. He believed that the individual's experience of will gave birth to the knowledge that one is endowed "with an inevitable and inalienable property, that of its individuality." All notions of riches and deprivations, of justice and injustice, he wrote, should, therefore, be seen as dependent on the idea of personality and the anterior awareness of self.[45] Drained from this analysis were the distinctions of class and rank whose balancing played so central a role in classical republicanism. Instead, Tracy started with natural rights and concluded that because all contracts by definition yielded gain to the

[41] Adams to Jefferson, Feb. 2, 1817, in Lester J. Cappon, ed., *The Adams-Jefferson Letters: The Complete Correspondence between Thomas Jefferson and Abigail and John Adams* (Chapel Hill, N.C., 1959), II, 506.

[42] Jefferson to Duane, Apr. 4, 1813, in Lipscomb and Bergh, eds., *Writings of Jefferson,* XIII, 231; Jefferson to Joseph C. Cabell, Feb. 2, 1816, *ibid.*, XIV, 419; Jefferson to Cooper, Jan. 16, 1814, *ibid.*, 62-63; Jefferson to Tracy, Jan. 26, 1811, *ibid.*, XIII, 13.

[43] In a different assessment of Tracy's influence on Jefferson, Drew R. McCoy describes Tracy as passing on to Jefferson his fears about European overpopulation (*The Elusive Republic: Political Economy in Jeffersonian America* [Chapel Hill, N.C., 1980], 253). Actually this analysis plays a very small part in Tracy's overall social theory and, unlike the long passages on Montesquieu, this section from the *Treatise* is never mentioned by Jefferson.

[44] See, most recently, Morton White, *The Philosophy of the American Revolution* (New York, 1978); Garry Wills, *Inventing America: Jefferson's Declaration of Independence* (Garden City, N.Y., 1978); and Ronald Hamowy, "Jefferson and the Scottish Enlightenment: A Critique of Garry Wills's *Inventing America: Jefferson's Declaration of Independence,*" *WMQ,* 3d Ser., XXXVI (1979), 502-523. Homowy's critique of Wills and the issue of the relative influence of Locke and the philosophers of the Scottish Enlightenment raises many points not resolvable here, but it is relevant that Tracy was unequivocal in his natural rights philosophy and on the priority of property rights to government.

[45] Tracy, *Treatise,* 35-36, 46-47. Madison anticipated Tracy on this point when he wrote that "as a man is said to have a right to his property, he may be equally said to have a property in his rights" (Hunt, ed., *Writings of Madison,* VI, 101-103; this line appeared originally in the *National Gazette* [Philadelphia], Mar. 29, 1792).

contracting parties, society itself rested on voluntary commitments. Rejecting out of hand Montesquieu's elaboration of cultural traits, he insisted to the contrary that "men everywhere hold to their interests, and are occupied with them." Far from being bad, this created an essential identity of interests among men that was founded on their dual and private capacities as producers and consumers.[46]

Clearly something had gone awry with society as it actually was, and Tracy explained this as the consequence of tendencies toward inequality and injustice that could be corrected by eliminating formal privilege and protecting the equality of rights established in nature. More specifically, he detailed how government could free economic life and liberate the active, desiring nature of man by discountenancing paper money, bank companies, and public credit. But unlike the Country party critics of England's funded debt, Tracy fired at his target with guns newly cast in the foundry of modern utilitarianism. The interests of society lay with the interests of the poor, and the interests of the poor lay with greater productivity. Government could contribute to progressive economic development by freeing trade and protecting property rights—those of the worker who owns himself and those of the capitalists who set others to work. In this, as in much else, Tracy exulted in having cleared up the confusions of Montesquieu. "Great talents," he declared, "belong only to our time." An appreciative Jefferson placed the phrase in capitals.[47]

It is against this background that the recent scholarly effort to construe the Jeffersonians as an American version of the English Country party must be judged. This new interpretation rests on the foundation laid in Bernard Bailyn's *The Ideological Origins of the American Revolution*. Bailyn traced the resistance movement of the 1760s to the colonists' peculiar conception of reality. Having absorbed a view of politics from the resonating rhetoric of the English opposition, the Americans considered the new British measures evidence of a conspiracy to destroy their rights. For Bailyn, however, the Revolution was a transforming event that triggered a "critical probing of traditional concepts." In *The Creation of the American Republic* Gordon S. Wood pushed forward the emergence of a native political idiom to 1787, when Americans abandoned their earlier "devotion to the transcendent public good" and accepted Madison's brilliant solution to the problem of majority faction.[48] In the scholarship of the last ten years, the date for the Americanization of politics has been delayed yet another score of years, and the celebrated clashes between Alexander Hamilton and Jefferson have been reinterpreted as a transatlan-

[46] Tracy, *Review of Montesquieu*, 192-205, *Treatise*, 162, 117.
[47] Tracy, *Treatise*, 185.
[48] Bailyn, *The Ideological Origins of the American Revolution* (Cambridge, Mass., 1967), 56-58, 101-109, 161; Wood, *The Creation of the American Republic, 1776-1787* (Chapel Hill, N.C., 1969), 93-97, 179, 418-425, 471-475.

tic mirroring of the battle between the great Court politician, Robert Walpole, and his Country opponent, Bolingbroke.

Pointing out the course others were to follow, Pocock noted in 1972 that if the Federalist-Republican debates are viewed as a replay of English Court and Country struggles, this would necessitate postponing the demise of the Country style in America until the end of the first party system. Turning this reflection into an affirmation, Pocock went on to name Jefferson as the conduit through which a civic concept of virtue entered "the whole tradition of American agrarian and populist messianism."[49] Writing four years later, John M. Murrin made the adoption of the Court-and-Country model an imperative: "The continuing unity and viability of the United States depended, ironically, upon its ability to replicate both sides of the central tensions that had afflicted Augustan England."[50] In a study of the "Jeffersonian persuasion," Lance Banning has discovered a persistent polarity between Court and Country throughout the entire early national period. He attributes the Country cast of Jeffersonian thought to the fact that Americans still lived in "a universe of classical political perceptions."[51] Focusing more tightly on the fiscal alternatives endorsed by Jeffersonians and Federalists, E. James Ferguson has argued that the reaction to Hamilton's policies followed the lines it did because of the pervasiveness of Country-mindedness in America.[52] To Forrest McDonald, the affinities between the Jeffersonians and the English Country party are even closer: they borrowed "*in toto* from such Oppositionists as Charles Davenant, John Trenchard, Thomas Gordon, James Burgh, and most especially Henry St. John, First Viscount Bolingbroke." Warming to his subject, McDonald concludes that "just about everything in Jeffersonian Republicanism was to be found in Bolingbroke."[53] Thus these historians have depicted the thought of Americans in the 1790s as encapsulated in the conceptual world of Montesquieu's civic humanism.

Banning has made the greatest effort to demonstrate the influence of classical republicanism on the polemics of the 1790s, and his study illustrates the problems involved in the enterprise. The power of English opposition thought is frequently asserted but nowhere traced through the body of any particular man's thought. The prior existence of Country-mindedness, detailed by Bailyn and Wood, forms the principal proof for

[49] Pocock, "Virtue and Commerce," *JIH*, III (1972), 133-134, and *Machiavellian Moment*, ix, 529-533.

[50] Murrin, "Great Inversion," in Pocock, ed., *Three British Revolutions*, 406.

[51] Banning, *Jeffersonian Persuasion*, 17-18, 92-93, 273-274.

[52] Ferguson, "Political Economy, Public Liberty, and the Formation of the Constitution" (unpubl. paper, Organization of American Historians, New Orleans, 1979), 24.

[53] McDonald, *Presidency of Jefferson*, 19-20, 161-163, ix. See also James H. Hutson, "Country, Court, and Constitution: Antifederalism and the Historians," *WMQ*, 3d Ser., XXXVIII (1981), 337-368, and Robert E. Shalhope, "Republicanism and Early American Historiography," *ibid.*, XXXIX (1982), 334-356.

the continuation of classical politics down to 1815.[54] So pervasive was this inherited mode of thought, Banning says, that newspaper writers could communicate with loose analogies or a suggestive word. "The most telling and ideologically most fundamental criticism of Federalist government was carried by a cryptic code." Corruption, for instance, "conveyed to friends and enemies alike an entire language about social and governmental degeneration." Hamilton's program inevitably provoked concerns in men "shaped by British opposition thought" because certain worries "were never very far beneath the surface of revolutionary minds." Writers in 1792 hammered home the opposition themes in a "few phrases loaded with the apocalyptic connotations" already familiar to Americans. "Without a fully systematic explication, they were comprehended and assented to in every corner of the land."[55] The subliminal aspects of Country ideology thus rendered unnecessary a search for confirming evidence. Banning's assertions, however, are plausible only if one accepts his basic assumption that eighteenth-century British opposition ideas acted as the "structured medium through which Americans continued to perceive the world and give expression to their hopes and discontents."[56] It is precisely this contention that must be proved.

Nothing in Jefferson's statements or policies suggests that he adhered to the agrarian conservatism implicit in classical republican thought. Rather, early in his political career, Jefferson saw in rising food prices the promise of flourishing American trade in grains. Unlike slave-produced staples, foodstuffs could be raised through the mixed husbandry of the family farm. The prosperity of ordinary farmers, Jefferson believed, would form the economic base for a democratic, progressive America. Also unlike the previously dominant staples, wheat could be grown in a wide arc that extended northward from the upper South through the middle states to the Connecticut Valley. On the issue of exploiting the commercial opportunitites in this vast area, Jefferson showed little hesitation. Indeed, in a rather callous appraisal of attitudes toward the War of 1812, he informed Madison that all he need do to shore up popular support was to seize Canada and secure markets for American flour. "The great profits of the wheat crop have allured every one to it; and never was such a crop on the ground. . . . It would be mortifying to the farmer to see such an one

[54] Banning, *Jeffersonian Persuasion*, 93. The only scholarship on the substance of English Country thought is Pocock's *Machiavellian Moment*, to which the historians of the Country interpretation refer. See, for example, Murrin, "Great Inversion," in Pocock, ed., *Three British Revolutions*, 382, 417, 448-449, n. 109; McCoy, *Elusive Republic*, 42, 60-61; and Berthoff, "Independence and Attachment," in Bushman *et al.*, eds., *Uprooted Americans*, 124, n. 96. Pocock himself appeals to Banning's work to refute Wood's contention that classical politics came to an end in 1787 (*Machiavellian Moment*, 527-531).

[55] Banning, *Jeffersonian Persuasion*, 185, 128, 177.

[56] *Ibid.*, 92, 273-274.

rot in his barn. It would soon sicken him to war."[57] The statement measures Jefferson's distance from the Harringtonian view of property as the means to stability and leisure, a possession, according to Pocock, that "anchored the individual in the structure of power and virtue, and liberated him to practice these as activities."[58]

Although Banning recognizes that it would be "an error to conceive of the Republicans as foes of either capital or wealth," he leaves unexplored the way in which their commercial attitudes either exemplified or modified the classical paradigm he finds reigning supreme in late eighteenth-century America.[59] A more empirical and hence more satisfying account of the Jeffersonian stance on economic issues is Drew R. McCoy's *The Elusive Republic*. McCoy finds the Republicans working consistently and aggressively to secure outlets for American produce. He also concludes that their economic program was tied to "an intense concern with the autonomy . . . of the individual." But he starts with the premise that Jeffersonianism reflected "an attempt to cling to the traditional republican spirit of classical antiquity" and turns Jefferson's well-known enthusiasm for westward expansion into a way of reconciling "classical republicanism with more modern . . . realities." Thus what was once seen as the basis for Jefferson's optimism now becomes a reflection of pessimism and anxiety about the future, a device for postponing the day of corruption and degeneration by throwing space in the way of time. Similarly, McCoy imputes to Jefferson a "continuing concern with the natural threat presented by the biological pressure of population growth," a view wholly at odds with Jefferson's repudiation of Malthus's dire projections.[60] Not until the Missouri crisis and his own bankruptcy did Jefferson, at age seventy-six, express apprehension about the fate of the nation that he had so willingly nurtured.

Jefferson was as absorbed with the details of his free-trade policies as with the grand plans for continental expansion. Free land and free trade spelled progress and prosperity. He was fascinated with scientific advances in farming. The scope of his activities as diplomat, secretary of state, and president pointed to the future, and as Thomas M. Cragan has written, "far exceeded the commercial developments needed to carry away normal American agricultural surpluses."[61] While Jefferson associated luxury with

[57] Jefferson to Madison, June 29, 1812, in Ford, ed., *Writings of Jefferson*, IX, 364. Jefferson's enthusiasm for international free trade can be traced back to his *Notes* (p. 174), and cannot be attributed to his French sojourn as asserted in James H. Hutson, "Intellectual Foundations of Early American Diplomacy," *Diplomatic History*, I (1977), 6.

[58] Pocock, *Machiavellian Moment*, 389-391.

[59] Banning, *Jeffersonian Persuasion*, 204-205.

[60] McCoy, *Elusive Republic*, 131, 10, 253, 189-195; Jefferson to Say, Feb. 1, 1804, in Lipscomb and Bergh, eds., *Writings of Jefferson*, XI, 2-3; Jefferson to David Williams, Nov. 14, 1803, *ibid*., 430-431.

[61] Cragan, "Thomas Jefferson's Early Attitudes Towards Manufacturing, Agriculture and Commerce" (Ph.D. diss., University of Tennesee, 1965), 310. See

unjust concentrations of wealth, he expected and approved of a rising standard of living, not the frugality so esteemed in the classical tradition. This distinction is nicely captured in a letter to Adams written when they were both in Europe. Reviewing Adams's draft of a commercial treaty with Spain, Jefferson urged that the word "necessaries" be replaced by "comforts."[62] If the Republicans' promotion of international commerce and westward expansion did in fact reflect a Country-minded concern about escaping the terrors of history, we would see them monitor the pace of economic development. Instead, at critical junctures Jefferson and Madison rushed the pace of growth by facilitating access to land, by protecting the reexport trade, and by hastening the market penetration of frontier areas. McCoy's fine research provides a wealth of information about the economic policies and practices of the Jeffersonians, most of it difficult to reconcile with an ideological resistance to social change. The central historical question has been begged: Rather than inquire if the Jeffersonians were Country thinkers, Banning and McCoy begin by asking how the Republicans' Country-mindedness helps explain their political decisions.

Starting with the latter question, Murrin has also examined the modifications in Country ideology between the Revolution and the end of the War of 1812. The Revolution opened American politics to a broader range of questions, he says, but disputes after 1780 "fit neatly within the old Court-Country paradigm." Although the broadening of suffrage threatened to disrupt the classical republican balance between the few and the many, Murrin maintains that this innovation was accommodated intellectually by shifting the constitutional balance from actual groups in society to branches of government.[63] The Jeffersonians, however, did not want to balance government; they wanted to limit it. Their liberal sympathies in this regard were well underscored by Jefferson's remark that "Locke's little book on Government, is perfect as far as it goes."[64] In the eyes of the Country interpreters, however, neither the doctrine of popular sovereignty nor the novelty of limited government brought an end to the dominance of a classical mode in America. The specific formulations may have changed, but the emotional timbre endured because the Country-minded Republicans sought to preserve ancient values in a modern world. The American opposition, like its English model, Murrin concludes, "idealized the past more than the future and feared significant change,

---

also Richard Ellis, "The Political Economy of Thomas Jefferson," in Lally Weymouth, ed., *Thomas Jefferson: The Man, His World, His Influence* (London, 1973), 81-95, and Merrill D. Peterson's review of *The Papers of Thomas Jefferson*, XVIII, XIX, in *WMQ*, 3d Ser., XXXII (1975), 656-658.

[62] Jefferson to Adams, Nov. 27, 1785, in Cappon, ed., *Adams-Jefferson Letters*, I, 103.

[63] Murrin, "Great Inversion," in Pocock, ed., *Three British Revolutions*, 401, 404-407.

[64] Jefferson to Randolph, May 30, 1790, in Lipscomb and Bergh, eds., *Writings of Jefferson*, VIII, 31.

especially major economic change, as corruption and degeneration." This demonstrates for him that the rest of the world has little to learn from eighteenth-century republicanism, which, "even in its own day, remained more nostalgic than modernizing." McDonald reaches a similar conclusion: Jefferson, like Bolingbroke, sought a return to "some Edenic Past: when all men revered God, respected their fellows, deferred to their betters, and knew their place."[65]

The incompatibility of Country ideology and the positions that Jefferson affirmed throughout his life should be abundantly clear. Much as he equivocated on the questions of slavery and national power, his dislike of social distinctions and political privilege never wavered. Far from idealizing traditional society, he boldly imagined a world without formal hierarchy. The issue cannot be confined to a discussion of the suffrage, for Jefferson's egalitarianism grew out of radical assumptions about human nature. He was temperamentally at odds with the reverence for the past nurtured by civic humanism. He neither venerated old institutional arrangements nor feared experimentation with new ones, and he repeatedly insisted that his was the party of change. Writing to Abigail Adams during his first term as president, he characterized the Republicans as men who feared the ignorance of the people less than the selfishness of their rulers. He rephrased the distinction for John Adams in a letter of the following decade. Looking back on the partisan battles of the 1790s, he differentiated the advocates of reform, who placed no definite limits on social improvements, from the enemies of reform who considered their inherited institutions "the akme of excellence."[66]

The writings of Tracy that Jefferson so ardently promoted also undercut the interpretation of the Jeffersonians as a Country party, for Tracy explicitly attacked the civic-humanist tradition. When he ridiculed Montesquieu's concept of virtue, he rejected its civic character. "Simplicity, habits of industry, a contempt for frivolity, the love of independence," he said, were the endowments of all rational human beings. Against Montesquieu's elaborate formulas for "voluntary privations and self-denials" Tracy pitted the simplicity of innate virtue. His extended commentary on *Spirit of the Laws* points up the error of making virtue a code word in Country ideology. The American critics of classical republicanism did not abandon virtue as a cherished goal but rather redefined it. Their redefinition, however, permitted them to ignore traditional political solutions because they no longer accepted the conventional formulation of the problem. By giving society a natural economic character they were able to believe in virtue with commerce. Decoding old conceptual languages

[65] Murrin, "Great Inversion," in Pocock, ed., *Three British Revolutions*, 400-401; McDonald, *Presidency of Jefferson*, 19.

[66] Jefferson to Abigail Adams, Sept. 11, 1804, in Cappon, ed., *Adams-Jefferson Letters*, I, 280; Jefferson to John Adams, June 15, 1813, *ibid.*, II, 332. See also Jefferson to Johnson, June 12, 1823, in Ford, ed., *Writings of Jefferson*, X, 226n-227n.

helps us to reconstruct a past reality, but meanings can change while terms remain the same. Virtue is one example; liberty is another. In the eighteenth-century English lexicon liberty referred to constitutional rights, but the liberty that Republicans hurled at Federalists was that of individual self-assertion, tamed by a new conception of human progress. Nor were contemporaries unaware of these differences. "Your Taste is judicious," Adams commented wryly to Jefferson, "in likeing [*sic*] better the dreams of the Future, than the History of the Past."[67]

The first assertion that the Jeffersonians were acting like the English Country party came not from historians in the 1970s but from Federalists in the 1790s.[68] Therein lies a clue to the locus of classical politics in America. Both the Country-minded and the Court-tempered moved into the ranks of respectable Federalism because they shared a traditional political vocabulary. The archetypal Country leader, Adams, found his prefigured enemy in the classical Court politician, Hamilton. Neither understood the expectations for social change entertained by their Republican opponents. Adams's addiction to moribund theories is notorious; less well advertised are the limits of Hamilton's conceptual world. Two quotations help mark the boundaries of his imagination. In 1784 Hamilton wrote in disbelief that some people maintained that commerce might regulate itself. Such persons, he went on to say, "will imagine, that there is no need of a common directing power" and then labeled the idea "one of those wild speculative paradoxes, which have grown into credit among us, contrary to the uniform practice and sense of the most enlightened nations." Elsewhere he distinguished freedom from slavery by saying that free men consented to the laws by which they were governed.[69] Totally missing from his thinking was the idea that the powers consigned to government might be reduced. Like Hamilton, most Federalists presumed that the world would go on as their histories taught them it always had. When confronted with a passionate assault on these assumptions, they could understand it only by assigning their attackers the historic role of the English opposition.

[67] Tracy, *Review of Montesquieu*, 20. Adams to Jefferson, Aug. 9, 1816, in Cappon, ed., *Adams-Jefferson Letters*, II, 487. With uncharacteristic optimism Adams predicted that Jefferson and he would find a meeting of minds. See also Jeffrey Barnouw, "American Independence: Revolution of the Republican Ideal. A Critique of the 'Paradigm' of Republican Virtue," in Paul Korchin, ed., *The American Revolution and Eighteenth-Century Culture* (New York, 1982).

[68] Banning, *Jeffersonian Persuasion*, 91; Ferguson, "Political Economy," 1. For evidence of Warren's adherence to Montesquieu's position see Lester H. Cohen, "Explaining the Revolution: Ideology and Ethics in Mercy Otis Warren's Historical Theory," *WMQ*, 3d Ser., XXXVII (1980), 218. Less convincing is Cohen's claim (p. 217) that Madison was an exponent of mixed government and that Jefferson was concerned with civic virtue.

[69] Hamilton, *Continentalist No. V*. Apr. 18, 1782, in Harold C. Syrett *et al.*, eds., *The Papers of Alexander Hamilton* (New York, 1962-1979), III, 76; Hamilton, "A Full Vindication," Dec. 15, 1774, *ibid.*, I, 51-52.

The composition of the Republican party also indicates that the choice was not between a Jeffersonian *gemeinschaft* and a Hamiltonian *gesellschaft*, as the Court and Country interpretation of early national politics would have it. Commercial farmers, small planters, urban tradesmen, and aspiring professional men poured into Jefferson's party as soon as he sounded the alarm about Hamilton's program.[70] To be fearful, as the Jeffersonians were, of the corruption they saw in public stock speculation was not the same as making corruption part of the eternal human drama. Because they believed that special privilege had poisoned the natural social harmony, they could look optimistically to a future rid of monarchs and aristocrats. At issue in the nation's first partisan battles were two mutually exclusive but entirely plausible blueprints for national development. The nationalists of both Republican and Federalist persuasions could agree on the establishment of an effective, unified government—even on the major planks of Hamilton's fiscal program—because they both favored growth with commerce. Indeed, the liberal economic order that Jefferson espoused was sustained in part by the success of the Constitution in providing the essential framework for capitalist development: a national market, a uniform currency, and the protection of contracts. Where the nationalists parted company was on the question of whether American growth should be controlled at the center through the manipulation of public credit or should move in response to the private bargaining of ordinary men.

This examination of Jefferson's social thought has been prompted by the accomplishments of the Court and Country interpreters. If they err—as I believe they do—in describing the Jeffersonians as classical republicans, they are surely correct to insist that civic humanism shaped the terms of political debate in the early national period, uniting one group of men and provoking an alternative ideology in another. The close attention they have paid to the conceptual world of Anglo-America has left an indelible mark on historical scholarship. No longer can a mindless liberalism be ascribed to human beings, nor the liberal theory about what is natural be confounded with nature itself. The values and beliefs that informed Jefferson's "Americanism" must be located and made precise. Readily assented to by many, these views could not be taken for granted if only because they conflicted with a venerable political tradition.

In defiance of that tradition, Jefferson rallied his countrymen with a

[70] Alfred F. Young, *The Democratic Republicans of New York: The Origins, 1763-1797* (Chapel Hill, N.C., 1976); John A. Munroe, *Federalist Delaware, 1775-1815* (New Brunswick, N.J., 1954); Paul Goodman, "Social Status of Party Leadership: The House of Representatives, 1797-1804," *WMQ*, 3d Ser., XXV (1968), 465-474; Norman K. Risjord and Gordon DenBoer, "The Evolution of Political Parties in Virginia, 1782-1800," *Journal of American History*, LX (1974), 961-984; Frank A. Cassell, "The Structure of Baltimore's Politics in the Age of Jefferson, 1795-1812," in Aubrey C. Land *et al.*, eds., *Law, Society and Politics in Early Maryland* (Baltimore, 1977), 278-295.

vision of the future that joined their materialism to a new morality. An unstable combination in the classical model, this fusion proved particularly strong in American thought. And Jefferson affirmed it repeatedly. Writing in 1817 to the Frenchman for whom he had so long ago composed his *Notes,* he pointed to American progress as proof of his social theories: "When you witnessed our first struggles in the War of Independence, you little calculated more than we did, on the rapid growth and prosperity of this country; on the practical demonstration it was about to exhibit, of the happy truth that man is capable of self-government." Then, taking aim at his old target, he declared his confidence that "we shall proceed successfully for ages to come, and that, contrary to the principle of Montesquieu, it will be seen that the larger the extent of country, the more firm its republican structure, if founded, not on conquest, but in principles of compact and equality." America's economic base and the concept of a benign human potential sustained Jefferson's optimism, for, as he explained, his hope of an enduring republic was "built much on the enlargement of the resources of life, going hand in hand with the enlargement of territory, and the belief that men are disposed to live honestly, if the means of doing so are open to them."[71]

[71] Jefferson to Barré de Marbois, June 14, 1817, in Lipscomb and Bergh, eds., *Writings of Jefferson*, XV, 130-131. The confidence that Jefferson expressed here contrasts sharply with the depiction of his mood after 1814 in Robert E. Shalhope, "Thomas Jefferson's Republicanism and Antebellum Southern Thought," *Journal of Southern History*, XLII (1976), 537-545.

The Jeffersonians: Classical Republicans or Liberal Capitalists?

JOHN ASHWORTH

Joyce Appleby, *Capitalism and a New Social Order: The Republican Vision of the 1790s* (New York: New York University Press, 1984, $22). Pp. x, 110. ISBN 0 8147 0581 2.

In recent years American historians have been subjecting the ideas of Jeffersonian Republicans to an unprecedentedly close examination. Undoubtedly much of the impetus behind this scholarship comes from the pioneering work of J. G. A. Pocock, whose writings have emphasized the debt which the Jeffersonians owed to English "Country" thought with its Renaissance and classical republican antecedents. In 1978 this view received a full expression in Lance Banning's stimulating *Jeffersonian Persuasion*. Banning entitled the final section of his book, which dealt with the election of 1800, "The Country Comes to Power." Other scholars have endorsed this interpretation.[1] In 1982 however, Joyce Appleby, their main critic, advanced a very different view of the Jeffersonians when delivering the Anson G. Phelps lectures.[2] The publication of these lectures thus presents an

John Ashworth is Lecturer in the School of English and American Studies, University of East Anglia, Norwich NR4 7TJ. He wishes to thank Roger Thompson and John Zvesper for their comments on earlier drafts of this essay.

[1] J. G. A. Pocock, "Virtue and Commerce in the Eighteenth Century," *Journal of Interdisciplinary History* 3, (1972), 119–134, Pocock, *The Machiavellian Moment: Florentine Political Thought and the Atlantic Republican Tradition* (Princeton, 1975); Lance Banning, *The Jeffersonian Persuasion: Evolution of a Party Ideology* (Ithaca, 1978). See also the extremely interesting essay by John Murrin, "The Great Inversion, or Court versus Country: A Comparison of the Revolution Settlements in England (1688–1721) and America (1776–1816)," in Pocock (ed.), *Three British Revolutions: 1641, 1688, 1776* (Princeton, 1980), pp. 368–453, and Rowland Berthoff, "Independence and Attachment, Virtue and Interest: From Republican Citizen to Free Enterpriser, 1787–1837," in Richard L. Bushman et al. (eds), *Uprooted Americans: Essays to Honor Oscar Handlin* (Boston, 1979), pp. 97–124. Two good historiographical articles by Richard E. Shalhope are "Towards a Republican Synthesis: the Emergence of an Understanding of Republicanism in American Historiography," *William and Mary Quarterly*, 3rd Ser. 29 (1972), 49–80 and "Republicanism and Early American Historiography," ibid. 39 (1982), 334–56.

[2] Professor Appleby's earlier work includes *Economic Thought and Ideology in Seventeenth-Century England* (Princeton, 1978), "Liberalism and the American Revolution," *New*

Journal of American Studies, 18 (1984), 3, 425–435 *Printed in Great Britain*

opportunity to review this controversy as well as some of the other recent literature on the ideological struggles of the 1790s.[3]

In the work of Banning, Murrin and Pocock, Jeffersonian Republicanism emerges as a creed whose most distinctive features can be located in European and especially English thought; Professor Appleby, by contrast, insists that it is their "rejection of the past as a repository of wisdom that constitutes the most important element in the ideology of the Jeffersonian Republicans." The Republicans, she claims, expected a different future and they displayed a new optimism about human nature. What distinguished them from their opponents was their single-minded effort to refashion the political institutions of the United States; theirs was "the first truly American political movement" and it shifted the trajectory of American political development decisively and inexorably away from the path of the mother country.[4] In Professor Appleby's opinion it was not the Jeffersonians but the Federalists who "in all essentials...remained classical republicans." Both parties were capitalist but while the Federalists expected "orderly growth within venerable social limits," the Republicans were archetypal liberals who looked forward to "capitalism and a new social order."[5]

I

Contrary to the impression presented by many of the recent works on Republican ideology, the party that raised Jefferson to the Presidency was far from uniform in its beliefs and principles. Undoubtedly *one* reason why Joyce Appleby's Republicans differ so sharply from Lance Banning's is that they are, quite simply, different people. Recent scholarship has emphasized the ideological distance between the two major parties, but it has given too little attention to the divisions within them and especially within the Republican party. Yet, as Richard Ellis has shown, serious differences of opinion were visible in the Republican party from its very inception (although their practical importance was relatively slight so long as the party was in opposition and faced with a powerful enemy). Their presence is enough to create doubts about the possibility of some of the generalizations which historians are now offering. As Ellis has pointed out, the Madisonian (moderate) wing of the party must be clearly distinguished from that represented by John Taylor of Caroline. Jefferson himself was in many respects midway between the two but it is as yet unclear how widespread and popular the specific ideas and beliefs expressed by each of these Virginians were within the party. In

---

England Quarterly, 49 (1976), 3–26, "The Social Origins of American Revolutionary Ideology," *Journal of American History*, 64 (1978), 935–58, "What is Still American in the Political Philosophy of Thomas Jefferson," *William and Mary Quarterly*, 39 (1982), 287–309. Some of the points in *Capitalism and a New Social Order* are, of course, anticipated in these writings.

[3] Perhaps because of limitations of space Professor Appleby does not always dispose of the evidence presented by her "opponents". In this essay I have tried to assess that evidence together with that which she and other scholars have presented in order to offer some suggestions about the current state of our knowledge on this subject.

[4] *Capitalism and a New Social Order*, pp. 79, 81, 86, 4, 14.

[5] Ibid. pp. 59, 94. See also p. 66.

short we do not yet know where the party's ideological centre of gravity lay, even in Philadelphia, the federal capital, let alone within each of the states. We need to know how typical a Jeffersonian Jefferson was.[6]

As far as the recent works on the Republicans are concerned, it is instructive to see which individuals the various scholars focus upon. Drew McCoy places great emphasis upon Madison's ideas, at least as much as upon those of Thomas Jefferson. He does not mention John Taylor of Caroline. Lance Banning, on the other hand, whilst not neglecting Madison, claims that Taylor's pamphlets "are probably the most important source for an understanding of Republican thought in the middle 1790s." Significantly, Joyce Appleby agrees that Taylor was "a country figure" but suggests that he was outside the mainstream of the party and concentrates her attention not upon the famous Virginians but upon Republicans from the middle states. Yet this dismissal of Taylor (along with John Randolph and Abraham Yates) is unsubstantiated by either fact or argument and it is significant that Banning and others are able to produce statements by other Republicans, including some from the middle states, which are quintessentially Taylorean. One suspects that a certain circularity of argument has entered Appleby's work here: the Jeffersonians were forward-looking and American, Taylor was a "country" republican; hence he was an atypical Jeffersonian. The likelihood is that a definitive explication of Republican ideology will have to take full account of the factional composition of the party and qualify its generalizations about that ideology accordingly.[7]

This need for qualification is apparent when we consider the extent to which the Republicans espoused what Appleby terms "the principle of hope." In her view the Jeffersonians were hopeful and optimistic about the future; the Federalists, as befitted classical republicans, were not. But this is problematic. It is certainly true that Polybius, whose theories were highly influential within the English country tradition, had asserted that most governments were doomed to an inevitable process of degeneration and decay. But even he had left open the possibility of an escape from this dismal fate and other thinkers in the "country" tradition, most conspicuously James Harrington, had explicitly claimed that a properly constituted commonwealth might be truly immortal. Hence it is not entirely correct to assume that pessimism about the future was always a feature of classical or "country" thought. Classical republicanism was not monolithic in this respect.[8]

When we turn to the partisans of the 1790s, simple generalizations are still more difficult. Even the apparently uncontentious association of Federalism with pessimism can be seriously challenged. For as John Zvesper points out in his excellent study of Federalist and Republican ideology, the Federalists in the late 1780s and early '90s were both confident and optimistic. It is true that this

[6] Richard E. Ellis, *The Jeffersonian Crisis: Courts and Politics in the Young Republic* (N.Y., 1971), pp. 19–24.

[7] Drew R. McCoy, *The Elusive Republic: Political Economy in Jeffersonian America* (Chapel Hill, 1980); Banning, *Jeffersonian Persuasion*, p. 193; Appleby, *Capitalism and a New Social Order*, p. 80.

[8] Banning, *Jeffersonian Persuasion*, p. 24; Pocock, *Machiavellian Moment*, pp. 77, 388, see also pp. 205, 297 (on Machiavelli and Giannotti).

confidence was swiftly dissipated when the Republican challenge was mounted but this is still enough to place a question mark against Appleby's assertion.[9] When we consider the Republicans the problem is still more complex. Undoubtedly Appleby's interpretation fits Thomas Jefferson himself, and fits him well. Jefferson's optimism does differentiate him from many classical republicans and Appleby has justly re-emphasized this. But as far as Madison is concerned her conclusions are far less satisfactory. For Drew McCoy has shown conclusively that Madison expected the United States to develop, as Britain had done, a surplus population of landless poor. This was a prospect which was most unwelcome and disturbing to him. But he believed that at best the nation could only postpone its degeneration. In McCoy's words, "Madison's republic was in a race against time."[10]

It is none the less possible that Madison here was at odds with his fellow Republicans. John Taylor's view was rather different. Essentially Taylor was hopeful about American society and the American economy but with the strict proviso that the government be conducted according to sound principles. His opinion as to the likelihood of this varied over time; in general he was neither confident nor despairing. Further research may well show that this attitude was the norm within the party as a whole.[11]

More central to classical republicanism than its optimism (or lack of it) is the emphasis its spokesmen placed upon virtue and their understanding of that term. Classical "virtue" denoted a willingness to place, on certain occasions at least, the common good ahead of private and personal gain. It meant not so much a renunciation of self-interest as an awareness that that interest was best pursued in accordance with social imperatives – in other words not on an individualistic calculus. Indeed the egotistical pursuit of self-interest narrowly defined, it was felt, would plunge a commonwealth or republic into anarchy. It is Joyce Appleby's contention that by the time Jefferson was installed as President a quite different perception of virtue was prevalent. "By the end of the century" she argues, "virtue more often referred to a private quality, a man's capacity to look out for himself and his dependents – almost the opposite of classical virtue." Clearly, this is an important claim. If substantiated it would go far towards proving Appleby's case for the novelty of Jeffersonian Republicanism.[12]

It appears, however, that partisan ideology is, once again, too complex to permit such a generalization. As is well known, Madison as Publius argued in the *Federalist* that it was necessary to balance the various interests in society. In so doing government would be using and even underwriting men's selfish passions. But this is a far cry from labelling such self-interest virtuous. For his part Jefferson hoped that good government (which for him meant a limited, inactive government)

[9] John Zvesper, *Political Philosophy and Rhetoric, A Study of the Origins of American Party Politics* (Cambridge, 1977), p. 40.

[10] McCoy, *Elusive Republic*, pp. 120–21, 131. McCoy agrees that Jefferson, except towards the end of his life, was generally optimistic – ibid. p. 249.

[11] These changes of mood are apparent in Taylor's *Inquiry into the Principles and Policy of the Government of the United States* (London, 1950), a work written over a period of many years. Taylor ends on a more pessimistic note than he begins on.

[12] Appleby, *Capitalism and a New Social Order*, p. 15.

would restrict the pursuit of self-interest; in the words of John Zvesper he sought to "cultivate man's natural sociality by subduing...those selfish passions that interfered with the operation of the socializing moral sense." Hence with good government "Republicans expected men's moral sense to flourish in society, [with] their selfish passions subdued and limited." As Jefferson put it, "every human being feels pleasure in doing good to another." But there is no reason to believe that Jefferson expected simple altruism to rule in the economy; it was rather that a good government would restrict the operation of self-interest within the economy and the polity to its "natural" sphere.[13] What was that sphere? At this point it is instructive to examine the thought of John Taylor of Caroline. Taylor argued forcefully that under a good government property would be acquired in accordance with industry. Self-interest would impel men to labour and this labour would in turn promote virtue. In this sense self-interest was a benign force. Equally Taylor insisted that a majority, even a corrupt majority, would have an interest in passing just laws and these would be such as to leave each individual free to enjoy the fruits of his labour. Virtue would be re-established. Only if government intervened so as to transfer wealth from some groups to others would vicious habits prevail. Taylor feared the self-interest of the minority who would gain from such laws; he welcomed that of the majority and viewed it as a source of moral virtue. This is certainly a view which differs from that of classical republicanism; equally, though, it is at odds with Professor Appleby's understanding of Jeffersonian Republicanism.[14]

What then of Federalist perceptions of virtue? There is no doubt – this is one of the few points upon which all scholars seem to agree – that in the 1780s the Federalists were convinced that there was too little virtue (understood in the classical sense) to sustain the Republic.[15] They proposed instead to accept the fact of Americans' self-interestedness. Nevertheless, as Zvesper shows, in the late 1780s and early 1790s there was a residual emphasis on virtue and this virtue was understood in two ways. First, the people clearly had to have the virtue necessary to place the wise and talented in government. Not surprisingly the Federalists were here referring to the Federalists. Equally unsurprising is the fact that the perception of this virtue grew dimmer as the Republicans gained strength. Second, the Federalists in the early 1790s believed that Americans possessed "an enterprising spirit." They held that with good government and in a properly functioning economy individual labour and enterprise would encourage virtue, specifically the qualities of "industry, oeconomy and a true spirit of patriotism." Like Taylor, therefore, they concluded that self-interest and virtue could be mutually reinforcing.[16]

Hence it seems difficult to argue that either party in the 1790s retained the traditional conception of virtue in the sense of believing in an overriding social

[13] Zvesper, *Political Philosophy*, pp. 103, 14, 104.

[14] Taylor, *Inquiry*, pp. 490, 362, passim.

[15] This is testimony to the debt of all scholars to Gordon Wood's *Creation of the American Republic* (Chapel Hill. 1969).

[16] Zvesper, *Politial Philosophy*, pp. 45–47. The social and political ideals of the Federalists were, of course, starkly different from those of Taylor. I am not seeking to minimize the ideological distance between Federalism and radical Jeffersonianism.

obligation. But it is equally difficult to accept that Republicans (or Federalists) believed that "a man's capacity to look out for himself and his dependents" actually constituted virtue. Spokesmen in both parties argued that such a capacity migh *promote* virtue but this is, of course, a very different claim. As far as virtue and self-interest are concerned, then, neither party was wholly classical – and neither was unambigiously liberal. The labels cannot be made to stick.

II

Similar problems are apparent when the concept of equality is considered. For Appleby classical republicanism seems a highly inegalitarian set of doctrines; she emphasizes its "assertion that society is divided between the few and the many – the elite and the common people." This was "an assertion of human inequality presumed to be rooted in nature and therefore unavoidable in social practice."[17] Clearly on this definition it is the Federalists who are more thoroughly classical than the Republicans. It was John Adams who argued most persistently for a separate chamber for the natural aristocracy and one can certainly find precedents for this in English republican thought of the seventeenth century. But there was another side to classical republicanism and it is this which other scholars, and in particular Banning, have stressed. It is possible to trace from Aristotle through Harrington to Trenchard and Gordon an insistence that republicanism could be subverted by a distribution of wealth that was too uneven. Indeed as Pocock shows, Trenchard and Gordon had to concede that England in their day was not yet ready for a pure republic because Englishmen were too unequal in their property holdings. Banning demonstrates conclusively that the Jeffersonians retained this suspicion of inequality but that the Federalists did not – at least not to the same extent. Who then were the classical republicans? Clearly the answer depends upon the definitions being used. If classical republicanism is inegalitarian in its thrust then it is plainly the Federalists, if egalitarian then of course the Republicans would more easily qualify. In fact it is Jefferson himself who emerges as the archetypal classical republican in this respect. For unlike John Taylor, for example, Jefferson wished to have the natural aristocracy in government. Yet he placed a heavy reliance upon social and economic equality as a necessary foundation for republicanism. Perhaps this combination of egalitarian and inegalitarian assumptions was unusual in the United States at this time; nevertheless this aspect of the Republican leader's thought places a large question mark over Professor Appleby's thesis.[18]

It does not, however, entirely vitiate her argument. At the very centre of her interpretation is her understanding of the relationship between Republicanism and capitalism and this clearly requires close scrutiny. Now for Professor Appleby, capitalism means little more than commerce, or, more specifically, production for

[17] Appleby, *Capitalism and a New Social Order*, p. 17.

[18] Banning, passim: Pocock, *Machiavellian Moment*, p. 473. Taylor's suspicion of "natural aristocracy" is evident in his *Inquiry*, pp. 223–24. Jefferson, of course, though keen to place the "natural aristoi" in government, opposed Adams' (and Harrington's) insistence that they be given a separate chamber. See Jefferson's famous letter to Adams of 28 Oct. 1813.

the market and for monetary gain as well as for subsistence needs. Undoubtedly, Republicans were in this sense capitalists since few if any of them ever condemned commerce or advocated individual self-sufficiency. Few scholars, however, have, in recent years at any rate, suggested otherwise. It is more important, though more difficult, to gauge the extent of Republican commitment to commerce and to determine how large a price the Republicans would pay for commercial development. Here the work of Drew McCoy is invaluable. McCoy shows conclusively that for Madison commerce, and indeed international commerce, was all-important. In order for the United States to remain predominantly agrarian, farmers would need foreign markets. Otherwise they would lack any incentive to labour and would become slothful and unfit citizens for a republic. This priority shaped much of Madison's thinking in the 1780s and '90s and beyond. As he wrote in 1786, "most of our political evils may be traced to our commercial ones, as most of our moral may to our political." But Thomas Jefferson's position is even more difficult to categorize. At certain times his thought paralleled Madison's. In 1785 he argued that "access to the West Indies," by which he meant to West Indian markets, "is indispensably necessary to us." But at other times he, like other Republicans, fretted that commerce was being overdone. For instance, in 1792 he voiced his opposition to the proposal for a national bankruptcy law – which was explicitly designed to foster commerce and enterprise – in the form of two questions: "Is commerce so much the basis of the existence of the United States as to call for a bankrupt law? On the contrary are we not almost [entirely] agricultural?" Here Jefferson was reaffirming that commerce should be the handmaid of agriculture. John Taylor's brand of Republicanism showed an even greater fear of some of the consequences of commercialization and it was this which informed his and other Republicans' attacks on banks, sinking funds and tariffs. It was not that Jefferson or Taylor desired to abandon commerce; rather that they wished for commercial progress to take place within traditional social, political and moral confines.[19]

This meant progress which would not remove the incentive to labour (which promoted virtue) and which would not undermine liberty and equality. In effect it meant a pre-capitalist commercialism. For it is surely a mistake to reduce capitalism to commerce. To do so is to overlook what is specific to capitalism, namely the relation between the capitalist who owns the means of production and the labourer who has little alternative but to work for him. It is, one may suggest, the dynamic of this relationship, rather than the mere fact of production for the market, which is responsible for the extraordinary increase in productive power which the modern era has witnessed. At any rate the Republicans of the 1790s were acutely aware of the importance of this relationship: they certainly did not miss the distinction between commerce and capitalism. There is no doubt that they were deeply suspicious of the dependence which capitalism (as I have defined it) entailed. For the whole classical tradition insisted upon the need for independence. Virtue and liberty required that the individual be free to exercise his own judgment; the wage labourer lacked this freedom. Similarly a capitalist economy would necessarily contain large inequalities and these too would subvert

[19] McCoy, *Elusive Republic*, pp. 114–24, 174, 181–82; Taylor, *Inquiry*, passim.

a republic. Hence the almost universal hostility of Republicans to manufacturers.[20] Their arguments can be traced back through the centuries to antiquity.[21]

The Republicans then welcomed commerce in that they associated it with progress and the advancement of humanity. But it is inappropriate to argue, as does Professor Appleby, that because the United States in the 1790s was undergoing rapid commercial expansion and because the Republicans did well in commercial states like Pennsylvania and New York they were quintessentially commercial in outlook. The relationship between economy and ideology is generally more complex than this deterministic model would suggest, and many Republicans were ambivalent about commerce. McCoy sums it up well: "American republicanism must be understood as an ideology in transition, for it reflected an attempt to cling to the traditional republican spirit of classical antiquity without disregarding the new imperatives of a more modern commercial society." It is true that the social ideal which they envisioned would prove fleeting and transitory; it is none the less one whose distinctiveness historians should recognize.[22]

In another sense too it is misleading to label the Republicans "capitalist." It is surely clear in retrospect that the United States in the 1790s had many of the characteristics of an underdeveloped economy. One of its chief problems was a chronic shortage of capital. It was against this that many of Hamilton's policies were directed. But the laisser-faire approach of the Republicans was one which would leave this central problem unresolved. The Republicancs were more concerned with acquiring land in order to preserve individual autonomy than with facilitating capital accumulation which they feared would ultimately subvert that autonomy.

One must not push this argument too far. As we have seen, it would be a mistake to argue that men like Thomas Jefferson believed that a golden age lay somewhere in the past; as Professor Appleby has shown, Republicans sought a new future. It would be a new, commercialized and as we can now term it, pre-capitalist future. And it would never arrive.

III

As many scholars have pointed out, the historiography of the early Republicans has suffered from a major defect. Whilst many works have focussed upon ideologies and the minority of the citizens who wrote as committed partisans, others have concentrated upon the broader changes that were taking place in American society and in the American economy at this time. Each of these schools has enormously advanced our understanding of the history of these years; the

[20] McCoy has brought out the fundamental difference between household manufactures, which Republicans welcomed, and the more modern manufacturing establishments employing wage labour, which they opposed fiercely. This is in fact the distinction between pre-capitalist and capitalist production, as I have defined the term, and further testifies to the centrality of that distinction in Republican thinking.

[21] See the fascinating analysis in G.E.M. de Ste Croix's *The Class Struggle in the Ancient Greek World* (London, 1983), pp. 179–204.

[22] McCoy, *Elusive Republic*, p. 10.

problem, however, is to reconcile their separate findings. In tracing Republican ideology to the commercial developments experienced in the middle Atlantic states Professor Appleby has attempted such a reconciliation. As I have already pointed out I believe the result can be seriously faulted. Is it possible to suggest an alternative?

Clearly any such hypothesis must be highly tentative; the present state of knowledge simply will not support any firm generalizations. Yet it is surely of interest that the Republicans drew a disproportionate amount of support from the South. In the words of Richard Buel "the essential division" in politics was "between a Republican South and a Federalist New England," with the middle Atlantic states divided. There were of course exceptions but the South undoubtedly provided the Republicans with disproportionate electoral support and with the great majority of their national leaders and spokesmen. In addition to the three Presidents of the Virginia dynasty, men like John Taylor, John Randolph and Nathaniel Macon were all Southerners. In this connection it is instructive to consider what would have happened to American politics from the 1790s if there had been no states south of the Mason–Dixon line. Historians would then doubtless have recorded the successful attempt of the Federalist elite to impose a republican but avowedly anti-democratic political system upon the nation. After the turbulence which often accompanies war a regime more akin to that of the British would have emerged. But in actuality the Republican party upset all this. Nothing is more striking in retrospect than the willingness of Republican leaders to take their case to the people. Jefferson himself always insisted that the Republicans "cherished" the people while the Federalists feared or despised them. In 1787, at a time when the Federalists (as they would become) were fearful of social unrest and political upheaval, Jefferson asserted that "a little rebellion now and then is a good thing, and as necessary in the political world as storms in the natural." Buel attributes this populism to the greater security which the Southerners enjoyed in their leadership roles. Ironically, "aristocratic" Southern leaders, perhaps because of the greater economic homogeneity of the South, could embrace democracy in the confident belief that their own positions would be safe.[23]

Buel's explanation is a perceptive one. Did Southern leadership give encouragement and organizational support to the northern Republicans? Did it make their views more popular and more respectable? As yet our knowledge is not sufficient to allow a firm answer to these questions. If they can be answered in the affirmative, however, it is difficult not to be reminded of Edmund Morgan's brilliant argument in his book *American Slavery, American Freedom*. Here Morgan claimed that it was in large part slavery which enabled Americans to embrace republicanism. Slavery created a "sense of common identity" among whites and altered the relationship between elites and masses. Because the slaveholders lived off the sweated labour of blacks the poorer whites were their allies rather than their antagonists. Similarly the main threat to republicanism, the fear of levelling if the poorer classes could vote, was much diminished if not entirely removed. As Morgan puts it: "Aristocrats could more safely preach equality in a slave

[23] Richard Buel, Jr., *Securing the Revolution: Ideology in American Politics, 1789–1815* (Ithaca, 1972), pp. 52, 76.

society than in a free one" since slaves would never be permitted to form levelling mobs. The labour force in Virginia "was composed mainly of slaves"; this was a major structural influence upon Virginian society and it paved the way for Jefferson's celebrated eulogy of the yeoman farmer.[24]

Morgan argues that slavery propelled Virginians and perhaps other Americans towards republicanism. His book is concerned primarily with the period up to and including the Declaration of Independence. Critics may reply that other nations before and since have embraced republicanism without slavery and that not all slave societies have generated republican sentiment. It is thus difficult to argue that slavery is either a necessary or a sufficient condition for republicanism. But is it not possible that Morgan's insights apply with greater force to the *democratization* of the republic in the half century or so after the adoption of the Federal constitution? For at this time the United States managed this remarkable transformation without any major political or social upheaval. The importance of Jeffersonian ideology, the role of Southern leaders and the importance of Southern voters in the Republican and Jacksonian Democratic parties are all so evident as to require little comment. In the 1790s the Republicans began to popularize American politics; historians need to ask what the precise function of American slavery was in this process.[25]

Recent studies of republican ideology have paid little attention to slavery. In one sense this is unsurprising; the ideologues themselves did not discuss the relationship between their ideas and the society which generated them. The hypothesis which connects democracy (or republicanism) with slavery cannot be tested by simple reference to partisan pronouncements since it need not assert that partisans were themselves aware of the connection. In another sense, however, the omission is rather startling. For classical societies were, of course, slave societies. Can it be a coincidence that the ideal of the autonomous and equal republican citizen should be generated in the slave societies of antiquity, and then rise to ideological dominance in the (partially) slave society of late eighteenth-century America?[26]

[24] Edmund S. Morgan, *American Slavery, American Freedom, The Ordeal of Colonial Virginia* (N.Y., 1975), pp. 364, 380. For a somewhat different view of Virginia at this time see Rhys Isaac, *The Transformation of Virginia, 1740–1780* (Chapel Hill, 1982).

[25] To put it rather differently, I am suggesting that the slaveholders were the dominant class in American politics and their enthusiasm for, or at least acquiescence in, the process of democratization made that process unusually smooth and harmonious. The price, of course, was that slavery was fixed even more firmly upon American society. See Murrin, "Great Inversion," p. 426. Referring to the debates over the constitution, Howard A. Ohline claims that "slavery and the fears of slaveholders acted to assure a more democratic political system for white men": Ohline, "Republicanism and Slavery: Origins of the Three-Fifths Clause in the United States Constitution," *William and Mary Quarterly*, 3rd Ser. 28 (1971), 562–84. The extent of Republican dominance in the South in the 1790s is suggested in Mary P. Ryan, "Party Formation in the United States Congress: A Quantitative Analysis," ibid. 28 (1971) 523–42, though it must be added that Rudolph M. Bell, *Party and Faction in American Politics: The House of Representatives 1789–1801* seeks to qualify this thesis somewhat.

[26] Ste Croix, *Class Struggle*, passim. As many writers have shown, the classical ideal of the independent citizen was important in many cultures at many times. In the United States

The suggestion is then that the relationship between classical republicanism and Jeffersonianism is a real and important one despite Professor Appleby's criticisms. It is clearly the case that some Jeffersonians did reject some of the ideals and assumptions of classical and country thinkers and Joyce Appleby has rightly drawn attention to this. But it seems to me that she fails in her attempt to depict the Republican as a liberal capitalist. Optimistic though Jefferson may have been and commercially-minded as Madison undoubtedly was, it is surely unwise to exaggerate the similarity between their thought and that of modern Americans. For republicanism, even as preached by the Republican party, was a highly complex creed. It contained some tenets which anticipated those of contemporary Americans and perhaps rather more which were redolent of the English "country" tradition. But Republicans sought a society and a policy which were different from those of past and future. Theirs was indeed an elusive republic.[27]

---

its dominance may perhaps be attributed to a combination of the English libertarian heritage and the social and political power of the slaveholding class.

[27] On the question of the continuity of Republican ideology into the Jacksonian era see John Ashworth, "*Agrarians*" *and* "*Aristocrats*"*: Party Political Ideology in the United States, 1837–1846* (London, 1983).

Sic et Non: THOMAS JEFFERSON AND INTERNAL IMPROVEMENT

Joseph H. Harrison, Jr.

During the intensive re-examination of the Founding Fathers' thought in which American historians have engaged for the past thirty years, economic questions have not been ignored. Scholars have been aware of the impact of commerce on the civic humanist tradition.[1] They have been sensitive to the problems that technology would raise for the devotees of a rural republic.[2] In the case of Thomas Jefferson, his followers, and his associates, it has been disputed whether they looked backwards to an idealized Arcadia of philosophical farmers or eagerly heralded modern capitalism.[3] Most recently it has been argued that

---

Mr. Harrison is a member of the Department of History at Auburn University, Auburn, Alabama. This article is based upon a paper presented at a meeting of the Society for Historians of the Early American Republic, Knoxville, Tennessee, July 25, 1986.

[1] J.G.A. Pocock, *The Machiavellian Moment: Florentine Political Thought and the Atlantic Republican Tradition* (Princeton 1975), 462-505; Ralph Ketcham, *Presidents Above Party: The First American Presidency, 1789-1829* (Chapel Hill 1984), 22-57, 188-193; Drew R. McCoy, *The Elusive Republic: Political Economy in Jeffersonian America* (Chapel Hill 1980), *passim*.

[2] See especially Leo Marx, *The Machine in the Garden: Technology and the Pastoral Ideal in America* (New York 1964), and John F. Kasson, *Civilizing the Machine: Technology and Republican Values in America, 1776-1900* (New York 1976).

[3] Joyce Appleby, *Capitalism and a New Social Order: The Republican Vision of the 1790s* (New York 1984), esp. 89-90, 103; see also her "Republicanism in New and Old Contexts," *William and Mary Quarterly*, 43 (Jan. 1986), 20-34, Lance Banning, "Jeffersonian Ideology Revisited: Liberal and Classical Ideas in the New American Republic," *ibid.*, 3-19, and the wealth of sources cited in these two articles. See also Gordon S. Wood's review of John Patrick Diggins, *The Lost Soul of American Politics*, in *The New York Review of Books*, Feb. 28, 1985, 29-32.

JOURNAL OF THE EARLY REPUBLIC, 7 (Winter 1987).

Jefferson's own philosophy, properly understood, offered a drastic modification of capitalism if not an actual alternative to it.[4]

Less attention has been paid—Professor John L. Larson is a notable exception—to the role of public works, especially of what were called internal improvements, in plans for the American future. Yet, as I hope to show elsewhere, such works evoked an enthusiasm, in the Europe of the Enlightenment, which poets and philosophers—not yet the "natural Luddites"[5] of the late Charles Snow—shared with statesmen and engineers. From the days of Pope and Voltaire to those of Goethe, great public works were viewed as the material counterpart of the Renaissance, the restoration of Europe to Roman levels. The spectacle of Peter the Great, cutting canals and summoning his "huge neglected empire . . . from Gothic darkness," moved James Thomson to enquire, "What cannot active government perform,/New-moulding man?"[6]

Thomson's fellow Scot, Adam Smith, was no friend to "active government." Yet even he allowed that, after defense and the administration of justice,

> The third and last duty of the sovereign or commonwealth is that of creating or maintaining those public works which, though they may be in the highest degree advantageous to a great society are . . . of such a nature that the profit could never repay the expense to any individual or small number of individuals, and which therefore it could not be expected that any individual or small number of individuals should erect or maintain.[7]

It was a dispensation of which Smith's American admirers, inhabiting so vast and lightly populated a land, had ample reason to avail themselves. It must have comforted Jefferson, first as a Virginia mercantilist and later as president, since he shared the prevailing zeal for

---

[4] Richard K. Matthews, *The Radical Politics of Thomas Jefferson: A Revisionist View* (Lawrence, Kan. 1984), *passim.*

[5] C.P. Snow, *The Two Cultures and the Scientific Revolution* (Cambridge, Eng., and New York 1959), 23 *et seq.* Larson's papers include " 'Bind the Republic Together': The National Union and the Struggle for a System of Internal Improvements," *Journal of American History*, 74 (Sept. 1987), 363-387, and "A Bridge, a Dam, a River: Liberty and Innovation in the Early Republic," *Journal of the Early Republic*, 7 (Winter 1987), 351-375.

[6] *The Seasons: A Poem.* "Winter," ll. 950-959, in *The Complete Poetical Works of James Thomson*, ed. J. Logie Robertson (London 1908), 221.

[7] *An Inquiry into the Nature and Causes of the Wealth of Nations*, ed. Edwin Cannan (London 1904), 681.

this form of progress as for almost all others. Yet, where the federal government was concerned, negative considerations kept breaking in.

For Jefferson internal improvement, like charity, began at home. The Rivanna River, or North Branch of the James as it was sometimes called, watered his own lands. At the age of twenty he explored its obstructions by canoe, set about raising a subscription of £200 for their clearance, and got Dr. Thomas Walker (his guardian and predecessor in the House of Burgesses) to obtain statutory authority for the project. At twenty-two he was named, with ten other Albemarle County magnates, as one of its trustees. The Rivanna was made "navigable for canoes and batteaux to its intersection with the South West mountains,"[8] and on the eve of his presidency Jefferson still considered this one of his principal achievements.[9]

As a fledgling legislator he had also been concerned with the repair of Virginia's roads and bridges.[10] By the end of the Revolution, as his *Notes on Virginia* show, he was thinking of connecting the James with the Ohio via the Kanawha or—just possibly—by the Shenandoah and Potomac.[11]

Persuaded that the last-named river was destined to compete with the Hudson for all but the bulkiest traffic of the Northwest (which would go down the Mississippi), he had wished Virginia to give highest priority to development of the Potomac-Ohio route. He had taken the lead in urging George Washington to resume its direction as "a noble amusement" for his latter years.[12] And though he was in France when the general and James Madison prevailed upon the Virginia Assembly to establish the "Patowmack" and James River companies, America's first mixed corporations, his interest in them did not lag.

In May 1787, while the Constitutional Convention was gathering at Philadelphia, Jefferson spent a week on the Languedoc Canal, the greatest European public work since Roman times. He enjoyed the

---

[8] Thomas Jefferson, *Notes on the State of Virginia*, ed. William Peden (Chapel Hill 1955), 6; "Project for Making the Rivanna River Navigable," [1771?], *The Papers of Thomas Jefferson*, ed. Julian P. Boyd, Charles T. Cullen, *et al.* (22 vols., Princeton 1950-1986), I, 87-88.

[9] *Writings of Thomas Jefferson*, ed. Paul Leicester Ford (10 vols., New York 1892-1899), IX, 163-166.

[10] "Amendments to a Bill concerning the Keeping of Roads and Bridges," [Apr. 1772?], in Boyd, ed., *Papers of Jefferson*, I, 88-90.

[11] *Notes on Virginia*, 6; a possible connection of the Kanawha and the Roanoke is also mentioned, *ibid.*, 13. For the Potomac-Hudson rivalry, see 15-16.

[12] Jefferson to Madison, Feb. 20, 1784, in Boyd, ed., *Papers of Jefferson*, VI, 544-551; the quotation is at 548.

nightingales but worked hard at prosaic data which might be useful to the Patowmack Company.[13] In supporting another favorite Virginia project, the Dismal Swamp Canal, he pronounced it "much better that these [works] should be done at public than private expence."[14] And, as a long-lost ledger of the James River Company has revealed, he owned ten shares of that corporation and was thus one of its ten largest private investors.[15]

His overriding purpose, however, was not personal gain. He and his friends were trying to enrich and strengthen Virginia—by internal improvements, by location of the federal capital on the Potomac, by favoring Norfolk as the state's primary port and Alexandria as "a rival in the very bosom of Baltimore."[16] Yet Virginia's improvements, except for the James River-Kanawha route, all extended beyond Virginia's borders; one on which Jefferson was especially keen, connection of the Ohio with Lake Erie, was entirely so.[17] For this the approval of Congress would be necessary. Pennsylvania controlled essential parts both of this and the Potomac-Ohio line. Maryland was a partner in the Patowmack Company and North Carolina's cooperation was essential for the Dismal Swamp Canal.

It was logical, then, for the Virginia delegation at Philadelphia to support Dr. Franklin's motion that Congress be empowered "to provide for cutting canals where deemed necessary." Madison tried to go further and authorize federal corporations. He failed, and Franklin got the support of Pennsylvania, Virginia, and Georgia only. On an earlier division the Virginians had fared better, their vote just carrying Elbridge Gerry's proposal that Congress be allowed to "establish" not only post *offices* but post *roads*.[18]

Yet when Madison moved in the House of Representatives nearly nine years later to survey the chief national post road from Maine

---

[13] Jefferson to Martha Jefferson, May 21, 1787, *ibid.*, XI, 369-370; to William Short, same date, XI, 371-373; to Washington, May 2, 1788, XIII, 124.

[14] Jefferson to Washington, May 10, 1789, *ibid.*, XV, 117.

[15] Ledger Book "A," 1785-1790, James River Company Papers (Virginia Historical Society, Richmond).

[16] Jefferson to James Monroe, Dec. 10, 1784, in Boyd, ed., *Papers of Jefferson*, VII, 562; see also "Documents concerning the Residence of Congress," (ca. Nov.-Dec. 1783), *ibid.*, VI, 361-370.

[17] Jefferson to Washington, Aug. 14, 1787, *ibid.*, XII, 36; same to same, May 2, 1788, XIII, 124.

[18] James Madison, *Notes of Debates in the Federal Convention of 1787* . . . (Athens, Ohio 1966), Friday, Sept. 14, 1787, 638-639. For the earlier adoption of the post road clause, Thursday, Aug. 16, see 470.

to Georgia, Jefferson immediately took alarm. His paramount fear was of corruption. He was not, we may presume, afraid of a single survey, but Madison had called his proposal "the commencement of an extensive work." Jefferson viewed it "as a source of boundless patronage to the executive, jobbing to members of Congress & their friends, and a bottomless abyss of public money." From the post office surplus, out of which Madison had proposed to appropriate five thousand dollars, they would move on to "other revenues . . . and it will be a scene of eternal scramble among the members who can get the most money wasted in their State; and they will always get most who are meanest."[19]

There were other objections, the most important of them constitutional. Jefferson thought the power to establish post roads merely that of choosing between roads already in existence. If "the term be equivocal, (& I really do not think it so,) which is the safest construction?"—especially in the absence of a constitutional "amendment, securing still due measure & proportion among us," and presumably assuring Virginia of her rightful share. He also wanted "some means of information to the members of Congress tantamount to . . . ocular inspection . . . ." America's roads Jefferson considered "the best in the world except those of France & England." He doubted that such expenditures on them were called for by "the state of our population, the extent of our internal commerce, the want of sea & river navigation . . . ." He did not think "our means adequate to it." Yet in the same letter he had looked forward to the time when "Mr. Gallatin would . . . reduce this [financial] chaos to order . . . ."[20]

Madison was apparently unmoved. He did

> not consider my proposition as involving any dangerous consequences. It is limited to the choice of roads when that is presented, and to the opening of them in other cases, as far only as may be necessary for the transportation of the mail. This I think fairly within the object of the constitution.

He added, cryptically, that "it had . . . become essential that something be done, and something would have been attempted, on a worse principle."[21] No doubt he explained himself to Jefferson in Virginia that summer. A Federalist critic suspected collusion between Virginia and

---

[19] *Annals of Congress*, 4th Cong., 1st sess., 297, 314-315; Jefferson to Madison, Mar. 6, 1796, in Ford, ed., *Writings of Jefferson*, 226.

[20] Jefferson to Madison, Mar. 6, 1796, in Ford, ed., *Writings of Jefferson*, VIII, 223-227.

[21] Madison to Jefferson, Apr. 4, 1796, Madison Papers (Library of Congress).

Pennsylvania, and it was almost certainly Federalist opposition that killed Madison's bill in the Senate the following month.[22]

Yet Jefferson was surely relieved at its demise. One must suppose that the fear of corruption, so natural to all readers of Bolingbroke and of *Cato's Letters*, had been intensified by his observation of real live congressmen in the 1790s. And his strict construction of the Constitution, which had led him at the beginning of the decade to consider the Tenth Amendment as its "foundation,"[23] was soon to express itself in the Kentucky Resolutions and in the suggestion that the "general government be reduced to foreign concerns only."[24]

Nevertheless, within a mere five years national roads and canals had assumed, along with a national university, a central role in Jefferson's policy. The story is familiar but some recapitulation of it may be useful. The change did not take place all at once. Early in his first term, the president agonized over the constitutional precedent set by federal erection of piers in the Delaware River under an amendment to the annual lighthouse bill; he also feared that it would "lead to a bottomless expense, & to the greatest abuses."[25] Yet he approved a bill on April 30, 1802, for admission of Ohio to the Union that included a much more elastic precedent.

As originally drafted by Secretary of the Treasury Albert Gallatin, this measure would have reserved ten percent of the receipts from public land sales for "turnpike or other roads, first from the navigable waters emptying into the Atlantic to the Ohio, and afterwards continued through the new State; such roads to be laid out under the authority of Congress, with the consent of the several States through which the same shall pass."[26]

The Senate reduced this fund from ten percent to five, and three fifths of that was earmarked the following year for expenditure by Ohio authorities within their own borders. The residue or "Two Per Cent

---

[22] Chauncey Goodrich to Oliver Wolcott, Sr., Feb. 21, 1796, in George Gibbs, *Memoirs of the Administrations of Washington and John Adams, Edited from the Papers of Oliver Wolcott, Secretary of the Treasury* (2 vols., New York 1846), I, 302-303. See also *Annals of Congress*, 4th Cong., 1st sess., 100, 104; and Jeremiah Simeon Young, *A Political and Constitutional Study of the Cumberland Road* (Chicago 1902), 40.

[23] "Opinion on the Constitutionality of the Bill for Establishing a National Bank," Feb. 15, 1791, in Boyd, ed., *Papers of Jefferson*, XIX, 276.

[24] Jefferson to Gideon Granger, Aug. 13, 1800, in Ford, ed., *Writings of Jefferson*, IX, 140.

[25] Jefferson to Albert Gallatin, Oct. 13, 1802, *ibid.*, IX, 398-399.

[26] Gallatin to William Branch Giles, Feb. 13, 1802, in *The Writings of Albert Gallatin*, ed. Henry Adams (3 vols., Philadelphia 1869), I, 78.

Fund" would be a precedent for the future states of Indiana, Illinois, and Missouri, and for federal road construction generally. It was the basis for the act of March 29, 1806, for a road from Cumberland, Maryland, to the Ohio.

That law was not approved, as Jefferson's successor later suggested, by oversight or in any end-of-the-session turmoil.[27] The head of a government that was having to administer Louisiana thought the new road would be "an important link in the line to St. Louis." He dreamed already of "a horse-post" which should make the trip from Washington to the Mississippi in six days.[28] He showed no uneasiness about the constitutionality of a national road that would require the consent of the states of Maryland, Pennsylvania, and Virginia, or concern about the validity of that consent when given. He had cause to hope that the question would be rendered moot, perhaps before the road was actually commenced, by constitutional amendment.

In his Second Inaugural he had already anticipated the redemption of the national debt. This wouldn't happen for another thirty years, but Gallatin's economies and Europe's wars, pouring revenue into the laps of neutral shippers, made it seem likely in a tenth that time. Subsequent surpluses could, "by a just repartition among the states, and a corresponding amendment of the constitution, be applied, *in time of peace*, to rivers, canals, roads, arts, manufactures, education, and other great objects within each state."[29]

This sounds like a strict constructionist version of Jacksonian distribution or the revenue sharing of more recent times. By late 1806 Jefferson was prepared to give the federal government a more active role. In his Sixth Annual Message he proposed to keep up the duties on foreign luxuries—he was gracious enough to assume that the rich who paid them would approve of this—and apply the proceeds

> to the great purposes of the public education, roads, rivers, canals, and such other objects of public improvement as it may be thought proper to add to the constitutional enumeration of federal powers. By these operations new channels of communication will be opened between the States; the lines of separation will disappear, their interests will be identified, and their union cemented by new and indissoluble ties.[30]

---

[27] Madison to James Monroe, Dec. 27, 1817, in *The Writings of James Madison*, ed. Gaillard Hunt (9 vols., New York 1900-1910), VIII, 403-407.

[28] Jefferson to Gallatin, July 14, 1806, in Adams, ed., *Writings of Gallatin*, I, 304-305.

[29] Ford, ed., *Writings of Jefferson*, X, 130.

[30] *Ibid.*, 317-318.

A number of elements, some permanent, some transient, combined to form this Jeffersonian nationalism. Three of these—westward expansion, reduction of the debt, and the profits of neutral trade—have already been noted. But the trade had its negative aspects: its "absorption of all our active capital," in the opinion of America's most professional engineer, B. H. Latrobe, was "the true reason . . . of the suspension of the internal improvements of the country." Turnpikes near Philadelphia, specifically, and "the Ch[esapeake]. & Del[aware]. Canal were children of the peace of Amiens. They sickened, & our canal indeed has died in consequence of the abstraction of pecuniary support . . . ."[31]

Private enterprise, then, seemed a weak reed to the supporters of public works. But the growing dangers of war—with England, France, or both—to which Americans were exposed by their neutral trade operated to revive a theoretical dislike of foreign commerce that Jefferson had long suppressed.[32] Joel Barlow, with whom the president was planning a national university, had collaborated with Robert Fulton, whom he brought to Jefferson's attention, in a justly unpublished poem called "The Canal."[33] Fulton's earlier *Treatise on the Improvement of Canal Navigation* had followed Adam Smith in stressing the prosperity of agricultural empires in Egypt, China, and India. He had observed that "in those countries where canals were most in use, they never encouraged foreign commerce, but seem to have arrived at their great opulence by a home trade, circulated through their extensive and numerous navigations . . . ."[34]

It was Fulton whom Jefferson chose to direct his program of road and canal building.[35] Constitutional amendment would avoid the danger of loose construction; administration by such as Madison, Gallatin,

---

[31] Benjamin Henry Latrobe to Christian Ignatius Latrobe, June 2, 1806, in Talbot Hamlin, *Benjamin Henry Latrobe* (New York 1955), 211-212.

[32] Henry Adams, *History of the United States of America During the Administrations of Thomas Jefferson and James Madison* (New York 1889-1891), III, 124, quoting Turreau to Talleyrand, Jan. 20, 1806. For more extensive discussion see Joseph H. Harrison, Jr., "The Internal Improvement Issue in the Politics of the Union, 1783-1825" (Ph.D. diss., University of Virginia 1954), 167-170.

[33] The manuscript is in the Beinecke Library, Yale University.

[34] *A Treatise on the Improvement of Canal Navigation: exhibiting the numerous advantages to be derived from small canals, and boats of two to five feet wide, containing from two to five tons burthen* . . . (London 1796), 16-17. Cf. Smith, *Wealth of Nations*, 348, 360, 462, 644.

[35] Barlow to Jefferson, Dec. 9, 1807, Jefferson Papers (Library of Congress); Jefferson to Barlow, Dec. 10, 1807, in *The Writings of Thomas Jefferson*, ed. Andrew A. Lipscomb and Albert Ellery Bergh (20 vols., Washington 1905), XI, 400-401.

and himself would obviate that of corruption. He was even persuaded by Gallatin to forego pressing his favorite idea that expenditure in the respective states be proportioned in the ratio of their representation in Congress.[36] Yet a select committee of the House, headed by Barnabas Bidwell, did nothing for the proposed amendments; the Senate fell to wrangling over particular projects but finally adopted a resolution of some value. Originally brought forward by John Quincy Adams and defeated, it was taken up by Gallatin's friend and land agent, Thomas Worthington of Ohio. It called on the secretary of the treasury for a comprehensive and constitutional plan of internal improvement, and information as to works already extant that might "require and deserve the aid of Government."[37]

By the time that Gallatin's Report on Roads and Canals, that documentary monument of Jeffersonian nationalism, was submitted to the Senate in April 1808, the Embargo had dried up the revenues needed to put its recommendations into effect. It had been hardly less fatal to Jefferson's popularity (and that of his party) in the Northeast. His constitutional amendments, in that last winter of his presidency, were effectively undercut by Joseph B. Varnum of Massachusetts, who had been placed in the speaker's chair to keep Nathaniel Macon out—and thereby keep John Randolph from the chairmanship of Ways and Means. Varnum, in Latrobe's opinion "one of the most ignorant and narrow-souled of men," consigned the amendments to a committee headed by Randolph. It was a death sentence: the committee never reported.[38]

Among the lesser troubles of Jefferson's final year in office was the insistence of the Pennsylvania Assembly and of Pennsylvania Congressman William Hoge that the surveyors' location of the route for the Cumberland Road be altered to take in three towns—Brownsville, Uniontown, and Washington—in the southwestern portion of their state. This so angered him that he toyed with the idea of instructing the surveyors to avoid Pennsylvania entirely. The state, however, was essential to James Madison's election as president—and Jefferson let Gallatin persuade him to give in.[39]

---

[36] Gallatin, Memorandum on Sixth Annual Message, in Ford, ed., *Writings of Jefferson*, X, 308n.

[37] *Annals of Congress*, 9th Cong., 2nd sess., 89-90, 95, 97, 114; *Memoirs of John Quincy Adams Comprising Portions of His Diary from 1795 to 1848*, ed. Charles Francis Adams (Philadelphia 1874-1877), I, 463, 471.

[38] B. H. Latrobe to William Tatham, Feb. 5, 1810, Latrobe Papers (Maryland Historical Society, Baltimore); *Annals of Congress*, 10th Cong., 2nd sess., 483, 485.

[39] Harrison, "The Internal Improvement Issue," 246-251.

Despite this unpleasantness, he clung to his "golden vision" for several years. To his physiocratic friend Pierre-Samuel Du Pont he wrote in 1811 that unless the government fell "into unwise hands," there would be a surplus for "canals, roads, schools, &c., and the farmer will see his government supported, his children educated, & the face of his country made a paradise by the contributions of the rich alone, without his being called on to spare a cent from his earnings."[40] And two years later he wrote John Wayles Eppes, himself a principled opponent of federal improvements, that "So enviable a state in prospect for our country, [had] induced me to temporize [with Great Britain], and to bear with national wrongs which under no other prospect ought ever to have been unresented or unresisted."[41]

This may have been, in part, a defensive rationalization, penned during a feckless war for which he had not prepared the country well. But the language is that of a decided nationalist, and if Jefferson had died at seventy he would have been so considered, at least by those unable to write him off as an opportunist. In his last years, however, he engaged in an ever more impassioned defense of state rights, and the issue on which he finally focused was internal improvement.

Again, the transition was gradual. If he declined a place, in 1816, on the newly created Virginia Board of Public Works, it was doubtless because he had decided to concentrate on the creation of a state university, and he knew that time and strength were running out.[42] If he supported Madison's veto of John C. Calhoun's Bonus Bill, he must have done so with the more assurance because he knew that Madison's position on federal post roads was more latitudinarian than his own; as to cutting canals, he was aware that the Philadelphia Convention had refused Congress that power.[43] Even as late as 1824, when Edward

---

[40] Jefferson to Du Pont, Apr. 15, 1811, *Correspondence between Thomas Jefferson and Pierre Samuel du Pont de Nemours, 1798-1817*, ed. Dumas Malone (Boston and New York 1930), 133-134. For the term "golden vision," see Henry St. George Tucker in the House of Representatives, March 6, 1818, *Annals of Congress*, 15th Cong., 1st sess., 1117.

[41] Jefferson to Eppes, Sept. 11, 1813, in Lipscomb and Bergh, eds., *Writings of Jefferson*, XIII, 355. For Eppes' scruples, see B. H. Latrobe to Joshua Gilpin, Jan. 7, 1810, Latrobe Papers.

[42] Philip Morrison Rice, "The Virginia Board of Public Works, 1816-1842" (M.A. thesis, University of North Carolina 1947), 263-265.

[43] Jefferson to Gallatin, June 16, 1817, in Lipscomb and Bergh, eds., *Writings of Jefferson*, XV, 131-135. His familiarity with the Philadelphia convention's rejection of the power to incorporate—advanced in specific connection with that of opening

Livingston sent him a copy of his own elaborate oration in behalf of the General Survey Bill, he could be conciliatory.

His constitutional doubts, he explained, were still unsatisfied, and among his fellow skeptics were "the Madisons, the Monroes [though Monroe signed the Survey Bill into law], the Randolphs, the Macons, all good men and true, of primitive principles." He reminded Livingston that "a government held together by the bands of reason only, requires much compromise of opinion; that things even salutary should not be crammed down the throats of dissenting brethren, especially when they may be put into a form to be willingly swallowed." Like his two successors, he still favored a constitutional amendment, in which provision for apportionment among the states—here his old disagreement with Gallatin came out—would "prevent that kind of abuse . . . so much practised in public bodies, I mean the bartering of votes. It would reconcile every one," and Jefferson supposed "there is not a State, perhaps not a man in the Union, who would not consent to add this to the powers of the general government."[44]

Livingston, reading this, must have concluded that the old man was wholly out of touch. The more vehement state-righters, like John Randolph and Philip P. Barbour, made no secret of the fact that they were as opposed to conferring the power as to inferring it; it was their intransigence, combined with that of their nationalist opposites, which had stifled every attempt at such an amendment thus far.[45]

By the end of his life, Jefferson himself had moved very close to their position. The program of John Quincy Adams bore a marked resemblance to that of his own second term, but the patriarch responded with a set of resolutions echoing those he had written for Kentucky in 1798 and 1799. His draft "Declaration and Protest of the Commonwealth of Virginia, on the Principles of the Constitution of the United States of America, and on the Violations of them" restated the compact theory of the Constitution, asserted Virginia's equal devotion to the rights of the federal and state governments, and accused the former

---

canals—is shown by the "Opinion on the Constitutionality of the Bill for Establishing a National Bank," cited above, n. 23.

[44] Jefferson to Livingston, Apr. 4, 1824, in Ford, ed., *Writings of Jefferson*, XII, 348-351.

[45] Cf. Barbour's speeches in the House of Representatives, *Annals of Congress*, 14th Cong., 2nd sess., 893-899; 15th Cong., 1st sess., 1151-1164; 18th Cong., 1st sess., 1005-1013; and Randolph, *ibid.*, 18th Cong., 1st sess., 1296-1311. See also Henry St. George Tucker, *ibid.*, 15th Cong., 1st sess., 1318-1339, for the futility of attempting an amendment against the combined opposition of uninhibited nationalists and uncompromising state-righters.

of "enlarging its own powers by constructions, inferences, and indefinite deductions from those directly given . . . ."[46]

Specifically, "They claim . . . and have commenced the exercise of a right to construct roads, open canals, and effect other internal improvements within the territories and jurisdictions exclusively belonging to the several States," a right that Virginia denied.[47] Yet the only national road so constructed had been authorized by Jefferson and begun under his successor. The only canal yet aided, and that solely by a subscription of its stock, was the Chesapeake and Delaware, approved by President Monroe.

Jefferson went on to attack an interpretation of the general welfare clause so broad that no responsible politician had ever put it forward. More pertinently, he denied the new president's doctrine "that the people . . . , by not investing their federal branch with all the means of bettering their condition, have denied to themselves any which may effect that purpose." The distribution of powers, he continued in phrases that echoed Adams' First Annual Message, had "completely secured the first object of human association, the full improvement of their condition, and reserved to themselves all the faculties of multiplying their own blessings."[48]

Virginia's attachment to the Union was such that she would resist only as a last resort, but she would not accept "submission to a government of unlimited powers." If most of the other states acquiesced in the Adams program, "we will be patient and suffer much, under the confidence that time, ere it be too late, will prove to them also the bitter consequences in which that usurpation will involve us all." Out of special respect for its "co-States," Virginia might even accept an amendment adding "the power of making roads and canals" to those "directly given to the federal branch . . . ." (There is no hint that he himself had ever desired such an amendment.) Even so, it must "be sufficiently guarded against abuses, compromises, and corrupt practices, not only of possible, but of probable occurrence." Meantime, Virginians should submit to these "usurpations" without admitting them as legal precedents.[49]

---

[46] Lipscomb and Bergh, eds., *Writings of Jefferson*, XVII, 442-448; the quotation is at 443. Cf., especially, John Quincy Adams' First Annual Message, in *A Compilation of the Messages and Papers of the Presidents*, comp. James D. Richardson (10 vols., Washington 1896-1899), II, 316-317.

[47] Lipscomb and Bergh, eds., *Writings of Jefferson*, XVII, 443.

[48] *Ibid.*, 494.

[49] *Ibid.*, 445, 446-447.

To Madison he suggested that the "olive branch" of an amendment might "be accepted, and the constitution thus saved at a moderate sacrifice."[50] To William Branch Giles he deprecated the thought that Virginians should "*stand to our arms*, with the hot-headed Georgian" (Governor George M. Troup) in his confrontation with Adams.[51] To another correspondent he acknowledged that an eventual change in "the free principles of our government . . . was to be expected." He had not thought it would come in a single generation or that "my favorite western country," so avid for internal improvements, "was to be made the instrument of change." He had always relied on the West "as a barrier against the degeneracy of public opinion . . . . But the bait of local interests, artfully prepared for their palate, has decoyed them from their kindred attachments, to alliances alien to them." Yet he "should not be for giving up the ship without efforts to save her. She lived well through the first squall, and may weather the present one."[52]

Fortunately, Madison—to whom he entrusted this draft—suppressed it, arguing tactfully that it was better for other states to take the lead, as New York and South Carolina eventually did.[53] Yet Jefferson's forebodings seem so apocalyptic, the whole business so strange a coda to his career, that the obvious explanations fail to satisfy. Why, especially in view of his singular friendship for old John Adams, should he have spent almost his last strength whipping up opposition to the administration of his friend's son?

He was old and sick, of course, and he had lived on the verge of complete financial ruin since the failure of Wilson C. Nicholas in the Panic of 1819. His sympathy, always limited, for the postwar nationalism may have lessened as tensions with Great Britain eased. His dislike of the United States Bank would not have been lessened by the fact that Nicholas had headed its Richmond branch. The protective tariff, briefly accepted as a necessity, was now viewed as a device for enriching manufacturers at the expense of debt-ridden planters like himself.[54]

---

[50] Jefferson to Madison, Dec. 24, 1825, in Ford, ed., *Writings of Jefferson*, XII, 417.

[51] Jefferson to Giles, Dec. 26, 1825, *ibid.*, 425.

[52] Jefferson to Claiborne W. Gooch, Jan. 9, 1826, in Lipscomb and Bergh, eds., *Writings of Jefferson*, XVI, 151-153.

[53] Madison to Jefferson, Dec. 28, 1825, in Hunt, ed., *Writings of Madison*, IX, 236-240.

[54] For good summaries of these influences on the attitudes of Jefferson's final years see Dumas Malone, *Jefferson and His Time* (Boston 1948-1981), VI, *The Sage of Monticello*, 301-361, 426-443, and Merrill D. Peterson, *Thomas Jefferson and the New Nation* (New York 1970), 988-1004. See also McCoy, *The Elusive Republic*, 248-252.

As an old man, he might be forgiven a proclivity to refight old battles. A political Manichaean, he believed in the perpetual division of more or less free societies between Whigs and Tories, those who trusted the people and those who feared them. In the election of 1824, he had identified William H. Crawford as the heir of the Revolution of 1800, John Quincy Adams as the champion of the other side.[55]

As a republican he feared corruption, and as a gentleman he loathed "log-rolling," its characteristic legislative form: "they will always get most who are meanest."[56] Perhaps, like John Bell a few years later, he foresaw a time when "an honest man will cease to have any business in" congresses preoccupied with the sharing out of public money.[57] It would be tempting to suppose that he was trying to draw the country back from the path that led on to the "Great Barbecue," to the political action committees (PACs) of our own time, to the blossoming of defense installations in the bailiwicks of senior members of armed services committees; that this lifelong prophet of progress had seen the future—and recoiled from it.

No doubt there was an element of this, but Jefferson hoped that his apportionment scheme could keep "log-rolling" within bounds. The primary motive for his *gran rifuto*, it appears to me, was a genuine devotion to the rights of the states, an attitude the twentieth century finds it difficult to imagine as anything more than an obstructionist pretext.

This had always been a central element of his political thought. He might dream of an "Empire of Liberty," preferably though not necessarily bound in a single union. He might wish to divide Virginia counties into wards and make it easier for every citizen to participate in his own government.[58] He had his macro-politics and his micro-politics. But the states were for him the basic political units and the principal guarantors of individual rights.

However wide the horizons of his mind, his political world had contracted steadily. With, ironically, the exception of John Adams,

---

[55] Jefferson to Richard Rush, Oct. 13, 1824, in Lipscomb and Bergh, eds., *Writings of Jefferson*, XVI, 78-79. See also Jefferson to Henry Lee, Aug. 10, 1824, *ibid.*, XVI, 73-74; to William Short, Jan. 8, 1825, *ibid.*, XVI, 92-97, where he speaks of "Whigs, Liberals, Democrats," as opposed to "Tories, Serviles, Aristocrats"; Jefferson to Samuel Harrison Smith, Aug. 2, 1823, to Nathaniel Macon, Feb. 21, 1826, in Ford, ed., *Writings of Jefferson*, XII, 300-302, 459-460.

[56] Jefferson to Madison, Mar. 6, 1796, in Ford, ed., *Writings of Jefferson*, VIII, 223-227.

[57] *Register of Debates*, 20th Cong., 2nd sess., 347-348.

[58] This point is ably set forth in Matthews, *Radical Politics of Thomas Jefferson*, 81-88.

he no longer had intimates who were not Virginians. The great public object of his latter years was the establishment of his university, and for this he worked closely with state politicians, including the state-rights rigorists of the Richmond Junto. Thomas Ritchie's *Enquirer* was the only newspaper read at Monticello, and Judge Spencer Roane had been the paladin of Virginia resistance to what Jefferson considered the dangerous encroachment of John Marshall's Supreme Court.[59]

He had been further driven in upon this world, in which his daughter and his grandchildren would be left, by his profound disturbance over the Missouri controversy. For him the "fire bell" must have continued to reverberate in the night.[60] The brusque contempt with which the younger Adams, while professing respect for his predecessors, dismissed their constitutional scruples as to internal improvement did not seem innocuous to him as it does to us.

It was not capitalism but "consolidation" that terrified him. For him as for Madison—and their agreement here counted for infinitely more than their philosophical differences[61]—the contractual rights of the states were the core of freedom, the essence of government by consent.

On his deathbed Jefferson exclaimed, "The Committee of Safety, it must be warned."[62] He even sat up and wrote out a message—presumably one of warning—on an invisible tablet. Was this a backward projection of the fears which shadowed his final months, or had he already escaped into the riskier but infinitely more hopeful days of the Revolution?

---

[59] For the Junto, its composition and influence, see Harry Ammon, "The Richmond Junto, 1800-1824" *Virginia Magazine of History and Biography*, 61 (Oct. 1953), 395-418; see also Joseph H. Harrison, Jr., "Oligarchs and Democrats: The Richmond Junto," *ibid.*, 78 (Apr. 1970), 184-198.

[60] Jefferson to John Holmes, Apr. 22, 1820, in Ford, ed., *Writings of Jefferson*, XII, 157-158. See, *e.g.*, Jefferson to Gallatin, Dec. 26, 1820, in Thomas Jefferson, *Writings*, ed. Merrill D. Peterson (New York 1984), 1447-1450.

[61] *Pace* Matthews, *Radical Politics of Thomas Jefferson*, 97-118.

[62] Thomas Jefferson Randolph to Henry S. Randall, n. d., in Randall, *Life of Thomas Jefferson* (3 vols., New York 1858), III, 543-544.

"Bind the Republic Together": The National Union and the Struggle for a System of Internal Improvements

John Lauritz Larson

On February 4, 1817, South Carolina Congressman John C. Calhoun rose to debate a bill pledging the "bonus" due the government from the new national bank to a fund for improving the nation's roads and canals. The idea was far from new: George Washington, Alexander Hamilton, Thomas Jefferson, Albert Gallatin, James Madison, and many other American founders had called for systematic internal improvements since before the creation of the Republic. At last, it seemed to Calhoun, the time was right to overcome all previous doubts and to step forward boldly with this great national objective. Hoping to disarm his detractors, he first observed that "it seemed the fate of some measures, to be praised, but not passed."[1] The comment was prophetic, for neither the Bonus Bill nor any other nationwide system of internal improvements passed into law in Calhoun's lifetime. Congress favored the bill in 1817, but the president condemned it as unconstitutional. Later Congresses failed to adopt a system or an amendment permitting one. Proposals for a system of internal improvements did not fail for want of merit. Scarcely any Americans doubted that internal improvements would strengthen and enrich their new country. Few denied that some works were too expensive or too risky for private or local authorities. Still, the general government never seized the initiative to direct and build an integrated network of roads and canals. Why?

Historians have long attended to this question, and their answers have reflected shifting attitudes toward business and government, as well as changing historical perspectives. Once most economic historians were satisfied to quote laissez-faire doctrine as the reason and to congratulate the founders and their descendants for resisting the temptation to interfere. In the New Deal era scholars like Oscar Handlin and Mary Flug Handlin and Louis Hartz rediscovered government intervention in the economy at the state and local levels, but they preferred to chart the rise of liberalism, rather than explain the failure of federal control. By 1960 Carter

John Lauritz Larson is assistant professor of history at Purdue University. An earlier draft of this article was read at the Organization of American Historians' annual meeting, April 1985. The author thanks Lester Cohen, Ronald E. Shaw, and Joseph H. Harrison, Jr., for critical advice and the Purdue Research Foundation for financial support.

[1] *Annals of Congress*, 14 Cong., 2 sess., Feb. 4, 1817, p. 851.

Goodrich had demonstrated that the failure of national planning derived, not from economic doctrines, but from conflicts over political power. "The real issue," Goodrich concluded, "was between national and state action." Fears of federal consolidation and optimistic assumptions about state and local capability to promote internal improvements doomed the general system long before private enterprise was strong enough to take the lead. Initiative passed to the states, and economic historians correctly turned their attention to state and local arenas where the real progress could be found.[2]

Goodrich laid the issue before political historians, who have concentrated on the constitutional objections of strict constructionists and states' righters to explain why federal systems repeatedly failed. Such accounts usually claim that improvements were universally popular and then attribute federal inaction to the constitutional piety of the Jeffersonians, the pettiness of party factions, or the interference in politics caused by Napoleon's wars. Specialized monographs discuss federal policy as a background to specific public works, invariably revealing a tangle of interests behind the promotions; case studies, however, cannot account for the system as a whole. Gallatin's *Report of the Secretary of the Treasury on the Subject of Roads and Canals* (1808) embodied the developmental hopes of the first generation's leaders for a national system of internal improvements that would bind the Republic together. But when the young nationalists in the postwar era, led by Calhoun and Henry Clay, pushed the Bonus Bill through Congress to realize that plan, Madison surprised them with a veto cast in the old-fashioned language of strict construction and limited federal power. Searching for reasons to explain that reversal historians find agrarian suspicions, reverence for the Constitution, and, finally, the emerging slavery question, which poisoned debates on a national plan.[3]

Those explanations are all true but incomplete. They stand at odds with much of what we know about Jeffersonian America, and they infuse the history of the internal improvements question with a hint of tragic loss: But for enemies of progress, the people might have had what the people must have wanted. A growing literature on Jeffersonian politics and ideology, however, portrays Republican leaders every bit as skilled at constitutional manipulations as any Hamiltonian Federalist. What once

[2] Carter Goodrich, *Government Promotion of American Canals and Railroads, 1800–1890* (New York, 1960), 44–47. See also Carter Goodrich, "American Development Policy: The Case of Internal Improvements," *Journal of Economic History*, 16 (Dec. 1956), 449–60; Carter Goodrich, "Internal Improvements Reconsidered," *ibid.*, 30 (June 1970), 289–311; Louis Hartz, *Economic Policy and Democratic Thought: Pennsylvania, 1776–1860* (Cambridge, Mass., 1948); Oscar Handlin and Mary Flug Handlin, *Commonwealth: A Study of the Role of Government in the American Economy: Massachusetts, 1774–1861* (Cambridge, Mass., 1969); Robert A. Lively, "The American System, A Review Article," *Business History Review*, 29 (Spring 1955), 81–95; and Ronald E. Shaw, "Canals in the Early Republic: A Review of Recent Literature," *Journal of the Early Republic*, 4 (Summer 1984), 117–42.

[3] See, for example, Charles M. Wiltse, *John C. Calhoun, Nationalist* (Indianapolis, 1944); Samuel Flagg Bemis, *John Quincy Adams and the Union* (New York, 1965); Ralph Ketcham, *James Madison: A Biography* (New York, 1971); George Dangerfield, *The Era of Good Feelings* (New York, 1952); George Rogers Taylor, *The Transportation Revolution, 1815–1860* (New York, 1951); and John Mayfield, *The New Nation, 1800–1845* (New York, 1982). For a considerable improvement on the story, see Harry N. Scheiber, "The Transportation Revolution and American Law," *Transportation and the Early Nation* (Indianapolis, 1982), 1–29. For the case study approach, see Ronald E. Shaw, *Erie Water West: A History of the Erie Canal* (Lexington, Ky., 1966); and Ralph D. Gray, *The National Waterway: A History of the Chesapeake and Delaware Canal* (Urbana, 1967).

appeared simple factionalism now looks like democratization and the building of the second party system. The rhetoric of 1798 notwithstanding, Jefferson and Madison remained nationalistic republicans still at war with the original antifederal forces. In 1801 they assumed guardianship over the future of the *nation*, not the states; they, not the Federalists, sought expansion, embargo, war, banks, tariffs, and internal improvements. The Republican "revolution" of 1800 promised, not an end to nation, but the triumph of nation in the hands of the "virtuous majority," and Americans seemed more inclined than ever to experiment with government to get what they wanted from liberty. As late as 1817 "states' rights" was still an anticonsolidation position, rooted in the struggle to create the Republic, not yet a southern, proslavery doctrine. In other words, in the era surrounding the War of 1812, constitutional reverence, factionalism, states' rights, and slavery were neither unequivocal enough nor strong enough to have blocked the Gallatin plan, if it was what the people wanted. Something in the plan itself explains its demise.[4]

The real barrier to a national system of internal improvements sprang, first, from that system's power to guide development from the center and, second, from Americans' lingering fear of just such consolidated power. They had staged a revolution against British imperial consolidation, and their instincts bristled at signs of centralized control. They had formed a union reluctantly, jealously preserving state sovereignty and forcing proponents of the 1787 Constitution to understate national power. All political theory and experience taught that government at a distance was corrupted easily. Thus the persistence of republican hostility to centralized power, a major inheritance from the Revolution, proved an obstacle to federal control of internal improvements.

The republicanism of the revolutionary era also affected the controversy over improvements in at least two additional ways. First, it spurred the Jeffersonians, like the Federalists, to advocate systematic internal improvements for the sake of liberty and union. The new nation—and therefore liberty itself—utterly depended on union for survival. Physical barriers to commercial and political intercourse threatened imminent disintegration, so roads and canals were required. But nothing promised to elevate union from a metaphor to a reality more convincingly than good communications, and if spatial barriers were shattered, the possibility of consolidation drastically increased. Could a central government be trusted to design and construct great works of national integration? In the Federalist era Jeffersonians said no. After their victory in 1800, however, leading Republicans remained committed to

[4] See Alexander De Conde, *This Affair of Louisiana* (New York, 1976); Drew R. McCoy, *The Elusive Republic: Political Economy in Jeffersonian America* (Chapel Hill, 1980); Burton Spivak, *Jefferson's English Crisis: Commerce, Embargo and the Republican Revolution* (Charlottesville, 1979); Ralph Ketcham, *Presidents above Party: The First American Presidency, 1789–1829* (Chapel Hill, 1984); Richard Hofstadter, *The Idea of a Party System: The Rise of Legitimate Opposition in the United States, 1780–1840* (Berkeley, 1969); Richard P. McCormick, *The Presidential Game* (New York, 1982); Lance Banning, *The Jeffersonian Persuasion: Evolution of a Party Ideology* (Ithaca, 1978); J. C. A. Stagg, *Mr. Madison's War: Politics, Diplomacy and Warfare in the Early Republic, 1783–1830* (Princeton, 1983); Joseph H. Harrison, Jr., "The Internal Improvement Issue in the Politics of the Union, 1783–1825" (Ph.D. diss., University of Virginia, 1954); and Robert H. Wiebe, *The Opening of American Society: From the Adoption of the Constitution to the Eve of Disunion* (New York, 1984).

national union and to the "general welfare." Doubting Adam Smith's new theory, that the clash of local and private interests produced the greatest general good, these elite republicans envisioned a planned system of improvements embodying statesmanlike regulation of development. But quickly spokesmen for a new liberal and democratic politics, with more faith in the free play of contending interests, dominated the campaign for internal improvements. State and local boosters scrambled for federal aid that would enlarge their resources but not dictate their designs. It mattered absolutely, local representatives believed, who designed and constructed the roads and canals, because that first conquest of space would fix forever the opportunities for growth enjoyed by distant places within the nation.

Second, as the new champions of improvements gained confidence in liberal competition and democratic politics they abandoned the classical republican belief that governments should guide or restrain private and local interests. As they did so, older leaders like Jefferson and Madison felt moved by their original republican scruples to oppose the new initiatives. Thus while everyone heralded the age of improvement, the field of public works became a field of battle where nationalistic vision and local autonomy, congeries of interests, and diverging views of the relation between the particular and the general welfare struggled for control of the new republic.

The idea of an integrated transportation network was older than the American union, and no individual better illustrates the original sweeping vision than George Washington of Virginia. As early as 1770 Washington proposed a subscription to improve the navigation of the Potomac River, and he pressed his neighbors to see the project as "the channel of commerce" for "the trade of a rising empire." After the revolutionary war, Washington toured the northern regions and completed his conception of a grand internal navigation: Connect the eastern waters to those that run westward; open the western rivers to the Ohio; link the Ohio with Lake Erie "and we shall not only draw the produce of the western settlers, but the peltry and fur trade of the lakes also to our ports . . . binding these people to us by a chain which can never be broken." Enthusiastic supporters of the general's views included Madison, who managed the Potomac Company's business in the Virginia legislature, and Jefferson, who wrote in 1784 that "Nature . . . has declared in favor of the Potomac and thro' that channel offers to pour into our lap the whole commerce of the Western world." The *Virginia Gazette* proclaimed the canal that enabled boats to bypass the Great Falls of the Potomac "one of the grandest chains for preserving the Federal Union."[5]

The story of the Potomac Company linked two important themes that would con-

[5] George Washington to Thomas Johnson, July 20, 1770, Corra Bacon-Foster, *Early Chapters in the Development of the Potomac Route to the West* (Washington, 1912), 18–21; Washington to Jacob Read, Nov. 3, 1784, quoted in Shaw, *Erie Water West*, 12; Thomas Jefferson to Washington, March 15, 1784, Bacon-Foster, *Early Chapters*, 37–38; *Virginia Gazette*, Dec. 4, 1784, *ibid.*, 45.

The Great Falls of the Potomac by T. Cartwright, after George Beck, 1802.
Courtesy Library of Congress.

tinue to mark the internal improvements issue. One was competitive localism and a tendency to see particular advantages as universal blessings. Washington's canal, for example, advanced the nation's destiny by enriching Virginia. Similar ambitions cherished by spokesmen for Philadelphia and New York, however, appeared to Washington as "foreign" interference in the Union's future. With equal scorn Washington condemned the "confined" views of other Virginians who preferred not to be taxed to improve a river they did not use, and he fulminated against the greedy Baltimore merchants who protested his "scheming" in their legislature for the purpose of "stealing" their commerce.[6]

The second theme was the close intermingling of private and public interests. Washington's fortune had been strained by the Revolution, and his best hope for recovery lay in developing his enormous holdings of western lands. In his mind the Potomac canal would open the West (his West) to settlers, increase the value of Continental veterans' land warrants, and secure the western country to the Union, thereby strengthening the nation's government, restoring its credit, and starting the flow of prosperity and happiness that the Revolution had promised. To the Marquis de Lafayette he wrote: "I wish to see the sons and daughters of the world in peace and busily employed in the more agreeable amusements of fulfilling the first and great commandment—'*Increase and multiply*,' as an encouragement to which we

[6] See Bacon-Foster, *Early Chapters*, 19, 68.

have opened the fertile plains of the Ohio to the poor, the needy, and the oppressed of the Earth."[7]

To accomplish that great work of public and private profit he needed only the forebearance of government and a favorable climate. Washington doubted that the taxpayers would ever support expensive works at fixed locations; therefore he wanted government only to suppress competition and to endorse his objective, so that "monied gentry" from outside the neighborhood could be induced to invest for profits. The combined prestige of great gentlemen and their governments would support the initial shares, while the success of the work and the prosperity that followed would secure to gentlemen and governments alike the hearts and interests of the people. It is hardly surprising, then, to find the interstate negotiations behind the Potomac canal intimately connected to the Annapolis Convention of 1786 and the call for a new, energetic, national government.[8]

The Virginians were not alone in their grand designs for opening the West or improving the commercial landscape. Robert Morris, the Philadelphia financier, was active in promoting a canal between the Susquehanna and Schuylkill rivers in order to capture the Baltimore trade. Pennsylvania improvers were also trying to cut a canal through Delaware and Maryland to Chesapeake Bay for much the same reason. At the same time New York's governor, George Clinton, threw the weight of government behind the ambitions of private investors to open communications between New York City and the Canadian and western waters. A three-way competition for the West had taken shape in promoters' minds. It pitted New York, Philadelphia, and the Chesapeake ports against one another for the right to play London to the rising American empire.[9]

Internal improvements had been much on the minds of the founders, and the Federalists uniformly approved them. Why, then, did the Federalists fail to implement a national system in the 1790s alongside funding, banking, and national defense? The answers lie in the political sensitivities of the constitutional period. The new federal government enjoyed at best marginal support in several states. Congress could not directly construct any one of the three main routes to the West without driving the rival states away from the Union. However, by fostering a stable political environment and promoting private franchises, the general government could take some credit for prosperity without threatening the sovereignty of the states. Hamilton, the most expansive of the Federalists, understood the delicacy of the matter: Federal authority dared not extend to things "confined to a particular spot." That was tragic, Hamilton believed, and he wished that Congress had the "liberty

[7] Washington to Marquis de Lafayette, July 25, 1785, *ibid.*, 66.

[8] Washington to Johnson, July 20, 1770, *ibid.*, 19. On the connection between the Potomac Company and the Constitutional Convention, see James Thomas Flexner, *Washington: The Indispensable Man* (Boston, 1969), 193–203; and Charles Royster, *Light Horse Harry Lee and the Legacy of the American Revolution* (New York, 1981), 57–113.

[9] See Julius Rubin, *Canal or Railroad: Imitation and Innovation in the Response to the Erie Canal in Philadelphia, Baltimore, and Boston* (Philadelphia, 1961); Gray, *National Waterway*; Shaw, *Erie Water West*; and Harrison, "Internal Improvement Issue," 68–134.

to pursue and promote the general interests" in just those cases where obstructive selfish interests might prevail. But such a power was, he knew, politically, if not constitutionally, denied.[10]

Federalist leaders thus hoped to bind the Republic together through the enterprise of the "monied gentry." There were others in government, however, who would use politics to link the interests of the people with the new federal government. In July 1789, for example, when Massachusetts Antifederalist Elbridge Gerry introduced a bill to establish and support at federal expense lighthouses, beacons, buoys, and piers, it sailed through both houses with little debate. The act called for spending federal money on local installations in the states with no more justification than to make navigation "easy and safe," yet no constitutional objection arose. Unlike transmontane canals or national systems, lighthouses and buoys were numerous, cheap, and easily distributed as patronage according to local influence. Even when tempers flared over coastal fortifications, it was more, not less, federal action that representatives demanded.[11]

More early congressional patronage derived from the postal service. Post offices and post roads were expressly reserved for congressional authority by the Constitution: Gerry had made a point of that detail in the 1787 convention. That he had in mind the perpetual distribution of legislative spoils was quickly confirmed in the second session of the First Congress, when the House refused to place the details of route selection in administrative hands. In denouncing this convenient delegation of authority, Gerry and his followers were fighting the old battle of the assembly against the magistrate. But Gerry's position had two meanings: To *antifederal* Republicans it meant keeping the union subordinate to the people and their states, while to *nationalistic* Republicans it meant checking the executive within the national empire. As long as Hamilton was a common enemy, all such partisans were brothers. Still, on the postal issue, Madison found himself squarely caught between his national vision and his opposition temperament. He urged his fellow legislators to use their power with forbearance and to place local jealousies behind them. In fact it was Madison who proposed the Maine-to-Georgia post road, the first unifying project that would have authorized federal road building in the states. Jefferson objected to Madison's highway expressly because it was a "source of boundless patronage to members of Congress and their friends."[12]

Consolidation of power was both an essential goal and a risky proposition in the Federalist years. Hamilton clearly intended his system to secure the interests of

[10] Harold C. Syrett, ed., *The Papers of Alexander Hamilton* (26 vols., New York, 1961–1979), X, 303, 310–11. James Madison, James Wilson, Benjamin Franklin, and others had tried to secure expressed powers over canals and improvements in the Constitutional Convention, but rival interests proved too likely to destroy the larger federal cause. See Harrison, "Internal Improvement Issue," 63–64.

[11] *Annals of Congress*, 1 Cong., 1 sess., July 2–Aug. 7, 1789, pp. 51–53, 619, 642–43, 659, 2160. For the discussion of coastal fortifications, see *ibid.*, 3 Cong., 1 sess., April 30, 1794, pp. 615–16; *ibid.*, 4 Cong., 2 sess., Feb. 20, 1797, pp. 2211–14.

[12] *Ibid.*, 1 Cong., 2 sess., June 16–July 22, 1790, pp. 1641–86; *ibid.*, 3 Cong., 1 sess., Feb. 17, 1794, pp. 455–56; *ibid.*, 4 Cong., 1 sess., Feb. 5–11, 1796, pp. 297–314; Jefferson to James Madison, March 6, 1796, quoted in Harrison, "Internal Improvement Issue," 127–28. See Max Farrand, ed., *The Records of the Federal Convention of 1787* (4 vols., New Haven, 1966), II, 308.

government through economic attachments that would soften the impact of politics, and it was specifically a system, not a random assemblage of laws, that Hamilton desired. Madison and Jefferson quickly rang the alarm of opposition to this attempted coup by the "monied gentry." In private they worried about logrolling, but in public they designated the overweening executive department as the greater enemy. Their "strict construction" stance originated in their opposition to the "design" (Madison's word) of Hamilton and the Federalists to "expound certain general phrases" in order to "consolidate the states" into a single sovereignty. Spelling out his fears in the Virginia Report of 1799, Madison explained how enlarging federal powers to promote "general welfare" necessarily led to greater *executive* prerogative, patronage, corruption, and tyranny. Jefferson equally condemned "transferring all the powers of the States to the general government, and all those of that government to the Executive branch." Yet each man carefully affirmed his dedication to the union because "country republicanism" easily reverted to chaotic jealous localism and disunion. The two Republican leaders sought popular sanction for their bitter opposition, while controlling the fury of the people and using it to recapture the edifice of federal power. A national union that was both federated and republican must find the middle way.[13]

In 1801 Jefferson heralded another "revolution" in government that would sweep out the usurpers, the monarchists in republican dress who, he said, had captured the federal establishment. In their place he promised true popular government, low taxes, small armies, responsible leadership, and minimal national control. His stereotypes of Federalists and Republicans were caricatures at best. Reality was more complex, and in the matter of federal internal improvements, positions were almost exactly reversed. Where Federalist leaders under Washington and Hamilton had scrupulously avoided pressing any centralized scheme for consolidation, the Jeffersonians urged comprehensive programs of public works to secure the general welfare against plunder and chaos at home and abroad. Rhetorical denials notwithstanding, after Jefferson's revolution the federal government took bolder steps toward a national system of internal improvements than Hamilton ever had dared. What accounts for the reversal?

Start with the fact that Jefferson was never opposed to internal improvements but had favored them all his life. True, he condemned Madison's post road in 1796 and an 1802 appropriation for piers in the Delaware River; but he put up no similar complaint in 1792 when Congress built a lighthouse on Chesapeake Bay, and his interest in Virginia improvements never flagged. He feared the pork barrel and corruption of the government, not the power to build nor the impact of the works themselves. As chief executive and leader of the "true" Republicans, Jefferson showed extraordinary confidence in national exertions—when they served correct

[13] [James Madison], "Report on the Virginia Resolutions," in Marvin Meyers, ed., *The Mind of the Founder: Sources of the Political Thought of James Madison* (Hanover, 1981), 237–42; Jefferson to Elbridge Gerry, Jan. 26, 1799, Paul Leicester Ford, ed., *The Works of Thomas Jefferson* (12 vols., New York, 1904–1905), IX, 17–18. See Dumas Malone, *Jefferson and His Time* (6 vols., Boston, 1948–1981), III, 395–409; and Forrest McDonald, *Alexander Hamilton: A Biography* (New York, 1979), 117–42.

ambitions. Thus in 1802 he approved Gallatin's scheme to fund a national road to Ohio from the proceeds of federal land sales in that state because it was good for the whole people, and his personal commitment to the project showed in his fury at the Pennsylvania localists who later tried to dictate the route of his national road through their wild western country.[14] Jefferson was no Hamiltonian Federalist, to be sure, but he was an expansive nationalist whose "empire of liberty" found room for Louisiana and much more. As the shade of Hamilton and his British-style politics dimmed, as the federal deficit shrank and taxes were repealed, as the Federalist judiciary sulked and the Republican party triumph grew more complete, Jefferson's positive vision of national grandeur overwhelmed once more his fear of government power.

Jefferson's second inaugural address, March 4, 1805, articulated his new confidence: "At home, fellow citizens, you best know whether we have done well or ill. The suppression of unnecessary offices, of useless establishments and expenses, enabled us to discontinue our internal taxes." Still the revenue poured in from taxes on imports. With current expenses met, the debt would soon be retired, and "the revenue thereby liberated may, by a just repartition among the States, and a corresponding amendment of the Constitution, be applied *in time of peace*, to rivers, canals, roads, arts, manufactures, education, and other great objects within each state." The message was cryptic. Even Madison wondered: "What is the amendment alluded to . . .?" Jefferson was sketching for his listeners an activist agenda of national development by republican means. In December 1806 the scheme was more fully revealed in his sixth annual message to Congress. Once more Jefferson insisted on a constitutional amendment enumerating new federal powers, but in doing so he sought clear sanction for national leadership that owed nothing to interpretation and stood above the inevitable logrolling that accompanied public works.[15]

Jefferson's program rode a wave of enthusiasm for internal improvements that by 1806 was already breaking at the feet of ambitious members of Congress. In addition to lighthouses, forts, and post roads, lawmakers considered new piers in the Delaware River, national roads to Ohio, relief to the Salem Turnpike Company, a post road to New Orleans, the Chesapeake and Delaware Canal, an Ohio River canal, a Merrimack River improvement, and a Lake Erie port bill connected with New Yorkers' plans for an interregional canal. The number of petitioners for federal aid crept steadily upward, and the number of projects in state and local hands that might reasonably appeal for help multiplied almost daily. Every petition originated

[14] Jeffersonian policy is closely traced in Harrison, "Internal Improvement Issue," 139–57, 246–51. Louisiana debates can be sampled in *Annals of Congress*, 8 Cong., 1 sess., Oct. 25–29, 1803, pp. 432–89, 497–515, 545–48; Ohio road arguments are in *ibid.*, 7 Cong., 1 sess., Jan. 28–April 28, 1802, pp. 258–96, 469, 985, 1097, 1155–62; and *ibid.*, 8 Cong., 1 sess., Nov. 28, 1803–March 24, 1804, pp. 254–301, 631, 986.

[15] Thomas Jefferson's Second Inaugural, March 4, 1805, James D. Richardson, ed., *A Compilation of the Messages and Papers of the Presidents* (20 vols., New York, 1897), I, 366–67; Jefferson to Congress, Dec. 2, 1806, *ibid.*, 397. See also Ford, ed., *Works of Thomas Jefferson*, X, 128–30, 147, 232–33, 317–19 (for Madison's question); and Harrison, "Internal Improvement Issue," 168.

in local ambitions, but proponents freely promised national benefits and the "cementing" of the Union if their particular schemes were funded. A competitive scramble for federal patronage was imminent, and Jefferson's fear of logrolling was well founded. In 1807 precisely the same concern caused Senator John Quincy Adams to begin the debate that ultimately called forth Gallatin's famous plan for a system of roads and canals.[16]

The Chesapeake and Delaware Canal was an old Philadelphia dream. Because the improvement lay in Delaware and Maryland but would benefit primarily Pennsylvania merchants, local cooperation and money had not come forward. In 1805 promoters of the canal appealed to Congress on the grounds that their interstate project served great national purposes. About the same time memorials arrived from Kentucky begging support for a canal around the falls of the Ohio at Louisville. When Kentucky Senator Henry Clay and Delaware Senator James A. Bayard discovered mutual advantages in pushing land grants for each project, John Quincy Adams sprang to his feet, charging his colleagues with shameless dealing. With a fervor that shocked even his friends, Adams accused the senators of "combining to divide the public lands, and public treasurers." Friends of the proposal cried out indignantly. The "integrity, the virtue, and the honor of the Representatives of the nation" precluded "even the idea of such a possibility." Adams found their virtue transparent. Rather than open such a pork barrel, he called for a full report from the secretary of the treasury on a national plan for internal improvements. Still smarting from the attack, Adams's colleagues voted him down, but a week later they adopted, twenty-two to three, the same resolution reworded by Ohio's Thomas Worthington.[17]

The *Report of the Secretary of the Treasury on the Subject of Roads and Canals*, published one year later by Albert Gallatin, lifted debate to a higher plane. Gallatin skillfully ignored the clash of jealous local interests, suggesting that confusion, not disharmony, inhibited progress. Neither private nor public capital was locally competent to invest where the fruits depended on simultaneous distant works: "The general government can alone remove these obstacles." Gallatin gathered detailed information on a host of existing or projected improvements, arranged them into an interlocking network, estimated their costs, and recommended the whole as a national blueprint for development. He acknowledged that the United States had no explicit authority under the Constitution to "open any road or canal, without the consent of the state" through which it passed. An amendment was in order to

[16] *Annals of Congress*, 9 Cong., 2 sess., Feb. 23–24, 1807, pp. 80–81. See also *ibid.*, 7 Cong., 1 sess., Jan. 28–April 9, 1802, pp. 465–70, 1097–1126, 1155–62; *ibid.*, 7 Cong., 2 sess., Jan. 31, 1803, p. 447; *ibid.*, 8 Cong., 1 sess., Nov. 28, 1803–Feb. 7, 1804, pp. 254, 631, 786, 986; *ibid.*, 8 Cong., 2 sess., Jan. 18–March 2, 1805, pp. 38, 43, 54, 70; *ibid.*, 9 Cong., 1 sess., Jan. 28–April 12, 1806, pp. 74, 192, 235, 448, 534–36, 827. John Quincy Adams's remarks were not recorded, but Samuel White's reply, quoted here, restated Adams's sentiments. See additional verification in Everett Somerville Brown, ed., *William Plumer's Memorandum of Proceedings in the United States Senate, 1803–1807* (Ann Arbor, 1923), 628–30; and John Quincy Adams, *Memoirs*, ed. Charles Francis Adams (12 vols., Philadelphia, 1874–1877), I, 460–61.

[17] *Annals of Congress*, 9 Cong., 1 sess., March 5, 1806, p. 537; *ibid.*, 9 Cong., 2 sess., Feb. 23–March 2, 1807, pp. 77–78, 97. See Gray, *National Waterway*, 1–27.

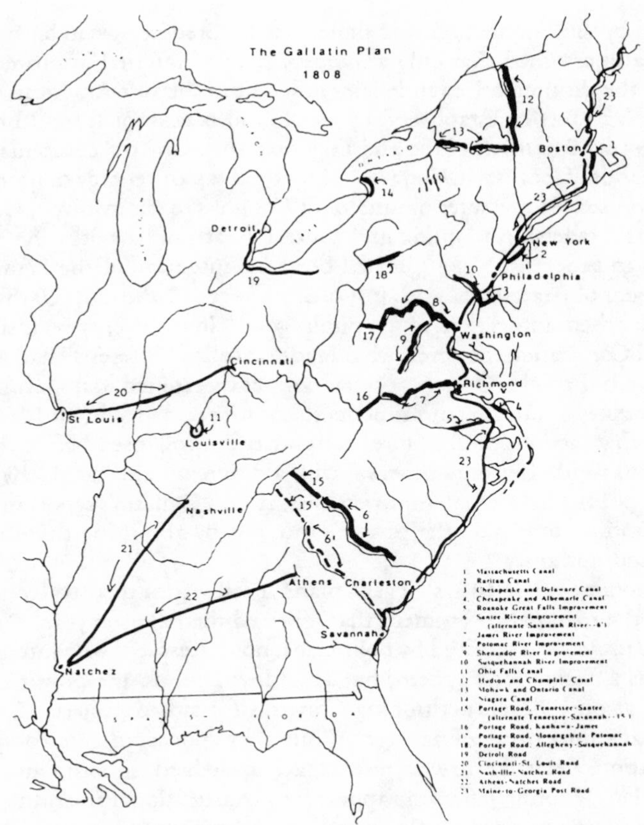

remove this "impediment to a national plan," but while constitutional reform was pending, there were ways to aid immediate works. He closed by reasserting that a national plan was "best calculated to suppress every bias of partiality to particular objects." "The national legislature alone," he concluded, "embracing every local interest, and superior to every local consideration, is competent to the selection of such national objects." Here Gallatin claimed for Congress the transcendent authority that Hamilton had thought it impolitic to seize, the power to neutralize local jealousies with a grand design.[18]

Gallatin's report embodied the Jeffersonian alternative to national development

[18] Albert Gallatin, *Report of the Secretary of the Treasury on the Subject of Roads and Canals* (1808; reprint, New York, 1968), 7, 73–75. The plan called for a great coastal waterway cutting the several barriers along the Atlantic shore, four interregional connections between Atlantic ports and the western rivers, and three canals connecting the Atlantic with the St. Lawrence River and the Great Lakes. Feeder lines of roads and canals could be added by local or private enterprise to fill out the network.

controlled by the "monied gentry" alone. Like his predecessors in both political parties, Gallatin assumed that only a *national* plan of internal improvements would overcome the disintegrative tendencies inherent in the vast American union. However, his plan must be established by republican means, or it would not be borne by the people. Popular rhetoric and lingering antipathy to "consolidation" played into the hands of localists in Congress who would tap the energy of union for narrow selfish purposes. As pressures mounted for Congress to get involved, Gallatin called for national leadership to guide and control great public works. As Madison had explained in Federalist No. 10, it had been the intention of the Framers to create a government of "statesmen" with just such a power to "adjust the clashing interests" and "render them subservient to the public good." In the twenty years since the Constitutional Convention, however, what Madison called "interests" had all but driven "virtue" from the field. Overtly popular politics threatened to undermine the legislative process with literal commitments to constituents' needs, and Madison's original hope that factions would cancel each other out collapsed before the likelihood that factions would buy each other off with aid to roads and canals. By substituting design for politics in internal improvements, Albert Gallatin's report sought to avert such corruption, to elevate the people's interests by absorbing them into national purpose and authority.[19]

What became of Gallatin's elegant plan? It fell victim to a steady erosion of authority in the national government that followed the Jefferson years. *The Report on Roads and Canals* was received by politicians, not statesmen, who interpreted it, not so much as a design for a system, but as an invitation to the public trough. Local improvers at once began petitioning Congress for aid to projects that served primarily local competitive advantages. While they sponsored true components of a transportation network, few improvers acknowledged subordination to an integrated plan. Ignoring Jefferson's appeal for a constitutional amendment, state and national lawmakers seized on the expedient devices suggested by Gallatin for immediate federal action, and the scramble was on.[20]

New York State, not surprisingly, was first in line in the campaign for federal aid. Possessed of an excellent harbor and port city, the penetrating Hudson River, and the water-level route to the Great Lakes, New York enjoyed a confidence about its future and an indifference to the Union that dated back to the Confederation. By 1808 state plans for canals to Lakes Erie and Ontario were well advanced, and while these projects were truly national works, they also promised New York City a permanent hold on America's rising commerce. Any federal aid to New York's canals was sure to inspire jealousy among rival Atlantic states. In 1810 Peter B. Porter, the state's westernmost congressman, urged the interregional canal as a *western* demand that,

[19] Jacob Ernest Cooke, ed., *The Federalist* (Middletown, 1969), 60, 64. See Harrison, "Internal Improvement Issue," 223.

[20] Petitions begging federal aid for local improvements (except postal petitions) were rare before 1808, but they increased steadily thereafter until the 1830s, when they exceeded fifty per year. Petitions were noticed, but not usually printed, in the journals of each house; many extant petitions for the Fourteenth Congress and after are collected in *American State Papers* (38 vols., Washington, 1832–1861).

unmet, might engender separation from the Union. The antidote lay in federal action. With the aid of the engineer Benjamin Latrobe, he assembled a bill for a system of roads and canals that patronized all geographical interests *except* those main water routes to the West that competed with New York's canal. In December 1811 the state's leading canal boosters, Gouverneur Morris (a Federalist improver of long standing) and De Witt Clinton (a Republican but no friend of James Madison), descended on Washington to line up support. President Madison received them cordially and forwarded their plea to the Congress, but he used the occasion to remind the legislature of the "signal advantages to be derived to the United States from a general system of internal communication and conveyance." The president's meaning was probably clear: No bill that ignored the Potomac route was really a "general system." The Erie Canal was primarily a New York improvement, and Congress, pleading penury and the threat of war, declined to grant it such exclusive favor.[21]

The enthusiasm for public works stimulated by Gallatin's *Report* extended far beyond New York. Among the projects whose supporters begged federal assistance before the War of 1812 were numbered the Middlesex Canal in Massachusetts; the New London Turnpike in Connecticut; the Erie Canal and Highland Turnpike in New York; the Union Canal, two turnpikes, and a bridge in Pennsylvania; the long-suffering Chesapeake and Delaware Canal; two bridges and a turnpike in Maryland; the Potomac Company and the Alexandria Turnpike Company in Virginia; the Catawba and Wateree river improvements in the Carolinas; the Ohio Canal Company; the Carondelet Canal at New Orleans; and a host of roads in the western states and territories. All of these petitioners conjured up national significance for their particular projects, but none recognized the selectivity and coordination that made Gallatin's plan a system. Narrow calculations of local interest undercut every design. Some residents of Detroit and upstate New York, for example, declined to support their own Erie Canal because trade through Montreal was good. Public enthusiasm for roads and canals was clearly not the same as commitment to a system or to the federal authority to create one.[22]

Deteriorating politics and war gradually paralyzed the Madison administration, while politicians seized influence where they could in Congress and outdoors. New England, stung by the Embargo Act of 1807, withdrew altogether over Madison's stubborn policy of commercial restriction. De Witt Clinton's New York Republicans had fused with the Federalists to promote canals and to challenge Virginia's dynasty. They demanded war instead of embargo, and they denounced Madison's intentions to conquer Canada (all the while trading through Canada with the British in violation of the embargo they said was ruining them). Pennsylvania Republicans dis-

[21] *Annals of Congress*, 11 Cong., 1 sess., Jan. 5–Feb. 8, 1810, pp. 522–25, 1388; Madison to Congress, Dec. 23, 1811, in Richardson, ed., *Messages*, II, 428. See also Shaw, *Erie Water West*, 45–48; and Harrison, "Internal Improvement Issue," 267–75.

[22] Evidence is scattered throughout *Annals of Congress*, 11 and 12 Congresses. For a coherent discussion of state and local progress, see Harrison, "Internal Improvement Issue," 300–378; the Detroit example is from Shaw, *Erie Water West*, 48.

solved into bitter factions, some driven only by a blind hatred for Gallatin. Madison had none of the charisma with which Jefferson had ruled his unruly followers. Westerners demanded war and protection from Indians, but they proved unwilling to take orders from Washington. Even Virginia Republicans quarreled openly. Young men in the capital city, like Clay and Calhoun, watched the Virginia gentry lose control of national politics, and they trimmed their sails accordingly. Madison's secretary of war, John Armstrong of New York, refused to defend the capital, and with the burning of Washington in August 1814, federal prestige collapsed. Congressmen demanded for their constituents local defenses at federal expense. Banks dictated terms to their sovereign government. Madison was forced in the end to distort military strategy and pay for state troops he could not command because local politicians abetted by local bankers would have it no other way. Behind it all lay a new style of politics, more "actual" in representation, more local in orientation, and more participatory than even before. The democratization that had frightened the founders into writing the Constitution was catching up with them once more, while the isolation achieved by distance in the "extended sphere of government" dissolved.[23]

The war brought near ruin to the national executive and wrecked the president's faith in politics, but peace gave Madison new hope. Determined to put the best face on his war and his leadership, Madison dismissed his own disgrace as proof that republican government could be led through world war without imperial abuses of power. He rebuilt his cabinet and tried once more to assert the kind of nonpartisan leadership that he identified as the genius of the American presidency. In his almost buoyant message to Congress in December 1815, he praised the conditions of peace and confidently asked for a new national bank, protective tariffs, a reformed and efficient military establishment, coastal defense works, a national university, and the construction of national roads and canals for the purpose of "systematically completing" the "inestimable" work begun in the states. It was a "happy reflection," he continued, that "any defect of constitutional authority" for building roads and canals, could be "supplied in a mode which the Constitution itself" provided. Madison hoped the last year of his presidency would be joyous.[24]

Madison's hope for the nation depended on restoring "disinterested" government, but his confidence was an illusion, and national politics were out of his control. Few high-minded statesmen stalked the halls of Congress, and no effort of the president's was likely to restore transcendent vision. Henry Clay had spent the war in the Speaker's chair in Congress and at the peace tables at Ghent, and he thought he understood the political climate. From the Battle of New Orleans Andrew

[23] The tenuous importance of the national government was first demonstrated in James Sterling Young, *The Washington Community, 1800–1828* (New York, 1966); it is reiterated in Wiebe, *Opening of American Society*. See also Gordon S. Wood, *The Creation of the American Republic, 1776–1787* (Chapel Hill, 1969), 571–78; Gordon S. Wood, "Interests and Disinterestedness in the Making of the Constitution," in *Beyond Confederation: Origins of the Constitution and the American National Identity*, ed. Richard Beeman et al. (Chapel Hill, 1987), 69–109; and Stagg, *Mr. Madison's War*, 1–176.

[24] Madison to Congress, Dec. 5, 1815, Richardson, ed., *Messages*, II, 552–53

Jackson had learned something quite different about the politics of victory. John C. Calhoun had been in Congress to the end, proving his own disregard for Madison's leadership by spearheading the movement *against* the bank the president wanted and *for* one he was compelled to veto. Madison had hoped to rule at last like Jefferson, by deferring to a Congress which in turn deferred to him—but it would never be. The Fourteenth Congress knew nothing of deference, and only when the voters themselves forcibly retired its members in punishment for the tactless Compensation Bill did anyone realize the extent to which power had exploded out of doors.[25]

The Bonus Bill of 1817, which climaxed the Jeffersonian movement for a national system of roads and canals, was a product of that political disintegration. National pride ran high that year, and the lessons of the late war impressed many congressmen with the frailty of the Union, but real power was now lodged firmly in state political establishments. When Calhoun announced his desire to "bind the republic together with a perfect system of roads and canals," he envisioned the old nationalists' dream of systematic development. But Calhoun must have known that a central plan would be harder than ever to win. His Bonus Bill, as proposed, did not even try to establish the system that Gallatin's plan designed. It called for a fund to aid improvements but not for the power to select, locate, or build public works in the states. Indeed Calhoun and his friends readily admitted that as soon as they brought in the map and specified the routes, the bill could not be passed. All Calhoun and his allies apparently wanted was a permanent fund from which they might support improvements without drawing fresh attacks by their enemies on annual appropriations bills. The Cumberland Road already suffered from possible extinction, and no larger system of roads and canals could proceed in the face of such uncertainty.[26]

During its first session, the Fourteenth Congress did not act on internal improvements, so in December 1816 President Madison reiterated his desires in his eighth annual message. "I particularly invite again their attention," he wrote, "to the expediency of exercising their existing powers, and, where necessary, of resorting to the prescribed mode of enlarging them, in order to effectuate a comprehensive system of roads and canals, such as will have the effect of drawing more closely together every part of our country by promoting intercourse and improvements and by increasing the share of every part in the common stock of national prosperity." After this explicit and forceful invitation the chief executive fell silent. Calhoun got up a committee and introduced his Bonus Bill two days before Christmas. The idea was to pledge the bonus due the government from the new national bank and the United States's share of the bank's dividends to a permanent fund for "constructing

[25] Stagg, *Mr. Madison's War*, 419–68; Young, *Washington Community*, 179–212; Ketcham, *Presidents above Party*, 100–123, 171–76; Wiebe, *Opening of American Society*, 7–20, 35–66; C. Edward Skeen, "'Vox Populi, Vox Dei': The Compensation Act of 1816 and the Rise of Popular Politics," *Journal of the Early Republic*, 6 (Fall 1986), 253–74.

[26] *Annals of Congress*, 14 Cong., 2 sess., Feb. 4, 1817, p. 854. See also Cumberland Road debates, *ibid.*, 14 Cong., 1 sess., Jan. 9–April 2, 1816, pp. 514, 1211, 1250–52, 1308.

The National Road near its eastern starting point, Cumberland, Md.
Courtesy National Archives.

roads and canals . . . subject to such specific appropriations, in that respect, as Congress may hereafter make."[27]

The House was slow to take up the bill. Finally, on February 4, Calhoun rose to present his case. The "indisposition" of the House even to take up the matter worried him, but the importance of the issue and a perfect constellation of conditions sustained his hope. Party and sectional feeling, he began, were "immerged in a liberal and enlightened regard to the general concerns of the nation." Peace prevailed and revenues abounded; the time was right to embark on internal improvements. Nothing promised so great advantage to the "wealth, the strength, and the political prosperity" of the country as good roads and canals. State and private efforts were important, but certain crucial projects were either too expensive or stimulated too much "rival jealousy of the States" to be completed without national direction.

According to Calhoun, pecuniary or commercial advantage was not the most compelling reason for establishing the system. The *political* health of the republic was at stake, and the experience of the late war had shown too well how fragmented and particular were the American people. "No country enjoying freedom, ever occupied anything like as great an extent of country as this Republic," he argued. Distance fostered the threat of disunion, and Calhoun felt a "most imperious obligation to counteract" every such tendency. Whatever impeded "the intercourse of the

[27] Madison to Congress, Dec. 3, 1816, Richardson, ed., *Messages*, II, 561; James F. Hopkins, ed., *The Papers of Henry Clay* (8 vols., Lexington, Ky., 1959–1984), II, 259; Robert L. Meriwether and W. Edwin Hamphill, eds., *The Papers of John C. Calhoun* (16 vols., Columbia, S.C., 1959–1985), I, 367–68, 372; *Annals of Congress*, 14 Cong., 2 sess., Dec. 16, 1816, p. 296.

extremes with this, the centre of the Republic"—whatever compromised the effectiveness of the federal government at a distance—weakened the Union. "To legislate for our country," he concluded, required, not the "selfish instincts of our nature," but "the most enlarged views" and a "species of self-devotion not exacted in any other" form of government.

What objections to a system could be raised? Some congressmen might feel the lack of constitutional authority to build roads and canals in the states. Out of order, ruled Calhoun. His bill appropriated money only: No real work was contemplated anywhere. But roads and canals were not enumerated among the objects of federal appropriations. Of course they were, replied Calhoun. The first power of Congress was to provide for the common defense and general welfare of the United States, and what more clearly served those objects than national internal improvements? The Constitution, he continued, "was not intended as a thesis for the logician to exercise his ingenuity on. It ought to be construed with plain good sense." Congresses since the very first had appropriated money for objects not enumerated but contributing to defense or the general welfare, and those precedents furnished "better evidence of the true interpretation of the Constitution than the most refined and subtle arguments." Another complaint was raised, that the bill wrongly placed the fund before the system, so that men knew not what they were buying. Calhoun disagreed. It was proper, or at least practicable, to set apart money first. "A bill filled with details would have but faint prospect of passing. The enemies to any possible system in detail and those who are opposed in principle, would unite and defeat it."[28]

Calhoun spoke sincerely in the developmental rhetoric republican nationalists had cherished since the Revolution, but two novel points emerged in his arguments. First, for the young Calhoun the Constitution was meaningful only if it facilitated the survival and practice of government. He could not imagine constitutional restrictions that endangered the Union itself. Many postwar nationalists in Congress agreed. Second, what was politically expedient was indistinguishable in his mind from what was natural and proper: The fund must precede the system because rival interests would lay waste any detailed design. Finally, in a shrewd blend of virtuous rhetoric and practical politics, he urged that the Fourteenth Congress get the credit for establishing the national system. "No body of men," he thought, "ever better merited the confidence of the country." They had been slandered by the public over the Compensation Bill, and Calhoun wished to restore their reputation (and, presumably, to rescue congressional prestige) by adding internal improvements to "the many useful measures already adopted." In much the same way Madison tried to rescue leadership by setting out a positive national agenda, Calhoun was trying to bind the people to their federal government before state and local politics completely mastered their allegiances.[29]

[28] *Annals of Congress*, 14 Cong., 2 sess., Feb. 4, 1817, pp. 851–58.
[29] *Ibid.*, p. 858.

The Old House of Representatives by Samuel F. B. Morse, 1821.
In the Collection of the Corcoran Gallery of Art, Museum Purchase, Gallery Fund.

Responses to Calhoun's arguments occupied the House all week. Friends of the bill identified different sources of congressional authority to undertake such activities: the general welfare clause, the commerce clause, or the several defense provisions. Some opponents complained bitterly that they had no system to vote on, even if they were favorably inclined to support specific improvements. Thomas Bolling Robertson of Louisiana blasted Calhoun's entire premise, pointing out that equal benefits had been offered by history's greatest tyrants. Expediency did not make the system safe or republican! Give the money to the states, he concluded, where people will know best what is to be done. That would prevent the "disgraceful scene" that surely would follow, "when we shall be called upon to designate the position and course of the contemplated roads and canals, when all our local feelings will be up in arms, and, under a pretense of a general benefit, we shall have in view exclusively the interests of the State or district which we represent." Penetrating even further to the heart of political anxiety, Robertson warned that this bill promised what was "anxiously wished by many—one grand, magnificent, consolidated empire."[30]

Robertson shaped his damaging comments into an amendment that distributed funds directly to the states according to population. Henry Clay descended from the speaker's chair to oppose the change. Proportional spending destroyed the potential for a system because funds could not be concentrated for national objectives. Clay was absolutely right, but Calhoun accepted the change in order to keep

[30] *Ibid.*, p. 865.

debate alive. Timothy Pickering of Massachusetts inserted "with the consent of the State" into a substitute motion, which Calhoun denounced as ruining the bill. State consent, like proportional spending, stripped away federal power to design and direct internal improvements, but Calhoun again relented. Even after thus destroying the bill's most powerful features, members still approached the idea cautiously. In the end the bill passed by only two votes.[31]

In its final form the Bonus Bill was almost useless as a basis for a national system of internal improvements, and yet Clay and Calhoun clung to it, heralded its passage, and proudly laid it before the president three days before his term expired. On March 2, at a farewell reception at the White House, Madison stunned the bill's young sponsor with news that he would veto it. The next day, in extraordinary desperation, Clay sent a confidential letter to Madison begging a reprieve: "Knowing that we cannot differ on the question of the *object* of the Internal Improvements bill, however we may on the Constitutional point, will you excuse me for respectfully suggesting whether you could not leave the bill to your successor?"[32] What Clay may not have understood, and what historians have always overlooked, was that he and Madison differed fundamentally on the *effect* of the new bill, if not its object. In their desperation to get authority into national hands in Congress, Clay and Calhoun had accepted a bill with no power to control local spoilsmen except by balancing their greed in legislative packages. Perhaps they believed the bill was the first step toward achieving Gallatin's plan, but Madison saw in it the worst of all possible corruptions.

Madison vetoed the Bonus Bill because he felt an "insuperable difficulty" in "reconciling the bill with the Constitution." The Washington community was justifiably surprised. The president's nationalism had risen steadily since Jefferson's election and seemed perfectly in tune with the same sentiments in Congress. His last several messages to Congress seemed to beg for energetic government, while his most recent veto had raised only tentative objections, which he invited Congress to override. As was his habit, Madison had said nothing while the bill was debated, and everyone assumed that Calhoun's work met with the president's pleasure. It did not. Madison attacked the Bonus Bill, not because it sought to build a system of roads and canals, but because it introduced a means to do so that placed in jeopardy once more the balanced federal system of government.[33]

According to the president, Congress possessed neither constitutional permission nor a strong enough precedent to construct roads and canals in the states. Such a power could not be "deduced," he argued, without an "inadmissible latitude of construction." Such latitude threatened the "definite partition" between the "General and State Governments" on which the "permanent success of the Constitution" de-

[31] *Ibid.*, Feb. 4–6, 1817, pp. 866–70, 876–94.

[32] Wiltse, *John C. Calhoun*, 137; Henry Clay to Madison, March 3, 1817, Hopkins, ed., *Papers of Henry Clay*, II, 322.

[33] "I console myself with the reflection that if [these objections] have not the weight which I attach to them they can be constitutionally overruled." Madison to Congress, Jan. 30, 1815, Richardson, ed., *Messages*, II, 540. See also Madison to Congress, March 3, 1817, *ibid.*, II, 569–70.

pended. This time Madison did not invite Congress to override his scruples; instead he directed them to the "safe and practicable mode" of constitutional amendment. Such rigid strict construction hailed from the bitter days of opposition to the centralizing Federalists, and it did not harmonize with Madison's confident and flexible republicanism of the past sixteen years. Just two years before he had dismissed constitutional objections to the national bank on the simple ground that legislators approved it, presidents and judges (all Federalists) upheld it, investors found it useful, and the "general will of the nation" seemed to concur. Suddenly in 1817 he denounced his own post road arguments of twenty years past, Jefferson's Cumberland Road, and all the accumulated improvements in rivers, harbors, and fortifications as inadequate precedents to sustain a similar reading of the Constitution. The positive spirit of nationalism that had brought him and Jefferson to embrace protective tariffs and the second bank abruptly disappeared behind a firm conviction that the Bonus Bill gave to Congress a "general power of legislation" that no state, no court, no executive could restrain.[34]

What had triggered Madison's reaction? Part of the answer lay in the provisions of the bill itself. Specifying no plan or projects to be funded, and guaranteeing proportional spending according to population in the states, the bill could not discriminate among improvements or unify the network. It was a bad bill, which could accomplish almost none of the control and design the older improvers wanted. Madison called it "very extraordinary" in a brief letter to Jefferson. Gallatin later denounced it. Jefferson, busy singing the praises of American improvements to his friends around the world, condemned the Bonus Bill as threatening to "loosen all the bands of the constitution." Jefferson believed (wrongly) that once asked for an amendment, the states would "certainly concede the power." In the meantime, he explained to Gallatin, a limited reading of the general welfare clause was "almost the only landmark which now divides the federalists from the republicans."[35]

Here was a mirror image of the crisis of 1798. At that time Jefferson and Madison had feared the usurpation of authority by the executive for purposes that contravened their own visions of the nation. They had sought refuge in the states and in the legislative branch of the federal government, where their influence happened to be growing. Now in 1817 they saw usurpation by the Congress, which was using Hamilton's broad construction to advance a bill that did not achieve the object of their nationalist dreams. To Madison the risk outweighed the gain. From the beginning of the Republic he had placed his faith in the balance of powers and interests. In the federal Constitution national power exactly matched the jealous sovereignties of the states, while internal checks on power among state and federal branches minimized the chances for corruption. Outside constitutional control lay the passions of the people, but here Madison seized on the large size of the republic as

[34] Madison to Congress, March 3, 1817, *ibid.*, 569–70.

[35] Madison to Jefferson, Feb. 15, 1817, *The Letters and Other Writings of James Madison* (4 vols., New York, 1884), III, 35. See also Henry Adams, ed., *The Writings of Albert Gallatin* (1879; reprint, 3 vols., New York, 1960), II, 54; Ford, ed., *Works of Thomas Jefferson*, XII, 58–59, 61–63, 69, 71–73.

its saving feature. "Factious leaders may kindle a flame within their particular States," he wrote in Federalist No. 10, but they could not "spread a general conflagration." The equipoise was precise and easily disturbed. Against elite consolidation in the Federalist years, Madison and Jefferson had launched their opposition, a "general conflagration" that swept them into office. Once in power they struggled with diminishing success against the "factious" independence of the people out of doors. Madison shifted with the times, but only to preserve the balance. After thirty years his faith was still tentative. He wrote to John Adams in 1817 that the "great question now to be decided" was whether there were "checks and balances sufficient for the purposes of order, justice, and the general good" in the rapidly growing republic. More than ever outdoor partisan behavior looked like factious combination, while special interest issues like banks, tariffs, and internal improvements everywhere corrupted the legislative process.[36]

The Bonus Bill threatened the balance that was the heart of Madison's constitution. Nothing prevented lawmakers from using the funds it would establish to cultivate majorities and to dominate the Congress contrary to public interest. Proportional spending protected nothing and even fostered something-for-everyone distributions. State consent was equally absurd: What state could long refuse benefits that flowed toward its neighbors? Presidents and experts would be powerless to impose order or fairness on the networks of trade. The strong would crush the weak, and while states plundered the federal treasury, politicians would erect nationwide factions on the backs of public works. The only check on such conspiracies was the constitutional limit on federal sovereignty, enforced by executive veto or judicial review. The Bonus Bill, as Madison interpreted it, claimed complete legislative authority over the welfare of the people. If his interpretation was true, all powers touching the general welfare, "not specifically exempted," belonged supremely to Congress, and the balance was destroyed. Consolidation and corruption must follow. Madison's veto called up the spirited language of 1798 because he thought he saw the enemies of liberty returning.[37]

Madison's fears were not unfounded, but they were cast in terms that were rapidly losing their meaning. The very potential for "corruption" that worried Madison so was the only plausible reason Calhoun and Clay wished to see the Bonus Bill survive. Earnest nationalists at this juncture, both men wanted to consolidate the Union with a system of roads and canals, and they would play the game of politics to achieve that end. They had seen the nation suffer in the War of 1812. They understood the petty localism that blocked important measures for defense, cooperation, and growth. They genuinely believed that the Union would collapse if its parts were not soon forcibly bound together. They were less inclined than their elders to mea-

[36] Madison to John Adams, May 22, 1817, in *Letters and Other Writings of James Madison*, III, 42; Cooke, ed., *Federalist*, 64. On contrasting political models, see Ketcham, *Presidents above Party*; Hofstadter, *Idea of a Party System*; and Richard P. McCormick, *The Second American Party System: Party Formation in the Jacksonian Era* (Chapel Hill, 1966).

[37] Madison to Congress, March 3, 1817, Richardson, ed., *Messages*, II, 569–70. See also *Annals of Congress*, 14 Cong., 2 sess., Feb 4, 1817, p. 179; *ibid.*, Feb. 26, 1817, pp. 862–70.

sure the Constitution against classical ideals and abstract truths, and they said so bluntly in Congress. They were not afraid of popular politics because they knew how they worked. Progress was their goal, and both men believed that progress for themselves and their nation depended on quick, energetic federal action. In the Fourteenth Congress there were enemies enough to a general system of roads and canals that no single design or constitutional amendment could be passed. The way to break the combination of antiprogressive ideologues and jealous localists was to lure them in with money. With the Bonus Bill in hand, skillful politicians like Clay and Calhoun hoped to bind the republic together with public works, federal patronage, and political influence. In the language of the past, that was corruption, to be sure; now they called it politics, and nearly all the people played.

A national system of internal improvements promised to consolidate the union of the United States, and that is precisely why no program ever passed. Too few people desired such a national union. Neither the Federalist image of benevolent gentry endowing their people with roads and canals, nor the Republican alternative of a government plan defining the field for local competition, survived the experiment in self-government that began with the Constitution. Rapidly expanding economic opportunities and the decline of social hierarchy and deference stripped liberty of its classical restraints. As freedom spread to the many ranks and places in American society, the imposition of order from the top became impossible. The national system of roads and canals was designed to impose such order and control, and even the Bonus Bill in its original form looked toward national objectives greater than the sum of local desires. Fearing consolidaton at the hands of distant elites, or jealous of local advantages, most congressmen refused to vest that authority in the president or any other agents who might injure their interests at home.[38]

Why people feared the national system is somewhat more complex. From revolutionary rhetoric and the partisan campaigns of Jefferson's Republicans, congressmen had learned to fear consolidation. While they were defending liberty against an overbearing empire, that revolutionary instinct had served Americans well, but during Washington's era it seemed as much a menace to union as a guardian of freedom. To wrest power from the Federalists, Jefferson once more denounced government and sought unity out of doors among the people. The speed with which democratization followed astonished everyone, and by 1817 genuine nationalists like Clay and Calhoun believed that federal power itself was in jeopardy. In the coming age a democratic people would only follow governments that met popular needs without infringing on popular liberties. Roads and canals were among those needs; if such improvements were to serve national, not local, purposes, then the federal government had better pay for them and take the credit. When national systems like the Gallatin plan continually failed in Congress, Clay and Calhoun settled for a scheme they thought gave them influence, if not control, in developmental poli-

[38] My arguments here complement the larger synthesis offered by Wiebe, *Opening of American Society*, 194–252.

tics. On the edge of victory they were stopped by the president, whose dread of corruption was older than their worries of disunion.

Madison vetoed, not the Gallatin plan, but the political alternative to gentry leadership and national design that Clay and Calhoun had crafted. The kind of interest group politics that the Bonus Bill invited was the last thing Madison wished to see in his ideal federal union. He could not distinguish between democratization and corruption, and the readiness of men like Calhoun to sacrifice theory to the clamoring of interests horrified the author of the Constitution. Madison's vision of the nation had always been focused through Virginia's special lens, and he faltered at the prospect of power in other people's hands. He went home to the Old Dominion, where politics was still a gentleman's game. There he moved steadily toward an insistence on the Framers' intent as the one sure guide to the Constitution; yet he of all people knew there was no single voice at that convention, only compromise and politics. Like Jefferson he took refuge in the states' rights bias that swept Virginia and the South, pretending it was true orthodoxy and not the selfish particularism that, in the hands of local "quids," it had been all along.[39]

After 1817 Congress debated internal improvements almost every year for a generation. Roads and canals were built everywhere, some with federal aid in the form of land grants and stock subscriptions. In 1824 a General Survey Bill (which had been Gallatin's first step) charged the army engineers with laying technical foundations for an integrated network. But Congress never let the experts' designs interfere with politics and popular sentiment, which ran the other way. Americans never did adopt a purposeful *system* of internal improvements the object of which was to secure the Union or perfect the national republic. Instead they built a multitude of public works serving local and private profit-seeking interests. Clay tried to build a national party around his integrated vision, but his system was condemned as elitist, Federalist, and antiliberal. As secretary of war, Calhoun seized an opportunity to build roads and canals "for defense" without congressional approval, before he turned against the nation altogether. James Monroe confused the issue further when he sustained Calhoun's administrative projects while vetoing bills for the repair and extension of Jefferson's National Road. Monroe produced a paper, twenty-five thousand words long, explaining his excruciating views on internal improvements, but he never comprehended the essential point.[40]

[39] See, for example, Madison to Spencer Roane, May 6, 1821, *Letters and Other Writings of James Madison*, III, 217–22.

[40] Henry Clay's efforts can be traced best in the *Annals of Congress*, with bitter commentary provided in Adams, *Memoirs*, ed. Adams, IV, 31, 38; and Worthington Chauncey Ford, ed., *Writings of John Quincy Adams* (7 vols., New York, 1913–1917), VI, 338–39. Calhoun's program as secretary of war appears in Meriwether and Hemphill, eds., *Papers of John C. Calhoun*, I, 410–13; II, 17, 78, 226, 325; III, 66, 173, 315, 479; see also Forrest G. Hill, *Roads, Rails, and Waterways: The Army Engineers and Early Transportation* (Norman, 1957), 3–56. For James Monroe's veto of the Cumberland Road Bill and his state paper on internal improvements, see Richardson, ed., *Messages*, II, 711–52. For a sketch of later congressional action, see Curtis Nettels, "The Mississippi Valley and the Constitution, 1815–29," *Mississippi Valley Historical Review*, 11 (Dec. 1924), 332–57.

It was John Quincy Adams who eventually recaptured the question in its original terms: Foreign nations, "less blessed with that freedom which is power," he told the Nineteenth Congress in 1825, had made "gigantic strides" in public improvements, and if we folded our arms and proclaimed to the world "that we are palsied by the will of our constituents," we would be casting away the "bounties of Providence" and dooming the United States to "perpetual inferiority." In his private correspondence, Adams imagined a strong national government and systematic improvements that would forge a continental republic "filled with a mighty people, marching under one flag, speaking one language, living one way of life and liberty, with capabilities of freedom and power such as associated man had never before witnessed on this earth." The rhetoric recalled the nationalist hyperbole of the 1780s, but unlike Washington's hazy images of humble farmers flooding the Ohio Valley, Adams's vision posed a stark and real alternative to the "palsied" confederation the nation had become. Furthermore, by 1825 southern conservatives like John Randolph of Virginia had already identified dangers in consolidation more palpable than Madison's fear of corruption: Mr. Adams's kind of Congress could "emancipate every slave in the United States."[41]

Adams's vision failed where the nationalism of his father's generation succeeded for two important reasons. First, the nation he envisioned was more tangible and present than anything imaginable at the founding of the Republic. The Erie Canal was a reality, and crews of engineers swarmed across the nation plotting waterways and turnpikes. Fears that conspirators might exploit federal power unfairly and gain a permanent advantage in the geographic universe of the new Republic daily gained credibility. Gallatin's plan had been scrupulously designed to allay just such fears. But even then Virginians had seen only the Potomac as the centerpiece of union, the New Yorkers only the Erie route, while representatives of other places had feared the triumph of either. A *general* plan reflecting a true national consensus would eliminate the danger, but as politics evolved toward more literal democracy, elite leaders such as Madison saw nothing but corruption in the legislature's work.

The second reason developed from the first. As the transportation revolution became daily more manifest, the contest for advantage grew more desperate. If a national design were ever to prevail, Congress would require sufficient power to impose without permission those links and components that jealous neighbors resisted for purely local reasons. In a paper union governed by elite gentlemen whose word one presumed to be binding, such a power might be trusted to the general government. But technology increased the force with which the union might be bound. In a clamorous democracy, where representatives responded to the passions of majorities at home, such a power in Congress too easily was turned on other topics of local jealousy—like slavery. Compromises hammered out by gentlemen now dead offered

[41] Adams to Congress, Dec. 6, 1825, in Richardson, ed., *Messages*, II, 882; Ford, ed., *Writings of John Quincy Adams*, VII, 312. See Bemis, *Adams and the Union*, 55–70; and Mary W. M. Hargreaves, *The Presidency of John Quincy Adams* (Lawrence, 1985), 165–88. John Randolph's words are from *Annals of Congress*, 18 Cong., 1 sess., Jan. 30, 1824, p. 1308.

scant protection from those rising possibilities. With Madison and Jefferson back in opposition, the original nationalist vision expired. Their true heir was John Quincy Adams, but when he told the Nineteenth Congress to use all the authority the Framers had intended in behalf of public works the people seemed to want, both the aging Framers and the people denounced him. Frightened by progress and popular rule, the first Republicans turned their backs on the confident national vision they had long ago inspired. In a final act of deference to the rhetoric of old, the people did the same.

The Bonus Bill veto alone did not cause Adams's discomfort, nor did it ruin Clay or Calhoun, nor did it destroy the Gallatin plan. What Madison's veto did was to turn once more that revolutionary fear of corruption and consolidation against the crumbling remains of energetic national government on which hopes for development of the Union rested. Through the Monroe, Adams, and Jackson years local interests still hounded Congress for grants-in-aid to all kinds of internal improvements, but as each part of the network progressed they saw less need for integrated design. Capitalizing on the lesson of the Bonus Bill, Andrew Jackson seized the Jeffersonian persuasion and made local autonomy the great virtue of his creed. He flattered the sentiments of a free electorate with the rhetoric of liberty. He made war on the bank and systematic tariffs, leaving Clay's American System in tatters, while he delivered such particular tariffs, roads, canals, and improvements as his loyal voters required. Under Jackson national purpose became little more than a license for local development, and he shrewdly lodged custody of this conviction in a political party that lay wholly outside the Constitution. The Bonus Bill veto did not bring Andrew Jackson to power. But he rode into office on precisely those forces that the Bonus Bill and the national system of roads and canals originally sought to restrain, before the national government lost control of the real work of the age.

The Founding of West Point

JEFFERSON AND THE POLITICS OF SECURITY

THEODORE JOSEPH CRACKEL
Army War College

In light of the extensive historiographic debate concerning the presidency of Thomas Jefferson, it is quite remarkable that with regard to his military policy historians have found themselves in substantial agreement. This is all the more remarkable because a president and his military policy are topics that usually invite debate. In this case, however, historians have so uniformly subscribed to a single view that it has become a commonplace. Jefferson—that interpretation goes—out of fear of a standing army and with a Republican regard for economy, reduced the regular establishment, consigned the remnants to the frontier, and then ignored it while trusting the defense of the nation to the militia he had always preferred.[1]

As popular as that design has been, not all the evidence can be made to conform. Some issues have been particularly troublesome to historians. Among them is Jefferson's establishment of a military academy—the quintessence of the regular army Republicans feared; a development they had resisted to a man when proposed by earlier administrations. It could not be made to fit the Republican mold historians had created for Jefferson's military establishment. It was a "Hamiltonian institution created by Jefferson," wrote one historian. It was "a curious turn of the wheel," an "ironical" circumstance, wrote others—that Jefferson should create a military school.[2]

When obliged to account for Jefferson's motive in creating the military academy, most modern writers have relied on either or both of

ARMED FORCES AND SOCIETY, Vol. 7 No. 4, Summer 1981 529-543

two related themes. It was a national academy that emphasized science instead of the classics; or it was a school that would provide trained engineers (military and civil) for the new nation. "[Jefferson] was eager" writes Stephen E. Ambrose "to found a national institution that would eliminate the classics, add the sciences, and produce graduates who would use their knowledge for the benefit of society. Within this framework Jefferson realized that a military academy had the best chance of success."[3] Dumas Malone argues that Jefferson was "little concerned about the professional training of army officers in a time of peace, [but that] he fully recognized the usefulness of engineers in peace or war and valued the infant Academy chiefly for its potential scientific contribution."[4] Some authors have placed more emphasis on the military nature of the school.[5] Others have stressed the peaceful benefits it produced, particularly from the engineers it trained.[6] But none have proceeded far beyond the limits of the two basic themes of science and engineering.

Under close scrutiny, each effort to explain Jefferson's founding of the military academy proves unpersuasive. The evidence indicates that he did not consider it to be a key institution of scientific learning, though no doubt he would have liked to have seen one established. Similarly, formal engineering training was neither the sole nor the primary goal, nor was it even a fact until nearly a decade after Jefferson left office. If Jefferson had intended West Point to be an important element of a national scientific school, he certainly would have chosen differently in terms of a student body, faculty, and curriculum. Nearly two years after he had ordered the military academy into being, the President's efforts to create a school that would promote science were (as they always were) focused on Virginia. Toward that end, he indicated that he was still "endeavoring to procure material for a good plan," and his perfunctory call for a national university three years later (1806) contained no suggestion that his school at West Point should be linked in any way to it. But then, his military school made no pretense of being an institution of higher learning.[7]

The extent of scientific training conducted at the military academy in its early years is easy to exaggerate. The administration, in fact, resisted efforts to increase the school's emphasis on science. When the first Superintendent, Jonathan Williams, requested new books on science, he was put off with the excuse that scientific thought was changing so fast that they would soon be useless.[8] The faculty would have been better characterized as laymen with interests in science and mathematics than as professional scientists such as were beginning to emerge in faculties at the better colleges.[9] The early curriculum at West Point clearly showed the very limited extent of either scientific or engineering instruction. In 1802 and for several years thereafter, when many other schools were offering higher mathematics, astronomy, natural philosophy, and chemistry as basic fare, the military academy offered only the rudiments of mathematics and military fortification.[10] The mathematics text, C. H. Hutton's *Mathematics*, (so basic that it was sometimes used in country schools) was the core of the cadet educational experience. In many ways the curriculum was more like that of a secondary or even an elementary school than a college—and for good reason. Some cadets, upon arrival, could neither read nor write; a larger number had little skill with either basic arithmetic or grammar.[11] Consequently, instruction was designed to impart only the most basic, practical knowledge needed by army officers of that day; sufficient mathematics and practical skills to lay artillery correctly, to construct simple fortifications, and to make rudimentary maps. Even that limited goal proved difficult to attain. After six years of effort, Williams conceded, "that mere mathematics would not make either an artillerist or an engineer." French and drawing had already been added, but a real remedy proved elusive.[12] It was not until after Sylvanus Thayer took charge of the school in 1817 that it began to produce truly qualified engineers. At "the elementary school at West Point," reported one early graduate, cadets "so fortunate as to render themselves serviceable either in the artillery or engineers" must have done so by "their own industry, and not in the education received by them at West Point, which was barely sufficient to excite a desire for military enquiries and of military pursuits."[13]

It has sometimes been suggested that the school (as a part of the new Corps of Engineers) was intended to produce only engineers, but the facts indicate otherwise. The law creating the new Corps of Engineers provided that as engineer ranks were filled with commissioned officers, the number of engineer cadets would decline from 10 to 4. However, in one of his first communications concerning plans for the academy, Secretary of War Henry Dearborn indicated a need for "rooms for twenty or thirty pupils." Obviously the academy was intended to train more than just the small number of engineer cadets authorized. In point of fact, the first cadet appointed under Jefferson was an artillery cadet and he was ordered to West Point immediately. From the beginning the school had regularly graduated both artillerists and engineers (more, by far, of the former), and from 1806 onward it graduated officers of infantry (and soon dragoons) alongside them. Of the 50 graduates commissioned during Jefferson's two terms, 14 were engineers, 27 artillery, 8 infantry, and 1 a dragoon. One additional cadet was graduated but not commissioned. In 1808, both Jefferson and Williams called attention to the training in both artillery and engineering that the academy offered. Later, in 1821, Jefferson referred to West Point simply as a school of instruction for artillery, noting that even the instruction in fortification was "for the artillery."[14] Engineering alone was never the intent.

Efforts to explain Jefferson's founding of the military academy at West Point as a manifestation of his Enlightenment interest in science (and engineering) and education simply cannot be made to square with the evidence. As Richard H. Kohn puts it, "the new President's motives [in founding the military academy] have never been convincingly explained." "Yet," Kohn continues, "Jefferson must surely have understood after a decade of debate the larger meaning of a military academy."[15] Such an academy would obviously promote the interests of the regular army and this could not have escaped Jefferson's attention. In his carefully reasoned universe such an institution would only have been created as a part of a broader scheme that took this concern into account.

The founding of the military academy needs to be seen as part of a comprehensive Jeffersonian plan for the military establishment. The keystone of that plan was the Military Peace Establishment Act of 1802, which not only formalized the military academy that Jefferson already had in place, but reorganized the staff functions, eliminating Federalist domination of the army's internal hierarchy, and reducing and reorganizing the offer corps in a way that allowed the removal of many of Jefferson's most persistent political critics within the army. The army had to be made compatible with the views of the new administration. The creation of the military academy is no paradox when viewed within its domestic political context—the creation and safeguarding of the new Republican regime.[16]

By the end of the highly charged campaign of 1800 Jefferson was convinced that the long-run success of the Republic and the Republican cause required a new direction. The success of this enterprise seemed to require the reconciliation of the men of both parties and his inaugural address outlined a policy of moderation and conciliation. The pattern of this conciliation as it related to federal offices was established early and followed in all agencies of the government over which the President had control. Removals were made with great care. Whenever possible moderate Federalists ("Republican Federalists," Jefferson called them) were reconciled to the cause, though as vacancies occurred appointments were made from among men of Republican persuasion. Jefferson applied himself, as he put it, to "the new establishment of republicanism."[17]

The place of the regular army in the new establishment received careful consideration. Republicans, who had long feared the misuse of military power, had been particularly concerned about the enlarged army that Hamilton had gathered for the Quasi War. This army, consciously officered from Federalist sources, seemed more likely to be turned on the Republicans than the French. When these regulars were used to suppress resistance to new taxes that paid for the larger force, Republicans were certain that their fears were justified.[18]

Regular troops were obviously necessary in their traditional mission on the frontier (and in coastal defense), and to relieve the militia in case of foreign attack, but another role was pointed out that might demand a loyalty to the administration that Jefferson could not take for granted. "I think your attention," wrote the ubiquitous Elbridge Gerry,

> should extend to the security of fortresses, magazines, and arsenals; by placing them under the protection of *faithful* officers and corps, and preventing by proper defenses their seizure or destruction. This precaution seems necessary even if the country was not infested by a desperate faction.[19]

Jefferson, he implied, had to be prepared to use the army to secure the Republic against a monarchist faction that still threatened it. How would the army respond in that situation? The army that Jefferson had inherited might turn out to be unreliable in the face of such factional conflict. Only a small number of the officers were identified with the Republican cause. Most were Federalists and more than a few (some in positions of great responsibility) were "opposed most violently to the administration and still active in its vilification."[20]

To Jefferson the solution was as obvious as the need; he would Republicanize the army and bring it into accord with the political philosophy of the new administration. He lost no time getting started. "The Army," he reported to Nathaniel Macon, just two months after his inauguration, "is undergoing a chaste reformation."[21] All vestiges of monarchical Federalism had to go. The army had to be rid of Federalist domination and supplied with officers whose Republican credentials assured their loyalty to the new administration.

Finding qualified men of proper persuasion for the new Republican army was not always an easy task. Federalists, on the average richer and more likely to have obtained a college education, held the advantage. "The children of illustrious families," wrote John Adams, "have generally greater advantages of education . . . than those of meaner ones, or even those in middle life."[22] Jefferson discovered, writes Sidney H. Aronson, that he could not effectively "break the upper-class monopoly of office until something was done to break the upper-class monopoly of education."[23] If the commissioned ranks were to be accessible to all classes of citizens; if the aristocracy of wealth and birth was to be replaced in the army with a natural aristocracy of virtue and talent; if men were to be used who lacked the advantages that wealth and position offered; then education and training would have to be provided that would equip them for leadership.

The new establishment of Republicanism in the army necessitated the military academy that Jefferson created at West Point—a school that would prepare Republican sons for military service. Far from being a school of science or engineering, the academy was created to provide selected young men with the skills they needed to officer Mr. Jefferson's army. In the early years of the nation Washington, Hamilton, Knox, and others had made attempts to obtain legislation that would create a military academy, but Republicans had always opposed them vigorously. Cadets were authorized for companies in the regiments of artillery and engineers in 1794, but few were appointed and no academy was provided for their training. Just before the end of his term as President in 1801, John Adams appointed a small number of these cadets, and made some preliminary arrangements for their instruction. Jefferson adopted this fledgling group and shortly after his inauguration ordered the "immediate" creation of a formal academy.[24] Congress, taking its cue from the President, incorporated the school into the new military establishment of 1802.

Some Republicans put considerable faith in the ability of educational institutions to reshape men. ("I consider it is possible to convert men into republican machines," wrote Benjamin Rush.)[25] But Jefferson's aim for the academy was made of simpler stuff. His new military school would train men from the good Republican stock of the country for positions of leadership in the new army. The school was not intended to politicize. It would not, as Rush might have suggested, make Republicans of army officers, but it would make army officers of Republicans. For many it would provide the education they could not otherwise acquire, and a change at West Point was immediately noticeable. Joseph Swift, an Adams appointee and first graduate of the new institution, reported that after the new administration had come into power, "appointments to military office were made from families of prominent Democrats and of less Educated Persons than had been heretofore appointed."[26] The new academy was a key component in Jefferson's new military establishment. Its creation was the conscious, thoughtful act of an eminently and consistently political man.

Jefferson had not always been so warm to the notion of a military academy. In 1793 he had opposed Washington's call for such an institution on grounds that it was unconstitutional, and in April 1800 he had noted with apparent satisfaction that Federalist-sponsored legislation to create an academy had been effectively killed. Yet, barely a month after his inauguration, he announced his decision to establish a military school at West Point.[27] His earlier opposition presupposed the kind of school that would have perpetuated a Federalist army that Republicans felt they had good cause to fear. In his hands there was no such concern. This new establishment posed no threat to the Republic. Certainly his academy was not the grandiose affair that had recently been proposed by the Federalists. Nevertheless, it could prepare young men for officership. If drawn from Republican families and trained under officers carefully selected for the task, these young men would form an officer corps that would be thoroughly attached to the Republican principles they were sworn to defend.

The administration was diligent in its effort to select cadets from within the country's Republican ranks. The political affiliation of applicants to the military academy (or their family's) was a common and important subject of mention in letters of recommendation. "His father . . . is a Republican and I am informed the young man is also," reported one correspondent.[28] "He is . . . of reputable parentage, the family have all be[en] considered as thoroughly attached to republican principles," wrote another.[29] "His political tenets accord with the principles of our political institutions and with the men and measures of the present administration," reported still another.[30] The failure to obtain an appointment was also subject to political interpretation. One applicant, whose letter had met with silence, complained that "perhaps I may be suspected in my politics." This young man, the editor of a generally

Republican newspaper, had supported a gubernatorial candidate whose political indiscretions had earned administration rebuke. In the factional disputes within the Republican party of New York the candidate had not only failed to gain administration support but allied himself with certain Federalist elements. The young editor was convinced that his secondhand indiscretion had disqualified him in the President's eyes. "I was always a friend of his administration," he pleaded, but the appeal fell on deaf ears. The young man's brother, who suffered no such disqualification, received an appointment to West Point.[31] The President went to unusual lengths to ensure that his new academy achieved the desired results.

The Military Peace Establishment Act of 1802 which created the academy, and which was proposed and supported by the Administration, was carefully drawn to provide the President with exceptional powers over the new Corps of Engineers and the military academy. The officers of that new branch were placed in a peculiar beholdence to him. The act called for a tiny engineer corps of seven officers and ten cadets—one major, two captains, two first lieutenants, and two second lieutenants—but added that

> the President is . . . authorized, when he shall deem it proper, to make such promotions in the said Corps, with a view to particular merit, and without regard to rank, so as not to exceed one colonel, one lieutenant colonel, two majors, four captains, four first lieutenants, four second lieutenants, [a total of sixteen officers] and so as that the number of the whole corps shall, at no time exceed twenty officers and cadets.[32]

In this Corps Jefferson was not bound by the traditional promotion by relative rank and seniority that was the rule in the balance of the army. The Corps, more than any other, belonged to him. A clue to the necessity for this very liberal arrangement lay in Jefferson's desire for particular control over those to whom he planned to entrust the preparation of the army's new officers. The same law provided that this new Corps of Engineers would establish and operate the military academy.

Jefferson took an active interest in the initial development of both curriculum and faculty. "On the subject of your Book, Instruments, etc.," wrote Secretary of War Henry Dearborn to Jonathan Williams, "I will consult the President and will write you an answer." A month later the Secretary instructed Williams that before making any purchases he should "observe the notes made by the President on the Margin of [the] list." The original curriculum approved by the President consisted simply of mathematics (including algebra and geometry), the fundamentals of fortification, and the use of surveying instruments. Instruction in the French language and in drawing were added a year later. Changes to the program were cleared through the President before they were implemented.[33] In his choice of faculty, Jefferson took care to avoid the selection of men whose strongly Federalist sympathies might hazard the project. It would surely not do to have strongly anti-administration role models. Nevertheless, the same shortage of qualified Republicans that prompted the school in the first place made it necessary to cast a broad net in the search for instructors. Jefferson could not avoid choosing some whom he labeled "Republican Federalists," but he did carefully avoid officers identified with the Hamiltonian faction. He organized the academy months ahead of the congressional sanction which he sought and received in 1802.

The first member of the new faculty to be chosen was Jonathan Williams, who was appointed Inspector of Fortifications and subsequently Superintendent of the military academy. Williams, a nephew of Benjamin Franklin, was a lay scientist and an officer of the American Philosophical Society. Jefferson had been acquainted with him in both capacities for a number of years. He had corresponded with Williams both in reference to society business and scientific endeavors. It is likely that the President had no concerns about Williams's politics—he had had more than sufficient opportunity to assess them—but if he had, Williams himself made an effort to dispel them. In a solicitous letter to the new President just days after the inauguration, Williams took pains to assure Jefferson that his recent appointment to the army by Adams had had no political basis. Dearborn, who interviewed Williams for the new post, took less than thirty minutes to offer him the job. Lieutenant Colonel Louis de Tousard, a former French officer and one of the few officers in the American army trained in a military academy, may have been considered for the job but it is likely that his close ties to Hamilton and his aristocratic background disqualified him. The same factors likely weighed in his dismissal the next year.[34]

In the beginning, the balance of the faculty taught mathematics. Jared Mansfield, another member of the American Philosophical Society, was commissioned a Captain and appointed Acting Professor of Mathematics. Mansfield had once been a member of the faculty at Yale, but seemed to prefer practical application to theorizing or teaching. He spent more time surveying in the west than he did instructing at West Point. A strong Republican, he was the most politically active of the instructors at the military academy. His correspondence, even that with Jeferson, demonstrated an interest in and knowledge of Republican affairs. His colleagues seldom broached political subjects publicly, and particularly not in communications with the President.[35] Captain William Amhurst Barron appears to have been a moderate Federalist of the ilk Jefferson thought compatible with Republican institutions and a Republican administration. Barron, who had been serving with the artillerists and engineers since 1800, was a Harvard graduate and had tutored there in mathematics. He joined Mansfield, and in the temporary absence of the latter as Surveyor General, also served as Acting Professor of Mathematics.[36] Joseph Garner Swift, the first graduate of the military academy, joined the faculty as an instructor in mathematics upon graduation. Swift came from a moderately Federalist family, but noted that "politics, were not generally discoursed upon at the Point, although the political opinion of every person there was well known, and newspapers of both parties were taken." Swift noted in his memoirs a personal interrogation by Jefferson concerning his politics, and a Presidential admonition that the Republican party was the "rising power".[37]

The Republican experiment at West Point met with as much success as might reasonably have been expected, but was not without problems. The new class of youths, without wealth and the income it provided, had some difficulty subsisting on the low pay and allowances. Williams reported that both pay and ration allowances were "swallowed up in food and they have nothing left for clothing." Before the end of a year, some were "literally in rags."[38] In addition, there were complaints of favoritism involving the newer element. One report that reached Jefferson alleged that "a young man from the country, uneducated, and who had been with the corps but three months, and had acquired little there, was lately made an ensign to the prejudice of much superior qualifications." This, if true, was carrying things a bit too far and Jefferson ordered Dearborn to investigate the matter.[39] Despite such minor problems the experiment promised quite satisfactory results and in 1808 Jefferson called upon Congress to enlarge the academy. Congress responded by increasing the authorized number of cadets from 44 to 200.[40]

It was no coincidence that Jefferson's announcement to Nathaniel Macon of a "chast reformation" of the military establishment came just two days after the War Department's first formal report indicating the contemplated establishment of the military academy.[41] The academy was an integral part of Jefferson's effort to Republicanize the army. The new school would equip young Republicans for commissioned service in the new establishment army. By 1806 the academy was providing the majority of the engineer and artillery officers needed by the army and was beginning to commission officers into the other branches. Jefferson was apparently pleased with the results. "The State and interests of the military academy shall not be forgotten," he assured Williams in 1808.[42] Years later he wrote Jared Mansfield, "I have always considered [the] Establishment [of the Military Academy] as of major importance to our country."[43] Quite contrary to his earlier staunch opposition,once in the presidency he gave active support to the academy he created. When it proved successful as a key element of his program, he unhesitatingly sought to enlarge it.

As President, Jefferson was faced with two security requirements: security of the Republic and security of the Republican regime. His actions vis-à-vis the military academy illustrate the importance he attached to the creation of a military establishment compatible with his conception of the nation's political institutions. His founding of the school was but one element of that program, but it suggests a level of concern and involvement in military affairs that far exceeds that usually attributed to Jefferson. Likewise, the political nature of that involvement, though consistent with his actions in other areas of the executive, has largely been ignored. For his new administration, however, security was as much a political as it was a military concern, and the founding of West Point was an important aspect of the Jeffersonian politics of security.

Notes

1. An exception is Mary P. Adams, "Jefferson's Military Policy with Special Reference to the Frontier, 1805-1809" (Ph.D. diss. University of Virginia, 1958), who "confounded the conventional wisdom on the subject by troubling to read military archives instead of drawing deductions from Jefferson's reputation for military idiocy" (Marshall Smelser, *The Democratic Republic, 1801-1805* [New York: Harper Torchbooks, 1968], p. 161n.). The mainstream includes Dumas Malone, "Jefferson the President, Second Term 1805-1809," in *Jefferson and His Time*, Vol. 5 (Boston: Little, Brown, 1974), pp. 507-523; James Ripley Jacobs, *The Beginning of the U.S. Army 1783-1812* (Princeton: Princeton University Press, 1947), pp. 244-343; Walter Millis, *Arms and Men, A Study of American Military History* (New York: New American Library, 1956), pp. 53-57; Russell F. Weigley, *History of the United States Army* (New York: Macmillan,

1967), pp. 103-111; and Leonard D. White, *The Jeffersonians: A Study in Administrative History, 1801-1829* (New York: Macmillan, 1951), pp. 211-264. White devotes four chapters to the Republican administration of the military but never gets beyond this simplistic analysis of Jefferson's relationship with the army.

2. Russell F. Weigley, *Towards an American Army: Military Thought from Washington to Marshall* (New York: Columbia University Press, 1962), p. 28; White, *The Jeffersonians*, p. 252; Malone, "Second Term," p. 510.

3. Stephen E. Ambrose, *Duty, Honor, Country, A History of West Point* (Baltimore: Johns Hopkins Press, 1966), p. 18. Why Jefferson should think a military academy had a better chance of success than a civil school among Republicans who had always opposed it, is not explained. See also Thomas J. Fleming, *West Point, the Men and Times of the United States Military Academy* (New York: William Morrow, 1969), p. 16; and Dorothy J.S. Zuersher, "Benjamin Franklin, Jonathan Williams and the United States Military Academy" (Ph.D. diss. University of North Carolina at Greensboro, 1974), pp. 90-91.

4. Malone, "Second Term," 5: 510. Malone, in Vol. 6 of his *Jefferson and His Times*, scheduled for release in 1981, discusses Jefferson's design for military training for all male college students—a theme Malone sees played out in Jefferson's autumn years.

5. See Jacobs, *Beginning of the U.S. Army*, p. 297; and Arthur P. Wade, "Artillerists and Engineers, the Beginning of American Seacoast Fortifications, 1794-1815" (Ph.D. diss. Kansas State University, 1977), p. 138. It has been suggested by Sidney Forman, ("Why the United States Military Academy was Established in 1802," *Military Affairs* 29 [Spring, 1965]: 16-28), that it was needed to provide the practical training not available at other schools. That, however, seems to have been limited to drill, a bit of surveying, and occasional lectures by Williams on fortifications. Most practical experience was gained "on-the-job."

6. See Weigley, *Towards an American Army*, p. 27; and Forest Garrett Hill, *Roads, Rails and Waterways, The Army Engineers and Early Transportation* (Norman: University of Oklahoma Press, 1957), pp. 12-13.

7. Jefferson to (Marc August) Pictet, February 5, 1803. *The Writings of Thomas Jefferson*, ed. Albert Ellery Bergh, Vol. 10 (Washington, DC: The Thomas Jefferson Memorial Association, 1907), p. 74. On Jefferson's proposals in 1806 see G. Brown Goode, "The Origin of the National Scientific and Educational Institutions of the United States," *Annual Report of the American Historical Association for the Year 1889* (Washington: Government Printing Office, 1890), pp. 74-75; 92-93. Joel Barlow had proposed in 1806 that the military academy should be attached to a central university in Washington and placed under the direction of a national scientific institution. (Ibid., p. 143.) Jefferson, who better than anyone knew the purpose of the academy, paid the idea no heed.

8. Henry Dearborn to Williams, March 24, 1806. Letters Sent by the Secretary of War Relating to Military Affairs, 1800-1899, U.S. National Archives, Record Group 107, M6.

9. George H. Daniels, *American Science in the Age of Jackson* (New York: Columbia University Press, 1968). The U.S. Military Philosophical Society founded by the early faculty—once called "the first national scientific society" (Goode, p. 68)—should be viewed more as a remnant of Enlightenment science than as a precursor of the kind of professional scientific societies that came a few decades later. It got only token support from Jefferson.

10. James William Kershner, "Sylvanus Thayer: A Biography," (Ph.D. diss. West Virginia University, 1976), pp. 10-14; Jonathan Williams, "A report on the progress and

present state of the Military Academy, March 14, 1808," in *American State Papers, Military Affairs*, 1: 229-230. See also "Statement of the examination of Cadets, 1806," Jonathan Williams Papers, U. S. Military Academy Library, West Point, NY.

11. Kershner, "Sylvanus Thayer," p. 47; Williams, "Military Academy, 1808," pp. 229.

12. Williams, "Military Academy, 1808," p. 229.

13. From an 1819 report by Colonel William McRee (USMA 1806) and Brigadier General Simon Bernard quoted in "Military Academy at West Point," *American Quarterly Review* 22 (September 1837): 91-92. The increased emphasis on civil engineering coincides both with the arrival of Thayer (1817) and the new national interest in internal improvements; it is not certain which had the greater influence. On the influence of the latter, see Rufus King to Christopher Gore, June 22, 1821, in *The Life and Correspondence of Rufus King*, Vol. 6, Charles R. King eds. (New York: G. P. Putnam, 1900), pp. 393-394.

14. Dearborn to Captain George Fleming, May 12, 1801. Letters Sent, Secretary of War, M6; "Military Academy, 1808" p. 228; and Jefferson to John Adams, September 12, 1821 *The Adams-Jefferson Letters* Vol. 2, ed., Lester J. Cappon (Chapel Hill: University of North Carolina Press, 1959), p. 575.

15. Richard H. Kohn, *Eagle and Sword, the Federalists and the Creation of the Military Establishment in America, 1783-1802* (New York: Free Press, 1975), p. 303.

16. Theodore J. Crackel, "Jefferson, Politics and the Army: A New Look at the Military Peace Establishment Act of 1802." Presented at the SHEAR Conference on the History of the Early Republic, Annapolis, Aug 10-11, 1979.

17. Jefferson to Albert Gallatin, August 14, 1801. *The Writings of Albert Gallatin*, Vol. 3, ed. Henry Adams (New York: Antiquarian Press, 1960), p. 37. Jefferson to Livingston, December 14, 1800. *The Writings of Thomas Jefferson*, Vol. 7, ed. Paul Leicester Ford (New York: G. P. Putnam 1892-1899), pp. 464-465.

18. Alexander DeConde, *The Quasi-War, The Politics and Diplomacy of the Undeclared War with France, 1797-1801* (New York: Charles Scribner, 1966), pp. 196-199. For the Federalist view see Kohn, *Eagle and Sword.* On the background of Republican fears see Lawrence Delbert Cress, "The Standing Army, the Militia and the New Republic, A Study of Attitudes Toward the Military in American Society" (Ph.D. diss. University of Virginia, 1976.)

19. Gerry to Jefferson, May 4, 1801. Thomas Jefferson Papers, Library of Congress. (My emphasis)

20. Officer's Roster, July 24, 1801. Jefferson Papers, 19697-19699, and 19705. This roster was annotated by Captain Meriwether Lewis, the President's private secretary, to show both the military qualifications and political sentiments for all officers for whom they could be ascertained. Though the roster was produced earlier, the annotations were probably supplied in early 1802. The nature of the annotations is in itself revealing. Symbols were used to identify each of the following categories:

(1) "1st Class, so esteemed from a superiority of genius and military proficiency."
(2) "Second Class, respectable as officers, but not altogether entitled to the first grade."
(3) "Unworthy of the commissions they bear."
(4) "Republican."
(5) "Opposed to the administration, otherwise respectable officers."
(6) "Opposed to the administration more decisively."
(7) "Opposed most violently to the administration and still active in its vilification."

(8) "Professionally the soldier without any political creed."
(9) "Political apathy."
(10) "Officers whose political opinions are not positively ascertained."
(11) "Unknown to us."

Two entries were usually made—first, military qualifications, then political sentiment. Those unknown were often very junior officers with little service.

21. Jefferson to Macon, May 14, 1801. Bergh, Vol. 10, p. 261.

22. John Adams, *A Defense of the Constitutions of Government of the United States of America*, Vol. 1 (Philadelphia: Budd and Bartram, 1797), p. 110.

23. Sidney H. Aronson, *Status and Kinship in the Higher Civil Service* (Cambridge, MA: Harvard University Press, 1964), p. 9.

24. Dearborn to General (James) Wilkinson, May 12, 1801. Letters Sent, Secretary of War, M6.

25. Rush quoted in Linda K. Kerber, *Federalists in Dissent, Imagery and Ideology in Jeffersonian America* (Ithaca: Cornell University Press, 1970), p. 109. Joel Barlow wrote to Jefferson that one objective of the national university that Barlow proposed was "to cultivate a strict adherence to republican principles." (See n. 7)

26. Joseph Gardner Swift, Joseph Gardner Swift Papers (U.S. Military Academy Library, West Point, NY, p. 34.

27. Ford, Vol. 1, p. 270; Jefferson to Edward Livingston, April 30, 1800. Bergh, Vol. 10, p. 164; Dearborn to Commanding Officer, West Point, April 15, 1801. Letters Sent, Secretary of War, M6.

28. I. Wingate to Dearborn, July 18, 1806. Moses Elliott File, U.S. Military Academy Cadet Application Papers, 1805-1866, U.S. National Archives, Record Group 94, M688.

29. Israel Smith to Dearborn, December 5, 1808. John Reed File, Cadet Application Papers.

30. John Willard to Dearborn, September 17, 1808. David B. M. Heil File, Cadet Application Papers.

31. Sylvester Roberts to Dearborn, December 8, 1807. Erastus Roberts File, Cadet Application Papers.

32. "An act fixing the Military Peace Establishment of the United States," March 16, 1802, *The Debates and Proceedings in the Congress of the United States* 7th Cong., 1st Sess. Washington, DC: Gates and Seaton, 1852), pp. 1306-1312.

33. Dearborn to Williams, May 31, 1802 and July 9, 1802. Letters Sent, Secretary of War, M6. Williams's complaint that he had "not received from the Secretary of War one word descriptive of the plans of the Institution and the Education expected," was written in a fit of pique (Williams to Major W. W. Burrows, July 17, 1803. Williams Papers, USMA). As he must have realized, the instructors that Jefferson and Dearborn handpicked, and the texts they approved, determined the curriculum. In 1808, when Williams submitted recommended changes relating to the academy, he noted suggestions made by Dearborn and went so far as to clear a rough draft of the document with the President (Williams, "Military Academy, 1808"; Williams to Jefferson, March 5, 1808. Jonathan Williams Papers, Lilly Library, Indiana University).

34. Williams to Jefferson, March 7, 1801. Jefferson Papers; Williams to Major W. W. Burrows, July 17, 1803. Williams Papers, USMA. Williams's politics were unknown to Meriwether Lewis who annotated Jefferson's roster of officers (see n. 20)—an indication that he was not vocal in his attachment to party. In fact, he had close friends and associates in both parties. Jefferson knew Williams personally; the two (and Wilkinson) had served

together in important roles in the American Philosophical Society. On Tousard, see Norman B. Wilkinson, "The Forgotten 'Founder' of West Point," *Military Affairs*, 24 (Winter 1960-1961). See also Ambrose, *Duty, Honor, Country*, p. 34; Wade, "Artillerists and Engineers," p. 110.

35. Samuel E. Tillman, "The Academic History of the Military Academy, 1802-1902" in *The Centennial of the United States Military Academy at West Point, New York 1802-1902*, Vol. 1 (Washington: Government Printing Office, 1904), p. 261; Ambrose, *Duty, Honor, Country*, p. 25; Mansfield to Jefferson, May 9, 1807. Jefferson Papers.

36. Tillman, "Academic History of the Military Academy," p. 242.

37. Joseph Gardner Swift, *The Memoirs of General Joseph Gardner Swift* (n.p., 1890), p. 31, 34. 42.

38. Quoted in Fred W. Sladen, "The Uniform of Cadets, 1794-1902," in *Centennial History* 1: 509. Cadet pay varied from ten dollars per month for artillery cadets to sixteen for cadets of engineers. Usually cadets were appointed (and paid) in artillery during their tenure at the academy. Then, if made engineer, they were transferred to that Corps just in time to be commissioned. This procedure offered two advantages: it saved the government six dollars a month for each month they were at West Point and allowed an opportunity to pick only the best for the small Corps of Engineers.

39. Jefferson to Dearborn, August 6, 1808. Bergh, Vol. 12, p. 116. This minor uproar may have concerned Samuel C. Mabson who had attended the military academy from July 1804 to October 1805 and was appointed an ensign on July 1, 1808. Dearborn was apparently satisfied that no impropriety had occurred and Mabson stayed in the service until discharged in 1815 as a captain.

40. "American State Papers," *Military Affairs*, 1: 228, 248. At the time Congress acted (in 1808), all 16 engineer officers authorized had been appointed, leaving only 4 openings for cadets. These, added to the 40 artillery cadets authorized, totaled 44. To this number Congress added 100 cadets of infantry, 20 each of light artillery and riflemen, and 16 of dragoons, bringing the grand total to 200. The faculty was not reorganized until 1812.

41. War Department, May 12, 1801, "Statement of Fortifications, Public Buildings, Military Stores, Quartermasters Department, Manufacture of Cannon, Indian Affairs, State of the Army, and Military Bounty Lands," Jefferson Papers.

42. Jefferson to Williams, October 24, 1808. Jefferson Papers.

43. Jefferson to Mansfield, February 13, 1821. Bergh, Vol. 15, p. 313.

THEODORE J. CRACKEL, Lieutenant Colonel, U.S. Army, has taught history and the formulation of military strategy and policy at West Point, the Army Command and General Staff College, and currently at the Army War College. He is now at work on a book on politics and the army under Jefferson.

Pell-Mell: Jeffersonian Etiquette and Protocol

By

ROBERT R. DAVIS, JR.*

DURING the presidential campaign of 1800, the Federalists predicted that a Jeffersonian victory would bring in its train an American equivalent of the French Reign of Terror. Taking advantage of Jefferson's avowed sympathy for the Revolution in France and his alleged infidelity and atheism, the Federalists painted an awesome picture of "dwellings in flames, hoary hairs bathed in blood, female chastity violated . . . children writhing on the pike and halberd."[1] New England clergymen, imbued with Federalist principles and outraged at the prospect of a freethinker in the White House, beseeched their flocks not to support this "howling atheist" and "confirmed infidel." Adding fuel to the fire, the *New England Palladium* warned professing Christians that "our churches will be prostrated, and some infamous prostitute, under the title of the Goddess of Reason, will preside in the Sanctuaries now devoted to the worship of the Most High."[2] When Jefferson was at last elected, most Federalists, resigned to their fate, prepared for the worst. The more bitter of their lot, according to Nathan Schachner, foresaw "the end of the world, the subversion of orderly government and the trampling of the breechless mob through the streets of cities; while their even more embittered adherents among the New England clergy prophesied the reign of Antichrist and the death of all religion."[3]

Notwithstanding the pounding hearts and trembling knees of the Federalists, the revolution of 1800 was hardly revolutionary. Where Jeffersonian republicanism departed from the Federalist tradition, the difference was often largely a matter of style and emphasis. Moreover, this difference was motivated almost entirely by political considerations. Throughout the administrations of Washington and Adams, not to mention the mudslinging melee of 1800, the Republicans had ranted and raved as to what they considered affronts to republican

*The author is Professor of History at Ohio Northern University.

[1]Cited in John C. Miller, *The Federalist Era, 1789–1801* (New York: Harper and Row, 1960), 265.

[2]Cited in Nathan Schachner, *Thomas Jefferson, A Biography* (New York: Yoseloff, 1957), 640–41.

[3]*Ibid.*, 659.

simplicity. A Pennsylvania radical had snorted during the campaign of 1800, for example, "Etiquette! Confound the word, it ought not to be admitted into an American dictionary. Ought we to follow the fashions and follies of old corrupt courts? Are we not a young Republic? And ought we not be plain and honest, and to distain all their craft, pageantry and grimace? It is . . . to be hoped, that the next President will discontinue ridiculous levees, squaring the heel and toe and bowing like a country dancing master . . . aping old worthless sovereigns and courtiers and all! . . . for the sake of etiquette. Mr. Jefferson, should he be our next President, will doubtless trample under foot these baubles. . . . He is elevated far above the nonsense of parade—mere adulation and asiatic servility are not to his taste."[4] Once elected, Jefferson could hardly turn his back upon nearly a decade of anti-Federalist propaganda. He therefore pushed the doctrine of republican simplicity to its logical extreme in a system of etiquette and protocol which he laconically dubbed "pell-mell."

As president-elect he did away with several of the niceties which had characterized the inaugurations of his two predecessors. On March 4, 1801, a parade of artillery and riflemen appeared before Jefferson's lodgings at Conrad's boardinghouse and released a salvo of guns and cannon. Thereupon, at twelve noon, the tall Virginian emerged from the dwelling. The manner of his dress and appearance, according to the sympathetic *National Intelligencer*, "was, as usual, that of a plain citizen, without any distinctive badge of office."[5] Spurning the pomp and formality of the state carriage with its six horses and outriders, Jefferson walked on foot in the company of several Republican colleagues and "an anonymous following of citizenry" from Conrad's to the Capitol, where he delivered his inaugural address in a low-pitched, near inaudible voice, to a joint session of Congress.[6]

Immediately after the inaugural ceremonies had been completed, the new president returned on foot to Conrad's boardinghouse, where "he lived on a perfect equality with his fellow boarders, and [ate] at a common table."[7] During his stint as vice president in the Adams administration, Jefferson and his democratic friends had soundly rejected attempts to establish a seating arrangement based upon rank at the common table. One observer remarked that the wife of John Brown, the senator from Kentucky, had suggested that a seat be provided for Jefferson at the upper end of the table, near the fire, "if not on account

[4]Cited in W.P. Cresson, *James Monroe* (Chapel Hill: University of North Carolina Press, 1946), 202–3.

[5]*National Intelligencer*, 6 March 1801, 2.

[6]Schachner, *Jefferson*, 661; Bernard Mayo, *Jefferson Himself: The Personal Narrative of a Many-Sided American* (Boston: Houghton Mifflin, 1942), 219–20.

[7]Margaret Bayard Smith, *The First Forty Years of Washington Society in the Family Letters of Margaret Bayard Smith*, ed. Gaillard Hunt (New York: Unger, 1965), 12.

of his rank as vice-President, at least as the oldest man in company." But this offer was politely refused, "and he occupied during the whole winter the lowest and coldest seat at a long table at which a company of more than thirty sat down." Mrs. Brown, however, was determined that Jefferson be accorded his due respect. On the evening of March 4, therefore, seeing that none of the gentlemen sitting at the table felt predisposed to relinquish his seat to the new president, Mrs. Brown rose and offered her place. Jefferson "smilingly declined it, and took his usual place at the bottom of the table." Mrs. Brown, her feathers a bit ruffled, was reported to have "felt indignant and for a moment almost hated the leveling principle of democracy, though her husband was a zealous democrat."[8] Even Margaret Bayard Smith, the wife of Samuel Harrison Smith, the Republican editor of the *National Intelligencer*, remarked that "this was carrying equality rather too far; there is no incompatibility between politeness and republicanism; grace cannot weaken and rudeness cannot strengthen a good cause, but democracy is more jealous of power and priviledge than even despotism."[9]

If these actions were not enough to shock Federalist sensibilities, Jefferson immediately upon taking office initiated the presidential practice of shaking hands instead of bowing, as his predecessors had done.[10] Moreover, the new president created somewhat of a sensation by the ungentlemanly habit of riding horseback *alone*. Federalist critics were quick to pounce upon the president's riding habits as being detrimental to the "respectability" of his office. Chief among these critics was the newly elected senator from New Hampshire, William Plumer, whose daily *Memorandum* gives valuable, if somewhat biased, accounts of Jeffersonian manners. Plumer was mortified to learn that Jefferson generally rode his horse unattended by a groom or servant. "I do not know the cause of this singularity," Plumer remarked, "for gentlemen of rank & consequence here are usually attended when they ride, by their servants—It may proceed from affectation—& it may arise from other causes. The appearance ill accords with the dignity of the chief of a great nation."[11]

The New Hampshire senator was further disturbed by the manner in which Jefferson invited guests to dine with him at the White House. Presidents Washington and Adams had sent invitation cards issued in the name of *The President of the United States*, whereas the new president simply used his own name. "The following is the form established by Mr. Jefferson—*Th: Jefferson* requests the favor of Mr. Plumer to dine with

[8] *Ibid.*, 12–13.

[9] *Ibid.*, 13.

[10] Bess Furman, *White House Profile, A Social History of the White House, Its Occupants and Its Festivities* (Indianapolis: Bobbs-Merrill, 1951), 37.

[11] William Plumer, *William Plumer's Memorandum of Proceedings in the United States Senate, 1803–1807*, ed. Everett S. Brown (New York: Macmillan, 1923), 550.

him on Monday next at half after three, or at whatever later hour the house may rise." Plumer later discovered that Jefferson addressed his cards in this fashion because he "meant it should be considered more as the invitation of a private gentleman, than of that of the President."[12]

When Plumer finally met Jefferson in person he expressed surprise and disgust at the undignified manner in which the president presented himself. Accompanied to the White House by General James Varnum, a Republican acquaintance from Massachusetts, Plumer described his meeting with Jefferson in a letter to Jeremiah Smith: "In a few moments, a tall highboned man came into the room; he was drest, or rather *undrest*, with an old brown coat, read waistcoat, old corduroy small clothes, much soiled—woolen hose—& slippers without heels. I thought this man was a servant, but Genl. Varnum suprised me, by announcing that it was the President. Never, never rally me again upon my inattention to dress—I certainly dress as well as the first officer of the nation."[13]

Hoping to suppress "all those public forms and ceremonies which tended to familiarize the public eye to the harbingers of another form of government," Jefferson next abolished the weekly presidential levees, which had figured so prominently in Washington social life during the administrations of his two predecessors.[14] This action was greeted with indignation on the part of those social gadabouts who relished nothing better than the weekly visitations to the presidential mansion. The disquiet provoked by Jefferson's suppression of leveeday had the effect of deterring the president from infringing any further upon the "rights" of the people: he therefore retained the established custom of throwing open the doors of the White House to the general public twice a year, on New Year's Day and on July 4.[15]

But this concession was insufficient in the eyes of many Washington socialites, and they persisted in their efforts to persuade Jefferson to reestablish the cherished levees. On one occasion, a group of ladies and gentlemen arrived *en masse* at the White House at the same time that the regular levees had been held under Washington and Adams. Much to their dismay, Jefferson was out horseback riding. Persisting in their determination, they decided to wait until the chief executive returned, hoping thereby to convince him as to the advisability of reopening the levees. "When he returned at three o'clock, and learned

[12]*Ibid.*, 211–13.

[13]Cited in Lynn W. Turner, *William Plumer of New Hampshire, 1759–1850* (Chapel Hill: University of North Carolina Press, 1962), 94–95.

[14]Jefferson to General Thaddeus Kosciusko, 2 April 1802, in Thomas Jefferson, *The Writings of Thomas Jefferson*, ed. Andrew A. Lipscomb and Albert E. Bergh, 20 vols. (Washington, D.C.: Thomas Jefferson Memorial Association, 1903), 10: 310.

[15]Katherine Anthony, *Dolly Madison, Her Life and Times* (Garden City, N.J.: Doubleday, 1949), 123.

that the great rooms were filled with company waiting to see him, he guessed their object, and frustrated it gracefully, and with perfect good humor, by merely going among them, all accoutred as he was, booted, spurred, splashed with mud, riding whip in hand, and greeted them as though the conjunction of so many guests were merely a joyous coincidence."[16] In pursuing this particular line of conduct, Jefferson succeeded in transforming a potential public levee into a coincidental private meeting between himself and a group of citizens who just happened to be passing by.

Abolishing the presidential levees did indeed have a positive effect. Much to the dismay of foreign diplomats and Washington socialites, who thrived on the punctilio of such affairs, Jefferson's action decreased the formality and idle ceremony which, according to the Republicans, had characterized the preceding administrations. On the other hand, the president's decision had a negative effect—one hardly anticipated by the chief executive. With the abolition of levees and the adoption of informality as a basis for social intercourse, the president soon found (as Washington had found a decade earlier) that much of his valuable time was being preempted by "coincidental" gatherings such as the one described above. Citizens began coming and going as they saw fit, while foreign ministers and other dignitaries began popping in at the White House unexpectedly, demanding to see the president. Despite the obvious drain on his time, Jefferson remained undaunted and stood steadfast in his determination to resist levees. Moreover, this was only the opening skirmish in the president's full-scale offensive against etiquette and protocol. He next turned his sights upon the diplomatic corps, hoping thereby to strip diplomatic etiquette and protocol of its legendary formality and punctiliousness.

In November 1803, Jefferson formulated his "Canons of Etiquette," which were directed primarily, though not exclusively, at the diplomatic corps. "In order to bring the members of society together in the first instance," the president began, "the custom of the country has established that residents shall pay the first visit to strangers, and, among strangers, first comers to later comers, foreign and domestic; the character of stranger ceasing after the first visits." There was one notable exception to this rule, however, and this was that foreign ministers, "from the necessity of making themselves known, pay the first visit to the ministers of the nation, which is returned." If this requirement annoyed foreign ministers, Jefferson's second decree infuriated them: "When brought together in society, all are perfectly equal, whether foreign or domestic, titled or untitled, in or out of office."

The remaining rules were, as Jefferson explained, merely "exemplifications of these two principles." To compensate the members of

[16]Anne Hollingsworth Wharton, *Salons: Colonial and Republican* (Philadelphia: J.B. Lippincott, 1900), 189.

the diplomatic corps, who were expected to make the first visit to cabinet members, Jefferson decreed that the "families of foreign ministers, arriving at the seat of the government, receive the first visit from those of the national ministers, as from all other residents." Yet this "compensation" was nothing more than a few crumbs thrown to the diplomatic corps, as the remaining "canons of etiquette" were distinctly unfavorable to foreign ministers accustomed to European court customs. In the first place, titles were not to be recognized in the transaction of diplomatic business or as a basis of creating social distinctions. Secondly, "differences of grade among diplomatic members, gives no precedence." In other words, Jefferson was maintaining that a minister plenipotentiary, for example, was entitled to no more or no less attention, socially or officially, than that accorded to a chargé d'affaires.

"At public ceremonies, to which the government invites the presence of foreign ministers and their families," the president continued, "a convenient seat or station will be provided for them, with any other strangers invited and the families of the national ministers, *each taking place as they arrive, and without any precedence.*" Finally, and perhaps most significantly, Jefferson directed that "to maintain the principle of equality, or of pele mele, and prevent the growth of precedence out of courtesy, the members of the Executive will practice at their own houses, and recommend an adherence to the ancient usage of the country, of gentlemen in mass giving precedence to ladies in mass, in passing from one apartment where they are assembled into another."[17]

Although Jefferson's "canons of etiquette" seemed harmless enough, the president little realized that he had just composed the libretto for nineteenth-century America's most farcical comic opera. Moreover, while Jefferson was formulating his rules of pell-mell, the British Foreign Office conveniently, though obviously unwittingly, provided the president with a male lead for his *opéra bouffe* in the person of Anthony Merry, who had recently been chosen to fill the vacant British ministerial position in Washington.

Merry's predecessor in America was Robert Liston. Liston was recalled on November 28, 1800, and from this time until late in 1803, British affairs in America were managed by Edward Thornton in the capacity of chargé d'affaires.[18] Finally, in 1803, the Foreign Office began considering candidates to fill Liston's vacated position. According to Henry Adams, the final decision as to who would receive the coveted position was made by Rufus King, the American minister at the

[17] Thomas Jefferson, *The Writings of Thomas Jefferson*, ed. Paul Leicester Ford, 10 vols. (New York: G.P. Putnam's Sons, 1892–99), 8: 276–77.

[18] S.T. Bindoff et al., eds., *British Diplomatic Representatives, 1789–1852* (London: Royal Historical Society, 1934), 185.

Court of St. James. Apparently the Foreign Office, in a conciliatory gesture, suggested to King the names of two possible choices—Francis James Jackson and Anthony Merry. King, in turn, expressed his preference for the latter.[19] "As I have had the opportunity of knowing both these gentlemen during my residence here," King later wrote to Secretary of State Madison, "it was not without some regret that I heard of the intention to appoint Mr. Jackson in lieu of Mr. Merry. Mr. Jackson is said to be positive, vain, and intolerant. He is moreover filled with English prejudices in respect to all other countries. . . ." In short, King let it be known that the appointment of Jackson would be undesirable and not particularly in the interests of amiable relations between the two countries. "On the other hand," King continued, "Mr. Merry appears to be a plain, unassuming, and amiable man, who having lived for many years in Spain is in almost every point of character the reverse of Mr. Jackson. . . ." Perhaps most important, concluded the American minister, "Mr. Merry wishes for the mission with the view of obtaining what he believes will prove to be an agreeable and permanent residence."[20]

In view of later developments—developments which seemed to contradict the expectations of the American minister—it might reasonably be alleged that Rufus King was a poor judge of character. But this was hardly the case. Anthony Merry was indeed "a plain, unassuming, amiable man"—providing, however, he remained within his milieu. Once out of it, he became as "positive, vain, and intolerant" as King feared Francis James Jackson would have been. Moreover, King was not alone in his praise of and confidence in the new minister. Secretary of State Madison, for example, maintained that Merry "appears to be an amiable man in private society, and a candid and agreeable one in public business,"[21] while Jefferson himself confessed that the Englishman was "personally as desirable a character as could have been sent us."[22]

For his part, Anthony Merry came to the United States with good intentions. He was indeed looking for a residence which would be both "agreeable and permanent," and he believed that the United States was the answer to his quest. The new minister's knowledge of American conditions, however, proved to be extremely limited. His chief source of information had been ex-Minister Liston, who had made his residence at Philadelphia, the temporary capital and perhaps the most

[19]Henry Adams, *History of the United States of America during the Administrations of Thomas Jefferson and James Madison, 1801–1817*, 9 vols. (New York: Antiquarian Press, 1962), 2: 360.

[20]King to Madison, 10 April 1802, cited in Adams, *History*, 2: 360–61.

[21]Madison to James Monroe, 26 December 1803, in James Madison, *The Writings of James Madison*, ed. Gaillard Hunt, 9 vols. (New York: G.P. Putnam's Sons, 1900–10), 2: 189.

[22]Cited in Mayo, *Jefferson Himself*, 234.

cosmopolitan city in North America, and who had departed long before Jefferson's pell-mell system of etiquette had been initiated.[23]

Arriving in Washington on November 6, 1803, Mr. and Mrs. Merry quickly discovered that the national capital was far from being a cosmopolitan urban center.[24] In point of fact, it was hardly even a city. One visitor remarked that Washington was "nothing more than distinct groups of houses, scattered over a vast surface, and has more the appearance of so many villages, than a city,"[25] while another complained about "the neighbourhood of the capitol particularly, where you may look in vain for fresh meat at the single houses of farmers along the road side, or for wine or beer, and think yourself lucky if you can get some indifferent whisky to qualify the bad taste of the water."[26] Even Gouverneur Morris, recently returned from France and filling out an unexpired term in the Senate, sarcastically noted that "we want nothing here but houses, cellars, kitchens, well-informed men, amiable women, and other little trifles of the kind to make our city perfect."[27] One French diplomat, upon discovering that he was expected to live in this material and cultural wasteland, exclaimed, "My God! What have I done, to be condemned to reside in such a city?"[28]

In one of his first despatches to the Foreign Office, Merry bitterly related the inconveniences which he had encountered upon arriving in Washington. "I cannot describe to you the difficulty and expense which I have to encounter in fixing myself in a habitation," he wrote to George Hammond. "By dint of money I have just secured two small houses on the common which is meant to become in time the city of Washington. They are mere shells of houses, with bare walls and without fixtures of any kind, even without a pump or well, all which I must provide at my own cost." If this were not enough to dismay the new minister, there was also the remoteness of Washington to consider: "Provisions of any kind, especially vegetables, are frequently hardly to be obtained at any price." In fact, Merry concluded, "everything . . . in the federal City is . . . perfectly savage."[29]

[23]Merry to Lord Hawkesbury, 6 December 1803, in Great Britain, Foreign Office, *F.O.-5, Foreign Correspondence: United States*, 41: 25 (Library of Congress photostat) (hereafter cited as *F.O.-5*).

[24]Bindoff, *British Diplomatic Representatives*, 185.

[25]Anne N. Royall, *Sketches of History, Life, and Manners, in the United States* (New Haven: privately printed, 1826), 130.

[26]Augustus John Foster, *Jeffersonian America: Notes on the United States of America Collected in the Years 1805–6–7 and 11–12 by Sir Augustus John Foster, Bart.*, ed. Richard Beale Davis (San Marino, Calif.: Huntington Library, 1954), 21.

[27]Cited in Gerald Carson, *The Polite Americans: A Wide-Angle View of Our More or Less Good Manners over 300 Years* (New York: William Morrow, 1966), 96.

[28]Cited in Helen Nicolay, *Our Capital on the Potomac* (New York: Century, 1924), 70.

[29]Merry to Hammond (private), 7 December 1803, *F.O.-5*, 41: 28–29.

The British minister's wife appears to have been an aggressive, overbearing woman, intent upon being treated with all those civilities and enjoying all those conveniences commonly enjoyed by English women of her station. Margaret Bayard Smith, whose notebook provides one of the best guides to the social and intellectual history of Jeffersonian America, observed that Mrs. Merry was "a large, tall, well-made woman, rather masculine, very free and affable in her manners, but easy without being graceful." More important, Mrs. Smith observed that she was "a woman of fine understanding and she is so entirely the talker and actor in all companies, *that her good husband passes quite unnoticed.*"[30] Merry's diminutive stature aside that of his domineering wife was noticed by Senator Plumer, who concluded that he was "a feeble inefficient man,"[31] and even by Jefferson, who observed that it was Merry's misfortune to be "unluckily associated with one of an opposite character in every point."[32] Viewing with dismay the inconveniences of the national capital, Mrs. Merry lamented that "this is a thousand times worse than the worse parts of Spain."[33]

When the Merrys landed at Norfolk harbor on November 4 and began their northward journey to the federal city, the diplomatic corps in America was hardly what one could call impressive. It consisted of only four individuals—the Marques Don Carlos Martinez de Yrujo, envoy extraordinary of Spain, Edward Thornton, chargé d'affaires of Great Britain, Louis A. Pichon, chargé d'affaires of France, and Peter Pederson, chargé d'affaires of Denmark—only one of whom (Yrujo) had full ministerial rank and powers.[34]

Although schooled in Old World diplomacy, Yrujo had been Americanized somewhat by his marriage to Sally McKean, the lovely daughter of Republican Governor Thomas McKean of Pennsylvania. Moreover, his "intimate relations at the White House had given him family privileges," and he therefore tended to quietly conform to Jefferson's canons of etiquette.[35] According to Henry Adams, however, Yrujo resented Jefferson's code of pell-mell intensely and demonstrated these sentiments by "living mostly in Philadelphia disregarding the want of what he considered good manners at Washington, according to which he was placed on the same social footing with his own secretary of legation."[36]

The remaining members of the diplomatic quarter—Thornton,

[30]Mrs. Smith to Mrs. Kirkpatrick, 23 January 1804, in Smith, *Washington Society*, 46.

[31]Plumer, *Memorandum*, 448.

[32]Cited in Mayo, *Jefferson Himself*, 234.

[33]Statement by Dolly Madison, cited in Anthony, *Dolly Madison*, 126.

[34]Editorial note in Thomas Jefferson, "Jefferson to William Short on Mr. and Mrs. Merry, 1804," *American Historical Review* 33, no. 4(July 1928): 832.

[35]Adams, *History*, 2: 362.

[36]*Ibid.*

Pichon, and Pederson—were less disturbed by Jeffersonian etiquette than was their colleague from Spain. In fact, they were probably quite enthusiastic about a system which accorded them more social recognition and mobility than they would have been entitled to in the precedence-encrusted courts of Europe. The rank of chargé d'affaires in the early nineteenth century was distinctly an inferior and subordinate position, especially in the eyes of those rank-conscious courtiers and diplomatic gadflies who fashioned the Old World handbook of diplomatic etiquette and protocol. In Russia, for example, the royal family refused to even speak to chargés d'affaires,[37] while in France, as William Short discovered, chargés d'affaires were not accorded the privilege of an official audience upon taking leave.[38] But in Jeffersonian America it was quite different. Chargés d'affaires distinctly benefited from the liberal official etiquette, being able thereby to mingle pell-mell with their superiors.

Merry's first official act upon reaching Washington was to notify Secretary of State Madison of his arrival and to make the necessary arrangements with him for the presentation of his credentials to the president. Madison, giving the new minister no hint that the ceremony would differ from standard European court procedure, arranged for an audience with Jefferson on November 29.[39] On the appointed day, Merry, dressed in his finest diplomatic attire, called upon Madison, who escorted him to the White House. Upon being presented to the president, Merry was silently mortified, as he later recalled, at the manner in which Jefferson was dressed to receive the distinguished minister of His Majesty George III. Blushing at the president's state of slippered undress, Merry later reported to the Foreign Office that the chief executive "received me in his usual Morning Attire, contrary to the Ceremony observed by his Predecessors."[40] Aside from this irritating point of difference, the remainder of the interview seemed to be agreeable to Merry, although he did express some surprise (but not indignation) at the relative simplicity and brevity with which it was conducted. "At the Audience," he wrote Lord Hawkesbury, "Nobody was present but Mr. Madison, who retired immediately after I had accompanied the Delivery of my Credentials with a short Speech . . . and after Mr. Jefferson had made a Reply to it. . . . This ceremony, which the President rendered as short as possible, being concluded, he desired me to sit down, when we conversed for some time upon general Affairs."[41]

[37]John Quincy Adams, *Memoirs of John Quincy Adams*, ed. Charles Francis Adams, 12 vols. (Philadelphia: J. B. Lippincott, 1874–77), 2: 95.

[38]Short to Jefferson, 15 May 1792, in William Short, *The Papers of William Short* (manuscripts), 52 bound volumes, 20:3462–63, Library of Congress.

[39]Adams, *History*, 2: 365.

[40]Merry to Hawkesbury (separate), 6 December 1803, *F.O.-5*, 41: 24.

[41]Merry to Hawkesbury (no. 1), 6 December 1803, *F.O.-5*, 41: 1–2.

Soon after the audience had been concluded, Merry appealed to Madison for some explanation as to why Jefferson was dressed so "shabbily" during the official interview. Madison informed the bewildered British minister that "the President did not observe those distinctions of dress, more than others in this country, and that he had received a Danish minister [Pederson] . . . in the same plain manner." This explanation hardly satisfied Merry, for he quickly pointed out that Pederson, the Danish chargé d'affaires, was only of the third rank, while he, being a minister plenipotentiary, was of the second rank—therefore entitled to additional consideration. Madison, in turn, reminded Merry that Jeffersonian etiquette did not recognize distinctions of diplomatic rank or precedence and that all diplomatic personnel stationed in the United States, at least in the eyes of the administration, were on an equal social and official footing.[42]

Finding little comfort or satisfaction in Madison's explanations, Merry was further appalled when he learned that *he* was expected to pay the first visit to the members of Jefferson's cabinet. Although this feature of Jeffersonian etiquette was common throughout western Europe, including his native Great Britain, Merry had been previously informed by Liston that American usage provided that the cabinet members, not the foreign minister, were to assume the initiative and pay the first call. In this regard, he resented what he obviously considered a personal affront:

> Mr. Liston had furnished me with a particular Account in Writing of all the Rules of Distinction which had been observed towards him and Mrs. Liston. They consisted in his receiving the first Visit from every Person, except the President and Vice-President, the Members of the Senate and the Secretary for foreign Affairs. . . .
>
> Now, for the first Time, Mr. Jefferson has required that I should make the first Visit to the Heads (as they are termed here) of all the other Departments as well as that of State. . . .[43]

Merry once again appealed to Madison, only to discover that the visiting requirement was an integral part of Jefferson's canons of etiquette. The secretary of state subsequently wrote to James Monroe, who at that time was the American minister at the Court of St. James, explaining what had occurred: ". . . the custom here as in England and elsewhere, was for the foreign minister, on his arrival, to pay the first visit to the Heads of Department. Mr. Merry had understood the custom to have been different, at least as it related to his predecessor. . . . The explanation given, and the appeal to the practice in his own

[42]Madison to Monroe, 19 January 1804, in James Monroe, *James Monroe Papers* (Library of Congress, Presidential Papers Microfilm, ser. 1, reel 3) (hereafter cited as *Monroe MSS*).

[43]Merry to Hawkesbury (separate), 6 December 1803, *F.O.-5*, 41: 25.

country reclaimed him from this pretension."[44] The perplexed minister really had no alternative but to acquiesce to the Jeffersonian rule, for to have done otherwise might have placed him in a state of social isolation. Sir Augustus John Foster, British secretary of legation under Merry, later confessed that "in such a desolate spot as Washington there was no choice but to submit unless one was to live quite in solitude especially during the recess."[45]

To make matters worse, Merry then learned that the Senate had recently voted overwhelmingly in favor of a resolution which denied congressional privileges to foreign ministers. During the administrations of Washington and Adams, diplomats had been accorded the privilege (if they so desired) of occupying specially designated seats on the right side of the podium in both houses. Owing "to some indiscretion of Yrujo in the House of Representatives," Vice President Aaron Burr later told Merry, it was decided to withdraw this privilege from the diplomatic corps *en masse*.[46] Although this action obviously was not meant as a personal affront to Merry, the British minister chose to regard it as such, listing it high on the list of those grievances which he reported to the Foreign Office on December 31.[47]

Suspecting that Jefferson's object was to place foreign ministers "on a Level with the lowest American Citizen," Merry nonetheless cordially accepted an invitation to dine with the president at the White House on December 2.[48] What Merry did not know was that Jefferson had invited several other guests to attend this presidential fête—the Madisons, the Yrujos, and, perhaps most significant, the Pichons. Believing that this affair was a private gathering intended to honor his wife and himself, Merry was evidently surprised to discover this assemblage when he and Mrs. Merry arrived at the presidential mansion on the appointed day. The presence of the Pichons, moreover, especially distressed and visibly irritated the British minister. When two nations were at war, neutral governments generally avoided inviting the representative of one belligerent to meet the representative of the other unless, of course, the occasion was a formal gathering of the entire diplomatic corps.[49] As England and France were at war, the presence of Pichon at the dinner was interpreted by Merry as a calculated insult—not only to himself but also to Great Britain.[50] When he approached Madison once again for an explanation, the secretary of state responded by indicating that the dinner

[44]Madison to Monroe, 19 January 1804, *Monroe MSS*, ser. 1, reel 3.

[45]Foster, *Jeffersonian America*, 54.

[46]Adams, *History*, 2: 367–68.

[47]Merry to Hawkesbury (separate), 31 December 1803, *F.O.-5*, 41: 46–47.

[48]*Ibid.*, 46.

[49]Adams, *History*, 2: 368.

[50]Merry to Hawkesbury (private), 7 December 1803, *F.O.-5*, 41: 28–29.

was not a private affair but rather an official diplomatic gathering. Merry remonstrated, pointing out that the Danish chargé d'affaires, Pederson, was not in attendance and that therefore the dinner was by its very nature private. In this regard, he informed Madison, "the presence of a hostile character was justly objectionable." Madison, however, endeavored to point out that Pederson had not been invited because "he had dined with the President two days before, and having no family was the more likely to be left out of a party made up for the most part of husbands and their wifes," and that therefore the present assemblage was of a diplomatic or official nature, not private as Merry had supposed.[51]

Upon the announcement that dinner was being served, Jefferson further alienated the British minister by offering his arm to Dolly Madison, thereby leaving an astonished Mrs. Merry standing in the lurch. The president proceeded to seat Mrs. Madison on his right, while Sally McKean Yrujo occupied the seat on his left. "Mrs. Merry was placed by Mr. Madison below the Spanish minister," Merry reported to the Foreign Office. "With respect to me," he added, "I was proceeding to place myself (though without Invitation) next to the Wife of the Spanish Minister, when a Member of the House of Representatives passed quickly by me and took the Seat without Mr. Jefferson's using any Means to prevent it, or taking any Care how I might be otherwise placed." Merry finally found a seat at the lower end of the table—far removed from the center of attraction and the seats of distinction which he apparently coveted.[52]

Shortly after this embarrassing episode, the Merrys accepted an invitation to dine at the secretary of state's home on December 6. It is most probable that they accepted this invitation under the impression that Madison had found the events at the White House disagreeable and that he would try to rectify the matter by according them those privileges and courtesies befitting their station in his own home. The English minister had apparently been informed by Yrujo that the secretary of state invariably yielded precedence to foreign ministers, despite Jefferson's canons of etiquette. (Yrujo had written to his government observing that "my wife and I had enjoyed in the houses of Cabinet ministers the precedence of which we had been deprived in the President's house."[53])

But Madison, on this occasion, had other plans. He had no choice, he later told Monroe, than to follow the example set by Jefferson—an example, he explained, which "could not with propriety be vi-

[51]Madison to Monroe, 19 January 1804, *Monroe MSS*, ser. 1, reel 3.

[52]Merry to Hawkesbury (separate), 6 December 1803, *F.O.-5*, 41: 26; Adams, *History*, 2: 369–70; Dolly Madison, *Memoirs and Letters of Dolly Madison*, ed. Lucia B. Cutts (Boston: Houghton Mifflin, 1886), 49.

[53]Yrujo to Don Pedro de Cevallos, 7 February 1804, cited in Adams, *History*, 2: 371.

olated."[54] Therefore, when the guests—which included the Merrys, the Yrujos, the Pichons, and the other cabinet members and their wives—assembled in the room adjoining the dining hall, Madison casually offered his arm to Mrs. Gallatin, the wife of Jefferson's secretary of the treasury, and proceeded to lead her to the honored position on his right. "This unexpected conduct," Yrujo reported to his government, "produced at first some confusion, during which the wife of the British minister was left without any one giving her his hand, until her husband advanced, with visible indignation, and himself took her to the table."[55] Even the amiable Pichon remarked that Madison's actions were unusual and constituted a profound innovation from previous procedure: "There is no doubt that Mr. Madison in this instance wished to establish in his house the same formality as at the President's, in order to make Mr. Merry feel more keenly the scandal he had made; but this incident increased it."[56]

In a stinging message to the Foreign Office, the British minister bitterly alleged that these actions were provoked "evidently from Design, and not from Ignorance and Awkwardness (though God knows a Great Deal of both as to Matters even of common Etiquette is to be seen at every Step in this Part of the Country)." He then related the embarrassing circumstances of the Madison fête:

> I experienced the same Want of any Kind of Distinction in a still stronger Degree from the Subordinacy of Mr. Madison's Situation compared with that of the President, for on this Occasion also the *Pas* and the Preference in every Respect was taken by, and given to, the Wives of the Secretaries of the Departments (a Set of Beings as little without the Manners as without the Appearance of Gentlewomen), the Foreign Ministers and their Wives being left to care of Themselves.
>
> In short, the Latter are now placed here in a Situation so degrading to the Countries they represent, and so personally disagreeable to Themselves, as to have become almost intolerable. The case Yesterday was so marked and so irritating that I determined to hand Mrs. Merry myself to the Table, and to place Ourselves wherever we might conveniently find Seats.[57]

Thereafter, the Merrys decided to "put themselves in coventry," according to Jefferson, and thereby to avoid attending official gatherings which might again infringe upon their honor and precedence. Writing to Hawkesbury, Merry explained that "I have thought it advisable to avoid all occasions where I and my wife might be exposed to

[54]Madison to Monroe, 19 January 1804, *Monroe MSS*, ser. 1, reel 3.

[55]Yrujo to Cevallos, 7 February 1804, cited in Adams, *History*, 2: 371.

[56]Pichon to Tallyrand, 5 and 13 February 1804, in France, Archives Nationales, *Affaires Etrangers, Correspondence Politique*, 56 (1803–04): 342–51 and 372–73 (Library of Congress photostat) (hereafter cited as *AECP*).

[57]Merry to Hammond (private), 7 December 1803, *F.O.*-5, 41: 28–29.

a repetition of the same want of distinction toward us until I shall have received authority from you to acquiesce in it, by a signification of his Majesty's pleasure to that effect."[58]

Not only did the Merrys succeed in withdrawing from official Washington society; they also managed to persuade the Yrujos into following their example. Yrujo himself had never been an enthusiastic admirer of Jeffersonian etiquette. Hoping to remain in the good graces of the president, however, the Spanish minister had submitted to pell-mell. But the recent affront to the entire diplomatic corps at Madison's, coupled with the acquisition of the Louisiana territory and the mounting determination of the United States to acquire the Floridas as well, actions and motives bitterly denounced by the Spanish government, had the effect of uniting Yrujo and Merry in a common bond. The defection of Yrujo, according to Madison, was "not a little awkward," since he had "acquiesced for nearly three years in the practice against which he now revolts."[59] A furious social war, affecting all of Washington society, quickly ensued.

The initiative was largely assumed by the wives of the two ministers. Mrs. Merry took advantage of Jefferson's ban on levees by instigating the practice of weekly drawing rooms, "with dancing and cards for the frivolous, and the honor of her conversation for those who could appreciate it."[60] More significant, it was decided that whenever the Merrys or Yrujos gave dinner parties, the ministers would lead their own wives to the table, thereby letting the wives of cabinet members fend for themselves in the scramble which would inevitably ensue. "This resolution," according to Pichon, who remained aloof from the social embroglio, "was carried out at a dinner given some days afterward by M. Yrujo." In addition, it was agreed that Mrs. Merry and Mme. Yrujo would boycott all presidential and cabinet affairs until the obnoxious pell-mell rule was dropped. Pichon reported to his government that neither Mme. Yrujo nor Mrs. Merry attended the traditional White House levee on New Year's Day, 1804, and that Yrujo himself "took care to answer everyone who inquired after his wife's health, that she was perfectly well."[61]

Jefferson was furious at what he considered an insult to the dignity of the presidency and an impediment to harmonious diplomatic accord

[58]Merry to Hawkesbury, 31 December 1803, cited in Adams, *History*, 2: 374.

[59]Madison to Monroe, 16 February 1804, in James Madison, *Letters and Other Writings of James Madison, Fourth President of the United States, Published by Order of Congress*, 4 vols. (Philadelphia: J. B. Lippincott, 1865–67), 2: 197 (hereafter cited as Madison, *Letters*).

[60]Nicolay, *Our Capital*, 80.

[61]Pichon to Tallyrand, 5 February 1804, in *AECP*, 56 (1803–04): 342–51. For newspaper comment, see *Gazette of the United States*, 17 January and 14 and 17 February 1804, and *Philadelphia Aurora*, 28 January 1804.

between the United States, England, and Spain. "The principle of society with us, as well as of our political constitution," he defensively wrote William Short, "is the equal rights of all; and if there be an occasion where this equality ought to prevail preeminently, it is in social circles collected for conviviality: nobody shall be above you, nor you above anybody, pele-mele is our law."[62] Convinced that Mrs. Merry was a "virago" and that she was directly responsible for the farcical social controversy, the president determined to maintain his principles of etiquette at all costs. "If [Merry's] wife perseveres," he wrote Monroe, "she must eat her soup at home, and we shall endeavor to draw him into society as if she did not exist. It is unfortunate that the good understanding of nations should hang on the caprice of an individual who ostensibly has nothing to do with them."[63]

The Merrys, therefore, continued to bear the brunt of Jefferson's canons of etiquette, and the subsequent Jerome Bonaparte affair added fuel to the fire. Jerome, Napoleon's brother, had recently married Elizabeth Patterson, the niece of Jefferson's first secretary of the navy, Samuel Smith. Upon visiting Washington, the newlyweds were wined and dined by the Jeffersons, who sponsored a gala celebration dinner for them. At this fête, Jefferson, contrary to his own rules, led the glamorous Mme. Bonaparte to dinner, giving her the honored position on his right. When the Merrys and Yrujos heard of this, of course, their indignation rose anew.[64]

The crowning blow, according to one writer, "came when Mrs. Merry, beginning to relent, accepted an evening invitation to the Madisons' and found her haberdasher and his wife to be among the company invited to meet her."[65] By this time, Mrs. Merry was beginning to recognize the utter hopelessness of her situation. Either she had to swallow her pride and submit to democratic manners and etiquette or withdraw from society completely. She chose the latter course, remaining in a state of social coventry until her husband's recall in 1806. Sir Augustus Foster, himself bitterly resenting American manners, sympathetically described the trials and tribulations endured by this proud but somewhat foolish English lady:

> In one way or another, either by remarking on her dress or diamonds or treading on her gown, they wearied Mrs. Merry to such a degree that I have sometimes seen her on coming home burst into tears at having to live at such a place, particularly on seeing the affected impoliteness of those who should have known better, but who, being ratters from the

[62]Jefferson to Short, 23 January 1804, in *American Historical Review* 33, no. 4 (July 1928): 832.

[63]Jefferson to Monroe, 8 January 1804, in Mayo, *Jefferson Himself*, 235.

[64]Adams, *History*, 2: 374, 377ff.

[65]Irving Brant, *The Life of James Madison*, 6 vols. (Indianapolis: Bobbs-Merrill, 1941–61), 4: 169.

Federal party seeking favour and place, made use of her assemblies in order to render their boorish humors, as well as their concurrence with the systematic manners of Mr. Jefferson, more conspicuous.[66]

Although Mrs. Merry's withdrawal from Washington society was construed in many quarters as being a serious matter, it could in no way compare with the sinister intrigues of her husband, first with the New England Federalists and then with Aaron Burr. Whether Merry was motivated by the social embarrassments suffered at the hands of Jefferson is difficult to determine. Nevertheless, it seems more than coincidental that he soon "became the confidant of all the intriguers in Washington, and gave to their intrigues the support of his official influence."[67] Both he and Yrujo "listened with a ready ear to the Federalist conspiracy for the secession of New England," while Yrujo himself instigated a vigorous newspaper campaign with the sole intention of embarrassing the administration.[68] Much more significantly, Merry soon became involved in the Burr Conspiracy.

Ten days following his fatal duel with Alexander Hamilton, Vice President Aaron Burr fled from New York. On July 23, 1804, he reached Philadelphia where Merry was vacationing. Recognizing their mutual animosity towards Jefferson, Burr immediately contacted Merry, informing him of his plot and requesting the aid of the British government in its execution. Merry quickly transmitted this startling information to the Foreign Office.[69] But contrary to Merry's expectations, his government responded only with silence. Shortly thereafter, Merry again beseeched the Foreign Office to support his scheme: "I have only to add," he wrote to Foreign Secretary Harrowby, "that if a strict confidence could be placed in him, he certainly possesses, perhaps in a much greater degree than any other individual in this country, all the talents, energy, intrepidity, and firmness which are required for such an enterprise."[70] But once again Merry was met with only silence on the part of his government, and the Burr conspiracy was left to proceed without British aid—much to the apparent chagrin of Minister Merry.

Although the social war between the foreign ministers and the Jefferson administration did have profound domestic repercussions, it caused scarcely a ripple overseas. Both Madison and Jefferson wrote lengthy letters to Monroe in London, advising him of the Merry affair and warning him to expect reprisals from the British government. Madison's fourteen-page letter is perhaps the best source available on

[66]Foster, *Jeffersonian America*, 55.

[67]Adams, *History*, 2: 390.

[68]Schachner, *Jefferson*, 787.

[69]Merry to Lord Harrowby (Dudley Ryder), 6 August 1804, cited in Adams, *History*, 2: 395.

[70]Merry to Harrowby, 29 March 1805, cited in Adams, *History*, 2: 403.

the *opéra bouffe* which engulfed Washington society. The secretary of state, explaining that Merry's "feelings had been deeply wounded," described the social war as being "nauseous" and "frivolous" and in conclusion apologized to Monroe for "having put so much trash on paper."[71] But Madison and Jefferson worried themselves needlessly; the British government was not about to provoke an international incident over American diplomatic etiquette and protocol.

In point of fact, Merry's communications and despatches describing the uncivil manner in which he and Mrs. Merry were being treated in Washington were not even answered by the Foreign Office. Nevertheless, Monroe reported a sequence of events that he and Mrs. Monroe experienced in London which may or may not have been connected with the Merry episode. On March 3, 1804, for example, he informed Madison that "the Queen, at the time the Etiquette story was in circulation, I thought passed me in the crowd intentionally. It might not be so," he added, "as her drawing room is without order, a confused multitude. . . ."[72] In a later letter, Monroe reported several earlier slights and incivilities that he and Mrs. Monroe had been subjected to but concluded that "all this preceded the affair of Mr. Merry, and had no connection with it."[73] On several other occasions, however, he had reason to believe that perhaps Merry's despatches provoked more irritation than he had originally supposed. At a dinner at Lord Hawkesbury's, for instance, he referred to flower festivals in South Carolina which brought out "a great concourse of people with gay equipages." At this point, Lord Castlereagh sarcastically asked the American minister what kind of equipage he was referring to. "I could not but be surprised at the enquiry," Monroe wrote, "nevertheless replied, such as I saw here."

> Sir Wm. Scott then remarked that he had lately read an acct. of a grand fête at the cape of good hope, which concluded with that all 'the beauty taste & fashion of Africa were assembled there.' This occasion'd some mirth as you will suppose at our expense, in which I could not well partake. . . .[74]

Although these mocking gestures were barbed in nature, Monroe finally came to the conclusion that they were not connected with the Merry affair and presumed "that there was no disrespect intended us."[75]

Although the long-range effects of the social conflict were largely inconsequential internationally, the realization that his extremism in

[71]Madison to Monroe, 19 January 1804, *Monroe MSS*, ser.1, reel 3.

[72]Monroe to Madison, 3 March 1804, *Monroe MSS*, ser. 1, reel 3.

[73]Monroe to Jefferson, 15 March 1804, *Monroe MSS*, ser. 1, reel 3.

[74]*Ibid.*

[75]*Ibid.*

matters of diplomatic etiquette and protocol may have pushed Merry and Yrujo to the brink of conspiracy must have had a sobering effect upon Jefferson. Evidently realizing that the alienation of foreign ministers by social or any other means was not the best method of promoting international harmony, the president somewhat modified his strict adherence to republican simplicity following his reelection in 1804. This was especially apparent in his dressing habits during diplomatic audiences and receptions. When the president gave an official audience to Turreau, the new French envoy sent to replace Pichon, his appearance was far different than on the occasion of Merry's initial presentation. "He has improved much in the article of dress," Senator Plumer reported; "he has laid aside the old slippers, red waistcoat, and soiled corduroy small-clothes, and was dressed all in black, with clean linen and powdered hair."[76]

But this was as far as Jefferson chose to depart from his pattern of simplicity in regard to diplomatic etiquette and protocol. Pell-mell remained the rule, and the president continued to slight foreign ministers throughout his second administration. On New Year's Day, 1806, for example, it seemed to the Englishmen that he went to great lengths to snub Merry, whose tour of duty in the United States was nearing its end. Sir Augustus Foster reported that among the guests at this reception was a number of American Indians. Jefferson, "who was so much attached to them from philanthropy and because they were savages as if they were his own children, . . . appeared wholly taken up with his natives." Merry and Foster believed that the president was intentionally slighting them and they decided "not to stay and be treated so and we went away after remaining five minutes."[77]

Jeffersonian diplomatic etiquette, at least when the cases of Merry and Yrujo are considered, clearly worked to the nation's disadvantage. Accordingly, future presidents of the United States would refrain from pushing republican simplicity to the extremes that Jefferson had. Strict pell-mell would retire with Jefferson to Monticello. The question remains, however, as to why Jefferson departed so far from the more polished and highly successful policies of his predecessors.

Several writers have maintained that Jefferson's canons of etiquette were his way of announcing a "cool" policy towards Great Britain and Spain.[78] This supposition, however, is extremely hypothetical and at a distinct variance with the evidence available. In point of fact, both Jefferson and Madison went out of their way to dispel any notion that their social actions were related to international political motivations. Writing to Monroe, for example, Madison strongly affirmed "that the

[76]Cited in Adams, *History*, 2: 405.

[77]Foster, *Jeffersonian America*, 22–23.

[78]See, for example, George Morgan, *The Life of James Monroe* (Boston: Small, 1921), 263, and Anthony, *Dolly Madison*, 127.

Government of the United States is sincerely and anxiously disposed to cultivate harmony between the two nations. The President wishes to lose no opportunity and spare no pains that may be necessary to satisfy the British administration on this head, and to prevent or efface any different impressions which may be transmitted from [Merry]."[79]

The foreign ministers themselves were convinced that Jefferson's behavior was designed, according to Pichon, "to sacrifice everything for the sake of his popularity."[80] Pichon's analysis was echoed by two future British ministers to the United States—Stratford Canning and Augustus Foster. Canning remarked that Jefferson's "bearing appears to have been very much that of a political coxcomb. Among his competitors were some whom he could hardly have expected to surpass by genuine merit, and it is allowable to presume that he sought to give weight to his own scale by popular manners and revolutionary principles."[81] Foster was even more explicit in his assessment of Jeffersonian protocol: "The President's popularity was unfortunately connected with his manners as well as with his acts and he and his party seemed sometimes to be on the look-out how best to humble us and run counter to all our received notions of propriety and etiquette."[82] Moreover, according to Foster, Jefferson was merely "playing a game for retaining the highest offices in a state where manners are not a prevailing feature in the great mass of society."[83]

A more reasonable explanation for the president's actions has been advanced in James Sterling Young's account of the social structure of the national capital during the Jeffersonian era. Young maintains that the diplomatic corps was a highly pompous lot and that their actions, sentiments, and manner of living were resented by the Americans. "In a society where most executive employees lived in poverty or on the brink of it, they strutted in ruffled shirts and silver spurs, or tiaras and ropes of diamonds, and sent fifty miles to Baltimore for table delicacies." Such flamboyance, Young concludes, probably accounts for the negative reaction produced. Although many cultural antipathies existed in Washington during the early national period, "none were so deep or irreconcilable as those between the Old World and the New, thrown into intimate confrontation in the executive community."[84]

Jefferson himself never specifically explained the reasons which prompted his departure from the diplomatic manners established

[79]Madison to Monroe, 16 February 1804, in Madison, *Letters*, 2: 196.

[80]Pichon to Tallyrand, 3 September 1804, cited in Adams, *History* 2: 404.

[81]Cited in Stanley Lane-Poole, *The Life of the Right Honourable Stratford Canning, From his Memoirs and Private and Official Papers*, 2 vols. (London: Longmans, 1888), 2: 315–16.

[82]Foster, *Jeffersonian America*, 51.

[83]*Ibid.*, 9.

[84]James Sterling Young, *The Washington Community, 1800–1828* (New York: Columbia University Press, 1966), 220–21.

under Washington and Adams. It seems reasonable to believe, however, that he was at least partially motivated by his personal aversion toward diplomacy and diplomatic procedure in general. "I have ever considered diplomacy as the pest of the peace of the world," he wrote William Short, "as the workshop in which nearly all the wars of Europe are manufactured."[85]

Whatever the motivation, it is clear that Jeffersonian diplomatic etiquette and protocol was largely a facade. In truth, the president was a Virginia aristocrat accustomed to the niceties and fineries common to the upper stratum of American society. He was not a yeoman farmer but rather the proprietor of a large plantation. Although his official wardrobe consisted in part of heelless slippers, red corduroy vests, and soiled linen, his private wardrobe—worn in the privacy of Monticello—included the finest and most expensive European garments available.[86] Moreover, as his earlier diplomatic career demonstrates, he was not a stranger to the intricacies of European diplomatic etiquette and protocol. In fact, Jefferson went a step further than most American diplomats abroad in his submission to European usage when he accepted a token gift from the French court upon his recall in 1789. More significant and perhaps ironical in view of his later attitude in regard to diplomatic manners, Jefferson even supported the brief American experiment of bestowing gifts upon foreign ministers during his term as secretary of state.[87]

[85]Jefferson to Short, 23 January 1804, in *American Historical Review* 33, no. 4 (July 1928): 833.

[86]Schachner, *Jefferson*, 721.

[87]American diplomatic gift-giving is discussed in Robert R. Davis, Jr., "Diplomatic Gifts and Emoluments: The Early National Experience," *Historian* 32 (May 1970): 376–91.

"OF BIGOTRY IN POLITICS AND RELIGION"

Jefferson's Religion, the Federalist Press, and the Syllabus

by CONSTANCE B. SCHULZ*

"WHAT an effort, my dear Sir, of bigotry in Politics & Religion have we gone through!" wrote Thomas Jefferson to Joseph Priestley on 21 March 1801. In writing to congratulate Priestley on his escape from persecution and to assure him of the demise of the alien law ("that libel on legislation, which, under the form of a law, was for some time placed among them"), President Jefferson was optimistic that "our countrymen have recovered from the alarm into which art & industry had thrown them."[1] His confidence in the returning good sense of his countrymen was reflected in the placating tone of his inaugural address. He was convinced that his fellow citizens were indeed ready to "unite with one heart and one mind" to banish both religious and political intolerance under the bond of "our own Federal and Republican principles." He exempted of course the "desperadoes of the quondam faction in & out of Congress" whom he considered as "incurables, on whom all attentions would be lost, & therefore will not be wasted."

Jefferson, though he spoke of tolerance, actually expected conversion of the opposition to his own point of view. He believed that the actions of his administration would disarm his critics, lead to correct principles all but the most misguided and perverse of the Federalist opposition, and bind the nation in "perfect consolidation" to provide "a standing monument & example for the aim & imitation of the people of other countries."[2] His expectations failed to materialize as rapidly as he had predicted. The continued strength of Federalist sentiment, particularly in New England and most markedly in Connecticut, and the "quondam leaders'" persistent political persecution of him in the press and Congress had a profound effect on Thomas Jefferson as a president and party leader. What has been relatively little explored is the extent to which this political criticism continued

*Ms Schulz is a visiting associate professor of history at the College of Wooster. This article was first presented in a shorter version at the July 1980 meeting of the Society for Historians of the Early American Republic in Urbana, Ill.

[1] Jefferson to Joseph Priestley, 21 Mar. 1801 (Paul Leicester Ford, ed., *The Works of Thomas Jefferson* [12 vols.; New York, 1904-5], IX, 217-18 [hereafter cited as Ford, *Works*]). In the margin, next to the phrase "that libel on legislation," is written "Alien law" in Jefferson's hand.

[2] From Jefferson's first inaugural address (Henry S. Randall, *The Life of Thomas Jefferson*, II [New York, 1858], 631-32); Jefferson to William B. Giles, 23 Mar. 1801 (Ford, *Works*, IX, 223-24); Jefferson to John Dickinson, 6 Mar. 1801 (ibid., pp. 201-2).

to be tied after 1801 to attacks on Jefferson's religious philosophy.[3] That combined attack had an important impact on his own perception of his faith and changed his expression of it.

During the election of 1800 Jefferson experienced religious persecution as a form of political attack. The charges were grounded in his pronouncements in the *Notes on Virginia.* He questioned the literal truth of the biblical story of the deluge; his opinions on the differences between blacks and whites seemed to deny the brotherhood of man; he opposed reading of the Bible by school children; he had the temerity to proclaim that "it does me no injury for my neighbor to say there are twenty gods, or no god." Federalists playing on religious fears could add other innuendos to the evidence of Jefferson's irreligion in the *Notes*. From his initial support of the anticlerical French Revolution was extrapolated his sympathy for the destruction of Christianity. His friendship with Thomas Paine, author of the deist apology, *The Age of Reason,* was cited as proof of his own heretical theology. His authorship of the Virginia statute for disestablishment of the Church of England was construed as enmity to organized religion. Such attacks, which had begun as early as 1792 when Jefferson was accused of having "no Conscience, no Religion, no Charity," continued through the election campaign of 1796 and reached a crescendo during the election of 1800.[4]

Jefferson was annoyed by these charges, which both confirmed his distrust of the Federalist press and fed his growing anticlericalism. But he was determined not to honor them by replying. "As to the calumny of Atheism, I am so broken to calumnies of every kind, from every department of government . . . that I entirely disregard it," he responded to James Monroe in May 1800 when Monroe, begging him to defend himself, wrote in some alarm of charges made against Jefferson by Supreme Court Justice Samuel Chase. "It has been so impossible to contradict all their lies, that I have

[3] See especially Dumas Malone, *Jefferson the President: First Term, 1801-1805* (Boston, 1970), chaps. 5, 12, 13; Dumas Malone, *Thomas Jefferson as Political Leader* (Berkeley and Los Angeles, 1963); Merrill D. Peterson, *Thomas Jefferson and the New Nation: A Biography* (New York, 1970), chap. 9; Robert M. Johnston, Sr., *Jefferson and the Presidency* (Ithaca, 1978), chaps. 6, 7; Gilbert Chinard, *Thomas Jefferson: The Apostle of Americanism* (Boston, 1929), bk. 5, chap. 1. Chinard alone noted the continued attack on Jefferson's religion during his first term but concluded, "We can only express the hope that some day it will receive due attention" (pp. 390-92).

[4] See Charles O. Lerche, Jr., "Jefferson and the Election of 1800: A Case Study in the Political Smear," *William and Mary Quarterly*, 3d ser., V (1948), 467-91; Fred C. Luebke, "The Origins of Thomas Jefferson's Anti-Clericalism," *Church History*, XXXII (1963), 344-56.

determined to contradict none; for while I should be engaged with one, they would publish twenty new ones."[5]

Jefferson expected that the New England clergy would continue such attacks, but that after his election, when his behavior would prove that he was no foe of religion, their influence over reasonable citizens, even in New England, would diminish. "I was always satisfied that the great body of those called Federalists were real republicans as well as Federalists," he wrote to Henry Knox in March 1801. To Gideon Granger in May 1801, he wrote a letter of congratulation over "the regeneration of Rhode Island," in what he hoped would be "the beginning of that resurrection of the genuine spirit of New England which arises for life eternal." The clergy, of course, "who have missed their union with the State, the Anglomen, who have missed their union with England, and the political adventurers, who have lost the chance of swindling & plunder in the waste of public money, will never cease to bawl," but, concluded Jefferson, "among the people, the schism is healed."

To Elbridge Gerry he confided that he was "not deluded by the eulogiums of the public papers in the first moments of change." When removals of Federalists from office began, he predicted, a "hue and cry" would ensue. "A coalition of sentiments is not for the interest of printers. They, like the clergy, live by the zeal they can kindle, and the schisms they can create. It is contest of opinion in politics as well as religion which makes us take great interest in them, and bestow our money liberally on those who furnish aliment to our appetite."[6] Even as Federalist criticism continued and was tailored to persistent religious qualms about Jefferson's fitness to be president, he bravely prophesied (against what must have been overwhelming evidence to the contrary) that "the tory papers will still find fault with everything. But these papers are sinking daily, from their dissonance with the sentiments of their subscribers, & very few will shortly remain to keep up a solitary & ineffectual barking."[7]

The Federalist press did not sink into oblivion but barked effectively at Jefferson's decision to remove Federalists from office. To define why such removals were sometimes necessary and to counteract charges that he had violated the pledges made in his inaugural address on 4 March 1801,

[5] Luebke, "Anti-Clericalism," *Church History*, XXXII (1963), 344-56; Monroe to Jefferson, 25 May 1800, Thomas Jefferson Papers, Library of Congress; Jefferson to Monroe, 26 May 1800 (Ford, *Works*, IX, 135-36).

[6] Jefferson to Knox, 27 Mar. 1801 (Ford, *Works*, IX, 236); Jefferson to Granger, 3 May 1801 (ibid., p. 249); Jefferson to Gerry, 29 Mar. 1801 (ibid., pp. 242-43).

[7] Jefferson to William Short, 3 Oct. 1801 (ibid., p. 308).

Jefferson decided to make an official answer to a remonstrance from the merchants of New Haven. They had protested the removal of midnight appointee Elizur Goodrich from the lucrative post of collector of the port of New Haven. Connecticut was a particularly galling state for beleaguered New England Republicans, for its congressmen had exhibited a bitter intransigence in the balloting between Jefferson and Burr. Moreover, after Jefferson's inauguration when a few ardent Federalists were replaced with Republicans in other states, the Federalist majority in Connecticut maintained a stranglehold on officeholding and proclaimed that Jefferson did not dare remove any Federalists in their state. Pierpont Edwards, grandson of Jonathan Edwards and a Republican leader in New Haven, reported that Goodrich's continuance in office

> instead of reconciling his friends, or any part of the federalists to republicanism, and to your administration will strengthen them in their Opposition. . . . They say "Mr. Jefferson has displaced no Officer in Connecticut; he has in other States; . . . the true cause of his thus conducting is, *he dare not trust a republican in Connecticut,* he knows they are, what we assert them to be, *disorganizers.*"

Edwards blamed the phalanx of clergy and monarchists for disseminating this charge: "The throne and the alter have here entered into an alliance offensive and defensive." Nor did he expect southerners to understand the strength of this coalition. "The malignity of the federalists here is wholly inconceivable to any, but such as are eye and ear witnesses to all." This was an opinion concurred in by Gideon Granger, who bitterly reported in 1801 that "with us in Connecticut the prospect is not pleasing, the exertions of our Clergy and Aristocracy at yesterday's election have exceeded every thing before known. The torrents of abuse from the pulpits were incredible." Edwards recommended Samuel Bishop, because of his sober civic, republican, and religious credentials, to replace Goodrich. Bishop was "Mayor of our City Chief Judge of our County Court, and a Decon in one of our established churches. . . . In him will be embraced respectability, integrity, religion steady habits and firm republicanism." When Jefferson removed Goodrich and appointed Bishop, the merchants of New Haven wrote a formal remonstrance to the president, protesting Bishop's age (seventy-eight) and infirmity. (He could not, they said, see well enough to write his name.) It was this protest that Jefferson used as "an opportunity . . . to come forward and disavow the sophistical construction on what I had declared on the 4th of March."[8]

[8] Edwards to Jefferson, 12 May 1801; Granger to Jefferson, 15 Apr. 1808 (Gaillard Hunt,

Jefferson carefully designed his answer to placate the political anxieties of more moderate Federalists and to reassure Republicans who feared that too few of their own would be rewarded with public office. But the Federalist press, ridiculing his justifications at great length, added an unexpected twist to its criticism. The underlying design of Jefferson's appointment of Bishop, argued the *Washington Federalist,* was not redress of the balance between Federalist and Republican officeholders in Connecticut, but the destruction of religion in that state. The appointment of the obviously incompetent Samuel Bishop was a cover for rewarding his deist and free-thinking son Abraham, "a flaming street orator, a bawling Lazaroni, a monstrous and most shocking patriot, a blazing meteor of republicanism, and a violent enemy of Christianity. . . . The character of the son is so notorious as a reviler of religion . . . that the President hesitated openly to reward. It must be done sideways, covertly."[9] Abraham Bishop's crimes, in Federalist eyes, were multiple. He had opposed adoption of the Constitution; he had divorced his wife; he had published during the 1800 election campaign a "virulent political pamphlet" attacking the clergy; and he had celebrated Jefferson's election with a feast and speech of thanksgiving in Wallingford on 11 March, where he was reported to have compared Jefferson to Jesus Christ and boldly to have proclaimed "that the cause of Mr. Jefferson requires the downfall of the clergy."[10]

To the Federalist press, which solemnly announced that "without morality no free government can be long sustained, and without religion there can be no security to morals,"[11] the appointment, even by proxy, of such a man was proof of Jefferson's continued hostility to religion. Nor was the character of Bishop the younger the only testimony to that hostility. It did not take long for pious critics to notice that Jefferson's response to the New Haven remonstrance had been penned on the Sabbath. "If individual evils are consequent on the neglect of the duties of the Lord's day, may we not expect national calamities when the rulers of the Land treat the day with irreverence? When we see the Chief Magistrate employed in his official

"Office-Seeking During Jefferson's Administration," *American Historical Review,* III [1898], 273-76); Jefferson to Edwards, 21 July 1801 (Ford, *Works,* IX, 279).

[9] *Washington Federalist,* 5 Aug., 21 Oct. 1801.

[10] On Abraham Bishop, see the sketch in Franklin Bowditch Dexter, *Biographical Sketches of the Graduates of Yale College . . .,* IV (New York, 1907), 17-24. Bishop's "Oration delivered in Wallingford, on the 11th of March 1801, before the Republicans of the State of Connecticut, at their General Thanksgiving, for the election of Thomas Jefferson to the Presidency and of Aaron Burr to the Vice Presidency of the United States of America" was reprinted as a pamphlet in New Haven, 1801.

[11] From the *Gazette of the United States,* reprinted in *Washington Federalist,* 26 Aug. 1801.

duties on the Sabbath?" editorialized the *New Hampshire Courier*. Surely such activities were but a prelude to the horrors of the French Revolution. "The persecution of the Clergy—a disregard of the Sabbath, followed by its total abolition—were among the first effects of the revolution in France," Federalist readers were reminded.[12]

If the appointment of Samuel Bishop (and through him of Abraham) suggested to Federalists Jefferson's hidden designs against Christianity, the return of Thomas Paine to the United States confirmed their suspicions. Rumors that Jefferson had invited him circulated as early as July 1801, although Paine did not arrive until the fall of 1802. The instigation of his coming was not Jefferson's invitation, but Paine's own request for safe passage.[13] This gave Federalist editors a full year in advance to fulminate against Paine and Jefferson.

> The President of the United States has, publicly, in the face of day, cordially, nay affectionately invited the most infamous and depraved character of this or any age to take refuge in our country—a man who, to please a French atheist, prostituted what talents he had, and wrote a public and daring attack on the Christian religion—who while an intimate with Gov. Monro wrote and published a letter to General Washington, containing the most infernal slander his crooked and unprincipled cunning could contrive.[14]

Although Paine's attack on Washington inspired some of the outrage against him, most criticism centered on the irreligion in *The Age of Reason*. A violent deist tract, bordering at times on the obscene in its criticism of scripture (particularly in passages dealing with the Virgin birth), the work nevertheless affirmed Paine's own faith in a God of nature and of reason.[15] Jefferson's invitation to Paine, the Federalists presumed, confirmed his sympathy for Paine's attacks on both Washington and religion. "How great must be the satisfaction of this fraternal pair, when released from all

[12] *Washington Federalist*, 28 Aug. 1801. The twin specters of Abraham Bishop and Jefferson's Sabbath exertions continued to rise in the *Washington Federalist* throughout Jefferson's first administration (3, 5, 7, 21, 28 Aug., 18 Sept., 2, 9, 21 Oct. 1801, 11 Apr. 1803).

[13] Malone, *Jefferson the President*, pp. 192-200; Jerry W. Knudson, "The Rage around Tom Paine: Newspaper Reaction to his Homecoming in 1802," *New-York Historical Society Quarterly*, LIII (1969), 34-63.

[14] From the *New York Evening Post*, reprinted in the *Washington Federalist*, 16 Aug. 1802.

[15] Begun while he was in prison, completed while he lived with James Monroe in Paris, *The Age of Reason* was published by Paine in two parts in 1794 and 1796. Although the first part went through seventeen editions in America by 1796, there is no evidence that Jefferson owned a copy at that time. He was certainly familiar with its reputation and must have known Paine's opinions on the subject. Gary B. Nash argues that *The Age of Reason* had the greatest effect on revealed religion of all Enlightenment writings in America, influencing clerical dislike of France long before the events of Adams's administration ("The American Clergy and the French Revolution," *WMQ*, 3d ser., XXII [1965], 402).

restraint, they can give full scope to their feelings; then they can unite in scoffing at the suffering of a Savior, making jest of his holy precepts," editorialized the *Washington Federalist* after informing its readers that "Citizen Ego has become quite domesticated at the President's; he dines there 3 or 4 times a week." Paine himself thought the welcome at Jefferson's home far less cordial than he might have wished. He wrote early in 1803 chastizing Jefferson for a "sort of shyness, as if you stood in fear of federal observation." The Federalists needed no such pretext for their charges, and Jefferson responded rather bitterly to Paine of "federal calumny" that, "as to fearing it, if I ever could have been weak enough for that, they have taken care to cure me of it thoroughly."[16]

Although Jefferson's appointment of Bishop and his hospitality to Paine gave the Federalists excuses to attack his religion, they frequently initiated criticism of his faith without any excuse. Events that had little or no connection to Jefferson were construed to illustrate the constant threat that an atheistical president posed to public morals and religious safety. A case in point was the widely reported trial of Jason Fairbanks for the murder of Eliza Fales. Fairbanks had been courting Eliza and possibly had been spurned. The newspapers reveled in the gory details. The finding of Eliza's mutilated body, the appearance of the murderer drenched in her blood, his trial and conviction, his escape from prison, recapture, and execution, and the trial of friends who aided his escape, titillated readers far from Dedham, Massachusetts, the scene of the crime.[17]

For Federalist editors, there was a solemn warning in the story. Two years before the murder, Fairbanks was reported to have "been seduced . . . by some European travellers; and joined with a society of Jacobin deists." Among the more dangerous of their beliefs was their avowal "that a rigid observance of chastity in man or woman was ridiculous." A Dedham correspondent assured readers that Fairbanks had been so lost to principles of morality and virtue that he had tried to seduce poor Eliza by loaning her the works of William Godwin. To Federalists, Godwin's name had become synonymous by 1800 with irreligious "philosophy," radical Jacobin revolutionary ideology, and amoral rejection of chastity and marriage.[18]

---

[16] *Washington Federalist,* 19 Nov. 1802; Paine to Jefferson, 12 Jan. 1803 (Malone, *Jefferson the President*, p. 198); Jefferson to Paine, 13 Jan. 1803 (Paul Leicester Ford, ed., *The Writings of Thomas Jefferson* [10 vols.; New York, 1892-99], VIII, 189 [hereafter cited as Ford, *Writings*]).

[17] *Washington Federalist,* 1 June, 2, 18 Sept. 1801, 17 Feb. 1802.

[18] An uncompromising radical intellectual, Godwin despite his views against matrimony married Mary Wollstonecraft for the sake of their daughter, Mary Wollstonecraft Shelley. An anarchist, Godwin rejected all contemporary forms of government and organized religion as a denial of man's nature.

Within a few weeks of the detailed reports of Eliza Fales's murder and its attribution to the baleful influence of Godwin, the *Washington Federalist* informed its readers that a "Bookselling Company and Literary Society" formed in the new capital city had as its chief intention the American printing of Godwin's works. Although this project was as yet incomplete, the society had established a circulating library. At the head of the list of subscribers for the library was Thomas Jefferson. The editor claimed that it was the great object of all "conspirators against the Christian religion, to have printed on course paper, and in the cheapest manner, immensely large editions of their atheistical philosophy that they might fall into the hands of every man, woman and child." There could be no mistake, he continued, that "with certain high characters . . . similar motives have operated, the destruction of Christianity, and the diffusion of Jacobinism." A contributor to the *Commercial Advertiser* made the connection more directly; in a satirical parody of a supposed debate between Jefferson and the New Haven merchants, Jefferson could not take an oath because he had lost his Bible and could not procure another in all Virginia. "To ease your doubts, however," said Jefferson, "I can substitute *Godwin's Enquirer*, and that in this part of the country, is of much greater authority than the Bible." [19]

If Jefferson's religious opinions were linked by insinuation to Godwin's freethinking philosophy on religion and marriage, they became the subject of direct ridicule in the episode of the mammoth cheese. In the summer of 1801 Elder John Leland induced his Baptist congregation in Cheshire, Massachusetts, to manufacture an enormous cheese, which he presented to President Jefferson for his Republicanism and support of religious liberty. Made from the milk of 900 cows, formed in a "cyder press," measuring four feet in diameter, fifteen inches in height, and weighing 1,235 pounds, the cheese was delivered to the president on New Year's Day, 1802, and presented with a suitable exchange of speeches between Jefferson and Leland.[20]

[19] *Washington Federalist*, 30 Sept., 7 Aug. 1801; see also in the issue of 7 Sept. 1801 a "New Political Primmer" satirizing Jeffersonian Republicanism with an introductory catechism as "an entering wedge, or accidence, to the Age of Reason and Godwin's Political Justice" (reprinted from *Columbian Centinel*).

[20] The cheese was pulled to Washington from Baltimore harbor in a wagon drawn by five horses. Jefferson paid Leland $200 for it on 4 Jan. A large part of the interior of the cheese had to be removed because of spoilage, but enough remained that Jefferson paid an additional $23 on 26 Nov. for transportation of the cheese (Jefferson account book, pp. 146, 159, Jefferson Papers). During the course of the year, he doled out pieces of it to various Republican celebrations (*Washington Federalist*, 7 July 1802). For accounts of this episode, see Malone, *Jefferson the President*, pp. 106-8; L. H. Butterfield, "Elder John Leland, Jeffersonian Itinerant," *Proceedings of the American Antiquarian Society*, LXII (1952), 214-29; *Washington Federalist*, 31 Aug., 12 Oct., 31 Dec. 1801, 2, 5, 11 Jan. 1802.

The first Federalist reaction to the project was surprise "to find a clergyman engaged in this business." The citizens of Cheshire were advised to "change their plan and present the cheese to a man of religion, of wisdom, and unfeigned patriotism, to Mr. STRONG, the Governor of their own state."[21] Others were less piously solemn, however, and the cheese became for one Federalist poet a metaphor for Jefferson's agony over his irreligion.

(From the *Portfolio*)

Reflections of Mr. Jefferson, Over the Mammoth Cheese

In this great cheese I see myself portray'd,
My life and fortunes in this useless mass,
I curse the hands, by which the thing was made,
To them a cheese, to me a looking-glass.

Once I was pure—Alas, that happy hour,
E'en as the milk, from which this monster came,
Till turn'd by philosophic rennet sour,
I barter'd virtue for an empty name.

Then *press'd* by doctrines from the Gallic school,
A harden'd mass of nameless stuff I stood,
Where crude confusion mindless without rule,
And countless seeds of foul corruption bud.

E'en the round form this work of art displays,
Marks the uncertain, endless path I tread,
Where truth is lost in falsehood's dreary maze,
And vice in circles whirls the giddy head.

Delusive view! Where light is cast aside,
And principles surrender'd for *mere words*,
Ah me, how lost to just and noble pride,
I am indeed become *a man of curds*.

Like to this cheese, my outside, smooth and sound,
Presents an aspect kind and lasting too;
When nought but rottenness within is found,
And all my seeming rests on nothing true.

Fair to the view, I catch admiring eyes.
The nation wonders, and the world applaud.
When spread beyond my *just and nat'ral size*,
I seem to them an earthly demigod.

. . . .

[21] *Washington Federalist*, 31 Aug. 1801.

Go, hated Mentor, blast no more my sight,
I would forget myself, and heaven defy,
Inur'd to darkness, I detest the light,
Would be a suicide, but dare not die.[22]

Throughout the first years of Jefferson's presidency, the Federalist press took great care to keep the question of Jefferson's faith, or lack of it, constantly before its readership, by printing letters to the editor on the subject. While the election of 1800 still hung in the balance, "Lucius," writing "To the Federal Members of the House of Representatives," warned that

> Mr. Jefferson is believed to be a Philosopher of the school of Voltaire, a school in which were instructed his former friends, Brissot, Condorcet, and the other infidel Philosophers of France who have in that nation endeavored . . . from deep rooted hatred to eradicate every principle and efface every vestige of the Christian religion.[23]

Despite Jefferson's silence on religion, his careful attendance at divine worship while president, and the continued safety of the churches, "Fidelis," writing to the *Columbian Centinel* nearly a year later in an "Address to Thomas Jefferson," told him that

> a large proportion are distressed with the apprehension that you belong to that class of philosophers who think the extirpation of the christian religion would be a benefit to mankind, that this is part of that plan of improvement upon which your heart is set, and that to aid you in the persecution of it, you have sent to France for the assistance of the author of the Age of Reason.[24]

"Recantator," in a long letter "To Thomas Jefferson, President of the United States" in March 1802, proclaimed that he had reverted from republicanism to opposition to the president because of his own religious scruples, that Jefferson's silence on the matter proved the president to be both an unbeliever and a hypocrite who deluded his friends and enemies alike.[25]

---

[22] Ibid., 2 Apr. 1802. A satirical editorial, "Anticipation of the Message," poking fun at Jefferson's policy of delivering his annual message to Congress in writing rather than making a speech, was devoted entirely to a report on the cheese (ibid., 13 Jan. 1802). The editor was so delighted with his own wit that he repeated himself with a similar "Anticipation of the Message" on 6 Dec. 1802.

[23] Ibid., 10 Feb. 1801.

[24] Ibid., 18 Sept. 1801. The same writer also found proof of Jefferson's designs against religion in the appointment of Bishop, in Jefferson's response to the New Haven merchants, and in the actions of his secretary of war in calling for a military review in Rhode Island on the Sabbath.

[25] Ibid., 8 Mar. 1802.

A Virginian, "Republicus," in a letter "To professors of the Christian Religion throughout the United States," asked,

> Is a man who despises religion, and the memory and the politics of Washington, qualified to govern Christians and the children of our great political father? We as orphans of our deceased father, Washington, have chosen Mr. Jefferson our guardian; and however approveable and fair his conduct may appear to some, yet when we have reason to suspect that his religious and political principles are averse to our late father's, we have cause at least to pause and examine.[26]

A "plain old countryman," who signed his letter "True Penny," wrote to the Federalist editors of his outrage that Jefferson had invited Paine to America. That "this Satanic disciple, this moving lump of infamy and rottenness, this vile libeller of Washington, this Blasphemer of our Saviour, would be the intimate of Jefferson . . . is too much for the American character to bear with."[27]

These are but a sampling of the types of assault on Jefferson's supposed religious philosophy that appeared in the Federalist press during Jefferson's first administration. The attacks occurred at a time when the press was increasingly the source of the community's knowledge of national and local politics.[28] Letters to the editor, responses in Republican papers that were in turn taken up again in the Federalist columns, satirical poetry, reports of toasts at Federalist celebrations of Washington's birthday, or at Republican feasts on the anniversary of Jefferson's inauguration—all kept the issue of Jefferson's religion constantly before the reading and voting public. Though by 1803 he was used to the abuse of his faith for the sake of his politics, Jefferson must have been discouraged by the tenacity of his opponents. In his later years he insisted that the only sound policy was to "Say nothing of my Religion: it is known to my God and myself alone."[29] That had been in general his policy before 1800. Given the persistence of the religious issue, the president and his party may have found silence unnecessarily risky as they prepared for the next election.

Of his knowledge of these lampoons there can be little doubt. Jefferson

[26] Ibid., 24 Dec. 1802.

[27] Ibid., 25 Feb. 1803.

[28] See Thomas C. Leonard for a discussion of the growing role of newspaper reporting as a source for partisan political information in the late eighteenth century ("News for a Revolution: The Exposé in America, 1768-1773," *Journal of American History*, LXVII [1980], 26-40).

[29] Jefferson to Charles Thomson, 29 Jan. 1817 (Ford, *Writings*, X, 75-76). Jefferson is here quoting a letter he had written to Mr. Delaplaine in response to the latter's accusations based on a 9 Jan. 1816 letter of Jefferson to Thomson. There is a 26 July 1816 letter to Delaplaine, but nothing in it is on this subject (Ford, *Works*, X, 55).

was an inveterate and careful reader of newspapers. His account books for the period 1798-1803 record his subscriptions to nineteen different newspapers, most of them Republican.[30] The Federalist paper he saw most often and read most completely while president was the *Washington Federalist;* between 1801 and 1803 he could have seen in its pages long diatribes against his religion reprinted from the *New England Palladium,* the *Port-Folio,* the *Fredericktown* (Virginia) *Herald,* the *New York Evening Post,* the *Connecticut Courant,* the *Richmond Recorder,* the *Gazette of the United States,* the *Charleston Courier,* the *Utica* (New York) *Patriot,* and the *Commercial Advertizer,* to mention only a few. Clearly the attacks were not confined to New England but were spread throughout the nation. Their political danger was heightened by the scurrilous charges against his sexual morality, published first by the disgruntled James Callender in 1802. Jefferson was determined not to countenance them by responding to the stories of his supposed liaison with Sally Hemings and the insinuations concerning his alleged adultery with Mrs. Walker.[31] But with the ongoing connections being drawn between his philosophy and that of Paine and Godwin, the Sally Hemings stories were doubly damaging.

Jefferson believed that "I am a Christian, in the only sense he [Jesus] wished anyone to be; sincerely attached to his doctrines, in preference to all others; ascribing to himself every *human* excellence; & believing he never claimed any other." Indeed the very persecution against which he wished to defend himself had in part stimulated Jefferson to a series of conversations and correspondence about matters of faith. Jefferson later recalled that conversations with Benjamin Rush during the height of the paranoia over the quasi war with France in 1798-99 "served as an anodyne to the afflictions of the crisis through which our country was then laboring," and that "the Christian religion was sometimes our topic."[32] References to religion are relatively sparse in Jefferson's correspondence before 1800, but even dis-

[30] Jefferson account book, pp. 101-67, Jefferson Papers; E. Millicent Sowerby lists twenty bound volumes of newspapers he had systematically collected (*Catalogue of the Library of Thomas Jefferson* [5 vols.; Washington, D.C., 1952-59], I, 267-85). On Jefferson's keeping newspapers for a record, see Jefferson to James Madison, 6 Apr. 1798 (Ford, *Works,* VIII, 403). On the *Washington Federalist,* see Jefferson to Levi Lincoln, 24 Mar. 1802 (Ford, *Works,* IX, 357-58).

[31] Malone, *Jefferson the President,* pp. 212-16; Fawn M. Brodie, *Thomas Jefferson: An Intimate History* (New York, 1974), pp. 348-56. The *Washington Federalist* had editorialized as early as 14 Sept. 1801, "That it has long been currently reported that a man very high in office, has a number of yellow children, and that he is adicted to golden affections. It is natural to suppose it possible that personal or political enemies of Mr. J. might raise such reports, when they are wholly unfounded—and on the other side it is observed that, what everybody says must be true. . . . If they are false and malicious they ought to be contradicted."

[32] Jefferson to Rush, 21 Apr. 1803 (Ford, *Works,* IX, 457).

counting the scathing dismissals of the clergy and their power, such references are far more numerous afterwards, increasing with the severity of the attacks on his faith.

During the height of the 1800 campaign, Jefferson wrote to Bishop James Madison a brief critique of a book on the philosophy of Wishaupt, the founder of the Masonic doctrines of Illuminism. This philosophy, Jefferson reported, is "the indefinite perfectibility of man," which "you know is Godwin's doctrine. . . . Wishaupt believes that to promote this perfection of the human character was the object of Jesus Christ. That his intention was simply to reinstate natural religion, & by diffusing the light of his morality, to teach us to govern ourselves." Jefferson's analysis of Wishaupt's Christian beliefs shows a clear parallel with the doctrines he later described as his own.[33] In 1801 he expressed to Moses Robinson his hope that once the clergy were cleansed of their political hatreds, "the Christian religion, . . . divested of the rags in which they have enveloped it, and brought to the original purity and simplicity of its benevolent institutor" would then be revealed as the faith "of all others most friendly to liberty, science, and the freest expansion of the human mind." To Priestley, to Elbridge Gerry, to Isaac Story, Jefferson wrote in some detail his admiring evaluation of the "mild and simple principles of the Christian philosophy."[34]

The question was how to convey such conviction to those loyal Republicans, particularly Republicans in New England, who might be sensitive to or confused by the joint attacks on Jefferson's immorality and irreligion. Jefferson claimed that if he were to answer one lie "twenty new ones" would be raised against him and that the newspapers were "a bear-garden field into which I do not chuse to enter." Nevertheless, he found ways of making his true political views known to those who could be reasonably persuaded. As president, he had used official responses to citizen petitions as a means of publicly stating important principles. The answer to the New Haven remonstrance was one such. An address from the Danbury (Connecticut) Baptists praising the separation of church and state provided another "occasion, by

[33] Jefferson to Bishop James Madison, 31 Jan. 1800 (ibid., pp. 108-9). Many of Jefferson's contemporaries would have been appalled at his approval of Wishaupt's ideas, for the Bavarian Illuminati, which he founded, enjoyed a reputation in 1801 not unlike that of the Communist party in 1950-53. For a scholarly treatment of that furor, see Vernon Stauffer, *New England and the Bavarian Illuminati* (1918; reprint ed., New York, 1967).

[34] Jefferson to Robinson, 23 Mar. 1801 (Albert Ellery Bergh, ed., *The Writings of Thomas Jefferson*, X [Washington, D.C., 1907], 236-37); Jefferson to Priestley, 21 Mar. 1801 (Ford, *Works*, IX, 216-19); Jefferson to Gerry, 29 Mar. 1801 (ibid., pp. 240-44); Jefferson to Story, 5 Dec. 1801 (ibid., pp. 319-21).

way of answer, of sowing useful truths and principles among the people, which might germinate and become rooted among their political tenets."[35]

Jefferson was also skilled in using private communications to sympathetic friends as a way of circulating opinions without implicating himself. During 1798-1800 when he feared prosecution under the Sedition Act and was almost paranoid about the possibilities of being misquoted, he continued to express himself in vivid language, proclaiming his political principles. He arranged for distribution of political propaganda, urged supporters to action, but insisted "do not let my name appear in the matter."[36] In a long letter to William Giles in 1801, he outlined his ideas on the removal of Federalists from office. Jefferson warned, "I sketch them to you in confidence. Not that there is objection to your mooting them as subjects of conversation, and as proceeding from yourself, but not as matters of executive determination." In July 1802 Jefferson candidly detailed his policy in a letter to Governor Hall of Delaware in response to a request from Republicans in that state that a Federalist be removed from his post for cause. Jefferson concluded,

> Our opponents are so disposed to make a malignant use of whatever comes from me, to torture every word into meanings never meant in order to gratify their own passions and principles, that I must ask the favor of you to communicate verbally the sentiments of this letter to those who forwarded their addresses through you, not permitting the letter or any copy to go out of your hands.[37]

In spite of the press of official business in early 1803—the negotiations for the purchase of Louisiana, the arrangements for Meriwether Lewis's expedition to the Pacific Northwest—and concerns over his health and

---

[35] Jefferson to James Monroe, 26 May 1800 (Ford, *Works*, IX, 136); Jefferson to Jeremiah Moor, 14 Aug. 1800 (ibid., p. 144); Jefferson to Levi Lincoln, 1 Jan. 1802 (Bergh, *Writings*, X, 305). Jefferson was dissuaded by his attorney general from using his January 1802 response to the Danbury Baptists to explain his scruples against proclaiming fast days, for fear that drawing attention to his actions would further alienate the clergy and any possible faithful New England Republicans (draft of Jefferson's "Address" to the Danbury Baptists, Jefferson Papers; Lincoln to Jefferson, 1 Jan. 1802, ibid.; Malone, *Jefferson the President*, pp. 108-9).

[36] On the need for anonymity or secrecy, see for instance Jefferson to John Page, 24 Jan. 1799 (Ford, *Works*, IX, 13-15); Jefferson to James Madison, 5 Feb. 1799 (ibid., p. 34); Jefferson to Archibald Stuart, 13 Feb. 1799 (ibid., pp. 40-45); Jefferson to James Callender, 6 Oct. 1799 (ibid., pp. 83-85). Jefferson proclaimed that he made no secret of his political principles: "On the contrary I wish them known to avoid the imputation of those which are not mine," but he requested that "no uncandid use" be made of his letter spelling them out (to Jeremiah Moor, 14 Aug. 1800 [ibid., pp. 142-44]). For similar reluctance to have his views explicitly known, see Jefferson to Dr. Hugh Williamson, 10 Jan. 1801 (ibid., pp. 167-69); Jefferson to Gideon Granger, 13 Aug. 1800 (ibid., pp. 138-41).

[37] Jefferson to Giles, 23 Mar. 1801 (ibid., pp. 222-23); Jefferson to Benjamin Rush, 24 Mar. 1801 (ibid., pp. 229-32); Jefferson to Hall, 2 July 1802 (ibid., pp. 377-78).

family,[38] Jefferson must have been searching in the back of his mind for a way out of the dilemma presented by the ongoing attacks on his religion. He must have wished to justify himself at least to his friends and family. In the middle of March 1803 Jefferson retired to Monticello for some much-needed rest. As he prepared to return to the capital on 6 April, he received from his old friend Joseph Priestley a small book entitled *Socrates and Jesus Compared*. The trip back to Washington gave Jefferson time to study thoroughly the comparison his friend had made; it suggested to him a format for outlining the tenets of his own faith. With characteristic deliberateness, Jefferson determined to prepare a description of his estimate of Christianity that he had promised Benjamin Rush in 1798. He first outlined his ideas for Priestley, thanking him for the gift of his book, then repeated them in a letter to Edward Dowse, a Massachusetts shipmaster.[39] Finally, in mid-April he composed a brief, closely written, two-page summary, "A Syllabus of an Estimate of the Merit of the Doctrines of Jesus, Compared with those of Others."[40]

The syllabus was the most complete statement of his faith that Jefferson ever wrote. It reflected the critical deism that formed the basis of Jefferson's approach to matters of faith throughout most of his adult life. Two aspects of the statement are important in the context of its creation. In comparing the ideas of Jesus, the Jews, and the ancient philosophers, Jefferson's overriding concern was with the question of morality. His preoccupation with that issue is revealing; it was precisely on the grounds of moral laxity that

[38] Jefferson suffered from a chronic diarrhea, which caused him some discomfort, and required him, as a cure, to spend much time riding (Jefferson to Rush, 20 Dec. 1801 [Ford, *Writings*, VIII, 126-27]; Rush to Jefferson, 12 Mar. 1802, Jefferson Papers; Jefferson to Rush, 28 Feb. 1803 [Ford, *Writings*, VIII, 219-21]; Jefferson to Rush, 23 Apr. 1803, Jefferson Papers).

[39] Jefferson to Priestley, 9 Apr. 1803 (Ford, *Works*, IX, 458-59); Jefferson to Dowse, 19 Apr. 1803 (Bergh, *Writings*, X, 376-78). Jefferson first met Dowse in October 1789, and they carried on a sporadic correspondence, with Dowse occasionally accepting a commission to purchase goods abroad for Jefferson (Julian P. Boyd, ed., *The Papers of Thomas Jefferson*, XV [Princeton, 1958], 527 n., 563). Dowse had written enclosing a sermon by Bennett on the moral precepts of Jesus, the reprinting of which he wanted Jefferson to sponsor.

[40] The syllabus is printed in Ford, *Works*, IX, 457-63; as a photographic facsimile in Sowerby, *Catalogue*, II, facing pp. 172 and 173. Both those sources surround the text with relevant correspondence. The syllabus is discussed in Malone, *Jefferson the President*, chap. 11; Brodie, *Jefferson*, pp. 370-73. Analysis of the intellectual sources for Jefferson's theological ideas in the syllabus is a task that has not yet been undertaken by scholars and is outside the scope of this paper. In general, scholars who have written on the subject of Jefferson's faith and the place of the syllabus in it, including most recently William B. Huntley ("Jefferson's Public and Private Religion," *South Atlantic Quarterly*, LXXIX [1980], 286-301) approach that belief system as if it were an inorganic whole, unchanging over time. Ideas expressed in Jefferson's retirement correspondence with John Adams are juxtaposed in a conceptual scheme with ideas that appeared in the *Notes on the State of Virginia*. I find Huntley's conceptual organization a useful one but ultimately misleading, even in its analysis of the syllabus, because of its failure to account for change, development, and the impact of external political and personal events upon Jefferson's faith.

Jefferson was currently being most viciously attacked. Moreover, the importance of the moral sense as the basis of Republican virtue lay at the heart of his own philosophy.[41] Jefferson wished his friends to know that the moral principles he most admired were those at the foundation of the Christian faith, whatever his critics might say of him.

Contained in the syllabus also are poignant reflections of Jefferson's sensitivity to relentless criticism. When he analyzed Jesus's career, Jefferson remarked that "the disadvantages under which his doctrines appear are remarkable." Chief among them was that "according to the ordinary fate of those who attempt to enlighten and reform mankind, he fell an early victim to the jealousy & combination of the altar and the throne." And the fragmentary doctrines that did survive this jealousy "have been still more disfigured by the corruptions of schismatising followers." Such language reflects a bitter awareness of Jefferson's own persecution from the "altar and the throne." When he spoke of Jesus's doctrines being committed to writing and "disfigured" by unlettered and ignorant men, he may have been remembering the overenthusiastic perversions of his own policy by such uninhibited Republican editors as William Duane of the Philadelphia *Aurora* or the betrayal by his former supporter Callender.

This is not to suggest that Jefferson saw himself as Christlike, whatever Abraham Bishop said to those faithful Republicans in Wallingford, Connecticut, or the reverence expressed by some of his modern biographers. But Jefferson had a special sympathy for those he saw as unjustly persecuted. It was no coincidence that he had bitterly complained in 1801 to one correspondent, "If revealed language had not been able to guard itself against misinterpretations, I could not expect it." To another he wrote that the clergy "crucified their Saviour, who preached that their kingdom was not of this world; and all who practise on that precept must expect the extreme of their wrath." The anticlericalism explicit in these letters and implicit in the syllabus became after 1803 increasingly evident in Jefferson's expression of his faith.[42]

In addition to sending the syllabus to Rush and Priestley and to outlining the ideas of it to Edward Dowse, Jefferson also discretely distributed it to

---

[41] See Adrienne Koch for a discussion of the importance to Jefferson of the "moral sense" and its relationship to his religion (*The Philosophy of Thomas Jefferson* [New York, 1943], esp. chaps. 3, 4).

[42] Ford, *Works*, IX, 461-62; Jefferson to Isaac Story, 5 Dec. 1801 (ibid., pp. 319-20); Jefferson to Levi Lincoln, 26 Aug. 1801 (ibid., p. 290); see also Luebke, "Anti-Clericalism," *Church History*, XXXII (1963), 344-56.

others. One of the three manuscript copies of it in the Library of Congress is accompanied by a short note:

> I am desirous it [the syllabus] should be perused by three or four particular friends, with whom tho' I never desired to make a mystery of it, yet no occasion has happened to occur of explaining it to them. It is communicated for their personal satisfaction & to enable them to judge the truth or falsehood of the libels published on that subject.[43]

The note does not say (and perhaps it did not need to) whether or not these "particular friends" could use the information in the syllabus as a basis for defending Jefferson to sympathetic doubters—without attribution, of course.

Although there is no mention of who those friends are, one copy of the syllabus was sent to Jefferson's secretary of war, Henry Dearborn, and another to his attorney general, Levi Lincoln. By no small coincidence Lincoln was a frequent advisor on policy affecting New England. Dearborn replied to Jefferson in May, suggesting a few changes of wording in the syllabus should it ever be put into print. Under the signature of "A Farmer," Lincoln had defended Jefferson's religious ideas in a series of "Letters to the People," published in the Worcester *Massachusetts Spy* between August and December of 1801 and reprinted by a Philadelphia printer in pamphlet form in 1802. Lincoln thanked Jefferson profusely and asked Jefferson's permission to keep his copy, which Jefferson granted. If the president sent copies to the other members of his cabinet, they considered the matter confidential and made no reply.[44]

On 25 April Jefferson finished distributing the syllabus for the time being by sending copies to both of his daughters with a similar covering letter:

> A promise made to a friend some years ago, but executed only lately, has placed my religious creed on paper. I have thought it just that my family, by possessing this, should be enabled to estimate the libels published against me on this, as on every other possible subject.

---

[43] Dated by another hand, 21 Apr. 1803, Jefferson Papers; Ford, *Works*, IX, 459.

[44] Dearborn to Jefferson, received 4 May 1803, Jefferson Papers; Lincoln to Jefferson, 24 Apr. 1803, ibid.; Jefferson to Lincoln, 26 Apr. 1803 (Ford, *Works*, IX, 459). The ten "Letters" appeared on 19 Aug., 9, 16, 23 Sept., 21, 28 Oct., 11, 25 Nov., and 2 Dec.; they were widely reprinted in New England and inspired answering attacks on Jefferson and "the Farmer" from such anonymous correspondents as "Quintilian," "Clericus," and "Fidelis." Contemporaries guessed that Lincoln was "the Farmer." See a letter addressed to "the Farmer, a writer of Great length and wonderful Obscurity . . . Supposed to be a Great Officer of State" (*Salem* [Massachusetts] *Gazette*, 5 Jan. 1802). *A Farmer's Letters to the People* (Philadelphia, 1802) was also published separately as a pamphlet in Salem in 1802.

Fawn Brodie was undoubtedly right that Jefferson intended to reassure his daughters by this roundabout way that the moral charges brought against him by Callender (which he could not bring himself to address directly, even to them) were as false as those religious charges controverted by the syllabus.[45] He must have been gratified to have Rush respond, "I have read your creed with great attention, and was much pleased to find you are by no means so heterodox as you have been supposed to be by your enemies."[46] The testament was indeed serving a dual purpose, satisfying its author of the rationality of his own creed and reassuring his family and friends that he was not the heretical atheist so graphically depicted by the Federalist press.

The syllabus was a turning point in Jefferson's approach to the questions that religion attempts to answer. He wrote far more about his beliefs after his compilation of it than he ever had before. It was as if the political interference of the theologians had opened the door of theology to one who had been primarily a politician. He pursued his reawakened curiosity on matters of doctrine in two characteristic ways. Through an extensive correspondence he expounded upon religion to friends who shared this interest. This culminated in his retirement with the long and rewarding exchange with John Adams. And he filled his library with books on the subject. During Jefferson's stay in Europe he had sporadically collected books on religious topics. His renewed interest in such purchases began as soon as he sent the syllabus off to Rush and Priestley. In the same post he wrote to his Philadelphia bookseller with a request for copies of the rest of Priestley's works, particularly his *A Harmony of the Evangelists* (in English and in Greek) and *An History of Early opinions Concerning Jesus Christ.*[47] These works and others reinforced and enriched, but did not substantially change, Jefferson's assessment in the syllabus of the centrality of the moral doctrines of Jesus of Nazareth to the true religion of nature. Preparing the syllabus, which served as an anodyne to the "bigotry in politics and religion"

[45] Jefferson to Martha Jefferson Randolph, 25 Apr. 1803 (Edwin Morris Betts and James Adam Bear, Jr., eds., *The Family Letters of Thomas Jefferson* [Columbia, Mo., 1966], pp. 243-44, where it is mistakenly dated 23 Apr. [see MS of this letter, Jefferson Papers]); Jefferson to Mary Jefferson Eppes, 25 Apr. 1803 (Betts and Bear, *Family Letters*, p. 245); Brodie, *Jefferson*, pp. 370-73. Late in 1803 Jefferson borrowed Mary's copy of the syllabus to loan it to his old friend, John Page (Jefferson to Mary Jefferson Eppes, 26 Dec. 1803 [Betts and Bear, *Family Letters*, p. 250]).

[46] Rush to Jefferson, 5 May 1803, Jefferson Papers. Rush did not agree "in your account of the character and mission of the author of our Religion" and promised "you shall receive my creed shortly."

[47] Sowerby, *Catalogue*, II, 121, 104-5.

that Jefferson suffered under between 1800 and 1803, was also a bridge to Jefferson's reinvolvement with questions on the nature of the universe that engaged him in lively debates with a number of correspondents during his retirement.

The Political Economy of John Taylor of Caroline

DUNCAN MACLEOD

After years of comparative neglect John Taylor of Caroline has recently begun to receive again a degree of attention more in keeping with his true importance. That his impact upon both his own generation and upon subsequent generations of historians has always been less than it might have been is due largely to his tortured style of writing and the tortuous thought processes it reflected. John Randolph of Roanoke once commented that Taylor needed only a translator to make an impact, and Thomas Jefferson, replying to a communication from John Adams in 1814, wrote that a book received by Adams must have been Taylor's *An Inquiry into the Principles and Policy of the Government of the United States*: "neither the style nor the stuff of the author of Arator can ever be mistaken. [I]n the latter work, as you observe, there are some good things, but so involved in quaint, in far-fetched, affected, mystical conceipts [*sic*], and flimsy theories, that who can take the trouble of getting at them?"[1] Taylor himself appeared to hold a fluent style in contempt, commenting that "A talent for fine writing is often a great misfortune to politicians."[2]

Although Taylor's style renders study of his writings far from congenial, the consistency of his purpose and thought make it relatively easy to extract the main thrusts of his arguments. Far from a rigorous theorist he provides a running commentary upon the politics of his times. In that capacity, however, he never felt compelled to define clearly, even to himself perhaps, some of the

Duncan MacLeod is a Fellow of St. Catherine's College and a Lecturer in History at the University of Oxford.

[1] Russell Kirk, *John Randolph of Roanoke: A Study in American Politics* (Chicago, 1964), p. 65; E. Millicent Sowerby, *Catalogue of the Library of Thomas Jefferson* (Washington, D.C., 1952), **1**, 371.

[2] "John Taylor Correspondence," in *The John B. Branch Historical Papers of Randolph-Macon College*, **2** (June 1908), 344.

Amer. Stud. **14**, 3, 387–406 *Printed in Great Britain*
0021–8758/80/BAAS–3002 $01.50

central premises from which his arguments derived. Writing over a period of some three decades and against a rapidly changing economic and political backcloth his extraordinary consistency has subjected him to surprisingly little actual misrepresentation. But he has suffered in one crucial respect, especially at the hands of more recent interpreters, who have paid too little attention to an examination of his underlying assumptions. The historians of the 1930s and 1940s did try to treat Taylor whole: today, one detects misleading stress upon a single if important, aspect of his work – what might be called his opposition side. This stress derives in part from the focus of many of his interpreters upon the events of the 1780s and 1790s. Conceiving of American politics in those decades in terms of court and country, administration and opposition parties, they have found a ready place for Taylor amongst the opposition.[3] But even the more comprehensive studies have tended to treat him similarly in terms of his oposition to trends in American society rather than in terms of any espousal of positive positions.[4]

That they have done so is not altogether unreasonable, for Taylor was in fact always opposing something or other and went so far as to suggest that he probably always would be. He wrote to Monroe in 1811 that he hoped Monroe would some day become President but he warned him that when that day came there would

> probably be an irreparable breach with the republican minority ... because you must in some measure suffer yourself to be taken in tow by an administration party; and I do not recollect in the history of mankind a single instance of such a party being republican. Should I live to see that day, I hereby give you notice, that you are not to infer from my espousing your election, that I will join a party yell in favor of your administration; No, no, the moment you are elected, though by my casting vote, carried an hundred miles in a snow storm, my confidence in

[3] See, for example, the various treatments of Taylor in Gordon Wood, *The Creation of the American Republic* (Chapel Hill, 1969); John Zvesper, *Political Philosophy and Rhetoric: A Study of the Origins of American Party Politics* (Cambridge, 1977); Lance Banning, *The Jeffersonian Persuasion: Evolution of a Party Ideology* (Ithaca, 1978); Eugene T. Mudge, *The Social Philosophy of John Taylor of Caroline* (New York, 1939). Professor Banning's treatment of Taylor suffers from being extensively illustrated by references to a pamphlet Taylor almost certainly did not write, *An Examination of the Late Proceedings in Congress Respecting the Official Conduct of the Secretary of the Treasury* (Richmond, 1793). (For evidence of James Monroe's authorship see Edmund and Dorothy Smith Berkeley, "'The Piece Left Behind'. Monroe's Authorship of a Political Pamphlet Revealed," *The Virginia Magazine of History and Biography*, **75** (1967), 174–80. The sentiments expressed in that pamphlet were, however, such that Taylor could easily have expressed them and they could have been illustrated by reference to the works Taylor did write.)

[4] See, for example, C. William Hill, Jr., *The Political Theory of John Taylor of Caroline* (Rutherford, N.J., 1977).

you would be most confoundedly deminished [*sic*], and I would instantly join again the republican minority.[5]

So Professor Banning and others are right to emphasize Taylor's fear of power, of privilege, and of corruption and to cast his thought in terms of an oppositional ideology. And Professor Hill and others are right to stress the division of powers, both within and between the state and federal governments, as a fundamental means by which Taylor sought to maintain the liberty of the people. They are only wrong in stopping there and in failing to seek the positive vision of society also entertained by Taylor.

The problem will not be solved, however, merely by returning to the formulations of earlier commentators who stressed Taylor's agrarianism rather more forcefully than have their successors. All have agreed upon that agrarianism but all have erred in deducing it almost entirely either from his politics or from some republican, romantic vision of a pastoral society.[6] The truth of the matter is, Taylor's thought rested not upon a single foundation, as most of his interpreters have suggested, but upon twin foundations, which were, variously, complementary, interactive, and conceptually autonomous:

A nation is both a natural and a moral being. Its natural powers we call physical, its moral, metaphysical or political. If it is deprived of its physical powers, it is like a man possessed of reason, bound; if of its intellectual only, it is like a maniac, unbound. If a nation is allowed the uninterrupted possession of either, it will get the other. Yet if it loses one, it will lose both; because usurpation is never safe with one only. Therefore an attempt to deprive it of either, confesses an intention to deprive it of both.[7]

From such reasoning Taylor derived a conviction that national happiness depended upon a joint commitment to agricultural prosperity and to republican liberty as it had emerged from the revolutionary struggle with England. That joint comitment was exemplified in two books: *Arator, Being a Series of Agricultural Essays, Practical and Political* (4th ed. 1818 – first published as newspaper articles in 1803) and *An Inquiry* (1814). They were intended to be complementary. "Arator is chiefly confined to agriculture, but it contains a few political observations. The Enquiry, to politics; but it labours to

[5] "John Taylor Correspondence," p. 316.

[6] The pastoral theme has been emphasized most significantly by Loren Baritz, *City on a Hill: A History of Ideas and Myths in America* (New York, 1964), pp. 159–203, and by M. E. Bradford in his introduction to the Liberty Classics edition of *Arator* (Indianapolis, 1977).

[7] John Taylor, *An Inquiry into the Principles and Policy of the Government of the United States* (Fredericksburg, 1814), p. 395.

explain the true interest of the agricultural class. The affinity between the subjects, caused them to be intermingled."[8]

Taylor wrote a number of other pamphlets and books, especially during what he conceived to be the critical situations of the 1790s and 1819–21. But although directed at particular targets there was nothing in these other works which was incompatible with the arguments of *Arator* and *An Inquiry*, nor, save in their applications, did he do much to elaborate those arguments. Yet it would be wrong to deduce from the vastly greater volume of Taylor's political works that his twin foundations were of unequal importance. Only circumstances dictated a greater emphasis upon the achievements of political ("moral") goals, than upon agricultural ("physical") ones:

> To save our sorry crops from free quarter sinecures, is even more important and more urgent, than to amend our agriculture....And the author ventures to assert, that whilst the readers of Arator will unanimously agree that its tendency is to improve our crops, those of the Enquiry ... will concur in the tendency of that book, to save them from becoming a prey to political frauds.[9]

Circumstances dictated political priorities.

> The plough can have little success, until the laws are altered which obstruct it. Societies for improving the breed of sheep or the form of ploughs, will be as likely to produce a good system of agriculture, under depressing laws, as societies for improving the English form of government under their depressing system of corruption.[10]

In his earlier pamphlets, in *Arator* and, for example, in an 1821 address to the United Agricultural Societies of Virginia, Taylor advocated the priority of political lobbying and action.[11] He did so because it appeared to him that the benefits to be derived from agricultural improvements were miniscule compared with the size of the levies imposed by government upon agriculture. In the defence of republican liberty political action was primary; although in the promotion of agricultural prosperity it was but a means to an end, the end was as dear as republican liberty itself.

[8] John Taylor, *Arator, Being a Series of Agricultural Essays, Practical and Political: In Sixty-Four Numbers*, Fourth Edition (Petersburg, 1818), p. iv.

[9] Ibid., p. v.

[10] Ibid., p. 42.

[11] John Taylor, *A Definition of Parties; or the Political Effects of the Paper System Considered* (Philadelphia, 1794), *An Enquiry into the Principles and Tendency of Certain Public Measures* (Philadelphia, 1794), *A Letter on the Necessity of Defending the Rights and Interests of Agriculture, Addressed to the Delegations of the United Agricultural Societies of Virginia* (Petersburg, 1821).

II

Although commentaries on Taylor's works differ in their balance and emphasis it is fair to say that his politics are fairly well understood. He opposed privilege, concentration of power and corruption particularly when they appeared in conjunction with banking and commercial interests; he advocated a strict separation of powers within the federal government and the rights of states as against those of the federal government; he pressed the interests of agriculture. The focus here, however, will be on Taylor's description of the "physical" world and the conclusions he drew from it, what might properly be called his economics. One must, however, begin by specifying his commitment to agriculture. Profound though it was it but reflected an even more fundamental commitment: to a labour theory of value. A labour theory of value penetrated both his twin foundations, the "moral" and the "physical," the political and the economic. It was a basic premise from which he deduced a number of political axioms; but it was also a theory he believed could be derived, or at least verified, by reference to the physical world. It thus served as both a metaphysical and a scientific theory. The significance of agriculture stemmed from two factors. First it was a "natural" activity operating directly upon land and land was "the unde derivatur of all products for man's use. It comprises the stock for trade and commerce. Its true interest, is the interest of the whole social and natural life."[12] Secondly, land constituted the majority interest of the nation.[13] These are recurring themes in Taylor's works and by no means unique to him.

Taylor's emphasis on land ran parallel to that of the French physiocrats although their paths never converged. For all the similarities of detail, all the mutual dependence upon agriculture, all the mutual commitment to *laissez faire* doctrines with respect to economic activity, Taylor and the physiocrats had different and incompatible objectives. Physiocrats might wish to free economic endeavour from state direction but they were not anti-statist in their orientation: their analysis derived from the need to generate a more substantial and secure governmental revenue.[14] Taylor on the other hand, was anti-statist and wished to avoid the generation of a revenue which he considered must inevitably become a fund for corruption extracted from the true producers of wealth. "Labour," he wrote, "in the erection of a government, after deducting the necessary expence of

[12] Taylor, *A Definition of Parties*, p. 8; Taylor, *Arator*, p. 190.

[13] See, for example, *Arator*, pp. vi, 20, 34.

[14] Elizabeth Fox Genovese, *The Origins of Physiocracy: Economic Revolution and Social Order in Eighteenth-Century France* (Ithaca, 1976).

supporting it, designed to secure safety to itself, in the enjoyment of its own fruits." He later stated the maxim "that national prosperity and liberty, are safe, endangered or lost, in proportion as individuals retain, or governments acquire, the investiture or disposition of the earnings of industry."[15]

Similarly, the notion that the agricultural interest, being the majority interest of the nation, could not oppress the nation, an idea which permeates Taylor's writings, was a commonly held view. Mercantilist and other writers had put forward this and many other of his arguments both within and without America. Taylor derived from the mercantilist tradition, for example, the idea that national wealth was a function of the net exports of the nation, an idea which underlay most of his almost incomprehensible calculations of agriculture's contributions to national prosperity.[16] Nevertheless, Taylor was not content merely to repeat the arguments of others: he fused them into a personal amalgam.

Taylor was writing at a time when the science of economics in the United States was still very primitive. The works of Adam Smith and David Ricardo were regarded there as difficult and abstruse. Familiarity with their ideas was more often gained through commentaries and secondary accounts than by reference to the originals.[17] Taylor had little in the way of American authors to guide him even had he been so inclined. Academic works on economics began to appear in the United States largely as a consequence of the interest eventually generated by Ricardo, the first edition of whose work appeared in America in 1819; Daniel Raymond's *Thoughts on Political Economy* appeared in 1820; The Reverend McVickar, of Columbia, published *Outlines of Political Economy* in 1825; works by Thomas Cooper, George Tucker and Jacob Cardozo appeared during the next two or three years.[18] All these were too late to be of any use to Taylor. His own writings were in the style of

[15] Taylor, *An Enquiry into the Principles . . .*, p. 31; *Arator*, p. vi.

[16] See the discussion in J. E. Crowley, *This Sheba, Self. The Conceptualization of Economic Life in Eighteenth-Century America* (Baltimore, 1974), pp. 86–91 and *passim*.

[17] For evidence that *The Wealth of Nations* was thought to be difficult to comprehend, see *American Monthly Magazine*, I (1817), p. 234; those familiar with Smith's ideas had often come to them through J. B. Say's *Traité d'économie politique*, described by Jefferson as an easy version of *The Wealth of Nations*, *The Writings of Thomas Jefferson*, Andrew A. Lipscomb and Albert E. Bergh, eds. (Washington, D.C. 1903), II, 223; see also Joseph Dorfman, *The Economic Mind in American Civilization* (New York, 1946–49), I, 513–14.

[18] Daniel Raymond, *Thoughts on Political Economy* (Baltimore, 1820); John McVickar, *Outlines of Political Economy* (New York, 1825); Thomas Cooper, *Lectures on the Elements of Political Economy* (New York, 1826); (George Tucker), "Political Economy," *American Quarterly Review*, I (1827), 309–31, Jacob N. Cardozo, *Notes on Political Economy* (Charleston, 1826).

the precursors of a scientific approach to the subject, and his analysis was never truly rigorous even when it involved a rather crude empiricism.

In its purist, most unqualified form the labour theory of value asserts that the value of any commodity reflects the quantity of labour required to produce it. The theory has been advanced to serve a variety of purposes but in and before Taylor's time its asertion was more often normative than analytical. When treated analytically it was almost invariably diluted. Mercantilists and their opponents often had recourse to the idea in order to refute or make the charge that a reliance upon bullion theories and their like was both materialistic and inhumane. Adam Smith stated such a theory but elaborated analyses quite at variance with it, as also did Tench Coxe in America. For all these, and other writers, the theory constituted a useful political statement or else a useful approximation to reality: Smith, for example, believed it to be approximately valid for pre-capitalist societies but not for more advanced ones.[19] The only contemporary of Taylor who might appear to have elaborated the theory in anything like its pure form was David Ricardo. Actually, however contemporaries interpreted him, Ricardo presented a cost-of-production theory of value in which labour was merely the most important element. There were other costs than labour involved and the final value of any commodity was the sum of all the costs.[20] Most of the Americans who published works on economics in the 1820s did so with specific reference to Ricardo's ideas. None of them was willing to accept what they understood to be his labour value theory. Cardozo came closest to being a Ricardian but even he rejected Ricardo's formulations on this issue.[21] Taylor, on the other hand, treated the theorem as one the validity of which was demonstrable by reference to experience and he regarded it not as an approximation but as absolutely true.

[19] Adam Smith, *An Inquiry into the Nature and Causes of the Wealth of Nations*, ed. E. Cannan (London, 1904), p. 49; Tench Coxe, *Observations on the Agriculture, Manufactures and Commerce of the United States: In a letter to a Member of Congress. By a Citizen of the United States* (New York, 1789). I have found particularly useful the following works on the economic theories of the eighteenth and early nineteenth centuries: Mark Blaug, *Economic Theory in Retrospect*, 3rd edn. (Cambridge, 1978); D. P. O'Brien, *The Classical Economists* (Oxford, 1975); and, more provocatively, Ronald L. Meek, *Studies in the Labour Theory of Value*, 2nd ed. (London, 1973).

[20] There has been considerable debate as to the exact nature of Ricardo's value theory. That debate has been reviewed in Blaug, *Economic Theory in Retrospect*, pp. 95–102, and O'Brien, *The Classical Economists*, pp. 84–91; see also Sraffa's introduction to the *Works and Correspondence of David Ricardo*, ed. P. Sraffa with M. H. Dobb (Cambridge, 1951–55).

[21] Jacob N. Cardozo, *Notes on Political Economy* (Charleston, 1826; reprint, New York, 1960), pp. 5–8, 64–71; Cardozo, "Political Economy – Rent," *The Southern Review*, **1** (Feb. 1828), 192–218; Melvin M. Leiman, *Jacob N. Cardozo. Economic Thought in the Antebellum South* (New York, 1966), pp. 20–35.

In discussing Taylor's theory of value, and the use he made of it, the best place to start is the question of property. A catch-phrase of eighteenth-century whiggery, at least until the French Revolution, "life, liberty and property" was transformed by Thomas Jefferson in the Declaration of Independence into "life, liberty and the pursuit of happiness." There can be little doubt, however, that he intended the phrase "pursuit of happiness" to incorporate the "means of acquiring and possessing property" which was associated with it in the Virginia Bill of Rights. Taylor certainly subsumed that sense of it when he wrote of the "happiness" of the nation.[22] Whether Jefferson recognized the difficulty of coming to a satisfactory definition of property and was unwilling to use a phrase associated generally with a particular form of property, land, is not clear. What is clear is that other types of property soon became the focal points of political controversy. Taylor had no doubts as to what *he* meant by property and he noted that

> Here it is probable that a disagreement will occur, between the disciples of corporation, monopoly and orders, and myself. It is acknowledged that I do not include under the idea of property, any artificial establishment, which subsists by taking away property; such as hierarchical, kingly, noble, official and corporate possessions, incomes and privileges; and that I consider those possessions as property, which are fairly gained by talents and industry, or are capable of subsisting, without taking property from others by law.[23]

An emphasis upon "natural" property runs throughout Taylor's works. "As nature compelled man to acquire in order to exist, his acquisitions from his own labour are his property, according to the law of his maker; since man must have existed before society." Natural property is "fairly gained by talents or industry." It is the "earning of labour, the reward of merit."[24] Industry, talents, merit: the notion of a pure labour theory of value would be compatible with this idea of property only if talents and merit were deemed to be themselves the fruits of industry. Of that Taylor had little or no doubt. The "acquisitions of useful qualities are genuine private property,"[25] he argued, and he dismissed the idea that talents are rare. The whole idea of a natural aristocracy of merit was anathema to him:

> [r]are talents, like a natural aristocracy, are created by ignorance. . . . Ignorance is the source of slavery, and knowledge of liberty, because the first begets, and the other explodes the errour, "that some men are endowed with faculties, far exceeding the general standard."[26]

Taylor's ideas respecting the nature and acquisition of natural property did

[22] *Arator*, pp. v, 191, 235, 237.
[23] *An Inquiry*, p. 124.
[24] Ibid., pp. 546, 124, 258.
[25] Ibid., p. 258.
[26] Ibid., p. 224.

not derive simply from his attack upon unnatural property although they served that purpose well. They stemmed as much from his consideration of the "physical" as of the "moral" world. The essays in *Arator* which are concerned with the generation of improved methods of farming constitute the core of the book and won Taylor a contemporary reputation as an expert on farming. Taken as a whole, they emphasize the labour input into agriculture.

The context within which Taylor was writing is here significant. Hume, Wallace and Smith, in Scotland, had all suggested that populations were limited by the possibilities of providing the means of subsistence. Malthus had given the idea form, and an appearance of rigour, in his *Essay on Population*, first published in 1798. Malthus had focused upon the limited supply of land which implied a limited population. A by-product of his theories was a concern about the supply and fertility of soil. The so-called classical economists in England were led further to argue for a law of inevitably diminishing returns as population pressure made increasing demands upon the land. Increased inputs into the cultivation of the land failed ultimately to generate equivalent outputs.[27] Most of these responses to Malthus were published in 1815 or after, rather too late to have influenced Taylor in the writing of either *Arator* or the *Inquiry*. Nevertheless, Malthus's work had excited speculation everywhere. In 1815 four independent works on the subject appeared almost simultaneously in England suggesting the extent to which the ideas they adumbrated were in the air.[28] Taylor appears to have grasped the connection between Malthus's basic theory and the possibility of diminishing returns. He rejected the argument that land was a free gift of nature subject to a law diminishing returns. He dismissed out of hand Malthus's political arithmetic:

> [T]he fact is, that with or without civil government, population has never been able to overtake the capacity of the earth to yield subsistence; and therefore it is probable, that all the operations of food and population, or of mind and matter, upon each other, are regulated by some unalterable natural law. At both extremities of man's moral state, the urban and the savage, we find its traces. Rather an excess than a want of food, is generally met with in cities; and where a want of food is met with in a savage state, it is never owing to an incapacity of the country

[27] Blaug, *Economic Theory in Retrospect*, Chapter Three; O'Brien, *The Classical Economists*, pp. 56–61, 124–31.

[28] T. R. Malthus, *An Inquiry into the Nature and Progress of Rent and the Principles by which it is Regulated* (London, 1815); Sir E. West, *Essay on the Application of Capital to Land, with Observations Shewing the Impolicy of any Great Restriction of the Importation of Corn* (London, 1815); R. Torrens, *An Essay on the External Corn Trade* (London, 1815); D. Ricardo, *An Essay on the Influence of a Low Price of Corn on the Profits of Stock* (London, 1815).

to produce it. The checks upon population in both states are therefore moral. Countries, in which a few savages starve for want of food, afford abundance for an hundred fold population, of a different moral character, as has been demonstrated in America.[29]

It is somewhat ironic that Taylor's refutation of Malthus should derive from the American experience since it was that selfsame experience which had provided Malthus with his own starting point. A free gift of nature land might be; but the free gift was also originally a wilderness and it was only too obvious to Taylor that what turned that wilderness into capital was labour; through labour the wilderness was given value; through labour its value could be maintained and enhanced; it could not therefore be subject to a law of inevitably diminishing returns. It was one of the prime objects of *Arator* to establish that fact. Indeed, Taylor stood Malthus on his head and argued that original fertility could be increased and the additional means of subsistence made to bear an increased population. As he wrote in the preface:

The thin soil of the United States, renders political frauds particularly grievous to agriculture, from its insufficiency to bear them; and the thin population, exposes us particularly to the evils of invasion. The population, necessary to contract or prevent these evils, can never be obtained, except by enriching the soil, and the soil cannot be enriched, except by legislative cooperation with individual industry, by forbearing to transfer wealth from an application to these great national objects, to the encouragement of doubtful projects. . . .[30]

Above all else, Taylor was concerned to arrest the declining fertility of the soil and to promote techniques which would enhance the capital values of farms and plantations. It was a concern for *settled* land, a concern to refute those who saw its deterioration as inevitable, which pushed Taylor beyond the positions occupied by Locke more than a century earlier and beyond those occupied by his contemporaries. Locke had likewise invoked the American experience to advance arguments very similar to those of Taylor regarding the legitimacy and naturalness of property. He, too, had stressed the input of labour as the factor which legitimated the acquisition of property, but he was never prepared to see the value of the property so acquired in terms solely of the labour input. He persisted in regarding the land as having some intrinsic, albeit small value. His goals were, of course, different from those of Taylor: he was concerned to account for the *origins* of property and to assert the existence of legitimate property rights.[31] Taylor was attempting to establish

[29] *An Inquiry*, p. 470.
[30] *Arator*, p. vi.
[31] John Locke, *Two Treatises of Government. A Critical Edition with an Introduction and Apparatus Criticus by Peter Laslett*, 2nd ed. (Cambridge, 1967), pp. 314–17.

the *nature* of property. Determined, moreover, to reject the views of those who saw land as a free gift of nature subject to diminishing returns, the value of which must therefore correlate ever less closely with labour inputs, he came to express the value of land entirely in terms of labour. Writing in 1823, at a time when he might have achieved some familiarity with the economic debate raging in England and beginning in America, Taylor revealed to what extent he was prepared to take the argument for the identity of property and labour. He wrote:

Man, by nature, had two rights; to his conscience, and to his labour; and it was the design of civil society to secure these rights. In the case of religious freedom, we have seen one right; in that of the freedom of property, our vision is not so clear; yet both, as natural rights, stand on the same foundation.

By suppressing the distinction between occupations, and covering all by the inclusive term, labour, we at once discern the natural equality of the right. The occupations of men are the men themselves.[32]

Taylor had adopted a vantage point rejected by those of his contemporaries who wrote on the same subject. Malthus differentiated between the *cause* of value and its *measurement*. As he put it: "The labour worked up in a commodity is the principle *cause* of its value.... It is not a measure of it."[33] The law of supply and demand would determine its measurement. In America, Daniel Raymond argued similarly that land was the *source* of wealth, labour was the *cause* of its acquiring value. The value it acquired through the input of labour would be determined by the law of supply and demand.[34] Jacob Cardozo insisted, like Locke, that Nature itself contributed directly to value: land possessed an intrinsic value over and above any contributed to it by an input of labour.[35] Even Ricardo and his followers were unable to leave the issue without further qualifications. Since different pieces of land had different natural fertilities they would produce different levels of output for equivalent inputs. Out of that insight they developed the theory of differential rents. The problem was intimately related to Malthus's population theory: pressure of population would compel recourse to relatively infertile soils. Rent then became the difference between an actual return on the investment of labour and capital and the return achieved by the marginal farmer. The English economists had as their prime objective an analysis of the English agricultural system then obtaining and, in particular, the current

[32] Taylor, *Construction Construed and Constitutions Vindicated* (New York, 1970), p. 203. First published 1820. Note how easily Taylor moves between labour and property as the selfsame natural right.

[33] Thomas Malthus, *Principles of Political Economy* (New York, 1951), pp. 72–73.

[34] Danield Raymond, *Elements of Political Economy* (Baltimore, 1823), I, 97–102.

[35] Cardozo, *Notes on Political Economy*, pp. 8–9, 84.

problems of wheat prices and the corn laws. Their target was the protected role of the landlord class.[36]

Taylor, on the other hand, was confronted by a situation in which the supply of naturally fertile land appeared almost limitless and the problems of agriculture appeared to stem from the actions of a government which leaned towards the interests of the commercial and manufacturing sectors, including those of land speculators. He perceived a situation in which agriculture suffered diminishing profitability and fertility and attributed that loss to excessive taxation and government-induced prospects of unearned income elsewhere. The capital value of farms and plantations was the embodiment of the labour which had been expended upon them; that capital value was being eroded by the government-sponsored exactions of other sectors of the economy and as a consequence of the fact that the labour required to sustain and increase it was being lured away by fresh lands in the west. But the attraction of those lands was artificially enhanced by the boosterism of speculators and by the investment of commercial capital – itself extracted from existing landholders – in creating systems of transportation. The greater attraction of western over eastern lands was, in other words, a function of an undesirable form of economic activity – speculation – and of capital transfers imposed by governmental action. The consequent drain of capital (embodied labour) and labour from east to west rendered impossible the preservation and improvement of eastern farms. One of the consequences of these tendencies was to promote in America an extractive view of agriculture which led to the consumption of land rather than its nurture. It was one of Taylor's prime objects in life – both through his writings and his promotion of agricultural societies – to transform that psychology.[37]

Jacob Cardozo was to argue that economic theories should and do reflect the circumstances and needs which give rise to them.[38] As far as Taylor was concerned, then, there was no need to elaborate or qualify his theory of value

[36] Blaug, *Economic Theory in Retrospect*, pp. 79–85; O'Brien, *The Classical Economists*, Ch. 3.

[37] *Arator*, pp. vi–vii, 19, 20, 22, 28, 31, 37, 39, 40. Some historians have likewise argued that too rapid settlement of the west was harmful not merely to eastern farmers but to agricultural profits as a whole; see, R. P. Swierenga, "Land Speculator 'Profits' Reconsidered: Central Iowa as a Test Case," *Journal of Economic History*, **26** (1966), pp. 1–28; G. Wright, "An Econometric Study of Cotton Production and Trade, 1830–1860," *Review of Economics and Statistics*, **53** (1971), 111–20; P. Passell, "The Impact of Cotton Land Distribution on the Antibellum Economy," *Journal of Economic History*, **21** (1971), 917–37; P. Passell and G. Wright, "Effects of pre-Civil War Territorial Expansion on the Price of Slaves," *Journal of Political Economy*, **80** (1972), 1188–1202.

[38] Cardozo, "Political Economv – Rent," p. 199.

as embodied labour, nor to generate notions of rent or profit. The American experience suggested to him that land was indeed a free gift of nature and also that nature was not niggardly in its offerings. Fertility was not something once granted and subject to erosion over time – to consumption, as it were. It was, or should be, a permanent benefit. Almost all the recommendations contained in *Arator* were designed to make it such and nearly all of them were labour-intensive. Hedging, ditching, deep ploughing, manuring, and fertilizing, were all intended to secure the value of the fixed capital of agriculture even more than to generate an increased income from the sale of its produce.[39] It has been argued that Taylor's prescriptions were no more than a reflex of the growing surplus of slave labour in eastern Virginia. Engaged in a less labour-intensive form of farming than tobacco cultivation and forced by soil-exhaustion to recommend a fallow period in his four-phase crop rotation cycle, he was no more than rationalizing the labour surplus of the area. But Taylor denied that his objective was simply one of absorbing labour and attacked the "error of making the mode of cultivation subservient to fluctuating labour, instead of adapting the labour to permanent land." He insisted that more labour was "necessary to build than to destroy" and argued for its use in improvements rather than in direct cultivation. The outcome would be greater fertility, higher productivity and enhanced capital values. Far from simply finding employment for surplus labour Taylor argued for an efficient and cost-effective application of labour. Thus he urged hedging instead of ditching because of its lesser labour demands; he recommended that animal pens be constantly shifted around the farm in order to avoid excessive labour in the distribution of animal manure.[40] The ideas of an economy of labour and of a labour theory of value stemmed therefore not merely from the requirements of political opposition and debate; nor merely from the demands of a small slaveholding class; but also from a concern with matters nowadays more associated with economics than with politics.

III

Taylor is usually, and rightly, described as an agrarian. But the nature of that agrarianism takes on a slightly different character when we view it in the context of a commitment to a labour theory of value. It cannot be understood

[39] *Arator*, pp. 59–187.

[40] Keith M. Bailor, "John Taylor of Caroline: Continuity, Change and Discontinuity in Virginia's Sentiments towards Slavery, 1790–1820," *Virginia Magazine of History and Biography*, **75** (1967), 290–304; *Arator*, pp. 99–101, 59–61, 73–5 – the quotations are from pp. 99 and 100–1.

in terms of its pastoral or republican associations alone. He did indeed write a section in *Arator* devoted to a description of the "Pleasures of Agriculture" and he certainly regarded agriculture as a character-building activity. But he never suggested that it was the only valuable or legitimate kind of economic pursuit, nor did he a.gue that those who followed different occupations were in any sense necessarily inferior to farmers. On the contrary,

> The words "agriculture, manufacture, commerce, profession and science" have produced artificial distinctions, which have obscured the reach of the inclusive word "labour." ... Workers upon the land, or upon the ocean, who give things new forms or new places, are all manufacturers; and being comprised in one essential character, are entitled to the same freedom in free societies.[41]

He recognized that in some occupations, especially in commerce and manufacturing, accumulations of capital were necessary and he insisted that provided the term capitalist was properly understood he was not himself anti-capitalist:

> I freely admit that capitalists, whether agricultural, commercial or manufactural, constitute useful and productive classes in society; and by no means design, in the use of the term, to insinuate that it contains an odious allusion. It may even be applied to the man whose bodily labour is his sole capital. But I also contend, that capital is only useful and reproductive, when it is obtained by fair and honest industry; and that whenever it is created by legal coercions, the productiveness of the common stock of capital is diminished, just as it is diminished by the excessive expenses of a civil government.[42]

A major portion of Taylor's political and literary energies was directed against governmental intervention in economic affairs because it produced capital which did not derive from "fair and honest industry." Note, also, that Taylor was not worried simply by the prospect of the government or its creatures growing fat on taxes, one of Locke's main concerns, although this prospect did alarm him. He was also opposed to all monopolies, banks and other corporations, bounties for private manufacturers, tariffs and heavy taxation caused by such excrescences as a large naval or military establishment. He opposed them in part because they constituted a form of privilege equivalent to aristocracy. He argued that the "cause of reasoning pursued by this essay (*An Inquiry*), results in the definition, *that a transfer of property by law, is aristocracy, and that aristocracy is a transfer of property by law.*"[43] In this he revealed himself to be a true heir to the traditions of the English opposition so well described by, amongst others, Caroline Robbins and

[41] *Construction Construed*, p. 208.
[42] Ibid., p. 234.
[43] *An Inquiry*, p. 352.

Bernard Bailyn.[44] His attack derived also, however, from his labour theory of value. All imposts fell ultimately upon labour, whether in the form of taxes to finance the national debt; of high prices to finance the tariff; or of interest to replace specie with paper as the circulating medium. The profits of all these imposts, drawn from labour, accrued to monied capital. They constituted a transfer of property from the labouring class, including all the poor, to a small, privileged class, which was coming increasingly to include all the rich. The basis of his opposition can best be illustrated by reference to two examples, namely the questions of tariffs and the public debt.

Taylor noted the arguments of tariff proponents to the effect that protective duties were intended to be temporary expedients designed to promote a shift in employment from one sector of the economy to another. But this argument appeared to him to demonstrate the essential falsity of their position. It "admits that the privilege and monopoly it is striving to obtain [is] bad; by asserting that it ought to be granted, because it will in time cease to operate partially and unjustly upon the other occupations of society."[45] He was scornful of the proposition that a new equality could be achieved by first departing from that naturally obtaining and insisted that to "direct the labour of the people, is extremely analogous to the relation between master and slave."[46] Moreover, it was the poor, being the majority of the nation and thus of the mass of consumers, who would pay the tax whilst the rich, that is the merchants and manufacturers, would appropriate the proceeds to themselves. The argument that labourers would benefit through higher wages he rejected, for these would seduce workers from the land and thereby reduce wages again.[47] Taylor never directly addressed the question whether accumulations of capital might have a gearing effect on the economy. But the inference is clear: the true value of manufacturing output could rise no faster than the quantity of labour input and that input could be no more productive of true value in manufacturing than in agriculture because the true value of labour was itself invariant. An increase in manufacturing output resulting from a

[44] Caroline Robbins, *The Eighteenth Century Commonwealthman: Studies in the Transmission, Development, and Circumstances of English Liberal Thought from the Restoration of Charles II until the War with the Thirteen Colonies* (Cambridge, Mass., 1959); Bernard Bailyn, *The Ideological Origins of the American Revolution* (Cambridge, Mass., 1967); see also Banning, *The Jeffersonian Persuasion*, esp. pp. 21–90.

[45] *Construction Construed*, p. 211.

[46] *A Pamphlet Containing a Series of Letters, Written by Colonel John Taylor, of Caroline, to Thomas Ritchie, Editor of the "Enquirer" . . . Richmond. In Consequence of an Unwarranted Attack Made by that Editor upon Colonel Taylor* (Richmond, 1809), p. 25.

[47] *Construction Construed*, pp. 224–30.

draft to its service of labourers hitherto engaged in other activities could not, therefore, lead to an increase in the nation's total wealth. All it did was interfere in the free market for labour and impose an artificial exchange rate by which manufacturers gained "two measures for one."[48]

When we turn to a consideration of the public debt we find Taylor arguing in an essentially similar manner. The mass of taxpayers pay the interest accruing to the privileged few who hold the debt. Thus "Taxation transfers wealth from a mass to a selection. It destroys the political equality which can alone save liberty."[49] Taylor argued that the impact of the debt was more evil than that of slavery because it expropriated the profits of labour more completely:

> In Rhode-Island, bank stock, to the amount of four millions is said to have been created. She has near seventy thousand people. Allowing her eighteen thousand actual labourers, and her stock to collect in expense, perquisites and dividends, ten per centum, her labour pays a capitation tax of above twenty-two dollars annually to banks.... If the stock interest in Rhode-Island, draws more nett profit from banking, than the Virginia masters do from eighteen thousand Negro slaves, banking approaches in substance to a mode of selling freemen. Arthur Young calculates the profits of English West-India slaves, at five pounds each. The banking mode of converting the labour of one to the use of another, is more profitable than this personal slavery.[50]

When Taylor wrote in terms of a labour theory of value he had a very concrete sense of what he was arguing. He believed in a free exchange of labour because all labour devoted to useful purposes was equal in value. His objections to the course adopted by successive governments in the United States arose from this conception as powerfully as they did from any considerations of political liberty in a more abstract sense.

IV

There is no form of labour organization more antithetical to the dictates of a labour theory of value than that of slavery. Yet it will not have gone unnoticed that Taylor was himself a substantial slaveholder who in his writings exhibited little or no squeamishness about slavery. On the contrary, far from denying, concealing or apologizing for his slaveholding he was prone to making comparisons between the plight of slaves and the plight, under some circumstances, of freemen. All such comparisons were designed to show slavery in a *relatively* good light. Thus he quite consciously used slavery as a benchmark against which the iniquity, or otherwise of certain policies and

[48] Ibid., p. 209.
[49] "John Taylor Correspondence," p. 275.
[50] *An Inquiry*, pp. 316–17.

their consequences could be measured. How can one square the acceptance of slavery with the advocacy of a labour theory of value? The answer is that one cannot; there is a contradiction which can neither be explained away nor even fully understood. Insofar as Taylor himself recognized and tackled the problem he did so through three mechanisms. First, an implied apologia for slavery runs through his works: it was less iniquitous than other means of expropriating the product of labour because a lesser share of that product was in fact taken. Whereas George Fitzhugh was later to compare the exactions of chattels and wage slavery Taylor's comparison was with the exactions of banks, tariffs, and taxes. Secondly, his belief in the intellectual and moral inferiority of blacks emerges from his every comment upon them. Logically, his denial of a natural aristocracy is incompatible with a belief in natural slavery but logic does not always dominate human affairs. He admitted that aristocracy, being dependent upon a monopoly, or near-monopoly of knowledge, might be beneficial if the majority of the population was ignorant. But it was a matter of choice. Spreading knowledge would erode the position of the aristocracy: what, however, if the population was incapable of imbibing that knowledge and morality? The definition of the problem reflected Taylor's racism and the solution was self-serving but there can be doubt as to the depth of his psychological commitment to it. Thirdly, Taylor's republicanism placed great emphasis upon social and political homogeneity. If freed, blacks would constitute a landless proletariat, a clearly marked faction, and would thereby destroy that homogeneity obtained by excluding them from the body politic. Emancipation, in other words, would impose too great social and political costs. Taylor never addressed himself to a comparison of the well-being of slaves in America with free blacks in Africa. He no doubt shared, however, the dominant view of his class that the labour devoted by whites to the transportation, training and supervision of blacks resulted in the enhancement of the value of black labour to blacks. Taylor, moreover, nowhere dealt explicitly with the inequalities amongst whites generated by the possession by some of slaves. But he did argue that "slavery is a misfortune to agriculture, incapable of removal, and only within the reach of palliation."[51] Responsible masters, in other words, gained little or nothing from their labour: on the contrary they paid a price for their possession of slaves. Whether Taylor regarded that price as commensurate with the market value of slaves is not clear.[52]

[51] *Arator*, p. 48.

[52] For a fuller discussion of Taylor and slavery see, Duncan J. MacLeod, *Slavery, Race and The American Revolution* (Cambridge, 1974), pp. 65–69, 82–89. For a different view see, Bailor, "John Taylor of Caroline."

The general question of unequal accumulations of wealth amongst whites posed no problems for Taylor. Granted, as he saw it, the inevitability and desirability of most people being engaged in agriculture unequal accumulations of capital could arise only slowly so long as no intervention occurred by government to accelerate income and capital flows. In the absence of laws of entail, primogeniture and incorporation, moreover, Taylor was confident that the inheritors of wealth could be relied upon to dissipate it.[53]

Some further general observations about Taylor's value theory are in order. First, it was undeveloped and unsophisticated. Indeed, his writings were never directed towards explicating any such theory. On the other hand, his very consistency and the coherence of his ideas justify the inference. That his theories were undeveloped owed something to his environment and purposes as well as to his intellect. Thus he never found it necessary to distinguish between different sorts of capital and capital-employment beyond the ways noted above. He did not develop theories of profits, rent or wages as different modes of employing money. On the contrary, he took for granted the supply of fertile lands in America, and the identity of farmers and landlords, and thereby disposed of the problem of rent; he saw capital solely in terms of its labour content and thereby disposed of the problem of profit – all that distinguished the wage labourer from other labourers was that he did not enjoy a return from his previous input of labour, now embodied in capital. The wide distribution of land ownership and the even wider opportunities for it blinded Taylor to the needs to make such distinctions.

Secondly, and as a consequence, he failed to make the kind of distinction English and American economists were making between wealth and value, between natural value and exchange value, or between the source, cause or measurement of value. As far as Taylor was concerned wealth was legitimate or illegitimate insofar as it embodied labour and its true value was in exact proportion to that embodiment.

Thirdly, it is clear that his value theory was a labour-embodied rather than a labour-commanded one. Like Ricardo, he rejected Adam Smith's idea that value was determined by the quantity of labour it could command in the market place. Like Smith, Taylor argued for the freedom of commerce and exchange but he did so confident that only governmental or other artificial interference could prevent an equal exchange of labour. Under conditions of freedom labour-embodied and labour-commanded values would be identical. Interestingly, Cardozo took an intermediate position, insisting that the market would determine the price of labour itself as well as of the commodities it

[53] *An Enquiry*, p. 30.

produced.[54] Taylor's approach denied a role for differential views of utility. Both Smith and Ricardo had tried, for example, to deal with the impact upon value of different degrees of utility. Taylor merely assumed that all useful labour was of equal utility and that labour which was not useful did not, in any case, produce real value. The whole body of Taylor's economic ideas rested upon the assumption that labour had a value which was invariant. That was an assumption rejected by pretty well every economist of his day with the exception of Ricardo. Even Ricardo was able to support it only by recourse to some further unreal assumptions and, in any case, advanced the view largely as a means of entering upon a discussion he regarded as far more significant, namely his theories of distribution.[55]

Taylor's economic ideas were presented without the accompaniment of rigorous economic analysis, although not without recourse to empirical data. He falls rather more easily into that category of writer described by William Letwin as pre-scientific than into that of those economists we associate with the classical school.[56] His theories were pre-capitalist in content and were advanced in an age of growing capitalism in large measure with a view to warding off its advances and the kind of society it seemed destined to produce. He regarded as iniquitous the idea that social classes could or should be defined in terms of the sources of their incomes: profits, rents, or wages. Social utility determined what occupations were legitimate and labour determined their value. He spoke for those Americans who doubted the benefits of the growing commercialism of the age in a way which the professional economists did not. Almost to a man the latter were concerned to explain, to justify, or to promote economic growth, whilst Taylor was concerned to describe and justify moral and poiltical value systems. His labour theory of value was a powerful preservative of stability and of an old social order.

[54] Cardozo, *Notes*, pp. 22, 33, 84 and "Political Economy – Rent," pp. 216–17.

[55] Blaug, *Economic Theory in Retrospect*, pp. 100–02; O'Brien, *The Classical Economists*, pp. 90–91.

[56] W. Letwin, *The Origins of Scientific Economics* (London, 1963).